HAUNTED
BY
EMPIRE

AMERICAN ENCOUNTERS/GLOBAL INTERACTIONS

A SERIES EDITED BY GILBERT M. JOSEPH

AND EMILY S. ROSENBERG

HAUNTED

BY

GEOGRAPHIES OF INTIMACY
IN NORTH AMERICAN HISTORY

EMPIRE

EDITED BY ANN LAURA STOLER

DUKE UNIVERSITY PRESS   DURHAM AND LONDON   2006

Designed by Rebecca Giménez

Typeset in Minion by Tseng Information Systems, Inc.

Library of Congress Cataloging-in-Publication Data

appear on the last printed page of this book.

"Tense and Tender Ties: The Politics of Comparison in North
American History and (Post) Colonial Studies" originally
appeared in the *Journal of American History* 88 (December
2001): 829–65. Copyright © Organization of American Historians.
Reprinted with permission.

AMERICAN ENCOUNTERS/GLOBAL INTERACTIONS

A SERIES EDITED BY GILBERT M. JOSEPH
AND EMILY S. ROSENBERG

This series aims to stimulate critical perspectives and fresh
interpretive frameworks for scholarship on the history of the
imposing global presence of the United States. Its primary
concerns include the deployment and contestation of power, the
construction and deconstruction of cultural and political borders,
the fluid meanings of intercultural encounters, and the complex
interplay between the global and the local. American Encounters
seeks to strengthen dialogue and collaboration between historians
of U.S. international relations and area studies specialists.

The series encourages scholarship based on multiarchival
historical research. At the same time, it supports a recognition
of the representational character of all stories about the past and
promotes critical inquiry into issues of subjectivity and narrative.
In the process, American Encounters strives to understand the
context in which meanings related to nations, cultures, and political
economy are continually produced, challenged, and reshaped.

Contents

Haunted by Empire describes both the cast that imperial formations spread over people's intimate social ecologies and the shadowy pall of U.S. empire over those of my generation who have studied the colonial and found U.S. intrusions to subjacently shape their intellectual choices and academic lives. I first began work in Indonesia in the early 1970s, near the end of the war in Vietnam, and it was U.S. imperialism as I then understood it that held my political and scholarly attention. I identified it with the undeclared violence of "strategic hamlet" operations in Vietnam, as boldly embodied in the "Green Revolution," the introduction of insecticides, fertilizers, and high-yielding "miracle" rice varieties that were hailed as boosts to agricultural production and—for the land poor of Indonesia, Malaysia, and the Philippines—drastically reduced labor opportunities; in family-planning policies introduced by the Agency for International Development (AID) and the World Bank; and, not least, in what "everyone knew" but about which few dared to speak publicly: the CIA-backed coup that deposed Indonesia's socialist president, Soekarno, and resulted in the slaughter of hundreds of thousands of alleged communist sympathizers and the annihilation of Asia's second-largest communist party. Still, there were no immediate signs of U.S. empire in rural labor relations that I could easily name.

For my dissertation research in the late 1970s on Dutch colonial and multinational agribusiness in North Sumatra, U.S. empire had a stronger presence. Uniroyal and Goodyear's vast holdings loomed large in my political vision, if less in my ethnographic work on the ground. While I combed the colonial and postcolonial plantation company archives housed in Medan and in the Netherlands, those of Goodyear's in Akron, Ohio, eluded my archive map. Uniroyal's palatial complex in Kisaran was at the center of my ethnographic orbit, but U.S. pursuits were overshadowed by the more attention-getting presence of corroding Dutch infrastructure and of the Indonesian military — thick, palpable, and cut into the very fabric of government-run complexes or legally hidden behind private Chinese-owned estates. My dissertation was titled "In the Company's Shadow," but it was equally shadowed by U.S. empire. The history that stretches between Route I-94 outside Detroit, where Uniroyal's eighty-foot-high tire (a former Ferris wheel for the 1965 New York World's Fair) now stands, and the intimate management of race that pervaded North Sumatra's rubber belt in 1917, when Goodyear (then the largest tire producer in the United States) began to acquire its holdings, is severed by historiography but held taut by imperial ligaments. It is a history haunted by the real and the unseen, both the invisible signs of exposure and those damages boldly marked as indelible ones.

Edward Said's *Orientalism* (1978), the book that was to launch postcolonial studies, had just appeared as I was writing my dissertation in Paris, as work on colonial effects was shifting from a focus on economic interventions to those embedded in the social fabric of the everyday. Said's insights confirmed what the plantation archives iterated at every turn: that racial hierarchies underwrote European rule and that white colonial communities were built on and dependent on those distinctions. But it was the obsession of the state and plantation bureaucracy with the intimate coordinates of racial categories — who slept with whom, who could marry and who could not, whose children were recognized as legitimate — that held me fast. At the time, Said's insistent claims about U.S. imperial power's specific cultural and political configurations had less resonance than the residual architecture of Dutch rule and the intimate artifacts of its colonial culture. The latter were evident in the strategic labor policies of agribusiness, in a history of managed domestic arrangements for Javanese workers and European managers. Not least, the plantation economy continued to be buttressed by the implicit insight and sometimes explicit knowledge that sexuality was a "dense transfer point of power." Colonial actors and agents knew it: students of colonialism did not.

It is difficult to study plantation economies of rubber, sugar, oil palm, and tobacco *without* attending to the similar forms of labor recruitment, coercion, and sexual management that agribusiness deployed recurrently throughout the world. North and South American histories of mixing, miscegenation, and illegitimate children were on the radar of the companies themselves, and they recognized the import of those comparisons. The imperial imaginaries that produced the *White Women's Protection Ordinance* in Papua New Guinea in the 1920s, the "black peril" in South Africa, and what Jacquelyn Dowd Hall has described of lynching and white chivalry in the U.S. South were more than resonant discourses — they echoed similar racialized logics and a familiar distribution of affective states.

Common to all was a focus on the disquieting presence of those "misplaced" and displaced in the colonial order of things — mixed-bloods, poor whites, abandoned "mixed-blood" children. The Dutch colonial commissions that so astonished me with their microphysical precisions about moral dangers, racial degeneracy, and political threat of "European paupers" were not particular to that Indies locale. Nor did administrative anxiety correlate with the number of persons imagined to occupy those categories. Similar government investigations were carried out in South Africa, British India, and British Malaya, all concerned with boring into the domestic, familial, and sexual lives of people stranded on the ambiguous racial borders that colonial situations produced.

The South African Carnegie Commission of the 1930s on the status of "poor whites" exemplified these studies. I was struck by the detailed attention to physical comportment and domestic space when I first read the commission's reports in 1985 but also by the number of U.S. sociologists, psychologists, doctors, and other race experts involved in the assessments. It took some twelve years before I went to Columbia University's Carnegie Corporation archives to trace the entanglements of U.S. social science and eugenic thinking in South Africa's protoapartheid policies. The nomenclatures of "white trash" in the United States, "poor whites" in Johannesburg, and "European paupers" in the Indies carried their own specificities, but they did not deter comparison across that imperial spectrum: preoccupation with the sentimental affiliations and disaffections of those on the margins drew my own comparative attention.

In the end the project of *Haunted by Empire* hovers at the quiet center, the violent vortex, and the frayed edges of people's lives. The structures of feeling and force described by these authors invoke the blur between care and coercion, respect and neglect, and in the muffled silence between consent and rape. Haunting occupies the space between what we cannot see and what we know. It wrestles with elusive, nontransparent power and, not least, with attunement to the unexpected sites and lineaments that such knowledge requires.

ACKNOWLEDGMENTS

Haunted by Empire is a volume of a peculiar and awkward sort: one whose form, content, and timing reflect the circuits of exchange it embodies and the unconventional process of its making. As an anthropologist and student of European colonial cultures for some decades, I had never thought to edit a book on U.S. history nor imagined myself positioned to do so. The initial impetus came from Linda Gordon's invitation to organize a plenary panel of the Organization of American Historians for spring 2000 that might speak comparatively to intimacies of empire. Vince Rafael, Peggy Pascoe, and Ramón Gutiérrez — all participants on the panel — shared generously in that opening conversation. Spurred by an enthusiastic audience and encouraged by some avid interlocutors, most notably Nancy Cott and Estelle Friedman, my essay went to the *Journal of American History*, a forum for which I would not ordinarily write nor, as it turned out, did I know how to address. The *JAH*'s editor, Joanne Meyerowitz, provided exacting and enabling counsel, pushing for a firm grounding of the essay's comparative claims and then inviting a diverse range of historians to respond to them.

When it appeared in January 2002, Ken Wissoker, editor-in-chief of Duke University Press, proposed something further: a slim book of essays elicited by my own. I approached Nancy Cott, Linda Gordon, Amy Kaplan, and Martha Hodes, who generously sat down at NYU one hot day that spring to imagine who might contribute and how to foster an organic exchange rather than a dispersed edited volume. Five contributors mushroomed to fifteen and a specific commission for them: not responses to my initial foray but essays that would take directions — resonant or dissonant — that their own historical contexts and disciplinary concerns might compel or suggest. We requested rough precirculated papers for a workshop the following December and asked each contributor to come prepared to comment on someone else's draft.

That two-day marathon meeting in Ann Arbor was key. It congealed around recurrent debates over which we mulled and disagreed rather than sought to resolve: over different understandings of the politics of intimacy, what was to be included in it, whether and how empire mattered, and what constituted imperial effects. For the final essays we again read one another's work. Some people visited (Vicente Diaz, Penny van Eschen, and Kevin Gaines), some departed (Amy Kaplan), some joined late (Tiya Miles and Warwick Anderson), and others revised the nature of their participation along the way (Linda Gordon). All are to be thanked for the open and spirited scholarship with which they graced and embraced this project.

Others contributed to the volume in crucial ways. Eva-Marie Dubuisson and Monica Patterson, then graduate students at the University of Michigan in anthropology and in anthropology and history, respectively, organized and coordinated the Ann Arbor workshop. Natalie Rothman, also of Michigan's doctoral program in anthropology and history, and later Smoki Musaraj of the New School for Social Research's anthropology department each gathered in and formatted an unwieldy eight-hundred-page manuscript for submission. David Bond, also of the New School, made the index and with Imogen Bunting deftly saw the manuscript to completion. Joe Abbott copyedited the whole with care and finesse. An anonymous reader for Duke University Press posed queries that sharpened our arguments. Special thanks go to Vince Rafael, the other Duke reader, who urged a foregrounding of "the haunting" that titled the introduction and that has since become the title of the volume. Gwenn Miller and Alexandra Stern each independently inspired the subtitle. During 1999 and 2000 the Center for Advanced Study in the Behavioral Sciences in Palo Alto provided the space and cherished time to pursue this venture. Fellow sojourners Anna Tsing and Ed Ayers offered sustained inspiration. My greatest debts are to Lawrence Hirschfeld, Jay Bernstein, Nancy Hunt, Gwenn Miller, Julie Skurski, Doris Sommer, and Alexandra Stern, each of whom challenged my limits while easing my doubts and exhilarations.

This book is dedicated to my children, Tessa and Bruno, who enter adulthood at a moment when U.S. empire continues to bear down deftly and crudely, in so many places, with enduring force. Let us hope that their generation recognizes the rhetorical and material forms in which U.S. empire sustains itself, that they don't confuse imperial stretch for compassion, that their understandings of empire's intimacies confront its tortures, and that their working vocabularies can identify those gradations of intervention and sovereignty that call themselves by so many nonimperial names.

HAUNTED
BY
EMPIRE

ANN LAURA STOLER

Intimidations of Empire:

Predicaments of the Tactile and Unseen

Haunted by Empire explores the familiar, strange, and unarticulated ways in which empire has appeared and disappeared from the intimate and public spaces of United States history; how relations of empire crash through and then recede from easy purview, sunder families, storm sequestered spaces, and indelibly permeate — or sometimes graze with only a scarred trace — institutions and the landscapes of people's lives. To haunt is "to frequent, resort to, be familiar with," to bear a threatening presence, to invisibly occupy, to take on changing form. To be haunted is to reckon with such tactile powers and their intangibilities. To be haunted is to know that such forces are no less effective because of disagreement about their appropriate names. *Haunted by Empire* is a book steeped in such predicaments. It works through — and rests uncomfortably in — the fierce clarity of intimacies and in those ambiguous zones of empire that refused or refuted colonial appellations. To be haunted is to be frequented by and possessed by a force that not always bares a proper name.

This volume seeks to carve out a common ground of conversation between United States history and postcolonial studies. It rests on the claim that these fields share more points of comparative reflection than either field has recognized or allowed. Its focus is neither on the applicability of colonial studies to North American history in general nor on a comparison of colonialisms in the abstract. Rather, it attends to what I have called the *politics of comparison*: what students of North American history and postcolonial studies have chosen to compare and what scholarly commitments, historiographic conventions, and political investments have dissuaded or encouraged them to do so.[1]

For more than two decades studies of the colonial have thrived on an analytic wave across the disciplines concerned to trace the social construction of difference and the historical production of social categories.[2] A sustained assault on the politics of knowledge orients the postcolonial field. Poised at the forefront of both impulses, postcolonial scholarship has sought to understand how the macrodynamics of colonial rule worked through interventions in the microenvironments of both subjugated and colonizing populations and through the distinctions of privilege and opportunity made and managed between them.[3]

Students of European colonialisms understand the concept of race as a central colonial sorting technique. Like other classificatory techniques, it establishes categories and scales of comparison. Racial thinking secures racial designations in a *language* of biology and fixity and in the quest for a visual set of physical differences to index that which is not "self-evident" or visible—neither easy to agree on nor easy to see. Scientific taxonomies of race stress the "concrete" measures of racial membership, but they, like social taxonomies, depend implicitly on a belief in the different sensibilities and sensory regimes imagined to distinguish human kinds. Within these racial grammars distinct affective capacities get assigned to specific populations. This comparative imagining does not necessarily ascribe a different repertoire of sentiments to different groups. Rather certain groups are imagined to have more limited emotive capacities or are endowed with more intense displays of affective expression.

Recognition of the power of classification is more familiar to studies of empire than is attention to how those categories work on the ground. Classificatory schemes may be instruments of reason, but their content is not. Colonial authority depended on shaping appropriate and reasoned affect (where one's sympathies should lie), severing some intimate bonds and establishing others (which offspring would be acknowledged as one's own), establishing what constituted moral sentiments (family honor or patriotic duty); in short, colonial authority rested on educating the proper distribution of sentiments and desires.[4] Domains of the intimate are not the only place to register the hierarchical terrain on which such comparisons get played out. But they are strategic for exploring two related but often discretely understood sources of colonial control: one that works through the requisition of *bodies*—those of both colonials and colonized—and a second that molds new "structures of feeling"—new habits of heart and mind that enable those categories of difference and subject formation.

The belongings of race, religion, and citizenship in part dictated colonial entitlements. But those in turn were decided by local knowledge and close encounters. Racial affiliations varied with who slept with whom, who lived with whom, and who acknowledged doing so; who was recognized as one's child and by whom one was nursed, reared, and educated; who was one's spiritual light and by whom one was abandoned. In the case of those labeled "mixed-blood" or "half-caste" children — an imperial icon in itself in Australia, French Indochina, Samoa, the Dakotas, and the Dutch East Indies — a demonstrated disaffection for one's native culture and native mother were critical gatekeeping criteria for European membership. Evidence of disdain or estrangement and sympathy for thoughts and things native were basic to the white community's entry requirements. Those thresholds of racial membership, sexual access, and colonial status were not "private" sites of respite or retreat. In recluse and repose race was put to the test. In these "tense and tender ties" of empire, relations of power were knotted and tightened, loosened and cut, tangled and undone. These ties are not microcosms of empire but its marrow.

French, British, Belgian, German, and Dutch colonial administrations in Southeast Asia, the Pacific, Asia, and Africa instituted labor regimes, social policies, urban planning, and medical protocols that produced and marked off social kinds, consolidated racial taxonomies and actively reordered the intimate spaces in which people lived. Understanding why those who governed cared so much about those spaces — what they imagined they could control and what they imagined occurred there — has altered our sense of governance and of how people defied it. Those tense and tender ties played out in beds, kitchens, nurseries, and schoolrooms were secured and subverted by too much knowledge and not enough, by newly acquired tastes, cadences of speech and movement within and outside what people at particular times considered private or called "home."

Those who governed the Netherlands' Indies, British Malaya, and French Indochina saw concubinage between European men and Asian women as a problem when they worried about political subversion. It is *they* who proposed the establishment of segregated nurseries in the Indies when anxious about European political loyalties, they who launched repeated commissions investigating domestic arrangements between women of color and colonial men when they feared growing political disaffections among subordinate whites. It was among those ministers of colonies, directors of education, labor, and public health who ran racialized states and their reformist institutions, operating within *their* racialized regimes of truth, not those of postcolonial scholars, that matters of the intimate were squarely identified as matters of state.

This volume summons these insights to work through — and push on — a basic set of premises: that matters of the intimate are critical sites for the consolidation of colonial power, that management of those domains provides a strong pulse on how relations of empire are exercised, and that affairs of the intimate are strategic for empire-driven states. To pose these as points of reference is not to suggest consensus on what counts as the intimate and why it matters. Few of the essays concur on *how* domains of the intimate relate to the structured violences of imperial states. Similarly, if there is some accord on the relevance of the concerns of colonial studies to North American history there is less on *how* these histories converge — and why their historiographies should as well. Such dissonance provides the grit and grist of the volume.

What is shared is an analytic disposition to extend our historical imaginations in often unrehearsed and awkward ways — to consider social imaginaries of high and low, colonial subjects, agents and architects that spanned continents and traversed empires and national borders.[5] What is also shared is a willingness to think about the *distribution of sentiments* within and between empire's subjects and citizens as part of imperial statecraft, to envision the interior landscapes of ordinary women and men caught in the movements that dislocation and dispossession coerced or cajoled. Not least is a shared commitment to think the intimate through and *beyond* the domestic and through and beyond the management of sex. We ask — in very different ways — how habits of the heart and comportment have been recruited to the service of colonial governance but never wholly subsumed by it. We attend, again with different emphasis and consequence, to those proximities of power — close encounters, unspoken knowledge, in close quarters — in which racialized differences might be recessed or held in brutal relief.

Some senses and sites of the intimate are foregrounded over others. Domestic space, schooling, and public hygiene figure prominently in this volume; the pungent, violent intimacy of prisons, barracks, and detention centers does not. Abu Ghraib and Guantánamo Bay haunt the edges of these pages, pressing for further attention. Unexplored here, they declare the limits of our collective purview, reminding us that the colonial intimacies are first and foremost sites of intrusive interventions.

4   Ann Laura Stoler

Attention here is on the social categories that comparison demands and the explicit and tacit commensurabilities that acts of comparison require. Colonialism was at once a comparative endeavor and a protracted war of assessments over what could be measured by common principles of right and rule—and who should be exempt or excluded from them. What Ian Hacking calls "making up people" is a critical colonial project—a racially laden measuring of what is thought to distinguish human kinds.[6] Such assessments were dependent on what could and could not be seen, on visible markers of distinction as well as nonvisible ones, on evaluations of implicit cultural competencies as much as a mastery of public recognized norms.[7] The management of bodies and dispositions—and racialized thinking about them—underwrote the most benevolent reforms. Social reform enlisted the participation of agents to distinguish social categories and to assign which intrusions and interventions of body and person could be foisted on them: on a subject population (but not a republican citizenry), on a colonized population (but not on colonizing whites), on impoverished poor white settlers (but not well-heeled "real" Europeans), and on enslaved black groups (but not on Native Americans).

If comparison is a scholarly, analytic task, it is also a historical and political one. We begin with the observation that colonialisms' actors and agents critically reflected on analogous governing practices and on those earlier and contemporary contexts from which lessons might be learned. Attending to their practices of comparison opens to their personal and professional trajectories—and sometimes to unexpected and subjacent connections. Looking to "other littorals" than the Atlantic hub of U.S. history takes us with a French slave manager in eighteenth-century Louisiana away from the Yankee continent to the "proper caresses and prudent distance" he culled from across the Caribbean.[8] Russians moving eastward to Alaska in the 1780s worried over the activities of "North American Republicans" in the Northwest and thought about their own colonial projects in relation to some European models of settlement and not others. But it was their prior Siberian experience that shaped immediate strategies to produce progeny and profits—as well as their comparative imaginations. The specific nature of the fur trade, not St. Petersburg mores, guided which kinds of domestic unions the local Russian Orthodox Church sanctioned for Aleut and Alutiiq women and Russian men.[9] Some, like the U.S. protestant missionaries in the Middle East, brought their notions of tolerance with them. In the 1840s they sought to Christianize Ottoman Arabs just after failing to do so among Native Americans at home.[10]

Some comparisons were *between* empires, not *within* them. Alexis de Tocqueville's understanding of democracy and imperialism derived in part from the double vision he maintained throughout the 1830s and 1840s, from what he knew of democracy and Amerindian annihilation in America and French colonial policies in North Africa.[11] And in the nineteenth-century Pacific, with its convergence of German, French, and U.S. empires, officials competed to assign sovereignty by identifying individual subjects, making every move in relation to "half-castes," what Damon Salesa aptly describes as "an intimate manifestation of an international frontier."[12]

Attuning our historical senses to these movements and exchanges allows us to consider principles of comparison of historical actors themselves — what they conceived as equivalent contexts, glossed over as common features or marked off as wholly uncommon ground. In short, histories of what was rendered comparable and/or incommensurable at any one time have a story to tell of their own. The U.S. senator who noted in 1850 that comparison becomes impossible when you change the criteria of category inclusion as did the census every few years got just the point.[13] Incomparability compels forgetting, just as comparison prescribes some lessons and effortlessly disavows others.

Attention to the historical categories of comparative practices refuses the comfort of discrete cases, highlighting instead those uneven circuits in which knowledge was produced and in which people were compelled to move. Not least, it brings into "sharper resolution" the kinds of knowledge generated — and on which people might draw — across imperial terrains and within them.[14] But global circuits of knowledge production were never abstract. They were peopled with those who moved, changed identities, were captivated by alien cultural forms that they borrowed to reinvent their own. Actual people dismantled some aspects of colonial cultures, but many more did not. Those thresholds of inside and out were *not* confined to those people caught on the margins — as if "mixed-bloods" and "half-castes" were the only categories of people wrought with interior battles of bitterness and grief. Thresholds of inside and out were spread throughout the population and a fundamental feature of colonial situations, not unlike the dissociations Albert Memmi describes for French colonials in North Africa, who were quick to criticize the colonial administration, and to distinguish their own good works and intentions from it, while enjoying the privileges and pleasures it conferred.[15]

Treating governance through the microphysics of daily lives has redirected historians to new readings of familiar archives and to new genres of documentation. It also has changed *how* we read—for discrepant tone, tacit knowledge, stray emotions, extravagant details, "minor" events. These elements can index how people made sense of these colonial conditions, what they successfully navigated or failed to maneuver. And they should train what ethnographic sensibilities we bring to our accounts. Orphanage records, housekeeping manuals, treatises on domestic hygiene, school medical reports, debates over breast-feeding, nurseries, and kindergartens (long part of the repertoire of feminist and family historians) now pertain to understanding the distances that separated imperial prescriptions from governing practices in ways they previously had not.

That new roster has drawn students of the colonial to subjacent histories wedged in the folds of dominant ones and to "dense transfer points of power" lodged in the proximities of socialization, crystallized in the distance between proper sentiments and misdirected affections, and caught in the interstices of elaborate state inspection systems for prostitutes that detailed the defects of diseased bodies but could not manage desire—much less sex.[16] New notions of the political—where it is located and how it might be expressed—have revised whose stories count, what kinds of stories count, and who is considered among empire's key, if not principal, agents and actors.

This sort of focus and the trajectories traced are familiar to U.S. historians. Students of U.S. social history (long committed to histories from below) and those of U.S. gender history (formative proponents of why and how the personal is political) have drafted some of these maps. What collectively compels us here is how attention to these sorts of intimate spaces may refigure what are taken to be common features of imperial regimes. Do relations in these "transfer points of power" tell new stories of North American empires that resonate differently with colonial practices elsewhere? And if so, how might those insights recast our accounts and reframe what we take to be admissible narratives?

Recastings are under several constraints, not least because some of the defining concepts developed in studies of the "ur" European imperial states sit awkwardly on North American terrain: "Metropole" and "colony" may "work" to describe the distance and difference separating the American Philippines and the United States in 1898, but the dichotomy seems "unsuited" when applied to the enmity lines that separate Native American residential schools from their surroundings or poor whites, Mexicans, and blacks from white ranchers on the Mexico-Texas border.[17] And how to understand New Mexico in the late nineteenth century—the last state incorporated into the continental United States and the only one with no prohibition on interracial marriage—that was inside the boundaries of the United States but, with respect to understandings of racial categories and sexual unions, was geared to "other littorals."[18]

North America's interior annexations, containments of peoples, "non-colonial" expansions, and outright occupations that run from Guam and Samoa to Puerto Rico and Cuba, from the Philippines to Tennessee, and Oklahoma to the Middle East neither respect the territorial transparency of the dichotomy between domestic and overseas nor conform to the metropole/colony model. The categories of "colonizer" and "colonized" are rendered "forced" as well. The fact that there were and are such gradations of sovereignty in U.S. expansions should not undermine the rationale for referring to these diverse spaces as part of a U.S. imperial formation. On the contrary, technologies of colonial rule have depended on that variation.

Students of European colonialism have questioned the simplicity of these dichotomies for some time. Indeed, the once conventional notion that British, French, and Dutch empires were made up of a "centralized bureaucracy operating as an imperial center," now seen through the lens of misinformation, mistranslation, and bungled reports, has been largely abandoned. In the Dutch East Indies, as in French Indochina, the administration was often "manned" by people with limited social and linguistic knowledge of those they were there to manage, who were rattled by dissensions in their own ranks and by inept prescriptions for rule.

But the fulsome entry of the history of U.S. sovereignty into the analytic and political fray of imperial studies—the entry of this "aberrant" empire that intermittently has refused to call itself by that name—raises new

Ann Laura Stoler

questions about the ubiquity of the frame. At issue for some is whether the broader band of territorial annexations, occupations, and hemispheric divisions make the United States an "empire" or not. "Empire," like "frontier," may be "an unsubtle concept in a subtle world"; nevertheless, it marks the interlaced forms of economic and cultural impositions and holdings that such an unsubtle macropolity allows.[19] The slippage between what is "colonial" and what is "imperial" in the U.S. context is more than a fraught scholarly debate. It is part of the very histories we seek to retrace here and their politics of comparison.

These uncertainties are not conceptual liabilities but entry points for analysis. They serve to challenge what constitutes colonialisms "proper" as much as what constitutes the U.S. "exception." Blurred genres invite better questions. What is taken for the fuzzy sovereign status of U.S. "dependencies," "trusteeships," and "unincorporated territories" may render U.S. empire more opaque. But opaque declarations of authority, "epistemic murk," and "semblances of sovereignty" are all part of the deep grammar of restricted rights and entitlements in the imperial world.[20] Most important, those who inhabited those indeterminate places and who were subjected to those ambiguous spaces were neither beyond the reach of imperial force nor out of imperial bounds.

As I have argued elsewhere, blurred genres are not empires in distress but imperial polities in active realignment and reformation. A combination of high-profile treaties, unwritten agreements, unacknowledged coercive tactics, financial bodies, and agribusinesses serving as surrogate states are empire's common features.[21] The "intimate connection" that Hannah Arendt observed "between imperialist politics and rule by 'invisible government' and secret agents" is fundamental to imperial architectures.[22] Some might argue that being an effective empire has long been contingent on partial visibility—sustaining the ability to remain an affective and unaccountable one.

Distinctly marked boundaries and transparent transfers of property represent a limited range of imperial forms and their orientations. Thus a starting point may be *not* to begin with a notion of empire based on a British imperial steady-state, a color-coded school map with fixed, clearly bounded units, but with a notion of empire that puts movement and oscillation at the center: to see them instead as states of becoming (and, for those ruled, as states of deferral), as polities with protean rather than fixed taxonomies and mobile populations whose designated borders at any one time were not necessarily the force fields in which they operated or even their sovereign limits. The United States is not a phantom empire just because it is a flexible one.

Which leads back to another question: why the imperial frame seems "forced" to some and the rubrics and vocabulary of postcolonial scholarship "contrived" in U.S. contexts? Do these terms seem forced because they have been made not to fit, because historical actors refused the term *empire* while practicing its tactics? Or was the United States an empire of a different sort, supported by what W. E. B. Du Bois called an "educated ignorance," what Neil Smith has described as a dissonant history of formidable state geographic intelligence and "popular geographical illiteracy" that has figured the nature of U.S. empire and its forms of expansion?[23] And is the "uniqueness" of U.S. empire built not on a difference from European modes but on a willful compartmentalization of its entangled parts?

Or have the refusals been located more squarely in U.S. historiography, where students asking what bearing Native American history may have had on the annexation of the Philippines might be redirected within domestic borders and chided for spreading themselves too thin? Tunnel vision also constricts queries the other way around. Students of early-nineteenth-century French colonial policies in Algeria only recently have been encouraged to consider its racial policies in light of those established in the United States. Nor would the British residential school system as initiated in Canada in 1879, which so assiduously attempted to reorder the sensory tastes and intimate spaces of its charges, be viewed up against the activities of the YMCA in South Africa, or the forced separation of half-caste Aboriginal children from their parents — Australia's "stolen generation" in the same years.[24]

The specific "dangers" of conjecture, superficial similarity, noncontextualized practices, and arbitrary comparison are clear. Trait-based comparison evokes the worst of early anthropology and warrants disparagements of historians disdainful of a generic generalizing enterprise rather than a peopled, context-driven one.[25] Here we are more interested in concomitant *constellations* of practices and convergent effects and, most important, with re-envisioning what circuits of knowledge production are considered as "context."

Still, one cannot help but wonder if those "dangers" of conjecture invite exposures of another kind: of ensnared relations between democracy and empire, liberalism and colonialism, compassion and race that still remain outside some national master narratives. A politics of sympathy generated by domestic and overseas empire runs deep and strong throughout U.S. history, much as "a little romance of misery" excited the sympathies of British antislavery advocates on tour in the 1820s of points in the southeastern United States.[26] And as Laura Briggs argues here, the contemporary international adoption industry rests on the maintenance of a sharp disconnect between transnational adoption, as a project of child rescue for white consumers from the North, and direct U.S. involvement in Guatemalan and Nicaraguan violences. That disconnect in part has made possible these children's "availability."[27] When Michael Ignatieff warns that "in becoming an empire the U.S. risks losing its soul as a republic," the assumption is that these are—*and have been*—mutually exclusive categories in the history of U.S. expansion.[28]

But any number of students of U.S. history or colonial studies could argue otherwise. Edmund Morgan has taught us that the very basis of republican ideals and practices consolidated exclusions and set in motion a whole new set of them; Uday Mehta has shown that the exclusions generated through liberalism's principles were foundational to the social discriminations of the British Empire.[29] Lisa Lowe's analysis takes us further, arguing that "degrees of unfreedom," rather than freedom or not, "unevenly distributed across the globe" were the norm rather than the exception. Degrees of unfreedom made it possible to affirm certain liberties at the expense of refusing their applicability to other populations.[30] These are political issues grounded in epistemological ones: how we know and the bases of that knowledge "suspend" some histories and make others hard to think, frame, or tell.

Still, our analytic quandaries over the comparative treatment of imperial formations may also lie elsewhere: not only in the compartmentalization of knowledge in the archives or historiographies but in an analytic vocabulary inadequate to the task of making these comparisons. If reasoning is impossible without comparison, as Hume argued, and if comparisons are always theory driven, as Wittgenstein claimed, then how do we understand a pervasive vocabulary of race and reform, of inclusion and exclusion that cuts across the globe without being "global," that was consolidated by colonial polities but not confined to them, and that displays a durability and portability that exceed colonial empires and their exemplary cases? Macropolities may share in technologies of rule that work through people's bodies and hearts in recognizably similar ways *without* necessarily sharing the same grids of intelligibility that make common sense of those practices.

In the design of the 1890 U.S. census, Martha Hodes finds "imperialist concerns within domestic borders," prompting us to ask whether what Ben Anderson calls the "confusedly classifying mind of the colonial state," to which Hodes alludes, was also shared by national polities but with a different force and weight.[31] The ambiguities of the census categories fortified state authority in the United States. Such ambiguities, as in other colonial contexts, like that of colonial Indonesia, were not necessarily vulnerable links in a system of exclusion but part of the plasticity of a power apparatus.

Challenges to what constitutes the principles of empire are coming from new positions and new locations. Students of the Japanese, Chinese, Russian, and Ottoman empires argue that the organization and policing of differences in these empire-states are clearly "colonial" but often bear little resemblance to racially infested European models. Others contend that contiguous and continental imperial expansions bore different social relations of tolerance and dominance as well.[32] Students of the Spanish Empire argue that Northern European racialized states were built on the inquisitorial, terror tactics of sixteenth-century Spain;[33] U.S. and Canadian historical studies are reconsidering cultures of empire forged at the violent *thresholds* where internal enemies were conflated with external ones. The interior frontiers of the nation-state, as evinced in the treaties with Native Americans, were as dependent on colonial relations of dominance as were any of Europe's external incursions.[34]

Similarly, the terrain and tenor of postcolonial scholarship have also changed to consider afresh how we think about empire, what histories have been suspended, and how we might write differently about them.[35] Forms of empire once outside its purview, deemed aberrant or "quasi empires" (like the "temporary" British occupation of the Falklands that lasted two hundred years or the "temporary" use of Guantánamo as a U.S. military way station at the start of the twenty-first century), no longer look like exceptions. Global events have placed empire under new scrutiny, helping to remind us that "exceptionalism" is a shared self-description of imperial forms and that every empire imagines itself an exception. Hodes's use of the phrase *domestic colonialism* to include the postslavery conditions of African American populations, the "internal colonialism" of Native Americans, and border relations in southern states, as well as Linda Gordon's insights that recoup "internal colonialism" for a broader swath of U.S. history counter that trend.[36]

Locating the boundaries of what and who was "inside" and "out" is not an abstract administrative task. Nor did it ever reduce to a legally prescribed territorial one. The threshold between inside and out cuts through families and across them, traces through selective genealogies and adoption agencies, "degrees of blood" and dense webs of fictive kin. And the effects of blood quanta could cut many ways. Evidence of a "drop of blood" could bar African Americans from citizenship, marriage, and mobility; starting in the 1880s Japanese and South Asians alternately won and lost access to citizenship based on determinations of their inclusion or exclusion from the category of Caucasian or Aryan. In the 1920s evidence of being less than one-half Indian conferred citizenship on "mixed-blood" Indians, reducing the size of tribes and making their subjection contingent on how state officials assessed their individual and collective capacity for self-governance.[37] But there is nothing linear about this history. Who had what "percentage" of blood that was labeled black, white, red, or brown may have been given credence in a language of scientific measurement, but it was recognition of sexual unions, silences about rape, acknowledgment of kinship, genealogies of affiliations, and knowledge of intimacies that mattered more to where the "color" line was drawn.

Where one "belonged" was reckoned, in part, by the cultivation of the self — by one's desires and by that for which *one ceased to long*. John Demos has brilliantly taught us what made an "unredeemed captive" in early America like the young Eunice Williams — an eminent minister's daughter who took a Mohawk husband and chose to remain with her captors.[38] Those in colonial Indonesia in the 1880s who did not "go native" but did choose a Javanese over a Dutch husband lost their rights to Dutch citizenship and often their cultural prerogatives to be considered really European. But "going native" was a white category — like "playing Indian." As Tiya Miles writes, when the African American reverend John Marrant refused a black identity in favor of an Indian one, he was staking important personal and economic claims on those intimate associations.[39]

This is not a choice between "trendy" topics and less "sexy" ones. *To study the intimate is not to turn away from structures of dominance but to relocate their conditions of possibility and relations and forces of production.* Foucault's "biopolitics" — the notion that power relations are played out in how bodies are aggregated and individuated, healed, buried, made indistinguishable, and marked—provides not an abstract model but one analytic tool for asking grounded questions about whose bodies and selves were made vulnerable, when, why, and how—and whose were not.[40] Rather than serve as a "distraction" from the "blood, sweat and tears" of colonial relations (as Ramón Gutiérrez chided in an earlier exchange), it may do exactly the opposite. Refocusing on the intimate opens to what haunts those social relations, to the untoward, to the strangely familiar that proximities and inequalities may produce.[41] Affective histories open to the uses and abuses that unsolicited and even desired intimacies may incite—lessons that feminism long has schooled us to identify and to which many of this volume's authors have been key contributors. Not least, it reminds us how central the emotional economy of sexual access, parenting, and domestic arrangements have been to colonial policies of labor recruitment and pacification—and the touchstone of noncompliance with them.

Intimacy is obviously not the only transfer point of colonial relations, nor is Foucault's concept of biopower the only tool we might use to understand how the intimacies generated from imperial contexts work. The strangely familiar "uncanny" intimacies alluded to above may leave room for relations that promise something else, that activate desires and imaginaries less easily named. An attentive reader might want to think with and beyond these essays to relations and spaces askew to those we present: to the ecstatic intimacy of religious conversion, to the crushing scent of torture, to what gets shared in disaster, involuntary dependence, or deprivation in contingent moments and unpredicted events.

A focus on "tense and tender ties" may lead to more "palatable" histories of interracial contacts if it rehearses an understanding of the affective heavily weighted to the "tender" and not to the range of sentiments and *ressentiments* of outrage and violation that the authors in this volume make mandatory for consideration. Paul Kramer does not let us forget that *rough riders* referred to those U.S. soldiers with venereal disease in the Philippines and that it was foot soldiers engaged in the occupation of the Philippines who cast that invasion as acts of "rough sex"—connecting the politics of sexuality to the politics of empire.[42]

What government strictures regulated the movements of household servants, what legal dictates made it impossible for a native woman to demand child support from the European father of her mixed-blood offspring, what social norms made domestic rape of a native housekeeper by a European man a private issue and the "attempted rape" of a European woman by a native man an incitement to stricter labor laws and a public call to arms touched those at the top and bottom. Distinctions made between the public and private were among a host of categories fundamental to how racialized empire states managed their agents and subjects—and what was shared in how they were differently ruled. As Damon Salesa writes about Samoa, intimate relations were indeed "occasioned by imperialism yet initially beyond its effective jurisdictions."[43] Even those intimacies that were outside the formal jurisdiction of the state could not, in the end, remain beyond it; state regulations impinged on how people as subjects were formed. These relations are not merely good illustrations, "microcosms" of how colonial privileges and deprivations were unequally distributed. They were the ground of contestations.

A striking feature of our collective engagement with the intimate is how differently we use it. What counts as the intimate—aside from "authenticity or ultimate belonging"—is part of our collective query.[44] For some it glosses the sensory, the affective, and domestic space. For others domains of the intimate build borders, create distances, mark off knowledge and shared forms of it. As Svetlana Boym puts it, intimacy does not inhabit the "outskirts of the social" but rather provides the terms of its definition. For Warwick Anderson the making of intimacy encompassed the expert and habituated benevolence of the state, which in the name of public health was "licensed to palpate, handle, bruise, test, and mobilize individuals," refashioning intimacies within these populations.[45] Colonial intimacies engender "precarious affections": awkward familiarities, unsolicited attentions, uninvited caresses, probings that cannot be easily refused.[46]

For others intimacy has less to do with the privileged secrets close encounters are thought to bestow than with something akin to Heidegger's notion of "nearness"—not something that can be measured by physical distance so much as the degree of involvement, engagement, concern, and attention one gives to it.[47] Whether that involvement be sexual relations or other bodily contact or tactile relations, whether it be in kitchen, field, school, or home—we explore how and why these offer strategic sites for assessing the contingent and convergent strategies of governance of both a wide range of colonizing regimes and the agents of their macropolities.

Because expressions of intimacy are so implicated in the exercise of power, they provide strategic nodes of comparison, unevenly laced with state effects. But giving weight to the intimate is not to suggest that these are the sites of deeper truths where the secrets of the state are stored. What it does allow is a call to question cherished assumptions: that the intimate is located primarily in the family, that the family is a ready model for, and microcosm of, the state, and that affective ties are inherently tender ones.

Instead, these authors work different senses of the intimate that hover in the proximities of personhood, the nearness of others, the closed space in which unspoken knowledge is shared. Tiya Miles shows how the Reverend John Marrant staked his claims on belonging to Native American culture on his corporal and emotional closeness to it. Laura Wexler's symptomatic reading reminds us that the hermeneutic of intimacy might actually rest on the inaccessible and unseen — and that haunted memory and dream space are parts of it.[48] Alexandra Stern traces the desire to make the latent something patent and measurable to lead us through the imperial coordinates of intelligence testing and through the circuits by which that scientific knowledge was produced. As she shows, racialized assumptions about the inner person were first rejected by Mexican scientists only to be later implicitly embraced by them.

HAUNTED BY EMPIRE: CONJUNCTURES
AND CRITICAL IMAGINARIES

Some edited volumes are disparate collections; some are truly collective projects. This one is neither. Rather, it reflects crosscutting and convergent conversations among its authors — sustained within disciplines, spirited across them, and sometimes contending with one another. Not least, the volume reflects the ongoing process of its formation — and in the end bears a shape of its own. What marks this venture is what it spans: the political conjuncture, the persons involved, the scholarly moment. It could be read as a set of responses or reactions to the essay I wrote (that appears here as the "archival" next chapter) in 1999 for the *Journal of American History*. The volume centers on three conceptual themes of that essay: (1) the politics of comparison, (2) proximities of power and their affective bonds, and (3) circuits of knowledge production between and within imperial projects.

But several things should become quickly clear. While these contributions are joined by that essay, they are never mere commentaries, neither elaborations nor "illustrative," of it. Each works through and against deep currents in North American historiography, cutting through, revolving around, and moving beyond those issues that motivated mine. Perhaps because students of the colonial have so long insisted that empire is a gendered history of power, my essay assumed that frame and placed its emphasis less squarely in that direction. But these essays return us to gender and sexuality with deliberate intent and renewed rigor. Scales and practices of comparison are rethought, circuits of knowledge production are traced through their creators and carriers, senses of the intimate are reworked and challenged.

Initially prompted by an invitation from Linda Gordon, my essay addressed two pointed questions: one, how readily the concerns of those studying domains of the intimate in colonial studies might speak to new ways of understanding what is colonial and imperial in the history of the United States? And two, a question that, as the project developed, turned the first query around: how might the messy distinctions in the United States, the very discomfort and overlap between imperialism and colonialism in U.S. contexts, help us think the tacit assumptions about European empire elsewhere? The questions were not mine alone. Conversations (about race and sexuality and empire) were in progress, global connections were being pursued (particularly in environmental studies and gender history), and (interdisciplinary) "introductions" had already been made. In scope, scale, and critical imagery these essays speak to an intellectual exchange that precedes and exceeds my own intervention.

"Tense and Tender Ties" was written as an essay before September 11, 2001, and conceived as a volume prior to the 2003 occupation of Iraq. Its contributions were completed before this round of U.S. military interventions, which in the familiar name of patriotic protection and moral obligation were celebrated and given credence with carefully culled Roman and British comparisons. More explicitly than in my *JAH* essay, the violence of colonial intimacies marks these contributions, giving deep historic resonance to the Abu Ghraib prison-abuse scandal that plastered digital images across the globe of a woman military officer pointing at the genitals of a hooded Iraqi prisoner. Gwenn Miller, Shannon Dawdy, Laura Briggs, and Alex Stern speak to the affective violences of sovereign stretch. Not least, the volume takes up what has been richest in both U.S. history and colonial studies—historiographic operations that move between a wide angle and close-up lens.

Some might argue that John Demos has already schooled us to understand that the iconic narrative of colonial encounter was a searingly intimate one—one that pushed bodies into new habits and limbs into new kinds of clothes, forced senses to respond to new smells and tastes. He has shown us what it meant to be captured by native culture and captivated by it, to be seized by its hidden force, to be lured away—to be educated to new dispositions and desires. The fine-grained focus is similar, but now we seek a broader frame. "Captivity narratives," like child rescue, are an imperial genre, albeit not a uniquely North American one.[49]

Together these authors take critical license with conceptual content and creative license with form. In so doing they press on my *JAH* essay's themes and move beyond them. Writing different histories of the United States and the subterranean veins of empire requires innovative historiographic operations, a vivid historical imagery, unfamiliar juxtapositions of archives, new content, and new forms. In these essays the "global" and the "local" seem flat compared to the layered set of circuits these authors track and the thickening and thinning of them. Interdisciplinary promises are often celebrated in the abstract but less often carried out. Here the conversations are among historians, anthropologists, and students of literature, philosophy, and public health. Alexandra Stern urges and demonstrates experiment with an "informed imagination" about what inter-American circuits of knowledge production are not readily visible and why they are not. She points to imperial movements "below the radar" of obvious complicities and connections to conflicts over inner disposition written into the very frame of intelligence testing and their multiple-choice questions.

Martha Hodes takes us on an imaginary nineteenth-century journey between the Caribbean colonial Grand Cayman Island and the domestic United States through the census categories of a family, examining how each member would have been made to "fit" smoothly into census parameters. She offers us the possibility of imagining people whose biographical and familial traces took them through imperial locations, of census takers whose "take" on race was shaped by civil war, of a husband whose race shifted when he was in the British Caribbean and not the United States. Emily Rosenberg follows the peregrinations of U.S. financial advisers and the imperial practices embodied in their services. She reminds us that circuits of knowledge production are not immobile routes comprising well-worn paths but are roadways under construction, traveled by individual carriers who use and reroute them.

Others, like Laura Wexler and Kathleen Brown, have sought ways to identify the imperial filaments of a world that informed their actors, when the latter only vaguely and in passing noted those connections. Laura Wexler works with nonverbal evidence to imagine the subliminal histories of a woman haunted by empire. Kathleen Brown fills out the habitus of a woman that empire only seemed to graze. Shannon Dawdy reads "how-to" manuals inside out for unruly sentiments, scents, and differences designed to be managed. Warwick Anderson stretches his own and our comparative imaginations across "apparently unrelated homologies" through the governing logic of the "transcolonial taxonomy of hygiene" that produced distressed and estranged liminal beings—lepers in the Philippines, half-castes in Australia—in what otherwise might be read as disparate contexts. Lisa Lowe invokes multiple notions of the intimate to reimagine histories of Asian, African, and native people in the Americas entangled in a tight embrace rather than careening in different forgotten directions. Nayan Shah rethinks the sovereign stretch of what is in and outside U.S. jurisdiction through marriage documents, birth records, and civil suits and not least by tracking the "waves of silence" interspersed with letters and telegrams that passed between the Punjab and the Southwest.[50]

CONCLUSION: ON CONTENTION, EXTENSION,
AND COMPARISON

If there is a commitment that both postcolonial historical scholarship and U.S. social historians share, it is an effort to write histories from the bottom up, histories that confront both the systemic constraints under which people live and the forms in which they redefine those constraints or move around them. Still, some students of U.S. history have queried whether a focus on empire and its broad-scale movements can allow historians to be attentive to both and, concomitantly, whether a "theoretical disposition that privileges processes of domination" and "policies of imperial states" may sideswipe social history and the ties between popular refusals and imperial design.[51] Both warnings share a common concern that "the small voices of history" may not receive their due. This "romance of resistance" models "agency" on the side of the colonized, and the inert structural weight of state institutions on the side of the colonizer.

Impatience comes from many quarters.[52] Historians of colonialism cannot write against the grain of imperial history and state-endorsed archives without attending to the competing logics of those who ruled and their fractious ranks.[53] It is not necessarily reworked subaltern histories of the "intimate desires of colonial subjects" that meets that challenge so much as histories that run askew into official paper trails and cut across the legal bonds of marriage and family. That state scripts speak in the metaphors of family is less interesting than the alienations of affection that state institutions produce and endorse. As Warwick Anderson shows for eugenic policies and Laura Briggs shows for international adoption strategies, these practices demand two things: that subjects forget "darker," impoverished family ties and that they show their "natural" desire for cleaner, more modern, and whiter ones. Tracking these affective redistributions means working "along the grain" of political rationalities that were not confined to any one nation and understanding their logic first.

Doing so restores to colonial cultures the ambiguous affiliations and ambivalent allegiances of those living in them. It renders the exclusionary practices of social reform, not as historical, quaint forms of racism but as uncomfortably familiar and at hand. As long as these phenomena are treated as realities of an Other moment, and empire as something on which domestic history and prosperity does not depend, ethnographies of empire will remain safely out of relevant bounds rather than what they should be — implicated histories in the disquieting present.

NOTES

1. On "the politics of comparison" see Stoler, "Tense and Tender Ties."

2. For an early formulation see Berger and Luckman, *The Social Construction of Reality*. On social constructionism and power see Dirks, Eley, and Ortner, *Culture/Power/History*, 3–47. On analytic turns from the "making" of class to the "imagining" of [national] community to the "making of race" see my "[P]Refacing Capitalism and Confrontation in 1995." And for a critique of all the above see Hacking, *The Social Construction of What?*

3. Stoler, "Genealogies of the Intimate."

4. On the "distribution of sentiments" as the substance of colonial governing projects see Stoler, "Affective States."

5. On the "social imaginary" see Taylor, *Modern Social Imaginaries*, 23–26.

6. See Hacking, "Making Up People."

7. On the patent vs. latent markers of race see Stoler, "Racial Histories and Their Regimes of Truth," 369–91, 417–21.

8. See Dawdy, this volume.

9. Miller, this volume.

10. Makdisi, "Bringing America Back into the Middle East."

11. Tocqueville, *Writings on Empire and Slavery*.

12. Salesa, this volume.

13. Hodes, this volume.

14. Stern, this volume.

15. Memmi, *The Colonizer and the Colonized*.

16. Kramer, this volume.

17. See Foley, *The White Scourge*.

18. Shah, this volume.

19. Limerick, *Legacy of Conquest*, 25.

20. On "epistemic murk" see Taussig, "Culture of Terror–Space of Death"; on the sliding scale of sovereignties see Aleinikoff, *Semblances of Sovereignty*. On explicit contests over degrees of sovereignty see Osborne, "Empire Can Wait."

21. Stoler, "Degrees of Imperial Sovereignty."

22. Arendt, *The Origins of Totalitarianism*, xx.

23. Du Bois, "Darkwater," 503; Smith, *American Empire*, 3.

24. On the abuses of the Canadian residential school system see Milloy, *A National Crime*. On the "stolen generation" in Australia see Anderson, this volume.

25. Kramer, this volume.

26. As Frances Trollope wrote in 1828 in *Domestic Manners of the Americans*, 3. On the "deep history" of "American" charity and philanthropy see Friedman and McGarvie, *Charity, Philanthropy, and Civility in American History*.

27. Briggs, this volume.

28. Ignatieff, "The American Empire," 24.

29. Morgan, *American Slavery, American Freedom*; Mehta, *Liberalism and Empire*.

30. Lowe, this volume.

31. Hodes, this volume.

32. For explicit attempts to think with and through colonial categories see, e.g., Bassin, "Inventing Siberia"; Bassin, *Imperial Visions*; Burbank and Ransel, *Imperial Russia*; Tamanoi, "Knowledge, Power, and Racial Classifications"; "Native Peoples and Colonialism"; Sunderland, *Taming the Wild Field*. On tolerance, see Makdisi, "Bringing America Back into the Middle East" (forthcoming).

33. Silverblatt, *Modern Inquisitions*. Also see Kammen, *The Spanish Inquisition*.

34. Kaplan, *The Anarchy of Empire in the Making of U.S. Culture*. Also see Hall, *The American Empire and the Fourth World*; Seed, *American Pentimento*.

35. See Stoler, "Introduction: Reassessing Imperial Terrain"; "Refractions off Empire."

36. See Hodes, this volume; Gordon, this volume.

37. See Biolsi, "The Birth of the Reservation." This is again an issue of historical comparisons and congruencies: differential treatment presumed assimilability of some and not others. The assimilability of African and Indian "blood" has a long history in the Spanish Empire. See Silverblatt, *Modern Inquisitions*. See also Ngai, *Impossible Subjects*; and Lopez, *White by Law*. I thank Alex Stern for urging me to flesh out the Asian American part of this blood quantum equation.

38. Demos, *The Unredeemed Captive*.

39. Miles, this volume; also see her "Uncle Tom Was an Indian."

40. On biopolitics and empire see my *Race and the Education of Desire*.

41. See Gutiérrez, "What's Love Got to Do with It?"

42. Kramer, this volume.

43. Salesa, this volume.

44. Boym, "Diasporic Intimacy," 252. For studies of "intimacy" that move deliberately away from its private coordinates see Herzfeld, *Cultural Intimacy*; Berlant, introduction, 1–8; and Shryock, *Off Stage/On Display*, all of which refer to Habermas's discussion in *The Structural Transformations of the Public Sphere*, 141–59.

45. Anderson, this volume.

46. Boym, "Diasporic Intimacy," 252.

47. Heidegger, "The Thing," 175; Weinter, *Tree Leaf Talk*, 28.

48. I thank Lisa Lowe for sharing this observation about Laura Wexler's essay.

49. On the British imperial version see Colley, *Captives*.

50. Shah, this volume. Some, like Paul Kramer, were more wary of both the "counter-intuitive" and the rich historical imaginary that others in this volume call on to trace unarticulated histories of what was and of what might be.

51. See Renda, "Sentiments of a Private Nature"; and Ginzburg, "Global Acts, Local Acts."

52. Jean and John Comaroff, for example, have argued that "histories of the repressed in themselves hold [no] special key to revelation if not situated in the wider worlds of power and meaning that gave them life" (Comaroff and Comaroff, *Ethnography and the Historical Imagination*, 17). Also see Fernando Coronil, "Listening to the Subaltern," 649.

53. See my *Along the Archival Grain*.

2

ANN LAURA STOLER

Tense and Tender Ties: The Politics

of Comparison in North American History

and (Post) Colonial Studies

This chapter takes as its subject two distinctive historiographies, one in post-colonial studies and the other in North American history, that both address how intimate domains — sex, sentiment, domestic arrangement, and child rearing — figure in the making of racial categories and in the management of imperial rule. It examines two prevailing trends: on the one hand, an analytic convergence in treatments of, and increasing attention to, intimacy in the making of empire; on the other, recognition of the distinctive conceptual commitments and political investments that shape the fields as separate disciplinary ventures and historiographic domains.[1] Throughout the chapter I call for more reflection on the history and politics of comparison, encourage doing a certain kind of comparative colonial history, and urge attention to practices of colonial comparison by colonial governments themselves.

This chapter comprises three parts. Part 1 looks briefly at recent attention to the intimacies of empire in colonial studies and in research on North America. Part 2 turns to four colonial moments in U.S. history and European expansion that have been extensively compared on some fronts — and that could be compared on others. Part 3 focuses on comparisons that both reinforce recent claims about the limitations of nationally focused comparative history and point to circuits of knowledge production and strategies of racial differentiation with wide resonance. The examples in part 3 are of three kinds: (1) an analysis of mid- to late-nineteenth-century debates about nurseries that addressed the making of sensibilities, citizens, and race; (2) a comparison of vocational schools in the nineteenth-century Dutch East Indies and those designed for Native Americans; and (3) a tracing of the expert knowledge that went into the South African Carnegie Commission of the late 1920s. I draw on these sites to illustrate the value of looking comparatively at circuits of knowledge production, governing practices, and indirect as well as direct connections that informed imperial rule. Each part raises questions about what categories are taken to be commensurable in historical analysis.

For some two decades my work on Indonesia's Dutch colonial history has addressed patterns of governance that were particular to that time and place but resonant with practices in a wider global field. My perspective is that of an outsider to, but an acquisitive consumer of, North American historical studies and one long struck with the disparate and congruent imperial projects in Asia, Africa, and the Americas.[2] This chapter invites reflection on those domains of overlap and difference as it registers the profusion of new insights about "becoming colonial" that students of North American history and colonial studies increasingly share. It looks to the mutual relevance of the two historiographies and grounds for further conversation.

Such projects are already underway. Comprehensive reviews of historians' treatment of empire and efforts to internationalize U.S. history and to trace its transnational linkages have been high on the agendas of students of North American history during the last decade: they are not my task here.[3] This is not an essay against notions of exceptionalism, though it substantiates the reasoning of those who have argued that United States history is not unique. Nor is this chapter a review of the vast range of research on gender and colonialism that cuts across both fields.

My interest is more specifically in what Albert Hurtado refers to as "the intimate frontiers" of empire, a social and cultural space where racial classifications were defined and defied, where relations between colonizer and colonized could powerfully confound or confirm the strictures of governance and the categories of rule. Some two decades ago, the historian Sylvia Van Kirk urged a focus on such "tender ties" as a way to explore the "human dimension" of the colonial encounter. As she showed so well, what Michel Foucault has called these "dense transfer point[s]" of power that generate such ties were sites of production of colonial inequities and therefore of tense ties as well. Among students of colonialisms, the intimacies of empire have become a rich and well-articulated research domain. A more sustained focus on the relationship between what Foucault referred to as "the regimes of truth" of imperial systems (the ways of knowing and establishing truth claims about race and difference on which macropolities rely) and those microsites of governance may reveal how North American histories and those of empires elsewhere compare and converge.[4] Pursuing connections between the broad-scale dynamics of rule and the intimate domains of implementation may suggest more lines of overlapping inquiry and a rethinking of our respective frames.[5]

My examples sketch ways intimate matters and narratives about them figured in defining the racial coordinates and social discriminations of empire. Common to all was a fashioning of moral policies that shaped the boundaries of race. Each points to strategies of exclusion on the basis of social credentials, sensibility, and cultural knowledge. Foucault defined such technologies of rule as "biopolitics"—as part of the political anatomy of states, governing techniques that relied on "the disciplining of individual bodies and the regulations of the life process of aggregate human populations."[6] For those impatient with Foucault, let us say they joined the making of an imperial social policy to the making of persons who were marked as particular sexualized and racialized selves.

Colonial state projects, such as those in the nineteenth- and early-twentieth-century Dutch East Indies, attended minutely to the distribution of appropriate affect (what sentiments could be shown toward, and shared with, whom), to the relations in which carnal desires could be safely directed, to prescriptions for comportment that could distinguish colonizer from colonized, and, as important, to those that finely graded the distinctions of privilege and class among colonizers themselves. My own interest has been in the relation between prescription and practice, in those domestic arrangements, frequently entered into, that could blur distinctions of color and culture but also those that reiterated relations of dominance in kitchens, bedrooms, and nurseries—and behind the barely screened partitions of the colonial army's "family" barracks.[7]

But there is still much more to ask about how civility and racial membership were measured less by what people did in public than in their private lives—with whom they cohabited; who slept with whom, when, and where; who suckled which children; how children were reared and by whom; what language was spoken to servants, friends, and family members at home. When Dutch children in the colonial Indies were forbidden to play with the children of servants lest they become too comfortable "babbling and thinking in Javanese" or when Javanese nursemaids were instructed to hold their charges away from their bodies so that the infants would not "smell of their sweat," more was going on than peevish squabbles over cultural style. Such standards were designed to ensure that European children in the colonies learned the right social affiliations and did not "metamorphose" into Javanese. They were part of the colonial state's investment in knowledge about the carnal, about sensibilities and familiarities, its preoccupying commitment to what I call "the education of desire."[8]

Historians of European expansion in North America as distinct from Asia and Africa often subscribe to a different conceptual vocabulary to describe cultural and racial mixture, the sexual opportunities afforded to colonizing men, the ways native women parlayed their services into private advantage, and the categories designating the children they produced. In turn, my Foucauldian identification of this domain as part of the "microphysics of rule" may be very different from vocabulary current in North American scholarship, whether Gary Nash's "intimate contact zones" or variations on Richard White's richly evocative "middle ground."[9] But those differences in lexicon should not get in the way. Both fields are concerned with the nature of this contested terrain, with fundamental sites of power in the making and unmaking. Both are attentive to the fixity and fluidity of racial taxonomies and those sexual and affective transgressions that formed and refigured the distinctions between ruler and ruled.

CROSSCURRENTS IN COLONIAL STUDIES
AND NORTH AMERICAN HISTORY

Students of colonialism might all agree that gender and race have been high on the agenda of historians studying the United States. We might also all agree that William Appleman Williams's 1955 observation that American empire is absent from American historiography no longer applies. Few would argue that American exceptionalism with respect to colonialism remains a prevailing paradigm. Nevertheless, many historians who take the United States as their subject are still unfamiliar with the new currents in scholarship that have animated colonial studies over the last fifteen years. Students of colonialism, for their part, still pay insufficient attention to early North American history and to the work on "tensions of empire" that historians of the United States have long produced.[10]

Some reasons for this disjuncture are suggested in Amy Kaplan's introduction to *Cultures of United States Imperialism*, published in 1993. As she described it, a "resilient paradigm" of United States domestic and foreign scholarship of the 1950s and 1960s cordoned off empire as a "mere episode" in American history, little more than a twenty-year blip on the democratic and domestic national horizon. In her formulation the denial derived from three phenomena: an absence of culture from the study of U.S. imperialism, an absence of empire from the study of American culture, and an absence of the United States from postcolonial studies of empire.[11] While some historians adamantly disagreed, Kaplan's point was instructive and productively disquieting at the time. Her citations were from an earlier historiography that often conceived American empire as a short-lived moment and a contained project. For that earlier generation the Philippines, Fiji, Cuba, Puerto Rico, and certainly the informal empire that gave U.S. capital, products, and personnel a strong presence throughout the European colonial world of Indonesia, Malaysia, and Indochina were outside United States history proper, unregistered in public memory, and off the popularized map.

But Kaplan's timely assessment was of another moment. A whole generation of social historians, historical anthropologists, and students of American culture have begun to reconsider what in United States domestic history relates to its expansionist strategies of empire, where studies of empire speak to the concerns of United States history, and—not least—what is colonial about "colonial America."[12] Students of Filipino history are demonstrating the parallels between American empire in the Philippines and within U.S. borders, as well as between the U.S. and British empires, bridging what they describe as a sustained separation between historiography on the Philippines and on mainstream America. Edited volumes such as *Close Encounters of Empire* have turned away from how United States imperialism "consolidated" North America and how empire influenced domestic policy to view racial politics from the regions that were colonized. They look to the "representation machines" to which colonized populations were subject, that is, to the ways colonizing populations depicted and categorized them, with emphasis "on the ground." Others have found colonial inflections elsewhere: on the borderlands of Mexico or in regions of western expansion and in the sexualized contact zones of Texas and Arizona, where poor whites, Native Americans, and African Americans met, producing what Jeremy Adelman and Stephen Aron have referred to as "hybrid residuals of these encounters."[13]

Gary Nash's presidential address to the Organization of American Historians in 1995, "The Hidden History of Mestizo America," marks a cusp, the moment of recognition of U.S. history as a "zone of deep intercultural contacts" understood as a space of cultural merging and conjugal relations more than a battleground. But it is the quantity and quality of edited volumes on the intimacies of empire appearing in the last few years that is staggering. All attest to the activity of scholars—both those of a new generation and those already established—who are reframing their questions to consider as fundamental the proposition that if race matters to the history of United States empire, then, as John D'Emilio and Estelle B. Freedman insisted a decade earlier, intimacies must matter as well. American historians across a wide spectrum have sought to understand how political authority was secured and how it worked through the management of marriage, domesticity, child rearing, and sex. More telling still, even in volumes not explicitly devoted to intimacies, a focus on domestic life, miscegenation, and family signals both a broadening trend and a new understanding of why and how those sites are political.[14]

Still, what is striking from the perspective of colonial studies is the circumscribed purview of even some of the best of the new historical scholarship. Nash's elegant and sweeping survey of United States historiography, which places mixing at the heart of American history and recognizes race and the affective as a potent political terrain, has a political agenda—directed more at the present than at the past. It reads as an originary narrative of the deep-rootedness of multiculturalism, rather than biracialism, on the North American landscape. Despite his reference to Salman Rushdie and obliquely to ethnic dislocations elsewhere in the world, Nash's story of crossing racial boundaries remains a celebration of "hybridity" as a source of national redemption and of "mixedness" in the making of the contemporary United States.

To an outsider looking in, Nash's luminous essay invites more than a genealogical reworking of the national narrative. It invites inquiries that engage both the historical specificity of mixedness and its widely varied political coordinates. Such approaches must work productively off the distortions of a close-up and wide-angle lens, reaching for distant and counterintuitive transnational comparisons, as well as those more obvious and oblique to national borders. It invites a wider treatment of "mixedness," showing debates about mestizos, métis, "Indos," and "half-bloods" as sites of imperial anxieties in colonial contexts much farther afield than the Spanish Americas: in Dutch-ruled Indonesia, in British India, in French-ruled Vietnam and Reúnion.[15]

From the Indies to South Africa, mixed unions not sanctified by the state, as well as those legally sanctioned in marriage, were condoned and actively encouraged as part of the strategic tactics of conquest. Only later were they condemned as encroachments on and threats to the privileges of an over-seas colonizing settler population. How being mestizo played out elsewhere raises other questions: mixing could provide access to some privileges but sharply blocked access to others. Carl Degler's notion that a "mulatto escape hatch" marked the difference between the racial politics of Brazil (where it existed) and the United States (where it did not) downplays a more com-plicated set of racialized practices and representations. It also flattens out colonial histories in which claiming to be of "mixed" origin at one histori-cal moment and being designated as "mixed" by those who ruled at another moment produced a range of different political practices. In those histories mixedness itself was a moving and strategic category.[16]

Sumptuary laws tell a tale of their own. Laws in the colonial Spanish Americas, where being mestizo was often equated with illegitimate birth, legally excluded those who were mixed from holding public office, owning property, and adopting elite forms of transport and dress. In the Indies, on the contrary, seventeenth-century and eighteenth-century sumptuary laws "standardized personal vanity" by regulating visible symbols of wealth that valorized the Javanese markers of status of the Dutch East India Company's mestizo elite.[17]

This is not to belabor the obvious point that mixedness meant different things in different places at different times. As Craig Calhoun warns in a study of contemporary social theory, "translation adequate to comparative analysis requires an interpretation of a whole organization of activity, not just the matching of vocabulary." Rather, it is to argue that shifts in the den-sity, frequency, and sequence of state attention to mixed unions should turn us to the historical specificities of a social category's occurrence, the rules that governed its appearance, the ways a set of relations and discourses about them could "arouse opposing strategies" and make it possible, "with a par-ticular set of concepts, to play different games."[18] In some colonial contexts, such as British India, mixedness was conceived as a threat to the state's racial taxonomies and was heavily policed. Elsewhere, as in the early-twentieth-century Netherlands Indies, discourses about the dangers of mixing pro-vided the contexts in which mixed unions continued to thrive. Clearly, dis-courses about the political hazards of mixing did not necessarily have the same effects. As in the profusion of scientific debates about the perils of mix-ing in French Indochina, such debates could serve as forceful reminders of the validity and purity of those racialized categories of persons who were clearly "native" and firmly "white" and knew where they belonged.

But discourses about mixedness were requisitioned to more than the service of colonial regimes, their agents, and those who produced their expert knowledge. Scholars have placed an ideology of *mestizaje* at the core of Latin America's varied nationalist narratives, with elites embracing mixedness to render nationalist rhetorics—which were ostensibly inclusionary, equalizing, and popularizing—as projects that targeted indigenous Indian populations for exclusion. Doris Sommer and Vera M. Kutzinski more specifically regard the sexual and erotic dimensions of *mestizaje* as at the heart of Latin America's national paradigms.[19]

My point is *not* that Nash's argument about mixing was amiss. The more interesting issue raised by his piece has to do with the breadth of comparison. When historians of the United States look in a transnational direction, it often tends to be south, to Latin America and to border crossings at the historical and contemporary frontiers of the United States.[20] But comparisons with historical studies from elsewhere highlight other features of mixing and of discourses about it that emphasize the tactical mobility of concepts, how mixed marriages and unions were used in strategies of governance that joined sexual conquest with other forms of domination. As North American history is becoming more international, the imperial politics of intimacies begs for broader comparisons as well.

Feminist scholarship has made important moves in that direction. Despite the bracketings that Kaplan noted in earlier scholarship—of culture out of empire, empire out of history, and United States empire out of postcolonial studies—feminist scholars have sought to document the interlocking of sexual and racial patterns of dominance that crisscross historical fields. The insistence that the "personal is political" has informed efforts to address how specific colonial conditions made that so. The direction set by Verena Martinez-Alier's research on interracial marriage in Cuba's nineteenth-century slave society, like that of Patricia Seed's on marriage choices in eighteenth-century colonial Mexico, helped those working in other colonial contexts appreciate how regulations on marital choice were transformed as those societies became increasingly racially organized and racially diverse. Recent work, such as Sharon Block's on comparative sexual coercion in early America, does what we need more of. Block questions what counted as sexual coercion by examining accounts of such acts and the discursive categories of accusation. She treats the coercion of slaves and servants, that is, of African American and white women, in a comparative frame that tells more than either instance could alone about the historical relationships between social and sexual power.[21]

But even in feminist scholarship, borrowings have often been of a particular kind. Students of American history may avidly reference postcolonial *theory* (that of Edward Said, Benedict Anderson, Homi Bhabha, and Gayatri Chakravorty Spivak, to name only a few of the luminaries) and its founding fathers (Frantz Fanon, Aimé Césaire, Albert Memmi), but they seem to consider less relevant the specific colonial *histories* in which colonial relationships and their gender dynamics were produced. Similarly historians of sexuality and race in the United States, although aware of theory, do not seem conversant with the studies of whiteness that feminist historians of the Pacific and Southeast Asian colonial contexts have been carrying out for some time.[22]

But borrowing in the other direction can be similarly selective and problematic. When students of colonial studies have drawn on Jacquelyn Dowd Hall's work on racial violence and white women's quest for suffrage, Patricia Grimshaw's on Hawaii's nineteenth-century missionaries, or Mary P. Ryan's and Nancy F. Cott's on domesticity, we have often done so for the conceptual form rather than the historical content of their analyses. Postcolonial scholars of British empire in India avidly read U.S. scholarship on whiteness, but they still treat North America's racial history as a case apart. Feminist scholars may push shared analytic concepts up against gendered political relations in other times and places, but the history of American imperial expansion usually remains another story.[23]

Still, the exceptions are instructive. Laura Wexler's analysis of photographs taken by middle-class white women during the war in the Philippines places the violence of United States empire up against the shaping of a gendered domestic space overseas and in the racialized space of the United States. Transnational histories of social movements, such as Ian Tyrrell's work on missionaries and cultural imperialism or Susan Thorne's on "missionary-imperial feminism," have demonstrated with striking consistency that such transnational global ventures "rested on the existence of a degraded female Other in the colonies and at home." Donna Guy's examination of the discourses about "white slavery" in Argentina shows how perceptions of emigrant women as "loose," and their own practices, "affected the rights and inherent restrictions of citizenship beyond national frontiers." Sometimes connections emerge from unlikely places. Elizabeth van Heyningen's interpretation of the Contagious Diseases Acts in South Africa's Cape Colony in the late nineteenth century as *imperial* legislation moves her to look to the unexpected agents of their implementation: local branches of the Young Men's Christian Association, the Salvation Army, and institutions staffed by American women and affiliated with the Mount Holyoke Female Seminary in Massachusetts. So what dissuades more archival ventures in such directions? Is it because archival sources make such connections difficult to pursue, because disciplinary convention ignores them, or because our paradigms render these histories as noncommensurable nation-making projects?[24]

COLONIAL COMPARISONS; OR, WHAT'S "COLONIAL" ABOUT NORTH AMERICA?

The task of comparing the racial and sexual entanglements that preoccupy students of colonial studies and those that preoccupy historians of North America raises questions about what is "colonial." One issue is clear: depending on how "the colonial" is defined, both the possible terms of comparison and the issues are different. By way of illustration we can look briefly at four moments in U.S. history for which extensive comparative work has been done. All could be construed as colonial in that they involved European settlement, exploitation, and dominance of separate "others" that transformed social organization, cultural convention, and private life. All produced "structures of dominance" that depended on the management of sex in the making of racialized forms of rule. Such structures figured prominently both in North American history and in Europe's Asian and African colonial expansions.[25]

An obvious point of departure is the first of the four moments, "colonial America." There is no period for which historians have more thoroughly detailed the convergent and competing strategies that pitted French, British, and Dutch in distinct ways against Native American populations and against each other. Similarly, the Spanish roots of colonial American policy have been richly documented. Still, the cultural critic Michael Warner blames the disjuncture between that history and postcolonial scholarship on "the old Imperial school" (which he identifies with Charles Andrews and George Louis Beer, among others), whose commitment to teleologies of nationalist narratives rendered what was colonial in colonial America irrelevant to those studying the colonial elsewhere. In Warner's telling, the conflicting agendas of historians of "colonial America" concerned a "future nation" rather than the characteristics of a historically specific "colonial culture." Instead, he urges a rethinking of British colonialism in the broader context of all the European empires, an approach that would be "attentive to the cultural patterns by which such disparate ventures were able to elaborate, for all their differences, a European colonial project, distinct from each of its manifestations but necessary to each." Indeed Warner points to common imperial concerns over reproduction, domestic space, and identities forged in the process of settlement (suggesting parallels with Anne McClintock's work and my own) that could draw students of North American history beyond the nation to a broader colonizing world.[26]

Still, the onus of rethinking the scope of analysis should not fall on North Americanists alone. Students of Southeast Asia, South Asia, and Africa have also subscribed to models that privilege metropolitan-colony exchanges rather than circuits of people, produce, and knowledge that might track common gendered principles of governance through this broader global frame. If they ignore North America, it is not because colonial America lacks resonance with other colonial contexts, nor is it because the concerns of American historians are so differently posed. The sheer volume of work on sexuality and race relations in early America, as well as the rich sources on domestic arrangements, of those in mixed-marriages and those outside legal union, invite, at the very least, mutual recognition.

For these early periods Ramón A. Gutiérrez has shown how marriage structured racial inequalities in New Mexico, as Jennifer L. Morgan, in her survey of sixteenth-century travel literature, has detailed how gender was imbricated in the racial ideologies and strategies of rule. Such studies as Kathleen M. Brown's on gender, race, and power in colonial Virginia speak directly to Jean Gelman Taylor's ethnographic history of the same issues in seventeenth-century colonial Java, halfway around the world.[27] Both document the centrality of women in shaping the contact zones of colonial cultures that became increasingly distinguished by race. Tracing genealogies of kith and kin five generations deep, Taylor showed how the political alliances of Dutch rule were forged by men through female networks that placed domestic arrangements, parenting styles, and education at the center of administrative efforts to shape cultural norms and secure authority. Her focus on the dislocations that colonialism imposed on both colonizers and colonized is a forceful reminder that innovation and improvisation, rather than the mere import of European norms, characterized the cultural ground on which racial differences were consolidated and the terms on which people met.

Parallel patterns of colonial intimacies in early America are well documented. Those that depended on "tender ties" between fur traders and Native American women in the Canadian Northwest and those that produced a vast mestizo population under Spanish rule to the south suggest manipulations of sexual access that resonate with the ways colonial administrations in South Africa and Southeast Asia watched over those intimacies — and the ways colonized women turned them to their own needs. An older historiography that sustained the myth that New England colonists and Native Americans did not mix has little currency today, as scholars have detailed their sexual arrangements, the children they produced, and the affections and disaffections that grew out of those encounters.[28]

If comparisons between early American contacts and other European colonial contacts are still to be made, a larger literature addresses the second moment, comparing the eighteenth- and nineteenth-century plantation societies of the "Old South" with plantation societies in British, French, and Dutch colonies of Asia, Africa, and the Caribbean. As Eugene D. Genovese, among others, has shown, plantation households in Georgia and South Carolina were similar to those in the West Indies on which they were initially modeled.[29]

Indeed, United States economic and social historians such as Genovese have clearly sought to write against American exceptionalism in comparisons with the West Indies and Spanish America. But the labor processes that created such plantation households, as a generation of scholars devoted to world-systems analysis has shown, were realized in congruent ways in other parts of the world. The long-distance displacements of people that split up families and took persons as property in the pursuit of white profits were not unlike the later forced recruitments of workers from Java and China to Malaysia and Sumatra, of indentured workers from south India to Fiji, and of workers from Jamaica to Costa Rica, to name but a few. Much depended on managing the domain of the domestic, on adopting differential pay scales for women and men, on encouraging concubinage and paid-for sex, on condoning sexual coercions, and on policing sexual access and intimate encounters. Workers responded with despair, desertion, and violence toward Europeans, other populations against whom they were pitted, or even their own families.[30] Women were compelled to sell their bodies and give up their children. Others used illicit unions with European men in exchange for more educational opportunities for their children and economic security for themselves. Racialized assessments of ability and worth structured these plantation societies across the board.

Although the plantation households of the Old South depended on slave labor and the colonial households of the Dutch, French, and British in Asia employed "contract coolies" and wage labor, anxieties within European colonial communities over intimacies and fear of contaminations by those who performed domestic service were strikingly similar. Those who worked as nursemaids, cooks, and houseboys were keen and critical observers as well as objects of fear and desire.[31] In this domestic sphere they were seen to transgress the protected boundaries of the very white homes whose cultivated cultural space they made possible: the leisures, ailments, and sensibilities that defined class privilege and distinctions of race.

Representations of and reactions to those domestic subversions and transgressions derived from local tensions and produced very different historical effects. But local explanations alone may occlude the powerful parallels expressed in discourses around sex, contamination, and colonial vulnerabilities that fears about racialized intimacies evoked. The domestic morality that American slaveholders saw as so tied to the subject of sex, described by the American historian Willie Lee Rose, was the object of vigilant attention in the Dutch East Indies and South Africa in the same period. Nor was the "culture of dissemblance" — Darlene Clark Hine's phrase, borrowed by the historian Michelle Mitchell to describe the "code of silence around intimate matters" that African American women developed during Reconstruction — so different from Javanese women's practice of recounting their memories of domestic work in Dutch colonial homes in ways that "protected their 'inner lives and selves.'"[32]

White men used the protection of white women as a defense against imagined threats — "the red peril," "the black peril" (in Africa), "the yellow peril" (in Asia). They imposed — and women actively participated in — protective models of womanhood and motherhood and prescriptions for domestic relations that constrained both the women and men in servitude and those who ostensibly ruled. Nor were such "perils" abstract fears. Invocations of the threat of sexual assaults on white women by native men in British India, South Africa, and New Guinea repeatedly returned to incidents of male servants — washermen, sweepers, cooks, and houseboys — poised at bedroom doorways or at thresholds of European homes, intruders into the very domestic spaces where they worked, where women were confined, and where white children were reared. At issue were servants who did not know their "places" and white (often young or working-class) women who did not know the standards for keeping theirs. All confirm Albert Memmi's insistence that colonialism produced both its colonizers and its colonized in the banal and humble intimacies of the everyday.[33] Such sites were neither metaphors for empire writ large nor metonyms of broader patterns of rule. The politics of intimacy is where colonial regimes of truth were imposed, worked around, and worked out.

A third moment inviting further comparison is highlighted in the model of internal colonialism used to describe the contact zones of the Native American colonial encounter. Whereas some American scholars mark the "imperialist epoch" as spanning the period from 1870 to 1920, others note that as early as the 1850s "evidence of empire was widely apparent in many forms." Still others, such as Francis Jennings, set North America's "empire of fortune" earlier. Indeed, such scholars as anthropologist Eleanor Leacock and historian Theda Perdue have long treated the dislocations of Native Americans and the warping of their domestic arrangements as a colonization process in which women have played a key role. The "internal colonialism" model has been applied broadly to describe modes of interaction between Mexican farmworkers and Anglos in the cotton culture of Texas, Mexican miners and Anglos in the copper towns of Arizona, and black sharecroppers and the dominant white culture in the South.[34]

If the debate over whether the United States could be characterized as a context of internal colonialism waned by the 1990s, attention to the political import of comparing the colonialism of the United States to that of other colonial regimes did not; indeed, that debate has escalated into the present. Linda Gordon's treatment of the Arizona orphan train scandal in the first decade of the twentieth century — a struggle over which women of which color were more appropriate foster mothers — reflects anxieties over rearing and race that echo concurrent discourses in a wider colonial field.[35] The struggles were much like those in the Dutch East Indies, which revolved around family life, sexual access, and mixed-race children who were abandoned, absconded with, or adopted or who remained precariously perched on societies' racial divides. White women were again charged with maintaining racial prestige, while women of different hue were seen as a threat to it.

Mary P. Ryan's observations about nineteenth-century urban America apply equally well to many European colonies. Gender "supplied the sexual prohibitions, codes of segregation and rhetorical power with which to mortar the rising wall of racial segregation." White women were subject to, and joint wardens over, strictures that made investments in racial uplift and reform—rather than social equality between races—the principle of their acceptance and participation in social life. Indeed, in the nineteenth-century Netherlands Indies, white women could lose their legal rights to European status if they married native men, on the argument of colonial lawyers that their feelings (rather than acts) betrayed cultural dispositions that were less Dutch than Javanese.[36]

Elaborate codes of conduct that affirmed manliness and virility arose from colonial cultures of fear—white men making unfounded claims to legitimate rule saw their manhood bolstered by equally unfounded claims to racial superiority. The displays of manliness in French Indochina, the Dutch East Indies, and Victorian India shared features with those described by Gail Bederman for the United States and by Kristin L. Hoganson for the gender politics that "provoked" the Spanish-American and Philippine-American wars.[37]

But there were differences. When white men in British New Guinea promulgated a *White Women's Protection Ordinance* in 1926 to guard their women against the threat of sexual assault by native men, there was no Ida B. Wells to mount a campaign that turned the discourse of manliness against itself. Nor was there a movement of white women in the Indies or New Guinea to galvanize revolt against the duplicitous chivalry of their protective, insecure, and racially fretful men. On the contrary, in India, when the Anglo-Indian press reported rumors of native assaults (and more often "attempted" ones) on white women, middle-class white women successfully led the boycott of a bill that would have allowed such cases to be tried by high-placed functionaries who were native men. Similarly, in colonial Sumatra, when a Dutch planter's wife was murdered "with a butcher's knife" by a Javanese worker in 1929, the 167 planters' wives who signed and dispatched a letter to the queen of the Netherlands called on their "womanly instincts" to beseech her to "change the regime"—*not* to investigate labor abuses but to tighten the rein of a "laboring people . . . on the road to unruliness and insubordination."[38]

If some comparisons entail a stretch, the fourth moment, the conventionally defined "age of American imperialism," starting with the Spanish-American War, lends itself to more obvious commensurability. Between 1898 and 1914 the United States acquired territories in Cuba, Puerto Rico, Hawaii, Guam, the Philippines, and Eastern Samoa. In the Pacific, Micronesia, Palau, and the Caroline Islands were brought into the American empire thirty years later. This was the heyday of European colonial ventures, if somewhat longer than Eric Hobsbawm's "Age of Empire."[39] The British, Dutch, French, and German empires were moving rapidly in two seemingly contrary directions: toward more social reform, education, and philanthropy (as in the Dutch Indies "Ethical Policy" and the French "civilizing mission") and toward increasing attentiveness to racial distinctions and social policies that consolidated those distinctions. Racial discrimination and social reform, as students both of colonial studies and of "benevolent colonialism" in United States history have learned, were not contradictions but complementary political impulses created out of the same cloth.

Like the American republic at the time of its making, as Edmund S. Morgan described it, nineteenth-century European colonialisms founded their inclusionary visions on exclusionary practices.[40] As colonial states expanded the scope of moralizing missions, their administrators worried over the numbers of impoverished Europeans in the colonies and particularly in the civil service ranks. Emergent debates over the state's responsibility for social welfare reworked the mid-nineteenth-century discourse that marked off the "deserving" from the "undeserving" poor. Now the goal was also to distinguish "subjects" from "citizens," the "real" Dutch and French from their "fabricated" variants of local origin, and poor natives from pauperized Europeans.

For some historians the tactics of rule that have concerned postcolonial scholars become relevant to the United States only with the winning of the Spanish-American War. For others the parallels seem apparent over a longer period and suggest comparisons of a longer *durée*. Both American and European empires produced their overseas others as they monitored the nation's "interior frontiers." Those sites of affiliation making allowed "enclosure and contact as well as passage and exchange." The discriminations made by agents of empire drew on assessments of moral attitude, cultural competence, and racial disposition to determine who should be granted citizenship and who should not. Both American and European imperial discourses subscribed to universalist principles and particularistic practices. In the Indies, Dutch administrators rejected the principle of racial inequality, but they made access to legal European equivalency dependent on whether applicants "felt at home" in a European milieu. Entrance exams for European schools in the Indies did not discriminate by race but by cultural and linguistic proficiency. What the student of French colonial policy Gary Wilder calls the "colonial humanism" of the late nineteenth century was not an oxymoron, but a defining feature of imperial rule.[41]

A comparative project should identify key topics of comparison and explicit criteria of commensurability. Why compare the manipulation of domestic arrangements in the making of race? Would it not be more fruitful to compare the governing strategies of colonial regimes or "the regimes of truth" that informed colonial cultures in different times and places? Should we consider only moments when a specifically colonial language was used or a formal taxonomy of race was operative?[42]

Doing so creates new obfuscations of their own. Legal acts may help produce racial taxonomies, but they alone are not the measure of social facts. The Dutch East Indies experience makes that point clear. In 1854, when racial classification of the Indies population was first established in government regulation, it was mapped onto discriminations that had long been culturally common sense. And in 1892, when new Dutch nationality laws made all native Indonesians and "Foreign Orientals" (that is, Chinese) residing in the Netherlands Indies "foreigners," race had long informed the practical reason of rule. Sites of comparison should not be tied to legal acts alone but to the conditions of possibility, the narrative frames and the particular practices that made those laws possible. Colonial governance in Southeast and South Asia show repeatedly that in the absence of legal demarcations, the cultural coordinates of race could produce and secure exclusions without putting into law distinctions based on chromatic visual markers. Such extralegal distinctions were common in the United States as well. Ronald Takaki notes a similar logic: one that racialized Native Americans not by law alone but by how they were culturally marked.

Critics of the comparative method have long suggested that methodological and analytic problems lie in the very assumptions of comparison. Raymond Grew, a historian of modern France, argued, and more recent critics have agreed, that the problem may be in "a tendency to make the nation (and the nation as defined by the state) the ultimate unit of analysis."

Such comparisons preserve the notion of "the [discrete] case," take the political territoriality of the emergent nation or full-fledged state as the historiographic directive, and privilege nation-making priorities and projects. The historian Robert Gregg makes the appeal yet again, urging that we "go beyond the boundaries of the nation-state to understand the larger dimensions of the imperial system."[43]

The challenge is of several kinds. First, to acknowledge colonial state projects without writing histories shaped only by state-bound archival production, state legal preoccupations, and realized state priorities; second, to use comparison, as the historian Frederick Cooper and others have advocated, as a window onto *specific* exchanges, interactions, and connections that cut across national borders without ignoring what state actors do and what matters about what they say.[44] Refocusing on an imperial field highlights the contradictions between universal principles and the differentiated imperial spaces and particularistic ways in which they were applied.

But it may also do something more, help identify unexpected points of congruence and similarities of discourse in seemingly disparate sites. It may prompt a search for common strategies of rule and the sequence of their occurrence that questions the relationship between imperial expansion and nation building and that asks why sex was a politically charged "transfer point" for racisms of the state. It may point to techniques for managing the intimate that spanned colony and metropole and that constrained or enabled both colonizer and colonized. Not least, such an exercise may challenge cherished distinctions between American empire and European overseas ones — or undo those distinctions altogether.

Another key comparison might turn on the relation of core to periphery — a relationship preinterpreted by that skewed analytic language. Increasingly, colonial studies has recognized a richer set of transnational connections. Transnationalism, however, as historians of early empires have shown, is neither a postmodern phenomenon nor a postmodern discovery. Colonialisms of the seventeenth, eighteenth, and nineteenth centuries drew on and animated circuits of movement that crisscrossed metropoles and peripheries, that disregarded official histories and national borders. Akira Iriye describes the Asia-Pacific region in the first half of the twentieth century as replete with cross-national figures — moving between cultures as journalists, students, artists, scholars, and musicians — who forged notions of internationalism that existed alongside, and despite, hostile relations between governments and nations. Similarly, colonial regimes recruited and dismissed colonizers who saw themselves as "world citizens," who followed career itineraries and personal trajectories that led them in and out of explicitly racialized contexts, from imperial to domestic missionizing projects, through locations where modernity was differently conceived and across imperial maps.[45]

Growing attempts in colonial studies to treat metropole and colony as one analytic field, as Frantz Fanon, George Balandier, and Bernard S. Cohn each urged decades ago, have yielded new ways of imagining and documenting how knowledge was produced along paths that went from metropole to colony and the other way around. Arguing that the colonies were "laboratories of modernity," Gwendolyn Wright has suggested that the principles of French urban planning were first played out on a colonial "experimental terrain." Elizabeth van Heyningen has made a strong case that the British Contagious Diseases Acts were "pre-eminently imperial legislation," implemented more directly in South Africa, India, and Malta than in Britain itself. Others have emphasized other aspects of the exchange between colony and metropole. Mary Louise Pratt's work disrupts commitments to unidirectional historical framing by showing how eighteenth-century bourgeois notions of social discipline may have first developed in seventeenth-century imperial ventures. Similarly, I have sought to identify the colonial etiologies of European bourgeois sexuality and social reform. A strong current of scholarship now is bent on showing that innovations in political form, and social imaginary, and in what defined the modern itself, were not European exports but traveled as often the other way around.[46]

These postcolonial insights have bearing on etiologies of race in North America. Not all American historians might agree with Kaplan's statement "that foreign relations do not take place outside the boundaries of America, but instead constitute American nationality." Still, few would deny the import of asking how best to study the relation between nation making and empire building and of questioning what scope and level of comparison with other colonial contexts enable doing so. Hazel M. McFerson has argued that the United States "exported to overseas territories racial attitudes at home." Robert W. Rydell has portrayed the rampant racisms of world's fair expositions in Chicago and St. Louis as instrumental in assuaging class tensions in the United States.[47] Despite the different emphases, both retain a myth of the United States steered by its own political rudder and on its own racial course.

Others disagree. Models of race relations in early America suggest that they, too, went the other way around. Peter H. Wood's observation that the Carolina lowlands were a "colony of a colony," modeled on Barbados in the late seventeenth century, resonates with arguments that New Orleans be construed as a colony of St. Domingue. Edward L. Ayers also doubts that domestic race relations in the United States were a template for America's overseas racial policy. Rather, the character of U.S. race relations tracked other colonial models, first of Spain and post-Restoration England, later of Victorian Britain and the social reform policies of colonial France. Ayers writes that "in the 1850s, white Southern nationalists eagerly pored over the newspapers, journals and books of Britain and Europe, finding there raw material with which to create a vision of the South as a misunderstood place. . . . The founders of the Confederacy saw themselves as participating in a widespread European movement, the self-determination of a people to be contained." In Ayers's view the segregation policy forged during Reconstruction took its precepts from British colonial rule and its rule of law. Local struggles to retain southern power in the face of those bent on increasing northern profits were only part of the story. Those patterns of segregation were produced, as Winthrop D. Jordan argued for an earlier period, through notions of servitude and strategies of racial domination refracted from elsewhere. But sometimes the refractions were in directions we have not been schooled to expect. Jennifer Pitts looks to Alexis de Tocqueville's letters and essays of the 1830s on Algeria to show that he considered America a "model" for the imperial project in French Algeria.[48]

Such lines of inquiry suggest that circuits of knowledge production and racialized forms of governance spanned a global field. The section that follows turns to three registers of comparison that involve two different sorts of connections: one, concerning child care, has elements of both direct and indirect connection; the second, concerning vocational schools, suggests no direct connection; and the final case, that of the South African Carnegie Commission, entails the most sustained convergence. All the comparisons invite attention to *parallel principles* and modes of governance. Each invites closer readings of the relationship between racial categories and state intervention in intimate practices. Each suggests that the power and authority wielded by macropolities are not lodged in abstract institutions but in their management of meanings, their construction of social categories, and their microsites of rule.

On Empire, Nurseries, and the Cultivation of Race

Would not such a nursery school be a heaven on earth for the child of the Indies' popular class who often vegetates amidst chickens and dogs in a village hut tended—not raised—by a mother, who does not know what rearing is?—D. W. Horst, "Opvoeding en onderwijs van kinderen van Europeanen en Indo-Europeanen in Indies"

Colonial regimes based on overseas settlements did more than produce their overseas others. They also policed the cultural protocols and competencies that bounded their "interior frontiers." In monitoring those boundaries they produced penal and pedagogic institutions that were often indistinguishable—orphanages, workhouses, orphan trains, boarding schools, children's agricultural colonies—to rescue young citizens and subjects in the making. Such colonial institutions, designed to shape young bodies and minds, were central to imperial policies and their self-fashioned rationalities. Colonial states had an abiding interest in a sentimental education, in the rearing of the young, and in affective politics. Antonio Gramsci was only partly right when he defined the function of the state as the education of consent. To educate consent to a colonial rule of law, to educate colonial and colonized women and men to accept, conform to, and collaborate with the colonial order of things, the state had first and foremost to school their desires.[49]

Nowhere was this concern for the schooling of desires and the learning of social place more baldly stated than in the nineteenth-century debates that surrounded the creation and failure of nurseries for children of European descent in the Dutch East Indies. Strict surveillance of domestic servants was one way to protect children; removal of them from the home was another. In the Indies, concerns for children's moral environments and for their sense of racial affiliation were deeply meshed. To trace the embeddedness of race in discourses about morality, sentiment, and sensibility, prescriptive child-rearing manuals are a useful resource. As Emile Durkheim insisted, "moral maxims are actually living sentiments."[50] If to be white and respectable meant to acquire behaviors that demanded restraint and civility, they also proscribed something else; racial and class "lower orders" did not share the prescribed attributes. Becoming adult and bourgeois meant distinguishing oneself from what was uncivilized, lower-class, and non-European.

Anxieties over European identity were amplified in anxieties about the young. In the Indies debates about rearing surfaced in sundry places: in classified state documents, public addresses, and scientific proceedings. And debates about nurseries were dominated not by women but by men. These nurseries were like those in the United States, imagined as a crucial step in the eradication of prostitution and crime. Both were about how to make subjects of a particular kind. As Nancy F. Cott observed about antebellum child-rearing manuals and as I have suggested about such manuals in colonial Java, these prescriptive texts were directed at schooling young citizens in a sense of morality and a proper tempering of their desires.[51] What seems different is the racial emphasis. In the Indies it is on the effects of *native* nursemaids on the sexuality of children, on the contaminations that those servants might convey. But how different were these assessments?

The Indies situation produced an unremitting and fearful refrain about "the damaging influence of the native nursemaid." One colonial doctor, in an 1898 handbook for European mothers in the Indies, warned of the "extremely pernicious" moral influence of native nursemaids and advised that "children under no circumstance should be brought to bed by them and should never be permitted to sleep with them in the same room." But "the threat of irreparable damage [done] to the child" by servants — incanted in Dutch colonial child-care manuals — was a central theme of American child-care manuals that warned against "bad handling." When the American observer Lewis Hough wrote in 1849 that "the coarse hugging, kissing, etc. which the children are sure to receive in great abundance from ignorant and low-minded domestics are certain to develop a blind precocious sexualism of feeling and action," how different were his concerns?[52]

At issue were more than competing definitions of "parental neglect." When Charles Loring Brace wrote in 1880 in *The Dangerous Classes of New York* about the orphan children of Irish and German immigrants, comparing them to children at the French reformatory of Mettray, he noted that the majority were the progeny of "concubinage" and that "the tendencies and qualities of their parents" encouraged them toward moral destitution and crime. Child-saving reformers in the United States held that the working classes did not know "what love really is," much as reformers in the Indies thought mixed-blood and native mothers did not know "what rearing is." Child savers of whatever name, in metropole and colony, in the Indies, England, the United States, and France, worried loudly over inadequate parenting, feared the desires of their young, and distrusted the influence of class and racial others on them.[53]

Such concerns were not new to the nineteenth century nor limited to

Europe. On South Africa's Cape of Good Hope, in the eighteenth century, new models of the domestic family dictated that the widespread use of slave wet nurses be replaced by mothers' nursing their children themselves. As in upper-class England, "it was claimed that the nurse imprinted her personality on the child and won his strongest affection."[54] Nurseries were designed to protect the sexual innocence of small children from the immoral influence and possible predations of domestic servants but also to cultivate sensibilities that underwrote their identification as white and privileged and, in the Indies, to ensure their distance and disaffection from those once charged with their care.

Class-specific theories of child development were exemplified in the first kindergartens and nurseries that emerged in Germany and England in the late 1820s and in the Netherlands in the 1850s. As distinct from the first nurseries for working-class children, called *bewaarscholen*, the kindergartens developed by Friedrich Froebel in the 1830s appealed to the patriotic sensibilities of the middle class and had a strong nationalist bent. Spurred by the conviction that bourgeois households were providing "poor child management," the Froebel movement recommended that toddlers and even infants were better off in kindergartens than in an unschooled nursemaid's or servant's care. Kindergartens were envisioned as "microcosms of the liberal state," stressing not only independence but also self-discipline, citizenship, and "voluntary obedience to general laws"—qualities that lower-class servants could not be expected to value, nurture, or protect.[55]

Experiments in social reform and child welfare were played out across a transnational and imperial field. Nor did they necessarily follow the administrative channels that joined metropole and colony. Some followed circuits of knowledge production and exchange carved out by philanthropic organizations; others moved along the shipping lines that rounded the Cape of Good Hope in South Africa. Some followed mail boats that collected news on what transpired in 1848 in France when they docked in Marseille. The French government education official Joseph Chailley-Bert culled his lessons on how to deal with "les métis" in Indochina from Dutch counterparts in Batavia and bypassed the metropole altogether.[56] Agents of empire were themselves rarely stationary. They moved between posts in Africa and Asia, schooled their children in international Swiss boarding schools, read avidly about other colonies, visited colonial expositions in Paris and Provence, came together in colonial hill stations around the globe, and had a passion for international congresses where their racial taxonomies were honed and their commonsense categories were exchanged.

Educating for Empire and the Politics of Race: Native American
Boarding Schools and Vocational Schools in the Indies

Were I to fix the date of completion of the carceral system, I would choose not 1810 and the penal code, nor even 1844, when the law laying down the principle of cellular internment was passed. . . . The date I would choose would be 22 January 1840, the date of the official opening of Mettray. Or better still, perhaps, that glorious day, unremarked and unrecorded, when a child in Mettray remarked as he lay dying: "What a pity I left the colony so soon." . . .

. . . In the arrangement of a power-knowledge over individuals, Mettray and its school marked a new era. — Foucault, *Discipline and Punish*

Some "cases" seem so strikingly commensurate that they make one ask why they have not been compared. But more elusive circuits of knowledge production are instructive as well. Successive state commissions on European poverty in the Indies in the second half of the nineteenth century looked to one of Europe's most acclaimed experiments with agricultural poor colonies, that instituted in the 1840s in France and the Netherlands and widely know as Mettray. In this model of reform a rural setting and a disciplinary structure and layout emphasizing moral and physical surveillance played a key role.[57]

Part of a wider campaign to rescue orphaned children or those who were subject to "parental neglect," Mettray resembled the new reformatory rural institutions scattered throughout Germany, England, the Netherlands, France, and the United States. But Mettray is quintessential in its detailed disciplinary design. Foucault singled it out as the beginning of the "carceral archipelago" of discipline and punishment in its modern European form. Similarly, in England the Red Hill reformatory was to bring rural reform into the "modern age," as were the many new corrective and industrial schools lauded as the "truest and noblest glories of [the United Kingdom's] island empire."[58]

As in Europe's colonies, debates about the need for and management of such schools revealed specific concerns. The debates were about mental capability and moral worth, about tempering aspirations, about which classes, ethnic groups, and races should be schooled to work with their hands. The frame of reference was Lamarckian notions of race, environment, and character. The focus was on the moral benefits of schooling young men for craft and artisan work that required limited industrial know-how and of schooling young girls in domestic science—to sew, cook, and care for homes.

Dutch sociologist Abram de Swaan's observation that many industrial and artisan schools in the eighteenth century failed because their purpose was "not so much to prepare children for the labor market, but to render them virtuous, patient and industrious through the practice of traditional arts" takes on a different political meaning in relation to nineteenth-century reformist projects.[59] They were less about the production of labor markets than about disciplining aspirations and policing the boundaries of race.

The parallels between the debates about vocational schools for the impoverished mixed-blood population in the Indies in the 1870s and 1880s and those about boarding schools for Native American girls and boys in the same period are striking. As Dutch officials so clearly argued, the colonies needed "not imitation Europeans, but perfected natives"—the creation, out of a mixed-blood population mired in poverty, of those who would no longer be objects of pity and agents of threat.[60] Under adverse conditions they loomed as "white haters" (*blanken-haters*); under proper tutelage they would be the future vanguard of a modernizing colonial rule.

Decades of debate about creating *ambachtscholen* (artisan/vocational schools) tied to the Indies' orphanages centered on recurrent themes, such as the inherent capabilities of such a population and what could be expected of its members. Lodged within detailed discussions of curriculum, food expenditures, building costs, and the preparedness of the prospective pupils were the calibrations of other "costs." At issue was the racial scope of social reform (who should be included), the moral scope of the state (whom it should assist), and, not least, the management of appropriate sentiments as a part of social policy. Participants in the debate shared a notion that indolence and insolence had to be checked, that skilled manual labor could craft respectable subjects and transform political beings. Reformers were convinced that a "desire to work" was the ingredient lacking; it was sentiment that had to be kindled and redirected, not opportunity that needed to be changed.

But the "desire to work" had to be of a specific kind. Efforts to teach crafts or trades were based on a common contention that the colony's economic and political viability depended on educating the hearts and minds of those who were a danger to it, on managing their aspirations in an Indies world. As the director of the Indies department of education put it in 1869, the impoverished "mixed-bloods" who were partial descendants of Europeans "must not [conceive of themselves] as *heeren* (bosses/masters), they must not be burdened with more skills than they need, but only practical know-how for the tasks to which they are geared."[61] Whether this population should be provided theoretical knowledge and practical instruction divided policy planners. But in all cases the debates returned to unresolved questions: Could this precarious population be incorporated into the Dutch fold without being granted other costly political and economic entitlements? Could they be offered economic incentives and participation in a modernizing economy without being granted any political rights? Self-worth in labor and political independence were seen to go dangerously hand in hand.

Striking in these conflicting and confused arguments is how much they changed. Between the 1840s and 1890s, different arguments were marshalled to evaluate whether orphaned and abandoned mixed-blood youths could become an artisan class. Craft schools, heralded in the 1860s as the solution to pauperism, were perceived twenty years later as badly misguided. By the 1880s both the artisan and industrial visions were sidelined by designs for discipline that looked more to agricultural colonies for boys and girls. Those visions focused less on remolding the recalcitrant than on shaping children in their tender years.

The institutions of the 1880s were modeled on Mettray and were guided by the notion that young vagrants and urban delinquents could be taught respect for religion and family by doing agricultural and domestic work. Such work would allow them to develop their skills and character and to learn self-discipline, while spartan conditions of labor and living would constrain expectations. Again, not everyone agreed. One Indies director of education thought the plans looked more like those for a penal colony, a "depot for delinquents," than anything else.[62]

Debates over federal policy toward Native American education in the same period were marked by similar principles if by differently framed concerns. Physical-labor schools were envisioned as a part of a moralizing mission, imparting policies of uplift that would wed citizens in the making to the "virtue of industry and the ability of the skillful hand." As in the policies directed at the Indies' mixed-blood population, the focus was less on labor than on instilling desire to perform it. As Commissioner of Indian Affairs John H. Oberly wrote in 1888, the Indian "should not only be taught how to work, but also that it is his duty [to do so]." As anthropologist Janet Finn notes, fears of the girls' "moral delinquency" occupied an inordinate amount of administrative time. Solutions were similar in part because the problem was seen as largely the same. In the Indies and among the Native American population, boarding schools, craft schools, and agricultural colonies were a means to remove children from the influence of their intimate environments — families on the reservations in the one case, native servants and their natal families in the other.[63]

School routines aimed to instill discipline of sundry kinds. As Richard Tennert writes of the boarding schools for Native American girls, school routines were organized in "martial fashion," with strict timetables. Nor were the similarities to penal institutions, as noted by the Indies director of education, coincidental. Richard Henry Pratt, founder of the boarding school system, was a military warden for Indian prisoners at Fort Marion from 1875 to 1878.[64]

Debates that made a "love for work," in the one case, and *werklust* (a desire for work), in the other, the test of innate capacity, constitution, and preparedness for citizenship join these distant projects as congruent strategies of reform. But their conclusions and outcome were not the same. In the Indies girls were trained to be competent marriage partners and mothers on modest family farms devoted to "agriculture, animal raising, butter and cheese production, and the tending of orchards" — a vision wildly out of sync with the reality of the Indies economy. The Native American girls trained in the boarding schools of Arizona, Pennsylvania, and Oklahoma were similarly educated for domesticity and trained for subservience but destined for a different fate: to use their skills as servants in Anglo households or as employees of the Indian Bureau.[65]

The differences between the cases are as important as the similarities. One could argue that one was a colony based on the extraction of labor and produce and the other a settlement or that the reservation system in the United States attempted to obliterate an entire culture while the Dutch East Indies variant did not. Still, the comparison warrants consideration. Both policies were elements of political technologies that crafted microenvironments to carry out public policy on race. Both reinforced inequities based on assessments of innate capacity and disposition. Both made children temporary wards of the state, removing them from their home environments while offering high doses of discipline and limited industrial skills. Both embraced reformist efforts for the remaking of racialized selves and the tempering of desires.[66] Not least, both suggest colonial genealogies of social welfare that were grounded in imperial concerns over the distinctions of race.

The Carnegie Commission on Poor Whites: Logics of Differentiation in South Africa and the United States

If circuits of knowledge production connecting boarding schools for Native Americans and vocational schools in the Indies seem difficult to trace, those that shaped the study of poor whites in the United States and South Africa between the 1880s and 1930s are clear. Nevertheless, comparative work done in the early 1980s treated the development of racialized social formations in South Africa and the United States as discrete cases, if highly relevant national stories, appropriate to compare. I think here of George M. Fredrickson's important comparative project on white supremacy and the essays that appeared in a volume edited by Howard Lamar and Leonard Thompson, *The Frontier in History*. More recent work underscores that the state racisms of the United States and South Africa both produced forms of resistance that cut across their borders.[67] What has been less noted is how much these racisms of the state produced their policy, expert knowledge, and racialized practices independently *and* in exchange.

The discourses used, the policies pursued, and the definitions of the poor-white problem were intimately tied through experts on race. Social scientists employed by and working for government agencies in the United States and South Africa compared and equated the two situations. The South African Carnegie Commission on the problem of poor whites of the late 1920s was a multiyear project fashioned by American-trained social scientists and funded with American dollars. Financed by Andrew Carnegie's Carnegie Corporation, established in 1913, the commission drew on the Dominions and Colonies Fund earmarked for educational and social research in British dependencies. Exactly how and where the particular fund was to be used was not specified at the start. But the fact that the corporation already funded the Eugenics Record Office in Cold Spring Harbor, New York, between the 1910s and 1939, endorsed the racist views of Madison Grant, and overtly sought to "preserve the racial purity of American society" shaped its scientific priorities and social policy. Charged with the fund's proper use, Carnegie's president, Frederick Keppel (former dean of Columbia College), and later James Russell (dean of Teachers College at Columbia University) made several reconnaissance visits to Australia, New Zealand, and South Africa in the mid-1920s. When Russell met one of his former students, E. G. Malherbe, who had already written on South Africa's poor-white problem in 1921, the commission began to take shape, with Malherbe as one of its prime architects.[68]

But it was not only Malherbe whose understanding of the poor-white problem was framed by his American contacts. The commission was staffed with American university social scientists. South African psychologists in its employ made visits to the psychology laboratories at Harvard and Yale. Most had received their PhDs or, at the very least, studied in Britain or the United States. Advisers to the Carnegie Corporation such as Kenyon L. Butterfield, who spent several weeks with the commission in 1929, identified "the Poor White question" as one of the "key problems" of South Africa and as an "economic menace," with an estimated three hundred thousand whites who fell into the category of the "very poor." To Butterfield the main issue was clear: "there can be little doubt that if the natives were given full economic opportunity, the more competent among them would soon outstrip the less competent whites." The recommendations of the Carnegie Commission were part of a broader set of plans to ensure that did not happen.[69]

The commission was presented as a South African initiative of local origin whose concerns were localized. But its scientific resources were not local, nor were its points of reference Cape Town Boers and South African Bantus alone. Its recommendations were drawn from studies of "feeblemindedness" in Appalachia, its experts from New Mexico, Georgia, and Tennessee. Its "intelligence surveys," based on eugenic testing honed in the United States, concluded "that the average intelligence of the poor whites was lower than that of the European population as a whole" and that "mental defect was an inborn condition." Grounded in the production of racialized knowledge in the United States, the Commission reports reflected efforts to identify commensurable kinds of persons who could be compared, differentiated, and then singled out for policy and prevention. Designed to deal with the poor-white problem in rural South Africa, the commission's work displayed priorities, principles, and solutions that grew out of a joint-venture project on segregation — out of production of knowledge and distribution of resources that were part of the consolidation of state racism in the United States.[70]

The Carnegie Commission offers a window onto the transnational currency of racial reform that circulated between such unlikely participants as officials in the Kimberly mining region of South Africa; the Commission on Interracial Cooperation in Atlanta, Georgia; and the state inspector of high schools in Nashville, Tennessee. But it also presages the conditions of possibility for a racialized welfare state. Prescriptions for family life, child rearing, and education were critical to it. The poor-white problem was fundamental to the making of apartheid, and the commission's recommendations laid its concrete foundations. At the heart of the investigation was one finding: "unrestricted competition on the labour market between the unskilled non-European and the poor white creates conditions of poverty which have a demoralising effect on the latter. Measures for restricting such competition should aim at counteracting this demoralisation." On the argument that the poor white "could not live like a white man without charitable aid" and without a built-in structure of differential access to employment, land, and social services, fundamental hierarchies of personhood *and* basic elements of a discriminatory welfare state were born.[71]

But as virtually every member of the commission noted, the problem of poor whiteism was poor whites themselves. R. W. Wilcocks, one of the commission's authors, concluded that "isolation" and the consequent "frequent intermarriage of blood-relatives" with "deleterious mental and physical effects among the offspring" were common denominators among poor whites in the Ozarks and Appalachia and constituted one "cause of poor whiteism" in South Africa and the United States. Commissioner M. E. Rothmann's detailed report, *The Mother and Daughter of the Poor Family*, noted that "much can be learned from the order or disorder in a home, from the attitudes of family members to each other, from the behavior of children." Psychological assessments took up much of the commission's time. Poor whites were not competitive with South Africa's native populations. They displayed a "lack of industriousness and ambition" and a "lack of self-reliance." Their "irresponsibility" and their "untruthfulness and lack of a sense of duty" were constant refrains. In the commission's language racial demoralization and white immorality went hand in hand. As the South African historian Saul DuBow has noted, "poor whiteism came to function as an important comparative discursive site for the expression of racial anxieties and the testing of racial theories." But these were neither generic nor abstract assessments of race, as the linking of "feeble-mindedness" to the incidence of masturbation by poor white children attests. Repeatedly, architects of national labor and welfare policy sought to do what Foucault has argued all racist states do: "defend society against itself" by remaking the domestic, by regulating appropriate intimacies, and by carefully monitoring the care and cultural grooming of the young.[72]

The commission returned again and again to the uplifting of "ignorant" women in poor-white households who were unable to equip "their children with a normal home and social training." In detailed analyses of "home conditions" schoolgirls were coded as "listless" and "fatigued," with "sagging" and "distended" abdomens from malnourishment caused by their mothers' ignorance of the simplest rules of hygiene. Children's health, commission members believed, was made worse by the native population on whom poor white families were dependent and with whom they lived. As the Carnegie commissioner W. A. Murray, senior assistant in the Health Office in Pretoria, reported, many of the home remedies in such families "bore the hallmark of the barbarism with which these people were in daily contact in the persons of their 'raw' native servants."[73]

The commission's conclusion was not that tropical climate created poor whites, a popular hypothesis that Malherbe disputed. Rather, the poor-white problem was due to competition with native labor and to contact with natives. To ensure the moral integrity of poor white young women, the commission made three strong recommendations: (1) introduction of "special training in home-making" on the argument that it was a "good investment for the state"; (2) establishment of boardinghouses for indigents to promote their "social education" and domestic skills, culminating in a "national housewife certificate" when they completed the course; and (3) encouragement of factory work in conditions set by Cape Town's "leading firms," "applying a wise and fair segregation of European and non-European female labour." Whites' willingness to live "cheek by jowl" with South Africa's black population and, worse, to engage in intimate relations with them were taken as "a clear indication of absence or loss of self-respect on their part."[74]

Built into the cultural machinery of empire in the 1920s were paradigms of progress that reverberated across a global field. Just as U.S. psychologists studying poor whites in the American South offered expert counsel to the British South African colonial state, the American managers of Uniroyal's and Goodyear's rubber estates worked with members of the Dutch colonial administration in the Indies to modernize estate management and to develop racially conceived systems of labor control. As the historian Frances Gouda has noted, U.S. State Department files from the 1920s document exchanges between the American consul general in the Indies and the United States secretary of state over "half-caste girls." Both worried that they posed a threat to racially bifurcated principles of governance. Gouda refers to a florid commentary on the beauty of Eurasian girls as an "undiplomatic flight of fancy," but as she would undoubtedly agree, such remarks were not generally outside diplomats' ken. Discourses around racial aesthetics, mixed unions, and people of mixed race appear too often to be considered aberrant indiscretions or archival asides. In high-level communications between governors-general and ministers of colonies and between ministers of colonies and whoever occupied the Netherlands' throne, they appear with a consistency that suggests they were the grist of governance, a site of vulnerability, and an integral element in the lexicon of rule.[75]

Comparative Connections and the Politics of Comparison

Politically, the Americans keep aloof from local issues and socially they are inclined to keep to themselves. America is too young in overseas enterprise and too full of opportunity at home to have developed a class with the true overseas point of view—such as the British have. The Americans all keep one eye on home and feel themselves temporarily in a strange land. —Consul General Coert du Bois, "The Problem of the Half Caste"

The breezy dismissal of American interest in intervention by the United States consul general in Java reads effortlessly as conventional wisdom and common sense. Indeed, his report of October 1928 expresses two widely shared sentiments: (1) the United States was a passive participant in an empire not its own; and (2) neither the United States nor its agents were imperial. But Consul General Coert du Bois's description of that "universal aim of the Dutch business group," namely, "to clean up a fortune in the fewest possible years and retire" home, was not so different from that of their American counterparts and colonialism's agents in other parts of the world. As Albert Memmi noted in *The Colonizer and the Colonized*, written on the cusp of the Algeria war, the prevailing definition of a colony for French nationals in North Africa was strikingly clear: "a place where one earns more and spends less," a place were "jobs are guaranteed, wages high, careers more rapid and business more profitable."[76] Profits and privilege came faster and in larger measures than in Akron, Delft, Toulouse, or Colmar.

The vocabulary was drawn from economics, but the cultural coordinates and intimate interventions that allowed it were not. It is no accident that Consul General du Bois's comments on "American aloofness" came in a classified report to the United States secretary of state on "the problem of the half castes." The report asserted that it was "the acutely race conscious . . . Dutch half-caste that constitutes a problem."[77] But United States agribusiness was "acutely race conscious" as well. For race mattered to Goodyear, Uniroyal, and the twenty-five thousand Indonesians whose jobs on their estates were racially scaled. Carefully monitored domestic arrangements and gender demographics were written into plantation strategies of labor control from the start. Labor and social policy fixed the lower, differential wages for Javanese women, who were then forced to "choose" prostitution and concubinage as not unreasonable options. Specific relations of dominance worked through a capitalist world economy and colonial technologies of rule. Both that economy and those technologies were founded on and thrived on racial differences and a sexual economy that depended on the learning of place and race and on the distribution of desires.

Such connections are less evident if we subscribe to colonial scripts themselves, if we abide by the strictures of national archives, state projects, and their historiographies. Indeed, research that begins with people's movements rather than with fixed polities opens up to subjacent histories less compelled to show the "natural" teleology of future nations, later republics, and future states. We might instead want to think, as Frederick Cooper and I have suggested elsewhere, about colonialism's modular qualities, how different regimes built projects with blocks of one earlier model and then another, projects that were then reworked by the colonized populations that those models could never completely master or contain. Rather than compare United States empire with a host of others, we might imagine nineteenth-century history as made up not of nation-building projects alone but of compounded colonialisms and as shaped by multinational philanthropies, missionary movements, discourses of social welfare and reform, and traffics in people (women in particular) that ran across state-archived paper trails.[78]

If comparison of discrete "cases" is so problematic, another line of inquiry might treat comparison not as a methodological problem but as a historical object. We might historicize the *politics of comparison*, tracing the changing stakes for polities and their bureaucratic apparatuses. What did agents of empire think to compare and what political projects made them do so? What did comparison as a state project entail? Scholars who have attempted to write against colonial histories have noted how our concerns have been contained by statist historiography, shaped by the archived grooves that colonial states carved out for themselves.

Colonial regimes were not hegemonic institutions but uneven, imperfect, and even indifferent knowledge-acquiring machines. Omniscience and omnipotence were not, as is so often assumed, their defining goals. I refer to them as "taxonomic states" whose administrations were charged with defining and interpreting racial membership, requirements for citizenship, acts of political subversion, and, not least, determining what intimate practices and what sorts of persons confirmed or threatened European notions of morality. Such states as that of the Dutch in the Indies demanded that their agents master not only ethnographic details but also broad sociological generalizations, encouraging their agents to pay less attention to detail than to sorting codes. In the Indies, social categories provided sociological short-hands that pared down what colonial recruits and residents thought they needed to master—what information and how much one needed to know.

Colonial bureaucracies were therefore invested in selective comparison with other polities: with highlighting their similarities to some and differ-ence from others. A case in point is the commensurabilities they found in such "folk" categories as "white prestige," "mixed-bloods," and "poor whites." Such category making was, as Ian Hacking notes of statistics, part of the moral science of statecraft, of the technology that created censuses and their commensurabilities in the eighteenth and nineteenth centuries.[79] Cate-gory making produced cross-colonial equivalencies that allowed for inter-national conferences and convinced their participants—doctors, lawyers, policy makers, and reformers—that they were in the same conversation, if not always talking about the same thing.

If the above is granted, historians of the colonial might move in another direction. Not to ask whether *métissage* (mixing) was similar in the Indies, India, the Caribbean, and the American Southwest, but to ask what distinc-tive work such a designation did to define empire and nation, and how af-filiation would be marked within those macropolities. We might equally ask how and why people could talk about what being mestizo entailed *without* agreeing on who was included in that category. Acts of comparison perform important political work as "weapons of reason" in the tactics of rule.[80] Com-parison produces truth claims about the attributes of race and the dispo-sitions that are purported to signal true racial membership. As such, com-parative frames provide rich ethnographic evidence of historically shifting strategies in the management of social kinds. Such a treatment turns focus on the political task of comparing as much as—or more than—on what was compared. We might ask not about the similarities of particular (racialized) entities but about the commonalities they were *made* to share and that made such comparisons pertinent and possible.

A focus on the relations of force lodged in specific comparative frames raises hard methodological questions: how to acknowledge similar configura-tions of rule without flattening out the historical specificity of their con-tent? How different do colonialisms look when varied colonial projects in the same place are compared rather than similar colonial projects at different points in time? What about comparisons from disparate moments and with-out common vocabulary that nevertheless speak to common technologies of intervention and common anxieties of rule? Should it be similar rhythms of rule to which we attend or similar sequences in how sexuality was politicized in the making of race, in how assessments of sexual morality were tied to racial worth?

To argue that management of the intimate defined the scope of colonial governance and its specific technologies is not to suggest that interventions were carried out with uniform intensity or uniform effects. It is to suggest that we focus on those political technologies that joined the cultivation of a social body to the cultivation of a self to rethink the boundaries of our analytic and historical maps. A question posed by one skeptical reader — "Were the intimacies vastly different *outside of imperial domains* at similar points in time?" — points to another: Was there an "outside of empire"? If colonialism is the "underside of modernity," as the Latin American social theorist Enrique Dussel held, and if the epistemic and political field has been shaped by an imaginary of the Occident since the sixteenth century, as Fernando Coronil and Walter D. Mignolo have separately argued in studies of Latin America's colonial history, then colonial differences and their sexual and affective entailments must pervade a far broader set of cultural and political practices than those captured by colonialism's most direct encounters.[81] Even unlikely comparisons may be instructive, for they prompt us to ask whether disciplinary conventions, sheer irrelevance, or different notions of empire and colonialism make sense of the conventions of comparison.

There are several choices, as I have argued here: to do better comparisons, to pursue the politics and history of comparison, or to reach for connections that go beyond comparison altogether. These are not mutually exclusive strategies, but they do place the analytic emphasis on different historiographic zones and archival places. One thing is increasingly clear as colonial studies reconsiders the breadth of its locations and its analytic frames. State machineries alone did not reshape the "interior frontiers" of the nation; people who moved within, between, and outside of imperial boundaries were doing so as well. Women may have been the boundary markers of empire.[82] But it was in the gendered and racialized intimacies of the everyday that women, men, and children were turned into subjects of particular kinds, as domination was routinized and rerouted in intimacies that the state sought to know but could never completely master or work out.

The colonies located in Asia and Africa were sites for experiments in urbanism, hygiene, and social reform but also sites where the vulnerabilities of imperial projects were in sharp relief and where bourgeois prescriptions for family life, morality, and sexual protocol were challenged and rejected. In the Dutch East Indies in the early twentieth century, creole Dutch, Indos (mixed-bloods), Chinese, Javanese were appropriating discourses, comportments, and communication networks—railways, telegraphs, telephones, and radios—to rework their possibilities for themselves. What was modern was not only exported from Europe nor invented in the colonial laboratories of public housing and estates landscaped by European colonial administrations. As students of colonialism insist, it was invented outside of those laboratories and in contradistinction to them.[83]

The incommensurabilities between North American empire and European colonial history diminish when the intimacies of empire are at center stage. Sexual violence was fundamental to conquest, but so was colonizing the hearts and minds of women, children, and men. A new generation of scholars in the making, if we attend closely to their bibliographies, citations, archival trajectories, and the multisited fashion in which they choose to work, are well aware of it. A scholarship looking to the affective strains of empire opens in two related directions: to rethink what political narratives inform our comparisons and to reassess what questions about the management of the intimate might produce differential knowledge of empire's racial politics. The task is not to figure out who was colonizer and who was colonized nor even to ask what distinguished metropolitan and colonial policy; rather, it is to ask what political rationalities have made those distinctions and categories viable, enduring, and relevant measures to distribute rights and resources in the world.

NOTES

This chapter grew out of a plenary panel, "Intimacies of Empire: Comparative Perspectives on Gender and Colonialism," at the Organization of American Historians meeting in spring 2000. I thank Linda Gordon for inviting me to put together this panel and for her encouragement, along with that of cofellows Ed Ayers and Michael Johnson, at the Center for Advanced Study in the Behavioral Sciences in Palo Alto, California. Julia Adams, Nancy Cott, Estelle Freedman, Lawrence Hirschfeld, Gwenn Miller, Julie Skurski, and Alexandra Stern pushed me to frame and broaden it for a wider conversation. I am also indebted to audiences at the Gender and History series at the University of Connecticut, the Department of History and American Studies at Yale University, the Social Science History Association presidential panel "Rethinking the Historical Sociology Project," the Frucht Memorial Lecture Series at the University of Alberta, and students in my history seminar, "Gender, Race, and Empire: The Politics of Knowledge," at the University of California, Berkeley, as well as two sets of anonymous readers for the *Journal of American History*, whose queries encouraged me to temper and refine my argument. I have attended closely to their suggestions and selectively drawn on their language. Joanne Meyerowitz's exemplary editorial guidance steered me through the perils of my interloper status in such a prolific field. Associate editor Susan Armeny copyedited the manuscript with unusual patience and finesse. What overgeneralizations and misrepresentations remain are of my own doing and my responsibility alone.

1. I use the phrases *postcolonial studies* and *colonial studies* interchangeably, although those who identify themselves with one do not always identify with the other. Some scholars use the term *postcolonial* to signal a cross-disciplinary political project, analytically akin to cultural studies, that rejects colonial categories and scholarship that takes them for granted. Others retain the phrase *colonial studies* to underscore more concern for the local and labor history of colonial societies while similarly acknowledging the continuing political, economic, and cultural landscape in which populations that have been colonized are subjugated and now live. The former tend to treat colonialism as a history of the present, to focus on the aftermath of empire and on contemporary hybrid metropolitan cultural forms that follow from it. The latter are less attentive to analytic orientation and more centered on the period of formal colonial rule. Here, I go back and forth between these literatures without close concern for these gradations of difference, which are neither consistent nor always substantive. Both designations indicate a concern, albeit differently framed, with the politics of scholarship and knowledge. On this issue see Chakrabarty, "Postcoloniality and the Artifice of History"; McClintock, "Pitfalls of the Postcolonial"; and Dirlik, "The Postcolonial Aura." On the lack of historical specificity in postcolonial theory see Kennedy, "Imperial History and Post-Colonial Theory."

2. See, e.g., Stoler and Cooper, "Between Metropole and Colony."

3. Readers of *Journal of American History* are familiar with the numerous issues over the last decade that have explicitly urged and explored a broader transnational perspective for United States historians. See, e.g., Thelen, "Interpreting the Declaration of Independence by Translation"; Thelen, "Rethinking History and the Nation-State"; and Thelen, "The Nation and Beyond." See also Tyrrell, "*AHR* Forum"; and Desmond and Domínguez, "Resituating American Studies in a Critical Internationalism."

4. Hurtado, *Intimate Frontiers*; Van Kirk, "*Many Tender Ties*"; Foucault, *The History of Sexuality*, 103. On "regimes of truth" (and "grids of intelligibility") see Dreyfus and Rabinow, *Michel Foucault*, 120–21. Sexual and affective intimacies are not the only microsites of governance from which to explore the relationship between metropolitan and colonial histories. Studies in public health and histories of deportment, labor, communication, and transport provide other nodal points. I thank James Vernon for making this point. Still, I would argue that sexual and affective intimacies are a privileged site on which those other sites invariably turn back and with which they converge.

5. For related arguments with different emphases see Appadurai, *Modernity at Large*, 48–65; and Burton, "Introduction."

6. On "biopower" as a political technology focused on individual and aggregate bodies see Foucault, *History of Sexuality*, 139–46. For a helpful explication of his historical treatment of biopower see Dreyfus and Rabinow, *Michel Foucault*, 133–42.

7. See, e.g., Ming, "Barracks-Concubinage in the Indies, 1887–1920"; Hansen, *Distant Companions*; White, *The Comforts of Home*; Clancy-Smith and Gouda, *Domesticating the Empire*; and Levine, "Orientalist Sociology and the Creation of Colonial Sexualities."

8. On the prescriptions placed on Javanese nursemaids in Dutch colonial homes, and how those former nursemaids now remember them, see Stoler and Strassler, "Castings for the Colonial."

9. See Stoler, *Race and the Education of Desire*; Stoler, *Carnal Knowledge and Imperial Power*; White, *The Middle Ground*; Nash, "The Hidden History of Mestizo America."

10. See Williams, "The Frontier Thesis and American Foreign Policy." For the contrary argument, that exceptionalism was "present at the very creation of America," not the imposition of later historians, see Greene, *The Intellectual Construction of America*, 6. As good an example as any of a colonial reader in which United States history does *not* figure is Cooper and Stoler, *Tensions of Empire*.

11. Amy Kaplan, "'Left Alone with America.'" As Kaplan put it, the absence of the United States from postcolonial studies "reproduces American exceptionalism from without" (17) — treats it as a phenomenon separate from imperial expansion rather than an interrelated form of it.

12. For recent statements see Canny, "Writing Atlantic History"; St. George, Introduction to *Possible Pasts*; and Warner, "What's Colonial about Colonial America?"

13. See, e.g., Rafael, *White Love and Other Events in Filipino History*; Jacobson, *Barbarian Virtues*; Kramer, "The Pragmatic Empire"; Joseph, LeGrand, and Salvatore, *Close Encounters of Empire*; Foley, *The White Scourge*; Gordon, *The Great Arizona Orphan Abduction*; Stern, "Buildings, Boundaries, and Blood"; Adelman and Aron, "From Borderlands to Borders." Patricia Nelson Limerick calls for more comparative focus on the West as a way to "cast a spotlight on both the common characteristics of colonies and the distinctive styles of particular empires." See Limerick, *Something in the Soil*, esp. 101, 355–56.

14. Nash, "The Hidden History of Mestizo America." See Linton and Gillespie, *The Devil's Lane*; Shoemaker, *Negotiators of Change*; Jameson and Armitage, *Writing the Range*; and Hodes, *Sex, Love, Race*. See also D'Emilio and Freedman, *Intimate Matters*. Even critical reviews confirm that D'Emilio and Freedman's work centered the intimate in a new kind of history and political conversation. See duCille, "'Othered' Matters"; and D'Emilio and Freedman, "Commentary." For an effort to put the intimate back into the making of U.S. foreign policy consult Costigliola, "'Unceasing Pressure for Penetration'"; and Costigliola, "'Mixed Up' and 'Contact'"; see also Matsumoto and Allmendinger, *Over the Edge*.

15. On mixedness, *métissage*, and *mestizaje* in other contexts see Taylor, *The Social*

World of Batavia; Vergès, *Monsters and Revolutionaries*; Stoler, "Sexual Affronts and Racial Frontiers"; La Cadena, *Indigenous Mestizo*; Stutzman, "El Mestizaje"; and Klor de Alva, "The Postcolonization of the (Latin) American Experience."

16. See Stoler, "Carnal Knowledge and Imperial Power." But contrast Antonia I. Castaneda's argument that sexual violence, rather than noncoerced unions, "functioned as an institutionalized mechanism for ensuring subordination and compliance" by Amerindian women in the seventeenth-century Spanish colonization of California (Castaneda, "Sexual Violence in the Politics and Policies of Conquest," 33). Degler, *Neither Black nor White*. For the classic study of how, when, and where races did and did not mix in the United States see Williamson, *New People*. For Latin America see Magnus Morner, *Race Mixture in the History of Latin America*. For a more recent treatment (and an excellent bibliographic essay on *mestizaje*) see Schwartz and Salomon, "New Peoples and New Kinds of People"; and Schwartz, "Spaniards, *Pardos*, and the Missing Mestizos."

17. Taylor, *The Social World of Batavia*, 66–68.

18. Calhoun, *Critical Social Theory*, 59; Foucault, *The Archaeology of Knowledge*, 36–37.

19. Not a small part of that expert knowledge elaborated the dangers of "racial hybridization," most starkly in eugenicist research. See Taguieff, *La force du préjugé*; and Vergès, *Monsters and Revolutionaries*. Eugenics figured in debates about Argentinian national identity in the 1920s and 1930s to give "biological currency to the idea of Latinity and thereby new life to scientific racism," according to Stepan, *"The Hour of Eugenics,"* 141. See also Stern, "Responsible Mothers and Normal Children." See Skurski, "The Ambiguities of Authenticity and National Ideology in Latin America"; Sommer, *Foundational Fictions*; Kutzinski, *Sugar's Secrets*, 13.

20. See, e.g., Saldivar, *Border Matters*; and Limon, *American Encounters*.

21. Martinez-Alier, *Marriage, Class, and Colour in Nineteenth-Century Cuba*; Seed, *To Love, Honor, and Obey in Colonial Mexico*; Block, "Lines of Color, Sex, and Service."

22. For a conceptual use of *métissage* in other contexts, see Spear, "'They Need Wives.'"

23. See Inglis, *The White Women's Protection Ordinance*; and Knapman, *White Women in Fiji, 1835–1930*. Hall, *Revolt against Chivalry*; Grimshaw, *Paths of Duty*; Ryan, *The Empire of the Mother*; Cott, *The Bonds of Womanhood*. For scholarship that gestures toward colonial and postcolonial histories that might be shared see Manderson and Jolly, *Sites of Desire/Economies of Pleasure*.

24. Wexler, *Tender Violence*; Tyrrell, *Woman's World/Woman's Empire*; Thorne, "Missionary-Imperial Feminism," esp. 60. Jane Hunter argues that "imperial evangelism's" entreaties to Chinese women to obey their husbands "tended to enhance missionary authority instead" (Hunter, *The Gospel of Gentility*, 177). Guy, "'White Slavery,' Citizenship, and Nationality in Argentina"; van Heyningen, "The Social Evil in the Cape Colony, 1868–1902."

25. See the definitions of *colonialism* in Hall, *Cultures of Empire*, 1–36. J. Jorge Klor de Alva notes a "profound shift" in the concept of colonialism since the late 1970s, from a "structural" focus on economics and politics to one highlighting "cultural, discursive

and power formation in everyday life." A more productive shift has recognized how economic and political structures are transformed *in* the power relations of the everyday. See Klor de Alva, "Postcolonization of the (Latin) American Experience," 263. See also Hall, "Race, Articulation, and Societies Structured in Dominance," 341.

26. Bailyn and Morgan, *Strangers within the Realm*; Greene and Pole, *Colonial British America*; Wood, "The Relevance and Irrelevance of American Colonial History"; and Daunton and Halpern, *Empire and Others*; Warner, "What's Colonial about Colonial America?" 57; McClintock, *Imperial Leather*.

27. Gutiérrez, *When Jesus Came, the Corn Mothers Went Away*; Morgan, "'Some Could Suckle over Their Shoulders'"; see also Trexler, *Sex and Conquest*; Taylor, *The Social World of Batavia*; and Brown, *Good Wives, Nasty Wenches, and Anxious Patriarchs*.

28. Van Kirk, *"Many Tender Ties."* For the argument that legitimacy played a central role in disputes between Native Americans and colonists over land rights in early New England see Plane, "Legitimacies, Indian Identities, and the Law"; see also Plane, *Colonial Intimacies*. For the argument that "collisions" over notions of propriety and property between Indians and English predominated over mixing see O'Brien, *Dispossession by Degrees*. See also Smits, "'Abominable Mixture'"; and Godbeer, "Eroticizing the Middle Ground." For a later period see Mandell, "Shifting Boundaries of Race and Ethnicity."

29. See Genovese, *Roll, Jordan, Roll*.

30. For a framing that has generated new kinds of non-nation-based histories, see Gilroy, *The Black Atlantic*. On the Indian plantation labor force of Fiji see Kelly, *A Politics of Virtue*. On the recruitment of Javanese and Chinese workers to Sumatra see Stoler, *Capitalism and Confrontation*. On colonial Malaya see Butcher, *The British in Malaya, 1880–1941*. For the Caribbean see Putnam, "Public Women and One-Pant Men." See Findlay, *Imposing Decency*.

31. Compare the sexual economy of domestic service and the racialized representation of servants in Smith, *Killers of the Dream*; Oyono, *Houseboy*; and McClintock, *Imperial Leather*, 75–131.

32. Compare Rose, "The Domestication of Domestic Slavery," with Stoler, *Race and the Education of Desire*, 137–64. African American women engaged in "a selective revelation of the personal that 'created the appearance of disclosure,'" according to Mitchell, "Silences Broken, Silences Kept," 436; see also Stoler and Strassler, "Casting for the Colonial," 14–17.

33. Compare the frequency with which accounts of alleged attacks from the late nineteenth century and early twentieth mention African, Asian, and Papuan male servants found in a bedroom, bathing area, or closet of a European home. See Sinha, *Colonial Masculinity*, 52–54; Hansen, *Distant Companions*, esp. 98–105; Etherington, "Natal's Black Rape Scare of the 1870s"; and Inglis, *The White Women's Protection Ordinance*. Memmi, *The Colonizer and the Colonized*.

34. For reviews of this debate see Hind, "The Internal Colonial Concept"; Cervantes, "Chicanos as a Post Colonial Minority"; and Hechter, *Internal Colonialism*. For a study of gender and internal colonialism without use of the latter term see Deutsch, *No Separate*

Refuge. See also Meinig, *The Shaping of America*, 170; Jennings, *The Creation of America*; Leacock, "Montagnais Women and the Jesuit Program for Colonization"; Rothenberg, "The Mothers of the Nation"; Perdue, *Cherokee Women*. For other uses of the internal colonialism model see note 13 above.

35. Gordon, *The Great Arizona Orphan Abduction.*

36. Ryan, *Civic Wars*, 296. On racial membership and mixed-marriage legislation in late-nineteenth-century colonial Indonesia see Stoler, *Tensions of Empire*, 198–237.

37. Bederman, "'Civilization,' the Decline of Middle-Class Manliness, and Ida B. Wells's Antilynching Campaign (1892–94)"; Hoganson, *Fighting for American Manhood.*

38. Inglis, *The White Women's Protection Ordinance.* This is not to exaggerate the breadth of the white women's antilynching movement or to ignore the fact that a much larger population of white women in the United States virulently upheld racist practice. Sinha, *Colonial Masculinity*, 52–63; "Political Report No. 6"; I thank Frances Gouda for calling my attention to this report.

39. On the conflicting cultural narratives from the 1920s about whether the United States was "imperialistic" see Rosenberg, *Financial Missionaries to the World*, esp. 131–37. Eric Hobsbawm, *The Age of Empire, 1875–1914.*

40. Morgan, *American Slavery, American Freedom.* On liberalism and its exclusions see Mehta, "Liberal Strategies of Exclusions." For a fuller account see Mehta, *Liberalism and Empire.*

41. On the exclusionary effects of "interior frontiers" see Balibar, *Masses, Classes, Ideas*, 61–87, esp. 64. See also Wilder, "The Politics of Failure."

42. On the legal system as a productive site of racial ideologies see Pascoe, "Miscegenation Law, Court Cases, and Ideologies of 'Race.'"

43. See Takaki, *Iron Cages*; McMichael, "Incorporating Comparison within a World Historical Perspective"; Somers, "'We're No Angels,'" esp. 758; Grew, "The Comparative Weakness of American History," esp. 93; Gregg, *Inside Out, Outside In*, 6.

44. See Cooper, "Review Essay"; and Cooper, "Le concept de mondialisation sert-il à quelque chose?"

45. For a related point see Tyrrell, "American Historians in the Context of Empire." See also Pratt, *Imperial Eyes*. On science and cross-imperial circuits of knowledge production see Grove, *Green Imperialism*. See Iriye, *Cultural Internationalism and World Order*. For example, Johannes van den Bosch's hand appears in the administration of poverty both in the Netherlands and in colonial Indonesia: see Schrauwers, "The 'Benevolent' Colonies of Johannes van den Bosch."

46. Fanon, *Black Skin, White Masks*; Balandier, "'La situation coloniale'"; Cohn, *An Anthropologist among the Historians and Other Essays*; Wright, "Tradition in the Service of Modernity"; van Heyningen, "The Social Evil in the Cape Colony"; Pratt, *Imperial Eyes*, 36; Stoler, *Race and the Education of Desire*, 95–135; Said, *Culture and Imperialism*, 32. On the political origins of modern English studies in the colonial education system designed for natives in nineteenth-century India see Viswanathan, *Masks of Conquest*. For the ar-

gument that colonialism is the "underside of modernity" in Latin America see Enrique Dussel, *The Underside of Modernity*.

47. Kaplan, "'Left Alone with America,'" 17; McFerson, *The Racial Dimension of American Overseas Colonial Policy*. For the argument that policy toward Native Americans "served as a precedent for imperialist domination over the Philippines" see Walter William, "United States Indian Policy and the Debate over Philippine Annexation," esp. 810. Robert W. Rydell, *All the World's a Fair*.

48. Wood, *Black Majority*. Ayers identifies a striking pattern in U.S. historiography on race: the racial thinking of an early-seventeenth-century moment is seen as borrowed and imported; the racial perceptions and practices of an eighteenth- and early-nineteenth-century period are seen as autonomously "American," internally induced and home-grown; America's domestic racial system in the third, early-twentieth-century "age of imperialism" is seen as exported overseas. See Ayers, "What We Talk about When We Talk about the South," 76. Jordan, *White over Black*; Tocqueville, *Writings on Empire and Slavery*.

49. See Hunt, "'Le Bébé en Brousse'"; Davin, "Imperialism and Motherhood"; and Comaroff and Comaroff, *Ethnography and the Historical Imagination*, 265–96. Gramsci, *Selections from Prison Notebooks*, 259. These points are developed more fully in Stoler, "Affective States."

50. Quoted in Corrigan, *Social Forms/Human Capacities*, 110.

51. Cott, "Notes toward an Interpretation of Antebellum Childrearing"; Stoler, "A Sentimental Education."

52. Pigeaud, *Iets over kinderopvoeding*; Synnott, "Little Angels, Little Devils," 88. For Lewis Hough's 1849 statement see Sunley, "Early Nineteenth-Century American Literature on Childrearing," 158. Bernard Wishy also notes the belief that masturbation was due to "the low and depraved character of nurses and 'licentious domestic[s].'" See Wishy, *The Child and the Republic*, 40.

53. Brace, *The Dangerous Classes of New York and Twenty Years' Work among Them*, 36, 43; Bellingham, "Waifs and Strays," 127–28.

54. McKenzie, *The Making of an English Slave-Owner*, 76.

55. Shapiro, *Child's Garden*; Allen, "Gardens of Children, Gardens of God," 437.

56. Seville, "*Les Métis Parias de l'Indo-Chine*," 228–31, 244–50, 261–63.

57. On the Europe-wide development of the Mettray model see Corssley, "Using and Transforming the French Countryside." On Mettray visions and disciplines see Dekker, *Straffen, Redden en Opvoeden*. On disagreements over this model in the Indies see Stoler, "Developing Historical Negatives."

58. Dekker, *Straffen, Redden en Opvoeden*, 55, 76.

59. Swaan, *In Care of the State*, 57.

60. KV March 28, 1874, no. 47, inv. no. 2668, General State Archives, The Hague, Netherlands.

61. Indies Department of Education to Governor General, KV March 13, 1869, General State Archives, The Hague, Netherlands.

62. Director of Education to Governor General, KV March 28, 1874, General State Archives, The Hague, Netherlands.

63. Oberly, "Indian Commissioners' Reports," 422. I thank Janet Finn for sharing her work in progress with me: Finn, "Boarding Schools and the American Indian Education Experience." On the coercive measures used to recruit Indian children for the boarding schools see Child, *Boarding School Seasons*, 13–15.

64. Trennert, "Educating Indian Girls at Nonreservation Boarding Schools, 1878–1920," 276; Finn, "Boarding Schools and the American Indian Education Experience," 6.

65. Lomawaima, *They Called It Prairie Light*. But Devon A. Mihesuah describes a differentiated "class system" in the school that distinguished between girls from "indigent," "traditionalist" families and those who were from "progressive," "mixed-blood" backgrounds. See Mihesuah, *Cultivating the Rosebuds*.

66. Such prescriptions for success were not embraced only by federal bureaus and colonial policy makers but also by some reformers within subordinated groups. See Polansky, "I Certainly Hope You Will Be Able to Train Her," 149; Washington, *Tuskegee and Its People*, 21; and Anderson, "Education for Servitude."

67. See Fredrickson, *White Supremacy*; and Lamar and Thompson, *The Frontier in History*. Even a study of segregation in South Africa and the American South that opens with the observations of Maurice Evans, a South African who wrote about American race relations, sets aside the fact that Evans, like many of the social scientists depicted there, traveled back and forth between the two locales. See Cell, *The Highest Stage of White Supremacy*; see also Gregg, *Inside Out, Outside In*, 1–26. If many early studies approached these cases as two-column entries, others were already challenging that frame: Stanley B. Greenberg treated racial formations in the two societies as the product of expanding capitalist process, producing similar practices and priorities. See Greenberg, *Race and State in Capitalist Development*. On the circuits of knowledge production in South Africa and the United States see Cuthbertson, "Racial Attraction." See also Campbell, *Songs of Zion*.

68. Nielsen, *The Big Foundations*, 32–33; Lagemann, *The Politics of Knowledge*, 30, 81. The Carnegie Corporation retracted its funding of the Eugenic Records Board in 1939 because of increasing condemnation of the board's overt racism, especially that of its superintendent, Harry Laughlin. I thank Alexandra Stern for pointing this out to me. This section is based on the published Carnegie Commission reports from South Africa, the Carnegie Corporation archives at the Rare Book and Manuscript Library, Butler Library, Columbia University, New York; and the Kenyon Butterfield Papers, Library of Congress, Washington, D.C.

69. The relationship to American social science is particularly clear in the case of Hendrik Frensch Verwoerd, a psychologist who received his PhD from the University of Stellenbosch and worked closely with members of the Carnegie Commission. See Miller, "Sci-

ence and Society in the Early Career of H. F. Verwoerd." I thank Grace Davie for pointing me to this article. Butterfield, *Report of Dr. Kenyon L. Butterfield on Rural Conditions and Sociological Problems in South Africa*, 9. The recommendations of the Carnegie Commission were aimed not simply at "replacing unskilled 'Native' workers with 'poor Whites'" but at establishing employment sanctuaries for white workers" (Ashforth, *The Politics of Official Discourse in Twentieth-Century South Africa*, 105).

70. See Wheeler, "The Intelligence of East Tennessee Mountain Children"; Wilcocks, "Psychological Observations on the Relation between Poor Whites and Non-Europeans"; Wilcocks, "On the Distribution and Growth of Intelligence." (Wilcocks was an investigator for the Carnegie Commission, but this subsequent research was carried out at the University of Stellenbosch and funded by the South African government.) On the prominence of "racial thinking . . . in the early years of Carnegie Corporation grant-making" see Lagemann, *The Politics of Knowledge*, 30.

71. The Carnegie grant for the poor-white study provided for participation by experts from the United States, and the study was later disseminated to educational facilities throughout the United States. Studies of "race crossing" were simultaneously carried out by the Carnegie Institute in Jamaica and Central America. See Davenport and Steggerda, *Race Crossing in Jamaica*; Steggerda, *Anthropometry of Adult Maya Indians*. I thank Alexandra Stern for providing these references and those to the Web site below. For studies by the Carnegie-funded Eugenics Records Office see Dolan DNA Learning Center, *Image Archive on the American Eugenics Movement*, http://vector.cshl.org/eugenics (accessed June 14, 2005). This is not to suggest that central premises of apartheid policy were not formulated earlier. See Martin Legassick, "British Hegemony and the Origins of Segregation in South Africa, 1901–1914," 43. Carnegie Commission, *Joint Findings and Recommendations of the Commission*, xix.

72. Wilcocks, "Rural Poverty among Whites in South Africa and in the South of the United States"; Rothmann, *The Mother and Daughter of the Poor Family*, 151; Carnegie Commission, *Joint Findings and Recommendations of the Commission*, x, xvii, xi; DuBow, *Scientific Racism in Modern South Africa*, 172, 173n20. See Michel Foucault's final 1976 Collège de France lecture on the birth of modern racism: Foucault, "Faire vivre et laisser mourir."

73. Wilcocks, "Rural Poverty among Whites in South Africa and in the South of the United States," xvi; Murray, *Health Factors in the Poor White Problem*, 7, 34.

74. Rothman, *The Mother and Daughter of the Poor Family*, xxiii, 206–7, 212. Wilcocks, *The Poor White*, 62.

75. On the Rockefeller Foundation's hookworm project in the colonial Philippines see Anderson, "Going through the Motions." For Gouda's "flight of fancy" comment see Gouda, "Nyonyas on the Colonial Divide," 335–36.

76. Du Bois, "The European Population of Netherland India," 12; Memmi, *The Colonizer and the Colonized* (1967), 4.

77. Du Bois, "The Problem of the Half Caste," 3.

78. On this modular quality see Cooper and Stoler, "Between Metropole and Colony." Robert Gregg, too, argues that the international traffic in women between London, South Africa, and the New York Bowery is a prime subject for studying intersecting histories. See Gregg, *Inside Out, Outside In*, 9–18.

79. Hacking, *The Taming of Chance*.

80. On the relationship between Friedrich Nietzsche's concept of a "will to knowledge" and Foucault's reworking of it see Sheridan, *Michel Foucault*, 118–23.

81. See Dussel, *The Underside of Modernity*; Coronil, "Beyond Occidentalism"; and Mignolo, *Local Histories/Global Designs*. Even though Siam was a noncolonized region, its "geopolitical" history as a nation was shaped by impingements of European imperial expansion and colonial discourses of race, according to Winichakul, *Siam Mapped*.

82. McClintock, *Imperial Leather*, 24. On the movement of some women between the positions of concubine, wife, trader, mother, and slaveholder see Chatterjee, "Colouring Subalternity."

83. Taylor, *The Social World of Batavia*, 155. See Mitchell, *Questions of Modernity*; Mrázek, "'Let Us Become Radio Mechanics'"; Chakrabarty, *Provincializing Europe*; and McGranahan, "Arrested Histories."

Convergence
and
Comparison

3

DAMON SALESA

Samoa's Half-Castes and

Some Frontiers of Comparison

Samoa may be largely overlooked in most historical discussions of U.S. empire, but for the last quarter of the nineteenth century it occupied more than its fair share of U.S. public attention. Samoa became the primary intersection of U.S., British, and German imperial interests in the Pacific, and a steady stream of usually bad, occasionally infuriating, and always complex news was published about the "Samoan trouble."[1] For Samoans this was a period of unprecedented foreign interventions, and although formal colonialism did not begin until Samoa was divided between Germany and the United States in 1899, indigenous sovereignty was not always honored in the actions beforehand of foreign militaries, missionaries, and businessmen.

Samoa had been a conscious unity for hundreds of years, speaking a single language and operating under a unitary political system.[2] No Europeans or Americans were resident there until after 1800, yet by 1875 Samoa housed the German commercial headquarters of the Pacific, a powerful group of British missionaries and traders, and some weighty U.S. interests and naval ambitions. In 1879 the three "Great Powers" were jointly ruling Samoa's most important port town, Apia. Samoa was one of the few places where these governments were in such proximity, and this situation proved dangerous. Germany, Britain, and the United States verged on war in Samoa during 1888 and 1889 and in 1899; hundreds of their soldiers and sailors were to lose their lives in Samoa. The causes were both local and imperial: geopolitical and economic concerns were implicated in Samoan politics and activities, particularly the ongoing civil wars. Bismarck, Gladstone, and Seward all came to regret their fraught involvement in "the Samoan tangle."[3] So although Samoa was not evenly significant in the histories of these empires, more than once it was critical.

By the time New Zealand made Samoa the first territory that Germany lost in World War I (in 1914), Samoa had been subject to four empires in fewer than twenty years. On the one hand, Samoa had remained a strongly contested imperial target; on the other hand, almost all Samoans continued to be autonomous, governed by a decentralized, yet unitary, indigenous political system.

The unity of Samoan culture and politics was maintained by a political economy of mobility and circulation that made Samoans seem, to some Euro-Americans, "travel happy."[4] This meant that the different networks of the various Euro-American empires that encountered Samoa intersected in complex indigenous networks operating in very different ways and for different reasons. By the last quarter of the nineteenth century these discourses and politics had become enmeshed in important, though partial and limited, ways.

Though traditional imperial histories have focused on diplomatic or high political matters in Samoa, many of the critical sites where these discourses and activities intersected were in the "domain of the intimate." In Samoa, as an archipelago contested by three different empires, this was to have some unusual dimensions. In particular, because there was generally no jurisdiction recognized by all parties, and because of the ways in which imperial discourse operated, jurisdiction, power, and sovereignty came to be substantiated not by territory or bureaucracy but individually, person by person. In this way the intimate frontiers also manifested "the frontier" in its larger sense. Making particular subjects and defining how they might be governed was not only a question of colonial administration but also an issue of imperial magnitude. For this reason I argue that in Samoa, and likely in analogous situations, there was a domain that was at once tactical and strategic, imperial and intimately local — a "strategic intimacy."

Equally, because of the proximity of these empires with each other, intersections in discourse and activity, and between indigenous and imperial circulatory networks, Samoa became a fertile ground for comparisons and cooperation between empires. All of these different dimensions can be accessed through the discourses surrounding half-castes. Half-castes embodied, both literally and figuratively, intersections between indigenous and imperial circulations. In half-castes and the discourses charged with identifying and managing them, the connections between the intimate and the strategic are also apparent. These people and discourses made apparent a number of different registers of comparisons. All of this makes the half-castes a particularly rich point of entry into the study of Samoa and its many imperial histories.

INTERNATIONAL FRONTIERS AND THE PROBLEM OF THE HALF-CASTE

One might begin by exploring how, in the last quarter of the nineteenth century, Samoa's half-castes came to be an intimate manifestation of an international frontier. That international frontier, the largest in the world, was the nineteenth-century Pacific Ocean and its islands, and it is necessary to think about its dynamics in order to appreciate many of the problems that half-castes seemed to cause. The Pacific was a frontier long before the U.S. invasion of Hawaii (1893), the Spanish-American War (1898), or the colonizing of eastern Samoa (1899). It was not only the "filling up" of the mainland that made the Pacific a U.S. frontier. In a sense the Pacific had long been a frontier, as the hundreds of New England ships in the Pacific showed. Americans were present in every major island group, and it was not unusual to encounter a Pacific Islander in a New England seaport, for neither Ishmael's nor Queequeg's experiences were unusual. Hawaiians, in particular, were a pioneering presence at certain places on both the west and east coasts of the U.S. mainland.[5] The United States was a notable presence in pre-1840 New Zealand, and the dispatching of American missionaries to places as distant as Hawaii and Ponape (Pohnpei) underlines the eastern U.S.'s Pacific connection. *Moby Dick* may be an American novel, but it is a Pacific novel too, and Melville was an American frontiersman.

Hawaii was an obvious, and key, site in the U.S. Pacific frontier, but Samoa as well.[6] Samoa took almost as much political energy as Hawaii after midcentury, despite being smaller in both land and population. The signal moment in this was a local treaty with a Samoan chief signed in 1872, and in the following three decades the empires of the United States, Britain, and Germany increasingly converged on Samoa. This first treaty led to a patchwork of treaties, and the United States, Britain, and Germany had soon each signed treaties claiming various extraterritorial rights in Samoa. In 1889 vessels from all three navies were crowded into Samoan harbors and often seemed destined for hostilities. Such entanglements made Samoa more comparable to situations like Treaty Port China than to most other Pacific Island groups. The intersection of empires, the competition between them, and their joint inability to either recognize indigenous Samoan sovereignty or relinquish their own claims meant the United States, Britain, and Germany were constantly in competing positions in Samoa. This meant that sovereignty, governance, and jurisdiction were severely complicated, paralleling what Eileen Scully has shown in her work on the United States and Treaty Port China.[7]

Indigenous Samoan sovereignty was never fully acknowledged by the Euro-American powers, who used it as an instrument of convenience. Samoan sovereignty was typically acknowledged only when it was being eroded, as in treaties. The giving away of extraterritorial rights was effectively the splitting of Samoan sovereignty, and its further division among the United States, Germany, and Britain meant that a "question always arose as to the limits of the respective jurisdiction of the various powers."[8] The most pronounced concession of Samoan sovereignty was the "municipality" of Apia, formally cleaved from the rest of Samoa and placed under the joint control of the three foreign governments.

Apia, however, was the exception. Because no single Euro-American power claimed to be sovereign in Samoa, none could extend jurisdiction through territorial sovereignty in Samoa. Each, instead, extended its sovereignty outside of Apia person by person, defining jurisdiction by identifying individual subjects. This was a critical step that implicated grand designs in local activity, measuring international frontiers in intimate ones. It was understood that jurisdiction could be created through individual nationals — the Englishman, to a greater or lesser extent, was believed to take English law with him; the American continued to relate to American law. There could be "a personal jurisdiction as in the case of the allegiance owed to the crown by British subjects over all the world."[9] As a U.S. consular agent explained, "American Citizens here [in Samoa] are Foreigners however long their term of residence they are still . . . sojourners owing fealty to the laws of their country and looking to them for protection."[10] This interest in the identity of individuals focused imperial attention on certain intimate domains in Samoa.[11]

This dependence on the identification of individual subjects was precisely why, for local imperial operations to be effective, certain elements of Samoa's population had to be fixed and identified.[12] The imperial frontier became not simply the place of Samoa but particular segments of its population. Instead of surveying, mapping, and marking land, similar techniques of inquiry were to be used on the population. Particular investments had to be made in distinguishing between and among mothers and fathers, different races, children of different ages, and different kinds of families. Strategic imperial interests were activated in family relations and lives, in people's private, sexual, and domestic arrangements. Repeatedly implicated in these concerns were the problems occasioned by half-castes.

The "frontier" setting of Samoa meant that the critical question became whether individual half-castes would be "recognized" and afforded subject status by one of the foreign governments. Such an approach was intended to clearly fix individuals (and thus the population), and it avoided the need for a formal "half-caste" category. Half-castes had proven difficult elsewhere, of course, and this Samoan activity was a clear indication of what Stoler has argued above—that "circuits of knowledge production and racialized forms of governance spanned a global field."[13] Imperial actions and practices in Samoa were often connected through knowledges and processes that connected elsewhere in interested empires or traversed their boundaries. Linking these various sites and instances were many different kinds of comparisons, which were at times broad or wide-ranging, at the level of geopolitics or strategy, as when Germany compared Samoa with Fiji and Hawaii or when Britain compared Samoa with neighboring Tonga.[14] At other times they could be deeply specific, as searches for comparable law, categories, or other analogues on which to directly model actions. This was true of American comparisons also, which on the one hand were strategic, such as comparisons that sought to use the "Samoan Tangle" to promote naval ambitions, and on the other might be very precise and limited, such as efforts to draw very specific legal comparisons.[15]

Various comparisons, not least those made during big diplomatic meetings such as the 1887 Washington Conference, bolstered and motivated U.S. activities concerning Samoa.[16] These activities, in turn, occasioned and conditioned the kinds of encounters U.S. empire was to have with Samoa's half-castes. It is enlightening to focus on such exchanges between the various different levels of discourse, from Washington to Apia, and encounters between these and indigenous Samoa. In these moments comparison was visibly a search for analogues, for transferable models, for examples with the potential to educate or inform action, practices, understandings—essential workings of the networks of empire. Moreover, in Samoa the difficulties presented by half-castes were a critical part of the motivation and process of making the intimate domains legible to empires.

The imperial officials based in Samoa were charged with implementing a set of imperial practices on a population that they had recurrent difficulties even identifying. It was work that would have taxed the most capable, and precious few of the officials working in Samoa were so capable. Officials had almost no established processes of discipline or management and for most of the year had to rely on cooperation or Samoan support to assert themselves, in conjunction with occasional, and oftentimes violent, visits by their navies.

There were very few docile subjects to be found in the archipelago. Even the officials themselves were usually at odds with each other or involved in competing factions. Consular cooperation was often hampered by outright antagonism and personal jealousies, and officials often used their positions in concert with their commercial or personal activities. Several consuls became so entwined with Samoan politics and people that involvement proved a further source of trouble. U.S. consuls, like those of Germany and Britain, wielded a very specific authority but very little specific power.[17]

If officials were difficult enough, other foreigners could prove even less willing subjects. It was by no means uncommon to be unsure of the origins of a given foreigner, and even if an official thought he was sure, it was not a matter that was easy to prove. In Apia there were often "persons going from one [Pacific] island to another, sometimes claiming protection from one consul, and again from another."[18] Some of these men endeavored to be recognized as British subjects because as French subjects they were liable for compulsory military service.[19] Some tried to change nations back and forth.[20] Others, such as James Nooney, sought almost to defy classification: "I am a private citizen of the United States, and not a *subject* of any nation."[21]

Such problems were compounded by the assumption of responsibilities by local officials that were well outside the bounds intended by their metropolitan governments. Samoans called consuls *fa'amasino*—the same word as that used for judge—yet with limited exceptions for German and British officials, these powers were denied to local officials, and U.S. officials talked enviously of their colleagues in China and Turkey.[22] As one complained: "I am so utterly unable to perceive in this place my true position. . . . [The consular officer in Samoa is] de facto Magistrate, and enshrouded with Judicial Authority, he is called upon to settle disputes, to preserve order, to enforce justice and compel recompense from the wrongdoer."[23]

The problem of sovereignty and jurisdiction, complicated by unruly subjects, was an everyday one. The machinations of petty colonial officials (Robert Louis Stevenson talked of the *"furor consularis"* in Samoa), as much as the grandiose ambitions of statesmen and diplomats, regularly caused international problems. This was why Samoa was an ongoing headache in Washington, Berlin, and London. Samoa may have been a small nexus of empires, but it was a busy one and one where the substance of jurisdictional and sovereign disputes was often the identities of certain individuals, their property, action, and relations.

The most problematic population proved to be the half-castes. Each of the different empires had protracted and intricate difficulties identifying and managing Samoa's half-castes — processes I have attempted elsewhere to more completely explore.[24] Most striking, however, is that although there were clear differences between the efforts of the different empires, there were greater similarities. Similar techniques were utilized: by the 1870s certain marriages in Samoa (involving foreigners) were being recorded, certain births and deaths were being marked down, and the first reliable censuses had been taken.[25] Enumeration and classification were being undertaken by all three empires, driven in part by both local and strategic necessities evident in Samoa. Importantly, the population that Britain, Germany, and the United States were attempting to construct by these techniques was not the native population (which would be poorly enumerated and classified until after formal annexation) but the population of "foreigners" (a subject status that included the select, "recognized" half-castes). The British consul, for instance, began registering all British subjects residing in Samoa, along with their families, using as compulsion the ultimatum that those who did not register forfeited their rights, their identity, as British subjects.[26] German consuls were similarly instructed to compile a register of Imperial German subjects.[27] Classifying Samoa's population of foreigners was an intersecting, even comparative, project.

The fundamental premise shared by all three powers was that foreign identity would be singular. None of the empires created a formal category of "half-caste"; rather, each was concerned with defining individuals as either subjects or nonsubjects. This approach paralleled efforts at fixing sovereignty and/or jurisdiction. The technologies of identity such as marriage certificates, letters of identity, and other bureaucratic instruments that "proved" nationality and naturalization were either designed or implemented in a way that they would not overlap.[28] In Samoa it was hoped that this procedure would resolve conflicting points of sovereignty and not simply relocate these troubles to the individual level. For instance, in 1857 the consuls and Samoan leaders reached a jurisdictional arrangement. When individuals had complaints, foreigners would go to their consul, and Samoans to their chiefs, and then these authorities would go to each other.[29] Such a method, for a time relatively effective, depended not only on the establishment of individual identity — of identifying "foreigners" and "Samoans" — but also on identifying to *which* foreign power they would be subject.

It was no coincidence that in that same year U.S. commercial agent Robert Swanston first made the dilemma of half-castes explicit. The inception of operations premised on clarity and fixity simply made the problem of those who were ill-defined more pressing. Swanston wrote to the State Department seeking advice:

> There are in this consulate a very great number of half caste children of American Citizens, and American Negroes, by Samoan women. Many of these children are Samoan to all intents, in education and habits, others again are comparatively civilized and follow the habits of the people of civilized nations. As it is very probable that at no distant day there may arise questions involving their rights as Samoans, or as Americans, I respectfully request that the Department will advise on this matter in order that all doubts may be settled.[30]

Swanston's inquiry was the first of many by U.S. officials explicitly concerned with fixing the position of half-castes. Similar requests for instructions regarding the "status" of half-castes were common among German and British officials, too, for similar reasons.

Such concerns with half-castes underlined that "racial" categories were artifacts of colonial encounter, visibly and knowingly manufactured and policed. The search for a kind of "general rule," one commonly sought by officials in Samoa, was, by and large, illusory.[31] Metropolitan governments, on the few occasions they offered advice, tended to focus on lawful marriage, the legitimacy of the children, or their ages as ruling criteria. In these instances it was quite clear that the precedents were drawn from other imperial sites, including domestically from the United States. Such rules were often difficult to apply in Samoa, where application was plagued by poor record keeping and unclear law, as well as matters such as polygamy and the widespread unavailability of legal marriage. The discretionary techniques that were established by these same practices also appeared to have been in use elsewhere and to resonate with both other empires, as well as some elements of domestic U.S. practice: the mode of life of the father, the degree of "civilization" of the children, oaths of allegiance, and wealth. This is not to say that Britain, Germany, and the United States approached Samoa's half-castes in the same ways.

The questions raised by concern with Samoa's half-castes were not just strategic or local to Samoa but were potentially of metropolitan significance. All three Euro-American powers seemed to share in more than one comparable predicament. On the one hand, they had entangled projects in Samoa, projects that came to hinge on stabilizing and mapping a human frontier and on creating a population that was singular and manageable. On the other hand, each of these governments was confronted with comparable problems in redefining the limits of domestic citizenship and the nation. If this second concern was crucially different between the three empires, it was not completely so. With slavery, the Civil War, and Reconstruction the process in the United States was marked, and much of the discourse circulating in Samoa was inflected with these concerns (as in Swanston's differentiation of citizens and "Negroes"). In Britain the problem of redefining the Victorian nation had begun in the 1830s, with the Reform Act, Catholic Emancipation, the Abolition Act, and Poor Laws, and continued with the further Reform Acts in 1867 and 1884. Class and gender, and to an increasing extent race, empire, and imperial locations, troubled previous incarnations of the citizenry and its meanings.[32] It was a process that was hardly foreign to other countries but, as is apparent with confederated and then imperial Germany, differed crucially from location to location. During this time the peculiarities and importance of German concerns with defining its citizenry were myriad.[33]

How citizenship might be acquired remained a fraught concern, as much domestically as overseas. Central in discussions was whether citizenship was acquired by birth (*jus soli*) or by descent (*jus sanguinis*). Each of the three Euro-American states involved in Samoa utilized both means, though in different ways, with varying qualifications. After 1871 Germany made it compulsory to register with an overseas consulate; otherwise, after ten years' residence outside of Germany citizenship would lapse.[34] In Samoa this gave the German consular officials a little more coercive weight than that possessed by their counterparts. As with the United States, immigration was an impetus for Germany to reconsider the way citizenship was assigned and managed, but Germans were also concerned with the ethnic Germans who lived outside state boundaries, the foreigners who lived within, and even the ways in which these concerns could be used to stabilize government.[35]

British citizenship could be acquired by either birth or descent but with the crucial limitation that children had to be born of a legitimate marriage.

Encounters between Samoa and the United States precipitated by half-castes foregrounded related concerns. As half-castes were coming to prominence in Samoa, in the late 1850s, a new U.S. citizenship law relevant to them was passed in 1855. This law made two provisions: that any woman married to a U.S. male citizen could take the nationality of her husband and that the children of U.S. citizens born abroad would themselves be citizens.[36] This signaled an important change from earlier U.S. law, which saw nationality as permanent. The passage of this legislation was to have important effects in Samoa, while in the United States it was dramatically to transform the substance of concerns over citizenship. As Nancy Cott has pointed out, the "reframing of American political society after the Civil War incorporated a preferred model for American marriage, which renewed emphasis on the spouses' being of the same race, highlighted the state's role in the marriage, and continued, as of old, to see the whole inspired by Christian principles."[37] These developments, in concert, showed how marriage continued to be a cornerstone in the production of citizenship, as much in the United States as abroad.[38]

During Reconstruction and afterward the U.S. federal government sought to impose what Scully has called "a new citizenship regime." These new federal assertions could at times be most fully articulated outside of the United States. "The chief accomplishment of late nineteenth-century federal policy in the extraterritorial zone [in Treaty Port China]," she argued, "was to unbundle the panoply of rights and responsibilities embedded in domestic citizenship."[39] To a lesser extent this was true also in Samoa, as State Department officials found new stresses in policy and law exposed by the predicaments of U.S. nationals in Samoa and their half-caste offspring.

U.S. officials in Samoa did not demand that offspring of U.S. citizens be legitimate to acquire citizenship. This contrasted with the policy of British officials in Samoa. Not only did this stem from the 1855 law, but it also reflected the wide gulf between U.S. law and English law in other respects, for instance concerning illegitimate offspring. By 1886 most U.S. states allowed such children to share in their maternal estates, and many states allowed them to share in their paternal estates. There was little such benefit in England, as seen in the notorious nineteenth-century "baby farms," which trafficked largely in "bastard" children, and the repeated parliamentary insistence that fathers need not support illegitimate offspring.[40] Though there was some uneasiness with the degree of recognition the United States granted illegitimate children, and the danger that this might undermine the institution of marriage, it was equally seen as "liberal and generous public policy."[41] The right of such children born in Samoa to U.S. citizenship was consistent with this approach.

The racial politics that informed U.S. domestic laws were very different from those confronted in Samoa. Yet these domestic laws were called on to work as analogues for many of the occurrences in Samoa. So it was in the letter quoted above, when Swanston separated out "American Negroes" as a category; in Samoa they were generally regarded as Americans, and there is no evidence that they were treated differently by authorities in an official capacity. At any rate, given the racial grammar furnished for them, there was not really much that could be held to directly guide U.S. officials in Samoa. This could well have been an advantage, an important discretion. In other places such matters could be counterproductive: laws intended to prevent Chinese women from becoming citizens after marrying an American in the United States prevented this from happening in China (even though these women formed an important part of American life there).[42] In the case of Samoa no domestic U.S. comparisons were used to clarify the racial status of indigenous Samoans. It was not clear whether Samoans might be considered white, Asian, black, or otherwise.[43]

With what, precisely, should Samoan cases be compared? This question remained open. From which body of law and policy should comparisons be drawn? International law or the laws of other nations? U.S. state or federal domestic law or law relating to U.S. subjects overseas? The answer to these questions was hardly clear, and an 1867 case in Samoa, involving William Barnes, his Samoan wife, and their half-caste children, made this particularly evident. In response to its complexities legal experts at the State Department cobbled together advice that was remarkably capricious. It called on, variously, the 1855 federal statute, New York state law, "the law prevailing in most of the states of the Union," and vague incantations of "*our* law."[44]

This was more than simple jurisprudence. Because the corpus of law appropriate to the case was not obvious, decisions about which laws and situations were comparable, and which were not, were vital. In retrospect, the nonapplication of domestic laws regarding miscegenation might seem surprising. But key distinctions prevented consistent application, one being that Samoa was regarded as "*foreign* soil" and another being that there was a lack of compelling straightforward racial comparisons between Samoa and the domestic United States. Indeed, citing the 1855 statute and *Kent's Commentaries*, the legal advice given in 1867 was that Barnes's Samoan wife was a woman who "might be naturalized," which was "*a periphrasis for free white person*."[45] Should she therefore be considered white, as that would allow her to be a citizen, especially when she was "probably of an olive complexion"? Ultimately, such anomalies strained the taxonomies themselves. The legal opinion concluded that it remained "an open question what the word 'white' . . . may be held to include."[46]

The status of half-castes was clearer: "*half-castes . . . are declared citizens*." But their citizenship was perforated with caveats. The State Department advised that half-castes "should therefore, at least during their minority, have the same protection . . . that their father would be entitled to expect." Once half-castes came of age, however, they were *sui juris*—outside of U.S. jurisdiction. Moreover, half-caste citizenship was only applicable inside a U.S. jurisdiction. "Outside of that . . . the rights of persons are to be determined by the law of the locality"—which remained a problem in Samoa because the United States had not finally decided whose or what laws applied. A final statement was revealing: "the precise condition . . . [of half-castes] is that they are subjects of Samoa with the faculty of becoming, at will, citizens of the United States by entering the jurisdiction with the intention of permanent residence." The disposition of half-castes with regard to the United States was hardly clear. They were in a state of "becoming"—a liminal position outside of the category of "Samoan" yet not fully, nor permanently, U.S. citizens. This is a position, strikingly enough, that parallels the modern-day condition of American Samoans, who are not *yet* subjects or nationals but are capable of becoming citizens.[47]

GENEALOGIES OF ORDER

Nineteenth-century indigenous Samoan understandings of half-castes make it clear that the difficulties empires had with half-castes were neither universal nor "natural." Although by the mid-twentieth century Samoan discourse regarding half-castes had partially begun to appropriate aspects of some colonial discourses, in the nineteenth century indigenous and imperial discourses were decidedly different. Half-castes were neither a necessary nor eternal problematic for Samoans; indeed, in Samoan discourses they were not originally even a category.

Before the mid-nineteenth century in Samoa, the Samoan language had no word for *half-caste*, and there was no analogous concept, either. The word became the one transliterated from English, *'afakasi*. Analogous situations that might have been seen by Euro-Americans as race mixing, such as marriages between Samoans and the non-Samoans who had visited or resided in Samoa for centuries (especially Tongans, Fijians, and those from Wallis and Futuna), were not understood in this way. Where colonial discourse and governance has been aptly described by Stoler and others as "taxonomic," the relevant Samoan discourses and governance might better be understood as genealogical.

Samoans, like other Polynesians, ordered much of their lives by means of genealogies (*gafa*).[48] Genealogies reaching back to the creation of the cosmos mapped out and connected both past and present, gendering, sequencing, and accounting for the universe and its people. Most Samoans could (and can) trace their genealogy, through both mother and father, through a dozen, often dozens, of generations. Samoan histories remember two supernatural brothers, Saveasi'uleo and Ulufanuasese'e, who on their final parting were destined to meet again in their descendants (*gafa*);[49] and in such ways lineages were connected to deities, to other worlds, to the creation of the earth and its future. It was through genealogy that one belonged to a family (*'aiga*); through a family that one belonged to a village (*nu'u*); and through villages and families that one gained rights, property, access, status. Tellingly, the organization of Samoan genealogies, through both mother's (*tama fafine*) and father's (*tama tane*) sides, meant that every child had two lines of descent. If a father's family was absent, as a half-caste's usually was, this was not unprecedented. It was not uncommon for Samoans to grow up and receive their status, property, and support from their mother's family. In one sense "half-castes" who lived in Samoan villages were as "whole" as their neighbors. In another sense every child was a kind of half-caste, even if both halves were Samoan. Individuals would trace their genealogy back to different villages and would often feel those ties in very different, practical, ordinary ways. One's identities were plural, and this was expected. This was the nature of Samoan genealogy: it was multiple, historical, and responsive to context.[50] Genealogy could also be adjusted by means of adoption, by the achievements of an individual or generation, or by other special events.[51]

For Samoans genealogy was a conditioner of living, not simply a pedigree or line of descent. More than this, genealogy itself was politics: better thought of as a network of relations than as a personal history. Even those who would have only the crudest idea of Samoan society would know the rudiments of Samoan genealogies, the principles of political legitimacy they confer, the political histories and connections they maintain, and the rules of political conduct they model.[52] One could make related observations about how genealogy conditioned gender relations, social interaction, or the conduct of ceremony. Genealogy was central to Samoan traditions and histories: one Samoan proverb remembers how even a clot of blood born to an important chiefly couple was given a name and a genealogical place.[53] To be without such connections was all but unthinkable. Genealogies gave order to Samoan lives, and they continued to do so after the arrival of foreigners.

Consequently, those considered in imperial discourses to be half-castes were seen very differently by Samoans. Imperial taxonomies sought to categorize such people in fixed and singular ways, as either Samoan or foreign, whereas Samoan genealogies allowed a fundamental duality within a relational, historical complex. In the nineteenth century, for most of Samoa, for most of the time, it was the genealogical order that pertained. Until imperialism made it otherwise, there is no evidence that Samoans treated half-castes differently from their Samoan relatives because they were half-castes, though if their father was or had been indispensable they were often accorded status or property. Half-castes (and other foreign subjects) who were not living near Apia were by and large living under exclusively Samoan authority, and it was that authority on which they relied for everyday order and safety.[54] The two main exceptions were the port-cum-municipality of Apia and the times of active imperial interventions, which were usually performed by warships and their shore parties.

In Samoa the capillaries of imperial power were consequently both spatially and temporally restricted. However, imperial incursions into Samoan realms were both occasioned by and gave occasion to challenges to the genealogical order. If people recognized as foreign subjects felt aggrieved by Samoan authority, they could turn to imperial officials. But even if they were left unsatisfied by Samoan authority, it was not always wise to approach imperial officials. For one thing consuls would decide which complaints to pursue. For another, imperial functionaries would decide what were appropriate punishments or recompense. Yet the potential power of this subjectivity was genuine, if potentially dangerous. One could not always expect to return to a village after challenging the dignity of chiefs, snubbing their authority, and damaging the well-being and order of villages.

Often these problems were further embodied by half-castes. As the century progressed, a number of half-castes were both foreign subjects and Samoan leaders, occasionally even important chiefs. In some cases this elevated status was due to the importance of their white fathers; in others it was premised on the genealogical claims of their mothers. In Manu'a, the easternmost islands of Samoa, the daughter of an American trader, Arthur Young, became the holder of perhaps the most ancient and revered chiefly title in Samoa, the *Tu'i Manu'a*.[55] (Another of his descendants, Chris Young, became the last *Tu'i Manu'a*, forcibly deposed by the U.S. naval administration in the 1920s).[56] For Samoans the recognition of such people as chiefs was based on traditional criteria, such as genealogy and *tautua* (service), and was a further expression of the genealogical order. In imperial discourse the foreign subject who was also an indigenous authority was recurrently disruptive, even confounding.

The spatial differentiations in power and discourse, and the punctuations of active imperial interventions, nurtured the complex topography of the half-caste population. In Apia the differences between Samoans, half-castes, and others and among the gradations of foreign subjects could be more carefully managed. Missionary societies, for instance, gave the more privileged foreign and half-caste students their own classrooms, even their own institutions.[57] In turn education, particularly fluency in English or German, increased opportunities. Half-castes found employment as clerks, interpreters, and policemen in disproportionate numbers in the new town.[58] In Apia alcohol was encoded with difference, and bars, bowling alleys, and billiard halls were places where half-castes clustered. More respectable were balls, polo matches, dancing clubs, and amateur theater, and half-castes frequented them also. Robert Louis Stevenson started a special dancing club solely for half-castes, and half-castes dominated other institutions from the tennis club and the public library to the church for foreigners (sometimes known as "half-caste church").[59] These were all facilities that were unavailable in Samoan villages and represented another vector, outside of official means, through which imperial distinctions might be constructed and made significant.

Although the exclusionary practices were present throughout Apia town, the half-castes that partook of this privileged social orbit were still the minority. Most half-castes, even in town, were not recognized as foreign subjects. Moreover, most half-castes did not have the social or economic resources to participate in the elite cultures of foreigners and half-castes, even if they desired to. It was often the case that "unrecognized" half-castes had to turn to their talents or their wits to get by: and for this reason half-castes often constituted the larger part of the economic individualists operating in Samoa (almost all other Samoans worked communally). Half-castes that could, might return to their villages, but an increasing number were born in the town. This meant that half-castes were often in search of work and opportunities in the small town of Apia. Half-caste women might aim to marry well, or even not so well, or otherwise to enter service for missionaries or well-to-do whites. Half-caste men who were fortunate would find an occupation such as boatbuilding, carpentry, blacksmithing, trading, or laboring. But half-castes were also well represented among less-reputable occupations, including prostitution, innkeeping, sly-grogging, gunrunning, and land dealing.[60]

Comparisons between Apia town and the villages throughout the rest of Samoa reveal how fraught concerns with half-castes could be. At the core was a striking contrast: the kinds of exclusions that were common in Apia by the end of the century mostly could not have been expressed in Samoan villages. This development reflected not simply the differences between genealogical and taxonomic orders but very different institutional and social circumstances. Of course these two different orders could not stand apart; they were entangled, and these entanglements were very often embodied in half-castes.

If the many different vectors for substantiating the differences "recognized" by the empires — schools, churches, employment — were unavailable in the Samoan villages, the increased exercise of imperial power, however crudely or irregularly, was making the category of half-caste more relevant for Samoans.[61] Whether a half-caste was recognized as a foreign subject or not placed (or potentially placed) tremendous strictures on the way he or she might be treated. At least in the eyes of Samoans and their leaders, too many half-castes used foreign officials and navies as a court of higher appeal to Samoan customary law. Any kind of sanction authorized by Samoan authorities, whether the destruction or taking of property, beatings, the taking away of land usage or other economic rights, or the levying of punishments on families rather than individuals, could potentially be contradicted. Such was the case when the chief Tuisila prevented a German half-caste, William Laban, from taking possession of a small islet. Though he had long been a resident of the district, living under Samoan authority, Laban turned to the German consul (and the German warship *Bussard*), who, in a thinly veiled show of force, installed him on the island.[62] When individuals were recognized as foreign subjects, any Samoan action, no matter how proper or justified, might bring a response if the aggrieved individuals turned to their officials.

The genealogical order indigenous to Samoa, and Samoan discourses, began to respond to the classifications of empire. In the 1850s the usual description was of *tagata Samoa* (Samoan people) or equivalent terms that captured differences in rank and gender. Yet by the 1890s Samoan discourse was clearly in dialogue, or at least inflected, with imperial taxonomies, especially in exchanges with officials. The term *'afakasi* (half-caste) was by this time commonly used, and it often differentiated between classes of half-caste, particularly those of foreign subjectivity, as with *'afakasi Peretania* (British half-castes), *'afakasi Siamani* (German half-castes), or *'afakasi Amelika* (American half-castes). Samoans even began to differentiate *'afakasi uliuli* (black half-castes).[63] These shifts in Samoan discourse were an index both of an increase in imperial relevance and interventions—the growing potency of imperial discourse—and of the entanglement of the indigenous and imperial.

An indication of just how imperial intervention had begun to alter Samoan life was apparent in the civil war of 1877–78.[64] By the time of these wars there were a number of half-castes fighting on either side. They were particularly valued as members of a war party because they were often accomplished in the use of firearms and well-versed in their maintenance.[65] In the heat of battle, particularly if they looked to be in trouble, many of these half-castes would assert their status as foreigners. They claimed that should they be harmed, warships would follow.[66] Only twenty years earlier such assertions, perhaps even the combatants' status as half-castes, would have meant little, and their safety would have been in doubt. But the capillaries of the different empires had begun to reach Samoan battlefields. The residents of Samoa evidently felt the leverage of imperial categories, and consequently a few half-castes could use their status as leverage, even on the battlefield. Half-castes had proven important yet anomalous within the taxonomies and practices of three different empires. This concern had made them potentially anomalous within Samoan discourses and lives.

NEW MORNINGS: THE UNITED STATES AND SAMOA

Today, in almost all formal Samoan speeches (*lauga*)—a highly allusive, specialized, and structured mode of speech—there is a section in which the speaker refers to *taeao*, or "mornings." These are a group of conventional allusions to the historical and mythical past, from which an able orator-chief (*tulafale*) should select one (sometimes more) appropriate for the occasion. They symbolize what are seen as the transformative and lasting moments in Samoan history.[67] "Mornings" refer to particular meetings or events, or particular locations, but the meaning of a taeao is always larger and functions as a kind of historical parable: as in English, "mornings" are beginnings. Although different parts of Samoa were at different times under the colonial rule of Germany, Britain, New Zealand, and the United States, only one common taeao refers to the colonial period. This is the taeao of Gagamoe. Gagamoe is the village green of Pago Pago, on which the sovereignty of the eastern part of the Samoan islands was ceded to the United States. Gagamoe is Samoa's American "morning."

Such mornings operate, among other things, as genealogies of the present. They characterize both the continuities and innovations of Samoan discourses more generally. These mornings are also histories, metonymies of Samoan life and values, parables of morality and identity. Most relevant for our purposes here is that this corpus of mornings is a matrix of a contemporary Samoan politics of comparison. For there are not many important taeao — not much more than a dozen or so — and the majority tell of ancient Samoan kings and queens, of legendary characters, the origins of plants and political divisions. Indeed, there are perhaps only four popular taeao that are "historical," in the limited Western sense that they might be verified by written texts. Three of these refer to the arrival in Samoa of the main religious denominations in the 1830s and 1840s: the Methodists, Congregationalists, and Roman Catholics. The fourth is Gagamoe, the American morning.

The select company it keeps makes the place of U.S. colonialism in the canon of Samoan public history even more intriguing. Although a Methodist Samoan is likely to invoke the Methodist morning where the Catholic might invoke the Catholic morning, the congregational morning, which commemorates the landing of the first Christian missionary in 1830, has a certain power for all. The year 1830 is held to divide all of Samoan history in two. Prior to the Word there is the time of Darkness and ignorance (*Pouliuli*), whereas after 1830 is the time of Light and understanding (*Malamalama*). The place of the American morning is revealing, as is the favoring of it by those who live in American Samoa. It tells of another division, though in space as well as time. Just as the Christian God still prevails, the eastern part of Samoa is still an American "territory." In Gagamoe we can glimpse the United States' Samoan genealogy.

In 2001 American Samoa governor Tauese P. F. Sunia told the United Nations that "the people of American Samoa take exception to the term 'colony.' In their unique relationship with the United States of America, they view themselves as an integral part of the U.S. family of states and territories. I once again respectfully request that the U.N. committee on decolonization remove American Samoa from the list of non-self-governing territories on which it was erroneously placed." This time the request was granted, and American Samoa was removed from the U.N. list.[68] As with Christianity, American rule has been appropriated, domesticated, and narrated by Samoans.

As Samoa's American morning commemorates, comparisons are hardly the work of imperialism alone. Equally, this "morning" is suggestive of how, in Samoan discourses, the intimate could also be entwined with larger formations. The domain of the intimate was not only one to be invaded and governed by colonialism but one that Samoans also sought to possess and have continued to construct and modify. This was relevant not only to the apparently increased "racialization" of Samoan discourses, for on the village green of Gagamoe Samoans have found a kind of intimacy with U.S. imperialism, one rendered legible in Samoan discourse. This is an important point, for one of the great dangers of pursuing imperial connections and comparisons is that of replicating imperial work—not only of privileging the questions, answers, and comparisons that imperial actors pursued but, more critically, of being seduced into studies only of elite actors and similarly elite terrains of discourse. Among the casualties of this seduction are often indigenous ways of knowing.

There is a certain power in comparisons, their histories and politics, that may reveal commonalities and modularities that might otherwise be hidden, such as "political rationalities." In this sense Samoa's half-castes suggest common political rationalities, turning on questions of sovereignty and subjectivity, that motivated three different empires to have comparable, at times even cooperative, taxonomies. These rationalities are cast into relief by different Samoan ones that operated genealogically rather than taxonomically. These rationalities are not, it seems, transient. If "foreign" and "indigenous" discourses are now even more closely entangled than they were one hundred years ago, the politics that lie behind contemporary Samoan comparisons continue to prove different, not only in conceptions of the intimate but in how these issues intersect with the historical and the present. The United States now has a wide range of new and effective taxonomies in Samoa, discursive projects that provide for a potency unthinkable in the nineteenth century. Yet, as the "morning" of Gagamoe reminds, the United States has a Samoan genealogy and is part of an intimate domain that is motivated by an impulse and genealogical rationalities that are still beyond its control.

NOTES

1. "The Samoan Trouble," 82.

2. For introductions to the history of Samoa's political system see Gilson, *Samoa 1830 to 1900*; and Meleisea and Meleisea, *Lagaga*.

3. See Kennedy, *The Samoan Tangle*.

4. See Salesa, "'Travel Happy' Samoa."

5. See Dodge, *New England and the South Seas*.

6. Frederick Jackson Turner explicitly mentioned Samoa in some of his earlier work. See LaFeber, *The New Empire*, 69–70. For discussion of Hawaii in these contexts see Merry, *Colonizing Hawai'i*; and Osorio, *Dismembering Lahui*.

7. See Scully, *Bargaining with the State from Afar*.

8. Ryden, *The Foreign Policy of the United States in Relation to Samoa*, 37.

9. Johnston, *Sovereignty and Protection*, 127.

10. Coe to Dept. of State, Nov. 15, 1866, District of the United States Consul, Apia (hereafter DUSCA), Vol. II, RG 84, National Archives and Records Administration, Washington, D.C. (hereafter NARA).

11. See Stoler, "Tense and Tender Ties," 832.

12. "Jurisdiction by legislation," the other seemingly distinct method by which jurisdiction was extended, remained dependent on the location of individuals. See Swanston to State Dept., April 20, 1857, DUSCA, Vol. I, RG 84, NARA; Gilson, *Samoa 1830 to 1900*, 358; Ryden, *The Foreign Policy of the United States in Relation to Samoa*, 35–38. Though it rested on individuals, if they were the victim, this kind of jurisdiction often extended to include the aggressor.

13. See Stoler, this volume, 65; "Tense and Tender Ties," 850.

14. Kennedy, "Bismarck's Imperialism"; Morrell, *Britain in the Pacific Islands*, 303.

15. *San Francisco Examiner*, March 8, 1889; Kennedy, *The Samoan Tangle*, 78–81.

16. Ryden, *The Foreign Policy of the United States in Relation to Samoa*, 354, 22–66.

17. Foster to State Dept., July 3, 1875, DUSCA, Vol. III, RG 84, NARA; Griffin to State Dept., Aug. 28, Sep. 3, 1877, DUSCA, Vol. V, RG 84, NARA.

18. Foster to State Dept., Oct. 19, 1874, DUSCA, Vol. III, RG 84, NARA.

19. Foreign Office to Swanston, Nov. 28, 1878, British Consulate, Samoa (hereafter BCS), Ser. 1, Vol. 2.

20. Foster to State Dept., May 20, 1875, DUSCA, Vol. III, RG 84, NARA; Coe to State Dept., Dec. 21, 1866, DUSCA, Vol. II, RG 84, NARA; Coe to State Dept., Aug. 4, 1868, DUSCA, Vol. III, RG 84, NARA; Foster to State Dept., April 21, 1875, DUSCA, Vol. III, RG 84, NARA.

21. Nooney to George Pritchard, Dec. 16, 1852, DUSCA, Vol. I, RG 84, NARA.

22. Swanston to State Dept., April 20, 1857, DUSCA, Vol. I, RG 84, NARA; Dirickson to State Dept., Sep. 25, 1857, DUSCA, Vol. I, RG 84, NARA.

23. Coe to State Dept., Nov. 15, 1866, DUSCA, Vol. II, RG 84, NARA.

24. See Salesa, "'Troublesome Half-Castes' Tales of a Samoan Border," MA thesis, University of Auckland, 1997.

25. The London Missionary Society (LMS) missionary Whitmee's census of 1875 was the most accurate census that had been taken in Samoa. See Foster to State Dept., Feb. 8, 1875, DUSCA, Vol. III, RG 84, NARA.

26. Pritchard, July 23, 1862, BCS, Ser. 3, Vol. 2. Though the original registers were seen in the 1970s by Caroline Ralston, they are currently inaccessible. Some copies are available in the microfilm collections of the Church of Jesus Christ of Latter-Day Saints; see, e.g., "Register of British Subjects Residing in the Samoan Islands, 1878–1882." See also Ralston, *Grass Huts and Warehouses.*

27. See "Law of November 8, 1867."

28. Williams to Foreign Office, Dec. 22, 1871, BCS, Ser. 3, Vol. 3, National Archive, Wellington, New Zealand. Foreign Office circular received Apia, April 22, 1871, BCS, Ser. 1, Vol. 2.

29. Swanston to State Dept., May 1, 1857, DUSCA, Vol. I, RG 84, NARA.

30. Swanston to State Dept., April 13, 1857, DUSCA, Vol. I, RG 84, NARA.

31. Foster to State Dept., Oct. 19, 1874, DUSCA, Vol. III, RG 84, NARA.

32. Hall, McClelland, and Rendall, *Defining the Victorian Nation.*

33. See Nathans, *The Politics of Citizenship in Germany.*

34. Brubaker, *Citizenship and Nationhood in France and Germany*, 114–37. Also see Hempenstall, *Pacific Islanders under German Rule*, 25–36; and Wareham, *Race and Realpolitik*, 23–27.

35. Nathans, *The Politics of Citizenship in Germany*, 128.

36. "Citizenship of Children Born Abroad and of Married Women."

37. Cott, *Public Vows*, 104.

38. Ibid., 133–43.

39. Scully, *Bargaining with the State from Afar*, 87.

40. Behlmer, *Child Abuse and Moral Reform in England, 1870–1908.*

41. James Schouler, quoted in Grossberg, *Governing the Hearth*, 224.

42. Scully, *Bargaining with the State from Afar*, 75.

43. Today a similar debate continues. Pacific Islanders had been categorized, until the

2000 census, with Asians. The most recent category was "Native Hawaiian or other Pacific Islander." Some Native Hawaiians and Samoans have even been pushing for federal classification as "Native American."

44. State Dept. to Coe, Jan. 31, 1867, "Note on inheritance," DUSCA, Vol. II, RG 84, NARA.

45. Ibid. As Nancy Cott has pointed out, this dated back to a 1790 statute. See Cott, *Public Vows*, 133.

46. State Dept. to Coe, Jan. 31, 1867, "Note on inheritance," DUSCA, Vol. II, RG 84, NARA.

47. Ibid.

48. For relevant historical discussions of genealogy in Polynesia see Dening, *Islands and Beaches*; Kame'eleihiwa, *Native Land and Foreign Desires*; Salesa, "Race Mixing," 63–100, 290–96; Salmond, *Two Worlds*.

49. Saveasi'uleo was the keeper of the underworld and had devoured all his other siblings. Only his youngest brother survived. The dynamics of relationships, and the significance of "o le va," have been highlighted and discussed by the Samoan historian and novelist Albert Wendt. See, for instance, "Tattooing the Post-Colonial Body."

50. Salesa, "'Troublesome Half-Castes,'" 29–56.

51. The Samoan proverb "o le gafa o le Tuia'ana ua o'o" (the succession of the Tuia'ana is assured) reminds of how adopted children could rise to the highest office, in the train of the adopted genealogy.

52. Tamasese, "The Riddle in Samoan History."

53. This proverb, "Tau o se mea e ala ai" (as long as the end is attained), is also a reminder of the ways that chiefs approached the practice of tradition, often respecting it only selectively. For an in-depth discussion of this proverb see Schultz-Ewerth, *Samoan Proverbial Expressions*, 101.

54. As was observed by John C. Williams in Williams to Foreign Office, July 23, 1862, BCS, Ser. 3, Vol. 2; Bull, *A Trip to Tahiti and Other Islands in the South Seas*, 29.

55. See Cusack-Smith to Foreign Office, Nov. 26, 1895, BCS Ser. 3, Vol. 7.

56. Gray, *Amerika Samoa*, 119, 207–10; Salesa, "'Troublesome Half-Castes.'"

57. Murray, *Forty Years' Mission Work in Polynesia and New Guinea*, 321. Phillips, Journal, Jan. 12, 1885; Salesa, "'Troublesome Half-Castes,'" 127–29.

58. A document that captures this well is Cusack-Smith's "Special Report," enclosed in Cusack-Smith to Foreign Office, Jan. 30, 1895, BCS, Ser. 3, Vol. 7.

59. The most accessible descriptions of this social orbit can be found in Stevenson, *The Letters of Robert Louis Stevenson*, vol. 8. For a discussion see Salesa, "'Troublesome Half-Castes,'" 146–54.

60. For example, Churchward, *My Consulate in Samoa*, 71; Gilson, *Samoa 1830 to 1900*, 341–42; Salesa, "'Troublesome Half-Castes,'" 110–13.

61. On different vectors see Comaroff, "Reflections on the Colonial State, in South Africa and Elsewhere."

62. Cusack-Smith to Foreign Office, Dec. 2, 19, 1895, BCS, Ser. 3, Vol. 7, National Archives, Wellington.

63. See, e.g., Eugen Brandeis to Palepoi, April 11, 1888, F. J. H. Grattan Papers, MS-Papers-4879-007, Alexander Turnbull Library, Wellington.

64. These were the wars between the two parliaments, the Ta'imua and Faipule who had been governing from Apia, and an opposition government, the Puletua, headed by Malietoa Laupepa.

65. *Samoa Times*, Oct. 20, 1877.

66. Ibid; the editor thought they should be stripped of their foreign status, should it be proven that they actually possessed it.

67. Regarding *taeao* see Papali'i, *'O Si Manu a Ali'i*, 354–58; Tatupu Fa'afetai Mataa'afa Tu'i, *Lauga*, 25. See also Linnekin, "'Mornings of the Country.'"

68. Sunia, "Statement by Governor Tauese P. F. Sunia on the Status and Wishes of the People of the United States Territory of American Samoa." The U.N. seminar on decolonization was held in Havana, Cuba, May 23–25, 2001. Both American Samoa's governor, Tauese Sunia, and congressman, Eni Faleomavaega, were in favor of retaining American Samoa's territory status (a plebiscite a decade earlier had indicated this was the popular view). See *Samoa News* (Pago Pago), May 14, 17, 23, June 1, 2001.

44

WARWICK ANDERSON

States of Hygiene: Race "Improvement"
and Biomedical Citizenship in Australia and
the Colonial Philippines

In May 1906 the Coast Guard cutter *Polilio* passed the massive limestone cliffs of Coron and negotiated a channel through the Calamianes Islands to the new leper colony at Culion, an isolated outpost in the far west of the Philippines archipelago. Almost four hundred leper pioneers disembarked there; most were young adults, and some were adolescents, but there were no infants. By the end of 1910 another five thousand had followed the same route, though more than three thousand died soon after arrival, and another 114 somehow escaped their doleful exile.[1] Inevitably, some leper women gave birth in the colony—sometimes the father was unknown, but between 1910 and the early 1920s the coupling was more commonly sanctioned by marriage at the old Culion church. American colonial officials had structured the leper colony as a laboratory of therapeutics and citizenship, a place where needy patients were resocialized, where they performed somatic recovery alongside domestic hygiene and civic pride. Thus Filipino leper families lived in small houses in the new "sanitary barrio," washing and scrubbing, tending their gardens, voting in local elections, making cheap goods for export, participating in baseball games, receiving regular injections of the new therapeutic agent chaulmoogra oil—and having children.

At first the medical authorities kept these exemplary families intact. But evidently fears of contamination had not completely evaporated in the tropical theater of hygiene, and from 1915 nonleprous children lived apart from their families at the Balala nursery. After 1927, efforts intensified to remove children at a younger age, though separation at birth remained rare. Every Sunday leprous parents could view their separated offspring through a glass barrier, until at the age of two the infants were either adopted or sent to the Welfareville Institution in Manila. Estela A., for example, was born in 1925, the daughter of two inmates: but in 1927 a middle-class Filipino family in Manila adopted her. A few months later her adoptive father wrote to the Protestant minister at Culion to reassure him that Estela was healthy and happy, and they were bathing her twice daily.[2] In the interests of medical and civic reformation the state had already taken lepers from their families and loved ones, subjecting them to a combined regimen of treatment and training; now it removed their nonleprous children and gave them hygienic middle-class identities in Manila.

In 1931 A. O. Neville, the protector of Aborigines in Western Australia, abducted three mixed-race Nyungar girls — Molly, Gracie, and Daisy — and placed them in the Moore River Native Settlement, away from their "uncivilized" family. In a total institution for the production of hygienic, self-possessed citizens they would, according to Neville, be subject to "a period of intense training in every sense of the word."[3] The "half-caste" children whom he collected would "sleep in their own exclusive dormitories, have their own classrooms, cooking, dining arrangements and playgrounds." They had entered an institution that focused on technical education, hard work, and compulsory sport, a place, too, where "matters of hygiene should be an essential part of an inmate's training." Above all, and everywhere, "the unseen sympathetic hand of Authority should be there to support and guide."[4] According to Neville, Aboriginal families were invariably incompetent, and only "Authority can teach their children the right way to live."[5] All colored children should therefore be treated as orphans. But the protector remained frustrated by "our easy-going, oft-times sentimental attitude towards the semi-civilised natives." He worried about the complacency and indifference that he thought caused some to hesitate to take children from their mothers. But if these potential partners for whites were not removed as infants, "they develop into weedy, undernourished semi-morons with the grave sexual appetites which characterise them." In contrast, "quadroons and nearer whites" who received correct training soon learned "to forget their antecedents" and seldom reverted.[6] Within a few generations Neville's plan for institutional assimilation would have "raised the social and moral outlook of the coloured people generally — instilled into them a sense of usefulness and a desire to create homes in accordance with white standards. . . . In short, it will complete their emancipation."[7] Residual blackness was the only thing preventing their recognition as citizens in the modern nation.[8] Authority would train this out of them and, Neville hoped, allow them to merge into whiteness. But Molly and Daisy, unlike hundreds of other children, soon escaped Neville's utopia and struggled back home, walking fifteen hundred miles along the rabbit-proof fence.[9]

The historian searches in vain for any specific link between these stories. Given that Neville was interested in tropical medicine and hygiene, he may have heard of the work of Dr. Victor G. Heiser, the director of health in the colonial Philippines and the architect of Culion. But Neville seems to have known little about leprosy policies in the Philippines and never referred to Culion as a model for his training centers. Moreover, there are obvious differences between these projects. At Culion the focus was on adult (though infantalized) lepers; in Australia it was on "half-caste" children, especially girls. Lepers in Australia were regarded as unreformable, untreatable; they were segregated and, for the most part, left alone.[10] On the other hand, Americans in the Philippines had no intention to make Filipinos, even mestizos, white—they had no formal plans for miscegenation. Yet the leper colony and the "half-caste" institution now appear to have followed a similar logic or political rationality: each was predicated on a form of biological and civic transformism in which the contaminated became hygienic and "savages" might become social citizens. In the ritual frame of the colonial, or protonational, institution, liberal medicos amalgamated supposed corporeal deficiency—whether sickness or racial difference—with perceived cultural failings, in particular a lack of civilization. They then sought to treat these fused conditions, to set their charges on a single trajectory from illness to health and from primitivism to civility.[11] That is, the identity of inmates, or patients, was assigned to one pole of a dichotomy, or more ambiguously to the ground between, and these figures were expected dutifully to traverse toward the further pole. In the twentieth century, medical progressivism and bureaucratic rationality therefore converged to make the copy more interesting than the fixed antithesis and mimicry more satisfying than opposition. The end point of this imagined modern trajectory was in practice unreachable: the leper was only in remission, and the "half-caste" girl was merely passing (or ensuring her descendants would pass). Despite its professed goals, the colonial reformatory thus produced—not eliminated—the in-between. It excelled in fashioning estranged, marginal men and women, in preserving contaminated bodies, and in making second-class citizens.

In state development projects in the Philippines and Australia, long-standing intimacies were to be reforged as abstract attachments to categories of progress, modernity, and nation. This was what the "emancipation" of lepers and "half-castes" really meant. White American medical officers and white Australian "protectors" urged their inmates or patients to forget traditional and affective ties to family and community; they warned against "nostalgia" and praised those who looked forward to the hygienic future — to incorporation into a whitelike, though allegedly generic, citizenry. An education in shame, delicacy, and disgust, this effort to train and reform also produced unexpected disclosures, proximities, and trajectories. In the late colonial reformatory, civic performance became more important than blood ties, hygiene more significant than kinship — or so the liberal medical vanguard in charge of these institutions would wish. In fact, neither they nor their charges would ever jettison completely their older — in a sense "nonmodern," or at least völkisch — attachments to community and race. And the new affective ties to state abstractions, or to the agents of the state, were rarely as intense as the progressive colonial intelligentsia had hoped. When Heiser began his leper-collecting trips in the Philippines, he claimed there was little resistance to the removal of the afflicted, in part, he thought, the result of successful inculcation of fear of the "loathsome" disease. "When it is remembered," Heiser wrote, that removal "often involved the lifelong separation of wife from husband, sister from brother, child from parents, and friend from friend, it will be appreciated that forbearance was necessary under such circumstances."[12] After having abducted them, Heiser regularly sought out the company of those lepers he meant to reform. On the day he left the archipelago, he confided to his diary his feelings for those he had so assiduously classified and displaced: "There is much sadness," he wrote, "that as yet I do not live in the hearts of the people. . . . I wonder if I will ever be understood and if the lepers will sometime look upon me as their friend."[13] His regret is a vivid expression of the pathos of the "progressive" colonial bureaucrat.

Ann Stoler has recommended that we examine the ways in which "intimate matters, and narratives about them, figured in defining the racial coordinates and social discriminations of empire."[14] Here I would like to consider colonial and protonational population policies — in particular, the institutional management of probationary national subjects in the American empire and on the Australian frontier — as examples of "the distribution of appropriate affect."[15] This requires an expansion of the historical understanding of the making of "intimacy" to encompass the expert and habituated benevolence of the state.[16] It is often forgotten that in the name of public health the state is licensed to palpate, handle, bruise, test, and mobilize individuals, especially with those deemed dangerous, marginal, or needy.

Moreover, in the twentieth century an emphasis on personal and domestic hygiene allowed an exceptionally intense surveillance and discipline of subject populations, which involved a refashioning of interactions and intimacies within these populations. Much of the prevailing attention to the quantity and quality of population — of which eugenics was just a small part — can thus be viewed as an effort to reshape identities and relationships, to reforge affective ties. Accordingly, I want to consider leper treatment and "half-caste" removal in terms of the making of intimacy *with* the colonizing state and the making of intimacy *for* the colonizing state.

THE PERSONAL HYGIENE OF THE MICROCOLONY

Michel Foucault has described how, gradually, "an administrative and political space was articulated upon a therapeutic space; it tended to individualize bodies, diseases, symptoms, lives and deaths; it constituted a real table of juxtaposed and carefully distinct singularities."[17] He was referring to the development of the modern clinic; lepers remained for him representatives of the unproductively confined. He wondered what would happen, though, if one was ever to "treat 'lepers' as 'plague victims,' project the subtle segmentations of discipline onto the confined space of internment, combine it with the methods of analytical distribution proper to power, individualize the excluded, but use procedures of individualization to mark exclusion."[18] At Culion, for the first time, lepers did become subjects of such intensive surveillance and discipline. In the past lepers might be segregated and excluded from civil society. Once isolated, they generally were neglected, except by missionaries who quickly discerned that they may be especially susceptible to the gospel. According to Megan Vaughan, leprosy had "offered to missionaries the possibility of engineering new African communities" for the performance of collective, tribal identities.[19] Such collectivization would seem to present an impasse to the engineering of individualized leper-citizens. The progressive medical officers who established the Culion colony tried instead to deregionalize and abstract Filipino lepers as separate national subjects. They fought against any grouping of lepers into Visayans, Tagalogs, Moros, and so on, preferring to figure their patients as individualized, if standardized, cases of leprosy. Rita Smith Kipp has remarked that during this period "new therapeutic approaches to leprosy lessened the evangelical uses" among the Karo people of Sumatra.[20] But in the Philippines the production of the individual civic subject — surely a form of evangelism — was predicated on such medicalization, on the spread of the "gospel of hygiene," and on modern chemotherapeutics.

For most of the Spanish colonial period in the Philippines, medical authorities had assumed that leprosy was hereditary. Accordingly, the rare instances of isolation of sufferers occurred more often for aesthetic and social reasons than for medical purposes. The disease was first identified in the archipelago in the early seventeenth century, and since then it had spread rapidly. The Franciscans took charge of charity work among lepers, building several asylums and hospitals for the severely afflicted. Institutions such as the San Lazaro Hospital, north of the old walled city of Manila, and the Cebu Leprosarium offered a refuge for those who sought it, along with palliative care in the last stages of their illness. In some of the larger towns groups of lepers often lived together in separate bamboo and nipa shacks. But the Spanish colonial regime did not try to isolate lepers from their communities in order to prevent the spread of the disease or to eliminate it entirely.[21]

Toward the end of the nineteenth century most medical scientists and clinicians came to favor social explanations of disease transmission, though hereditarian assumptions were never entirely abandoned. Sickness might now appear to spread from person to person, but the hereditary proclivities of certain groups still seemed to make them more likely to participate in this process. With the development of germ theories during this period, social explanations of disease transmission soon acquired greater pathological depth. Thus germs to which one group of people appeared especially susceptible might lodge covertly in the meretriciously healthy bodies of another group or race. One race might demonstrate immunity, relative or absolute, to a disease; another would seem utterly vulnerable to the same microbe.

The discovery of Hansen's bacillus, *Mycobacterium leprae*, in the early 1880s signaled the entry of leprosy into the emerging etiological mainstream. Its presence in the nasal scrapings of suspects — regardless of clinical signs — came to suggest, to the more scientifically inclined of medical and civic authorities at least, the need to isolate the victim, or carrier, and to engage in relentless efforts to remove the contaminating germ. Thus Heiser, on assuming control of public health in the Philippines, urged all medical officers to take a census of lepers in their region and report their findings to him. He estimated that there were more than six thousand lepers distributed over the archipelago, and each year some twelve hundred more contracted the disease. A review of the medical literature convinced him that only isolation and experimental treatment could accomplish the eradication of leprosy in the islands. "This policy," he observed, "at first sight seems to impose many hardships upon the lepers themselves and their immediate relatives and friends, but it is believed to be fully justified not only by the fact that hundreds may be annually saved from contracting leprosy, but also that the victims may be given as pleasant a life as possible."[22] He set Culion aside for the experimental station, and every year he traveled through the archipelago on his "leper ship," collecting eligible inmates.

In the Culion "museum" today one finds thousands of case histories, now dusty and insect ridden, piled on benches and on the floors. Each is prefaced with a photograph, followed by an account of the initial presentation, the family and social history, and "progress," which was correlated with treatment—usually with chaulmoogra oil—and laboratory findings. The case record of José E. tells us that he was admitted to Culion in 1913, at the age of twenty-three, having suffered from leprosy for eight years in Ilocos Sur. His "signs" were the white patches on his back and arms, thickening and contractures of the fingers, and an ulcer on his left foot. After receiving the new preparation of chaulmoogra oil for a decade, he became "bacteriologically negative" and was discharged two years later. Or take the case of Marcelo A., who in 1909 was taken from Batangas, at the age of fifteen, with nodules on his back, shallow scars on his legs, a fallen nasal bridge, and no eyebrows. For a while he was bacteriologically negative, but then in his early twenties he showed more "activity." After chaulmoogra oil and two years of negative findings he was discharged in 1926—but he had nowhere to go and was soon readmitted. Then there is the case of Alfredo F., who was born at Culion after his parents were sent there and soon acquired the disease, developing reddish patches on his cheeks and lower abdomen. In 1926, after years of chaulmoogra oil, the adolescent was ready for discharge—but he, too, had nowhere to go. Each person has become a distinct "case"; each has acquired a standardized individuality in the medical record. And in each of these cases the future has been structured as a prognosis.

In the hermetic world of Culion, in that infinitely detailed colonial miniature, lepers would repeatedly reaffirm their diagnosis, and demonstrate their responsibility, in the hope of the recognition that might confer both medical relief and moral elevation. Culion combined features of an American small town with aspects of an institutional reformatory or asylum. The government built a town hall, a store, a general kitchen, a jail, a school, and the Leper Club, which contained "a piano, a pool table, and many newspapers, some recent, and miscellaneous discarded 'charity' magazines and books unintelligible except for the pictures."[23] Most lepers resided in dormitories, segregated by sex, but celibacy proved difficult to enforce. As more leper women became pregnant, medical officers reluctantly decided it was best they marry the leper fathers of their children. These new families, along with the leper families that had arrived intact, and individuals who became bacteriologically negative, might occupy small houses in the "sanitary barrio." Life in the colony was organized around the routinized, yet individuated, treatment of leprosy. Every week the inmates went dutifully to the clinic, where they received an injection of chaulmoogra oil.

Rituals of modern citizenship pervaded the leper colony. "The lepers," Heiser observed, "are given all possible liberty, and are, to a large extent, controlled by regulations which they themselves make."[24] Medical facts and social potential were amalgamated: as part of the treatment, the diseased were supposed to govern themselves. The community elected its own mayor and council; from 1908 women voted—the earliest female suffrage in Southeast Asia. Leper police saw that the town was "kept in good sanitary condition" and made "arrests of offenders against their own ordinances."[25] Leper sanitary inspectors, under the command of a nonleprous chief, also helped to maintain sanitary order in the colony. A leper brass band greeted new arrivals and gave occasional concerts—Heiser once joked that they were so enthusiastic that they "literally played their fingers off."[26] Several times a year, the lepers put on a play; indeed, they "took eagerly to dramatics," recalled the director of health.[27] And twice a month patients would dress up to watch "very cheap films" in the large concrete theater.[28] Athletic gatherings, though held rarely, elicited considerable enthusiasm for baseball. "That they possess the true American baseball spirit," wrote Dr. John Snodgrass, "was demonstrated at one of the games when both teams attacked the umpire with ball bats."[29] The tiresome emphasis on performance animated social life and medical protocols throughout the colony: lepers at Culion were regularly onstage in therapeutic and civic dramas.

Medical authorities expected lepers to work diligently between their doses of chaulmoogra oil—indeed the treatment was supposed to enhance their industrial capacity. But Heiser lamented that "contractions of the limbs, destruction of tissue, losses of fingers and toes . . . and general debility" meant that only a few lepers performed sufficient physical labor to supply food for themselves. Some tried raising cattle or started "tiny sugar plantations." The bulk of the food was still prepared in a large kitchen by leper cooks. Many of the afflicted remained capable of carrying out simple domestic duties for a small salary: cooking, cleaning, dressmaking, taking care of streets, making repairs to buildings, and so on.[30] Still, it seemed to Heiser that most lepers remained "naturally apathetic" and dependent on government aid. Yet "the streets must be swept, the garbage cans emptied, assistance rendered at the hospital, and supplies carried."[31] The director of health hoped for more meticulous observance of medical protocols and civic responsibilities in the future.

Despite its flaws and disappointments, Culion became a model for "the making of men out of savages, the regeneration of a conquered people by the conquerors by teaching them the benefits of labor and industry." It was the progressive colonial official's "work of civilization . . . of regeneration and instruction," organized through a multitude of individual medical careers.[32] In the microcolony—in the controlled laboratory of subject formation—the supposedly docile lepers might thus be enrolled in American modernity in advance of the nonleprous. The diagnostic disciplines of the leper colony were not supposed to reproduce the denigrated Philippine social body but rather were meant to normalize American ideals of civic responsibility, to attach recovering lepers to the colonial state and its agents. Accordingly, exile to Culion was represented not as the deprivation of liberty but as its creation. Citizenship was linked symbiotically to corporeal metamorphosis, and the successful achievement of both was endlessly postponed. Even those discharged from Culion required continued monitoring: they were in remission, not cured, and "nationals," not full citizens. Their identities and relationships, their affective ties, were never as modern as hoped.

Those most rejected from a society that American officials sought to reform had seemed the most eligible for correct training. Lepers were selected for normalization not because they were especially delinquent but because they appeared more medically needy and desocialized. It should have been so much easier, Heiser thought, to remove lepers from their families and communities and to affiliate them with state abstractions such as "progress," "civilization," and "liberty." Heiser, too, longed for the personal affection of lepers and could not understand why it was withheld from him. Clearly, hygiene, industry and chaulmoogra oil never worked quite well enough to make amends for the sundering of old affective ties and relationships. Lepers at Culion continued to feel nostalgia, resentment, and regret; they pined for home, especially when they could not go back. The removal of non-leper infants from the colony was evidently an admission of this medical and civic failure. If the colonial reformatory had effectively refashioned bodies and personae, then little Estela A. would never have been sent to her new Americanized, middle-class family in Manila. We cannot now determine, of course, whether removing her from her leper parents was any more effective in meeting the reformist goals of the colonial state.

In 1911, while briefly protector of Aborigines in the Northern Territory of Australia, Dr. Herbert Basedow—an Adelaide physician who had trained in craniometry in Germany—proposed a "reformatory" or "industrial" school for part-Aboriginal children in Darwin.[33] The acting administrator of the territory, S. J. Mitchell, endorsed the anthropologist's suggestion and recommended the collection of all "half-caste" children. "No doubt the mothers would object and there would probably be an outcry from well-meaning people about depriving the mother of her child," Mitchell wrote, "but the future of the children I think should outweigh all other considerations. It is quite impossible to state the number that would so be gathered in."[34]

In the early twentieth century the growing numbers of "half-caste" Aboriginal children living on the fringes of outback towns presented a serious problem for the state and territory "protectors." Tribal Aborigines, or *myalls*, were scattered and few, occupying land of little value for whites; the "full-blood" fringe dwellers seemed destined for extinction through disease and miscegenation, but the numbers of mixed-race children just kept growing. In the Northern Territory the government began to separate "half-caste" children from their mothers, placing them in special quarters in the Kahlin compound in Darwin and at the Bungalow in Alice Springs.[35] In Western Australia mixed-race children lived in separate dormitories at the Moore River Native Settlement and other isolated institutions, while from 1933 those with lighter skin resided at Sister Kate's Quarter-Caste Children's Home.[36] (In Queensland, however, the state protector favored the segregation of whole Aboriginal families on large reserves, such as Palm Island, and rarely removed even the lightest children.)[37] Cook in the Northern Territory and Neville in Western Australia represented their policies as especially scientific, secular, and interventionist. Austere rationalists and progressives, both men controlled tens of thousands of Aboriginal people. At a time when white settlers still sent out occasional punitive expeditions to massacre troublesome natives—at Forrest River, in the north of Western Australia, in 1926; at Coniston, near Alice Springs, in 1928; and at Caledon

Bay, in Arnhem Land, in 1933 — Cook and Neville advocated instead the hygiene and correct training of "half-castes" and, later, from the early 1930s, the biological absorption of those so trained. At first they simply had gathered up the susceptible children near white outposts, but soon they began, with disturbing rigor and enthusiasm, to collect them far and wide.

With the federation of the six Australian colonies in 1901 the new nation had dedicated itself to the settlement of a prosperous, working white race across the whole of the continent, even in the tropical north and the arid center. For Australian nationalists the "menace of colour," as a leading geologist put it, was multiply threatening.[38] Colored labor would, it seemed, undermine industrial conditions; colored voters imperiled the legitimacy of universal franchise; and colored bodies, according to medical authorities, endangered white health.[39] Raphael Cilento, one of the leaders of tropical medicine in Australia, repeatedly warned that colored people inevitably coalesced into vast "reservoirs of disease," concentrating and distributing microbes to which they were indifferent but that proved especially dangerous to civilized whites.[40] Therefore, the health of the white nation must be predicated on quarantine and immigration restriction. Until the 1920s, Aboriginal Australians, although undoubtedly colored and hence pathogenic, appeared too scattered to present much of a hazard to the working white race as it diffused over the quarantined continent. In any case most experts had for a century or more predicted the demise of the natives, a consequence of their clash with a superior race. The growing presence of "half-caste" children challenged this forecast. When that plucky reporter Ernestine Hill traveled across the Top End and into the Red Center in the early 1930s, she lamented that "the future of white Australia looks very dark indeed."[41] A few years later, Dr. A. Grenfell Price, a leading Adelaide geographer, echoed her concerns: "Despite the 'white Australia' policy, a great part of the continent is black Australia still."[42]

Cilento and Cook — his former student — led the medical profession in discerning the pathological significance of "half-caste proliferation." In 1931 Cilento asserted that Aboriginal people in the tropics now "represent foci for the dissemination of hookworm, malaria and other diseases"; in 1934 he reported that leprosy follows "very roughly with the degree of prevalence of coloured persons in the population."[43] Protector Cook believed the native threat to white health was both more specific and more insidious: "The pernicious influences which the coloured races exercise upon the hygienic, social and economic development of races where white settlement is sparse and upon the public health where hybrid remnants concentrate in the poorer quarters of cities or on the fringes of country towns, continue for the most part unsuspected."[44] Cilento had recommended the segregation and medical policing of Aboriginal communities; Cook initially agreed that "the lack of any disposition towards interracial intercourse, which is a feature of Australian national character, has been a potent factor in protecting the whites in areas from which many coloured lepers have been reported."[45] In later years, after more experience in the management of Aboriginal communities and observation of the uncontrolled interactions on the frontier of white males and native women, Cook recognized his error. Instead, he came to promote "education of the native in citizenship" and other efforts to "adapt him to white civilization," in order to preserve white health and political security. Otherwise, "uneducated, bewildered, without any tangible point of contact with white citizenship and with no stable foothold in the social structure, psychologically unequipped for community life and outcast from white society, the native hybrid must remain a ready prey to agitators and a receptive field for subversive ideologies."[46] For Cook, as for Neville, somatic peril and civic menace were inseparable, and for both men it seemed that hygiene and correct training might eventually dissolve the fused threat.

From his appointment as protector in 1927 until his resignation in 1939 Cook sought to make mixed-race Aborigines into useful economic and social units, to teach them occupational skills, and to inculcate "a high appreciation of the principles of hygiene and industrial cleanliness."[47] The children assembled in the Kahlin compound and at the Bungalow learned English, the value of money, the significance of time, and the dangers of "going walkabout"; they also came to appreciate the importance of personal and domestic hygiene. Boys acquired skills needed in the pastoral industry; girls trained as housekeepers and domestic maids. In 1929, forty-four young inmates occupied the three rooms of the Darwin home; in the 1930s the Bungalow and its extensions housed more than one hundred "half-caste" children (Alice Springs, the attached town, could boast fewer than sixty permanent white residents).[48] According to Cook children were "removed from the evil influence of the Aboriginal camp with its lack of moral training and its risk of serious organic infectious disease. They are properly fed, clothed and educated as white children, and they are subject to constant medical supervision and in receipt of domestic and vocational training."[49] In fact, these institutions were overcrowded and filthy; the children were poorly fed and inadequately educated—but thoroughly regimented.

Conditions in Western Australia during this period were no better. Despite Neville's professed desire to infuse "scientific thinking" into the management of "half-castes," institutions like the Moore River Settlement remained impoverished and sometimes brutal places. Life there was dreary, repetitive, and restricted. In his 1932 report Neville admitted, "The enforced congregation of these people in communities in idleness is leading to undesirable results. Unwise mating and sex relationships, incest, gambling and such-like evils are prevalent." Still, he hoped that "half-caste" children might yet, through the regimen of hygiene and correct training, "be turned into self-respecting citizens rather than a race of outcasts."[50]

On arrival at the "half-caste" home the child was inspected, scrubbed, and given a set of clothes. Often she received a new name and date of birth; sometimes her head was shaved. Anna Haebich has described this process as "re-creating each individual anew," but in the eyes of the state it was their inauguration as individuals.[51] As "individuals" they slept together in single-sex dormitories, cordoned off from the world outside. As "individuals" the children learned new rituals of grooming and toileting, the intimate care of the body. And as "individuals" they assembled and marched in lines, the boys generally in khaki, the girls in blue uniforms — they would even bathe in line. The regimentation was relentless. June Barker remembered the bells at her institution: "Your life was governed by the bell. The first bell would go of a morning, you would have to go down to the treatment room: that's where you would get your cod-liver oil and eyes done every day. . . . The bell would ring for school; the bell would ring for rations; a mournful bell would ring for funerals. . . . You got to know the different sounds in the bell."[52] June and the other girls would spend the rest of the day cleaning, washing clothes, and sewing, while the boys learned station work, mechanics, and driving.

As a leading historian of Aboriginal assimilation has observed: "in place of resources to ensure good health there were endless inspections of bodies," especially the girls' bodies.[53] Through observance of personal and domestic hygiene the children were expected to conform to idealized "white standards." Hygiene in the "half-caste" home was always racial hygiene. "It was all about control, reform," Peggy recalled. "It was drummed into our heads that we were white," according to John. "It didn't matter what shade you were." A "civilizing" project had been fastened to corporeal reform, a refashioning or regrooming that was never expected, or allowed, to succeed fully. "They tried to make us act like white kids," Millicent — who grew up at Sister Kate's—wryly remarked, "but at the same time we had to give up our seat for a whitefella." Anne, who was eventually fostered in a white family in Sydney, put it differently. They were "to be trained to feel and think as if they were white, while living in the shadows of their Aboriginality ashamed of their black skin colour."[54]

The authorities frequently claimed that as "half-castes" the children, like lepers, were rejected by their Aboriginal families, and their mothers felt little remorse after their removal. But this was rarely, if ever, the case. Millicent was told to "forget about my past and my family," but she found it hard. As visits from Aborigines were forbidden, John and others at his home "didn't know we had a family." In 1936 Fiona, at the age of five, was passing through Ernabella with her mother when the police came and took her away. At Oodnadatta her head was shaved; she learned to eat new food, use a make-shift toilet, and sleep in a house. "I guess the government didn't mean it as something bad," she later reflected, "but our mothers weren't treated as having feelings."[55] Once separated, the children were exhorted to become more "whitelike" and "civilized" in habit and demeanor, to concentrate on making progress on the path from dark native to white citizen. But ordinary affective ties—to fellow inmates, to remembered family, even to local authorities—would supervene on mandatory devotion to abstractions like "civilization" and "progress." Nostalgia for mothers and camp life often was durable and appealing (though years later it would prove difficult to go back and restore affective ties). Some children came to call the women working in the institution "mother." Daisy Ruddick, who was taken to the Kahlin compound when she was six, fondly recalled a matron there who was "good at keeping us clean." Later, Daisy, too, became a nurse and married a white man.[56]

In the 1930s both Cook and Neville became fascinated by the prospect of the biological absorption of "half-castes" into a homogenous whiteness. The economic depression made further investment in "half-caste" training and hygiene ever less likely. At the same time, academic experts, mostly from Adelaide University, were suggesting that Aborigines might claim a remote Caucasian affiliation, which meant that a much larger European population could, in effect, digest them biologically without discomfort.[57] Eventually, Aboriginal genes would be swallowed up and disappear. Neville, in particular, seized this opportunity to "breed out the colour." Repeatedly he proclaimed the latest scientific findings: "half-caste" absorption presented no risk to whites since Aborigines were "a people already allied to us by association, consanguinity and ancestry"; and because they "predate us in some vague Caucasian direction," the mingling of blood presented "no marked antagonistic features." He was sure there would be no dark "throwbacks."[58] Light-skinned Aboriginal girls who mated with white men would produce even lighter offspring — in a few generations the family would appear white. What was the alternative? "Are we to have one million blacks in the Commonwealth," the protector asked in 1937, "or are we going to merge them into our white community and eventually forget that there were any Aborigines in Australia?"[59]

For Neville and Cook correct training and managed reproduction were different, though intersecting, routes to the same destination: racial absorption and disappearance. The rituals of the "half-caste" home could now be reinterpreted as preparing light-skinned girls for marriage to white men. "Experience shows," Cook declared in 1933, "that the half-caste girl can, if properly brought up, easily be elevated to a standard where the fact of her marriage to a white will not contribute to his deterioration."[60] Unfortunately a reluctance to invest generously in Aboriginal retraining and refashioning meant that not enough girls had been — as yet — properly brought up. Still, some were proving acceptable as partners for white men and were producing creditable nuclear families. Cook and Neville sought to increase the contact of "half-caste" girls with white families through fostering them or employing them as domestic servants; the protectors also continued to exercise their power to prevent mixed-race Aborigines from marrying "full-bloods." Reproductive intervention might thus cover for institutional tardiness or inadequacy: it would confirm and accelerate the process begun in the "half-caste" colony. After all, it was easier for a "half-caste" girl to develop affection for a white man and her own pale children than to demonstrate lasting devotion to institutional representations of white identity. Cook longed for the day when, instead of ad hoc, unsupervised coupling, a scientific breeding program would manage all Aboriginal reproduction (or rather, disappearance). He hoped that the state might intervene more often to substitute respectable working-class white men for disreputable white bushmen or perversely masculine "full-bloods." Managed breeding would thus complete and stabilize the work of the "half-caste" institution.

In the mid-1930s, as the Philippines moved toward self-government under U.S. guidance, the concentrating of lepers at Culion fell out of favor. New treatment stations scattered across the archipelago allowed lepers to lead responsible and healthful lives while still integrated in their community. (Some lepers, however, have hung on at Culion until the early twenty-first century.) In Australia the authorities would continue into the 1960s to assemble "half-caste" children in disciplinary enclaves, though after World War II most of these institutions fell under religious control. Gradually, a dispersive logic came to direct the management of Aboriginal populations too, with widespread educational and adoptive efforts eventually substituting for intensive retraining in a few microcolonies. Moreover, from the 1940s the linkage of biomedical "fact" with social or cultural potential, once so tight, began to be loosened. Thus "full-bloods" and intact Aboriginal families also became eligible for assimilation and integration into the Australian nation: that is, a biologically more generous notion of citizenship came slowly to prevail in Aboriginal affairs. An influential adviser to postwar governments, A. P. Elkin, the professor of anthropology at Sydney, argued for a "sane native education policy" that would help tribalized and detribalized Aborigines to understand white customs and the market economy.[61] His advice in the 1940s was "based on the hypothesis that the Aborigines (even of 'full-blood') could eventually become worthy citizens of the Commonwealth." "We must not be afraid to try new ways," Elkin wrote in 1944, "and trust to human nature — even if it be clothed in a dark skin."[62]

The same year that Elkin expressed his commitment to cultural amalgamation and adjustment, with or without miscegenation, the Western Australian parliament passed the Natives (Citizenship Rights) Act. It stipulated that an Aboriginal person who met certain criteria could apply for a Certificate of Citizenship and therefore no longer be classed as an Aboriginal native. The applicant must have served in the war, have avoided any tribal association for the previous two years, and have "adopted the manner and habits of civilised life." Two letters of recommendation also were required, along with evidence that the aspiring citizen was not suffering from any infectious disease, especially active leprosy. As John Chesterman and Brian Galligan, recent analysts of Australian citizenship legislation, point out: "That an individual's citizenship could be lost through contraction of a disease showed just how precarious the basis was on which some Aborigines were granted citizenship."[63] Regardless of Elkin's proposals, the linkage of biological characteristics — whether racialized, or pathologized more directly — with civic capacity or achievement would prove difficult to uncouple.

At both the Philippines leper colony and the Australian "half-caste" reformatory inmates were positioned as desiring and deserving "treatment" and "civilizing." As the most needy and most malleable members of a marginal or disparaged population they seemed the most eligible candidates for a coeval process of medicalization and civilization. In the controlled environment of the microcolony — in that exemplary space — scientific experts watched over the correct training, the bodily and moral reform, of those with "curable" yet chronic disease and those with concealable yet ultimately durable racial ambiguity. Liberal or progressive intellectuals in the colonial and protonational state regarded both these pathologies as remediable, so long as those so afflicted were prepared to learn supposedly "white" ways of relating to the body, to family, and to authority. For Heiser, Neville, and Cook the most intimate activities of the body and the most intimate of human interactions were open to view and available for refashioning. Moreover, these experts were convinced that any attainment of civic responsibility was predicated on an acceptable performance of somatic self-government and moral self-possession. The trajectory from native (or leper) to citizen thus implied a reconfiguring of intimacies with one's own body and the bodies of others — a remaking of the private. It entailed at the same time a realignment of affect away from maternal ties and other "traditional" family bonds and toward state abstractions, such as "progress," "modernity," and "nation." Of course, in practice the authorities were rarely willing to validate a passage from black to white or from leper to hygienic citizen. In each case the destination mattered, but individuals were not really expected to reach it. The "type" was never quite as movable as the nation demanded. As a result, the progressive colonizing state excelled at producing bodies that were merely in remission or passing, citizens that were second-class, and, eventually, nations that failed.

The juxtaposition of Culion and Moore River helps us to understand the full repertoire of the apparently benevolent or progressive modern state. It should not be forgotten that the same state was also operating through dispossession and terror, producing or condoning places of violence — a "deathspace in the land of the living," as Michael Taussig has called it.[64] But it is equally important to recognize that both the American colonial state in the

Warwick Anderson

Philippines and the emergent Australian nation-state worked concurrently through the production of life and the reorientation of affect and intimacy—primarily through the discipline of hygiene and the management of reproduction. Not surprisingly, the patterning of these modalities differs at each site. Yet comparison of the Philippines leper colony and the Australian "half-caste" reformatory draws attention to the mutual imbrication of breeding programs and hygiene regimens. Without such juxtaposition it is easy to assume that protocols of hygiene were alone responsible for the production of the "civic-minded leper" and to ignore reproductive arrangements at Culion. Similarly, the comparison helps us to view Aboriginal absorption in its wider frame, to see, that is, absorption as a more general program of racial hygiene and not simply a policy of "breeding out the colour." In other words, it makes us realize that welfare, treatment, and education are symbiotic with reproductive interventions—it thus becomes more difficult to separate "good" welfarist assimilation from "bad" breeding policies.[65] At some points "breeding" breaks through to the surface, becomes obvious, but at others it lies not far below the ordinary cultivation of racial hygiene and its attendant misery.

In the past I would have chosen to examine sites more closely connected than the Culion leper colony and the Australian "half-caste" home. Elsewhere I have argued for the tracing of genealogical ties between imperial center and colony, and between colonies, rather than resorting to the collection of apparently unrelated homologies.[66] Comparison of different models has often proven idle and unrewarding. What does it mean if one thing happens to look like something else? What does that tell us about cause and effect, about historical agency? Yet it now appears that a comparative study of sites as different as settler Australia and the Philippines under the American colonial regime can help us understand processes as elusive as the creation of national subjects—provided we hold constant our focus, that is, so long as we find a sensitive and specific "sampling device." Here I sampled the intimacy of hygiene reform, first in an administrative colony and then in a settler society that was emerging as a nation. Just as the Philippines was the borderland of U.S. empire, so was Australia the borderland of the British Empire—thus I might have attempted to find contact points between metropole and colony (or "dominion") in each case. Instead, I searched for a family resemblance—or better, a transcolonial taxonomy of hygiene—and not for actual evidence of kinship, though kinship there may be. I hope that this essay has demonstrated that a taxonomic gaze allows one to discern patterns and relationships that otherwise would remain obscure. Even so, such a gaze still seems to me a distancing, imperial optic—and therefore one that we should use with caution.[67]

NOTES

Some of the Philippines material has appeared in another form in Anderson, "Leprosy and Citizenship"; and the Australian material covers some of the same ground as chapter 8 of Anderson, *The Cultivation of Whiteness*. I am grateful to Hugh and Dawn Anderson for Australian research assistance. Adele Clarke, Richard Keller, Judith Walzer Leavitt, and James Vernon offered helpful advice on earlier versions of this chapter. I also benefited from lively discussion of the paper at a meeting of the San Francisco Bay Area Medheads.

1. On the history of the Culion leper colony see Burgess, *Who Walk Alone*; Thomas, *A Study of Leprosy Colony Policies*, chap. 7; Chapman, *Leonard Wood and Leprosy in the Philippines*; and Anderson, "Leprosy and Citizenship."

2. Mr. V. to Rev. Frederick Jansen, May 8, 1927, Culion Museum. On the transfer of Estela see Casimiro B. Lara, M.D., to director of health, Manila, Feb. 25, 1927, Culion Museum.

3. Neville, *Australia's Coloured Minority*, 42. See also Jacobs, "Science and Veiled Assumptions"; Jacobs, *Mister Neville*; Haebich, *For Their Own Good*; and Paisley, "Unnecessary Crimes and Tragedies."

4. Neville, *Australia's Coloured Minority*, 130, 131.

5. Ibid., 120, 141.

6. Ibid., 168, 174, 179.

7. Ibid., 182.

8. In "Citizenship and Social Class" T. H. Marshall defined social citizenship as "the right to share to the full in the social heritage and to live the life of a civilised being according to the standards prevailing in society" (10). For a critique of the nexus of biology and citizenship see Stepan, "Race, Gender, Science, and Citizenship." On citizenship in Australia see Chesterman and Galligan, *Citizens without Rights*; and Peterson and Sanders, *Citizenship and Indigenous Australians*. The status of Australia during this period is ambiguous: the colonies had federated in 1901, but the nation was still a dominion of the British Empire. White Australians until 1948 were Australian nationals and British citizens. It is thus difficult to establish when Australia became independent of Britain.

9. Pilkington, *Follow the Rabbit-Proof Fence*. The most influential and extensive documentation of the stolen generations is in Human Rights and Equal Opportunity Commission, *Bringing Them Home*. The report claimed that between one in ten and one in three Aboriginal children were removed from their families from 1910 to 1970 (37).

10. On leprosy in Australia see Saunders, "Isolation"; and Bashford and Nugent, "Leprosy and the Management of Race, Sexuality, and Nation in Tropical Australia."

11. See Elias, *State Formation and Civilization*. On the ambivalence of this project — with its barbaric corollary in Australia of child removal — see Van Krieken, "The Barbarism of Civilization." See also Bauman, *Modernity and Ambivalence*; and Burkitt, "Civilization and Ambivalence."

12. Heiser, "The Culion Leper Colony," 6.

13. Heiser, Diaries, July 13, 1914.

14. Stoler, "Tense and Tender Ties," 832.

15. Ibid.

16. I should emphasize that I am not suggesting here that the state was unified and coherent; rather, I want to look at examples of how some agents of the state sought to manage scientifically certain marginalized populations.

17. Foucault, *Discipline and Punish*, 144.

18. Ibid., 199.

19. Vaughan, "Without the Camp," 79.

20. Kipp, "The Evangelical Uses of Leprosy," 176. For another account of leper evangelizing see Kakar, "Leprosy in British India, 1860–1940." See also Deacon, "A History of the Medical Institutions on Robben Island, Cape Colony, 1846–1910," esp. chap. 6; Buckingham, *Leprosy in Colonial South India*; and Obregón, *Batallas contra la lepra*.

21. Victor G. Heiser claimed that the attitude of Filipinos "fluctuated between a great horror of [leprosy] amounting almost to a panic, and the greatest callousness" (Heiser, *An American Doctor's Odyssey*, 220).

22. Heiser, "The Culion Leper Colony." See also Victor G. Heiser to Secretary of the Interior, "Memorandum, 1911," RG 350–1972–31, National Archives and Records Administration, Washington, D.C.

23. Wade and Avellana Basa, "The Culion Leper Colony," 402.

24. Heiser, "Leprosy in the East," 10, 11.

25. Heiser, "Fighting Leprosy in the Philippines," 316–17.

26. Heiser, *An American Doctor's Odyssey*, 236. See Snodgrass, *Leprosy in the Philippine Islands*. Snodgrass was medical director at Culion.

27. Heiser, *An American Doctor's Odyssey*, 236.

28. Wade and Avellana Basa, "The Culion Leper Colony," 406.

29. Snodgrass, *Leprosy in the Philippine Islands*, 25.

30. Heiser, "Leprosy in the East," 17–18.

31. Heiser, "Fighting Leprosy in the Philippines," 318, 320.

32. Brownell, "What American Ideas of Citizenship May Do for Oriental Peoples," 975. Brownell claimed that the United States' policy was "the subject of scoff by every other colonizing nation" because it "considers each of the subject people to be a human being, entitled to certain unalienable rights, which we not only freely grant, but *teach to him*" (975; my emphasis). See also Brownell, "Turning Savages into Citizens"; and Jenks, "Assimilation in the Philippines."

33. Austin, *Never Trust a Government Man*. On earlier efforts toward "half-caste" adolescent assimilation in Victoria see Attwood, *The Making of the Aborigines*.

34. S. J. Mitchell to Minister for External Affairs, Sep. 12, 1911, quoted in Zogbaum, "Herbert Basedow and the Removal of Aboriginal Children of Mixed Descent from Their Families," 128.

35. On Northern Territory Aboriginal policies see Markus, *Governing Savages*; Austin, *Never Trust a Government Man*; and Parry, "Identifying the Process."

36. Haebich, *For Their Own Good*; Haebich, *Broken Circles*; and Jacobs, *Mister Neville*; Maushart, *Sort of a Place Like Home*.

37. Kidd, *The Way We Civilise*. For policies toward white Australian children during this period see Van Krieken, *Children and the State*; Howe and Swain, "Saving the Child and Punishing the Mother"; and Bessant et al., *Violation of Trust*.

38. Gregory, *The Menace of Colour*.

39. Anderson, *The Cultivation of Whiteness*.

40. Cilento, *The White Man in the Tropics, with Especial Reference to Australia and Its Dependencies*.

41. Hill, *The Great Australian Loneliness*, 121.

42. Price, *White Settlers in the Tropics*, 120.

43. Cilento, *Report of the Federal Health Council*, 5th sess., 1931; and Cilento, *Report of the Federal Health Council*, Appendix III, 1934; both quoted in Parry, "Tropical Medicine and Northern Identity," 93.

44. Cook, "The Native in Relation to Public Health," 569. Undoubtedly disease and malnutrition were common among Aborigines, but most white medicos in the 1930s and 1940s, if they recognized these conditions at all, would, like Cook and Cilento, see them primarily as risks for European settlers, or impediments to efficient native labor.

45. Cook, "Leprosy Problems," 802.

46. Cook, "The Native in Relation to Public Health," 569, 571.

47. Cook to R. H. Weddell (administrator of the Northern Territory), July 8, 1936, quoted in Austin, *Never Trust a Government Man*, 170.

48. In the late 1920s there were approximately three thousand Europeans, eighteen thousand "full-bloods," and eight hundred "half-castes" in the Northern Territory. Most of the Europeans huddled in Darwin.

49. Cook, April 28, 1931, quoted in Markus, *Governing Savages*, 98.

50. Neville, *Annual Report for the Aborigines Department* (1932), quoted in Jacobs, *Mister Neville*, 204.

51. Haebich, *Broken Circles*, 343.

52. Barker in Rintoul, *The Wailing*, 242.

53. Haebich, *Broken Circles*, 403.

54. Individual quotes are from Bird, *The Stolen Children*, 82, 56, 29, 89. See also Sabioni, Schaffer, and Smith, *Indigenous Australian Voices*; and Bain and McGowan, *Telling Stories*.

On Aboriginal "witnessing" as evidence see Watson, "'Believe Me'"; and Kennedy, "The Affective Work of Stolen Generations Testimony."

55. Bird, *The Stolen Children*, 32, 57, 96.

56. Ruddick, "'Talking about Cruel Things,'" 16.

57. See Anderson, *The Cultivation of Whiteness*, chap. 8; McGregor, "Representations of the Half-Caste in the Australian Scientific Literature of the 1930s"; McGregor, "An Aboriginal Caucasian"; and McGregor, *Imagined Destinies*.

58. Neville, *Australia's Coloured Minority*, 57, 63. See also Jacobs, "Science and Veiled Assumptions."

59. A. O. Neville, in Aboriginal Affairs Planning Authority, *Aboriginal Welfare*, 11. For comparative studies of interracial marriage during this period see Wolfe, "Land, Labor, and Difference"; and Ellinghaus, "Taking Assimilation to Heart."

60. Cook to Weddell, June 27, 1933, quoted in Austin, "Cecil Cook, Scientific Thought, and 'Half-Castes,'" 113.

61. Elkin, "Anthropology and the Future of the Australian Aborigines," 7.

62. Elkin, *Citizenship for the Aborigines*, 12, 90. See also Gray, "From Nomadism to Citizenship."

63. Chesterman and Galligan, *Citizens without Rights*, 133. The linkage of rights to hygiene has recently resurfaced in Australia as "mutual obligation," where in order to receive basic services and development aid, Aboriginal Australians must demonstrate improvement in personal hygiene. See Meaghan Shaw, "Hygiene Pact in Deal for Blacks," *The Age* [Melbourne], December 9, 2004, and Shaw, "No Deal on Our Right, Group Says," *The Age* [Melbourne], December 15, 2004.

64. Taussig, *Shamanism, Colonialism, and the Wild Man*, 4.

65. Robert Manne makes this distinction in "In denial."

66. See Anderson, "Where Is the Postcolonial History of Medicine?"; and Anderson, "Postcolonial Histories of Medicine."

67. Said, "Secular Interpretation, the Geographical Element, and the Methodology of Imperialism."

NAYAN SHAH

Adjudicating Intimacies on U.S. Frontiers

Empire-states and nation-states, in the processes of conquest, territorial expansion and labor migration, confront people with diverse understandings of the intimate and the commitments by which they live those ties. States administer intimate ties in legislation, in judicial trials, and in registration and licensing procedures. Judicial trials, in particular, produce flashpoints of controversy and uncertainty of which unions would be sanctioned by government. In the cases I explore here in the early-twentieth-century western United States, the unusual controversy over Hindu marriage reveals how states manage intimate ties and recognize human choices.

Interrelated notions of the intimate and intimacy shaped the characteristics of the human subject and the rights and abilities to engage freely in unions. In popular usage at this time, intimacy connotes sexual relations, sexual liberty, and close familiarity. As Ann Stoler and Lauren Berlant have underscored, intimacy can also reflect a person's innermost nature and character. Following the work of Carole Pateman, I examine how these two meanings of intimacy calibrate liberal societies' legal definitions of the capacity of self-possession and for the ownership of property. This relay between a person's innermost nature, sexual relations and the material world produces an optic that spotlights the relentless assessments of the human subject that undergird the state's scrutiny of intimate ties.[1]

In two court cases from starkly different localities in the northwestern and southwestern edges of the continental United States, the legitimacy of a "Hindu marriage" framed the outcomes of court proceedings and prison terms. Although marriage customs in British India, such as dowry, child brides and grooms, *zenanas* (harems), and *sati* (widow immolation), circulated widely in the print culture of late-nineteenth-century American evangelical Protestants, it was not until the early-twentieth-century migration of male laborers from Punjab that "Hindu marriage" emerged as a legal and political issue. In Gate, Washington, in February 1912, after an evening of drinking and socializing among a group of white and South Asian men in a sawmill bunkhouse, Clarence Murray was found by his brother and cousins that night unconscious and undressed in the room of Don Sing. Murray's drinking companions — Jago Sing, Bram Sing, and Don Sing — were arrested the next day on charges of sodomy and after a brief trial imprisoned. In Las Cruces, New Mexico, in 1933, two women — Soledad Garcia Jubala of New Mexico and Nami Singh of Punjab — claimed to be the wife of a deceased man, Julio Jubala, and the heir of his estate.

Although Hindu marriage became a central issue in both cases, what "Hindu marriage" meant — and how and why it was deployed as an issue for official judgment, differed markedly. Hindu marriage had different consequences in the sodomy and estate cases. In the first, the status of "Hindu marriage" helped commute a convicted man's sentence from a serious charge; and, in the second, the legitimacy of a "Hindu marriage" determined the inheritance of valuable agricultural property. Despite different legal outcomes, both cases unleashed broader questions about the legitimacy and illegitimacy of marital ties.

As U.S. women's historians and legal historians have demonstrated, gradations of legality and illegality were a cornerstone of the government management of the intimate.[2] In the United States, state legislators, federal bureaucrats, missionaries, and social critics created and defined the standard of Christian monogamous marriage and shored it up against an array of putatively deviant unions. As Nancy F. Cott has argued, assertions of differences of race and civilization buttressed the superiority of the marriage norm: "marital non-conformists most hounded and punished by the federal government were deemed 'racially' different from the white majority. They were Indians, freed slaves, polygamous Mormons (metaphorically non-white) and Asians. Prohibiting divergent marriages has been as important in public policy as sustaining the chosen model."[3] Christian monogamous marriage was the norm, with an array of "horrors" of sexual relations and "female degradation" on either side. Knowledge of nonnormative unions circulated culturally among evangelical Protestant Christians in North America and in what historian Joan Jacobs Brumberg has so dramatically called "characteristic atrocities" of Asia and Africa, including "concubinage and polygamy; bride sale; . . . consecrated prostitution and sacrifice; . . .

[and] child marriage," as well as sodomy, in all its possible nonprocreative forms.[4]

The liminal spaces of the early-twentieth-century Southwest Spanish American borderlands and the Pacific Northwest hosted the collision of multiple races, cultures, and customs and became laboratories for the elaboration of distinct interpretations of legal intimacy.[5] The management of marriage and sexuality that emerged regionally in the nineteenth century varied widely, but it mirrored British, French, Spanish, and Dutch imperial policies in regulating and recognizing marital, concubinary, and sexual relations of those under their rule.

The two court cases I treat here strategically invoked Hindu marriage to define what constituted legal unions. Both show the government's management of the intimate as a *process* that simultaneously shored up the norm as it scrutinized deviancy. The judges, attorneys, individual advocates, and prison wardens attempted to fit the particular circumstances of individual cases in the categories of monogamous marriage, concubinage, bigamy, polygamy, and sodomy. Christian monogamous marriage may have been the norm, but government agents and judges confronted a diversity of other arrangements that were made either legible, visible, and legitimate or the immoral opposite.

In governing multicultural societies, judges and attorneys sifted through local customs to understand how a particular marriage was religiously sanctified or legitimated by community acceptance. In adjudicating, a stream of questions arose. Was the social bond and duty maintained by the couple's sharing of household or by the vows they exchanged? Was it possible that the marriage could be dissolved by divorce, the distance or length of time the couple was apart, or by abandonment?

This chapter explores how new gradations and variations of legal unions were created based on particular cases brought for judicial review. In both of the court cases with which I am concerned here the implicit evaluation of a person's intimate properties affected the distribution and organization of land, labor, wealth, and status. In the United States, the transmission of property, citizenship status, and immigrant entry were worked through understandings of marriage, ideas of respectable family formation, and the clear designation of dependents and heirs. The local adjudication of these disputes reveals how the hard edges of taxonomy are muted by the ways in which sympathies are distributed and played out.

Political and cultural thought in the United States during the nineteenth century and early twentieth characterized migration from Asia as an "invasion," "subversion," and unwelcome "amalgamation" that threatened the establishment of European "civilization" in the western territories and states. White Americans and Canadians feared labor competition, interracial marriage, sexual seduction, disease, and immorality introduced by Asian male workers.[6] Migrants from British colonial India were a small portion of the stream of migrants from Asia and Europe who populated the territories and later states of the Pacific coast and the desert Southwest. South Asian migrants came to the United States and Canada to work in railroad construction, the timber industry, and agricultural harvesting. Nearly all came from Punjab, and many had served in the British military or worked as security guards and police in Hong Kong, Shanghai, and Singapore.

In the late nineteenth century and the early twentieth the western United States experienced rapid capitalization, uneven economic development, and shifts in political administration from territories to statehood. South Asian migrants came to work in the timber extraction and processing plants of British Columbia, Washington, and Oregon. South Asian men had left the sawmills of the Pacific Northwest for the irrigated farms, orchards, and vineyards of California, Arizona, and New Mexico. In the Southwest, speculative private and state-subsidized investments in rail transportation, water, electricity, and communication infrastructure had created uneven economic opportunities, fostering both large-scale corporate agriculture and sharecropping. More than twenty-five thousand Punjabi Sikh, Muslim, and Hindu laborers and farmers migrated to the United States and Canada before immigration restrictions in the 1910s stopped the flow. These migrants, despite their varied religious beliefs and practices, were referred to as "Hindu," which was short for Hindustani. Canadian and U.S. immigration laws made it nearly impossible for South Asian women to immigrate.[7] Prohibitions on interracial marriage, which were unevenly legislated and varied by territory and state, stymied legitimate unions for Asian migrants. A number of historians have demonstrated that variable racial taxonomies of marriage emerged in every western territory and state. As Peggy Pascoe has argued, antimiscegenation laws "in the West, not the South, reached their most elaborate, even labyrinthine development, covering the broadest list of racial categories."[8] However, these laws were irregularly enforced and creatively bypassed by individuals, clerks, and judges to suit local conditions.[9]

New Mexico was one of the last states admitted into the continental United States and one of the few states in the West and South that allowed interracial marriage. However, a court case in the Rio Grande Valley town of Mesilla, New Mexico, raised compelling questions about how the state interprets marriage and concubinage within a prism of ethnic, religious, and race differences. On the night of December 27, 1932, forty-five-year-old Julio Jubala was instantly killed when the truck he was driving was struck by a northbound freight train at the Mesilla Park crossing.[10] At the probate hearing in April 1933 two women claimed to be his wife. One of these women, Soledad Garcia Jubala, whom he married in 1929, lived in Mesilla; the second woman, Nami Singh, lived in India and claimed she and Jubala were married in 1898. Because of the claim of a prior marriage in India, a fairly routine probate case after a tragic death became a civil suit played out over two continents and over three years in the New Mexico court system.[11]

As the attorneys tried to probe and justify the competing claims of the two women, the legitimacy of the Hindu marriage and the Christian marriage came under dispute. First, Nami's attorneys developed their case that the deceased, Julio Jubala of New Mexico, was the same man as Jawala Singh, who Nami Singh married in Punjab in 1898 and who left India in 1907. They used immigration documents and testimony from family and friends to show that Julio/Jawala arrived in Mesilla, New Mexico, in 1910 after stops in Hong Kong, the Philippines, and Mexico. Nami's attorneys introduced testimony that verified that the marriage had been properly consecrated and recognized in British India. The New Mexico District Court enlisted the U.S. Consul in Karachi in British India to depose witnesses in Punjab. The consul summoned Nami Singh, her father, Jawala's father, and a Brahmin priest. They testified that the parents had arranged the marriage; Nami was twelve and Jawala was eleven when they married in a Hindu ceremony in her home village on June 3, 1898. Nami declared that the bride and groom "had not seen each [other] before the day of the ceremony," which was typical of arranged marriages. After the ceremony she lived in Jawala's father's house for six years. Jawala's father explained that "at the time of the marriage of my son to Nami, neither party were of puberty age," and three years later after reaching puberty they assumed the "relations of man and wife"—a euphemism for having publicly sanctioned sexual relations. Subsequently they lived together for approximately three more years before the departure of Jawala Singh for the United States (176–77). International treaties obliged the United States to recognize legitimate unions in Britain and its empire. The details of a properly arranged match, the preadolescent age of the bride and groom, and the timing of sexual consummation were elements in the narrative of legitimacy produced by Nami's attorneys. However, these very same details were deployed by Soledad's attorneys as indicators of a morally "repugnant" and thereby illegitimate system of marital unions.

Long-distance migration and the protracted separation of spouses and families across the Pacific created a different sense of time, marital duty, and the significance of kin networks in forging bonds of communication for Jawala's family in India. The distance and the length of time away were "perfectly normal procedure," according to Nami's father, who claimed that at the time "many Sikhs were leaving the Punjab for America to seek employment" (172). Although Jawala Singh had not written much to his family, his father received "news of his whereabouts and activities" from a network of "friends, neighbors, and acquaintances" that also migrated to the United States (172, 177). Principally through telegrams and mail, villagers in Punjab kept tabs on their relatives scattered in California and the Southwest. The same network delivered news by telegram of Jawala's death within days and had, within weeks, sent reports of the estimated value of his estate and information regarding local attorneys (100–102, 110–11). From the perspective of Nami's family, Julio/Jawala had abandoned neither her nor them.

The distance and decades of separation created waves of silence and insight in all the locations of transoceanic migration. Migrants kept some details of their intimate and social lives secret but revealed others to the kin at home, as well as to friends and kin who had also migrated. These fluctuating crests and eddies of silence and partial knowledge were most striking in who possessed knowledge about each union and where they lived. Julio/Jawala's friends and relatives from Punjab who worked in the Rio Grande Valley testified that they were aware of his dual marriages. For instance, when an El Paso friend, Bood Singh, quizzed him about having two wives, Julio responded, "There will be no trouble. I have a wife in both countries" (76). Julio was even intent on persuading Bood to do the same and marry a "beautiful girl" locally in addition to Bood's wife in India. Bood argued that it was against the law to marry unless you divorce your first wife in India. Julio said, "No body know I am married. Here you can marry here too; nobody tell it to the courts" (76, 113–16). Jawala was careful, however, to keep the knowledge of his marriage in India secret in his New Mexico home. His cousin Delip Singh, who had attended Nami and Jawala's marriage ceremony, became reacquainted with Jawala in 1929 when they met at an El Paso horse corral (104). After Delip learned of Soledad, Jawala begged Delip to keep his marriage to Nami secret: "Don't tell it so my Mexican wife will know it" (100–102). These promises of silence were kept; in Punjab no one admitted to know of Soledad, and in New Mexico no one but Punjabi friends knew about Nami.

While Jawala's practice of plural marriage was controversial among his friends and relatives in the United States, it was unclear whether the disputes between Jawala and his friends arose from the moral value of monogamous marriage in the Sikh-Hindu traditions or economic fears. Losing land through the dissolution of marriages in community-property states such as New Mexico and California was a fear that haunted many Punjabi men in the early twentieth century. For some the handful of divorces from marriages with Mexican American women had resulted in the loss of land and savings; these served as cautionary tales of the danger of marriages to women in the United States.[12]

The overwhelming evidence of Nami's legitimate marriage provoked Soledad's attorneys to argue that Julio must have divorced Nami prior to his marriage in the United States. In questioning Nami's family, however, they discovered that divorce was an illegitimate option in Sikh and Hindu communities in British India.[13] Both fathers were adamant that marriage under "Hindu religious rites" did not recognize "divorce granted to either party."[14] Soledad's attorneys insisted, nevertheless, that Jawala had petitioned for divorce sometime during his travels in Hong Kong, the Philippines, and Mexico. There was no documentation of divorce between Jawala and Nami in New Mexico records, and in Mexico divorce was not permissible until 1915. Interestingly, one could not even argue that Jawala was unfamiliar with divorce proceedings because a record search by the court revealed that Jawala had been legally married in 1917 to Maria Fierro, whom he divorced in 1929.[15]

There was no debate over the legality of Julio Jubala's marriage to Soledad Garcia. A marriage certificate was produced that revealed that six weeks after his divorce from Maria, forty-two-year old Julio married barely sixteen-year-old Soledad Garcia, who was nearly four months pregnant in March 1929. She married with permission of her father, Domingo Garcia, who worked on Julio's farms.[16] Julio and Soledad had three daughters in quick succession; the first, Alicia, was born five months after their marriage. Esther and Julia came quickly afterward. When Julio died, Soledad was pregnant with their first son, who was named Manuel.

Curiously, Nami's attorneys did not raise moral suspicions about the context of Soledad's marriage. Her youth, the generational differences in their ages, the advanced state of her pregnancy on the wedding day, nor her father's economic relationship with the groom elicited comment from the attorneys or the judge. Apparently, as an issue of the law, Soledad's father's permission and the proper legal documentation allayed any doubts about the morality of the union and gave it irreproachable legitimacy.

These issues appeared as stray details in the court transcript, and the historical actors of the time never raised them in the court record. Documentation from marriage licenses, birth records, and other civil suits substantiated these details and heightened the ambiguity of Soledad and Julio/Jawala's marriage. My interpretive approach is to juxtapose the judicial decision and attorney arguments against these details within the court transcript or in other court documents and registers in order to delve into uneven, ambiguous, and incommensurate discourses of legitimacy that the judicial decision and even the attorney's briefs often foreclose. The analysis that follows closely pursues these juxtapositions and incommensurate moments as they emerge in the strategic arguments employed by the judges and attorneys.

The shadow of bigamy influenced district court judge James B. McGhee's decision in 1934. McGhee wrote that the "the testimony is overwhelming that the claimant, Nami Singh, was lawfully married to the deceased in India."[17] The precedence of Nami's marriage, no evidence of divorce, and the principle of marital monogamy guided his decision. Since Nami married Jawala/Julio first, she was entitled to inherit. Judge McGhee knew the consequences of his ruling would "deprive the Dona Ana county widow, who married the deceased a few years since, her share of the property, and that it invalidates her marriage" (35). In following the rule of law on the precedence of marriage and abiding by the government principle of monogamy, the district court had put the estate's property in jeopardy and the Mesilla widow and her children at the mercy of government financial support. Nami Singh's status as an "Asiatic alien," however, prohibited her possession of the estate's 125 acres, according to the Alien Land Law (34).

Soledad's attorneys made an aggressive appeal to the New Mexico Supreme Court on grounds of the immorality and illegitimacy of Hindu marriage. They argued that New Mexico was not "bound by a law or custom that is repugnant to its established public policy; and the Hindu child marriage [consummated in India by a Brahmin priest] . . . is repugnant to the established public policy of the State of New Mexico" (54–55). The effect of Judge McGhee's decision would make Soledad Jubala "nothing more than a concubine and that would in the same breath bastardize the four innocent children"; the decision would take away five-eighths of Jubala's estate and "give it to a woman who contributed nothing to its accumulation" (54–55).[18]

Soledad's attorneys inveighed against what they subsequently called "infant marriage" and its affront to New Mexico age-of-consent laws passed from 1915 to 1929, which required parental consent for marriages of males under the age of eighteen and females under the age of fifteen. They insisted that the New Mexico Supreme Court must stand in solidarity with the British imperial government's crusade to eliminate the "custom of child marriages" in India and its "evil effects." They speculated that if the New Mexico Supreme Court upheld the judgment, then the floodgates of deviant marriages would be opened, and New Mexico would be forced to recognize "polygamous marriage" and "incestuous marriage" and "infant marriages of 7 year olds" if they were valid elsewhere. They argued that the sanctioning of "Hindu" marriages disrupted the "standards of morals in every Christian nation" (57, 61–62).[19]

In July 1936 the New Mexico Supreme Court reversed the lower court decision and found in favor of Soledad Garcia Jubala. Judge Blair, speaking for the court, argued that there was "insufficient evidence to overcome presumption that alleged marriages have been dissolved when deceased married in US" (312). The court accepted Soledad's attorneys' position that in order to marry in the United States, Jawala must have divorced somewhere. The court also doubted the validity of Nami's marriage and whether it had been truly consummated. Judge Blair denied any "unequivocal proof" that "the marriage in India, if it ever existed, was a bar to legal marriage in New Mexico" (313–14).[20]

Judge Blair accused Nami Singh of making "no effort to communicate" with the deceased in twenty years and opined that she "asserted no claim or right of wife during [Jawala's] lifetime, but her interest, or that of others ostensibly in her behalf, became apparent only when the opportunity arose after his death to claim a community interest in an estate she had no part in earning. In the meantime he had married appellant and reared a family of four children" (315). Blair linked the right to "community interest in an estate" to participation in the earning of the estate or in the rearing of children as evidence of a woman's unrewarded labor.[21] In their unsuccessful appeal for a rehearing, Nami's attorneys claimed that Julio/Jawala owned all property prior to his marriage to Soledad: "Soledad brought him nothing . . . and helped him acquire nothing" (7–8).[22]

The State Supreme Court's reversal in July 1936 made Soledad Jubala the "legal widow" of Julio Jubala and the recipient of his estate of 125 acres, valued at twenty-one thousand dollars.[23] She did not remain a widow for long. Three weeks after the conclusion of the suit, Soledad Garcia Jubala, at the age of twenty-one, married twenty-three-year-old Enrique Telles of San Miguel, New Mexico.[24]

In both the lower and Supreme Court ruling the judges had to actively delegitimize one union in order to recognize another. Since bigamy was impossible to countenance, Soledad's attorneys developed a compelling argument that the specter of Hindu "infant marriage" practices would disrupt the standards of the "Christian nation" of the United States. The category of "Hindu marriage" summoned analogies to an array of deviant marriages and injected into this case the heated political debates on polygamy of the late nineteenth century. This court case is an illustration of a broader dispute over legitimate marriage. In nineteenth-century political and legal debates Mormon polygamy was characterized as an "Asiatic custom" and "Mohammedan barbarism" in counter distinction to the "civilized" traditions of Western Europeans and white people in the United States.[25] The idea of Hindu marriage was represented as an arranged marriage and one between children, a practice that troubled notions of consent. In the early twentieth century, arranged marriages were a flash point of anxiety in U.S. immigration policy. Newspapers, missionary journals, and public policy debates emphasized the "coerced will" of Japanese picture brides and Eastern European Jewish child brides. These marriages were labeled as the uncivilized customs of Asian traditions that undercut American sexual modernity, liberalism, and the superiority of Protestant Christian values.[26]

In the nineteenth century and early twentieth the U.S. nation-state had intervened to prohibit and punish plural marriage, which appeared as a Native American social custom and a Mormon religious and social practice. State marriage laws categorically denied legitimacy to polygamy. Immigrants had to offer oaths to neither condone nor practice polygamy as a condition of immigration to the United States and naturalization to U.S. citizenship.[27] Polygamy was also the object of contentious regulation in the British Empire's management of intimate unions in India and of South Asian indentured and voluntary migrants in its African and Caribbean colonies.[28]

The New Mexico Supreme Court had resoundingly determined which marriage was legitimate and deepened a commitment to a core norm of Christian monogamous marriage. Yet from the perspective of Nami Singh and her kin and community in Punjab, the U.S. system was disquieting. In committing to monogamous morality the New Mexico Supreme Court countenanced the abandonment of women in "deviant marriages." From the perspective of her family Jawala had not abandoned Nami. However, the New Mexico Supreme Court made her an abandoned wife. Had the marriage failed? Or did the courts have to implicitly presume and condone that Julio/Jawala had abandoned his wife for the convenience of the state? Otherwise, Jawala/Julio's two unions in Mesilla would be perceived as serial concubinage. Although never explicitly stated in any of the testimony, it would be conceivable that concubinage is precisely how Jawala/Julio's relationship to Soledad was perceived in his community in Punjab during the trial. The Sikh-Hindu customs of the Punjabi village would not accept that a secular marriage license or even a Christian ceremony in the United States could trump the marriage bond solemnized by a Brahmin priest. Nami's attorneys' first settlement offer in probate was to split the estate between the legitimate wife, Nami, and his four children by Soledad. This offer appeared to be a tacit acceptance of Soledad as a "concubine" who held no rightful claims to inheritance; however, her children with Jawala might be potential heirs, despite their "illegitimacy" in the eyes of the Punjabi community. From its perspective Soledad could have been a temporary concubine, a "necessary" situation to offer comfort and care to a man who worked far from his home village. Such a concubine could also potentially produce heirs that might be recognized in both the succession of property and lineage. The possibility of migrant men with wives and children on either side of the ocean was a fairly common experience in both European and Asian migrations to the Americas in the late nineteenth century.[29] From the perspective of both home and host societies, it was usually at the moment of a migrant man's death that the implications of plural families would be confronted in the dispersion of property.

In the arguments that shaped the decision in New Mexico, Hindu marriage emerged as an "uncivilized" custom of ambiguous morality that obligated children to marital union. As such it could not be treated as a trusted social contract in U.S. society. However, the discourse of Hindu marriage could also be refashioned to produce very different results. In 1912, after the conclusion of a court trial for sexual crime in the sawmill town of Gate, Washington, the discourse of Hindu marriage was used to provide respectable status to a maligned migrant from India. A young South Asian college graduate in Portland, P. L. Verma marshaled Hindu marriage to protect a man, Don Sing, convicted of sodomy. Forty-year-old Sing had been arrested with two other South Asian men for sodomizing Clarence Murray, an eighteen-year-old white male whose father was a foreman in the sawmill where they all worked. All three men were tried together, and their attorney offered no substantive defense. The all-white, male jury swiftly returned a verdict of guilty, and all three men were sent to Washington State Penitentiary. The accusation of a drunk white male penetrated by South Asian men perhaps heightened the widespread antipathy toward South Asians who had since 1906 been repeatedly harassed, reviled, and driven out of a number of sawmill towns in Washington State by white laborers.[30]

Verma, who had served as a translator for part of the trial, orchestrated a campaign for Don Sing's clemency. In addition to raising questions about court procedure and unreliable eyewitness accounts of Don Sing's presence at the scene of the assault, Verma offered the parole board an explanation of the sexuality and morality of "Hindoo" men. Verma characterized sodomy as a "great and unnatural sin among Hindoos," and held that it was unlikely that "a good Hindoo citizen is addicted of that habit."[31] Yet he quickly set aside the disturbing affronts to white masculinity by the revelations of South Asian men sexually penetrating a white male, to focus on the status and behavior of married men. For Verma, a "good Hindoo citizen" was a married man who was religiously observant. Marriage was a deterrent to sodomy: "Don Sing is married and married men do not like things like that, they are never addicted to such unnatural habits. They have to look far into the future. They are tied down by the weight of marriage."[32] Verma presented the exemplary Hindu married men as possessing sexual self-restraint and monogamous morality, much like the images of respectable white American manhood. Sodomy was coded as a habitual practice that could be addictive to the unmarried man prone to unregulated behaviors and ruled by irrational passions. Future responsibilities loomed large for the married man, who must avoid the entanglements, distractions, and costs of transitory sexual encounters. The imperative against sodomy was less about steadfast heterosexual preference than the necessity of containment within and for marriage and the legitimate progeny that it would produce.[33]

Verma skillfully marshaled compassion for Don Sing and his predicament and invoked a sympathetic hearing for Don's wife. Verma included a letter from Don Sing's wife to bolster the appeal for his client's parole. She wrote, "Life to me is not worth living, I have no body to support me."[34] The pitiful wife was an archetype; her letter was translated for the parole board, but she was never named except as Don Sing's wife, his dependent. However, the success of the appeal to evoke pity demanded that she appear to be a worthy and helpless dependent. Verma created a scene of what Karen Halttunnen has called "spectatorial sympathy," which produced a "tableau of pitiful suffering," with a helpless woman's body bearing the "burden of the sympathetic gaze."[35] According to scholars of nineteenth-century Anglo-American sentimentality such a powerful scene could arouse sympathetic response and a "call to action."[36] So too in his letter Verma emphasizes the wife's "miserable condition" and her "cries for help" because she was without means of male support and would become destitute. Don Sing's "misfortune . . . has fallen on her head. She will be starved to death unheeded, if no steps are taken for granting Don Singh [sic] his liberty."[37]

Her letter's content and the choreography of Verma's appeal hinged on the asymmetrical power relations Amit Rai has analyzed in the British colonial context and Randall McGowen in the context of slavery abolition in the United States. She pleaded, "Is there any means of his getting out or the case is hopeless? People say he has been imprisoned for 20 years. . . . I hear many things which are incredible in connection with Don Singh."[38] Her own letter articulated both despair and powerlessness that invited the assistance of the empowered, both Verma and the parole authorities. As Amit Rai has noted, the "rule of sympathy" both marked and created "racial, gender and class inequalities" as it paradoxically "bridged them through identification."[39]

Verma's campaign for Don Sing was enhanced by the sympathetic portrait of the pitiable wife, as well as by a rehabilitation of Don's public reputation. Verma enlisted testimonials from Don's white employers and landlords in Portland, who praised him as an "honest, well-behaving gentleman" and "trustworthy," "reliable and industrious" worker who has a gentle and unassuming disposition.[40] Twenty men who had signed their names in either Punjabi or English endorsed a petition of the "Hindoos of Portland" for Don Sing, drafted by Verma. The petition characterized Don Sing as "always a law-abiding citizen," "from a good family," and possessing "temperate habits."[41] These qualities of honesty, temperance, and industriousness were certainly values that the warden and parole board would uphold as evidence of Don Sing's character. However, the petition of his friends also revealed Sikh communitarian values that may have demonstrated for them a different vision of his humanitarianism. His friends considered Don Sing a devout man who worshipped regularly and was treated as a "missionary" for his charitable work. With legendary generosity in his Portland community, he was known to help others financially in distress. The support of the community of South Asian laborers and Sing's employers created a credible portrait of a civic-minded and responsible immigrant in the United States and became crucial to Don Sing's appeal. The other two men who were convicted, Bram Sing and Jago Sing, had no such local support in Gate, Portland, or elsewhere.

The final and perhaps most crucial element in making Don Sing a subject for compassion was the assessment prison authorities made of his advocate, Verma. Certainly, Verma's English education and resourcefulness in soliciting and collecting testimonials, creating petitions, and meeting with Reed, the prison warden, made such an appeal strategically plausible. Yet as Ann Stoler has argued, the interplay of compassionate and reasoned administration placed a high value on assessing "good character" by observing an individual's "comportment" and "tastes" and by "cultivating the right sentiments."[42] Perhaps Verma's striving to be a trustworthy subject is nowhere more evident than in the florid conclusion of his appeal. Verma invoked the ideas of "American Justice . . . Equality and Brotherhood" to win the intercession of the warden, whom he personally thanked for his "kind and philonthropic [sic] words that you love our nationality just as you love your own. Your words that Hindoos are treated by you as brothers still ring in my ears."[43] The strategy of invoking American justice and cross-national brotherhood to dislodge racial antipathy was surprisingly successful. The sentiments Verma expressed may well have assured the warden that his account was reliable and that he could be trusted. If Verma's claims could be trusted, then perhaps sympathy for the plight of Don Sing and his pitiable wife could be addressed as well. The warden encouraged a review of Don Sing's case. In 1913 the prison board determined that there was grave doubt that Don Sing was present at the commission of the crime, and on October 14 Governor Ernest Lister commuted Don Sing's five-year sentence, of which he had served eighteen months.[44]

Verma had succeeded in winning Don Sing's release by casting the abstract category of "Hindu marriage" as moral and respectable and then reshaping Don Sing's status as an irreproachable example of Hindu married men. Verma analogized the Hindu married man as a copy of the white married man, characterizing such an individual as steadfastly heterosexual and faithful to his wife. The sympathetic judgment that favored Hindu marriage and its responsibilities simultaneously represented Don Sing as a "good family man" and protected the reputation of heterosexual married men generally as beyond reproach. It distinguished him from the two unmarried men who were convicted. The power of "sympathy and morality," as Amit Rai has shown, both created and targeted the heterosexual family for compassionate assistance.[45]

INTIMATE PROPERTIES

Verma's successful campaign enabled Don Sing to recover the property of a public self—his reputation. Sing's reputation was tied with the responsibilities of his overseas marriage and its demands of moral rectitude. It was a reputation that enabled the review of his conviction and his freedom from imprisonment. The status of public married man, however, was contingent and uncertain in Sing's experience as a migrant laborer. In his file at the Washington State Penitentiary a 1930 FBI report catalogues a litany of public drunkenness and disorderly conduct convictions in Washington, Oregon, and California during the 1910s and 1920s. Spellings of the man's name differ, but the FBI has catalogued them all as the same Don Sing who received clemency from a sodomy conviction in 1913.

Julio Jubala (a.k.a. Jawala Singh) was able to navigate effectively the social and legal landscape of Dona Ana County for twenty years until his tragic death in 1932. During his lifetime, and even afterward, he never had to entertain a criminal proceeding about bigamy or the Alien Land Law, which was approved as a constitutional amendment in New Mexico in 1921. As a successful farmer, he was able to seek assistance from the county clerk, lawyers, and bankers to obtain and retain property. He succeeded in holding two marriages simultaneously, as he boasted to his Punjabi friends in El Paso. The New Mexico Supreme Court upheld his actions; it preferred to presume that the marriage in India had been dissolved, even though there was no documentation to support such an assertion.

From the very beginning, the suit in New Mexico was about the ownership of land and the legitimate claims of inheritance. As the case moved from probate hearing to civil suit in the district court in Las Cruces to the New Mexico Supreme Court hearing in Santa Fe, a spiral of claims and questions about the ownership of land emerged. New Mexico laws regulating property were key to understanding Julio Jubala's success as a farmer in Mesilla. Marriage to Mexican American women appeared to be the strategy Julio used to hold and accumulate farmland and circumvent the restrictions of the Alien Land Law. Modeled after the California law first passed in 1913, the Alien Land Law in New Mexico was adopted by voters in 1921. The constitutional amendment prohibited an "alien, ineligible to citizenship under the laws of the United States," from owning or leasing land in New Mexico.[46] Chinese immigrants were explicitly denied naturalized citizenship, being neither "white persons" nor "persons of African nativity." The U.S. Supreme Court handed down decisions in 1922 and 1923 that denied "white person" status to Japanese and Hindus respectively. In the same period federal courts offered "white" status, and therefore the ability to naturalize and become property holders, to Syrians, Lebanese, Sephardic Jews, Turks, and Persians.[47]

Community-property law and familiarity with local officials enabled Julio to continue to acquire land even after Alien Land Laws applied to Hindus. Under the New Mexico community-property statute, husband and wife formed a legal partnership, agreeing that all accumulated property would be divided equally when death or divorce ended the partnership. Julio Jubala's attorney had manipulated the divorce settlement to Maria Fierro in 1929 in order to retain land ownership of 125 acres; he ceded all personal property, made a cash settlement, and promised to build her an adobe home.[48]

The question of how Julio had acquired land legally was raised several times in the court proceedings. Even the estate administrator and county clerk, J. F. Nevares, could not explain Julio's ability to circumvent Alien Land Laws despite having "handled business" for him on several occasions. Nevares's stance was disingenuous self-protection given that Nevares had been actively involved in helping Julio file real estate transactions, marriage certifications, and naturalization petitions.[49]

Race and citizenship requirements of property ownership in New Mexico and the United States threw another wrinkle into the lawful inheritance of the estate. Soledad's attorneys argued that the alien land constitutional amendment of New Mexico made it impossible for Nami Singh to inherit Julio/Jawala's real property. Nami's attorneys countered that treaty rights between the United States and Great Britain enabled Nami Singh to own land temporarily as a British citizen. According to a commercial diplomatic treaty between the two empire-states, which included imperial possessions in India, both British and U.S. citizens could inherit real estate in the other state's jurisdiction as long as that property was disposed of within three years.[50]

Citizenship and the possession of land were contentious issues in New Mexico. In the early twentieth century, New Mexico land had been leveraged away from Mexican American families through taxation burdens and intermarriage with Anglos.[51] Among a handful of successful Asian immigrants, Julio Jubala acquired land before and during his marriage with Mexican American Maria Fierro and retained it through a subsequent divorce. Soledad's attorneys and the Supreme Court judges framed Soledad Garcia Jubala as the local woman, whose claim to land might be drawn away by the claims of the foreign woman, Nami Singh. It was a twist to the more familiar story of how marriage to white men with Native American and Mexican American women had led to the "leaking out" of the land from indigenous communities in the midwestern and southwestern territories.[52] Ironically, Soledad's own U.S. birth citizenship status was precarious, potentially lost by her marriage to a foreign man. Within weeks of winning the suit and ownership of the land, Soledad, through her marriage to Mexican American Enrique Telles, regained her citizenship status as well.[53]

The intimate properties of citizenship and belonging were contested in discursive arenas of morality and civilization and through the policing of sex and marriage. The legislation of antimiscegenation, antipolygamy, landownership, naturalization and immigration laws, and the adjudication of particular legal disputes feasted on uneven and incommensurate racial taxonomies.

COMPASSION AND TAXONOMY
IN ADMINISTERING JUSTICE

Don Sing's status as a married man offered Sing an alibi of respectable sexuality and morality. The moral empathy generated by his good character and record and the pitiful condition of his incredulous wife in India may have loosened the suspicions of the parole board about the testimony in the trial. The judicial decision, however, was not made on the basis of the moral status of "Hindu marriage" alone. The decision was made on the basis of other legal criteria of evidence, testimony, and the purported role of Don Sing in the crime. The board reflected on the conspicuous absence of eyewitness testimony that placed Don Sing in the bunkhouse room when the two other South Asian men were identified. This encouraged doubt about the presence of Don Sing at the moment of the crime rather than implying guilt during the trial because he was discovered sleeping in the same room when the "white victim" was found. The sympathetic treatment that Don Sing received by the prison warden and the parole board did not disrupt the judicial certainty that Clarence Murray had been sodomized, nor did it temper the convictions of Jago Sing and Bram Sing.

The play between sympathy and taxonomy in the process of judgment paralleled the judicial decision of the New Mexico Supreme Court. In that case Soledad's attorney's appeals to sympathy for the "Dona Ana county widow," whose marriage had been delegitimized by the court and whose status had been summarily transformed from "widow" to "concubine," persuaded the judges to doubt the legitimacy of the "Hindu child marriage." Unlike the imperative of the district court to solve the local problem when presented with evidence of Nami Singh and Jawala Singh's marriage in India, the New Mexico Supreme Court wrestled with the precedent produced by Hindu marriage and its potential to legitimate a fearful cascade of deviant relationships—from "infant marriage," polygamy, and incest. The moral sympathy of Soledad's plight and the concerns of unwittingly validating "repugnant" foreign customs shaped the New Mexico Supreme Court's scrutiny of whether Nami Singh's marriage was ever "consummated" or "dissolved" to make her claim irrelevant to Julio Jubala's estate. Justice Blair's decision cast dubious light on Nami Singh's motives and the legitimacy of her relationship with Julio/Jawala. She and her "Hindu marriage" became Julio/Jawala's "past," with no relevance to the future disposition of his legacy and property.

It was through the juridical and administrative practices of governance, from the local to the national scales, that racial and sexual classifications developed their shapes. As Ann Stoler has argued, "taxonomic states" were charged with "interpreting what constituted racial membership, citizenship, political subversion and the scope of the state's jurisdiction over morality." Overall consistency of details and universal applicability of these taxonomies and hierarchies was less significant than the "sorting codes" and "technologies" that shaped the "circuits of knowledge production."[54]

The legal cases in Gate and Mesilla first did the work of performing and offering particular detail that intensified knowledge of the array of racialized immoral and degenerate sexual activities and relationships. The Gate case heightened the conflation of Oriental depravity and the sexual dangers of interracial sodomy. The Mesilla case confirmed suspicions about the cavalier disregard of U.S. prohibitions against polygamy among Asian and Middle Eastern migrants. Even where polygamy was tightly regulated or prohibited, the histories of transoceanic migration produced unsettling anxieties about the moral and social dangers of widespread concubinage as a counterfeit of legitimate marriage.

The cases did double work, as well, by consolidating and subtly diversifying the norm into a multicultural array underpinned by a shared value of monogamy. The court judgment in both the estate suit and the sodomy case depicted Christian marriage as an eternal social commitment and duty in a sea of transitory sexualities and encounters and as the legal container for legitimate sexual activity. The illegitimate container of sexualities, however, included a sliding scale of deviant heterosexuality and homosexuality. The standard of monogamous marriage encompassed tolerance zones of divergent practices. By time, place, and circumstance certain customs and practices could be grudgingly accepted or rejected as too far outside the norm. Concubinage might be tolerated in the "frontier" of state expansion and outposts of empire, but as societies became settled and property inheritance imperatives increased, the state pressured informal relationships to be "regularized" and "formalized" into marriage. Similarly, both concubinage and female prostitution were understood as "necessary evils" of empire, settler colonialism, and mass labor migration, tolerated as practices that would purportedly forestall male-to-male sexual relations.[55]

The international and imperial circuitry of customs and practices traveled from British imperial administrators, Anglo-American missionaries, and U.S. attorneys in translating one such category, "Hindu marriage," into a local lexicon in the United States. In both cases British renditions of Hindu marriage oscillated between "uncivilized" (because of practices of concubinage and prepubescent brides) and "civilized" (because of its capacity to prove the character of a man). In the cases explored here, Hindu marriage figured differently into the dynamic hierarchies of marriage and sexuality. In the Gate case Hindu marriage became a tolerable substitute for heterosexual marriage. In the Mesilla case Hindu marriage abroad became the reservoir of intolerable contradictions to the fidelity of the local registered marriage that produced four heirs. The particular context shaped how Hindu marriage was perceived contingently within and outside the norms of American society. Legitimating or delegitimating intimate unions, moreover, was a process that unfolded through a similar sliding scale of norms and deviance in British colonial India and, more expansively, in the British, French, Dutch, and U.S. empires, where South Asian migrant laborers added to the mix of "races" necessary to sustain intensive capitalist cultivation and resource extraction.

Marriage has been and is unstable yet central to the production of citizenship and peculiarly entangled in the formation of the racialized property-owning citizenship in the western United States. How the norm of marriage has been refracted through religion, ethnicity, and race is an important historical problem. Charting the comparative use of "sorting codes" in the governing strategies of the state — codes that shifted from the rule of taxonomy to the rule of sympathy — alerts historians to the variable dynamics of race and morality that compound and confound any easy hierarchy of sexual deviance. Legislatively and judicially, the state approached the variety of sexual and intimate relationships by recognizing the particular practice under a rubric of sympathy or by disallowing it as an example of irreconcilable difference.

Notwithstanding the narrow interpretive parameters of judicial and prison records, an investigation of government management of sex, race, and morality can also reveal lost and fragmented histories embedded within the archive of the state. Both cases contain suggestive detail in the telegrams and letters that were part of the communication network between Punjab villages and U.S towns. The social institutions of marriage and kinship may have held meanings that were incommensurate with the norm of legitimate marriage. For the people from the villages in Punjab, marriage had durability and ties that were far more expansive than the courts entertained. While the judges saw unwarranted influence in the actions of Jubala's uncle, father, and cousins, they imagined family as a broad umbrella of kin rather than as a space restricted to spouse and the progeny of the marriage union. The adhesive of kinship may also transform the social ties and protections among migrant men who shared religious values, caste, and community ties.

The management of intimacy and adjudication of what constituted legal unions had tremendous consequences for crafting human society. The issue was not just a matter of governing Hindu marriage as a site either of deviancy or of reform. Nor was it only a matter of how Hindu marriage was placed among a continuum of unions that were categorically nonnormative or that, through their "deviance," these nonnormative unions normalized and centralized Christian monogamous marriage as the only legitimate intimate union. Analyzing both of these cases and this process through the dynamics of compassion and judgment of the intimate demonstrates how the categories were profoundly about shaping the human subject. The evaluative process of assessing innermost character, judging the pathways of sexual and domestic relations, and defining the capacity to be a property-owning citizen provided what the administrators conceived as a broad liberal canvas. Yet through this processing of intimacy, the state elaborated a highly restrictive criterion of being human and a constricted vision of society, polity, and its legitimate participants.

NOTES

I presented versions of this chapter at the University of Michigan, the University of Chicago, and the University of Arizona. I greatly benefited from the questions and suggestions of Laura Briggs, Kathleen Brown, Nancy Cott, Sarah Deutsch, Neil Foley, Ken Foster, Adam Geary, Kevin Grant, Linda Gordon, Catherine Hall, Martha Hodes, Steve Johnstone, Miranda Joseph, Amy Kaplan, Lisa Lowe, Michael Meranze, Radhika Mongia, Alex Stern, Ann Stoler, and Leti Volpp. I received invaluable assistance from archivists at the New Mexico State Law Library in Santa Fe, New Mexico; Dona Ana County Courthouse, Las Cruces, New Mexico; and the Washington State Archives in Olympia, Washington. A UCSD Humanities Center grant and a Rockefeller Humanities Fellowship with the Project on Sex, Race, and Globalization at the University of Arizona supported the research and writing of this chapter.

1. Stoler, *Carnal Knowledge*; Berlant, *Intimacy*; Pateman, *Sexual Contract*.

2. The literature on this historical problem is vast. The following offer a sample of different interpretive and methodological approaches: Cott, *Public Vows*; Volpp, "Dependent Citizens and Martial Expatriates"; Grossberg, *Governing the Hearth*; Merry, *Colonizing Hawai'i*; Berry, *The Pig Farmer's Daughter and Other Tales of American Justice*.

3. Cott, *Public Vows*, 4.

4. Brumberg, "The Ethnological Mirror," 108–9.

5. See Adelman and Aron, "From Borderlands to Borders"; Gitlin, "On the Boundaries of Empire"; and Deutsch, "Landscapes of Enclaves."

6. See Lee, *Orientals*; Lowe, *Immigrant Acts*; Shah, *Contagious Divides*; and Okihiro, *Margins and Mainstreams*.

7. See La Brack, *The Sikhs of Northern California, 1904–1975*; and Dua, "Racialising Imperial Canada."

8. Pascoe, "Race, Gender, and the Privileges of Property," 216.

9. Leonard, *Making Ethnic Choices*; Volpp, "American Mestizo."

10. "Julio Jabala Killed by Train at Mesilla Park Crossing," *Las Cruces Citizen*, Dec. 29, 1932, 1; "Killed by Train," *El Paso Times*, 29 Dec. 1932.

11. See "In the Matter of the Estate of Julio Jubala." Transcript, Supreme Court of New Mexico, File No. 4137. New Mexico Supreme Court Law Library and Archives, Santa Fe. Parenthetical page citations in the following three paragraphs of the text proper refer to this document.

12. La Brack, *The Sikhs of Northern California, 1904–1975*, 187–88.

13. Divorce, however, was possible in Muslim communities. But neither the attorneys nor the judges researched the code of marriage and divorce in British India.

14. "In the Matter of the Estate of Julio Jubala," 179.

15. On 8 December 1917, at the age of twenty-seven, he had married twenty-eight-year-old Maria Fierro in her hometown of Guadalupe, New Mexico. Dona Ana County Marriage Record Book 4, 520, Dona Ana County Courthouse, Las Cruces, New Mexico. According to these records, Julio Jublio was born in "Las Indias."

16. Julio Jubala and Soledad Garcia registered their marriage on 30 March 1929. Dona Ana County Marriage Record Book 13, 310, Dona Ana County Courthouse, Las Cruces, New Mexico; Maria F. Jubala and Julio Jubala, Third Judicial District Court of Dona Ana County, Civil Court Case No. 5354, Dona Ana County Courthouse, Las Cruces, New Mexico. See also "Property Settlement Agreement between Julio Jubala and Maria P. Jubala" 12 Feb. 1929, Petitioners Exhibit #6, in "In the Matter of the Estate of Julio Jubala," 218–19.

17. "In the Matter of the Estate of Julio Jubala," 32. Parenthetical page citations in this paragraph of the text proper refer to this document.

18. "In the Matter of the Estate of Julio Jubala," Appellants Brief, 17 June 1935.

19. Ibid.

20. "In Re Jubala's Estate," *New Mexico Reports*, Vol. 40, 312–15.

21. Ibid.

22. Estate of Julio Jubala file, 7–8.

23. "Soledad Jubala Wins Suit," *Las Cruces Daily News*, 10 June 1936.

24. Enrique Tellez and Soledad Garcia registered their marriage on 27 July 1936; see Dona Ana County Marriage Book 25, 218, Dona Ana County Courthouse, Las Cruces, New Mexico.

25. Cott, *Public Vows*, 113–17; see also Gordon, "'The Liberty of Self-Degradation.'"

26. Haag, *Consent*.

27. Cott, *Public Vows*.

28. Mongia, "Always Nationalize."

29. Gabbacia, *From the Other Side*; Hsu, *Dreaming of Gold, Dreaming of Home*; Gilfoyle, "The Hearts of Nineteenth Century Men."

30. Don Sing, Washington State Penitentiary Inmate File #6453. Department of Corrections, Washington State Archives, Olympia. Joan Jensen, *Passage from India*. Peter Boag has also recently explored this court case in his illuminating study of rural and urban male homosexualities in the early-twentieth-century Northwest. See Boag, *Same-Sex Affairs*, 55–57.

31. P. L. Verma to the Board of Prisons, 4 Aug. 1912, Don Sing, Washington State Penitentiary Inmate File #6453. Department of Corrections, Washington State Archives, Olympia, 4.

32. Ibid., 8.

33. Ibid., 4, 8.

34. Ibid.

35. Karen Halttunnen, "Humanitarianism and the Pornography of Pain in Anglo-American Culture"; Rai, *The Rule of Sympathy*, 162.

36. Clark, "'The Sacred Rights of the Weak,'" 480.

37. Verma to Board of Prisons, 9.

38. Ibid.

39. Rai, *The Rule of Sympathy*, xviii; McGowen, "Power and Humanity, or Foucault among Historians."

40. John Kim to Whom It May Concern, Aug. 3, 1912; Louis Roberts to Whom It May Concern, 3 Aug. 1912; J. J. Russell to Whom It May Concern, 2 Aug. 1912; C. A Baxter to Pardon Board, Washington, 5 Aug. 1912; all in Don Sing file.

41. Petition from "Hindoos in Portland" to State Prison Board, 3 Aug. 1912, Don Sing file.

42. Stoler, "Affective States" (manuscript copy), 30.

43. C. S. Reed to Verma, Aug. 5, 1912, Don Sing file.

44. Charles Lopez to Mr. Jones, Washington State Board of Control, 16 Sept. 1913; "Commutation of Don Sing's Sentence," Washington State Prison Board, 14 Oct. 1913; both in Don Sing file.

45. Rai, *The Rule of Sympathy*, 162.

46. New Mexico Constitution, Art. II, sec. 22.

47. Lopez, *White by Law*; Jensen, *Passage from India*.

48. See Clark, "Management and Control of Community Property in New Mexico."

49. "In the Matter of the Estate of Julio Jubala," 82–84.

50. See ibid., 59, 61, 62.

51. In 1911, before the development of the Elephant Butte irrigation district, Hispanics had owned 70 percent of the valley's farmland, but by 1929 landownership had shifted to 60 percent Anglo, who leased the land to Hispanic and Asian tenants. See Jensen, "Farm Families Organize their Work, 1900–1940"; and Clark, "The Elephant Butte Controversy."

52. Purdue, *Cherokee Women*; Hurtado, *Intimate Frontiers*.

53. Cott, *Public Vows*; Volpp, "Dependent Citizens and Marital Expatriates."

54. Stoler, *Carnal Knowledge and Imperial Power*, 206–7.

55. Stoler, *Race and the Education of Desire*, 129; Stoler, *Carnal Knowledge and Imperial Power*, 48; Espiritu, *Asian American Women and Men*.

SHANNON LEE DAWDY

Proper Caresses and Prudent Distance:

A How-To Manual from Colonial Louisiana

In the 1720s and 1730s Antoine Simon Le Page du Pratz worked as a manager of a plantation owned by King Louis XV, located directly across the Mississippi River from New Orleans. Le Page du Pratz fancied himself a man of the Enlightenment. After his return to France he published a three-volume work entitled *Histoire de la Louisiane* in 1758, which was a combination of colonial memoir, natural history, ethnography, and how-to guide for future colonists and plantation managers. In a section titled "Maniere de gouverner les Négres" he wrote the following passages:

> When a negro man or woman comes home to you, it is proper to caress [*caresser*] them, to give them something good to eat, with a glass of brandy; it is best to dress them the same day, to give them something to sleep on, and a covering. . . . Those marks of humanity flatter them, and attach them to their masters.

> Prudence requires that your negroes be lodged at a proper distance, to prevent them from being troublesome or offensive; but at the same time near enough for your conveniently observing what passes among them . . . never to suffer them to come near your children, who, exclusive of the bad smell, can learn nothing good from them, either as to morals, education, or language.[1]

Caresser in French means, "to caress, fondle, stroke, make much of, to flatter, to pat."[2] Along this range of intimacy, what was practiced by Le Page du Pratz as an eighteenth-century slave manager? Did he offer the caresses of a father, a lover, or a good host? Which of his caresses were "proper" and why? How did he caress human beings he also claimed to find repulsive? Can we know how his caresses were received?

While the moral contradictions of slavery as an institution have long spurred scholarship and public debate, the apparent inconsistencies within one practitioner's own strategies for "managing" slaves demands explanation. Le Page du Pratz at once pulls slaves close and pushes them away. How can we understand a man who repeatedly exhorts his readers to recognize the humanity of slaves, to tend to their emotional, spiritual, and physical needs with "caresses," but who also designed New Orleans's first segregated neighborhood, obsessed about the "smell" of light-skinned Africans, and abhorred the idea of black nursemaids suckling white children? While to late modern ears such views sound dissonant and unlikely to reside in one individual, we need to understand Le Page du Pratz's cultural logic in its own terms — there may have been no contradiction.

In his treatise Le Page du Pratz embodies two sides of the Enlightenment applied to colonial slavery: "reason" and "sentiment." The rational, scientific impulse of the Enlightenment is reflected in Le Page du Pratz's aesthetics of segregation, activities of observation, and penchant for recording. The sentimental, or Rousseauian, side reveals itself in his effort to make slavery humane by cultivating affections, encouraging noble instincts, and offering Christian baptism. Both his "rational" and "sentimental" approaches are intended to make slaves manageable and useful; his justification rests on utilitarianism, the third leg of the Enlightenment.[3]

But why does this matter? How can a minor *philosophe* from French Louisiana help refigure U.S. history? The short answer is disciplinary. Some might consider that eighteenth-century Louisiana is stretching the subject of U.S. empire too far. The French Bourbons ruled the territory long before the United States was even a recognized nation, much less an empire capable of exerting its will over other nations. But if colonial Louisiana does not belong to the study of colonial America and the development of U.S. empire, to what field does it belong? French empire? Canadian studies? Caribbean studies? Perhaps all of the above. Many American historians might answer, "Borderlands." But the borderlands of what? Implicit in usage of the term is a bursting center located along the east-central coast of North America — the U.S. empire, either embryonic or a muscle-bound brute, depending on the time period. The borderlands framing serves national and nationalist narratives. From what point in time, and from which geographical vistas, do we begin a study of U.S. colonialism and U.S. empire? An Atlantic bias plays into the east-west directional arc of Manifest Destiny. We ought to be able to track and teach American empire from other littorals — from the Gulf of Mexico, the Gulf of Saint Lawrence, the Straits of Florida, the beaches of California. U.S. empire also emerged from these directions. The Atlantic society stretching from Boston to Charleston did not simply swallow up fragile and irrelevant remnants of other empires. In these territories away from the Atlantic, lessons were learned, patterns were established, lands were altered, and peoples were conditioned in ways that informed and facilitated U.S. empire after 1789. That is the short answer. The long answer to the question of relevancy will be explored through the rest of this chapter. I think a close reading of Le Page du Pratz's writing will show how Enlightenment values intersected with North American practices to develop two key strategies of racial rule strongly associated with antebellum slavery and its aftermath: paternalism and segregation. These ideologies are both diffuse and materially specific—they can be located in the discourse of Enlightenment texts but also in the ways people built their houses and touched one another's bodies. The principles of these strategies are also familiar to scholars of modern empire, suggesting fertile ground for comparison—and escape from U.S. exceptionalism.

The Louisiana Purchase of 1803 provides the earliest and clearest example of U.S. empire-building through territorial expansion.[4] Though a convenient date for textbooks, we ought to avoid seeing 1803 as a fault line separating an "untamed" Mississippi Valley from its American destiny. Thomas Jefferson did not imagine he was purchasing a vacant wilderness nor one occupied only by conquerable Indians. Part of what made the territory attractive was the fact that the French and Spanish had developed lower Louisiana into a major hub of transportation and trade, as well as a profitable plantation region. In fact, Jefferson originally aimed only to acquire the developed portion around New Orleans, the "Île d'Orleans." He was surprised and delighted when he learned Napoleon was willing to sell the whole territory, but the acquisition of vast tracts of potential farmland for American resettlement was an afterthought. Jefferson certainly planned to make significant changes in the government of Louisiana by introducing free trade and republican democracy. But he also planned on keeping some things the same and learning from locals what worked best in the region. He supported retention of the French language and assigned French lawyers to draw up a civil code that would preserve the "customs of the country." Long before the purchase, Jefferson had made a study of Louisiana and the writings of its European colonists. His library contained seventeen works on the colony. One of these was Le Page du Pratz's *History of Louisiana*.[5]

This chapter is more about Jefferson's purchase of Le Page du Pratz's little book than about his purchase of the Louisiana territory, but the two are related in critical ways. The smaller purchase illuminates not only how knowledge of natural history and "natives" circulated in the eighteenth century but also how ideas about human difference, proper intimacies, and strategies for social control moved about. In the case of Le Page du Pratz and Jefferson these ideas fed into, and rose out of, each man's direct involvement with the colonialism of slavery.[6] The ultimate origin of a particular idea such as architectural segregation is not important (nor often traceable), but its travels once loosed on the world are instructive to watch.

In the eighteenth century the "management of slaves" was not a national project; rather it formed an international and experimental field of inquiry, a dark subject taking place in the open light of philosophe dialogue.[7] These discussions only very slowly (and never completely) gave way to questioning the moral justification of the institution itself. While most scholars have focused on Le Page du Pratz's discussion of Native Americans, I am deliberately taking a magnifying glass to his overlooked passages on slaves and slavery. American colonialism involved both indigenous and imported subject populations. Precisely because slavery is sometimes held out as a factor in U.S. exceptionalism, I wish to set my sights on it and, for this moment, neglect the indigenous.

This chapter works off two central points made by Ann Stoler in "Tense and Tender Ties": (1) that the "domain of the intimate" is a critical site for understanding colonial and racial rule in North America; and (2) that at least some American strategies for controlling this domain were developed out of "circuits of knowledge production and racialized forms of governance [that] spanned a global field."[8] The first point will perhaps surprise no one familiar with either early American history or slavery studies, but the ways in which the "domain of the intimate" was a global space as early as the eighteenth century may be helpful to think about for both U.S. historians and scholars in colonial studies. Thus, the *how* of knowledge is more important here than the *what* contained in these two generalized strategies of colonial rule — segregation and paternalism. My methodology experiments at the extreme ends of the scale of historical analysis — close textual reading on the microhistorical level and some broad temporal and geographical sweeps at the macrohistorical.[9]

I want to turn to two specific ways that Le Page du Pratz made slavery an Enlightenment project through experiments of containment with houses and bodies. The rationalities and sentiments that inform his views on these topics show him to be a man of his times and show he and Jefferson to be men of the same place.

HOUSES

When it came to "prudence" and a "proper distance," Le Page du Pratz practiced what he preached. Fancying himself an architect, Le Page du Pratz set about designing slave quarters for the King's Plantation across the river from New Orleans. King Louis XV had acquired this plantation from the Company of the Indies when it surrendered its charter in 1731. Slaves based at the plantation were employed on public works projects around New Orleans, loading and unloading ships, and in growing a small amount of indigo and tobacco. During an inventory of the king's properties in 1732, a colonial engineer drew a plan of the "Camp des Negres" that Le Page du Pratz had built (Figure 1).

Le Page du Pratz's design became the model for his recommendations in *History of Louisiana*: "The negro camp ought to be inclosed all round with palisades, and to have a door to shut with a lock and key. The huts ought to be detached from each other, for fear of fire, and to be built in direct lines, both for the sake of neatness, and in order to know easily the hut of each negro."[10] Le Page du Pratz's own descriptions make it clear that the intent of his design was to keep a watchful eye on a tense (im)balance of power over slaves. He advised fellow planters "always to distrust them, without seeming to fear them." Le Page du Pratz's design for a slave village resembles the neat, linear quarters that planters began to build somewhat later in Virginia and the Carolinas, including "Mulberry Row," designed by Jefferson at Monticello.[11] Le Page du Pratz's decision to enclose the compound with a wall and locked gate, however, imposed an unusually strict control of slave movement within the plantation space.

In attempting to control behavior through architectural design, Le Page du Pratz was following the same principles used by the French engineers who designed New Orleans in the early 1720s. They had laid out the city's perfect grid and assigned public and private uses of space according to emerging ideals of the ancien régime. Clear, linear streets and public spaces overlooked by official buildings were intentionally designed to make surveillance of citizens easier.[12] In this respect Le Page du Pratz was applying principles developed to control free Europeans under absolutism to the control of en-

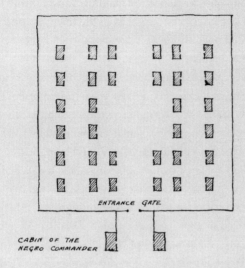

ENTRANCE GATE

CABIN OF THE
NEGRO COMMANDER

Plan of the negro camp with their cabins constructed on the plantation of the Company, of posts in
the ground covered with bark. Surveyed and drawn on
the spot the 9 January, 1732.
                                        De Batz

Figure 1. Drawing of Le Page du Pratz's slave village by Sam Wilson, after DeBatz 1732. Courtesy of Southeastern Architectural Archives, Special Collections, Tulane University Library.

slaved Africans and Indians. Le Page du Pratz and the engineers of New Orleans also implemented spatial segregation in their designs. By discouraging elements of the population from "mixing," crime and insubordination were supposedly prevented. In the city's first few years the majority of its European workers from the fourth estate (a mixture of soldiers, indentured servants, condemned exiles, and a handful of adventurous farmers and artisans) lived in large barracks buildings in the town center. These buildings were segregated not only between civilian and soldier but also between Swiss, German, and French.[13]

New Orleans's original design placed housing for most African slaves entirely outside the town's walls. In the early years the majority of slaves who worked in New Orleans lived at one of two communities: the governor's plantation to the west or the public plantation managed by Le Page du Pratz across the river (marked A and B respectively on Figure 2). The latter was a large enterprise operated first by the Company of the Indies and later taken over by the Crown in 1731. As a result, New Orleans began as a relatively segregated space reserved for free whites. Although in 1726 Europeans or Euro-Americans accounted for only 48 percent of Louisiana's colonial population, they accounted for 88 percent of New Orleans's population. Segregation, however, was not ultimately a successful strategy in New Orleans. Only six years later the number of people of color living in town had tripled. By the end of the French period the white majority had shrunk to 65 percent. The proportion of colored to white increased between 1726 and 1732 because both the number of slaveholding households and the average number of slaves per household grew. More New Orleans households became more multiracial. Native-born, or creole, New Orleanians of all colors grew up in more intimate quarters than had the founder generation.

Le Page du Pratz left the colony in the mid-1730s, just as Louisiana's first creole generation rose to prominence and the Crown abandoned the colony to its own devices. Deciphering the reasons Le Page du Pratz continued to advocate a segregation policy into the 1750s, although New Orleanians did not find it necessary to heed his advice, leads into some of his strangest thinking but also introduces the manner in which the creole generation managed slavery on intimate terms—through an illusion of bodily containment. With the creole generations, to cultivate the sentiments of disgust and parental love—which Le Page du Pratz also promoted—replaced architectural segregation as the prevailing strategy for controlling behavior and preventing "dangerous mixtures" in Louisiana.

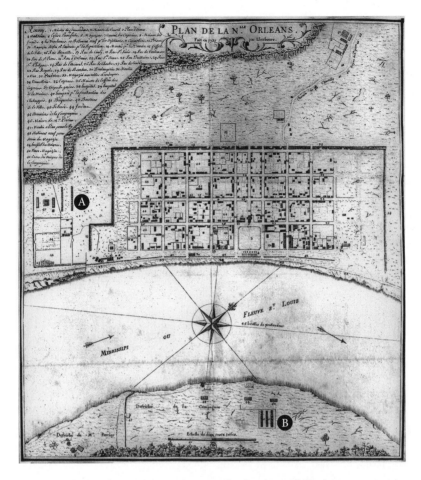

Figure 2. 1731 Plan of New Orleans and environs by L'Herbours. "A" is slave quarters at the governor's plantation; "B" is slave quarters at plantation managed by Le Page du Pratz. Courtesy of the Newberry Library.

BODIES

The recommendations Le Page du Pratz makes in his "how-to" manual represent a mixed strategy and a transitional period in the management of colonial slavery, shown in the way he combines rationalities about buildings and bodies. Although Le Page du Pratz himself claims to have uncovered a major Bambara slave conspiracy to revolt and take over the colony in 1730 (led by his own driver Samba), he does not cite security as a reason to keep the slave quarters well away from the master's residence. Instead, he says:

> When I say that they ought not to be placed so near your habitation as to be offensive, I mean by that the smell [*puanteur* = stench] which is natural to some nations of negroes, such as the Congos, the Angolas, the Aradas, and others. On this account it is proper to have in their camp a bathing place formed by thick planks. . . . That you may be as little incommoded as possible with their natural smell, you must have the precaution to place the negro camp to the north or north-east of your house, as the winds that blow from these quarters are not so warm as the others, and it is only when the negroes are warm that they send forth a disagreeable smell.[14]

Because of Le Page du Pratz's perception of a physical difference between Europeans and some Africans that can be noxious to the former, spaces should be segregated and designed to put a comfortable distance between the groups. What is so astounding about this "reasoning" is the way in which Le Page du Pratz completely disregards the physical conditions of over-worked, sweating bodies in the Louisiana heat. Separating himself from the fact of their coerced labor and his dependency on it, Le Page du Pratz can only ascribe a "natural" smell, not an induced one.

But Le Page du Pratz does not cut a simple black-white line of differ-ence. He finds a brown middle ground more disturbing: "The negroes that have the worst smell are those that are the least black; and what I have said of their bad smell, ought to warn you to keep always on the windward side of them when you visit them at their work."[15] These lighter-colored slaves, whom he employed in the fields and in other heavy labor tasks, were the ones he locked up at night in his walled slave town. In a segregating, classifying Enlightenment rationality, those people and things that did not fit into the emerging natural history schema were offensive and needed to be closely controlled. Underscoring his preferences, Le Page du Pratz recommends Senegalese people for housework because they can be trusted and have "the purest blood. . . . [They] are the blackest, and I never saw any who had a bad smell." Ignoring their lighter duties, Le Page du Pratz sees smells in color.[16]

Le Page du Pratz's imputation of an offensive natural odor to light-skinned Africans and mixed-race individuals exemplifies Mary Douglas's "abominations of Leviticus." She argues that in societies with a diverse popu-lation and a well-articulated authority, marginal individuals who threaten the basis of the social order will be considered polluted and dangerous.

American slave society was evolving in the early eighteenth century into "a total structure of thought whose key-stone, boundaries, margins and internal lines [were] held in relation by rituals of separation."[17] Douglas writes, "[A]ll margins are dangerous. . . . We should expect the orifices of the body to symbolise its specially vulnerable points. Matter issuing from them is marginal stuff of the most obvious kind. Spittle, blood, milk, urine, faeces or tears by simply issuing forth have traversed the boundary of the body. So also have bodily parings, skin, nails, hair clippings and sweat."[18] If we accept this relation, then Le Page du Pratz's obsession with odors emanating from slave bodies makes sense in light of the demographic changes he was witnessing in New Orleans in the 1720s and 1730s.

I would add to Douglas's calculus of pollution that activities producing or involving the contact of bodily fluids between two individuals at different positions in the grid would have also been the subject of abhorrence. "Caresses" such as breast-feeding, sex, and even perhaps medical care ought to be highly charged sites of potential contamination. In the context of slavery, "proper caresses" were of a distant, paternal kind, flowing one way — from "father" to slaves — that avoided contaminating contact.

Le Page du Pratz offers some uncharacteristically harsh social criticism when he addresses the subject of breast-feeding. Breast-feeding and the use of wet nurses were to become a significant focus of ideas regarding racial contamination and child rearing in nineteenth-century imperial regimes. A common thread is that milk was a form of blood that could create biological, as well as affective, ties of kinship and thus degrade the ruling group's claims to racial superiority. Wet-nursing was also a form of "caress" in which the relations of caresser and caressed were improperly reversed in the paternalist scheme.[19]

Closely following his passages about the scent of Africans, Le Page du Pratz expresses his disapproval of those white women in Louisiana who used black nursemaids: "I conclude that a French father and his wife are great enemies to their posterity when they give their children such nurses. For the milk being the purest blood of the woman, one must be a step-mother indeed to give her child to a negro nurse in such a country as Louisiana, where the mother has all conveniences of being served."[20] Le Page du Pratz believed that white children would be contaminated by contact with blacks. Cultural and physical contaminations were entangled: "[They] can learn nothing good from them, either as to morals, education, or language." Physically, they could not thrive with such "impure blood."[21] Le Page du Pratz's view that breast milk transferred the character and qualities of the woman was not unusual. Both English and French writers on the subject agreed on this score. Until the middle of the eighteenth century this meant that elite mothers were advised to select their nursemaids carefully. For Le Page du Pratz in a colonial context, where nearly all servants were dark skinned, it meant that they should not be used at all. Le Page du Pratz applied a racial meaning to established beliefs about bodily fluids and temperament.[22]

In 1758 Le Page du Pratz was a few years ahead of his time in his shrill condemnation of women who used nursemaids. He says, "I have no inclination to employ my pen in censuring the over-delicacy and selfishness of the women, who thus sacrifice their children; it may, without further illustration, be easily perceived how much society is interested in this affair."[23] Mother's milk did not become a popular movement in France until Rousseau's publication of *Emile* in 1761. One reading of the movement is that it registers growing class tensions and an anxiety over the relationship between the wet nurse and her employer. In the words of Michelet, "To the extent that the social war becomes more acute, there is danger in trusting a wetnurse. It means delivering oneself to the enemy. The wetnurse as well as the domestic servant becomes impossible."[24] Le Page du Pratz's discomfort with black nursemaids makes sense as a political tension between unequals, transformed into disgust and medical theory. The basic premise of paternalism, as expressed in both Le Page du Pratz's and Jefferson's references to slaves as children, is that masters were to act as good fathers to oversee childlike slaves, whose development had been stilted either by the conditions of servitude or by racial limitations. The use of a black nursemaid reversed this parent-child relationship in an uncomfortable way, as well as created a site of contact for bodily fluids.

Not only could the strategies of segregation and paternalism coexist in the same regime, but they could coexist within the same mind. Le Page du Pratz was one of the earliest exponents of "humanitarian" slavery and paternalism. He says, "I advise the planters to take great care of their negroes, I at the same time shew them that their interest is connected in that with their humanity. But I do no less advise them always to distrust them, without seeming to fear them, because it is as dangerous to shew a concealed enemy that you fear him, as to do him an injury."[25] Le Page du Pratz's Africans are quite human, though physical differences matter enough to repel him from "dangerous mixture." He does not explicitly condone sexual caresses between the races, but neither does he criticize this widespread colonial practice, in contrast to his sustained attack on breast-feeding. His only mention of cross-racial unions refers to the degradation of Indian women by immoral Frenchmen. Despite his focus on bodily fluids, he sees differences between blacks and whites as more cultural than racial: "The negroes must be governed differently from the Europeans; not because they are black, nor because they are slaves; but because they think differently from the white men." He goes on to describe their belief in white vampires and magical practices such as gris-gris charms. Although they are "very superstitious" and utterly lacking in enlightenment, he advises planters to permit them their own beliefs because it would upset them too much to interfere with these little comforts.[26]

Le Page du Pratz's practical theory is that "one may, by attention and humanity, easily manage negroes." His paternal "caresses" of attention and humanity include: giving them good food, shelter, clothing, and medical care; encouraging nuclear families; allowing some cultural independence; and punishing only in moderation. Pregnant and postpartum women are to be given an extra half-ration and allowed to rest when necessary. Le Page du Pratz also looks after what he sees as their spiritual needs and his "humanitarian" duty. Newborn children should be "baptised and instructed, since they have an immortal soul." A little later he makes it clear that this precept also applies to adults, having its utilitarian value: "If they are slaves, it is also true that they are men, and capable of becoming Christians: besides, it is your intention to draw advantage from them, is it not therefore reasonable to take all the care of them that you can?"[27] One difference between the paternal caressing of slaves and the paternal caressing of children is that one does the first out of self-interest and the second (which is made clear from his critique of wet-nursing) out of an ideal of selflessness.

Le Page du Pratz's paternalism is transparently utilitarian, but he also convinces himself that the emotional bond with his "children" is mutual. He consciously manipulates them with patriarchal psychology but believes their reactions are genuine:

> When I surprised them singing at their work, and perceived that they had discovered me, I said to them cheerfully, Courage, my boys [enfans = children], I love to see you merry at your work; but do not sing so loud, that you may not fatigue yourselves, and at night you shall have a cup of Tafia (or rum) to give you strength and spirits. One cannot believe the effect such a discourse would have upon their spirits, which was easily discern-

ible from the cheerfulness upon their countenances, and their ardour at work.[28]

Le Page du Pratz believes that his verbal and alimentary caresses of slaves instill an "ardour" for work, and perhaps for himself. On complimenting a slave that he is a "good negro," Le Page du Pratz reports that the man replied (in one of the earliest examples of Louisiana Afro-Creole), "Monsu, Negre mian mian boucou travail boucou, quand Negre tenir bon Maître, Negre veni bon" (Master, when a Negro is well fed, he'll work hard; when he has a good master, he'll behave).[29] Le Page du Pratz seems oblivious to the subtle challenge of the slave's voice, which interprets paternalistic gestures not as gratifying caresses but as concessions he expects. The enslaved man's response quickly stakes out the terms of a negotiated detente while he declines to agree that there is such a person as a "good negro." He tells his owner: if you want me to work hard and not give you any trouble, then you need to feed and treat me well. Who, exactly, is writing the text of paternalism? The improved material conditions brought about by paternalism may be viewed in part as a response to slave threats and demands. It is perhaps no coincidence that paternalism as the preferred rule of slavery became most pronounced after the Haitian Revolution.[30]

OF TWO MINDS

While we do not know Thomas Jefferson's opinions about Le Page du Pratz's how-to manual for slave management, Jefferson did share with Le Page du Pratz a conviction that slaves should receive a humane level of material care and were owed a father's duty. He wrote to another advocate of paternalist practice: "The inculcation [in your book] on the master of the moral duties which he owes to the slave, in return for the benefits of his service, that is to say, of food, clothing, care in sickness, and maintenance under age and disability, so as to make him in fact as comfortable and more secure than the laboring man in most parts of the world . . . gives great merit to the work."[31] Records of Jefferson's own plantation management show that he allowed his slaves a degree of comfort and self-determination liberal by the standards of the day and that he had a personal affection for many of them. He explained his hypocritical failure to manumit his own slaves as a matter of paternal loyalty: "As far as I can judge from the experiments which have been made to give liberty to, or rather, to abandon persons whose habits have been formed in slavery is like abandoning children."[32] Both he and Le Page du Pratz used "proper caresses" to lessen the discomforts of slavery — physically for their slaves and morally for themselves — at the same time they conducted Enlightenment experiments in architectural segregation. Paternalism has often been explained as a response to the closure of the slave trade in 1807, a way to improve the life expectancy and natural increase of the slave population. The writings of Le Page du Pratz and Jefferson suggest instead that it began much earlier, as a way to manage power within a fundamentally strained system.

We know Jefferson considered Le Page du Pratz a useful source on Louisiana's natural and political history. He referenced Le Page du Pratz extensively in notes he prepared at the time of the Louisiana Purchase.[33] He also thought enough of the book to recommend that Lewis and Clark pack it in their luggage on the first American expedition into new imperial territory.[34] Jefferson apparently valued Le Page du Pratz's descriptions of the geography, natural history, and Native American peoples of greater Louisiana. In fact, my concentrated focus on Le Page du Pratz's passages on Africans and slavery risks misrepresenting the fact that he devoted the great majority of his volume to Native Americans, particularly the Natchez, whom he greatly admired. As *les naturels*, they were embraced within the scope of Natural History. They had beautiful bodies and keen minds. Though some of their behavior (such as human sacrifice) was reprehensible, they were eminently civilizable and in many ways superior to Europeans, according to Le Page du Pratz. They represented "natural men" of almost enlightened sensibilities. Jefferson agreed. "I am safe in affirming, that the proofs of genius given by the Indians of North America place them on a level with whites in the same uncultivated state."[35] Jefferson also opined that the origins of both Indians and blacks demanded more serious study by Anglo-American scholars: "I advance . . . that the blacks whether originally a distinct race, or made distinct by time and circumstances, are inferior to the whites in the endowments both of body and mind."[36] Jefferson compares, more blatantly than Le Page du Pratz, the "inferior" mental abilities of blacks to those of Indians, a difference he locates in biology.[37] Whereas Le Page du Pratz was keenly aware of cultural differences and the effects of environment, Jefferson assigned differences in mental abilities to differences of origin and nature, offering as proof the "uplift" visible in black-white metissage.[38]

Despite this observation, and despite his relationship to Sally Hemings and his children by her, Jefferson, to the end of his life, publicly expressed disapproval of white-black mixture.[39] Sexual caresses between whites and blacks were "improper." Instead, he advocated the ultimate in segregated space—separate continents through recolonization of Africa, or even liberated Haiti.[40] "The amalgamation with the other color produces a degradation to which no lover of his country, no lover of excellence in the human character can innocently consent."[41] His stated distaste for black-white miscegenation ties him to Le Page du Pratz through that most peculiar belief in bodily smells:

> To these objections, which are political, may be added others, which are physical and moral. Whether the black of the negro resides in the reticular membrane between the skin and scarfskin, or in the scarf-skin itself; whether it proceeds from the color of the blood, the color of the bile, or from that of some other secretion, the difference is fixed in nature, and is as real as if its seat and cause were better known to us. . . . Besides those of color, figure, and hair, there are other physical distinctions proving a difference of race. They have less hair on the face and body. They secrete less by the kidneys, and more by the glands of the skin, which gives them a very strong and disagreeable odor. This greater degree of transpiration renders them more tolerant of heat, and less of cold than the whites.[42]

Despite their shared public abhorrence of black-white mixture, neither man objected to Indian-White sexual unions. Jefferson advocated them as a policy of assimilation, and Le Page du Pratz maintained such a union through his longtime relationship with an enslaved Chitimacha woman. His direct statements on the subject indicate that he only worried about the detrimental effects that lovers less noble than he might have on Native American women and their communities.[43] How can we understand the positive views of Native Americans and their bodies, and the negative views of Africans and theirs, as seen in Le Page du Pratz and Jefferson? One answer lies in sweat as a symbol of the very different terms of interdependence between Europeans and Native Americans and between Europeans and Africans in North America. Although a small number of Native Americans were enslaved in Louisiana and early Virginia, land and furs attained through trade were their resources that interested Europeans most. Native American "sweat labor" that produced pelts and prepared land for agriculture was less visible under the more contractual terms of Euro-Indian relations.[44] Africans and African Americans, on the other hand, were strangers unnaturally transported to the new world, their bodies directly exploited for sweat-producing labor. Their "natural resource" was acquired solely through a closely monitored form of coercion that engendered paranoia and constant ideological adjustment on the part of slave owners. As the Enlightenment began to question the right of despotic rule and to embrace universal humanism, rationalizations for slavery became more complicated and more vulnerable. Repulsion by sweat was a convenient reaction that dehumanized blacks and divorced them from universal rights. Sweat was a noxious by-product that reminded slave owners of the fragilities at the margins of their system—fragilities formed by tense and tender ties.

HISTORIAN HENRY STEELE COMMAGER claims that late-eighteenth-century Americans precociously took Enlightenment ideas and "wrote them into law, crystallized them into institutions, and put them to work. That . . . was the American Revolution."[45] Among these ideas, I would argue, were theories regarding methods of social management using both sentiment and a segregating rationality. While it is doubtful that many administrators of the "new imperialism" of the late nineteenth century and early twentieth read the works of Le Page du Pratz or Jefferson, their designs for segregated towns and workers' camps in Africa and their articulations of a paternalistic policy toward colonized natives in India are more developed versions of the same ideas.[46]

My purpose in reuniting Le Page du Pratz and Jefferson has not been to trace a genealogy of ideas specific to these two authors but rather to demonstrate that their minds were part of a larger field, and so was the empire they helped create. Both men practiced slavery "enlightened" by reasonable segregation and noble sentiment—they attempted to define a fine line between proper caresses and prudent distance. Both men conducted experiments with architecture, human bodies, and their own emotions, experiments made dangerous by their own vulnerabilities—a fear of violent revolt, the fragility of paternalist conceit, a contradictory desire for a rational yet humane system, and entanglements of sex, kinship, and perhaps even love. Each adjustment in strategy had the potential to unveil these vulnerabilities. Le Page du Pratz and later Jefferson were among the first to recommend "caresses" as a management tool for slavery. They recommended ministering the fatherly stroke and word of encouragement, in addition to being a good provider of housing, food, and clothing. Fussing, as a father would, over medical care and meting out discipline only in moderation were other components of a sensible approach to slavery, in both its meanings (practical and sensitive). Le Page du Pratz saw no contradiction between his recommendations for sensitivity to the needs of slaves and the crass utilitarianism that motivated his approach. He believed that managing slavery through sentiment did not represent an erosion of power but its enhancement.

Each man privately offered other types of "caresses" to their female slaves through long-lasting liaisons, the emotional terms of which are obscured from our view. The ground on which these men and women met was so uneven that from one perspective, all such concubinage constituted a form of violence. But even if many enslaved women were unable to use these relationships to improve their conditions or gain their freedom (as some did),[47] such physical intimacy at least symbolically threatened the racial boundaries of slavery. Jefferson and Le Page du Pratz did not recommend this type of caressing to others, but its prevalence in the experience of slavery suggests another reason for their efforts to create a public policy of "affective" slave management. Redirecting the caresses between slaveholders and slaves to the "proper" ones of a father to a child created an ideology in which cross-racial liaisons became equivalent to the abomination of incest, an arithmetic perhaps intended to prevent the "dangerous mixing" that threatened to topple the racial basis of slavery. Furthermore, Le Page du Pratz and Jefferson may have realized from personal experience that if the ties between slaveholder and slave became too tender — as lovers, spouses, or even mother-child relations in the case of black nursemaids — then discipline became difficult and the moral authority of the system confused. The recognition that intimacies were inevitable in domestic slavery, but ought to be of a certain kind, constituted a major step toward the retrenchment of slavery in the antebellum period. The rule of North American slavery came to rest on the controlled politics of sentiment.

My suggestions here intersect with three major fields of inquiry. First, Jefferson scholars have long placed him within the context of the Enlightenment and recognized the influence of French thought on his writings and life. They have also come to realize that Jefferson, like Le Page du Pratz, embodied contradictions of the Enlightenment, particularly between his ideals and his practices. His work to halt the slave trade and his stated wish to end slavery itself are difficult to reconcile with his failure to manumit his own slaves.[48]

Second, my observations touch on histories of the intimate, familial, and the domestic in slave society.[49] While the practices these studies reveal (such as Jefferson's relationship with Sally Hemings) may make the institution seem that much more "peculiar," this body of literature in fact has much in common with recent work on the intimate politics of modern colonialism. Slavery may represent an extreme case of the way in which race and intimacy get defined by economic desires and political anxieties, but American exceptionalism is unwarranted in this field. North America was not the only site where power worked its way along slippery racial boundaries between men and women, nursemaids and children, masters and servants.

Third, an argument can be made that plantation societies across the middle portion of the Western Hemisphere had more in common with one another, and had more communication with one another, than the colonies and their metropoles. Planters carried on correspondences across imperial boundaries and across the Caribbean. They eagerly consumed the same treatises on crops, slaves, and natural history. North Americans were neither peculiar nor isolated in the strategies they developed to "manage" slaves or other coerced laborers. South Carolina was established by Barbados planters. San Dominguan planters resettled in Maryland. Royalist Virginia planters moved to the Bahamas and Brazil. Other planter families moved back and forth between Louisiana and Cuba. More important, slaves themselves, as well as free blacks, moved across these protonational boundaries with even greater frequency prior to the shutdown of the Atlantic slave trade in the early nineteenth century. They also carried news and ideas from place to place, helping to create a cross-national African American world developing its own strategies of resistance. Planters scrambled to react to this growing challenge through cooperative agreements that reached a desperate pitch after the Haitian Revolution.[50]

Rather than seen as a curio of an aborted colonial history that ended with the Louisiana Purchase, Le Page du Pratz's writing should be read as part of a pan-national dialogue that continued long after. His work reflects two prevailing strategies used by an uncomfortable minority to rule a dangerous majority—segregation and paternalism. While the study of American slavery tends to associate paternalism with the "mature" antebellum slavery of the nineteenth century, and segregation with the retrenchment of Jim Crow, these were really just moments when one particular strategy was temporarily dominant and relatively successful.[51] These practices, nearly taken for granted in studies of nineteenth-century North American race relations, resonate with strategies of rule used in Victorian and early-twentieth-century India, South Asia, and Africa that have so much been the focus of colonial studies. Ann Stoler notes, however, that historians have privileged rationalizing, segregating practices in their critiques, to the neglect of practices that call upon sentiment such as paternalism. She suggests "another historical frame for understanding what made up colonial rule; not one that starts with the supremacy of reason in the nineteenth century and then traces it back to the roots of rationality in the Enlightenment. Rather one that sets out another genealogy of equal force—and of as long a *durée*. Such a genealogy . . . would register that sustained oscillation between reason and sentiment rather than the final dominance of the one and their definitive severance."[52] The writings of Le Page du Pratz and Jefferson show that North American strategies of colonial and racial rule formed an early branch of this genealogy. Segregation and paternalism date back at least to the era of the "enlightened," experimental slavery of Le Page du Pratz and Jefferson, when we hear the first clear articulations of these practices in North America.[53] The penchant for dissertating on any useful subject in the eighteenth century created the first "how-to-run-a-plantation" manuals that I suspect directly informed the "how-to-run-a-colony" manuals of the nineteenth century and early twentieth.[54]

The spread of paternalistic slavery coincided with the Louisiana Purchase, an expansion that was neither accidental nor unidirectional. It spread as much from Louisiana to Virginia as it did from Virginia to Louisiana, and it emerged out of a transnational exchange of ideas and practices. Generations later, the other side of Le Page du Pratz's and Jefferson's management theory—architectural segregation—was revived as a dominant strategy of racial rule. At the beginning of the Jim Crow era Louisiana again played an important role. In 1892 the case of *Plessy v. Ferguson* protested the spatial segregation of whites and blacks on a New Orleans train, but the court ruled that segregation was valid—a ruling that held until the civil rights era of *A Streetcar Named Desire*, set in one of New Orleans's interracial neighborhoods. While Elia Kazan's film of Tennesee Williams's drama played in segregated movie houses, the aesthetics of American power tilted once again toward sentiment and official empathy. Louisiana's "oscillation between reason and sentiment" reverberates within the theater of American colonialism, and beyond.

NOTES

This chapter has benefited greatly from the input and support of several individuals and institutions, including Ann Laura Stoler, Martha Hodes, and the other "Tense and Tender Ties" workshop participants, the Newberry Library, the Rackham School of Graduate Studies at the University of Michigan, the "Comparative Colonialisms" workshop participants at the University of Chicago, and the anonymous reviewers. Any improvements are to the credit of my colleagues; remaining delinquencies are my own.

1. Le Page du Pratz, *The History of Louisiana*, 380, 381; Le Page du Pratz, *Histoire de la Louisiane*, 3:340. When the correspondence is faithful, I use the reprint edition of the 1774 translation of Le Page du Pratz's 1758 French original; otherwise, I provide my own translations. Because of space limitations I will not in most cases transcribe the original French passages, although I will offer the original French citations when possible. It is important to note that Le Page du Pratz wrote these passages nearly twenty years after returning to France. I have written elsewhere on the implications of this fact and the context of his written project. See Dawdy, "Enlightenment on the Ground."

2. Baker, *Cassell's French-English, English-French Dictionary*, 128. A more parsimonious entry for *caresser* in the *Dictionnaire de L'Académie française* of 1762 (4th ed.) suggests a meaning quite close to its cognate in modern English, as a gesture of affection and caring. An interesting figurative expression speaks of a prince warmly receiving a subject: "Faire des caresses. Caresser un enfant, caresser un chien. On dit figurément, qu'Un Prince a bien caressé quelqu'un, pour dire, Que le Prince l'a bien reçu." (To make caresses. Caress a child, caress a dog. It is said figuratively that a Prince has caressed someone well, meaning, that the Prince has received them well.) The entry for *caresse* reads: "Témoignage d'affection que l'on marque à quelqu'un par ses actions ou par ses paroles" (248). (Evidence of affection that one shows to someone by their actions or words.)

3. See Jones, "Ruled Passions"; and Hirschman, *The Passions and the Interests*.

4. Note that I am emphasizing U.S. empire, in the sense of actions taken by the national polity that emerged in 1789 (as opposed to British empire and its expansion in North America prior to the Revolutionary War). I thus distinguish North American colonialism as a larger entity (temporally, spatially, conceptually) than U.S. imperialism, which I define in the narrower political and territorial sense.

5. Jefferson owned an extremely rare 1763 first edition in English (which appeared just five years after Le Page du Pratz's first French edition), suggesting Jefferson purchased Le Page du Pratz between 1763 and the second edition of 1774. He gave this copy to the Library of Congress in 1815. Library of Congress, *Catalogue of the Library of Thomas Jefferson*, 4:235–42.

6. I do not mean that slavery is *like* colonialism, nor that it is a component of colonialism, but that it *is* colonialism. A generation ago Philip Curtin defined *colonialism* as "a government by people of one culture over people of a different culture." He went on to describe a continuum of experience in terms of demographics and cultural domination, from that of free blacks in 1950s Nigeria ruled by a tiny European minority (.03 percent) in their own homeland to Africans from a patchwork of places brought together under white majority rule in North American slavery. Although their experiences were distinctly different (as they were for Native Americans under the same regime), the definition holds.

Curtin also makes clear that he means by *colonialism* not only the legal-political structures of "government" but its cultural, sociological, and psychological conditions. It may be more correct, but less elegant, to talk about North American colonialism*s*, which overlap discontinuously over time and space. See Curtin, "The Black Experience of Colonialism and Imperialism," 22.

7. Raynal, for example, devoted passages to the ethical and effective management of slaves in his *Histoire des deux Indes*. I argue elsewhere that these had a direct genealogy with Le Page du Pratz's writings. See Dawdy, "Enlightenment on the Ground."

8. Ann Laura Stoler, "Tense and Tender Ties," 850.

9. The "middle" is deliberately skipped over here—the social-historical setting of Le Page du Pratz's Louisiana, including dynamics of gender, race, and class. For that, see Dawdy, "*La Ville Sauvage*," esp. chap. 3. For an important biographical approach that echoes themes here, see Galloway, "Rhetoric of Difference."

10. Le Page du Pratz, *The History of Louisiana*, 381–82.

11. Vlach, *Back of the Big House*.

12. See Cleary, *The Place Royale and Urban Design in the Ancien Régime*; Harouel, *L'Embellissement des villes*.

13. Swiss mercenaries were commonly used by the Bourbons. The Company of the Indies actively recruited German immigrants to Louisiana in the 1710s and 1720s.

14. Le Page du Pratz, *The History of Louisiana*, 381–82.

15. Ibid., 382.

16. Le Page du Pratz's "disgust" for mixed-race individuals and preference for darker-skinned domestic servants contrasts notably with the domestic practices of the mid-Atlantic region, where lighter-skinned individuals were more commonly selected for the intimate details of housework. This could be Le Page du Pratz's subtle way of showing disapproval for sexual liaisons between whites and blacks.

17. Douglas, *Purity and Danger*, 41.

18. Ibid., 121.

19. On this topic see Stoler, *Race and the Education of Desire*, 145–47, 162–63; and Shell, *Children of the Earth*, 142–59.

20. Le Page du Pratz, *The History of Louisiana*, 382; Le Page du Pratz, *Histoire de la Louisiane*, 3:343.

21. Le Page du Pratz, *The History of Louisiana*, 382.

22. For background see Salmon, "The Cultural Significance of Breastfeeding and Infant Care in Early Modern England and America"; Senior, "Aspects of Infant Feeding in Eighteenth-Century France"; Davin, "Imperialism and Motherhood"; and Treckel, "Breastfeeding and Maternal Sexuality in Colonial America."

23. Le Page du Pratz, *The History of Louisiana*, 382. It would be interesting to have women's perceptions on breast-feeding and wet-nursing, but the few published accounts and letters by women from French Louisiana do not touch on the subject.

24. Michelet, "25 août 1850," 120.

25. Le Page du Pratz, *The History of Louisiana*, 385–86.

26. Ibid., 376–77; *Histoire de la Louisiane*, 1:333.

27. Le Page du Pratz, *The History of Louisiana*, 287, 381, 385.

28. Ibid., 384.

29. Le Page du Pratz, *Histoire de la Louisiane*, 1:349.

30. See Genovese, "Rebelliousness and Docility in the Negro Slave"; Mullin, *Africa in America*.

31. Thomas Jefferson to Clement Caine (1811), in Jefferson, *The Works of Thomas Jefferson*, 11:329.

32. Thomas Jefferson to Edward Bancroft (1789), in Jefferson, *The Works of Thomas Jefferson*, 5:66.

33. See Jefferson, "Extract and Notes on Louisiana," April 30, 1803.

34. Several references to Le Page du Pratz's work appear in the journals of the expedition. To the Western Ocean: Planning the Lewis and Clark Expedition (http://www.lib.virginia.edu/speccol/exhibits/lewis_clark/planning2.html).

35. Thomas Jefferson to Gen. Chastellux (1785), in Jefferson, *The Works of Thomas Jefferson*, 3:137.

36. "Notes on the State of Virginia (1782)," in Jefferson, *The Works of Thomas Jefferson*, 3:249.

37. Ibid., 245.

38. Ibid., 247.

39. On this aspect of Jefferson's life see Lewis and Onuf, *Sally Hemings and Thomas Jefferson*. Contributors to Lewis's and Onuf's collection vary in seeing Jefferson's relationship with Hemings from a hypocritical exploitation, that he wrote about with self-deprecating irony, to a committed love for a woman he perceived as basically white.

40. Thomas Jefferson to William Short (1826), in Jefferson, *The Works of Thomas Jefferson*, 10:362.

41. Thomas Jefferson to Edward Coles (1814), in Jefferson, *The Works of Thomas Jefferson*, 9:478.

42. "Notes on the State of Virginia (1782)," in Jefferson, *The Works of Thomas Jefferson*, 3:244.

43. The history of miscegenation practices and policies in colonial Louisiana is complex. See, e.g., Spear, " 'They Need Wives' "; and Spear, "Whiteness and the Purity of Blood."

44. See Harris, "Whiteness as Property"; Limerick, *The Legacy of Conquest*; and Wolfe, "Land, Labor, and Difference."

45. Commager, *The Empire of Reason*, xi.

46. See, e.g., Cell, "Anglo-Indian Medical Theory and the Origins of Segregation in West Africa," esp. 308; King, "Writing Colonial Space"; Wright, *The Politics of Design in French Colonial Urbanism*. For an example of paternalistic ideology in the period, a less studied subject, see Rai, *The Rule of Sympathy*.

47. On this topic in French Louisiana see Spear, "Colonial Intimacies."

48. Adams, *The Paris Years of Thomas Jefferson*; Commager, *Jefferson, Nationalism, and the Enlightenment*; Eze, *Race and the Enlightenment*; Shuffleton, *The American Enlightenment*; Weymouth, *Thomas Jefferson*; and Wilson, "Thomas Jefferson's Library and the French Connection."

49. Brown, *Good Wives, Nasty Wenches, and Anxious Patriarchs*; Bynum, *Unruly Women*; Cashin, "The Structure of Antebellum Planter Families"; Clinton, *The Plantation Mistress*; Clinton and Gillespie, *The Devil's Lane*; Fox-Genovese, *Within the Plantation Household*; Gutman, *The Black Family in Slavery and Freedom, 1750–1925*; Hodes, *Sex, Love, Race*; and Tate et al., *Race and Family in the Colonial South*. For the Jefferson-Hemings affair see Lewis et al., "Forum"; Lewis and Onuf, *Sally Hemings and Thomas Jefferson*.

50. Breeden, *Advice among Masters*; Landers, *Against the Odds*; Greene, Brana-Shute, and Sparks, *Money, Trade, and Power*; and Scott, "The Common Wind."

51. The classic work on antebellum paternalism is Genovese, *Roll, Jordan, Roll*. See also Rose, "The Domestication of Domestic Slavery"; Scarborough, "Slavery—The White Man's Burden"; Oakes, *The Ruling Race*; Gallay, "The Origins of Slaveholders' Paternalism."

52. Stoler, "Affective States," in *A Companion to the Anthropology of Politics*, ed. David Nugent and Joan Vincent, 10.

53. The movement toward paternalistic slavery appears similar to what Amit Rai calls "the rule of sympathy" that emerged in late-eighteenth-century British India. See Rai, *The Rule of Sympathy*.

54. Writers from the French islands were particularly prolific, and Jefferson owned many of their works in addition to his Louisiana collection, for example, Monnereau, *The Complete Indigo-Maker*; and Moreau de Saint-Méry, *Description topographique et politique de la partie espagnole de l'isle Saint-Domingue*.

TIYA MILES

"His Kingdom for a Kiss": Indians and Intimacy
in the Narrative of John Marrant

In the spring of 1785 an American-born evangelist described his return from an extraordinary sojourn among the Cherokee Indians:

> I now and then found, that my affections to my family and country were not dead; they were sometimes very sensibly felt, and at last strengthened into an invincible desire of returning home. . . . I had seventy miles now to go back to the settlements of the white people. . . . My dress was purely in the Indian stile [*sic*]; the skins of wild beasts composed my garments, my head was set out in the savage manner, with a long pendant down my back, a sash around my middle, without breeches, and a tomahawk by my side.[1]

Although this description may conjure images of Daniel Boone or Davy Crockett, the speaker was, in fact, a mild-mannered Methodist, born in New York, raised in South Carolina, and living in England under the patronage of a countess.[2] John Marrant, who was thirty years old in 1785, found God as an adolescent boy and dedicated his life to saving others, especially the natives of North America. Perhaps it should not surprise us that Marrant felt called to Christian evangelism, a process that Native American studies scholar Vine Deloria Jr. has noted went "hand in hand" with colonial land acquisition, for Marrant had experienced multiple imperial regimes in his lifetime: the English in America, the Americans in America, and the English around the globe.[3] Indeed, Marrant's fluency in the narrative forms that accompanied and rationalized colonization are evident in his articulated life story, rendered as an Indian captivity narrative, perforated by Indian princess and American woodsman tropes, and told in public preceding his ordination to the ministry.

But the most outstanding aspect of John Marrant's story need not have been spoken. For the "facts" were clearly in evidence to Marrant's British audience that the orator was black. The novelty of his racial assignment, coupled with his fantastical story of spiritual awakening, capture by Indians, and subsequent conversion of a Cherokee "kingdom," captivated John Marrant's eighteenth-century audience on both sides of the Atlantic. After hearing Marrant's account, Englishman S. Whitchurch published a poetic tribute, titled "The Negro Convert, a Poem; Being the Substance of the Experience of Mr. John Marrant, a Negro, As Related by Himself."[4] A written rendition of Marrant's own narrated life story would be published in 1790 under the editorship of the Reverend William Aldridge, who transcribed the tale. Within its first year of publication Marrant's unusual report went through four editions, and it would soon become one of the three best-selling Indian captivity narratives in the genre's history.[5] By 1835 Marrant's narrative had been republished at least twenty times.[6] But despite this strong early showing, the text saw a prolonged period of diminished public and academic interest through the mid-nineteenth century and the late twentieth, until the notice of African American literary scholar Henry Louis Gates brought it renewed attention.[7]

"A Narrative of the Lord's Wonderful Dealings with John Marrant" has confounded some scholars of the Indian captivity narrative and of early African American literature, and I am no exception.[8] John Marrant's rendering of his dramatic transformation during the Great Awakening and his ardent proselytism among the southeastern Indians includes strange and surprising features that led one scholar of early Native American literature to describe it as "opaque."[9] Chief among the stumbling blocks to our comprehension of what John Marrant conveys is the notion that Marrant, an African American man, has composed a life story devoid of racial consciousness and revelation. One ethnohistorian expressed frustration over this: "When one starts reading [Marrant's] narrative itself one would practically never even know that a black man was behind the pen."[10] Literary scholar Rafia Zafar, who has written extensively about Marrant's text, has observed that "virtually none of the narrative concerns issues of race or slavery" and has speculated that editor William Aldridge is likely responsible for this absence.[11] Critic Benilde Montgomery has argued that "because Marrant identifies himself as 'black' only twice in the narrative, his work apparently lacked interest for both nineteenth century abolitionists and certainly for Protestant nativists. Up to now, he has continued to be ignored or dismissed."[12]

Perhaps Rafia Zafar is correct in positing William Aldridge's role in excising black racial identification from John Marrant's memoir. Aldridge's function as Marrant's amanuensis, more common in early American Indian literature than in early African American literature, is certainly another barrier to "transparency" in Marrant's text. Though Aldridge's participation in the construction and production of Marrant's story has led critics to question Marrant's degree of authorial control, most acknowledge Marrant as the "author" of this work but note the tensions involved in white transcription and editorship of African American writings.[13] Adam Potkay and Sandra Burr chose to reprint the fourth edition of the text, which they note was originally published for the author.[14] Potkay and Burr point out that William Aldridge refused to sell this version, suggesting that Aldridge may not have approved of additions that Marrant made to the fourth edition.[15] Interestingly, this singular version of Marrant's narrative includes a sympathetic description of Native American experience of white settlement, as well as the addition of a white mistress's cruel treatment of African American slaves, but it does not include augmented references to Marrant's own identification as a black man.[16] The relative independence that Marrant seems to have had in this particular version of his narrative and the persistent lack of attention to his own racialization as black in the text suggests that John Marrant was not interested in positing his racial assignment as a central theme of his personal revelations and leads us to confront the possibility that Marrant was more interested in associating himself with Indians than with African Americans. If this is the case, the meanings of racial classification and identification in Marrant's narrative become more evident at the juncture of black and red racial signification than in the realm of black experience alone.

What John Marrant seemed to recognize, and what I seek to explore in this chapter, is that entering the sphere of cleric, citizen, and culture hero that is strictly reserved for white men in the transatlantic Enlightenment milieu means distancing oneself from blacks and drawing nearer to Indians. In claiming a relationship with native people, John Marrant enters into implicit dialogue with a prominent concept in late-eighteenth-century American and European thought that seizes on the Indian as a primary symbol of nobility, liberty, and national identity. Conscious of the sorting system that Europeans devised to categorize and assign value to diverse populations, and aware of the differential positioning of African Americans and American Indians within that taxonomy, Marrant "flips the script" of the colonial narratives that he employs, refusing to accept the subordination that his racial assignment dictates and projecting familiarity with Indians to enact a status for himself akin to that of an authoritative white man. Central to my interpretation here is the notion that the mechanism through which Marrant stakes his claim is knowledge of and closeness with native people. This idea takes multiple forms in his text and most often appears as corporeal, cultural, and emotional connection, as indicated by Marrant's adopting of Indian dress and habits, his sharing of Indian spaces, his capturing of Indians' spiritual passions, and his receiving an Indian's kiss. This link between expressions of closeness and the exercise of power in Marrant's tale echoes the tenor of indigenous and white relations in colonial and early American history, in which contact was "close but abrasive" and benevolence masked the threat of violence.[17]

EXPLORATIONS: BLACK AND INDIAN DIFFERENCE IN THE WORK OF JEFFERSON AND TOCQUEVILLE

In her new foreword to classic writings by women of color *This Bridge Called My Back*, feminist theorist Cherríe Moraga describes Indians and blacks as the "first and forced Americans."[18] Moraga's alignment of black and native historical experience locates her in a long line of intellectuals who have made this gesture of comparison, a gesture that posits a simultaneous sameness and difference in the position of African and indigenous peoples in America. As the joint objects of European and Euro-American exploitation, blacks and Indians are classed together in this gesture, but within this shared classification a key distinction is implied: American Indians are the "first" (or colonized) and Africans are the "forced" (or enslaved). It is this bifurcated association of Native Americans with land and African Americans with labor that inspires contrasting characterizations of blacks and Indians by Thomas Jefferson and Alexis de Tocqueville, two men whose political writings have deeply influenced the ways that the early American nation-state, its subjects, and its citizens have been understood.[19] Though the following tandem discussion of Jefferson's and Tocqueville's thoughts on race will be familiar terrain for scholars of early America, it structures a previously unexplored context for interpreting the narrative of John Marrant.

While Cherríe Moraga's modern-day foreword seizes on an Afro-Native comparison to mark a history of "internalized colonization" and to further a coalitional political vision, eighteenth-century American statesman Thomas Jefferson and nineteenth-century French traveler Alexis de Tocqueville examine African Americans and American Indians comparatively in a manner that highlights an insurmountable *difference* between these two populations.[20] The two men's separate treatments locate Indians and blacks at differential distances from whiteness, Americanness, and the promises of democracy, which in turn secures the idealized image of the Indian for use by the new republic even as it protects the American citizenry from the specter of black contamination. In *Notes on the State of Virginia* (1785) Thomas Jefferson concludes that Africans and Native Americans are antithetical in moral virtue, strength of mind, imagination, beauty, and self-possession. Jefferson first arrives at this bifurcated racial assessment while rationalizing his aversion toward blacks and arguing the necessity of African colonization.[21] In a second, related passage Jefferson begins with a discussion of black inferiority that shifts into a comparative discussion of Indian acceptability. While Jefferson observes that "in imagination they [blacks] are dull, tasteless, and anomalous," he comments that evidence of Indian artistry "prove[s] the existence of a germ in their minds which only wants cultivation."[22] Jefferson, it seems, is unable to explain his views on the bankruptcy of those designated as black without invoking the first Americans as a point of contrast.

Alexis de Tocqueville engages in a similar, though more sympathetic, act of comparison. In volume one of *Democracy in America* Tocqueville laments the black and Indian condition, noting the pathos and irony of black exclusion from white society and Native American pride in isolation: "The Negro, who earnestly desires to mingle his race with that of the European, cannot do so; while the Indian, who might succeed to a certain extent, disdains to make the attempt. The servility of the one dooms him to slavery, the pride of the other to death."[23] Tocqueville views both blacks and Indians as ill-fated races who can never be fully incorporated into white society. As political theorist Jennifer Pitts has noted, black and native populations represented two poles for Tocqueville, marking the outer limits of American democracy.[24]

Is it significant that Jefferson and Tocqueville both take this comparative turn in their interpretations of early America? As anthropologist and historian Ann Stoler has observed, constructing comparisons, or preserving particular subjects and modes of commensurability and incommensurability, was a strategy of meaning "management" employed by imperial regimes and their subjects. In Stoler's assessment "selective comparison was itself part of colonial projects that also served to secure relations of power."[25] Indeed, in the writings of Jefferson and Tocqueville relations of power between whites and nonwhites, citizens and noncitizens, were encoded and stabilized through the act of comparing African Americans and Native Americans, implicating the two men in a larger "politics of comparison" of which black evangelist John Marrant seems to have been all too aware.[26]

Though Thomas Jefferson and Alexis de Tocqueville were citizens of distant nations writing decades apart, they had a number of experiences in common. Jefferson was a statesman and scholar who served as governor of Virginia, secretary of state, and third president of the United States, and he was principally responsible for extending American colonialism into the West. Alexis de Tocqueville was a statesman and scholar who served as a parliamentary member and foreign minister for France, and he was essential to the planning and assessment of France's imperial interests in North Africa. Both men were profoundly shaped by the Enlightenment movement that intoxicated Europe and its colonies, inspired works of political theory and art, and catalyzed revolts against monarchic governments and aristocratic institutions. It follows, then, that the Enlightenment ideals of reason, knowledge, feeling, freedom, democracy, humanity, and justice informed and suffused Jefferson's and Tocqueville's writings. Each man, therefore, would confront in his master work the ulterior conflict that shadowed the Age of Enlightenment: namely, that the innovations and transformations of this era both disavowed and depended on systematic slavery and comprehensive colonialism.

Thus, Jefferson, who had earlier acknowledged the "unalienable rights" of human liberty and equality finds it necessary in *Notes on the State of Virginia* to rationalize his dislike of blacks, to confess his fear of a just God who would certainly punish America for the inhumanity of slavery, and to devise a plan for the eventual abolition of all bondsmen and women. Likewise, Tocqueville laments the destruction of native peoples at the hands of the "most grasping nation on the globe" in *Democracy in America*, even as he accepts the inevitability of the Indians' demise as the price of civilization.[27] Jefferson's and Tocqueville's comparative analyses of Indians and blacks seem to grow out of the implicit recognition that the conjoined presence of these populations whose exploitation and expulsion constituted the groundwork, or land and labor, of the American state chaffed at the very Enlightenment principles that each man held dear. Jefferson and Tocqueville were pressed, therefore, to address the "Indian plight" and "Negro problem" that were foundational to, if irreconcilable with, American nationhood.[28]

As de facto spokesmen for an American experiment that would model the enlightened present and "mirror" a liberated future, Jefferson and Tocqueville faced the unenviable task of interpreting the inherent rift between Enlightenment principles and American practices.[29] The politics of their comparison of blacks and Indians worked toward narrowing this gap by rationalizing the difficulties of black emancipation and the necessities of black expulsion from the national body, and by reiterating the image of the idealized Indian and the benefits of Indian incorporation into the national body. The continuation of slavery, though horrific in both men's view, could be understood, for the cost of black freedom would be catastrophic to the nation; and the history of colonization, though a tragedy, could be recompensed if only the Indian were willing to be assimilated. In actuality, these lines of thinking resulted in the continued dehumanization and abuse of African Americans and the ongoing dispossession and decimation of Native Americans. Symbolically, these lines of thinking reflected and created an elevated space for the Indian, but not for the African, in the increasingly racialized national and international imagination.

This necessity for separating blacks from Indians, for highlighting African inferiority in contrast to Indian superiority, for associating Indians with bountiful land and Africans with debased labor found ready expression in the shared symbolism of the European Enlightenment and American national identity.[30] Native American studies scholars Donald Grinde and Bruce Johansen have argued convincingly that the European "discovery" of American Indian peoples would later provide a living example of embryonic Enlightenment notions, for French and English philosophers of this period viewed Indians as existing in absolute liberty and contentment, with no constraints save the laws of nature.[31] The Noble Savage archetype took shape in these early interpretations, and the American Indian as imagined by Europeans "suffused enlightenment thought."[32] America's founding fathers saw in the idealized Indian not only an example of emancipated man but also of democratic principles in practice, and they viewed Indian peoples and Indian lands as the model and mechanism of the American experiment and as the intangible essence of American exceptionalism.[33]

That Americans were able to endure the cognitive dissonance of devastating native populations and usurping native land bases, even while valorizing the image of the Indian through their own appropriation of Indian-like ideals, appearances, and behaviors, is as central to the nation's founding as the irony of slavery. As American studies scholar Philip Deloria has pointed out: "Americans wanted to feel a natural affinity with the continent, and it was Indians who could teach them such aboriginal close-ness. Yet, in order to control the landscape they had to destroy the original inhabitants. . . . American social and political policy towards Indians has been a two-hundred-year back-and-forth between assimilation and destruc-tion."[34] American studies scholar Rayna Green has explained, further, that even as Euro-American settlers disappeared living Indians, white Americans stepped into that empty space, claiming the legacy of Indian nobility and freedom for themselves.[35] The tale of Daniel Boone, published for the first time in 1784, one year before John Marrant told his own life story, epito-mized this act of substitution and, as Richard Slotkin has observed in his classic work on American mythology, became the quintessential formula-tion of an American culture hero. Slotkin explains that "it was the figure of Daniel Boone, the solitary, Indian-like hunter of the deep woods, that yielded the most significant, most emotionally compelling myth-hero of the early republic."[36]

At the convergence of Enlightenment ideals, democratic longings, and land lust, European and Euro-American thinkers consistently called on the idealized figure of the American Indian. Both Thomas Jefferson and Alexis de Tocqueville reproduce this figure, albeit to different degrees, preserving Indians as the noble savage of the American wilderness and, by comparison, assigning Africans to the irredeemable category of debased and racialized labor. For Jefferson this distinction is a sharp one. Blacks are "inferior to the whites in the endowments both of body and mind" in his view, whereas Indians are "brave" and "keen" and possess a "vivacity and activity of mind . . . equal to ours in the same situation." Jefferson proclaims that "we shall probably find that they are formed in mind as well as in body, on the same module with the Homo Sapiens Europaeus."[37] For Tocqueville, however, the image of the idealized Indian in contradistinction to the debased African is subtler and more nuanced.[38] Echoing Jefferson, Tocqueville says of Native Americans, "The Indians, in the little which they have done, have unques-tionably displayed as much natural genius as the peoples of Europe in their greatest undertakings."[39] And in an extended scene with which he concludes his comparative discussion of Native Americans and African Americans, Tocqueville paints an intimate portrait of the multiracial American family:

> I remember that while I was traveling through the forests which still cover
> the state of Alabama, I arrived one day at the log house of a pioneer. I did
> not wish to penetrate into the dwelling of the American, but retired to

rest myself for a while on the margin of a spring, which was not far off, in the woods. While I was in this place . . . an Indian woman appeared, followed by a Negress, and holding by the hand a little white girl of five or six years, whom I took to be the daughter of the pioneer. A sort of barbarous luxury set off the costume of the Indian; rings of metal were hanging from her nostrils and ears, her hair, which was adorned with glass beads, fell loosely upon her shoulders; and I saw that she was not married, for she still wore that necklace of shells which the bride always deposits on the nuptial couch. The Negress was clad in squalid European garments. All three came and seated themselves upon the banks of the spring; and the young Indian, taking the child in her arms, lavished upon her such fond caresses as mothers give, while the Negress endeavored, by various little artifices, to attract the attention of the young Creole. The child displayed in her slightest gestures a consciousness of superiority that formed a strange contrast with her infantine weakness; as if she received the attentions of her companions with a sort of condescension. The Negress was seated on the ground before her mistress, watching her smallest desires and apparently divided between an almost maternal affection for the child and servile fear; while the savage, in the midst of her tenderness, displayed an air of freedom and pride which was almost ferocious. I had approached the group and was contemplating them in silence, but my curiosity was probably displeasing to the Indian woman, for she suddenly rose, pushed the child roughly from her, and, giving me an angry look, plunged into the thicket.[40]

I quote this passage at length because it seems to express in full not only Tocqueville's view of Indians and blacks but also the divergent characteristics associated with blackness and redness that have persisted in American thought. Here Tocqueville reprises his central suppositions regarding Native Americans and African Americans: Indians are strangely alluring, naturally fierce, overly proud, and too fond of their freedom, which locates them at the margins of white society; blacks are desperate, devoid of culture, self-effacing, indecorous, and despised by the Europeans whom they emulate, which locates them in a subjugated position within white society. In this scene Tocqueville fluently incorporates the racial and gendered iconography of early America to display what is ultimately a simultaneous interdependence and separation of white, black, and native inhabitants.

As is often the case in *Democracy in America*, Tocqueville's observations

here are layered. His decision to reconstruct a domestic scene as the ultimate illustration of his analysis of "the three races" indicates his recognition
that the power of the state to control racial meanings is reflected in and supported by intimate relations and that intimate relations are effectively expressed through representations of women's bodies and emotions.[41] Political theorist Laura Janara has asserted that Tocqueville shapes his argument
around a "symbolic family drama" that charts the maturation of a childlike American democracy, which, at a distance from its English "mother,"
is nurtured in the "'cradle' of a feminized North American nature."[42] In the
passage quoted above Tocqueville doubles his symbolism of Native America
as mother, figured here as both the land itself—the wood and stream that
succor him—and the materialized Indian woman, mother to the child who
is alternately described as "white" and "Creole." The native woman whom
Tocqueville portrays is a composite figure of the fierce yet noble Indian
Queen once symbolic of the New World and the beautiful and assimilable
Indian princess, epitomized in the American "origin story" of Pocahontas
and John Smith.[43] The woodland grove setting is also central to this scene,
as the woods have long been a site of metaphorical resonance in America.
Although Puritan and Quaker colonists feared the woods as a dangerous,
interstitial zone peopled by wild, demonic Indians, the American settlers'
growing knowledge of the Indians' woods ensured survival and paved the
way for national independence.[44] Tocqueville's presence in these woods, as
well as the presence of the settler's cabin, marks the penetration of whites
into Indian spaces and the subsequent taming of the wilderness. Though the
Indian woman flees Tocqueville's scrutiny by dashing deeper into the forest,
the nostalgic tone of this passage reveals this means of escape as transitory.
The enslaved black woman, ever subject and abject, remains a captive of
the grove, exposed to Tocqueville's imperial gaze even as the Indian woman
finds temporary refuge in her native nature.

If Tocqueville's use of familial symbolism can be applied to this single
moment, then the mixed-race Indian-white child represents democracy, the
naturalized American Indian woman is democracy's mother, the enslaved
black woman is democracy's handmaiden, and the American wilderness is
democracy's birthplace. It is notable that the father of democracy, the white
male pioneer whose prior actions of acquiring the Indian woman, Indian
land, and black slave have given rise to the scene that Tocqueville observes,
is an absent presence here, represented by his structural "improvement,"
the log cabin. In rendering this primal scene, Tocqueville makes two im-

plicit assertions that I want to emphasize—that American relations of power are organized through racial categories and embedded in intimate interactions, and that whites (especially men) and Indians (especially women) share a particular closeness, expressed geographically, physically, sexually, and symbolically, from which blacks are excluded. Tocqueville's cognizance of the intimate tenor of this scene is clear in his concluding statement: "But in the picture that I have just been describing there was something peculiarly touching; a bond of affection here united the oppressors with the oppressed, and the effort of Nature to bring them together rendered still more striking the immense distance placed between them by prejudice and law."[45] Affection notwithstanding, Tocqueville recognizes and reproduces a hierarchy of racial designation that is not only enforced by law but also in the private realm of interpersonal relations: the native woman who caresses a child begotten by a white settler, the black woman who sits at their feet and gazes up with fondness and terror, the white child who feels contempt for both women, and Tocqueville himself, who surveys the scene from a sentimental, yet authoritative, distance.

Alexis de Tocqueville's portrayal of this woodland respite recreates the longing for the Indian and loathing for the African that is prefigured in Thomas Jefferson's work. The politics of their comparison ameliorates the gap between Enlightenment ideals and American practices and underwrites the bifurcated metaphorical and material uses to which Indians and Africans have been put by the white republic.

In this way the writings of Thomas Jefferson and Alexis de Tocqueville reflect and consolidate the overdetermination of African and Indian positioning in America. As Vine Deloria Jr. has put it: "Because the Negro labored, he was considered a draft animal. Because the Indian occupied large areas of land, he was considered a wild animal. . . . Thus whites steadfastly refused to allow blacks to enjoy the fruits of full citizenship. . . . The Indian suffered the reverse treatment. . . . Everything possible was done to ensure that Indians were forced into American life. The wild animal was made into a household pet."[46] African American and American Indian intellectuals prior to and including Vine Deloria have long challenged their separate representations and abuses as inscribed in American letters and "commonsense" understanding. However, few works by black or native thinkers reveal the comparative and therefore associated nature of African American and Native American racial classification and valuation.[47] Considered in this context, John Marrant's attention to Indians in "A Narrative of the Lord's Wonderful

Dealings" provides a rare opportunity. While Marrant's story may lead us beyond the comfort zones of proper and expected African American subject matter, it leaves us with a record of one man's refutation of received racial classifications and offers a glimpse into the meanings of native people, cultures, and spaces to eighteenth-century African American subjectivity.

ERRAND IN THE WILDERNESS: READING JOHN MARRANT

"A Narrative of the Lord's Wonderful Dealings with John Marrant" borrows from proto-American literary forms — the spiritual conversion narrative and the Indian captivity narrative — to fascinating effect. The salient features of the text are Marrant's emotive acceptance of Christianity and his God-given ability to convert the savage Cherokees who hold him hostage. In the first paragraph of his preface to the narrative, Marrant's transcriber and editor, William Aldridge, highlights the wondrous quality of Marrant's singular experience: "He crosses the fence, which marked the boundary between the wilderness and the cultivated country. . . . He wanders, but Christ is his guide and protector. — Who can view him among the Indian tribes without wonder? He arrives among the Cherokee, where gross ignorance wore its rudest forms, and savage despotism exercised its most terrifying empire. Here the child just turned fourteen, without sling or stone, engages, and with the arrow of prayer pointed with faith, wounded Goliath, and conquers the King."[48] While Aldridge views the Cherokees as an imperial people controlled by a single, despotic royal, it is John Marrant, who, when he emerges from the wilderness near the end of his tale, wields the power of a monarch.

Marrant's narrated journey from sinner to saint, boy to man, and peasant to prince begins with a misstep. Marrant reports at the start of his life story that as an adolescent his love of playing the violin and French horn had "opened to [him] a large door of vanity and vice."[49] While walking with a friend along the streets of Charleston, Marrant, a free black boy who is nonetheless "a slave to every vice" (77), comes upon a meeting house in which the Reverend George Whitefield is preaching. The boys conspire to disrupt the service with a musical prank, but when they cross the threshold into the church, Marrant is paralyzed by the power of God. The reverend assesses Marrant's condition, saying, "JESUS CHRIST HAS GOT THEE AT LAST" (79). Marrant is then bedridden for days with a mysterious spiritual malady and does not recover until Whitefield dispatches a Baptist minister to pray for him. Marrant describes the effects of the reverend's ministrations: "and near the close of his prayer, The Lord was pleased to set my soul at perfect liberty, and being filled with joy I began to praise the Lord immediately; my sorrows were turned into peace, and joy, and love" (79).

Following his conversion, Marrant reads the Bible incessantly and is moved to tears when his family members refuse to behave like Christians. When his mother and siblings begin to "persecute" him and call him insane, Marrant seeks safety beyond the limits of the town (80). Like the Israelites escaping Pharaoh in the Old Testament, he wanders into the "desert" wilderness: "Accordingly I went over the fence, about half a mile from our house, which divided the inhabited and cultivated parts of the country from the wilderness. I continued traveling in the desert [sic] all day without the least inclination of turning back" (81). Marrant roams directionless for miles, suffers from hunger and thirst, and is threatened by wolves and bears. Along the journey God repeatedly saves Marrant by revealing deer grass and mud puddles for his sustenance and shielding him from animal attacks, just as he had shielded the biblical Daniel in the lion's den.

After Marrant has traversed fifty-five miles, surviving only by the grace of God, he encounters an Indian hunter who takes him in. Marrant travels with the man for ten weeks, learning hunting techniques as well as the Cherokee language. Much to his surprise, however, Marrant is told that he will be put to death for trespassing when he and his Indian friend approach the Cherokee village. Marrant's would-be executioner explains his torturous methods and then jails Marrant. Marrant is moved by God to pray in the Cherokee language, and the executioner, on hearing the fervent prayer, converts to Christianity. After this marvelous turn of events, the Cherokee "king" demands an interview with Marrant. An interrogation ensues, during which the king's daughter is mysteriously drawn to the black captive. Marrant tells us, "The executioner fell upon his knees, and intreated [sic] the king in my behalf, and told him what he had felt of the same Lord. At this instant the king's eldest daughter came into the chamber, a person about nineteen years of age, and stood at my right hand. I had a Bible in my hand, which she took out of it, and having opened it, she kissed it, and seemed much delighted with it" (86). After kissing the Bible a second time, the Cherokee princess is stricken with a spiritual illness. Marrant alone has the power to save her, so the king must spare his life.

As Marrant prays for the princess, the king accepts the Christian faith and releases the Cherokee people from his heathen rule: "The Lord appeared most lovely and glorious; the king himself was awakened, and the others set at liberty. A great change took place among the people; the king's house became God's house; the soldiers were ordered away, and the poor condemned prisoner had perfect liberty, and was treated like a prince. Now the Lord made all my enemies to become my friends. I remained nine weeks in the king's palace" (87). In the afterglow of his success among the Cherokees Marrant travels farther south to preach to the Creek, Catawba, and Housa tribes. Finally, he rejoins his Cherokee hunter friend and begins the journey back home to Charleston. When Marrant returns, draped in animal skins and carrying a tomahawk, his relatives do not recognize him. Marrant reports, "The singularity of my dress drew every body's eyes upon me, yet none knew me" (89). Finally, convinced that he is indeed kin, Marrant's uncle reveals that they had thought him dead. Marrant, the prodigal son now embraced by his family, says of the reunion: "the dead was brought to life again; thus the lost was found" (90).

Marrant continues his work for the Lord, traveling seventy miles from Charleston to teach slave children the catechism and witnessing their cruel treatment at the hands of their mistress. However, the American war for independence from England disrupts Marrant's preaching. He is impressed onto a British ship. When the ship encounters a ferocious storm, Marrant is first thrown overboard and is then miraculously rescued from sharks. It is at this moment that Marrant sees his "call to the ministry fuller and clearer" (95). He finds a patron in Selina Hastings, the Countess of Huntingdon, and is ordained in her chapel in Bath, England. Marrant's intention, at the conclusion of his narrative, is to travel to the British colony of Nova Scotia to spread God's word: "I have now only to intreat [sic] the earnest prayers of all my Christian friends, that I may be carried safe there; kept humble, made faithful, and successful; that strangers may hear of and run to Christ; that Indian tribes may stretch out their hands to God; that the black nations may be made white in the blood of the Lamb." (95).

John Marrant's life story as recounted in his narrative observes the hallmarks of the Indian captivity form. As scholars of the genre have explained, authors of the captivity narrative were understood by their contemporaries to have been chosen by God to undergo extreme experiences. Because English colonists viewed Native Americans as innately different and morally inferior, time among the Indians was the ultimate test and fortification of Puritan beliefs.[50] The author's successful passage through the trial of being taken by Indians, a passage evidenced by steadfast adherence to the faith in the direst of circumstances, proved the author's election by God. The repetition of this story line in early American writing gave rise to what literary scholar Tara Fitzpatrick has described as an American myth of the "imperiled but chosen pilgrim alone in the wilderness braving the savage 'other.'"[51] As is common in works of this genre, John Marrant's own salvation is tested and authenticated through his successful converting of the Indians. His ability not only to survive his ordeal in the "spiritual wasteland" that was the Indians' wilderness but also to transform the Cherokee town makes his narrative an overstatement of the genre's case.[52]

In addition to demonstrating the individual author's religious election, the Indian captivity narrative did the cultural work of reinforcing an English moral authority that was linked to the enforcement of imperial power over indigenous Americans. As literary scholar John Sekora explains, "From its beginnings the captivity had provided a theologically powerful as well as physically useful version of manifest destiny."[53] Indeed, the earliest text of America's first organic literary genre, Mary Rowlandson's 1682 narrative, "The Soveraignty and Goodness of God," was published in the aftermath of combat. King Philip's War, also known as Metacom's War, devastated native and Anglo communities in New England between 1675 and 1676. The conflict resulted in a massive death toll and extensive dispossession of Native American lands.[54] Rowlandson, who was kidnapped by Nipmuck Indians during the war, told her story of terror and triumph six years later. And as the title of Rowlandson's memoir implies, the sovereignty of a Christian God overcomes all forms of American Indian authority in this new genre. Rowlandson's narrative and others that followed served as ethnocentric records of Puritan-Indian relations and evidence of redemptive suffering that proved the Puritans, as a cultural and spiritual community, to be God's chosen people. The interrelationship of narrative form and imperial power encoded in these texts created what Rafia Zafar has called a "literary imperialism."[55]

The narrative of John Marrant is reminiscent of Mary Rowlandson's paradigmatic text, to which, as Benilde Montgomery has pointed out, Marrant's work "closely adheres [in] spirit and design."[56] For instance, vanity precipitates the need for spiritual purification for both Rowlandson and Marrant. At the conclusion of her narrative Rowlandson writes: "The Lord hath shewn me the vanity of these outward things. That they are the vanity of vanities, and vexation of spirit."[57] Similarly, Marrant's spiritual journey ensues after he has entered "a large door of vanity and vice."[58] Marrant's narrative, like Rowlandson's, emphasizes the role of landscape and carefully marks the boundary between civilization and the wilderness. While Rowlandson organizes her tale around a series of "removes" that take her deeper into the forest, Marrant tracks the number of miles that he travels into "uncultivated" country.[59]

These and other striking parallels between Marrant's tale and early expressions of the genre have led Rafia Zafar and others to question whether John Marrant is implicated in the imperial politics of the captivity narrative form. Zafar concludes that Marrant, like most black authors of his day, wrote for his own purposes, which diverged from the colonial project of demonstrating the "rectitude of Puritan rule" by "reinforc[ing] white views of Indians as inhuman."[60] At the same time, though, Zafar insists that Marrant's text yields dialectical readings. For when Marrant controls the Bible before the Indians, he "can be viewed as both the agent of a white, Protestant colonizing power and the colonial subject adapting and mimicking the sign of the colonizer."[61]

This moment and others like it, in which John Marrant presents himself as a colonial agent, deviate from the norm of early African American literature and therefore tap into the complexities of black subjectivity in the Age of Enlightenment. Critical here is that these acts of agency turn on the presence of Indians. For John Marrant—who, in the exactness of his narrative construction, evidences a familiarity with the relative positioning of Indians and Africans in the American and European imaginary, as well as a familiarity with American literary tropes of colonial expansion, African abjection, Indian disempowerment, and Indian negation—deploys this knowledge to reposition himself in the racialized scale of humankind.

In my attempt to understand Marrant's iterated relationship with Indians, I envision his narrative as a tripartite tableau, a set of three scenes that interpolate with one another *and* with familiar plotlines of conquest. From this perspective these moments in Marrant's text become "scenes of subjection," to borrow the language of literary scholar Saidiya Hartman.[62] However, the subjected person here is not the figure of the black slave, as is often the case in African American literature, but rather the figure of the tempered Indian. In these scenes Marrant achieves closeness with Indians—gaining their knowledge, guiding their spiritual lives, adopting their habits—in a manner that makes the Indians subject to Marrant's authority. In effect, Marrant trades on the idea of the idealized Indian to trade up his own position in the dominant racial hierarchy.

As historian James Merrell has elucidated, the notion of the woods as pernicious, mysterious spaces and as the natural abode of American Indians has long held sway in American thought.[63] Certainly, the captivity narrative and early works of American fiction express this deep-seated fear of the forest. But, as Richard Slotkin has pointed out, being forced into the wilderness against one's will also allows for the fulfillment of a hidden need for knowledge of the woods and its inhabitants. For the woods not only represent danger but also the possibility of transformation. The individual white captive, as well as the American colonies and future nation, must come to know the wilderness in their quest for survival and self-making. Slotkin explains that the captivity narrative "constitutes the Puritan's peculiar vision of the only acceptable way of acculturating, of being initiated into the life of the wilderness."[64] The initiator in this transaction is the Indian, who, in progressive stages of the development of this genre, teaches the European how to be an American. By the mid-1700s to early 1800s, Slotkin continues, "the captivity experience itself became an experience of adoption or initiation into the Indian's world."[65] John Marrant's use of the captivity narrative form, then, can be viewed as initializing his bid for closeness with Indians. The native woods become a transformative space for Marrant, a portal to his future self and a resonant setting for the narrative tropes that he enacts.[66]

The first scene of note begins just as John Marrant is being interrogated by the Cherokee king, who intends to have him killed. As the king is questioning Marrant, the king's daughter disrupts the proceedings, draws near to the captive, and kisses his Bible. The woman's contact with Marrant's potent appendage, coupled by his prayer, causes her to "cr[y] out."[67] And as Marrant is the only one capable of soothing her through the power of prayer, the king spares his life.

Marrant's inclusion of Indian royalty in his remembrances is not original, for the Indian queen figure, and her iconographic daughter, the Indian princess, had been associated with the "New World" since 1575.[68] The idea of the Indian princess was integrated with story in 1624, when Captain John Smith published his *History of Virginia*, in which Smith described his rescue by a young woman named Pocahontas, daughter of the Indian ruler Powhatan. Over the course of decades American writers, artists, and dramatists embellished the tale, emphasizing the romantic tenor of the lovely princess who saved the Englishman's life, throwing her body over his and protecting him from the fatal blow of her father's men.[69] As Rayna Green has convincingly argued, this image of the Indian princess, which turns on her betrayal of "the wishes and customs of her own 'barbarous' people to make good the

rescue, saving the man out of love and often out of 'Christian sympathy,'"
became a template for relations between Indians and whites.[70] Because the
native woman's body had come to symbolize American land in narratives
and images of colonial exploration, the Indian princess's action of offering
her body to the foreigner is at the same time an offering of indigenous terrain.[71]

When John Marrant describes the Cherokee princess, he rehabilitates a
story line that authorizes English and American conquest of native peoples.
The kiss of the princess, her invitation to intimacy, sets in motion a chain of
events that leads to Marrant's eventual influence over her nation. Like Pocahontas, whose bodily offering ensures and symbolizes the conquest of native
lands, the kiss of the Cherokee princess makes her people's conversion possible and refigures conquest as the fulfillment of native desires. John Marrant,
like John Smith, is the beneficiary of this transaction, as his encounter with
the Indian princess underwrites his authority in the Indians' homeland.

The scene in which the Indian princess kisses Marrant's Bible, and is
"much delighted with it," extends into a second key moment in this narrative.[72] The young woman, having bestowed her kiss, reaches for Marrant's
Bible again. Marrant reports: "His daughter took the book out of my hand
a second time; she opened it, and kissed it again; her father bid her give it
to me, which she did; but she said, with much sorrow, the book would not
speak to her."[73] It is this singular instance that led Henry Louis Gates to recover Marrant's text from obscurity in 1988, identifying it as a key work in
early African American literature. Gates cites Marrant's narrative as a primary example of what he terms the "trope of the talking book," arguing that
the recurrence of this trope in the narratives of Ukasaw Gronniosaw (1774),
John Marrant (1785), John Stuart (1787), Olaudah Equiano (1789), and John
Jea (1815) indicates a dialogic relationship among black-authored texts that
marks the emergence of an African American literary tradition. In tracing
out this lineage, Gates credits John Marrant with: "inaugurat[ing] the black
tradition of English literature, not because he was its first author but because
he was the tradition's first revisionist."[74]

An earlier occurrence of Gates's trope appears not in an African American context but in a Native American one. Ethnohistorian James Axtell
has described the "sense of wonder" and "almost totemic reverence" with
which nonliterate native peoples of North America first encountered the
books of European missionaries.[75] He suggests that in the late 1600s Jesuit
priests among the Huron and Iroquois met with greater success in their con-

version efforts in large part because of the native perception that a secret force existed within their Bibles.[76] And Axtell notes further that some native peoples in the Northeast expressed their reverence for the written word by kissing, fondling, and rubbing their bodies against the books of Europeans.[77] This pattern of white and Indian contact recorded in missionary writings, together with the similar pattern of white and black contact expressed in African American slave narratives, makes the "talking" or "wonderful" book a far-reaching and compelling motif.

The trope of the talking book as defined by Henry Louis Gates entails an illiterate person (black) viewing a literate person (white), reading a book (the Bible).[78] In this interaction the illiterate person feels impotent and marginalized because he cannot access the text and make it "talk" to him as the literate person can.[79] The repetition of this exchange in early black-authored texts points to what Gates calls "the problematic of speaking and writing," or the challenge of reconciling orality with literacy in African American experience.[80] As Gates notes, Marrant repeats and amends the trope of the talking book when he describes the Cherokee princess's reaction to his Bible.[81] Furthermore, Marrant augments and enlivens this African American trope by merging it with reiterated descriptions of northeastern Indians' early reverence for the book. While Ukasaw Gronniosaw's narrative depicts a white slave master holding the book and a black slave, Gronniosaw himself, standing bewildered, Marrant describes *himself* as having sole access to the written word. Because he borrows from the image of the awestruck native, Marrant's take on the trope of the talking book is unique within the African American literary tradition. Gates explains that unlike others in the tradition, Marrant: "seeks to reverse the received trope by displacement and substitution" and "restructures the trope such that it is the Cherokee who assume the perilous burdens of negation."[82]

Indeed, in Marrant's version—an amalgamation of African American and Native American archetypes—Marrant stands in the place of the literate white man, and the Indian woman stands in the place of the subjugated slave. Even as Marrant displaces the exclusion and subjugation of blackness onto Cherokees in this scene, he projects his own disempowered persona onto the Cherokee woman. She becomes the embodiment of the qualities that render Marrant weak and vulnerable early in the memoir. For it is in opposition to the Cherokee woman's feminized illiteracy that Marrant sheds his own boyish weakness and enters into the authority of manhood. His intimate exchange with the princess, which begins with a kiss, ends by positioning Marrant as reader, knower, and master or, in Gates's words, as a "substituted white man."[83]

The third scene in this tableau is a compilation of disparate segments that build to the moment when John Marrant returns to Charleston dressed "purely in the Indian stile."[84] The manner of his reentry to the civilized world reflects the influence of an extended sojourn among the Indians that has been a process of learning and self-transformation for Marrant, in which he takes on the characteristics of the Cherokees even as he converts them to Western beliefs.

When Marrant first enters the wilderness at the start of his tale, he is at a loss for how to survive until God provides him with food and drink and an Indian hunter, who offers him aid. It is through travels with the hunter that Marrant's initiation into Indian ways begins. By the time he is taken captive, Marrant is proficient in the Cherokee language and has learned how to hunt and skin deer, create bedding out of moss, and tend a fire to prevent the approach of wild animals. After he revives the princess and is released from prison, Marrant graduates from his position of Indian initiate and becomes a leader in Cherokee affairs. His elevated status is expressed through his clothing, which is as fine as the king's. Marrant says, "I had assumed the habit of the country, and was dressed much like the king, and nothing was too good for me. The king would take off his golden ornaments, his chain and bracelets, like a child, if I objected to them, and lay them aside. Here I learnt to speak their tongue in the highest style."[85] The black adolescent, who was at first bewildered in the woods, looks like a native, speaks like a native, and has significant influence over the native potentate.

Marrant's is a story of surviving the wilderness through an adoption of Indian ways that leads, circuitously, to mastery over indigenous peoples. This plotline, featuring a male woodland hero, is borrowed and adapted from a previous text. Embodied by the heralded eighteenth-century figure Daniel Boone and, later, Davy Crockett and James Fenimore Cooper's Natty Bumpo, the white man who acts like an Indian and evidences deep knowledge of the wilderness is a recurring character. Richard Slotkin discusses this figure at length, describing him as "the solitary, Indian-like hunter of the deep woods," who is the "archetypal American and mediator between civilization and the wilderness."[86] The Indian-like hunter, in the primary example of Daniel Boone, is also a consummate Indian fighter who clears the way for white habitation. John Marrant's rendition of this myth follows suit, demonstrating the author's ability to mediate between "civilized" and "uncivilized" cultures through familiarity with Indian ways and facility with Christian doctrine. When John Marrant returns to town, Indianized and triumphant, he catapults up the dominant racial scale, leaping from the status of black boy to the status of white culture hero, on the backs of red Indians.

Benilde Montgomery has observed about this narrative that "Marrant undergoes a complete change of identity, the fullness of his rebirth signified by his assuming the wardrobe of an Indian King."[87] Indeed, by the time he has exited the forest and inscribed these three familiar scenes, Marrant has undergone a miraculous transformation in both persona and caste. The new Marrant is a purposeful, self-possessed agent of God, whose perseverance and accomplishments rival those of John Smith and Daniel Boone. In the territory of the Cherokees, beyond the limits of Tocqueville's democracy, John Marrant does not perish but is instead empowered. Though unpredictable and at times unwieldy, the narrative of John Marrant reveals an astute awareness of the symbolic valuation of Indians and relative devaluation of Africans in Enlightenment thought, a familiarity with narratives of conquest that are enacted through closeness with Indians, and an employment of these same plotlines to subvert assigned racial categories.

Yet John Marrant's act of narrative subversion is something akin to rearranging deck chairs on the *Titanic*, as racial taxonomies and the meanings assigned to them proved arbitrary and changeable into the nineteenth century and beyond. Though imaginary American Indians would continue to be sporadically romanticized in American life and thought, living Indians were vilified, exploited, exterminated, and defined as others in an expanding white world. Nor does Marrant seem fully at ease with telling a life story that borrows much of its logic from colonial scripts. Although he acts as an agent of native conversion, Marrant evidences ambivalence. In the singular fourth edition Marrant reports the following after his return from preaching among the southern tribes: "When they recollect, that the white people drove them from the American shores, they are full of resentment. These nations have united, and murdered all the white people in the back settlements which they could lay hold of, men, women, and children. I had not much reason to believe any of these nations were savingly [sic] wrought upon."[88] This brief moment of introspection suggests not only the limits of Marrant's evangelical influence, and by extension God's power, but also implies a nascent connection with native peoples' motivation for resistance. Embedded in John Marrant's tale of triumph might be a seed of anticolonial sentiment that, to misapply the words of Thomas Jefferson, "only wants cultivation."[89] But in the ever-mystifying layers of meaning that characterize this text, Marrant's ambivalence at the conquest in which he has taken part might also be read as another hallmark of his memoir's resonance with foundational narratives of imperial desire.[90]

NOTES

I am grateful to Jean O'Brien and Catherine Griffin, whose comments in a graduate seminar shaped this essay in its earliest stages, and to Kathleen Brown, Ann Stoler, Alexandra Stern, and Vicente Diaz, whose later comments contributed greatly to my conceptualization and revisions.

1. Marrant, "A Narrative of the Lord's Wonderful Dealings with John Marrant," 88.

2. Potkay and Burr, "About John Marrant," 67–68. My essay does not delve into the specifics of Methodism in African American experience. John Saillant has written extensively about race and the Methodist Church in late-eighteenth-century and early-nineteenth-century America. He argues that white Methodist ministers who believed in divine providence saw slavery as part of God's design to test the righteousness of white Christians and to convert Africans. Though they supported emancipation, Methodist leaders believed that blacks were so different from whites that they would contaminate America if they remained there. For more on blacks and Methodism see Saillant, "Slavery and Divine Providence in New England Calvinism"; and Saillant, "Remarkably Emancipated from Bondage, Slavery, and Death."

3. Deloria, *Custer Died for Your Sins*, 102.

4. Potkay and Burr, "About John Marrant," 68.

5. VanDerBeets, "Introduction," 177.

6. Ibid.

7. See Gates, *The Signifying Monkey*, 142; see also Montgomery, "Recapturing John Marrant."

8. For a recent, innovative, and inspired study of Marrant's work see Brooks, *American Lazarus*.

9. Barry O'Connell, conversation with the author, Lannan Summer Institute, D'Arcy McNickle Center for American Indian History, Newberry Library, Chicago, Aug. 1, 2001.

10. Anonymous peer review, comments to the author for *Ethnohistory*, May 2002.

11. Zafar, "Capturing the Captivity," 29.

12. Montgomery, "Recapturing John Marrant," 105.

13. For more on the debate concerning Aldridge's role as editor and Marrant's role as author see Sekora, "Black Message/White Envelope"; and Zafar, "Capturing the Captivity."

14. Potkay and Burr, "About John Marrant," 72–73.

15. Ibid.

16. Ibid., 73.

17. See Nash, "The Image of the Indian in the Southern Colonial Mind," esp. 198, 204.

18. Moraga uses this phrase in a parenthetical comment and attributes the wording to a friend: "We recognized and acknowledged our internally colonized status as the children of Native and African peoples ('the first and forced Americans,' as a friend once put it)" (Moraga, "From inside the First World, Foreword 2001," xvi).

19. My thoughts on historical associations of Indians with land and Africans with labor have been influenced by conversations with Catherine Griffin. See Griffin, "'Joined Together in History.'"

20. Ibid.

21. Jefferson, *Notes on the State of Virginia*, 145. Though Jefferson was against black-white intermarriage, he supported Indian-white intermarriage. In an address to Delaware and Mohican Indians he clearly expressed this support: "You will unite yourselves with us, join in our great councils and form one people with us, and we shall all be Americans; you will mix with us by intermarriage, your blood will be in our veins, and will spread with us over this great island" (quoted in Padover, *The Complete Jefferson*, 503).

22. Jefferson, *Notes on the State of Virginia*, 147.

23. Tocqueville, *Democracy in America*, 332, 334–35.

24. Jennifer Pitts, introduction to *Writings on Empire and Slavery*, xv.

25. Stoler, "Tense and Tender Ties," 850, 863.

26. Ibid., 27.

27. Tocqueville, *Democracy in America*, 347, 342–43. Harvey Mitchell discusses Tocqueville's belief in the Native Americans' inevitable demise in Mitchell, *America after Tocqueville*, 80, 101.

28. I have derived my formulation of the "Negro problem" and the "Indian plight" from the work of W. E. B. Du Bois and Vine Deloria Jr.; see Du Bois, *The Souls of Black Folk*; and Deloria, *Custer Died for Your Sins*, 1.

29. May, "Tocqueville and the Enlightenment Legacy," 31.

30. The rhetorical segregation of Africans from Indians in Jefferson's and Tocqueville's work did not reflect the reality of New World configurations in which indigenous Americans, along with Africans, were enslaved in the first centuries of American colonization, and in which African lands, as well as Indian lands, were usurped and plundered for their natural resources. Nor does this rhetorical segregation reflect the findings of contemporary ethnohistorians who have documented integral cultural, social, and political relations between blacks and Indians in the Americas. These scholars include, among others, Littlefield (*Africans and Seminoles*); Perdue (*Slavery and the Evolution of Cherokee Society, 1540–1866*); Wright (*The Only Land They Knew*); Merrell ("The Racial Education of the Catawba Indians"); Forbes (*Africans and Native Americans*); and Brooks (*Confounding the Color Line*).

31. See Grinde and Johansen, *Exemplar of Liberty*. For more on the Noble Savage see Berkhofer, *The White Man's Indian*.

32. Grinde and Johansen, *Exemplar of Liberty*, 63. As Gary Nash, Karen Kupperman, and others have shown, English colonists' views of Indians varied, changing over time and differing between those who lived near native people and those who lived at a distance. In his classic article Nash traces three images of Indians that developed between the sixteenth and eighteenth centuries: the "guileless primitive of certain sixteenth-century writers," the "savage beast of colonial frontiersmen," and the " 'noble savage of eighteenth-century social critics' " (Nash, "The Image of the Indian in the Southern Colonial Mind," 197). Kupperman argues, in contrast, that English colonial gentry of the late sixteenth century and the early seventeenth did not view Indians as especially or irrevocably savage but rather saw Indians in similar terms as they did English commoners; see Kupperman, *Settling with the Indians*. For an analysis of European views of native women in America and Africa see Morgan, " 'Some Could Suckle over Their Shoulder.' "

33. Grinde and Johansen discuss in detail ways that the Iroquois Confederacy of the Northeast inspired and influenced American political thought and organization; see Grinde and Johansen, *Exemplar of Liberty*, 19–35, 141–68. However, other scholars have questioned the soundness of this claim; see, e.g., Richter, *Facing East from Indian Country*, 8, 259. For a gendered analysis of the influence of Six Nations social and political organization on American political life see Landsman, "The 'Other' as Political Symbol."

34. Deloria, *Playing Indian*, 5.

35. Green, "The Tribe Called Wannabee," 31.

36. Slotkin, *Regeneration through Violence*, 21.

37. Jefferson, *Notes on the State of Virginia*, 150, 63, 64, 66.

38. Jennifer Pitts has pointed out that Tocqueville had the luxury of observing rather than legislating in the United States, which shaped his reflections in *Democracy in America*. His attitude toward the native people in the French colony of Algiers was far less generous. See Pitts, introduction to *Writings on Empire and Slavery*, xxxi.

39. Tocqueville, *Democracy in America*, 349.

40. Ibid., 335–36.

41. Ibid., 331; see Stoler, "Tense and Tender Ties," 829, 832. For more on the intersection of race, power, and intimate relations in eighteenth- and nineteenth-century America see Bynum, *Unruly Women*; Brown, *Good Wives, Nasty Wenches, and Anxious Patriarchs*; Hodes, *White Women, Black Men*; and Pascoe, "Race, Gender, and the Privileges of Property."

42. Janara, *Democracy Growing Up*, 5, 18, 52.

43. For more on the Indian queen and Indian princess figures see Fleming, "Symbols of the United States"; Green, "The Pocahontas Perplex." I am borrowing the term "origin story" from Philip Deloria, who uses it to describe the Boston Tea Party; see Deloria, *Playing Indian*, 2.

44. For more on the meaning of woods and wilderness see Merrell, *Into the American Woods*, 19–41; Lepore, *The Name of War*, 71–96.

45. Tocqueville, *Democracy in America*, 336.

46. Deloria, *Custer Died for Your Sins*, 8. Deloria's observation echoes a similar notion of Tocqueville's—that "we should almost say that the European is to the other races of mankind what man himself is to the lower animals: he makes them subservient to his use, and when he cannot subdue he destroys them" (Tocqueville, *Democracy in America*, 332).

47. As is often the case with racial definitions, the relationship of blacks and American Indians within a hierarchical racial scale has sometimes been inverted. A primary example is the Indian Program at Hampton Institute, in which African American students were viewed as appropriate role models for Native American students because of their higher level of civilization attained through the experience of enslavement. For more on race relations at Hampton see Lindsey, *Indians at Hampton Institute, 1877–1923*; and Lovett, "'African and Cherokee by Choice.'"

48. William Aldridge, preface to "A Narrative of the Lord's Wonderful Dealings," 75–76.

49. Marrant, "A Narrative of the Lord's Wonderful Dealings with John Marrant," 77. Parenthetical page citations in the following four paragraphs of the text proper refer to this narrative.

50. For more on English views of Indians as expressed through the captivity narrative see Nelson, *The Word in Black and White*.

51. Fitzpatrick, "The Figure of Captivity," 1–2.

52. See Kolodny, *The Land before Her*, 20.

53. Sekora, "Red, White, and Black," 95.

54. For more on this conflict between the Wampanoag leader, Metacom, his native allies, and the English colonists see Lepore's *The Name of War*. Lepore argues that the label "King Philip's War" is a misnomer, suggesting instead that this war for Indian land should be called a "Puritan Conquest" (Lepore, *The Name of War*, xv).

55. Zafar, "Capturing the Captivity," 21.

56. Montgomery, "Recapturing John Marrant," 108.

57. Rowlandson, "The Soveraignty and Goodness of God," 90.

58. Marrant, "A Narrative of the Lord's Wonderful Dealings with John Marrant," 77.

59. For detailed comparative analyses of Rowlandson and Marrant see Montgomery, "Recapturing John Marrant"; and Zafar, "Capturing the Captivity."

60. Zafar, *We Wear the Mask*, 42.

61. Ibid., 59.

62. See Hartman, *Scenes of Subjection*.

63. Merrell, *Into the American Woods*, 20–25.

64. Slotkin, *Regeneration through Violence*, 102.

65. Ibid., 247.

66. I am grateful to Vicente Diaz, who asked pointed questions about the role of the woods, and to Alexandra Stern, who described the woods as a "portal" or "threshold." Both aided me in attempts to understand the relationship between John Marrant and the Cherokee wilderness. Vicente Diaz and Alexandra Stern, conversations among *Haunted by Empire* contributors, Ann Arbor, Mich., Feb. 28, May 20, 2003.

67. Marrant, "A Narrative of the Lord's Wonderful Dealings with John Marrant," 86.

68. Green, "The Pocahontas Perplex," 702.

69. Tilton, *Pocahontas*.

70. Green, "The Pocahontas Perplex," 704, 700. Clara Sue Kidwell offers an alternative explanation for Pocahontas's apparent "rescue" of John Smith. Reinterpreting this moment from the perspective of southeastern native peoples, Kidwell suggests that Pocahontas was performing a valued duty endemic to her community's rituals for adopting war captives or strangers into the tribe. See Kidwell, "What Would Pocahontas Think Now?" For a review of the historical debate about whether Pocahontas was in fact participating in an adoption ritual see Tilton, *Pocahontas*, 6. For more on the role of southeastern indigenous women and the adoption of outsiders see Perdue, *Cherokee Women*, 38–39.

71. For more on the Indian woman as symbolic of American land see Kolodny, *The Lay of the Land*; Sparks, "The Land Incarnate." The association of the native female with the action of "possessing the charms inherent in the virgin continent" was especially apparent during the American Revolutionary War, when the Indian princess repeatedly appeared in anti-British propaganda as the symbol of an independent and promising America. See Kolodny, *The Lay of the Land*, 4; Fleming, "Symbols of the United States," 3.

72. Marrant, "A Narrative of the Lord's Wonderful Dealings with John Marrant," 86.

73. Ibid.

74. Gates, *The Signifying Monkey*, 145.

75. Axtell, *The Invasion Within*, 102–3.

76. Ibid., 102.

77. Ibid; Axtell, "The Power of Print in the Eastern Woodlands."

78. Gates discusses the trope of the talking book in chapter 4 of *The Signifying Monkey*, 127–69.

79. It is interesting and perhaps suggestive of the need for further research that the trope of the talking book seems to be repeated only by African American men; Gates does not give examples of African American women writers who employ it.

80. Gates, *The Signifying Monkey*, 132.

81. Ibid., 143.

82. Ibid., 145.

83. Ibid., 150.

84. Marrant, "A Narrative of the Lord's Wonderful Dealings with John Marrant," 88.

85. Ibid., 87.

86. Slotkin, *Regeneration through Violence*, 21, 23.

87. Montgomery, "Recapturing John Marrant," 109. For more on the meaning of dress in the cross-cultural contact experience see Little, "'Shoot That Rogue, for He Hath an Englishman's Coat On!'"

88. Marrant, "A Narrative of the Lord's Wonderful Dealings with John Marrant," 88.

89. Jefferson, *Notes on the State of Virginia*, 147.

90. Nash, "The Image of the Indian in the Southern Colonial Mind," 202.

PROXIMITIES
OF
POWER

LISA LOWE

The Intimacies of Four Continents

My investigation begins in 1807, and extends to the surrounding years, in order to examine particular connections between Europe, Africa, Asia, and the Americas just after the Haitian Revolution, when the British abolished the slave trade and introduced Chinese indentured laborers into their West Indian colonies in the Caribbean. C. L. R. James observed in *The Black Jacobins* that the eighteenth-century slave society in San Domingo connected Europe, Africa, and the Americas: the fortunes created by the slavery-based societies in the Americas gave rise to the French bourgeoisie, producing the conditions for the "rights of man" demanded in the Revolution of 1789.[1] In *Cuban Counterpoint* Fernando Ortiz observed that "peoples from all four quarters of the globe" labored in the "new world" to produce tobacco and sugar for European consumption. Ortiz commented, "Sugar was mulatto from the start."[2] These understandings that the "new world" of Africans, natives, and Asians in the Americas was intimately related to the rise of European modernity are an inspiration for my investigation. Yet I begin with the premise that we actually know little about the "intimacies of four continents," despite available knowledge, however uneven, about their various constituent elements.

Historians, philosophers, and sociologists have written extensively about the origins of modern Europe, whether they focus on the French Revolution as a key event in the shift from feudal aristocracies to democratic nation-states or emphasize the gradual displacement of religious explanation by secular scientific rationalism, the shift from mercantilism to industrial capitalism, the growth of modern bureaucracy, or liberal citizenship within the modern state. There is also a distinguished historiography of the Atlantic slave trade and slave economies throughout the Americas.[3] There is work on indentured labor systems utilizing Europeans and Africans but sparser attention to the role of Chinese and Indian migrations to the early Americas, fewer that document the complex history and survival of native peoples in the Caribbean, and even fewer that examine the connections, relations, and mixings of Asian, African, and native peoples in the Americas.[4] I begin within this modern puzzle of the New World by observing the particular obscurity of the *figure* of the transatlantic Chinese "coolie," who first appears with some regularity in British colonial papers in 1803 in a plan to recruit the Chinese as contract laborers to work in Trinidad in the British West Indies. Yet because the Chinese are relatively absent in the historiography of the early Americas, and they seem to matter little in eighteenth-century and nineteenth-century liberal political philosophies, I query the particular loss of this Chinese figure, not in an effort to recuperate the loss but as an occasion to inquire generally into the politics of knowledge about "New World modernity." That is, I am interested in asking not simply about what we know and do not know of the links and interdependencies between Europe, Africa, Asia, and the Americas but also what the circumstances and conventions were for producing these distinctly shaped comparative knowledges. I argue that the particular obscurity of the transatlantic Chinese in these relations permits an entry into a range of connections, the global *intimacies* out of which emerged not only modern humanism but a modern racialized division of labor. By "modern humanism" I mean the secular European tradition of liberal philosophy that narrates political emancipation through citizenship in the state, that declares economic freedom in the development of wage labor and an exchange market, and that confers civilization to the human person educated in aesthetic and national culture, in each case unifying particularity, difference, or locality through universal concepts of reason and community. In my readings of the colonial archive, political philosophy, and historiography I observe that ideas of race, gender, and family reproduction were central to this humanism, as well as to the modern constructions of freedom, civility, and justice that are its consequences. Yet these definitions made universal the politics, culture, and society of republican Europe and North America, and they omitted the global relationships that comprised the very conditions for humanism, despite the displacement of these conditions by its political philosophy.

While *intimacy* is usually taken to mean romantic or sexual relations, familiarity, or domesticity, I employ the term against the grain to elaborate three meanings, which I place in relation to one another within the emergence of modern liberal humanism. First, I mean *intimacy* as spatial proximity or adjacent connection, and with "the intimacies of four continents" I hope to evoke the political economic logics through which men and women from Africa and Asia were forcibly transported to the Americas, who with native, mixed, and creole peoples constituted slave societies, the profits of which gave rise to bourgeois republican states in Europe and North America.[5] Reading British Colonial Office papers composed from 1803 to 1807 and from the peak years of Chinese emigration, 1852 to 1866, in tandem with antislavery and proslavery debates among British parliamentarians and West Indian planters—the "intimacies of four continents" emerge as a way to discuss a world division of labor emerging in the nineteenth century.[6] Colonial labor relations on the plantations in the Americas were the conditions of possibility for European philosophy to think the universality of human freedom, however much freedom for colonized peoples was precisely foreclosed within that philosophy.[7]

In 1807, as Britain abolished the African slave trade in its empire, the first Chinese were sent to Trinidad as a new labor force for the plantations. In a "Secret Memorandum from the British Colonial Office to the Chairman of the Court of Directors of the East India Company," written in 1803, just following the Haitian Revolution, a colonial administrator laid the groundwork for the introduction of Chinese indentured laborers into the British West Indies:

> The events which have recently happened at St. Domingo necessarily awaken all those apprehensions which the establishment of a Negro government in that land gave rise to some years ago, and render it indispensable that every practicable measure of precaution should be adopted to guard the British possessions in the West Indies as well against . . . the danger of a spirit of insurrection being excited amongst the Negroes in our colonies.
>
> . . . No measure would so effectually tend to provide a security against this danger, as that of introducing a free race of cultivators into our islands, who, from habits and feelings could be kept distinct from the Negroes, and who from interest would be inseparably attached to the European proprietors. . . . The Chinese people . . . unite the qualities which constitute this double recommendation.[8]

After two centuries of African slavery this British plan to import Chinese coolies marked a significant, yet largely ignored, shift in the management of race and labor in the colonies. The decision to experiment with a different form of labor was explicitly racialized—"a free race . . . who could be kept distinct from the Negroes"—but moreover it framed the importation of this newly "raced" Chinese labor as a solution both to Britain's need to suppress black slave rebellion and its desire to expand production. The context for the British desire to innovate sugar production in the West Indian colonies was the international or "transcolonial" rivalries with the French West Indies, the primary producer of sugar for the world market before the Haitian Revolution, and Spanish Cuba and Puerto Rico, who were quickly becoming more competitive since revolts there.[9] In this sense, while some historians explain the end of slavery in the Americas throughout the nineteenth century as a response to liberal abolitionists, many more now view the British decision to end the slave trade in 1807, and slavery in its empire in 1834, as pragmatic attempts to stave off potential black revolution, on the one hand, and to resolve difficulties in the sugar economy resulting from the relative "rigidity" of slave labor within colonial mercantilism, on the other.[10] The "Trinidad experiment" imagined the Chinese as a "racial barrier between [the British] and the Negroes," the addition of which would produce a new division of labor in which the black slaves would continue to perform fieldwork, and a "free race" of Chinese could grind, refine, and crystallize the cane. The British described the Chinese workers as "free," yet the men would be shipped on the same vessels that had brought the slaves they were designed to replace; some would fall to disease, die, suffer abuse, and mutiny; those who survived the three-month voyage would encounter coercive, confined conditions on arrival. In this sense the British political discourse announcing a decision to move from "primitive slavery" to "free labor" may have been a modern utilitarian move, in which abolition proved an expedient, and only coincidentally "enlightened," solution.[11] The representations of indentured labor as "freely" contracted buttressed liberal promises of freedom for former slaves, while enabling planters to derive benefits from the so-called transition from slavery to free labor that, in effect, included a range of intermediate forms of coercive labor—from rented slaves, sharecroppers, and convicts to day laborers, debt peonage, workers paid by task, and indentureship.[12] The Chinese were used instrumentally in this political discourse as a collective *figure*, a fantasy of "free" yet racialized and indentured labor, at a time when the possession of body, work, life, and death was foreclosed to the enslaved and the indentured alike. In other words, in 1807 the category of "freedom" was central to the development of what we could call, after Foucault, a modern racial governmentality in which a political hierarchy ranging from "free" to "unfree" was deployed in the management of the diverse labors of colonized peoples. In 1807, as Britain moved from mercantilist plantation production toward an expanded international trade in diversified manufactured goods, the Chinese coolie appears in colonial and parliamentary papers as a *figure* for this world division of labor, a new racial mode of managing and dividing laboring groups through the liberal promise of *freedom* that would commence with the end of slavery.

The second meaning of *intimacy* I examine is the more common one of privacy, often figured as conjugal and familial relations in the bourgeois home, distinguished from the public realm of work, society, and politics.[13] The Chinese emigrant to the Americas occupied a place, also, in the colonial discourses constituting bourgeois intimacy. While this distinction between private and public spheres emerged as a nineteenth-century ideal characterizing British, European, and northeastern American societies, the separation of the feminine home and the masculine world of work has been criticized by some feminist scholars as a liberal abstraction for ordering relations in civil society that is contradicted by the social realities of laboring women.[14] The paradigm of separate spheres, moreover, cannot be easily extended to colonial or slave societies, where the practice of private and public spheres was unevenly imposed: colonial households and districts may have aspired to such divisions in manners reminiscent of the European metropolis, but native-descendant peoples, African slaves, and indentured Chinese could be said to be at once differentiated from yet subordinated to regulating notions of privacy and publicity. Furthermore, in the colonial context sexual relations were not limited to a "private" sphere but included practices that disrespected such separations, ranging from rape, assault, domestic servitude, or concubinage to "consensual relations" between colonizers and colonized, what Ann Laura Stoler has termed the "intimacies of empire."[15] We must critically historicize this second meaning of intimacy, of sexual and affective intimacy within the private sphere, insofar as *bourgeois intimacy* was precisely a biopolitics through which the colonial powers administered the enslaved and colonized and sought to indoctrinate the newly freed into forms of Christian marriage and family. The colonial management of sexuality, affect, marriage, and family among the colonized formed a central part of the microphysics of colonial rule.[16] Bourgeois intimacy, as an effect of the private and public split that was the sociospatial medium for both metropolitan and colonial hegemony, was produced by the "intimacies of four continents" —

in the sense that the political economy of slave and indentured labor in the colonies founded the formative wealth of the European bourgeoisie *and* in the sense that the labor of enslaved and indentured domestic workers furnished the material comforts of the bourgeois home.

The British colonial archive is not a static, comprehensive collection of given facts or a source of recorded history. Following Foucault and Said, we must consider the archive as a site of knowledge production, "reading" it as a technology for administering and knowing the colonized population that both attests to its own contradictions and yields its own critique.[17] As Ann Stoler argues, the colonial archive became "a supreme technology of the . . . imperial state, a repository of codified beliefs that clustered (and bore witness to) connections between secrecy, the law, and power."[18] Reading British documents on the design of introducing Chinese women among the Chinese contract laborers in the West Indies, I have become especially interested in the *figure* of the Chinese woman, who recurs throughout the papers as a trope for the colonial imagination of the Chinese capacity to develop bourgeois intimacy. From the inception of the plan to introduce Chinese into Trinidad, and continuing throughout the nineteenth century, administrators state their desire to import Chinese women, but all documents indicate that Chinese female emigration was actually quite rare. Attorney-General Archibald Gloster wrote:

> I think it one of the best schemes possible; and if followed up with larger importation, and with women, that it will give this colony a strength far beyond what other colonies possess. *It will be a barrier between us and the Negroes* with whom they do not associate; & consequently to whom they will always offer formidable opposition. The substituting of their labour instead of Negro labour is out of the question, as to the common business of the plantation. They are not habituated to it, nor will they take to it in the same way, nor can we force them by the same methods; but their industrious habits, and constitutional strength, will I think greatly aid the planters. They will cut and weed cane. They will attend about our mills. They will act as mechanics.[19]

The introduction of the Chinese into the slave plantation economy was thus described in terms of a need for a nominally "free" labor force, one that would not "substitute" for the slaves but would perform different labors and would be distinguished racially and socially from both the white colonial planters and the black slaves. Gloster imagined the community of Chinese workers as an adjacent group that would form a "racial barrier between us and the Negroes." The British introduced the Chinese into the community of white colonials and black slaves as a contiguous "other" whose liminality permitted them to be, at one moment, incorporated as part of colonial labor and, at another, elided or excluded by its humanist universals. Neither free European nor the white European's "other" (the black slave), neither lord nor bonded, the Chinese were represented as a paradoxical figure, at once both an addition that would stabilize the colonial order and the supplement whose addition might likewise threaten the attainment of any such stability.[20] The Chinese woman figured as a colonial fantasy of the Chinese capacity for bourgeois family and "freedom."

That Gloster goes on in the same document to liken the Chinese to "our Peons, or native Indians . . . Mulattoes or Mestees" really indicates no similarity between the Chinese laborer and the mixed, part-native, or native descendant peoples with whom he may have worked. Rather, I understand this colonial association of the Chinese with various racially mixed figures as a moment in the history of modern humanism and racism in which the fixing of a hierarchy of racial classifications gradually emerged to manage and modernize labor, reproduction, and society among the colonized and to rationalize the conditions of creolized mixing and the range of potential "intimacies" among them.[21] With respect to the long history of black African and Native American interethnic contacts from the fifteenth century onward, Jack Forbes has argued that native, as well as part-African and part-native persons, were mostly misclassified with terms ranging from *loro*, *mestizo*, *gens de couleur*, or *mulatto* to *dark* or *brown*, to even *negro*, *noir*, or *black*. The late-eighteenth-century topographer of St. Domingue, Moreau de Saint-Mérys, presented eleven racial categories of 110 combinations ranked from absolute white (128 parts white blood) to absolute black (128 parts black).[22] We can explain the dramatic, encyclopedic proliferation of both racial classification and racial misattribution of this period if we observe that the racial governmentality continually innovated new terms for managing population and social spaces in the Americas.[23] The colonial relations of production, which required racial mixing, constituted what Fredric Jameson would call the "political unconscious" of modern European taxonomies of race; the relations of production were the absent yet necessary context that founded the possibility for racial classification yet the context with which such ordering was in contradiction.[24] Joan Dayan writes of Haiti: "If racial mixing threatened to contaminate, the masters had to conjure purity out of phantasmal impurity. This sanitizing ritual engendered remarkable racial fictions."[25]

The West Indian Governors' offices stated that needs of the plantation demanded male workers, but even in the early correspondence we see the Colonial Office rationalizing the idea of creating Chinese families through the desire for a stable racial "barrier" between the colonial whites and the enslaved blacks. Yet the idea of Chinese reproduction, which persists in the colonial correspondence and parliamentary debates throughout the peak years of emigration in the 1850s and 1860s, was a curious fantasy, contradicted by the fact that the Chinese in the Caribbean and North Americas did not establish family communities in significant numbers until the twentieth century.[26] The persistent mention of Chinese families suggests that for some colonial administrators, the "value" of the Chinese may not have been exclusively their labor but also the instrumental use of the *figure* of Chinese sexuality as resembling the "civility" of European marriage and family, in an implicit contrast to the sexualized representations of "the peculiar nature" of African and African-descendant mulatto peoples.[27] In the 1803–7 discussions before the British decision to end slavery this fantasy of Chinese family civility was a way of marking a *racial* difference between "Chinese free labor" and "Negro slaves," through imagining the Chinese as closer to liberal ideas of human person and society. Later, in the 1850s and 1860s, following the end of slavery in the British West Indies in 1834, by which time there were significant numbers of working "free" people of color and South Asian Indian laborers, this phantasm continued to figure as a part of a racialized classification of laboring cultures. In 1851 the agent in charge of Chinese emigration, James T. White, fantasized a *class* hierarchy among the groups of the "Chinese," "Bengalees," and "Negroes" based on the races' ostensive physical traits and capacities for forming families, stating the social potential of the Chinese to form "middle-class" families through Christian marriage and reproduction.[28] This required representations of "Chinese culture" that defined it as one whose traditions could be summarized by the protection of chaste virtuous women who would stabilize the laboring community; ironically, Chinese women could only be imagined as virtuous to the extent that "Chinese culture" would not permit them to migrate. As a figure that promised social order, the Chinese woman was a *supplement* who appeared to complete the prospective future society of the colony; yet her absence, around which desire was reiterated, marked the limit of a social field whose coherence and closure depended on ideas of racial purity and distinction. In contrast, while later nineteenth-century British colonialist and Indian nationalist discourses idealized middle-class upper-caste women in India, the *bhadramahila*, as "pure" and "chaste" symbols of the nation, both discourses represented migrant lower-caste Indian women in the indentured communities in the West Indies as licentious and immoral, precisely *because* they migrated.[29] The colonial archive reveals the altogether fantastic structure of racial imaginations based on ideas about Asian female sexualities. Throughout the nineteenth century the racialized sexual differentiation of Africans, East and South Asians, and native people emerged as a normative taxonomy that managed and spatially distanced these groups from the spheres within which "freedom" was established for European subjects.

For European subjects in the nineteenth century, this notion of *intimacy* in the private sphere became a defining property of the modern individual in civil society, and ideas of privacy in bourgeois domesticity were constituted as the individual's "possession" to be politically protected, as in "the right to privacy." We can trace this narrative of the modern individual, or Western man, who possesses interiority of person, as well as a private household, in the liberal political philosophical tradition from Rousseau, Kant, and Hegel through to its critique in Marx and Engels. Hegel's *Philosophy of Right* is arguably distinct in this tradition, however, for its impressive narrative synthesis that has defined the central forms of modern personhood, property, family, civil society, and state. Hegel's text pivots on the dialectical overcoming of "slavery" by modern human "freedom" to be resolved in the unity of human particularity with the universality of the state. Yet this "overcoming" depended on a concept of slavery that located its practice in the "Old World" of ancient Greece and Rome rather than in the "New World" of the Americas. Hegel employed freedom and slavery as primary metaphors in the dialectic of human self-realization elaborated in his *Phenomenology* and in the *Philosophy of Right*, but he significantly foreclosed mention of the slave revolts in Haiti going on at the time of the writing and publication of these works.[30] Michel-Rolph Trouillot has argued that the Haitian Revolution entered history with the peculiarity of being "unthinkable" even as it happened and then was forcibly forgotten within over a century of historiography.[31] The important Hegelian dialectic that established intimacy as a property of the individual man within his family in civil society enacted a series of influential displacements that rendered unavailable not only slavery per se but the relations I wish to signify with the concept of the "intimacies of four continents." Hegel's dialectic obscured Europe's dependency on the new world in a narrative of European autonomy and disavowed native, Asian migrant, and African work, resistance, and contribution to the emergence of European modernity.

In *Philosophy of Right* Hegel traced the dialectical development of the individual's self-consciousness through the political forms of property, family, civil society, and the state. We can think of Hegel's dialectic as a series of phases in which each subsequent phase emerges as a more explicit or more inclusive whole of which the former phase can be seen in retrospect as one moment. In this process of supersession, or sublation, what Hegel called *Aufhebung*, the initial contradiction is suppressed and reformulated in new terms, involving a preservation of its original terms in either a deferral or elevation of the contradiction to a higher level.[32] This movement encompasses Hegel's idea of negation comprehending difference, assimilating and overcoming opposition or relation. This dialectic is essential to understanding and to human being. Negation always takes place and operates within a unity; we conceive of nothing and have nothing without this totalizing unity. For Hegel this movement takes place both on the level of the individual person and through the movement toward self-consciousness, as well as through the evolution of the person and community in the ethical and political forms of family, civil society, and state. Property in oneself and in the objects one makes through will, labor, and contract — all are levels in Hegel's dialectical development that resolve in the unity of the particular will of the individual with the collective universality of the whole, or the state.

"Property" is the way that Hegel explained the individual initially investing will and work into nature, making that nature objective, transforming world and himself. Through property the condition of possibility of human self-possession — of one's body, interiority, and life direction — is established. Indeed, Hegel argued that property is an essential condition for the possibility of moral action because without property, without a locus of independence of the individual will, the person cannot be independent, thoughtful, or self-conscious; without property he will be dominated by others, by needs, and by nature. Thus, the individual's possession of his own person, his own interiority, is a first sense of *property*. The ethical contract of marriage and the development of the family are more complex social manifestations of "property" within Hegel's vision of the development of freedom. The individual man establishes his relation to "family" through marriage to a woman whose proper place is the "inner" world of the family, the family constituting the key intermediary institution between civil society and the state. Interiority of person and of the domestic sphere of the family are thus stages in Hegel's description of the progressive unfolding of the ethical life.

In this sense Hegel defined *freedom* as a condition achieved through a developmental process in which the individual first possessed him- or herself, his or her own interiority, then put his will in an object through labor, and then made a contract to exchange the thing. Marriage and the family were primary and necessary sites of this investment of will in civil institutions; the "intimacy" within the family was the property of the individual becoming "free." Property, marriage, and family were essential conditions for the possibility of moral action and the means through which the individual will was brought consciously into identity with the universal will, expressing the realization of true "freedom" rather than mere duty or servitude.

In 1834 Britain initiated the four-year period of "apprenticeship" in the West Indies that was to grant full "emancipation" to slaves in 1838. This "emancipation" was to promise slaves this set of institutions constituting "freedom": "emancipation" proposed a narrative development in which wage labor, contract, marriage, and family would be the formal institutions through which modern freedom could be attained and the condition of slavery overcome. Yet emancipation clearly did not establish freedom for black peoples in the British West Indies, many of whom were still confined to the plantation and others who left bound in economic servitude and poverty. Indeed, as Thomas Holt has argued, the socialization of former slaves into liberal promises of freedom in Jamaica was part of the gradual disciplining of blacks into wage work, which Marx would call "another form of slavery." Saidiya Hartman has argued that "emancipation" effectively inserted former slaves into an economy of social indebtedness. Catherine Hall has observed that the disciplining of former slaves in Jamaica likewise included their "civilization" into English bourgeois notions of gender, morality, and family, as well as inculcating in the newly freed the judgment that they were essentially "savage" and unable to adapt to the requirements of civilization. The British inserted the Chinese as so-called free laborers at the critical time of slave emancipation, calculating that they would occupy an intermediary position within this governmentality in which the colonized became human through development of economic and political freedom. In other words, the liberal promise that former slaves, natives, and migrant workers could enter voluntarily into contract was a dominant mode for the initiation of the "unfree" into consensual social relations between "free" human persons: in the crucible of American modernity, Amy Dru Stanley has observed, the contracts of labor and marriage became the very symbols of humanity and freedom.[33]

To appreciate the particular "plasticity" of the figure of the Chinese within liberal capitalist modernity, we need only realize that toward the end of the nineteenth century, U.S. discourses about the Chinese laborer contradicted the British discourse that portrayed the Chinese contract laborers as "free."[34] In the United States those arguing for the prohibition of Chinese female immigration in the Page Law of 1875, and the end to all further Chinese immigration in the Chinese Exclusion Act of 1882, emphasized that Chinese laborers recruited to work in mining, agriculture, and railroad construction in the mid-nineteenth century were "unfree" and therefore ineligible for citizenship.[35] Historian Moon-Ho Jung observes, of the nineteenth-century U.S. debates, that the Chinese "coolie" was opportunistically constructed as a transitional figure, midway between slavery and free labor, used both to define and to obscure the boundary between enslavement and freedom. The Chinese contract laborer occupied a liminal, ambiguous intermediary position throughout the nineteenth century, brought to the Americas to supplement, replace, and obfuscate the labor previously performed by slaves yet to be differentially distinguished from them. In the British discourse the Chinese laborer was a "harbinger of freedom," yet in the United States the Chinese was a "relic of slavery."[36] In Cuba, where the Chinese were indispensable to the modernization of the sugar industry, "coolies" were presented as a new source of tractable workers, a viable supplement to slave labor.[37] Whether in the British West Indies, where slavery was legally terminated in 1834; in the United States, where the Civil War ended slavery in 1865; or in Spanish Cuba, where slavery was not abolished until later in the 1880s, African, Asian, and mixed native workers labored and struggled together in the early Americas.

Finally, there is a third meaning of *intimacies* in the constellation to be elaborated. This is the sense of intimacies embodied in the variety of contacts among slaves, indentured persons, and mixed-blood free peoples living together on the islands that resulted in "the collision of European, African, and Asian components within the [Caribbean] Plantation, that could give rise to rebellions against the plantation structure itself."[38] The British colonial archive on Chinese emigration to the West Indies, includes a rich assortment of documents: letters from the West Indian governor's offices requesting specific numbers of laborers per year; documents describing measurements of ships, the water supply, the nature of provisions aboard; immigration agents' records of lengths of voyages, mortality and survival rates of the human cargo; ships' logs of abuses, mutinies, disease, and opium use. There are copies of the public notices posted in the Chinese ports to recruit workers with promises of freedom and copies of the contracts for five years of indenture at two to three dollars per month. As stated earlier, I approach the colonial archive not as a source for knowledge retrieval but as a site of knowledge production; in this sense one notes the explicit descriptions and enumerations but also the rhetorical peculiarities of the documents, the places where particular figures, tropes, or circumlocutions are repeated to cover gaps or tensions; these rhetorical ellipses point to illogic in the archive, as well. So although this third sense of *intimacies*—the volatile contacts of colonized peoples—is never explicitly named in the documents, it is, paradoxically, everywhere implicit in the archive in the presence of such ellipses. "Intimacies" between contracted emigrants and slaves and slave-descendant peoples are repeatedly referenced by negative means, in cautionary rhetorics and statements of prohibition with respect to possible contacts between the slaves and the indentured, all implying the fear and anxiety of racial proximity in a context of mixture and unstable boundaries. For example, White's 1851 letter to the governor of British Guiana warned, "The Chinese are essentially a social and a gregarious people and must be located in masses together, not scattered throughout the colony. They must be kept in the first instance distant and separate from the Negroes, *not only at their work, but also in their dwellings.*"[39] The repeated injunctions that different groups must be divided and boundaries kept distinct indicate that colonial administrators imagined as dangerous the sexual, laboring, and intellectual contacts among slaves and indentured nonwhite peoples. The racial classifications in the archive arose, thus, in this context of the colonial need to prevent these unspoken intimacies among the colonized. This other valence of intimacies, then, can be said to be the obverse of the intimacy of bourgeois domesticity. These intimacies are the range of laboring contacts that are necessary for the production of bourgeois domesticity; they are also the intimacies of captured workers existing together, the proximity and affinity that gave rise to political, sexual, intellectual connections, including subaltern revolts and uprisings: organizations and rebellions that included the Haitian Revolution, the Louisiana cane workers strike of 1887, or the cross-racial alliances that underlay the Cuban struggles for independence from 1895 to 1898.[40] This third sense of intimacies as cross-racial alliance is suggested in the work of James and Ortiz, who emphasized the connections of slave-based colonial societies in the Americas to the prosperity of Europe. Both Frederick Douglass and W. E. B. Du Bois also linked black slavery with a global system that used Chinese coolie labor. In his history of the colonial division of labor in Guyana that separated blacks and Asians and permitted the postemancipation exploitation of those divisions, Walter Rodney advanced an analysis that suggested that Asian indentured workers could have been part of a working class of color, which would have constituted what he called "a definite historical achievement."[41] Thus, defining *intimacies* as the relations of four continents critically frames the more restricted meaning of *intimacy* as the private property of the European and North American individual.

Interpreting the multivalence of *intimacy*, I have tried to identify the genealogy of the process through which the "intimacies of four continents" was rationalized and sublated by a notion of "intimacy" that defined the liberal individual's freedom. Reading the archive, I have observed that racialized ideas of family reproduction became central to early-nineteenth-century humanism and, reading political philosophy, observed that the racialized distribution of "freedom" was an equal part of this legacy. Modern hierarchies of race appear to have emerged in the contradiction between humanism's aspirations to universality and the needs of modern colonial regimes to manage work, reproduction, and the social organization of the colonized; the intimacies of four continents formed the political unconscious of modern racial classification. However, these intimacies remain almost entirely illegible in the historiography of modern freedom, making the naming and interpretation of this global conjunction a problem of knowledge itself. It has been estimated that between 1451 and 1870, 11,569,000 African slaves were brought to the New World[42] and that after the sixteenth century, out of eighty million native peoples in the Americas, there remained only ten million.[43] Between 1834 and 1918, half a million Asian immigrants made their way to the British West Indies, in the context of possibly another million going to Latin America, North America, Australia, New Zealand, and Southeast Asia.[44] But, while these numbers powerfully convey the roles of working peoples of color in the building of the "New World," I am less concerned with the significance in demographic terms than with the production of knowledge that might link the Asian, African, creolized Americas to the rise of European and North American bourgeoisie societies.

What we know of these links and intimacies has been rendered legible through modern methods of comparative study. Yet Europe is rarely studied in relation to the Caribbean or Latin America, and U.S. history is more often separated from studies of the larger Americas. Work in ethnic studies on comparative U.S. racial formation is still at odds with American history that disconnects the study of slavery from immigration studies of Asians and Latinos or that separates the history of gender, sexuality, and women from these studies of "race." Native Caribbeans have been rendered invisible by both the histories that tell of their extermination in the sixteenth century and the subsequent racial classifications in which their survival is occluded. While anthropological studies have focused on ethnic mixings of Asian and African peoples in the Caribbean, historians are just beginning to explore the braided relations of indenture, slavery, and independence among these groups.[45] Recently, scholars of the black diaspora have undertaken the histories of both forcible and voluntary African dispersion as means for understanding the longer global past of New World modernity. Eric Williams and Cedric Robinson both observed the centrality of black labor to the development of modern global capitalism, which depended on the vast labor of African slaves just as European labor moved from agrarian to factory work.[46] Later studies like Paul Gilroy's *Black Atlantic* illuminate the encounter between Europe and the New World; others bring to light the circuits and connections among Yoróban Africans, Afro-Caribbeans, and African Americans.[47] Yet Robin D. G. Kelley emphasizes that the significance of black diaspora projects to the field of U.S. history may be precisely their capacity to chart *more* than black identities and political movements, what he calls "other streams of internationalism not limited to the black world."[48]

Kelley's call to investigate "other streams" is suggestive with respect to reconstructing a global past in which Asia emerges both within and independently of a European modernity built on African slavery, in which Asian contract labor in the Americas is coterminous with the emancipation of African slaves. Like the intimacies of four continents, Kelley's "other streams of internationalism" require new inquiries that will uncover and interpret evidence of these relations, but they also mean that we must investigate the modalities of "forgetting" these crucial connections. I suspect that Asian indentureship in the early Americas has been "lost" because of its ambiguous status with respect to *freedom* and *enslavement*, polar terms in the dialectic at the center of modern political philosophy. Yet I would not want to discuss this loss as an isolated absenting of Asians in the making of the Americas. Rather, the loss is a sign of the more extensive forgetting of social violence and forms of domination that include but are not limited to indentureship: that reaches back into the slave trade and the extermination of native peoples that founded the conditions of possibility for indentureship; that stretches forward into the ubiquitous migrations of contemporary global capitalism of which Asian contract labor may be a significant early instance. Moreover, the loss of the figure includes the process of the operative forgetting itself, the way the humanist archive naturalizes itself and "forgets" the conditions of its own making.[49] In this sense my purpose in observing the elision of Asian actors in the modern Americas is not to pursue a single, particularist cultural identity, not to "fill in the gap" or "add on" another transoceanic group, but to explain *the politics of our lack of knowledge*. It is to be more specific about what I would term the "economy of affirmation and forgetting" that structures and formalizes humanism. This economy civilizes and develops freedoms for "man" in modern Europe, while relegating others to geographical and temporal spaces that are constituted as uncivilized and unfree. One of its histories is the particular manner in which freedom overcomes enslavement through a dialectic that displaces the migrations from and connections of "four continents" and internalizes it in a national struggle of history and consciousness. The social inequalities of our time are a legacy of this definition of "the human" and subsequent discourses that have placed particular subjects, practices, and geographies at a distance from "the human."

"New World" people of the British, French, Dutch, and Spanish colonized Americas created the conditions for modern humanism, despite the disavowal of these conditions in the liberal political philosophy on which it is largely based. Colonial racial classifications and an international division of labor emerged coterminously as parts of a genealogy that were not exceptional to, but were constitutive of, that humanism. *Freedom* was constituted through a narrative dialectic that rested simultaneously on a spatialization of the *unfree* as exteriority and a temporal subsuming of *enslavement* as internal difference or contradiction. The "overcoming" of internal contradiction resolves in *freedom* within the modern Western political sphere through displacement and elision of the coeval conditions of slavery and indentureship in the Americas. In this sense modern humanism is a formalism that translates the world through an economy of affirmation and forgetting within a regime of desiring freedom. The affirmation of the desire for freedom is so inhabited by the forgetting of its conditions of possibility, that every narrative articulation of freedom is haunted by its burial, by the violence of forgetting. What we know as "race" or "gender" are the *traces* of this modern humanist forgetting. They reside within, and are constitutive of, the modern narrative of freedom but are neither fully determined by nor exhausted by its ends. They are the remainders of the formalism of affirmation and forgetting.

We might pursue observation that liberal humanism is a formalism that translates through affirmation and forgetting in a variety of ways. Some have recovered lost or hidden histories to provide historical narratives for the "people without history," those forgotten in the modern tales of national development, or have challenged existing historiography with new studies of the political economy of British imperialism in nineteenth-century China and India that produced the impoverishment that led to the emigration of Asian laborers. In new ethnographies interpreting the syncretic cultures of Caribbean *créolité*, *mestizaje*, and *métissage*, anthropologists Aisha Khan and Viranjini Munasinghe have found other versions of person and society, beginning and end, life and death, quite different remnants of the earlier affirmation and forgetting.[50] We could study representations of the rise and fall of the plantation complex in the Americas in nineteenth-century Caribbean literature or its recasting in the twentieth century by Alejo Carpentier, Jean Rhys, or Maryse Condé.[51] We could look at how the problem of forgotten intimacies is thematized in recent Caribbean diasporic or postcolonial literature: Patricia Powell's *The Pagoda*, for example, imagines the coexistence of Chinese and Indian immigrants, blacks, whites, and creoles in nineteenth-century Jamaica; Cristina Garcia's *Monkey Hunting* imagines the late-nineteenth-century union of an escaped Chinese indentured laborer and the slave woman he buys and frees, and it follows their Afro-Chinese-Cuban descendants from China to Cuba to the United States and Vietnam. Each offers rich and worthy directions to pursue.

In my discussion, however, I have not moved immediately toward recovery and recuperation but rather have paused to reflect on what it means to supplement forgetting with new narratives of affirmation and presence. There is an ethics and politics in struggling to comprehend the particular *loss* of the intimacies of four continents, to engage slavery, genocide, indenture, and liberalism as a conjunction, as an actively acknowledged loss within the present. David Eng and David Kazanjian describe a "politics of mourning" that would "investigate the political, economic and cultural dimensions of *how* loss is apprehended and history is named—how that apprehension and naming produce the phenomenon of 'what remains.'" Moustafa Bayoumi, reflecting on the manuscript of Sheikh Sana See, an African Muslim slave in nineteenth-century Panama, observes that it "is at once a product of the modernity of slavery as it is a representation of how modernity obliterates that which stands in its way." Stephanie Smallwood, historian of the seventeenth-century Atlantic slave trade, has put it this way: "I do not seek to create—out of the remnants of ledgers and ships' logs, walls and chains—'the way it really was' for the newly arrived slave waiting to be sold. I try to interpret from the slave trader's disinterest in the slave's pain those social conditions within which there was no possible political resolution to that pain. I try to imagine what could have been."[52] The past conditional temporality of the "what could have been" symbolizes aptly the space of a different kind of thinking, a space of productive attention to the scene of loss, a thinking with twofold attention that seeks to encompass at once the positive objects and methods of history and social science and the matters absent, entangled, and unavailable by its methods. I have tried to suggest that understanding the relation of the intimacy of the "possessive individual" to the "intimacies of four continents" requires a past conditional temporality in order to reckon with the coeval violence of affirmation and forgetting, in order to recognize that this particular violence continues to be reproduced in liberal humanist institutions, discourses, and practices. However, in recognizing this reproduction, we do not escape the inhabiting of our present and the irony that many of the lost struggles we would wish to engage are not only carried out in the humanist languages of liberty, equality, reason, progress, and human rights—almost without exception, they must be translated into the political and juridical spaces of this tradition. Present struggles over the life and death of the "human" often only become legible in terms of those spaces authorized by political philosophical humanism.

Our contemporary moment is so replete with assumptions that freedom is made universal through liberal political enfranchisement and the globalization of capitalism that it has become difficult to write or imagine alternative knowledges, to act on behalf of alternative projects or communities. Within this context, it is necessary to act within but to think beyond our received humanist tradition and, all the while, to imagine a much more complicated set of stories about the emergence of the now, in which what is foreclosed as unknowable is forever saturating the "what-can-be-known." We are left with the project of visualizing, mourning, and thinking "other humanities" within the received genealogy of "the human."

Many people have assisted me in the research and writing of this chapter, especially Aisha Khan, Walton Look Lai, Stephanie Smallwood, Moon-Ho Jung, Grace Kyungwon Hong, Chandan Reddy, Roderick Ferguson, Judith Halberstam, David Eng, David Theo Goldberg, Rosemary Marangoly George, Nicole King, Lisa Yoneyama, Takashi Fujitani, John D. Blanco, Yen Le Espiritu, Shelley Streeby, and Nayan Shah. I hope my gratitude to others is understood in my citations of their work. Catherine Hall, Ann Stoler, Amy Kaplan, and Laura Briggs offered indispensable engagements with an early draft for this volume.

1. See James, *The Black Jacobins*.

2. Ortiz, *Cuban Counterpoint*, 58.

3. See Tannenbaum, *Slave and Citizen, the Negro in the Americas*; Elkins, *Slavery*; Patterson, *Sociology of Slavery*; Klein, *Slavery in the Americas*; Curtin, *Atlantic Slave Trade*; Davis, *Slavery and Human Progress*; Eltis, *Economic Growth and the Ending of the Transatlantic Slave Trade*. A new generation of scholars is asking different questions of these earlier studies. See, e.g., Johnson, *Soul by Soul*; Smallwood, *Saltwater Slavery*; Hartman, *Scenes of Subjection*.

4. See Saunders, *Indentured Labour in the British Empire, 1834–1920*; Lai, *Indentured Labor, Caribbean Sugar*; Lai, *Chinese in the West Indies, 1806–1995*; Helly, *The Cuba Commission Report*. For discussions of native peoples in the Caribbean see Forbes, *Black Africans and Native Americans*; Benitez-Rojo, *The Repeating Island*; Mignolo, *Local Histories/Global Designs*. For studies of the Chinese in the Caribbean see Jung, "*Coolies*" *and Cane* (forthcoming); and Yun, "'Coolie': From under the Hatches into the Global Age" (working paper; manuscript in possession of the author).

5. Among the definitions of *intimacy* offered by the *Oxford English Dictionary* are "state of being personally intimate"; "sexual intercourse"; "close familiarity"; "closeness of observation, knowledge, or the like"; "intimate or close connexion"; and "inner or inmost nature; an inward quality or feature."

6. I interpret primary documents from several historical periods: first, correspondence surrounding the introduction of the first Chinese workers into Trinidad in 1807; second, correspondence from 1850 to 1853 (U.K. Public Record Office [hereafter PRO], Colonial Office Correspondence, Colonial Office [hereafter CO] 885, 1/20); third, records from 1860 to 1862 (PRO, CO 111, vol. 327) and from 1861 to 1863 (PRO, CO 111, vol. 334); and fourth, discussions of the Chinese Passenger Act of 1855 (PRO, Foreign Office Correspondence, Foreign Office 97, vol. 101). See also *Great Britain Parliamentary Papers*; Burnley, *Observations on the Present Condition of the Island of Trinidad*. On Chinese indentured labor in the Americas see Lai, *Indentured Labor, Caribbean Sugar*; Helly, *The Cuba Commission Report*. On slave trade and global economy see Williams, *Capitalism and Slavery*; Robinson, *Black Marxism*; Tomich, *Through the Prism of Slavery*; Eltis, *Economic Growth and the Ending of the Transatlantic Slave Trade*.

7. I am not merely observing that philosophers employed freedom and slavery as meta-

phors, while disavowing the slave revolts in the Americas; nor am I only emphasizing that modern philosophy's definition of human freedom excluded women, slaves, and non-Europeans, or simply condemning Hegel's transparent racism toward the "dark races" of Africa, India, and China. Rather, it is my concern to identify dialectical supersession as the key logic that enacts the foreclosure of colonial slavery in the development of European freedom, an argument I develop further in "Race from Universalism," *TRACES* (Durham: Duke University Press, forthcoming).

8. PRO, CO 295, vol. 17.

9. See Tomich, *Slavery in the Circuit of Sugar*; Stinchcombe, *Sugar Island Slavery in the Age of Enlightenment*. Françoise Lionnet elaborates the concept "transcolonial" to stress the multiple spatialities of the colonized Caribbean. See Lionnet, "Narrating the Americas," 69.

10. See Mintz, *Sweetness and Power*; Eltis, *Economic Growth and the Ending of the Trans-atlantic Slave Trade*.

11. See Scott, *Slave Emancipation in Cuba*.

12. See Cooper, Holt, and Scott, *Beyond Slavery*; Holt, *The Problem of Freedom*.

13. See, e.g., Berlant, *Intimacy*.

14. On the history of gendered separate spheres see Wolff, *Feminine Sentences*; on feminist critique of separate spheres see Fraser, "What's Critical about Critical Theory?"; Brown, *States of Injury*. On feminists of color criticism of separate spheres as a concept that disregards racialized women's labor see Glenn, "Racial Ethnic Women's Labor"; Collins, *Black Feminist Thought*. Amy Kaplan's "Manifest Destiny," 23–60, discusses the extension of separate spheres of ideology through imperial projects.

15. Stoler, "Tense and Tender Ties"; see also Stoler, *Carnal Knowledge and Imperial Power*.

16. On the role of Christian marriage as a social form for assimilating ex-slaves into middle-class citizenship see Hall, *Civilizing Subjects*; and Cott, *Public Vows*.

17. Foucault, *The Archaeology of Knowledge*; Said, *Orientalism*.

18. Stoler, "Colonial Archives and the Arts of Governance," 87.

19. PRO, CO 295, vol. 17 (emphasis mine).

20. On the figure of the neighbor and the injunction to "love thy neighbor" see Reinhard, "Freud, My Neighbor."

21. On the historical periodization of scientific racial classification see Goldberg, *The Racial State*; Donna Haraway, *Primate Visions*; Moore et al., *Race, Nature, and the Politics of Difference*.

22. Joan Dayan has commented on Moreau's "radically irrational" racial taxonomy, saying that it was "stranger than any supernatural fiction" (Dayan, *Haiti, History, and the Gods*, 231–32). See also Cohen, *The French Encounter with Africans*.

23. The racial governmentality I trace is a normative taxonomy that defined the terms of civilization for both the colonizer and the colonized. Its classifications managed work and reproduction of the colonized, placing subjects within a discourse of civilization and a

regime of desiring freedom. This governmentality insisted on racial distinction and purity yet admitted an always already creolized and miscegenated population that required classification. The Chinese woman was a figure of impossibility signifying the limits of the taxonomy, a trope for the Chinese capacity for bourgeois domesticity within the context of its historical impossibility, and a sign of colonial desire for an indentured family community that would create a racial barrier between black and white. See Foucault, "Governmentality"; and Foucault, *Society Must Be Defended*." On racial governmentality see Ferguson, *Aberrations in Black*; Hesse, "Writing Racialized Modernity."

24. See Jameson, *The Political Unconscious*. Daniel Sherman employs Jameson's concept to discuss the nineteenth-century French museum; see Sherman, "Quatremère/Benjamin/Marx."

25. Dayan, *Haiti, History, and the Gods*, 190.

26. Representations of "Chinese women" varied remarkably in the contexts of immigration to the West Indies and the western United States. In the British discourses Chinese women appear as passively feminine and antiquated, unsuitable for work, while in the U.S. discussion of the 1875 Page Law "Chinese women" were represented as prostitutes, promiscuous and morally inferior. See Yung, *Unbound Feet*; Volpp, "Dependent Citizens and Marital Expatriates," paper presented at Rethinking Asian American History, Los Angeles, May 2002.

27. Dayan, *Haiti, History, and the Gods*, 197.

28. White wrote, "Chinese have sufficient intelligence and ambition to rise in the world, and in a short time would become useful and valuable as a middle class in the West Indies. . . . One difficulty . . . is the impossibility of obtaining women and families" (PRO, CO 885, 1/19).

29. On the "woman question" in Indian nationalism see Mani, *Contentious Traditions*; Sangari and Vaid, *Recasting Women*; Chatterjee, *The Nation and Its Fragments*; Chakrabarty, *Provincializing Europe*. On representing Indian indentured women's sexuality see Kale, "Projecting Identities"; Niranjana, "'Left to the Imagination,'" 111–38.

30. The San Domingo revolts occurred in virtually the same years that Hegel was writing the *Phenomenology of Spirit*. See Buck-Morss, "Hegel and Haiti," 42–70.

31. Trouillot, *Silencing the Past*.

32. The overcoming of the contradiction is elaborated in Hegel's dialectic of lordship and bondage in *Phenomenology of Spirit* and in the Bildung of the state in the *Philosophy of Right*. See also Kojève, *Introduction to the Reading of Hegel*; Kelly, *Idealism, Politics, and History*; Butler, *Subjects of Desire*.

33. Holt, *The Problem of Freedom*; Hartman, *Scenes of Subjection*; Hall, *Civilizing Subjects*; Stanley, *From Bondage to Contract*; see also Cho, "Narratives of Coupling in the Shadow of Manifest Domesticity."

34. In her study of Indian indentureship in the British Caribbean, Madhavi Kale argues that "free labor" was a "plastic" ideology, based on historically contingent, gendered, and raced assumptions about the nature of freedom and labor. See Kale, *Fragments of Empire*.

35. Lowe, *Immigrant Acts*; Glenn, *Unequal Freedom*.

36. Jung, *"Coolies" and Cane*. I am grateful to Jung for sharing this work.

37. Helly, *The Cuba Commission Report*.

38. Benitez-Rojo, *The Repeating Island*, 12.

39. PRO, CO 885, 1/19 (emphasis mine).

40. See Scott, "Fault Lines, Color Lines, and Party Lines," 61–106; Fu, "Rethinking Chinese Workers in Cuban History."

41. The Chinese coolie figured also in the antislavery and anticolonial thought of Frederick Douglass, W. E. B. Du Bois, and Walter Rodney. For example, Douglass wrote in 1871 about the "rights of the coolie in California, in Peru, in Jamaica, in Trinidad, and on board the vessels bearing them to these countries are scarcely more guarded than were those of the Negro slaves brought to our shores a century ago" (Douglass, "Coolie Trade," 262–63; and Douglass, "Cheap Labor," 264–66). Du Bois describes "that dark and vast sea of human labor in China and India, the South Seas and all Africa, in the West Indies and Central America and in the United States" and calls for "emancipation of that basic majority of workers who are yellow, brown, and black" (Du Bois, *Black Reconstruction in America, 1860–1880*). Walter Rodney, in *A History of the Guyanese Working People, 1881–1905*.

42. Database of Stephen Behrendt, David Richardson, and David Eltis at W. E. B. Du Bois Institute, Harvard University. See also Curtin, *Atlantic Slave Trade*.

43. Todorov, *Conquest of America*, 47–49.

44. See Lai, *Indentured Labor, Caribbean Sugar*; Helly, *The Cuba Commission Report*; Adamson, *Sugar without Slaves*; Tinker, *A New System of Slavery*; Laurence, *A Question of Labour*; Hu-DeHart, "Chinese Coolie Labor in Cuba and Peru in the Nineteenth Century"; Yun, "Under the Hatches."

45. Anthropological studies have richly interpreted the mixed cultures of Africans, South Asian Indians, and Chinese in twentieth-century Trinidad as expressing the longer braided histories of indenture, slavery, and independence. See Dabydeen and Samaroo, *Across the Dark Waters*; Yelvington, *Trinidad Ethnicity*; Wood, *Trinidad in Transition*; Khan, *Callaloo Nation*; Viranjini Munasinghe, *Callaloo or Tossed Salad?*

46. Williams, *Capitalism and Slavery*; Robinson, *Black Marxism*.

47. Gilroy, *Black Atlantic*; Clarke, *Mapping Yoróba Networks*.

48. Kelley, "How the West Was One," 124.

49. On the politics of memory see Yoneyama, *Hiroshima Traces*; see also Fujitani et al. *Perilous Memories*.

50. Khan, *Callaloo Nation*; Munasinghe, *Callaloo or Tossed Salad?*

51. See Johnson, "Migrant Recitals."

52. Eng and Kazanjian, *Loss*, 6; Bayoumi, "Moving Beliefs," 62; conversation with Stephanie Smallwood about "Saltwater Slavery," her work in progress.

KATHLEEN BROWN

Body Work in the Antebellum United States

In 1827 a butler in the household of Massachusetts governor Christopher Gore published a book of advice for men entering domestic service. Appearing a decade before the best-selling household management guides by Lydia Maria Child, Catharine Beecher, and Eliza Leslie, Robert Roberts's *House Servant's Directory* found a receptive audience, prompting two subsequent editions. In addition to being in the vanguard of the American house books, Roberts's manual stood out among antebellum advice manuals for its author's social and racial position. Roberts was not the master of the house, writing to assist other masters and mistresses in the task of running a household full of servants, but himself a domestic servant. He was, moreover, not a woman, as was the case with most domestic servants and the authors of most household guides, but a man. He was, most exceptionally, a free African American who had experienced the workings of a prominent northern household in a nation where his closest counterparts, racially speaking, were overwhelmingly enslaved and living in the South. Taking advantage of the status of his employer's household, as well as making use of his own literacy, Roberts dispensed household advice that depicted a disciplined and sanitized servant body navigating the intimate spaces of an upper-class white household. Translating Old World taste, manners, and standards into an American idiom, Roberts aimed at capturing the aura of elegance associated with European aristocracy for an audience of newly prosperous Americans who needed to know how to burn Lehigh coal as well as how to clean a japanned tea urn.

Roberts was a fastidious man who found bodily filth distasteful, especially if it broadcast vast social differences. Urging his imagined audience of young male readers to heed his advice, he warned, "How many have we seen going about a city, like vagabonds, diseased in mind and body, and mere outcasts from all respectable society, and a burthen to themselves?"[1] According to Roberts's interpretation of the urban scene, vagabonds threatened all who entered public spaces, but he might have considered them especially damaging to the integrity and respectability of working-class people, particularly those who constituted the servant class and needed to be seen as fit and trustworthy to enter middle- and upper-class homes.

This would have been a particular concern for African Americans in the North by the 1820s. The alchemy of southern slavery—the strong desire of white southerners to believe that they knew and could trust their enslaved domestics and the equally intoxicating belief that purchasing human property enabled an owner to refashion both his own and his new slave's identity—technically did not exist in northern states that had abolished slavery after the American Revolution. But the North had its own regional version of this alchemy nonetheless. The domestic employment of free African Americans in the postabolition North gave wealthy northern households an exotic cachet, enabling masters and mistresses to associate their own social standing with that of a planter aristocracy. Yet this cachet was only available to a handful of households—a northern aristocracy of sorts—and depended in large measure on the seeming exceptional character of their hired domestics. Racial divisions hardened in the North following the abolition of slavery, manifested and reinforced by discouragements to intimate contact across racial lines. African Americans in the North increasingly bore the stigma of racial difference that made them appear to lack the refinement necessary for laboring in the private chambers of white households. In contrast to their white laboring counterparts who rejected demeaning labels and insisted on being considered "help," moreover, African American domestics found it hard to distance themselves from the term *servant*. As the case of Robert Roberts suggests, however, at least until the 1820s certain black domestics marked wealthy households as aristocratic spaces, akin to large plantation households in the South and to the great houses of Europe's wealthiest families.[2]

Taking Roberts's unique contribution to the household management genre as its point of departure, this chapter considers how prosperous white northerners and their hired domestic laborers together produced the domestic culture—specifically the care and maintenance of bodies and domestic environments—that anchored transnational judgments about respectability and civilization. How did employers and servants negotiate the physical presence of their own bodies, distinguished by inequities of wealth, power, and cultivation, within intimate domestic spaces that served simultaneously as work spaces and domestic sanctuaries? To what degree did these negotiations make this dominant culture politically useful and transportable? Thinking about the physical interactions of employer and employee bodies as cartographies of domestic labor rather than as coincidental or merely pragmatic relationships helps us to understand the distinctions between servant and employer bodies resulting from those interactions and the attention of both parties to tiny details. Employers and employees helped to produce cartographies that reinforced the division of bodies into zones — upper and lower, public and private — and mapped them onto different domestic spaces. The bodies of entire groups of people might be similarly classified as upper or lower. Analyzing domestic labor, material culture, and care of the body — what historian of medicine Mary Fissell describes as "body work" — helps us to appreciate the mundane ways bodies acquired meaning as well as the crucial contribution of these meanings to emerging concepts of racial and ethnic difference.[3]

Servants in the antebellum North were increasingly likely to be Irish or African American rather than native-born white by the 1840s. They brought what many middle-class people saw as the most distasteful feature of democratic society — the disorderly mingling in public spaces of people of different races, classes, religions, and ethnicities — into the sacralized private spaces of the emerging white middle class. Yet servants also provided the labor indispensable to differentiating these domestic spaces from their public counterparts and imbuing them with the meanings that anchored the privileged social identities of their inhabitants. For middle-class women and children, in particular, domestic spaces consolidated social identities defined through privacy, purity, and a partial release from the manual labor that foreclosed the possibility of gentility. Although Roberts wrote about running an aristocratic home, both his volume of advice and the goals of gentility and privacy it advanced became central to bourgeois domestic agendas during the antebellum period.

Roberts's household guide provides the historian with a singular servant's-eye view, early in this antebellum transformation, of this process of domesticating the servant bodies that in turn lent grace and status to prosperous household spaces and persons. The other source considered in this chapter — the records of a wealthy employer — provides a view of this process from the opposite perspective. Sarah E. Lawrence, the mistress of a prominent Boston-area household, recorded the names, wages, and assigned labor of approximately three dozen servants in her employ between 1842 and 1864. Lawrence also commented briefly on their performance, character, and reasons for leaving. Her diary, in contrast, offers a view of her household from the perspective of her own reproducing body, her network of friends and relatives, and her efforts to live a Christian life by accepting God's will, providing religious instruction to her dependents, and supporting missionary work in Africa and China.

Taken together these sources allow us to glimpse the complex negotiations over the aesthetic and metaphysical dimensions of waged domestic work, as well as its better-known physical dimensions. What comes into view are struggles over the cleanliness of servant bodies — especially of feet, hands, and clothes — that inevitably became soiled as they labored to meet (or occasionally to challenge) elite and bourgeois domestic standards, as well as the suitability of those bodies for the increasingly refined and intimate zones of nineteenth-century bourgeois households. This was not simply a matter of domestic laborers' appearance but of the way their physical presence contributed to the smells, tastes, sounds, and appearance of the domestic environment, providing aristocratic and middle-class men and women with unwelcome reminders of their place in a larger world of unruly bodies of multiple races, ethnicities, classes, and religions. These sources also provide a view of how the bourgeoisie had begun to interpret the body's calling cards as evidence of moral condition. Employers like Lawrence dealt with this challenge less by scrutinizing each servant's appearance and deportment than by organizing female domestic labor to give certain trusted employees greater access to the bodies of her family while keeping others at further remove.[4]

Finally, this chapter is an attempt to expose the connections between the power relations producing these domestic cartographies and larger patterns of inequity in racial, class, and imperial power in the first half of the nineteenth century. Although I maintain that there are important analytical reasons to avoid an expansive definition of *colonial* such that all the power inequities within these households become examples of "colonialism," it is equally important that, as Ann Stoler, Amy Kaplan, and others have demonstrated, we recognize connections between these so-called home fronts and the conflicts and conquests that seem easier to classify as "imperial." Stoler's important research into the intimate forms of imperial power in the

Dutch East Indies, Kaplan's pathbreaking conceptualization of nineteenth-century domesticity as part and parcel of "Manifest Destiny" in the North American West, and my own work on how the seemingly natural foundations of intimate forms of power can obscure the history and politics of that power provide crucial conceptual and historical foundations for the essay that follows. Especially in domestic environments in which significant resources had been devoted to protecting domestic life from the vagaries and crass exploitation of the larger world, bodies became laden with political meanings that traveled well. Put somewhat differently, even as I hesitate to label Roberts's or Lawrence's nonfamilial domestic relationships "colonial," they took place in a larger imperial world that was mobilizing and redefining meanings for "self" and "other," "black" and "white," "civilized" and "savage," "clean" and "filthy," and "decent" and "degraded."[5] I conclude with some additional thoughts about how two individuals, situated on opposite sides of the employer-employee relationship, might both be interpreted as participating in the creation of a domestic culture that would prove so crucial to imperial projects. Although the antebellum United States lacked a formal empire in the European sense, it was no less seriously embarked on imperial cultural formations during the first half of the nineteenth century. Even in the documents of bourgeois domestic life, we find hints of the connections between intimate daily interactions and those larger formations underpinning the North's conflict with the South, the war with Mexico, the territorial expansion into the West, and missionary efforts overseas. What we must struggle to reconcile, however, is how persons with intentions and political stakes as different as those of Roberts and Lawrence might nonetheless appear as cocreators of the "civilized" domestic culture that served as imperialism's unstated premise.

ROBERTS SCRUPULOUSLY AVOIDED AUTOBIOGRAPHY in his guide to servants for reasons we will consider later. But the details of his early life help to explain his appeal for his elite northern white employers. Born and raised in South Carolina, in close proximity to slavery if not actually enslaved himself, Roberts acquired domestic skills and literacy before moving north. He may have symbolized the exoticism and aristocratic privilege of southern slavery to his first northern employer, Nathan Appleton, who visited Charleston between 1802 and 1803. Whether Roberts joined Appleton's household during that trip or after making the journey to Boston a few years later is not known. By 1805, however, he was in New England, married to the daughter of an African American Revolutionary War veteran, and likely employed in Appleton's household.[6]

Appleton was one of Boston's wealthiest and most influential merchant investors. He traveled abroad to England and the Continent between 1810 and 1812, possibly with Roberts in tow. Soon after his return, he joined a group of Boston investors who financed the textile mills in Lowell, Massachusetts. By the early 1820s, if not before, Roberts worked as a manservant for Appleton and Kirk Boott, another Lowell investor. In 1825, at about the age of forty-five, he left Appleton to work for former Massachusetts governor and senator Christopher Gore, who was then an ailing man in his sixties, presiding over a large country estate in Waltham. With its period furnishings and carefully groomed grounds, Gore Place is currently a tourist attraction for those interested in the elegant life enjoyed by this aristocratic family. Its material trappings remind us that one purpose of servant staff was to enable well-to-do families to live comfortably amidst material objects that broadcast refinement and good taste, not just to their Boston compatriots but to well-bred visitors from around the world.[7]

Both Appleton and Gore were staunch Federalists, although they differed in their opinions on slavery. Historian Graham Russell Hodges suggests that in Roberts both men found the combination of experience, competence, and seeming deference that many elite New Englanders believed could no longer be found among native-born whites. Elite Federalists like Gore and Appleton mourned the passing of a hierarchical social order that justified their own brand of paternalism — a world that had certainly disappeared with the abolition of slavery in Massachusetts, if it had ever truly existed — even as they engaged in the commercial activities that wrought its demise. Both men might have found consolation in Roberts, a middle-aged southern African American who brought extraordinary self-discipline to his domestic work. In different ways both men also likely found Roberts's connections to the slaveholding South soothing to their political sensibilities and useful to their projects of aristocratic self-fashioning. For Appleton, who supported slavery throughout his political career, Roberts might have embodied the alchemy of slavery so seductive to wealthy northern men for whom southern planters represented the nearest model of aristocratic life. Indeed, as social relations among white New Englanders moved further away from the hierarchical English model, as a vocal middle class emerged, and as animosities toward black New Englanders sharpened with the end to slavery, southern ways might have appeared even more attractive to wealthy Federalists like Appleton. In contrast, Roberts's presence might have allowed the antislavery Gore to mimic certain privileges of slave ownership without complicity in its evils. Literacy, freedom, and wages distinguished Roberts from the debased southern slave of the northern antislavery imagination. Yet his labor and his person still might have enabled Gore to indulge in a fantasy of aristocratic life.

Roberts's long career as an activist against slavery and on behalf of African American civil rights compels us to consider that he, too, might have had reasons for leaving Appleton's employ. Perhaps Gore's antislavery views made Gore a more attractive employer than Appleton. A shared political perspective on slavery might have provided important common ground for the two men, fostering the compatibility and seeming intimacy of their relationship until Gore's death in 1827.[8] Too, Roberts may simply have realized that Gore's patronage could enable him to achieve economic independence, making the cultivation of intimacy a worthwhile endeavor.

The House Servant's Directory reflected Roberts's experience as a servant in aristocratic households — he boasted of service in England and France, as well as in the United States — and anticipated the concerns of an upwardly mobile middle class eager to gentrify their domestic lives. The book's subtitle noted that, although "chiefly compiled for the use of house servants," it was "identically made to suit the manners and customs of families in the United States," many of whom could not procure the domestic labor to live in the style of Christopher Gore. Roberts's warnings about diseased vagabonds wandering city streets, an alarm that echoed similar refrains in cities throughout Europe, spoke to middle-class fears of contamination in public spaces and of the dangers of an unruly and potentially dependent underclass. His strictures to menservants to keep their persons free of dirt — including that honestly acquired through their domestic labors — were ostensibly designed to protect the genteel inhabitants of upper-class domestic spaces from similarly distasteful spectacles. To accomplish this sleight of hand, servants needed to discipline their bodies to rise early in the morning and immediately to take on the most unpleasant labor. Roberts advised readers to complete their dirtiest chores before ladies and gentlemen arose for breakfast. "There is nothing more disagreeable than to run about with dirty hands and dirty clothes," he pronounced, "and this must inevitably be the case if you defer this part of your work until every body is stirring and bustling about" (3).

"Disagreeable," in Roberts's use of the term, captured the sentiments of genteel employers at the sight of filth on the body and clothes of menservants, but it did not necessarily reflect the views of menservants themselves, as Roberts subsequently explained: "There is not a class of people to whom cleanliness of person and attire is of more importance to servants in genteel families. There are many servants, whom I have been eye witness to, through negligence as I must call it, who are a disgrace to the family that they live with, as well as to themselves, but appearing in their dirty clothes at a time of day that they should have all the dirtiest part of their work done" (4). Although early rising was crucial to avoiding this disgraceful spectacle, designating different clothes for different kinds of work was also important. Roberts recommended a separate outfit for dirty work, made of dark fabric so as to minimize the appearance of dust and dirt. Accessories such as vests, caps ("to keep the dust from your hair"), and aprons were essential. Having completed the dirty work of cleaning boots, shoes, knives, and lamps, and in winter, taking up ashes, cleaning grates, tidying up the hearth, and making fires, a good manservant carefully washed his hands before touching window shutters or breakfast place settings where dirty fingers were likely to leave unsightly smudges (28). Never, Roberts warned, should a manservant "attempt to wait on the family in the clothes" worn during this dirty morning labor (3). Rather, "before your family come down to breakfast," he advised, "you should have on a clean shirt collar and cravat, with a clean round jacket, white linen apron and clean shoes, with your hair neatly combed out" (4).

In addition to effacing any traces of this dirty morning work, Roberts urged servants to labor as silently as possible. Wearing slippers rather than shoes in the morning minimized the noise that would inevitably result from running about to accomplish morning tasks. Even when it might be acceptable to have a noisy footfall, however, after the family was awake, Roberts warned against wearing thick shoes or boots (62–63). Such footwear might be suitable for navigating city streets and muddy country lanes, but it was inappropriate for attending guests in the parlor or waiting on dinner. Indeed, his entire oeuvre of advice on these matters appeared to be aimed at maximizing the distinctions between the refined space of the middle-class dining room and the hurly-burly of city streets. Domestic laborers needed to take pains to efface any visual or auditory links between their own laboring bodies and those of the uncouth vagabonds who contributed to the filth and noise of public life.[9]

Roberts seemed almost painfully aware of the need for domestic laborers to efface traces of their own physical beings—through grooming and hygiene, as well as through changes of clothes—to minimize the conflict between who they were and where they worked. Washing the visible body was an important part of this effort, as it had been for respectable people for several centuries. "You must always be very clean in your person, and wash your face and comb your hair, &c," he admonished (63). Such cleanliness routines might have been sufficient for those who lived sedentary lives or for those less fastidious than Roberts and the employers he imagined for his readers. But, as Roberts observed, more attention to cleaning the body was necessary for people performing strenuous physical labor: "Wash your feet at least three times per week, as in summer time your feet generally perspire; a little weak vinegar and water, or a little rum is very good for this use, as it is a stimulant, and there is not danger of taking cold after washing in either. Servants being generally on foot throughout the day, it must cause perspiration, which makes a bad smell, which would be a very disagreeable thing to yourself and the company on whom you wait" (63).

Foot odor was not Roberts's only concern for the servant's olfactory impact on his or her immediate environment. Nor were his concerns always to protect employers from distasteful smells and sights. He also sought to protect servants from having their bodies used in evidence against them. Thus, for example, although he warned servants not to drink, he provided a remedy "to prevent the breath from smelling after drink" so that "no person can discover by your breath whether you have been drinking or not" (99). Recipes also allowed servants to make their appearances more appealing to employers. Roberts detailed a recipe for a wash "to give a luster to the face," a wash for the hair, "an excellent paste for the skin to firm it," and a hair dye to turn red hair black (100–101).

The portrait Roberts presented was of a dutiful, accomplished man-servant, who had mastered the challenges of his occupation through a combination of bodily discipline (early rising, washing the body, and treading softly in slippers), strategy (do the dirty work before anyone wakes up), and subterfuge (don't drink, but if you do, efface the traces from your breath). Was Roberts perhaps more scrupulous about the state of his clothes, hands, feet, hair, and breath than a white writer might have been? There is not much in his text to identify him as African American except perhaps this careful attention to areas of the body that represented the body's frontiers—the smells emanating from its mouth and its feet, the appearance of clothing that revealed the labor it engaged in, and the condition of the hair and skin on the visible body. In a climate increasingly hostile to black people and more committed to views of race as an innate, embodied condition, Roberts may have been more sensitive about his own physical presence in white middle-class households—both more self-aware and more self-conscious—than his white servant counterparts.

One tiny detail in his advice manual encourages this view of Roberts's heightened awareness of his position as an African American man working in close proximity to white middle-class female bodies. In the midst of instructions about how to black shoes, Roberts reminded readers that ladies' shoes required special treatment. As in other instances in which direct contact with the bodies of the white family necessitated that the manservant wash his hands (for example, when waiting on them at the breakfast table), a manservant who had been blacking men's shoes—shoes that were worn outside—needed to wash his hands before touching the shoes of the lady of the house. Ladies' shoes were not blacked but literally "whitened" with milk or egg whites. The linings of such shoes were also usually white, he explained, and so only clean hands should touch the inside of the shoe to hold it while polishing the exterior. To do otherwise would soil the white linings with dark finger and hand smudges, destroying the illusion that the wearer's feet were as pure and clean as the lining of her shoes and reminding her of her manservant's intimate access to accessories that were part of her social person. Did Roberts believe these telltale marks were especially problematic if the manservant were African American? Even when he was cleaning a lady's shoe, that all-important accessory that marked a boundary of the body and its movement across the threshold of the house, a black manservant had to be scrupulously careful to efface traces of his own physical presence, especially if that presence suggested intimate access to a potentially reproductive white female body.

One could also read race into Roberts's advice to servants to be deferential to employers in their speech as well as in their embodied behavior. Such a reading reinforces his appeal for his Federalist employers, but it does not explain how such a seemingly deferential text could be authored by a man who devoted the rest of his life to fighting racial injustice. A closer look at his text, however, reveals a more complicated view of the master-servant relationship, one that provided a religious context for deference and eschewed any association between domestic service and slavery. A few circumscribed examples showcasing the virtue of long-suffering Old Testament "servants" Joseph and Jacob suggest that Roberts deliberately employed this euphemism for slavery as part of his project to redeem domestic labor as an honorable and dignified occupation for free African Americans. In a pointed double entendre, moreover, he warned his readers "never to be a slave to passion." In addition, Roberts's advice to would-be servants departed from injunctions to be deferential and delivered a subtle moral indictment of their masters. Endowing the domestic laborer with the dignified obligations of the true Christian, he reminded readers to bestow charity on those less fortunate than themselves, to love their enemies no matter how unjustly they behaved, to choose honesty over flattery, and to resist the desire for riches, glory, and pleasure as a disease of the mind. "It is much better to be the oppressed than to stand in the place of the oppressor," Roberts observed, "for patience is ever acceptable in the sight of God, and in due time will be rewarded, for God hath promised that it shall be so; and when have his promises failed?" (lviii–lx).

Roberts remained silent about his race, his place of birth, and his possible former connection to slavery. Indeed, the message of his text appears to be that biographical details were irrelevant to the corpus of advice he dispensed. Did Roberts fear that his race would hurt sales of his book in a region where racism against African Americans was on the rise? Perhaps. But it seems more likely that he hoped to protect his brand of domestic professionalism and competence from both the stigma of slavery and white fantasies about slave deference. Indeed, the main reason scholars of Roberts's work don't know for sure whether he was a slave seems to be that he did not want them to know. His silence about his own life was not an effacement of his own black male body but an assertion of its irrelevance to professional standards for domestic service. In adopting this strategy, Roberts anticipated the self-protective silence of generations of African American women, hiding his self from view much as colonized peoples throughout the world did. For a man who made a career out of disciplining his body into silence and invisibility, dignity cohered in the refusal to expose the struggles of his inner life to the white gaze and in the patient endurance of injustice and oppression.[10]

AT FIRST GLANCE, Sarah Lawrence's perspective on intimate household routines could not have been more different from that of Roberts. Whereas Roberts calculated the impact of each footfall, breath, and grasp of an object — one almost imagines him moving balletically around the dining table, making his physical presence appear effortlessly unobtrusive — Lawrence calculated wages, physical strength, and character. She showed little concern for the bodily deportment and containment that absorbed Roberts. Indeed, her most pointed commentary about the bodies inhabiting her domestic space concerned her own and her children's bodies. Yet her journal and her book of wages also revealed a careful choreography of intimacy reflected in her division of labor and its allocation to different household spaces.

Sarah Elizabeth Appleton was twenty years old when she married Amos A. Lawrence, a man eight years her senior, in 1842. The marriage made her the mistress of a prosperous household located in the upper reaches of Boston society and united two of the region's wealthy and politically influential families. Appleton was the daughter of shipping merchant William Appleton and niece of Robert Roberts's former employer, Nathan Appleton. Indeed, it is likely that she and Roberts crossed paths when she was a small child and he worked in her uncle's household. From modest beginnings, her father, William, built a successful shipping empire based in textiles, raw cotton, grain, and lumber exported to China and the East Indies in exchange for tea, silk, rice, hemp, sugar, indigo, and coffee. Trade to Liverpool brought credit for the China market or iron and steel while trade in merchandise to California gained the company hides and gold. This fortune helped to launch Appleton's political career as a Whig congressman from the state of Massachusetts in 1851. He also served as president of the United States branch bank and a local Massachusetts bank and gave funds to various educational and charitable institutions.[11] Every year in his diary he reviewed his moral and financial accounts and expressed pleasure at his growing net worth. "My success in business is uncommon," he admitted; "no man in Boston of the Age, I am forty-five, has made as much, and only one, David Sears, possesses as much probably," he noted with pride.[12]

In Amos Adams Lawrence, Sarah found a man as wealthy and powerful as her father. Lawrence was the son and namesake of Amos Lawrence, a merchant who had built a lucrative shipping business with his brother. Although the elder Lawrence never left the North American continent, his trade networks and his fortune reflected a global reach. Self-conscious of his vast shipping empire, the older man donned a Turkish cap and robes in one portrait from his middle age. His fortune enabled his sons, moreover, to lay claim to a far more cosmopolitan experience of education and travel than their father had enjoyed. In his advice to his sons Lawrence stressed polished manners ("manners are highly important in your intercourse with the world") and careful accounts ("being accurate will have an influence upon your whole character in life") as the two habits that would ensure future success.[13] Indeed, as Sarah's father considered the virtues of his future son-in-law, he noted "he is a young man of good common sense, with business habits, a very safe man to entrust a daughter with."[14]

The younger Lawrence was a Harvard graduate, a merchant, an investor in the textile industry, and an antislavery sympathizer who would leave his mark mainly through various nation-building projects. His business and philanthropic interests took him to Europe and the southern and western United States. He supported the New England Emigrant Aid Company, an interest that sponsored antislavery immigrants to Kansas following the Kansas-Nebraska Act in 1854. His land speculations, as well as this work to encourage immigrants, led to his financing Lawrence University in Appleton, Wisconsin (the town was named after Sarah), and the University of Kansas in Lawrence. He also became involved in the Utah Emigrant Aid Company, which sponsored non-Mormon immigrants to Utah. During the Civil War he helped to raise a Union cavalry and infantry unit. In addition, he was a generous benefactor of Harvard University. In all of these projects he pursued a vision of a modern nation — one committed to free labor, Protestant monogamy, and the possibility of higher education for leading citizens.[15]

Tracking the cosmopolitan experiences of her closest male relatives is a most imperfect method for placing Sarah Appleton Lawrence in a larger world. Yet it can help us imagine how national politics and global trade shaped the domestic priorities of this young woman as she began her married life. Although we know little of Lawrence's own travel experiences before her marriage, we know that she grew up among men and women whose horizons extended to Europe and beyond. William and Nathan Appleton and Amos A. Lawrence had all traveled to Europe. Indeed, her father and her future husband had met at that quintessential site for male sociability and business, a London coffee house. All three men profited from the China trade and the global market in slave-produced cotton and textiles. All three men played signal roles in bringing about the industrial transformation of New England textile production, a development that would have far-reaching implications for the rest of the United States and for its place in a global economy. Lawrence accompanied her parents on trips to New York, Philadelphia, and Washington, D.C. She also had the benefit of corresponding with her mother, Mary Ann Appleton, who traveled extensively. The elder Appleton took tea at the White House with President Andrew Jackson and Secretary of State Martin Van Buren. She also visited White Sulphur Springs, Virginia, to enjoy its healing waters and traveled to Europe with her husband. Her mother's cosmopolitan worldview certainly shaped Sarah's sense of her own place in a wider world. Her mother, moreover, contributed to Lawrence's budget for domestic labor during the first few months of her marriage, a crucial material condition that set the tone for Lawrence's domestic life.[16]

From the moment she became the mistress of her own household in 1842, Lawrence was fortunate to be able to employ a full complement of servants to perform a wide range of household labors. Her book of wages listed "chamber maids" and "parlor girls," who were paid the least of her employees, as well as "trusty and industrious" men, who usually earned three times that amount and were paid monthly rather than weekly. For twenty-two years, until she was forty-two, she kept a journal describing household and family events and a book of wages that recorded employment tenures, dates and amounts of payment, and miscellaneous comments about ability and character. Keeping two different records, Lawrence attempted to separate family relationships and reproductive life from household management. By making the latter matters of account, she attempted to rationalize and systematize the labors of her domestic employees, subjecting them to the discipline of the calendar and measuring them against standards that could be assigned a cash value. This decision to roster her household employees and keep an account of their weeks of labor is striking in light of her father's immersion in global accounts. To keep such a roster separate from the diary of family visits, shopping trips, illnesses, weddings, pregnancies, births, christenings, and deaths would seem to evacuate the economic sinews of household management from the emotional, spiritual, and social life of the household. But, in fact, her diary entries about the bodies under her care reveals a similar desire to rationalize and modernize.

Lawrence adhered to a gender division of labor in which women filled differentiated slots, notable for their different degrees of intimate contact with the bodies of the Lawrence family. Chamber maids and parlor girls, for instance, were defined by their responsibility for spaces that emphasized different regions of the body: the sleeping chambers, where one might encounter filled chamber pots, soiled sheets and undergarments, and the semi-dressed bodies of occupants, and the parlor, the most public room in the house, where codes of formal dress and social behavior emphasized the social "upper" body rather than the "lower" body that engaged in sexual activity and produced bodily waste. Whereas Lawrence expected the chambermaid to do the family's laundry — yet another indication of the undesirable and strenuous nature of the job and its focus on the family's intimate, lower bodies—the parlor girl would have been expected to display great discipline over her own body, much as Roberts recommended in his book. Cooks and nursery women also cared for the Lawrence family's bodies in intimate ways by preparing food and looking after the health and welfare of the Lawrence children. The greater the employee's access to and responsibility for actual bodies, the more trust Lawrence had to place in the employee herself.[17]

The hired men, in contrast, performed seemingly generic male labor, undifferentiated in Lawrence's account book and at least partially located out of doors. On leaving Lawrence's employ, at least one of these men took up farming, returning for seasonal employment during the slow winter months. The only exception to this divide between men and women occurred in 1853, when Lawrence noted that her parlor maid, Phebe M. Coombs, left after Lawrence "took a man," most likely a manservant to perform indoor work, and because Coombs "prefered to do chamber work—& live in town."[18]

The wages Lawrence paid her employees reveal that her own agenda for the household was often at odds with the larger currents of the labor market and the smaller currents of individual employee struggles to improve their situations. Although chambermaids performed the most strenuous female work in the household—weekly laundry—they were paid the least of Lawrence's employees. Lawrence's chambermaids made $1.75 per week until late 1853, when Lawrence contracted to pay Margaret Amos, a relative, $2.00. The turnover in chambermaids may have been one of the reasons Lawrence finally decided to raise their weekly wages. During the twelve years she kept accounts, Lawrence recorded employing twelve women for this job. Two of the women, Abby Foster and Mary Gutterson, left on account of "not being strong enough to wash." Mary Anne Dorety left to take up dressmaking, Laura returned home to continue her schooling, and Mary Ann Coburn and Maria Coburn, possibly sisters, each left paid domestic labor to perform work for their own households as married women (Maria returned briefly twice after her marriage). Another, Harriet Conant, left the Lawrence household to accompany Mrs. Freud to Savannah. More than half of her chambermaids, in short, revealed agendas at odds with Lawrence's for easier or more satisfying labor, or they placed priority on education or marriage over earning wages.[19]

Lawrence's parlor girls and cooks made at least $2.00 per week, with cooks earning an additional fifty cents if they provided the household with fresh butter. Lawrence employed even more cooks than chambermaids over the course of twelve years—fourteen—but comparatively few parlor girls.

The reasons for the turnover in cooks were similar to those for the chamber-maids. Jane Walter was too old to continue the work, and Susan Hayden found it too hard. Dorothea Lord and Julia Quinn each left to marry. Barbara Gifford was unwilling, after two years service, to continue accompanying the family to the north shore for the summer. Eliza Dimond gave up on going out to work. Betsy Chase left for Nauvoo in June 1843, where Mormon leader Joseph Smith had recently dictated his revelation on "Celestial Marriage." Sarah Roberts, who could well have been the daughter of Robert Roberts, proved to be an "excellent" cook, despite her "peculiar disposition," but wanted to return home. Mary Ann Pickett left in haste for more wages.

In contrast to the Lawrence household's female employees, the men were paid better and tended to stay longer. Joseph Whatney received $12.00 a month in 1842 and stayed for four months. "Flighty" Alvin Dugar earned $16.50 a month and remained a Lawrence employee for approximately the same interval. Simeon Le Strout and John Magee each made the $16.00 wage per month, with Le Strout staying for more than a year and Magee for just a couple of months. James Cate began his tenure with the Lawrences in 1846 at $16.00 and steadily received raises until 1850, at which point his wages peaked at $20.00 per month. His departure to marry and take up farming prompted Lawrence to comment, "very trusty & industrious man—sorry to lose him." Joseph Williams, paid $18.00 a month, left after a couple of months because he was "too fond of going out." Jacob Brown worked his wages up from $20.00 to $22.00 in just six months before he was dismissed for drinking.

Lawrence was much more concerned with physical strength, health, and pliability of temperament than with bodily deportment. We get little sense that Roberts's efforts to perform the part of the ideal manservant would have made a big impression on Lawrence except in the case of parlor girls, although this was, perhaps, the very outcome Roberts would have desired. The ideal manservant would have labored nearly unnoticed, making his work appear to have been done by magic. What Lawrence did notice were the gaps between her expectations for completed tasks and behavior and what the servants actually did. In addition to noting which women had not been strong enough to do the wash, Lawrence observed that she had to fire her cook, Lurania, one week sooner than her planned termination date for "refusing to comply with my wishes." After several weeks of looking for a cook in March 1849, Lawrence finally found Eliza Dimond but had to send her home a few weeks later for coughing. Boston was bracing itself for its second major cholera epidemic of the century, and Lawrence might have been extra cautious about her family's health. Dimond eventually left the Lawrence household in July, at the height of the epidemic, owing to "sickness" in her own home. Jacob Brown's inability to curb his tippling habit resulted in his dismissal in 1851.[20]

On the whole, Lawrence's comments about the men and women in her employ suggest that she was carefully sifting through evidence of morals and character as much as she was evaluating their work. Her positive judgments of the women tended to be more generous than those of the men — suggesting that she might have had an opportunity to observe and converse with them — and equally dismissive when they were negative. Successful female employees were "good," "clever," "neat," and "obliging," while the unsuccessful ones had "bad character," were "lazy" or "shiftless," or "tired of work." One exceptional young woman left her employ because the washing was too hard but subsequently benefited from the good impression she had made; in 1851 she traveled to Europe as a lady's companion to Lawrence's younger sister Nancy. Another "very good woman" who no longer wished to cook left to keep Lawrence's mother's house.

It is difficult to ascertain how much race and ethnicity entered into these judgments. Lawrence never made disparaging remarks about dirty "Bridgets" or lazy "Negroes," as some of her white New England contemporaries did. Was this a dimension of her own performance of elite authority, that it transcended the particularities of region or the race of local laborers? Or was she simply striving to make her daily dealings with laborers live up to her charitable ideals? In the absence of clear ethnic or racial labels in her account book, we guess about the ethnic-racial identities of her laborers at our peril. Julia Quinn and Mary Dorety likely were Irish. If Sarah Roberts was the daughter of Robert Roberts, she might have been the only African American working for the Lawrence household. When we correlate Lawrence's comments on morals and character with our guesses about ethnic backgrounds, we find Lawrence slightly more likely to judge girls with Yankee-sounding names and plans for marriage and education "good" and "clever" than their Irish-named counterparts or those leaving her employ for other reasons — dislike of hard work or desire for higher wages.[21]

But women from ethnic backgrounds similar to Lawrence's own may also have had some advantage in gaining and keeping the most intimate jobs in the household — those that involved care for the bodies of the Lawrence children. Mrs. Moulton, the children's nurse, was one of the best-paid women and the one with the longest tenure. Her duties revolved around relieving Sarah of the care of the Lawrence children. She remained in the household from 1843 to 1854 at the wage of $2.50 per week plus a quarterly bonus of $5.00. Lawrence also seemed more inclined to become involved in the lives of her wet nurses than those of other employees. When her daughter Sally became ill in the autumn of 1846, the doctor recommended a wet nurse. Lawrence convinced "Marianne" (a friend?) to wean her son early to pass the wet nurse along to Sally. When Sally refused to go near the hired woman, Lawrence (and likely her mother and Mrs. Moulton) arranged to have a puppy stimulate the woman's milk supply while they tried to secure her another position. When her fourth child would not stop crying, Lawrence successfully procured a wet nurse to supplement her own supply of milk. The birth of her fifth child in 1852 provoked a similar search for help. Lawrence set her sights on an "English girl," Hannah Brockway, whose baby was only two weeks old. A month into her employ, Brockway's child suddenly died. Both Lawrence and Mrs. Moulton went to see the dead baby. Brockway remained as wet nurse for the Lawrences until the following October, earning the following notation in Lawrence's book: "Left & lived as chambermaid at several places: turned out well." Examining the employment records of Lawrence's nurse and wet nurses reveals a subtle pattern of bringing Anglo-American women rather than Irish or African American women into the inner sanctum of labor centered on caring for the children's bodies as well as greater personal involvement in the lives of these trusted employees.

Indeed, comparing Lawrence's diary to the account book, we get the impression of a household that revolved around her own reproducing body and those of her children. During the first sixteen years of her marriage, she recorded the births of seven children: Mary Ann in 1843 (when her journal begins), Sally in 1845, Amory in 1848, Willie in 1850, Susan in 1852, Hetty in 1855, and a fifth daughter in 1858. In addition, Lawrence assumed responsibility for her deceased sister's twins, born in 1844, and an orphaned relative.[22] Lawrence's embodied experience of her own household was thus punctuated by multiple pregnancies, lyings-in, breast-feeding (which she seems to have done on her own for the most part for at least eighteen months after each birth), teething crises, weanings, and the inevitable bouts of illness. This cycle of childbearing lent a distinctive rhythm to the household's need for the midwives, doctors, wet nurses, nursery women, and cooks who appeared in the pages of the account book.

The focus on her own reproducing body and the regimes of care for the children help us to pinpoint Lawrence's medical politics. Mary Ann Appleton's trip to White Sulphur Springs during the 1830s suggests that Sarah's mother may have taught her to keep an open mind about medical care. Lawrence's willingness to try hydropathy and her commitment to summer bathing—the entire family relocated to Nahant, on Boston's north shore—appears to have been accompanied by a progressive view of the reproducing female body.[23] Although she relied on Doctor Warren for the illnesses of household members, she herself turned to a midwife during pregnancy and childbirth. Indeed, during the 1840s there appears to have been a brief resurgence in the popularity of midwives in Boston. When Lawrence missed her "turns" in 1851 while still nursing her fourth child, she visited Miss Alexander to rule out the possibility of pregnancy. Unfortunately, Alexander could not ease her mind, and Lawrence soon reported that she was expecting another child. Alexander attended the delivery of the healthy nine-pound baby in February 1852.[24]

Recording body weights, practicing hydropathy, and using a midwife rather than a doctor were all components of Lawrence's struggle to define a modern, reproductive female body during the 1840s and 1850s. The emotional counterpart to this effort was Lawrence's decidedly unsentimental approach to pregnancy and motherhood. Although her diary reveals her affection for her children and her concerns for their well-being, it lacks a sentimental view of childhood or motherhood: no descriptions of cherubic toddlers or pledges of connubial affection, although Lawrence did occasionally note that the children were "good" or brought her pleasure. Lawrence's own health and that of her living children, particularly of one-year-old Willie in the example that follows, dominated her account of her suspicions that she might be pregnant again:

> I am feeling quite anxious, lest I shall be obliged to wean my baby—not having [been regular crossed out] had my turns, & suspecting something, though I am perfectly well, & have had not thought of it until a day or two past, if so it must be, I think, two or 3 months I trust that it is not, & that shall soon feel my mind easy about it. I fear the result for Willie on account of teething & I want a little respite which I had hoped to have had but I will try & be submissive.[25]

When it became clear that she was indeed pregnant again, Lawrence struggled to reconcile her budding modernity—the agency of choosing hydropathy and midwifery over the services of a regular physician—with the resignation taught by her religious tradition: "I do not think I have felt properly about my condition, but was very much disappointed to find myself situated thus—I hope I shall indulge no more improper feelings, but act rightly; I had nothing for my baby & was obliged to wean him on Thursday I pray that no[w?] he may not suffer, but get through his summer in health." Lawrence spent the rest of the summer frequenting the bath. After her son was born, she commented several times in her diary that she thought he might be the "best" child she ever had.[26]

What happens to our image of the Lawrence household if we move beyond the boundaries of the nation to see the global inspirations and ramifications of its intimate domestic projects? Amos Lawrence's national preoccupations focused on creating a modern national body politic by fostering legal orthodoxy on questions of slavery and monogamous marriage, a set of interests consistent with his desire to help the United States take its rightful place among other imperial nations, as well as with his involvement in overseas trade. Sarah's version of these projects included her practice of a modern female politics of the body, centered on hydropathy, midwifery, childbearing, and breast-feeding. But her struggle to accept her pregnancies offers a clue to what was perhaps her most important contribution to her family, made possible in part by the extensive labor provided by her domestic staff and in part by her religious training: her ability to inhabit her class and gender position gracefully, despite the burgeoning size of her household, in ways that confirmed the righteousness of the paths chosen by the men in her life. Men such as William Appleton and Amos Lawrence, situated at the cutting edge of global commerce and national politics, required seemingly endless affirmation that they were living Christian lives. In addition to the material and familial comforts she provided, Sarah's orderly management of family life and production of domestic pleasure made them feel that they were good men. "Dear Sarah is as loving & lovable as ever," her father observed in 1851. "All agree she is a worthy pattern for her sex."[27] Ten years later, he was still struck by his daughter's wonderful qualities: "Sarah is one of the best of wives, Mothers, friends & housekeepers," he noted approvingly, "all order & not fuss."[28] After forty years of marriage, husband Amos effused, "Dear, good wife she has been to me, the light of my life and my chief worldly support. May we live together in the hereafter forever!"[29]

Cheerful acceptance of duty also marked Sarah's recognition of her privileged place in the world—a domestic practice that meshed with her global politics. In January 1849, for example, Lawrence attended a sewing circle at the home of Miss Phillips, a missionary to Africa. While they sewed, the group read two letters, presumably from missionaries, as well as an essay by Miss Beecher on Education. Beecher was a leader in creating educational opportunities for white women and in her youth had been active in the effort to prevent the removal of Cherokee Indians from Georgia. In subsequent writings, however, she revealed a dim opinion of Native American culture, immigrant intelligence, and women's political involvement in issues like slavery. Indeed, with her effort to rationalize housekeeping and health and make both more scientific, Beecher engaged in her own modernizing project — an effort that depended on classifying some groups of people as less civilized than others based on criteria rooted in certain domestic and bodily practices.

Like Beecher, Lawrence placed great stock in the transformative power of education, which she saw as a tool for improving class relations at home and securing missionary progress abroad. She reported listening to sermons that solicited support of overseas missions and visiting with missionaries recently returned from China. She also noted meeting a sixteen-year-old Chinese boy brought back to Boston ostensibly to be educated but also to provide tangible evidence, crucial to fund-raising, of the mission's charitable objectives.[30] Seen in the context of Beecher, whose work she knew, Lawrence's careful accounts of employees, her record of her own reproducing body, and her willingness to experiment with progressive medical regimes suggest that she was no less dedicated to modernizing than her husband, although her focus was on the domestic realm. Sponsorship of education and foreign missions represented the public face of this emerging modern identity.

IMPERIAL RECKONINGS

Both Roberts and Lawrence exemplified patterns that could be found in other metropolitan places. With the exception of references to local conditions, like the use of Lehigh coal, Roberts's guide to American servants and families could be appreciated by any reader — New Englander, white southerner, or Englishwoman in South Asia — who aspired to the quality of life produced by servant (or slave) labor. Lawrence's struggles to resign herself to pregnancy, as well as her efforts to produce healthy, well-educated children and an orderly domestic environment, echo the stories of women beyond her own century and locale, even as the details of illnesses, labor markets, and material environments reflect the specific conditions of life in antebellum Brookline. They were both, in short, participants in a domestic cultural formation that provided imperial powers with a litmus test for civilization and a rationale for intervening in the lives of those with different domestic sensibilities.

Just as the patterns they exemplified pointed to larger global trends in domestic life, Roberts and Lawrence were clearly products of a wider world. Roberts was the leading edge of a post-Atlantic slave-trade labor market in which African Americans would try to stake their claim as free laborers and distance themselves from the degradations of slavery. In a world marked by transnational flows of goods, money, missionaries, and business communications, Lawrence met with missionaries recently returned from China and Africa and faithfully attended church services where ministers exhorted their congregations to support these missions. She was also an avid shopper, who likely filled her house with tangible proof of her proximity to the China trade, dressed her children in fine imported cloth, and delighted her guests with labor-intensive dishes containing imported ingredients.

Yet different perspectives on antebellum body work also emerge from these texts, compelling us to distinguish between participation in the production of domestic gentility, which Roberts and Lawrence had in common, and their distinct intentions. Their positions on opposite sides of the employer-employee divide suggest that the "civilized" domestic culture they both helped to create accommodated a diversity of agendas. As an employee who hoped to make domestic service an honorable profession for free African Americans, Roberts believed that mastery of domestic skills promised to confer dignity on laborers, especially if they could keep their bodies from offending their employers. As an employer attempting to preside over a genteel household, Lawrence strived to reduce the unpredictability of her employees' personal circumstances to fit the regular entries of the account ledger. Was it the plastic nature of this domestic culture—its ability to accommodate different local and personal objectives—that insulated Roberts and Lawrence from its larger use to judge nonwhite, non-Protestant peoples uncivilized?

Genteel standards for domestic life created new demands for domestic labor that men like Roberts perceived as an opportunity for African Americans to establish themselves in a profession. His ideal for the servant body was one that few could live up to. Indeed, Roberts's regime of bodily discipline for laborers who faced the early morning groggily, perspired as they worked, got dirt on their hands and under their nails, and dust in their clothes and hair distinguished those servant bodies from run-of-the-mill domestics in lesser homes. Instructed by Roberts's guide, a servant could distance himself from the dirt and sweat that marked his laboring body even as his labor enabled his bourgeois employers to do the same. In the interstices of his silence about his own identity, his insistence on the manservant's full bodily self-mastery and his vision of labor in a refined aristocratic rather than merely bourgeois home, Roberts depicted the career servant as dignified, professional, and self-disciplined. No African American who met this standard could be easily confused with a slave.

Lawrence's account book and diary take us from the public spaces of the aristocratic Gore household to the kitchens and childbeds of the subsequent generation of elite New England entrepreneurs and reformers. While her husband pursued a vision of a legally uniform and unified nation, purged of slavery and the Mormon menace and with its western territories continually peopled by like-minded Yankee emigrants, Lawrence struggled to reconcile this modern vision with the white female reproducing body necessary for such a diaspora. In the first twelve years of her marriage, repeated pregnancies, births, and the demands of breast-feeding and child care consumed her, determining many of her needs for hired domestic help. She appeared to care more about the physical stamina and character of the people she hired than about the aesthetics of their body work, although this might reflect the fact that reproductive labor rather than other forms of class display dominated her experience as mistress of the household. Whereas Roberts focused his attention on the bodies of laborers, Lawrence focused on the needs of her own pregnant body and the children it produced.

Lawrence appears aloof from imperial circuits of knowledge when one compares her to her male relatives. Her diaries and account books emphasized local conditions—the supply of domestic labor, the children's health, and social, political, and religious networks—but the books memorializing her father, husband, and father-in-law emphasized their global and national concerns. The details of transnational activity contained in these published sources highlight the traditional sinews of empire—the shipping fleets; the China trade; the desire for stable trading partners; the speculation on cargoes; the intuitive processing of news about fluctuating currencies, military conflicts, poor harvests, and property values; and the need to trust the judgments of trusted merchant friends and business partners with whom one communicates by letter.

Working with such sources, the historian appears to have a choice between documenting the male creation of traditional structures of empire—manifested in military, commercial, communication, financial, and educational institutions—or the female saturation with the nitty-gritty details of local, daily life. Connecting these nitty-gritty details to imperial formations *feels* like a greater leap of imagination when one's subject is a Yankee mistress presiding over a prosperous New England household in the 1840s, than when one's subject is a European woman resident in the Dutch Indies, a Quaker missionary to Native Americans, or the mistress of a slave household in the Caribbean. But is it?

Several patterns apparent in the Roberts and Lawrence texts disrupt this overly neat gender division of imperial labors and point to the interconnectedness of domestic and imperial cultures within even these relentlessly domestic sources. First, there is the undeniable concern, reflected in both Roberts's and Lawrence's texts, with body work. The daily labors that occupied both Lawrence and Roberts contributed to producing both the bodies that would eventually take their place in global commercial networks and the standards by which certain bodies and domestic lives would be judged deficient. The silent labor of the servant, like the cartography of domestic labor in the Lawrence house, ultimately produced bodies that felt affinity with others who displayed similar manners, education, and cosmopolitan experience. Amos Lawrence, Sarah's father-in-law, acknowledged this in his reminders to his sons that nothing would secure their place in "the world"—a loaded term that referred to his European commercial contacts—faster than good manners.

The fact that the historian can reconstruct Amos's advice to his sons reflects another aspect of Sarah Lawrence's body work: her duties as wife and mother produced filial persons who would be stirred to memorialize their fathers as self-made, pious men whose ventures in shipping and manufactures made the family's name, as well as its fortune. No descendant has been inspired to excerpt her diary to illustrate an exemplary life of childbearing and household management. Memories of her success as a mother, household manager, and employer seem to end with her life, with the exception of a few abstract effusions recorded by her male relatives in their memoirs. Subjected to the light of historical inquiry, a mother's and mistress's calculated efforts dissolve into the ethereal expressions of daughterly deference, wifely devotion, and biologically based maternal love. The emotional recollections of domestic life thus effectively contained it within the household—

kept it in the family, so to speak — and masked its connections to larger in-equities of class, race, and ethnicity.

Second, there were the religious devotions, given direction and meaning by the Episcopal Church and shared by the members of the Appleton and Lawrence families, regardless of gender, that anchored their identities in re-lation to peoples less fortunate (and less powerful), whether they be poor white Bostonians, African American slaves, or African and Chinese "hea-then." Religious feelings and religiously motivated acts of charity, such as the distribution of American Sunday School Union tracts to the poor or the decision to school half a dozen poor boys in the exquisitely decorated Apple-ton parlor, existed in tension with the accumulation of worldly goods — in the case of Sarah Lawrence's father, a personal worth of more than a million dollars that he boasted about proudly and uneasily in his diary and peri-odically resolved to give away to charity. Through acts of benevolence, such wealthy Christians tried to turn worldly comforts and privileges into virtues. Although Sarah shared this religious worldview with her male relatives, she struggled more than they to resign herself to circumstances she could not change: an unplanned pregnancy or her sister's terminal illness.

Christian resignation had a different inflection across the divide of race and class. Roberts, in contrast to Lawrence, revised a rich vein of Christian consolation to the oppressed by turning Old Testament slaves into servants and comparing the virtuous forbearance of faithful domestic laborers with the diseased, capricious demands of their unjust masters. God rewarded patient servants who behaved righteously, contended Roberts, but he also granted them happiness in an integrity that he denied to their enemies (lviii–lix).

Finally, there is the confounding, resistant fact of the documents them-selves that connects imperial and domestic cultural formations: a guide to managing an aristocratic household, European-style, written by an African American man, that would become a domestic bible of sorts for several gen-erations of white American housewives; a prosperous woman's record of servant wages, labor, and character, kept in that quintessential form of com-mercial reckoning, the account book; and the memorials to the Appleton and Lawrence men, justifying their political and economic accomplishments with references to domestic lives marked by impeccable morality, dedication to family, and diligent spiritual housekeeping. Such men looked to families and domestic environments for a source of disinterested moral purity that would prove the righteousness of their commercial and political triumphs over others less worthy. As Roberts knew all too well, however, rather than being temples of moral purity, such households offered the unwary servant injustice and oppression as conditions of employment. Ultimately, the politics of producing so-called civilized bodies and homes were not so different from those producing empires, even if Roberts and Lawrence could not or would not see the connections.

NOTES

1. Roberts, *The House Servant's Directory, or a Monitor for Private Families*, lxi. All subsequent citations of Roberts's book refer to this edition and are given parenthetically in the text.

2. See Johnson, *Soul by Soul*; Melish, *Disowning Slavery*; Sweet, *Bodies Politic*; Bushman, *The Refinement of America*; Dudden, *Serving Women*, esp. 33.

3. Conversation with Mary Fissell, Johns Hopkins University, April 2003.

4. Lawrence, Diaries and account book (cited hereafter as SEL diary).

5. See Stoler, *Race and the Education of Desire*; Kaplan, *The Anarchy of Empire in the Making of U.S. Culture*; Brown, *Good Wives, Nasty Wenches, and Anxious Patriarchs*.

6. My discussion of Roberts leans heavily on Graham Russell Hodges's introduction to Roberts, *The House Servant's Directory*.

7. Appleton subsequently authored an account of this venture, *Introduction of the Power Loom, and Origin of Lowell*, for the proprietors of the locks and canals on the Merrimack River, whose waters powered the textile mills.

8. Hodges, introduction, xx–xxiv.

9. Bushman, *The Refinement of America*. For an important discussion of the structural dependence of the refined and the pure on the disgusting and the tainted see Stallybrass and White, *The Politics and Poetics of Transgression*, esp. 139–40, on the repression of smell. See also Bakhtin, *Rabelais and His World*, chap. 5, for Bakhtin's concept of the grotesque body.

10. See Hine, "Rape and the Inner Lives of Black Women in the Middle West"; Scott, *Domination and the Arts of Resistance*, lviii–lx.

11. Information on the Appleton and Lawrence families comes from the William Appleton and Company Collection in the Harvard Business School Archives; and the Appleton Family Papers, Massachusetts Historical Society; see also Appleton, *Selections from the Diaries of William Appleton*; Lawrence, *Life of Amos A. Lawrence*; and Appleton, *Introduction of the Power Loom, and Origin of Lowell*.

12. Appleton, *Selections from the Diaries of William Appleton*, 8.

13. Lawrence, *Extracts from the Diary and Correspondence of the Late Amos Lawrence*, 89.

14. Appleton, *Selections from the Diaries of William Appleton*, 85.

15. See Gordon, *The Mormon Question.*

16. On the culture of the southern springs see Lewis, *Ladies and Gentlemen on Display.*

17. Stallybrass and White, *The Politics and Poetics of Transgression*, 20.

18. SEL Account Book, vol. 14, entry for Phebe M. Coombs.

19. On at least one occasion Lawrence noted her expectation that a healthy chambermaid would relieve her of child care; see SEL diary, vol. 6, Jan. 5, 1851. See also SEL diary, vol. 7, Oct. 11, 1851, for yet another search for a cook and chambermaid.

20. See SEL diary, vol. 6, July 10, 1850, for Lawrence's search for a new parlor girl. See also Rosenberg, *The Cholera Years*, 101–20.

21. Lasser, "The Domestic Balance of Power," 5–22.

22. SEL diary, vol. 6, Oct. 14, 1850.

23. See SEL diary, vol. 6, Dec. 22, 1850, for Sarah's application of warm water to Amory's feet when he had a bad cold; see ibid., Sep. 6, 1851, for her use of homeopathy on Amory before Dr. Lyman diagnosed asthma.

24. Lawrence's midwife, Miss Alexander, may have been related to her more celebrated counterpart, Mrs. Alexander, whose death in 1845 was noted by the Boston press. For information on Mrs. Alexander see Gregory, *Man-Midwifery Exposed and Corrected*. Sarah had been plagued by worry during previous pregnancies; see SEL diary, vol. 6, April 28, 1850, for her inability to concentrate during church out of worry about her "situation."

25. SEL diary, vol. 7, June 29, 1851.

26. SEL diary, vol. 7, July 13, 1851.

27. Appleton, *Selections from the Diaries of William Appleton*, 150.

28. Ibid., 225.

29. Lawrence, *Life of Amos A. Lawrence*, 272.

30. SEL diary, March 27, Nov. 3, 1850, March 9, 1851.

10

MARTHA HODES

Fractions and Fictions in the

United States Census of 1890

In 1869 in Massachusetts, a white working-class widow named Eunice Richardson married an African Caribbean sea captain named William Smiley
Connolly. Eunice's first husband had died in the Civil War, and her two
children began to address the captain as "Father" even before the wedding.
Within a week of the ceremony Eunice and Smiley (as he was called), together with the children, sailed to Smiley's home on Grand Cayman Island
in the British West Indies. The family settled in the district of East End,
where the Connolly family had lived since emancipation in the 1830s. Over
the years in Cayman, Eunice gave birth to two more children, and every so
often the couple ruminated about returning to the United States. "I would
like to have one good sleigh ride," Eunice sighed from the tropics one January, promising to stay for a year if her relatives would teach Smiley how to
farm New England's rocky soil. The family never did return to the United
States, but this chapter imagines just such a journey. They would set sail in
late fall, after hurricane season but in time for Eunice to enjoy her sleigh
ride, or maybe at the start of North American springtime so as to avoid the
shock of winter. Either way, they would arrive by June of 1890, in time to
be recorded in the eleventh census of the United States. Eunice and Smiley
would have been near sixty that year, the children in or near their twenties.[1]

Such an imagined voyage offers a starting point from which to reflect
on the "intimacies of empire," in the words of Ann Laura Stoler. Stoler
and others have demonstrated that empire builders across time have expressed anxiety about the mixing of their own citizens with colonial subjects,
whether in everyday life (say, between white women and their servants) or in
sexual relations (usually between white men and native women).[2] The design
of the 1890 census reflects a version of these kinds of imperialist concerns

within domestic borders. As the color line steadily became more rigid in the post-Reconstruction United States, Congress designed the federal census to employ more categories than ever before in efforts to describe people of African descent. The "one-drop" rule was not yet firm in 1890, a historical moment preceding full-fledged Jim Crow segregation, so a series of fractional categories seemed necessary to identify all people of any African ancestry whatsoever in order to prevent those people from claiming membership in the presumably monolithic category of "white." The making of the most rigid legal binary thus at first required the most detailed articulation of fractions. Benedict Anderson writes of the "(confusedly) classifying mind of the colonial state," counting "the objects of its feverish imagining," a vision that well describes U.S. census taking in 1890. "The fiction of the census," Anderson writes, "is that everyone is in it, and that everyone has one — and only one — extremely clear place. No fractions." But the enumeration of people of African descent in the census of 1890 was all about fractions. Of course fractions of blackness implied complementary fractions of whiteness; the difference was that to qualify for the designation of "white," no fractions of blackness were formally permitted. For the maintenance of white supremacy in the United States, whiteness had to be an impassible divide.[3]

The census of 1890 was the first and only U.S. census to divide people of African descent into four categories: "black," "mulatto," "quadroon," and "octoroon." Because the mathematical equations that defined each term obviously derived from sex between people of African descent and people of European descent, most especially as the legacy of racial slavery, it might appear that the state was more willing than ever before to recognize the history of sex between blacks and whites. At the same time, however, the fact of sex across racial lines remained almost entirely veiled in the voluminous analysis of the nation's population that officials produced from the 1890 census data. This near-silence stood in sharp contrast to concurrent American displays of intense white anxiety over sex and race: ideas about "race suicide" understood the falling birthrate of native-born white Americans as a threat to U.S. global superiority; more directly, virulent white discourses advocating the lynching of black men for the alleged rape of white women make the census officials' neat categories and subsequent circumspection almost comical, if that comedy were not overtaken by the tragedy of lethal white violence that reached its height in the early 1890s.[4]

In this chapter I invoke the imagined journey of a white New England woman, her African Caribbean husband, and their children to argue that the fractional divisions in the census of 1890 ultimately worked not to illuminate, or even to acknowledge, the history of sex between people of African ancestry and people of European ancestry but rather to mark Americans of African descent in efforts to exclude them from the nation in the aftermath of the destruction of racial slavery. A generation after emancipation, these fractional designations were intended to bar African Americans from the national project — a contested and intensely debated project, to be sure — of absorbing supposedly inferior peoples and molding them into citizens, in direct counterpoint to the fact that African Americans had won the constitutional rights of citizenship (and for men, the right of suffrage) following the Civil War. Racial classifications are unstable constructs, and that inherent instability always leaves room for resistance and defiance, most obviously in the form of "passing." But there is another facet to classificatory instability and confusion that becomes apparent here: just as the most imperious force is called "arbitrary" power, I argue that the very arbitrariness of census categories could work to fortify state authority. The proliferation of official racial designations at century's end, and the very confusion generated by those labels, worked to advance the demarcation and oppression of African Americans, thereby strengthening this particular manifestation of domestic colonialism.[5]

Silences about sex on the part of census analysts are easily matched by the silences of our protagonists on matters of race. We know the story of Eunice and Smiley Connolly from a collection of letters written among the members of Eunice's family between about 1850 and 1880, including a handful posted from Grand Cayman Island. Eunice was not a plantation mistress, a missionary, or a Victorian lady voyager — the kind of traveler who left the United States or Great Britain to observe a strange or seemingly depraved culture. Her letters offer few descriptions of climate and fewer still of complexions. If Eunice's narratives were atypical of nineteenth-century white travelers, so, too, was her life, not only because she married across the color line but also because that marriage resulted in an elevation of status. Eunice's first husband had done poorly in New England's industrializing economy, and after his death Eunice eked out a living as a domestic servant. In the British West Indies, by contrast, where the Connolly family belonged to the elite "colored" class, Eunice stayed home to care for her children and hired a servant of her own. Yet atypical as her life may have been, Eunice's imagined homecoming in 1890 serves well to expose the ways in which racial classification and the mission of white supremacy intersected with nation-building and the policing of intimacy within the borders of the United States on the eve of imperial expansion.

THE PROLIFERATION OF RACIAL CATEGORIES

The U.S. census of 1890 is significant not only for its unprecedented and unduplicated system of classification but also for its resonance both backward and forward in the nation's history. Census questions necessarily express earlier concerns that become more sharply articulated over time; accordingly, the 1890 categories reflected issues that began to brew not simply with emancipation but also with the possibility of black freedom that accompanied the rise of abolitionism in the 1830s. That movement's literature often invoked the specter of sex across the color line in the slaveholding South, and white opponents frequently accused northern black and white reformers of intimacy across racial lines. Such concerns became most dire in the aftermath of emancipation, and congressmen who designed the 1890 census attended to this anxiety in their scheme of racial classification. Moving in the other direction, census categories also have ramifications beyond the decade they are intended to describe; 1890 population counts would thus become the basis for quotas established by the 1924 National Origins Act. Sponsored by a senator who headed the Eugenic Research Association, this law limited immigration to 2 percent of each nationality as counted in the 1890 census, specifically to reduce the number of southern and eastern European immigrants entering the United States.[6]

The information sought on census forms, the order and wording of the questions, the pool of acceptable responses — all are presented as an objective gathering of facts, yet each constitutes inventions and interpretations. Simply to divide and count by categories of race serves to make race seem an observable, tangible characteristic. Yet the idea of race as real and recognizable is negated by the very history of the census itself, since the categories pertaining to race have changed so frequently that, invoking the census as evidence, it would be impossible to tell a coherent story about any of those categories. The category of "mulatto," for example, first appeared in 1850, disappeared in 1900, then reappeared in 1910 and 1920. The 1870 census, meanwhile, instructed enumerators to list American Indians in the column for "color," and from that year forward, categories of nationality also appeared under the designation of "race" or "color" (Chinese in 1870, Japanese in 1890, Filipino and Korean in 1930), as did categories relating to religion (beginning and ending with Hindu in 1930 and 1940). "By changing the mode of making the return every ten years," one senator commented astutely as early as 1850, "you destroy the whole value of the statistics for reference and comparison."[7]

The history of racial categorization in the United States began, of course, with a fraction. The purpose of the national census, as stipulated by the U.S. Constitution, was to determine the population of each state for the purposes of taxation and representation: a state's total population was to be calculated as all free people, with the exception of Indians living on reservations; in addition to that number, each enslaved inhabitant would count as three-fifths of a person. Between 1790 and 1840 the census counted whites, slaves, and free people of color, but significant changes came at mid century. In 1850 the census consisted of two separate schedules, one for free people and one for the enslaved. Now the census asked specifically for each individual's "color." The choices for free people were "white," "black," and "mulatto" and for slaves "black" and "mulatto," thereby acknowledging sex between African Americans and European Americans in the implicitly fractional term *mulatto*. Between 1850 and 1880 the census continued to ask not for each person's "race" but rather for "color," a term that betrayed reliance on perception rather than any truly measurable feature.[8]

The mid-nineteenth-century census also marked the first appearance of instructions regarding racial designation. "In all cases where the person is white, leave the space blank; in all cases where the person is black, insert the letter B; if mulatto, insert M," marshals were ordered in 1850 and 1860. As if personal observation could effortlessly make such determinations, the marshals were also cautioned, "It is very desirable that these particulars be carefully regarded"; it was imperative, too, that the "color of all slaves should be noted." In 1870, the year of the first postemancipation census, blank columns ceased to be acceptable ("It must not be assumed that, where nothing is written in this column, 'White' is to be understood"). Following the demise of racial slavery, census officials added definitions to their imperatives. Although the terms *quadroon* and *octoroon* would not appear on the census form proper until 1890, those words made their debut in the instructions for 1870. The designation of "mulatto," marshals were informed, should be recorded for "quadroons, octoroons, and all persons having any perceptible trace of African blood." As well, the categories of Chinese and Indian were added under the column for "color," though without accompanying definitions. The same five categories, instructions, and imperatives prevailed for

1880, but now the language of fractions intruded into the process of counting American Indians. Those living outside of reservations were to be included in the regular population, "whether full-bloods or half-breeds," and a special schedule for reservation Indians would further record whether each individual was "of full or mixed blood." From 1850 forward, then, census instructions came with imperatives of precision yet maintained that a person's classification could be determined by personal visual assessment.[9]

This hundred-year prelude exposes an ongoing revision of racial categorization and organization according to the intertwined political stakes of monolithic whiteness and African American exclusion. In the census of 1890, question number four on schedule number one, "Population and Social Statistics," reads: "Whether white, black, mulatto, quadroon, octoroon, Chinese, Japanese, or Indian." Whereas the term *mulatto* had previously included anyone in whom a census taker believed he could discern African ancestry, enumerators in 1890 had to comply with more complicated briefings. Following the imperative to "be particularly careful to distinguish between blacks, mulattoes, quadroons, and octoroons" came a narrative of fractions: "The word 'black' should be used to describe those persons who have three-fourths or more black blood; 'mulatto,' those persons who have from three-eighths to five-eighths black blood; 'quadroon,' those persons who have one-fourth black blood; and 'octoroon,' those persons who have one-eighth or any trace of black blood." Such figures implied precise genealogy, but the phrase "or any trace" gestured toward the subjective criterion of appearance that overlay the entire project.[10]

At the same time, the division of people of African descent into four fractionally defined categories had no effect on legal status: those designated as "octoroon" possessed no more federal rights than those marked as at least three-quarters Negro. Why, then, the proliferation of labels? In part, this step was related to the advancement of the census as a tool of science at century's end. The census first took on an aura of science in 1840, when the government gathered statistics regarding the mentally ill and impaired ("insane" and "idiots"), and when analysts asserted that people of African descent suffered higher rates of insanity in the free states than in the slave states. It was the census of 1850, however, that "marked the beginning of scientific census inquiry in the United States" (in the words of the director of the 1900 census). Of the "mulatto" category the instructions for 1870 announced, "Important scientific results depend upon the correct determination of this class," for Congress was impatient to move census taking into the age of "advanced statistical science," a shift propelled, as we will see, by a fixation on questions of racial fertility and endurance. Thus, the census of 1890 — the nation's centennial census, after all — would be a modern, efficient, endeavor of objective information gathering and processing. Administered by the Department of the Interior, the 1890 census was "enlarged, amended, and improved," with "nothing like it ever having been carried out under any government."[11]

The old system of marshals was now replaced with a massive bureaucracy. A staff of fifty thousand division chiefs, supervisors, special agents, experts, special experts, enumerators, special enumerators, computers, stenographers, copyists, and clerks would account for each and every one of the nation's nearly sixty-three million inhabitants. According to one admiring description, the staff formed a "great census army" engaging in "field operations" comparable to Union and Confederate generals in the Shenandoah Valley during the Civil War. Military metaphors abounded; taking a census was like "raising an army" or "mobilizing troops," and "surveying the field" was akin to a "great battle" — perhaps casting the nation's population as the enemy.[12] More than simple compilation was demanded, and the census of 1890 was the first to employ mechanical punch cards, capable of counting facts either in isolation or in combination, processed at the rate of ten thousand cards per day. Thousands of pages of statistics and analysis would ultimately be produced in an eleven-million-dollar operation that strived for virtually error-free results. Nonetheless, the 1890 census came under attack for organizational disarray, poorly trained workers, and an excess of patronage. As early as 1891, a high-ranking official called the whole process "bungling, unwieldy, and unproductive of scientific results."[13]

None of the critics, however, considered the clumsy and troublesome nature of the racial definitions. "This seems to be an inexpensive inquiry, to be accomplished by a check-mark in the schedule, and is desired by scientists," Congress pronounced in justifying the new categories for 1890. Indeed, the congressmen enjoined enumerators to exercise the "very greatest care" in obtaining "accurate information" for "the negro race." In particular, the question of whether "the mulattoes, quadroons, and octoroons are disappearing and the race becoming more purely negro, is a question which can not be settled by observation," they insisted — an ironic statement, given the reliance of those very statistics on the personal perceptions of census takers. In addition to trying to figure out whether blacks and whites were still having sex with each other after emancipation ("the race becoming more purely negro"), another goal was, according to the superintendent of the 1890 census, to study "the influence of race upon fecundity and mortality," including "the birth and death-rates of mulattoes as distinguished from negroes on the one hand, and whites on the other."[14]

This was not the first time that the state had raised such inquiries. In 1850, as sectional strife over slavery escalated, congressmen had debated recording the number of children born to each enslaved woman. One draft had marshals counting each child's "degree of removal from pure blood," and the opposition was fierce from slaveholders, who argued that the "longevity" of "different races" was not for the census to determine. Popular wisdom held that people of mixed descent were more intelligent than those of "pure" African descent, though shorter lived and less fertile, and the other side countered that Congress needed to determine definitively "whether the really black race or the intermediate colors are the longest lived and the most prolific." Queries about "removal" from "pure" African "blood" were, of course, queries about sex. Specifically, the lawmakers in 1850 were talking about (or around) the rape of enslaved women by white men, even about sex between black men and white women, and fractions peppered their debates (did "two bloods . . . mixed in the proportion of one-half or one-quarter with three quarters" result in diminished longevity?). In the closest the lawmakers came to naming sex, one congressman asked if the advocates wanted to pass laws in which "these mixtures are hereafter to be prohibited or restrained?" A senator on the other side corrected himself: "I did not mean to say that it would be useful as a means of settling who should marry, and who should not marry," he insisted, invoking matrimony as a convenient cloak for rape and illicit sex. In the end Congress voted to omit the question, but the issue of longevity did not go away. By 1890 the main concern came to be the "relative rate of increase of the white and negro population . . . especially since the war." In fact, the later-revealed undercount of African Americans in the 1870 census had "aroused much needless anxiety" among whites over a seemingly substantial increase in the black population in 1880. Although it was safely understood by 1890 that Negroes were "increasing much less rapidly than the white element," the state was now more intent than ever on marshaling statistics to answer questions about racial survival.[15]

Fractions of ancestry, professedly intended to illuminate survival by racial category, were deeply bound up with the maintenance of white supremacy, betrayed most starkly in the fact that individuals who possessed mostly, but not exclusively, European ancestry could not be counted as "white."

The 1890 census counted as "black" those whose ancestry might be as much as one-quarter European ("three-fourths or more black blood"), perhaps stemming from the understanding that sex between people of African descent and people of European descent had been so widespread that any category defined as "full-blooded" or "pure" Negro would garner such low numbers as to make the fact of "amalgamation" all too apparent. In contrast, the category of "white" was predicated on purity: the absence of any African ancestry whatsoever. State laws continued to blur the lines of whiteness and purity into the first decades of the twentieth century, defining *Negro* by varying fractions of African ancestry (say, one-eighth or one-sixteenth "black blood"), whereas the federal census of 1890 wanted "any trace" of African ancestry to disqualify individuals from the category of "white." Was "a single drop of African blood . . . sufficient to color a whole ocean of Caucasian whiteness?" asked the lawyers for Homer Plessy, the man who challenged segregation on a Louisiana railroad, and who described himself as seven-eighths white and one-eighth black. The ensuing 1896 Supreme Court decision in *Plessy v. Ferguson* furthered the one-drop rule, establishing the doctrine of "equal but separate" (as it was phrased in the original opinion).[16]

Mixing—that is, sex—mattered, because if people of exclusively African descent produced children with people of exclusively European descent, their offspring might successively lighten so that census takers (and anyone else relying on visual perception) would erroneously count those offspring as "white": erroneously, only because whiteness was defined by absolute purity. "Mixture" thus had to be quantified in efforts to prevent passing, for the "pure" Negro population (or at least those who were three-quarters Negro) could reproduce itself only by uniting with the pure; any other combination whatsoever, whether with white people or with people of mixed ancestry, amounted to lightening, at least from the standpoint of the darker parent. Indeed, maybe white authorities embraced the idea that people of mixed descent were infertile because that scenario erased the danger of generational whitening. As the lawyers defending Homer Plessy phrased it, "Why not count every one as white in whom is visible any trace of white blood?" Their answer: "There is but one reason to wit, the domination of the white race."[17]

The additions of "quadroon" and "octoroon" were not the only fractional innovations in the U.S. census of 1890. For the first time, all Indians were to be counted. This included those "not in tribal relations, whether full-bloods or half-breeds," whether "found mingled with the white population, residing in white families, engaged as servants or laborers, or living in huts or wigwams on the outskirts of towns or settlements," as well as those "living on reservations under the care of Government agents or roaming individually or in bands over unsettled tracts of country." The 1890 *Report on Indians Taxed and Not Taxed* defined reservation Indians in colonial language, as "natives" but "not citizens"; "a ward of the nation"; "a subject, still not a citizen"; "in a dependent condition, a state of pupilage, resembling that of a ward to his guardian"; and "inferiors" under the "care and control" of "superiors." With all Indians presumably enumerated, the superintendent of the 1890 census declared the American frontier closed and celebrated approaching Anglo-American global dominance. "Up to and including 1880 the country had a frontier of settlement, but at present the unsettled area has been so broken into by isolated bodies of settlement that there can hardly be said to be a frontier line," proclaimed the *Report on Population* in an interpretation that at once erased Indians and inspired historian Frederick Jackson Turner to compose his influential address on the frontier as the progenitor of American democracy. Continental expansion from east to west pointed to "a century of progress and achievement unequaled in the world's history," the 1890 report asserted, an achievement that culminated in "our development into a great and powerful nation." The director of a previous census likewise marveled in 1891 that the "enterprise exhibited by the American people in thus overrunning and occupying, settling and cultivating a million and a half of square miles in the course of a single century, is absolutely unparalleled in the history of mankind."[18]

The possibility of international dominance that loomed so brightly in the minds of some Anglo-Americans in the late nineteenth century relied on the "absorption" of "inferior" peoples, even as American citizens of African descent were excluded from this supposedly uplifting process. As John Fiske wrote of Anglo-Saxons, "It is a race which has shown a rare capacity for absorbing slightly foreign elements and moulding them into conformity." The white American, he believed, had "absorbed considerable quantities of closely kindred European blood, but he is rapidly assimilating it all." The key lay in the modifiers *slightly* and *closely kindred*, descriptors intended to bar Americans of African descent, as well as Asians and Asian Americans. The Chinese Exclusion Act of 1882 prohibited further immigration, but African Americans were more problematic precisely because they were native born and legally entitled to citizenship. When Josiah Strong defined *Anglo-Saxons* as including "all English-speaking peoples," he did not mean to include African Americans, for qualified mixture also mattered in his scheme for world domination. "The marked superiority of this race is due, in large measure, to its highly mixed origin," Strong wrote, naming Saxon, Norman, Dane, Welsh, Irish, French, and German, among other strains. Likewise, according to James K. Hosmer in *A Short History of Anglo-Saxon Freedom*, "New blood, provided it comes from sources not too remote, and is without morbid taint, invigorates" — again, the modifiers ("not too remote," "without morbid taint") served to draw boundaries around those capable of assimilation. To be sure, in Strong's rendition of Darwinian natural selection, those unfit to participate in the American nation might find themselves subject to extinction. Such would be the case when Anglo-Saxons peopled the continent of Africa. American Indians, too, figured in these equations of eligibility. As Joseph Le Conte rationalized in *The Race Problem in the South*, people of African descent were "plastic, docile, imitative" and therefore could be subordinated, whereas "highly specialized and rigid" Indians had to be exterminated. Thus were imported people marked for subjugation, immigrants for possible blending, and natives for eradication.[19]

But these respective assignments were never entirely clear-cut, since African Americans stood somewhere between imports and assimilated natives, in the minds of worried white Americans. Some found increasing numbers of European immigrants to be a greater threat than free people of color, like the Chicago sociologist who based her conclusions on data from the 1890 census. "Colored" people, she asserted, were native-born English speakers under the "moulding influence of American institutions," whereas immigrants were foreigners under the influence of thoroughly alien institutions and parents alike. "Compared with our foreign problem, the negro problem is insignificant," she asserted in 1894. Other thinkers, however, equated African ancestry with foreignness. A commentator in 1895 wrote of "the South, where the possession of the suffrage by the negro has compelled the American population to choose between misrule and practical rebellion," thereby defining *American* as whites only. A northern newspaper in 1898 likewise opined, "We have evidently just begun the task of Americanizing the African."[20]

As white supremacists pondered the fate of those who stood outside of Anglo-Saxondom, the early 1890s witnessed both the beginnings of race-suicide discourses and the height of lynching in the United States. The inherent tensions in these ideas about civilization and barbarity were neatly captured in an 1893 issue of the *Nation*: white Americans, the supposed mis-

sionaries of civilization, participated in "the most brutalizing and barbar-
izing of all the processes by which humanity can be or ever has been degraded," an anonymous writer intoned in a condemnation of lynching. "The
Anglo-Saxon flag, wherever this occurs, goes down before that of the Congo
and Ashantee," he continued, equating American barbarism and presumed
African primitivism. The same issue of the magazine, however, contained a
report on the Chicago World's Fair, at which American visitors could find
"the various bodies of uncivilized natives," along with lessons on the arts
practiced by "savage and semi-barbarous people." Thus, people of African
descent living within the borders of the United States had to be described
by fractional equations in order to determine their fertility and longevity; in
order to prevent (if only that were possible) sex with Anglo-Saxons or those
deemed capable of absorption into Anglo-Saxondom; in order, ultimately,
to prevent participation in the full privileges of national citizenship. But
fractions proved dangerous and, as we will see, the national authorities could
not bring themselves to engage much further with such perilous numbers.[21]

A RETURN VOYAGE

Let us imagine, then, that Eunice and Smiley Connolly returned from the
Caribbean, setting sail in time to be recorded in the U.S. census of 1890. In
this imagined journey the couple is accompanied by Clara, Eunice's daughter from her first marriage, born in New England in 1862; Louisa Charlotta,
born in Cayman in 1871; and a second Cayman-born daughter whose name
and year of birth are unknown. Before we follow the census taker into the
Connolly's New England home, we must make a brief detour to Grand Cayman Island in order to understand more fully how the Connolly family
was classified in the British West Indies. As a well-to-do sea captain, Smiley
Connolly belonged to an elite class of "colored" men and women in the
British Caribbean who differentiated themselves from "black" laborers. ("I
live easy enough I tell you," Eunice wrote, informing her family in America
of the "black girl" who cleaned her house.) Living in a settlement of former
slaves, Eunice partook of the privileges of white, middle-class domesticity
in a way that she had never been able to do in her native land. Although
Eunice probably never thought of herself as anything other than white, her
West Indian neighbors may well have placed her in the intermediate category of "colored," the same as her new husband. Whereas the categories
of "mulatto" and "black" could be difficult to differentiate in the United

States, the categories of "colored" and "white" could appear equally indistinct in the racial hierarchies of the West Indies. (Missionary census takers in Cayman in 1855, taking their cues from islanders, constructed a single category for "white and coloured," noting that it was "impracticable to distinguish" between the two, whereas "black" constituted a separate category.) At home, then, Smiley was a man of color who could shade over into whiteness; his wife was a white woman who might shade over into the category of "colored."[22]

Back in New England in the summer of 1890, the census taker would have turned first to Smiley Connolly, the head of household. Congress had determined and defined the census's racial categories, but the translation from instructions to implementation brought inevitable loss of rigor. Because preference in the hiring of enumerators went to local men who had served honorably in the U.S. military, the Connolly family might well have opened their front door to a neighborhood Union veteran, perhaps one who had expressed (as had Eunice's own brother) bitterness about fighting for black freedom. As this man participated in the "field operations" of the "great census army," he could easily cast a family like the Connollys as the enemy.[23]

How this official judged Smiley's racial classification would depend on where the family resided. Let us imagine, first, that they settled just outside of Lowell, Massachusetts, where Eunice's mother had lived until her death the year before (perhaps that was the occasion for their return?). The local scandal that had surrounded the couple's courtship and wedding in Massachusetts back in 1869 probably intensified on their departure, eventually becoming a well-worn shred of neighborhood gossip. That, too, we can imagine: "The Richardson girl married a colored man after the War." "Eunice ran off with a Negro." "Two of her children were mulattoes." Eunice had captured the early versions of such talk in a few terse lines in her letters home from Grand Cayman. "I can't quite get over some of her slurs," she wrote in reference to a neighbor, and she explained that she could not have given up Smiley "even though public opinion was against *him* and against *me* on *his* account." In a white neighborhood that had treated him so poorly twenty years earlier, Smiley might now exercise some caution. We know from the couple's marriage license that he may have been able to pass for white: the clerk had left the column marked "color" blank for bride and groom alike, the same as for the vast majority of New England couples. Maybe Smiley always told government officials in America that he was white, further assisted by his Irish last name and British-sounding accent. In truth foreign-born people of African descent were something of an anomaly to white North Americans, and in some 1890 census tabulations, the machinery was set up to reject foreign-born Negroes. If Smiley Connolly was white, so were his wife and children, and the census taker was swiftly out the door.[24]

But maybe the family had already encountered neighbors who recalled the scandal, so Smiley thought better of telling what those adversaries would have considered a racial falsehood. The designation of "mulatto" was easiest all around, he would reason, since it could describe his status both in the United States and the British Caribbean. Or Smiley might have told the census taker to record "quadroon" or "octoroon," terms also familiar to West Indians. No matter which of these options he selected, however, it would complicate the classification of Eunice and the children. To avoid the possibility of an unpleasant reaction from the government official inside their house, Eunice (or Smiley for her) might have chosen to claim the same ranking for husband and wife, or perhaps a category designating Eunice as a shade or two lighter, though still of African descent. In that case the children, too, would have been designated from among those three categories (they would always have a "trace" of African "blood"), and again the census taker was briskly on his way.

Perhaps, though, Eunice did not wish to be recorded in the U.S. census as anything other than a white woman, and maybe Smiley wanted it known that he had married a white woman. In that case, after Smiley labeled himself as "mulatto," "quadroon," or "octoroon," Eunice (or Smiley for her) told the man that she was white. Had the enumerator felt any suspicion—why would a white woman marry a Negro?—he could have consulted his instructions, only to find that it was "not required" for a census taker "to accept answers which he knows or has reason to believe are false." Scrutinizing Eunice more closely, the man could see that her skin was dark—from the ocean voyage, perhaps, or maybe he perceived her skin as dark simply because her hair was dark, even if straight (a lone photograph can be found in the family papers), or just because her husband was not a white man. Turning from one to the other, and back again, it may have been difficult to say whose complexion carried the duskier cast. Back to the instructions, then, which reassured the enumerator that "no statement should be accepted which he believes to be false." This woman must be attempting to erase that last trace of Negro blood, the man now assumed, and so he recorded Eunice in the census of 1890 as "octoroon," maybe even as "quadroon" for good measure.[25]

On the other hand, if the family took up residence in one of Boston's "colored" enclaves, perhaps near some of Smiley's West Indian merchant associates, Eunice might have had an even more difficult time asserting whiteness. "Should any persons persist in making statements which are obviously erroneous," the instructions went on, "the enumerator should enter upon the schedule the facts as nearly as he can ascertain them by his own observation." Living among people of color, the Connolly family was colored, too. Any combination of "mulatto," "quadroon," and "octoroon" would do, and the census taker was down to the next house.[26]

But there is also the possibility that Smiley would have considered the question of race to have no straightforward answer; he had never been counted in a U.S. census before, and his puzzlement may have appeared to the agent as evasion. Luckily, the instructions included a final imperative: if the enumerator's "own observation" yielded no apparent answer, he could ascertain the facts "by inquiry of credible persons," including "inquiry from neighbors." This endeavor offers yet another range of possible scenarios. Still-vindictive white residents in the old neighborhood might gloat at calling Eunice colored; after all, she had forfeited the privileges of white womanhood when she disgraced herself by marrying across the color line. Conversely, a conversation about racial categories with West Indian immigrants would have made the official's job no easier; some may have agreed that Eunice was a colored woman, whereas others, mindful of the Connollys' high-class status, may have considered the whole family white. All in all there is a fair chance that Eunice Connolly's racial classification would have echoed that of her husband, illuminating the ways in which the determination of racial classification flowed through men, from census enumerators to heads of household.[27]

After the census taker finished with husband and wife, he had to contend with the children. We know from the letters that Clara called Smiley "Father," and had the census taker overheard such a salutation (we can imagine Clara descending the stairs, asking, "Who's at the door, Father?"), that may have settled the matter. If Smiley was white, so was his daughter; if Smiley was a Negro of any degree, so was his daughter. The same would go for Louisa Charlotta and the second Cayman-born daughter. Had Smiley tried to explain that Clara was his stepdaughter, the census taker might have chalked that up, again, to family attempts at passing. In fact, the presence of the children would cast a different kind of doubt on Eunice's whiteness. Consider the illustrations found in a 1900 southern pamphlet, *The Negro a Beast*, depicting a white woman cuddling an apelike black baby, a dark-

DID NATURE BLUNDER?

Would you believe that the above negro was the daughter of pure whites? Never, though it was written in letters of fire upon the face of the heavens.

This pamphlet, published in 1900, depicts various images of white women who bore children of African descent; here the man's suspicious glance implies that the woman either engaged in sex with a man of color or denied her own African ancestry until the child's birth. From Charles Carroll, *The Negro a Beast, or, in the Image of God* (196). Reprinted with permission of the General Research Division, Schomburg Center for Research in Black Culture, New York Public Library, Astor, Lenox, and Tilden Foundations.

skinned little girl walking in between a fashionably dressed white couple, and two white parents at the bedside of three children, one very dark. In one interpretation the husband — who in one drawing casts a suspicious glance at his wife — has discovered his spouse's illicit liaison with a black man. In a different interpretation, though, the husband has discovered that his wife had been passing for white and that her African ancestry emerged in their offspring. Thus if the census taker could not stand the idea that Eunice was a white woman married to a man of color, he could turn her into a woman of color attempting to pass for white.[28]

But let us suppose, alternatively, that the census official accepted Smiley's status as a man of color and Eunice's as a white woman. Barbara Fields has astutely described "the well-known anomaly of American racial convention that considers a white woman capable of giving birth to a black child but denies that a black woman can give birth to a white child." If the congressmen who designed the 1890 census were concerned with the lightening and possible passing of people of African descent, then Eunice and her children would raise concerns in the other direction: about the darkening of whites or, to be more specific, the darkening of the children of white women. Marriages between white women and men of color were troublesome precisely because they entailed — under a system in which whiteness conferred the absence of fractional ancestry — the assignment of mothers and their children to different racial categories. Late-nineteenth-century ideas about white women as "carriers of the race" meant that white women were capable of degrading the race in a way that white men were not (when a white man produced a child with a black woman, that child would be classified as Negro, like its mother, and, more likely than not, disappear into a black community). If Smiley Connolly passed for white, the census takers would have been content all around. If Eunice Connolly called herself a colored woman, that, too, would have been acceptable. But if the couple classified themselves and their children according to the rules of the U.S. racial system (Eunice and Clara as white, Smiley as fractionally black, and the children of Eunice and Smiley also as fractionally black), then the family would be contributing to the pollution and dilution, indeed the contamination, of the white race.[29]

By confounding the census taker, a transgressive family like the Connollys jeopardized the entwined national projects of white purity and white supremacy. Yet at the same time, the confusion unleashed by such an encounter worked also to confer power on the state. The Connollys' imagined encounter with the census taker reveals the ways in which the incoherence of racial classification worked not only to open wedges of resistance but also to seal off those possibilities. The racial definitions of the 1890 census could generate, at least for people of known mixed descent, a whole host of difficult questions. How did you define yourself? Did you know enough of your genealogy to fit yourself into the 1890 definitions? Did those mathematical calculations turn out to contradict what you thought you were? Did your complexion seem to defy that genealogy? What if you were classified one way at home but as something else away from home? Did the fractional 1890 definitions contradict state laws, some of which accorded legal whiteness to people who could prove a certain number of "generations removed" from "Negro blood"? If you had arrived in the United States from elsewhere, did those definitions contradict the racial schemes of your native land? For that matter, was your racial classification ambiguous within your own community or perhaps your own mind? Even if you arrived at satisfactory answers to these inquiries, what if the census taker challenged those answers based on his own perceptions? After all, the instructions gave the government official final say. For that matter, what if the census taker never even asked but rather simply marked the form according to his own interpretation of visual evidence?

The federal census represented a massive statistical aggregate of the nation's population, whereas an individual's racial designation in daily life depended on local knowledge and assessments. These macro- and microlevel undertakings converged in the act of census taking, when government officials visited communities and stepped inside people's homes. Such encounters between household and functionary took place within a political and ideological context that multiplied the factor of confusion. The project of sorting and ranking the nation's inhabitants brought with it another series of inquiries, this time in the minds of those who hoped to further Anglo-Saxon supremacy. Were America's citizens of African descent to be uplifted or subjugated? Were immigrants from certain parts of Europe more foreign than Americans of African descent? Shouldn't American Indians have been exterminated long ago? Since they were still present, though, should they be assimilated or subordinated, or did that depend on whether or not they lived in wigwams? Were people of mixed descent fertile and bright or sterile and stupid? Were they dying out or multiplying, or were immigrant families the ones reproducing at an alarming rate?

In the end, as we will see, the confusion proved too overwhelming for the census analysts, and the state's imperatives about precision turned into pronouncements of uselessness. In that move alone, the state gathered power to itself: the calculated decisions or necessarily immediate responses, the suspicions, accusations, and perhaps humiliations endured by a family like the Connollys in an encounter with the census taker came largely to be erased in the analysis of the 1890 data. The official's prerogative to mark the columns at his own discretion (and to seek validation from neighbors) could serve ultimately as an exercise in subordination. The arbitrary nature of racial categories complicated the process of classification, but inherent in that very arbitrariness, families like the Connollys could experience the weight of imperious power. Indeed, the fact that the fractionally defined categories of the 1890 census had no effect whatsoever on a person's federal legal status served to mock the imperatives of precision for all people of any African descent. Presumed fractional accuracy was meant only to maintain an invincible boundary between whiteness and African ancestry for the sake of upholding white supremacy.

THE ERASURE OF SEX ACROSS THE COLOR LINE

Despite all the instructions and imperatives that accompanied the census forms of 1890, the four fractionally defined categories for people of African descent rarely appeared in the subsequent manipulation of the data. Readers of the twenty-five volumes, three-part compendium, statistical atlas, and abstract would find those four categories invoked either inconsistently or, more often, not at all. Brimming just beneath the surface of the statistics and analysis—impartial-sounding narratives punctuated by innumerable tables complete with explanatory footnotes—readers would find a combination of randomness and incoherence that nurtured the authority of the state. Household members in conversation with census officials could extract a measure of resistance through categorical defiance, but the design and workings of the 1890 census also expose what I have elsewhere called "the mercurial nature and abiding power of race." In this case, within the arbitrary nature of racial constructs lay the authority of the state to divide, count, mark, and erase. Those initiatives in turn fostered the intertwined national projects of subjugation, assimilation, and extinction at the turn of the century, in the interest of white purity and supremacy.[30]

In the analysis of the 1890 census data, people of African descent were occasionally divided into four categories, as in a table entitled "The Colored Population Classified as Blacks, Mulattoes, Quadroons, Octoroons, Chinese,

Japanese, and Civilized Indians" in the *Compendium of the Eleventh Census*. Most often, however, the single category of "colored" or "Negro" served to encompass all people of any African descent. In the *Statistical Atlas*, for example, the categories under "color and race" were enumerated as "whites, negroes, Indians, and Asiatics, the term negroes including all persons of negro descent." Some tables noted that the term *colored* referred to "persons of African descent only," whereas elsewhere the term *colored* encompassed anyone outside the category of "white." The *Report on Population*, for example, noted that numbers for the nation's "colored element" included Chinese, Japanese, and Indians; tables in the *Compendium* headed "Colored" likewise referred readers to a footnote indicating that the term included "Persons of negro descent, Chinese, Japanese, and civilized Indians."[31]

If people of African descent were rarely broken down into fractional categories for the purpose of analysis, white people were frequently divided into categories of nativity. Yet here, too, it remains difficult to decipher patterns. In the *Report on Crime, Pauperism, and Benevolence* some tables divided native-born whites according to whether their mothers or fathers were native born, while dividing the category of "colored" into Negroes, subdivided into "pure" or "mixed," followed by Chinese, Japanese, and Indians. Other tables divided the category of "white" according to whether one or both parents were native or foreign (without specifying which parent) and divided the category of "colored" into Negroes, Chinese, Japanese, and Indians. The *Report on the Insane, Feeble-Minded, Deaf and Dumb, and Blind*, in yet another arrangement, divided whites by nativity but divided the category of "colored" into "black" and "mixed blood," likely because percentages of African ancestry mattered to statistics on mental health. In short, any uniformity of divisions and subdivisions remained beyond the grasp of discerning readers because no such rigor existed at all.[32]

If perusers of the volumes doubted the arbitrary nature of racial classification, they needed only to scan the footnotes that accompanied the tables concerning schools, prisons, and charitable institutions. Sometimes the category "white" was footnoted as "Includes unseparated colored," but most strikingly, census officials were unable to fit Asians on the Pacific Coast into schemes fabricated in the context of the nation's East Coast populations. For the city of Los Angeles the category of "white" was footnoted as "Includes 12 Japanese," whereas for San Diego, the category of "colored" included a number of "Mongolians." For Washington State, where one table listed twelve Chinese, the footnote indicated that five were actually Japanese. A table of female prisoners in California recorded two Chinese, except that a footnote indicated that the number "Includes 1 Japanese." In a table of inmates the number 2 under the column "Chinese" for Washington State was footnoted simply as "Japanese." And a footnote for a table of city prisoners in Washington indicated that the five Chinese "includes 5 Japanese." These conflations become particularly conspicuous in contrast to the initial obsession with fractional definitions of African ancestry.[33]

If the federal government was concerned with measuring sex across black-white racial lines—as is evident in the definitions of *black, mulatto, quadroon,* and *octoroon* in the census instructions—then the analysis of marriage statistics should have been important. "Statistics of conjugal condition are presented for the first time as part of the United States census," the analysts noted proudly, yet when it came to marriage across racial lines, they retreated. The term *condition* (indicating single, married, widowed, or divorced) was key, for the analysts recorded only whether or not someone was or had been married, not who was married to whom. Thus even if census takers had recorded Eunice and Smiley Connolly as respectively "white" and "colored," Eunice would have been counted under "Females—Native White, Native Parents—Married," and Smiley would have been counted under "Males—Colored—Married," with no indication that the two were husband and wife.[34]

The closest indication of sex across the color line can be found in two tables respectively counting prisoners and paupers. Labeled "Analysis of Mixed Parentage," and invoking categories of nationality, the first chart indicated one person with an African-born mother and an English-born father and another with an African-born mother and a New Zealand–born father; the second noted one person born to a West Indian mother and an English father. Thus the census analysts marked only three couples out of almost sixty-three million inhabitants of the nation as having crossed the "blood" of Africa and Europe (and produced criminals and beggars at that). Other tables for prisoners and paupers, moreover, divided whites by nativity and invoked the term *colored* to encompass Negro, Chinese, Japanese, and American Indian. "The Chinese and Japanese were, of course, born abroad," the analysts explained, though this was hardly the case for all people of Asian descent living in the United States in 1890, "while the Negroes and Indians may be supposed to have been born in this country." This oddly tentative phrasing regarding the nativity of Indians and African Americans (recall that foreigners of African descent were dismissed in the 1890 analysis) perfectly

TABLE **25.**—INMATES OF BENEVOLENT INSTITUTIONS, PUBLIC AND PRIVATE, IN THE UNITED STATES IN 1890, EXCLUSIVE OF PRISONS, ALMSHOUSES, HOSPITALS FOR THE INSANE, AND SCHOOLS FOR THE DEAF, THE BLIND, AND THE FEEBLE MINDED, BY STATES AND TERRITORIES, SHOWING THE NUMBER OF MALE INMATES IN THE AGGREGATE AND BY COLOR, NATIVITY, AND RACE.

STATES AND TERRITORIES.	Aggregate.	WHITE.						COLORED.		
		Native.				Foreign born.	Nativity unknown.	Negroes.	Chinese.	Indians.
		Parents native.	One parent foreign.	Parents foreign.	One or both parents unknown.					
The United States ..	55,316	11,485	2,490	11,283	12,062	13,141	2,167	2,135	a41	512
North Atlantic division...	31,382	7,112	1,693	7,516	5,232	7,716	890	898	15	310
Maine	106	63	3	3	21	15	....	1	....	....
New Hampshire	182	43	13	59	37	28	2	....	....	....
Vermont	129	47	3	28	33	9	8	1	....	....
Massachusetts	2,858	539	214	683	508	757	94	61	....	2
Rhode Island	478	77	10	33	164	133	44	17	....	....
Connecticut	666	116	25	185	158	93	51	31	6	1
New York	18,189	3,399	768	4,827	3,285	4,853	503	541	7	6
New Jersey	1,348	267	52	383	195	403	35	13	....	....
Pennsylvania	7,426	2,561	605	1,315	831	1,425	153	233	2	301
South Atlantic division...	2,991	734	60	278	979	531	71	338	....	....
Delaware	107	20	2	9	64	4	7	1	....	....
Maryland	1,226	256	42	206	312	321	16	73	....	....
District of Columbia..	717	127	8	41	269	106	23	143	....	....
Virginia	147	43	1	3	7	55	15	23	....	....
West Virginia	22	7	....	5	10	....	....	....	....	....
North Carolina	110	91	....	....	9	3	....	7	....	....
South Carolina	309	34	2	1	193	13	1	65	....	....
Georgia	313	147	4	13	108	20	9	12	....	....
Florida	40	9	1	....	7	9	....	14	....	....
North Central division....	14,440	2,355	426	2,206	4,438	3,368	1,026	457	16	148
Ohio	4,422	1,191	188	697	1,409	561	159	205	12	....
Indiana	1,430	238	26	103	628	193	106	106	....	30
Illinois	3,285	434	83	397	910	1,195	226	36	4	....
Michigan	855	69	20	77	222	263	164	29	....	11
Wisconsin	919	58	10	240	248	183	168	10	....	2
Minnesota	786	33	6	51	270	193	36	6	....	105
Iowa	427	23	6	51	273	62	12	....	....	....
Missouri	1,924	263	74	478	314	607	133	55	....	....
North Dakota	7	1	....	....	....	6	....	....	....	....
South Dakota	3	....	....	....	....	3	....	....	....	....
Nebraska	153	19	3	24	65	29	12	1	....	....
Kansas	229	26	....	12	99	73	10	9	....	....
South Central division....	3,146	787	99	427	638	730	78	386	1	....
Kentucky	658	135	24	80	156	195	21	47	....	....
Tennessee	449	133	10	45	105	31	4	121	....	....
Alabama	139	34	10	6	50	12	23	4	....	....
Mississippi	116	42	....	....	33	7	3	31	....	....
Louisiana	1,377	332	45	250	192	383	21	144	1	....
Texas	379	102	9	35	98	90	6	39	....	....
Arkansas	28	9	1	2	4	12	....	....	....	....
Western division	3,357	497	212	856	775	796	102	56	a9	54
Montana	51	7	4	10	2	28	....	....	....	....
Wyoming	18	3	2	2	1	10	....	....	....	....
Colorado	317	58	12	23	113	104	4	3	....	....
New Mexico	40	6	1	2	1	13	....	....	....	17
Arizona	15	6	....	2	....	7	....	....	....	....
Utah	28	7	4	3	....	9	5	....	....	....
Nevada	28	....	4	8	13	1	....	....	....	2
Idaho	....	....	....	....	....	....	....	....	....	....
Washington	216	23	8	19	50	92	19	3	b2	....
Oregon	82	14	1	5	24	32	5	1	....	....
California	2,562	373	176	782	571	500	69	49	c7	35

a Includes 3 Japanese.   b Japanese.   c Includes 1 Japanese.

The three footnotes to this table indicate the conflation of the category "Japanese" with that of "Chinese" in the U.S. census of 1890; both categories are further subsumed under the heading "Colored." U.S. Census Office, *Compendium of the Eleventh Census: 1890* (2:206).

ANALYSIS OF MIXED PARENTAGE.

NATIONALITIES.	Total.	BIRTHPLACE OF FATHERS.													
		Can-ada, En-glish.	Can-ada, French.	Bra-zil.	Cuba.	Mex-ico.	En-gland.	Scot-land.	Wales.	Ire-land.	Aus-tria.	Azore isl-ands.	Ba-varia.	Bel-gium.	Cor-sica.
Total......	1,274	77	11	1	5	2	288	196	22	341	4	1	2	2	1
Canada, English .	134		7		1		27	12		70					
Canada, French..	7	1					1			2					
Mexico	3							1		1					
South America ..	1														
England.........	226	13	1					46	7	118					
Scotland.........	159	7			1		36		2	92					1
Wales	14						7	1		5					
Ireland	484	51	3		2	1	171	118	10		1	1		1	
Austria..........	3						2								
Bavaria..........	1														
Belgium..........	2									1					
Bohemia..........	1									1					
Denmark	3						1			1					
France	79	1				1	16	7	2	19					
Germany	113	3		1	1		22	10	1	25	2		1	1	
Greece...........	1														
Holland	8						1						1		
Italy	4														
Norway	2						1								
Portugal.........	1									1					
Prussia..........	2										1				
Russia...........	2														
Spain............	9						2	1		2					
Sweden	1									1					
Switzerland	6	1													
Africa...........	2						1								
Australia........	6									2					

(Row label at left margin: BIRTHPLACE OF MOTHERS.)

In a rare acknowledgment of sex between people of European descent and people of African descent in the government's analysis of the U.S. census of 1890, this table, concerning prisoners and paupers, records a single individual of mixed African and English ancestry. U.S. Census Office, *Compendium of the Eleventh Census: 1890* (2:166).

reflects the conviction that those outside the category of "white" were not really Americans at all and thus undeserving of citizenship.[35]

In sum, the four fractionally defined categories put forth to describe African Americans were derived from proportions of ancestry (in turn derived from sex between people of African and European descent), yet despite the earnest entreaties to the scientific urgency of this information, analysts made very little use of those categories. The irony, of course, is that had census officials endeavored to grapple with the frequency of sex across the color line, they would have found themselves even more hopelessly mired in the kinds of uncertainties that must always accompany efforts to classify people by invented categories of race. A 1915 Census Bureau report admitted as much, pointing out that the categories of "black" and "mulatto" could measure only "with some uncertain degree of accuracy" the infusion of "white blood" in those "classified as Negro." Specifically invoking the 1890 definitions, the report pondered the infinite range of fractions, noting that if six individuals of varying proportions of "Negro blood" were to intermarry, their great-grandchildren "would be represented by approximately 70 fractions having 128 as a denominator and numbers ranging between 17 and 100 as numerators." As the African American intellectual Kelly Miller put it in 1924, "Various enumerations of the Negro population by the Census Office since 1860 have not been very flattering to the scientific reputation of that bureau"; those enumerations, he averred, were "conflicting and inconsistent," even "whimsical," and characterized by "unaccountable capriciousness." If the division of people of African descent into four categories proved too confusing, that powerful confusion ultimately proved dangerous. "These figures are of little value," the 1890 *Report on Population* announced, after listing the numbers for each category, adding, "as an indication of the extent to which the races have mingled, they are misleading." Perhaps it was during the analysis of the data that census officials realized how unseemly, even disruptive, it would be to think about the meaning of "mulattoes," "quadroons," and "octoroons" in a government forum at the hopeful start of an era of imperial power.[36]

At the dawn of the new century the government retreated yet further from questions about sex across the color line. In 1900 the census listed the single category of "black," defined as "Negro or Negro Descent." At the same time, however, census officials attempted to define American Indians in ways that paralleled—though with a crucial distinction—the 1890 categories for African Americans. "If the Indian has no white blood, write 0," the instructions read. "If he or she has white blood, write, 1/2, 1/4, 1/8, whichever fraction is nearest the truth." If the 1890 categories were intended to mark "black blood" in efforts to bar people of African descent from absorption into the white world, then the 1900 categories were intended to mark "white blood," in efforts to facilitate the absorption of American Indians, a project predicated on the appropriation of native land.[37]

Still, the U.S. census would not jettison fractions of African ancestry for two more decades. In 1910 and 1920 the category of "mulatto" reappeared, defined as anyone "having some proportion or perceptible trace of negro blood." The classification of "black" was reserved for "all persons who are evidently fullblooded negroes," a category that purported to count people of "pure" African ancestry (as the census of 1890 had not) but that hedged on precision with the dismissive modifier *evidently*. Yet if the terms *perceptible* and *evidently* acknowledged just how fickle racial classifications could be, that same awareness did not influence the enumeration of American Indians. In 1910 all Indians, both on and off reservations, were to be counted on a special schedule, in three columns labeled respectively "Indian," "white," and "negro." Enumerators were to divide each person into "the fractions which show the proportions of Indian and other blood," making sure each sum added up to "1" — necessary to determine who qualified as a federally recognized Indian for the sake of retaining land. The census of 1920 marked the final usage of the category of "mulatto" and hence the last attempt at an official fractional division of people of African descent on the national level. In 1890 the Jim Crow laws that would rule by 1930 had not yet become pervasive, and the U.S. government was laboring mightily to figure out how to exclude a whole generation of free people of African descent from the newly invigorated American mission of assimilating supposedly inferior "races." By the early decades of the twentieth century federal officials had discovered another kind of potency in the now-entrenched laws of racial segregation. Enforced separation of "white" and "colored," especially in the South, where most African Americans resided, but also in the North, would, they hoped, work to maintain Anglo-Saxon purity and white supremacy at home.[38]

CODA: THE REST IS FICTION

If the Connolly family arrived in the United States to be counted in the census of 1890, the records would not be available, for most of those returns burned up in a fire in 1921. Eunice, Smiley, and the children had no opportunity to contemplate a visit to New England near the end of the century anyway, for the entire family drowned in a hurricane on the Mosquito Cays off the Coast of Nicaragua in 1877. Nonetheless, let us extend their imaginary lives a moment longer. Had the family lived, and had their descendants moved back and forth between the United States and the British Caribbean, marrying and producing children, some of Eunice and Smiley's great-great-great grandchildren would have encountered the U.S. census of 2000, a census that reflected crucial historical developments both in civil rights and in developing national debates about the nature of race. Most notably, respondents in the year 2000 were for the first time permitted to check off more than one category to describe themselves. In other ways, however, the census of 2000 also reflected the history that had come before. "What is this person's race?" the form inquired, and the alternatives presented were visually striking. Immediately under the question came a box next to the word "White." Directly underneath that, a box matched up with "Black, African Am. or Negro," and beneath that, a box indicated "American Indian or Alaska Native," followed by a line in which the respondent was instructed to "Print name of enrolled or principal tribe." Clearly, then, the order was neither alphabetical nor historically chronological. Farther down still, came columns of options—Asian Indian, Chinese, Filipino, Japanese, Korean, Vietnamese, Native Hawaiian, Guamanian or Chamorrow, and Samoan—followed by "Other Asian" and "Other Pacific Islander." Arrows from these last two options led the respondent yet farther down the page to an additional line, with the instructions to "Print race." Finally, underneath that, came the notation "Some other race," followed by another line and the same instructions to "Print race."[39]

Those who defined themselves exclusively as white got to check off the first box and move swiftly on to the next question. Those who considered themselves black checked off a box underneath that, and moved on; American Indians moved yet another row down, with the added burden of claiming a single tribe. Individuals who did not fit themselves exclusively into any of those categories had to read through an array of options until they had traveled a full three inches from the category of "White." In short, the farther a person moved "down" from whiteness, the more confusion ensued. As one scholar has noted, the "colonial practice" of "putting Europeans at the top of the list in the census" served as "a marker of the status differential between the ruling whites" and the "subordinate" populations. Such a description pertains to the U.S. censuses of 1890 and 2000 alike.[40]

Most especially in the census of 1890, we see the pretension to measurable categories of race and to fraction-free whiteness. Sex between those deemed worthy of citizenship and those deemed unworthy spurred white anxieties about the corruption of Anglo-Saxonism, which in turn circled back to uphold convictions about inclusion and exclusion in the nation-state. We see, too, in the analysis of the 1890 data, the erasure of sex between people of European descent and people of African descent, leading eventually to the decree of a single census category for all people of any African descent, no matter how many white ancestors could be counted. The design and implementation of the 1890 census, and the subsequent interpretation of that data, reflects a transitional moment between black freedom and Jim Crow segregation, in which the federal government invoked a proliferation of racial categories in efforts to maintain white supremacy. In the imagined encounter between the Connolly family and a federal official in the summer of 1890, we see, too, the ways in which the arbitrary nature of racial classification could translate into arbitrary power. That power—of illusion and confusion—remains palpable, even if the rest is fiction.

NOTES

I thank audiences at the "Tense and Tender Ties" workshop, the College of William and Mary, and Hunter College High School. For close readings I thank Paul Kramer, Barbara Krauthamer, Ann Laura Stoler, Laura Wexler, and especially Bruce Dorsey.

1. Eunice Connolly to Lois Davis, East End, Grand Cayman, Jan. 5, 1873, Davis Papers; some punctuation has been added for readability. The full story, traced from the Davis Papers, will be told in a forthcoming book, under contract with W. W. Norton.

2. Stoler, "Tense and Tender Ties," 831. On anxieties see, e.g., Stoler, *Race and the Education of Desire*, 95–164; Stoler, *Carnal Knowledge and Imperial Power*, 67–70, 112–39; Rafael, "Colonial Domesticity: White Women"; Kaplan, *The Anarchy of Empire in the Making of U.S. Culture*, 23–50.

3. Anderson, *Imagined Communities*, 165, 169, 166. On domestic and imperial parallels see Painter, *Standing at Armageddon*, 141–69; Gatewood, *Black Americans and the White Man's Burden, 1898–1903*; Aptheker, *Toward Negro Freedom*, 88–95. On the U.S. one-drop rule see Davis, *Who Is Black?*, esp. 51–80.

4. By "sex" I mean reproductive sex, as nonreproductive sex across racial categories is uncountable. As I argue in *White Women, Black Men*, whites in the antebellum U.S. South could tolerate liaisons between white women and black men until the production of children blurred the equation of blackness and slavery by producing free children of partial African descent.

5. For a different component of this argument see Hodes, "The Mercurial Nature and Abiding Power of Race." Paul A. Kramer has noted tensions between "racial-exceptionalist" defenses of U.S. colonialism and "national-exceptionalist" anti-imperialist discourse; see Kramer, "Empires, Exceptions, and Anglo-Saxons."

6. Goldberg, *Racial Subjects*, 32–33. Harris, "From Abolitionist Amalgamators to 'Rulers of the Five Points'"; Dorsey, *Reforming Men and Women*, 150–54. On the 1924 law see Jacobson, *Whiteness of a Different Color*, 83–90.

7. U.S. Congress, *Congressional Globe*, vol. 19, 31st Cong., 1st sess., 1850, 678. Nayan Shah points out that "Hindu" was "more a reference to their 'national' origin—Hindustani" (Shah, *Contagious Divides*, 313n48). On census forms see Starr, "The Sociology of Official Statistics." On changing categories in the U.S. federal census see Goldberg, *Racial Subjects*, 27–58, but note that Goldberg incorrectly omits the categories of Chinese and Indian for 1880 (36); and Nobles, *Shades of Citizenship*, 25–84.

8. Anderson, "Counting by Race." The two best sources for census questions and instructions are Wright, *The History and Growth of the United States Census*; and Gauthier, *Measuring America*. On 1850 see Anderson, *The American Census*, 32–57.

9. Wright, *The History and Growth of the United States Census*, 128–29, 152–54, 157, 158, 166, 168, 171; Gauthier, *Measuring America*, 10, 12, 13, 14, 15, 18, 20, 21. Thornton, *American Indian Holocaust and Survival*, 186–224. Note that Nobles, *Shades of Citizenship*, misstates the 1870 instructions regarding blank columns (52). On the visual nature of race see Hodes, *White Women, Black Men*, 96–122; Smith, *American Archives*, esp. 177–86.

10. U.S. Census Office, *Report on Population of the United States at the Eleventh Census*, 1:cciv; Wright, *The History and Growth of the United States Census*, 177, 187; Gauthier, *Measuring America*, 27.

11. Merriam, "The Evolution of American Census-Taking," 839; Wright, *The History and Growth of the United States Census*, 157; Stone, "The Census of 1880," 110; Wright, "Lessons from the Census," 725. On science and the census see Cohen, *A Calculating People*, 175–204; Anderson, *The American Census*, 83–102.

12. Wright, "How a Census Is Taken," 730–31; U.S. Congress, *Permanent Census Bureau*, 66, 72, 68. For overall procedures see Wright, "How a Census Is Taken," 727–37; "The Census of the United States," 132; Adams, "How the People Are Counted," 473–76; Wright, "Lessons from the Census," 721–28; "The United States Census of 1890"; Wright, *The History and Growth of the United States Census*, 69–76, 84–88, 92; Merriam, "The Evolution of American Census-Taking," 831–42; Holt, *The Bureau of the Census*, 27–31.

13. Truesdell, *The Development of Punch Card Tabulation in the Bureau of the Census, 1890–1940*, 26–56; Austrian, *Herman Hollerith*, 58–73. Wright, "Lessons from the Census," 75. For criticisms see also "The Census Muddle"; "The Misfortune of the Census"; Du Bois, *Some Notes on Negro Crime, Particularly in Georgia*, 9–18.

14. U.S. Congress, *Congressional Record*, vol. 20, 50th Cong., 2nd sess., pt. 3, 1889, 2244, 2246. Porter, "The Eleventh Census," 328.

15. U.S. Congress, *Congressional Globe*, vol. 19, 31st Cong., 1st sess., 1850, 674, 676. U.S. Census Office, *Report on Population of the United States at the Eleventh Census*, 1:xciv-xcv. On mixture see Nott, "The Mulatto a Hybrid"; Hoffman, *Race Traits and Tendencies of the American Negro*, 177–88. On undercounting see U.S. Bureau of the Census, *Negro Population, 1790–1915*, 25–28; Anderson, *The American Census*, 78–81, 89–90.

16. Mangum, *The Legal Status of the Negro*, 1–17, 245–48. *Plessy v. Ferguson* 163 U.S. at 547; Olsen, *The Thin Disguise*, 98. See also Chesnutt, "What Is a White Man?"

17. Quoted in Olsen, *The Thin Disguise*, 85.

18. Wright, *The History and Growth of the United States Census*, 181; *Report on Indians Taxed and Not Taxed in the United States (Except Alaska) in the Eleventh Census*, 663, 664; *Report of Population*, 1:xxxiv, xxvii; Turner, "The Significance of the Frontier in American History"; Walker, "The Great Count of 1890," 408. On proving federally recognized Indian status through "blood quantum" see Churchill and Morris, "Key Indian Laws and Cases"; Jaimes, "Federal Indian Identification Policy"; Snipp, "American Indians"; Wilson, "Blood Quantum"; "Certificate of Degree of Indian or Alaska Native Blood" concedes that the "base rolls of some tribes are deemed to be correct by statute, even if errors exist" (20776).

19. Fiske, *American Political Ideas Viewed from the Standpoint of Universal History*, 105; Strong, *Our Country*, 161, 171–72, 175–77; Hosmer, *A Short History of Anglo-Saxon Freedom*, 325. Le Conte, *The Race Problem in the South*, 360–61. See also Hofstadter, *Social Darwinism in American Thought*, 170–92. On the encounter between Chinese immigrants and authorities, with parallels to the argument here, see McKeown, "Ritualization of Regulation."

20. Atchison, *Un-American Immigration*, 46, 54; Denison, "The Survival of the American Type," 17; *Philadelphia Record*, quoted in Aptheker, *Toward Negro Freedom*, 93. On fears of immigrants see, e.g., Smith, *Urban Disorder and the Shape of Belief*, 147–74.

21. "Judge Lynch as an Educator"; "The Columbian Exposition — IX." For early race-suicide discussions see Walker, "Immigration and Degradation"; Billings, "The Diminishing Birth-Rate in the United States"; Gordon, *The Moral Property of Women*, 86–104. On lynching see Wells-Barnett, *On Lynchings*; Hodes, *White Women, Black Men*, 176–208; Bederman, *Manliness and Civilization*, 45–76.

22. Eunice Connolly to Lois Davis, East End, Grand Cayman, Aug. 25, 1870, continuation of May 16, 1870, letter, Lois Wright Richardson Davis (hereafter LWRD) Papers; *Missionary Record of the United Presbyterian Church*, vol. 10, Nov. 1, 1855, 190. On the racial classification of Eunice and Smiley Connolly across national boundaries see Hodes, "The Mercurial Nature and Abiding Power of Race."

23. U.S. Congress, *Permanent Census Bureau*, 8.

24. Eunice Connolly to Lois Davis, East End, Grand Cayman, March 7, 1870, Davis Papers; Massachusetts Vital Records, Dracut, 1869, vol. 218, 166; Truesdell, *The Development of Punch Card Tabulation in the Bureau of the Census, 1890–1940*, 64, 67, 73, 74.

25. Carroll, *The History and Growth of the United States Census*, 179. These instructions technically pertained to the issue of encumbrances on homes and farms, but it is perfectly plausible that the dynamics were extended to the question of racial categories.

26. Ibid.

27. Starr notes that "ambiguities of classification" can result in misunderstanding, evasion, and lying ("The Sociology of Official Statistics," 34).

28. Clara Stone to Lois Davis, continuation of letter from William Smiley Connolly to Lois Davis, East End, Grand Cayman, Oct. 16, 1872, LWRD Papers; Carroll, *The Negro a Beast, or, in the Image of God*, 74, 196, 226; and see Larsen, *Passing*, 49–51, in which passing

women discuss fears of giving birth to dark children. Regarding the Mixed-Marriage Law of 1898 in the Netherland Indies, Ann Laura Stoler discusses the perception that European women (often lower-class) who married native men denied the privilege of European status to their children; see Stoler, "Sexual Affronts and Racial Frontiers," 217–22.

29. Fields, "Ideology and Race in American History," 149. On white women as "carriers of the race" see Hodes, *White Women, Black Men*, 198–202. In "Color, Classification, and Manhood" I argue that the design and implementation of the 1890 census, and the confusion inherent in its categories, served to compromise the agency and autonomy of men of color and that men of color were cast as the contaminators of white women and the white race.

30. Wright, *The History and Growth of the United States Census*, 75; Hodes, "The Mercurial Nature and Abiding Power of Race."

31. All categories listed: U.S. Census Office, *Compendium of the Eleventh Census*, 1:470; also U.S. Census Office, *Report on Population of the United States at the Eleventh Census*, 1:397. Single category for all people of African descent: U.S. Census Office, *Statistical Atlas of the United States Based upon Results of the Eleventh Census*, 17; also U.S. Census Office, *Report on Population of the United States at the Eleventh Census*, 1:ccii, 400, 402; U.S. Census Office, *Report on Population of the United States at the Eleventh Census*, 2:23, 43, 51, 52, 106, 108, 109, 113; U.S. Census Office, *Compendium of the Eleventh Census*, 2:182; 3:278, 309, 325; U.S. Census Office, *Report on Vital and Social Statistics in the United States at the Eleventh Census*, 2:81; U.S. Census Office, *Vital Statistics of Boston and Philadelphia*, 236–37; U.S. Census Office, *Report on the Insane, Feeble-Minded, Deaf and Dumb, and Blind in the United States at the Eleventh Census*, 15, 16; U.S. Census Office, *Abstract of the Eleventh Census*, 40, 47. "African descent only": U.S. Census Office, *Compendium of the Eleventh Census*, 1:473, 475–515. Anyone not white: U.S. Census Office, *Report on Population of the United States at the Eleventh Census*, 1:xciii, 397, 489, 524, 576, 681; U.S. Census Office, *Compendium of the Eleventh Census*, 3:5, 6, 72, 91, 112, 198, 277, 334, 349; U.S. Census Office, *Abstract of the Eleventh Census*, 43–45, 54, 58–65, 70–72. These references, and those below, do not exhaust all supporting examples.

32. U.S. Census Office, *Report on Crime, Pauperism, and Benevolence in the United States at the Eleventh Census: 1890*, 2: 3, 12, 18, 25, 127, 651; 148, 401, 490, 515, 821. *Report on the Insane, Feeble-Minded, Deaf and Dumb, and Blind in the United States at the Eleventh Census*, 18, 29, 36, 157. In another model, whites were divided by their own and their parents' nativity, whereas the category of "colored" was divided into Negroes, Chinese, Japanese, and Indians: U.S. Census Office, *Compendium of the Eleventh Census*, 2:161, 162, 170, 175. Elsewhere, "white" was broken down only into native and foreign, juxtaposed to monolithic "colored": U.S. Census Office, *Report on Population of the United States at the Eleventh Census*, 1: 733; U.S. Census Office, *Compendium of the Eleventh Census*, 1: 469, 3: 198–99, 268; U.S. Census Office, *Report on Vital and Social Statistics in the United States at the Eleventh Census*, 1:29, 2: 43, 44; U.S. Census Office, *Vital Statistics of Boston and Philadelphia*, 20; U.S. Census Office, *Abstract of the Eleventh Census*, 11; U.S. Census Office, *Re-*

port on the Insane, Feeble-Minded, Deaf and Dumb, and Blind in the United States at the Eleventh Census, 78.

33. U.S. Census Office, *Compendium of the Eleventh Census*, 2:214, 224, 253, 255; "Report on Education," in U.S. Census Office, *Report on Population of the United States at the Eleventh Census*, 2:51–52, 106, 124; U.S. Census Office, *Compendium of the Eleventh Census*, 2:253, 177, 179, 206, 184, 193. On the "eastern black-white binary" see Gordon, *The Great Arizona Orphan Abduction*, 356–57n88, and 96–106; on West Coast concerns about sex between Asians and whites see Yu, "Mixing Bodies and Cultures"; Shah, *Contagious Divides*, 97–104.

34. U.S. Census Office, *Compendium of the Eleventh Census*, 3:115, 149. U.S. Census Office, *Report on Population of the United States at the Eleventh Census*, 1:830–80.

35. U.S. Census Office, *Compendium of the Eleventh Census*, 2:166–67, 173; 164, 170–71.

36. U.S. Bureau of the Census, *Negro Population, 1790–1915*, 207, 208n1. Miller, *The Everlasting Stain*, 226, 228. U.S. Census Office, *Report on Population of the United States at the Eleventh Census*, 1:xciii.

37. Gauthier, *Measuring America*, 36, 44. On absorption see Powell, "Are Our Indians Becoming Extinct?" For two key analyses see Wolfe, "Land, Labor, and Difference"; and Harris, "Whiteness as Property."

38. Gauthier, *Measuring America*, 48, 55–56, 58, 59; Shoemaker, "The Census as Civilizer." On the historical development of segregation see Woodward, *The Strange Career of Jim Crow*; and, for a recent treatment, Litwack, *Trouble in Mind*.

39. Blake, "'First in the Path of the Firemen'"; Gauthier, *Measuring America*, 100.

40. On ranking see Yanow, "American Ethnogenesis and Public Administration"; Starr, "The Sociology of Official Statistics," 46; Hirschman, "The Meaning and Measurement of Ethnicity in Malaysia," 568. Self-definition began in 1960, with respondents choosing among a set of givens that mixed racial and national categories; see U.S. Census Bureau, *Census of the Population: 1960*, 1:xcix, ci. For parallels in recent British censuses see Owen, "'Mixed Race' in Official Statistics."

11

LAURA WEXLER

The Fair Ensemble: Kate Chopin
in St. Louis in 1904

Those who would put the negro race in supremacy would work against infallible decree, for the white race can never submit to its domination, because the white race is the superior race. But the supremacy of the white race of the South must be maintained forever, and the domination of the negro race resisted at all points and at all hazards—because the white race is the superior race. This is the declaration of no new truth. It has abided forever in the marrow of our bones, and shall run forever with the blood that feeds Anglo-Saxon hearts.—Henry Woodfin Grady, "The South and Her Problems"

Henry Woodfin Grady was born in Athens, Georgia, in 1851. He was the son of an Irish immigrant who served, and fell, in the Confederate forces during the Civil War and an American woman who raised their three children as a widow in the desolated South. After graduating from the University of Georgia in 1868, Grady became a popular journalist and newspaper editor devoted to the economic recovery and political resurgence of his state. His starstruck editor, Edna Henry Lee Turpin, considered that "no man ever did more to upbuild and develop a section than did Mr. Grady to the South, desolated by war and ravaged by reconstruction misrule."[1] Turpin substantiated this claim by fulsome praise of Grady's personal kindness to individuals (read, former Confederate soldiers) who had been harmed psychologically and economically by the ravages of the war, as well as on Grady's well-received writings and speeches and his years of economic boosterism of the region.

Joel Chandler Harris, another fan, also highlighted Grady's racist sentiments: "He had a theory that the rich who have become poor by accident or misfortune, suffer the stings of poverty more keenly than the poor who have always been poor, for the reason that they are not qualified to fight against conditions that are at once strange and crushing."[2] Grady addressed this problem by generous acts of charity, making Christmas celebrations possible in many homes that would otherwise have been dark and joyless at that season. In his own writings Grady also praised "the hero in gray with a heart of gold" who had the fortitude to "step . . . from the trenches into the furrow . . . [to] kiss [his] wife and raise a crop."[3] Grady believed in sentiment.

He also believed that restoration and renewal of the patriarchal character of white households was as crucial as economic activity for the South to regain its prosperity, and he detailed the gender relations that, as he saw it, were going to make this possible. For example, Grady saw—or thought he saw—"women reared in luxury cut up their dresses and made breeches for their husbands, and, with a patience and heroism that fit women always as a garment, gave their hands to work. There was little bitterness in all this. Cheerfulness and frankness prevailed."[4] In Grady's version of the ideal southern family, men wore the pants (though made from dresses), and women wore the virtue.

In other words the New South required a new private as well as public agenda. Grady believed that harnessing the energy of the domestic sphere was essential to the mobilization of white supremacy. The historical comparisons he habitually made in his writings—between black and white, slave and free, before and after—centered "intimacy" along with economy in his political and cultural analysis. For example, in "The South and Her Problems" he personified the South as "she" and explained the proper relation between the races in terms of gender. The metaphor he used was marriage, albeit in reverse. "The races and tribes of earth are of divine origin. Behind the laws of man and the decrees of war, stands the law of God. What God hath separated let no man join together."[5] He identified the South as a vestal virgin. "She must walk through the valley of the shadow, for God has so ordained. But He has ordained that she shall walk in that integrity of race that was created in His wisdom and has been perpetuated in His strength." He appealed to the "young men of the South" to protect the "truth" of the racial "integrity" of southern life by defending white supremacy as a chivalric token. "I declare that the truth above all others to be worn unsullied and sacred in your hearts, to be surrendered to no force, sold for no price, compromised in no necessity, but cherished and defended as the covenant of your prosperity, and the pledge of peace to your children, is that the white race must dominate forever in the South because it is the white race, and superior to that race by which its supremacy is threatened."[6] "The South and Her Problems" is a well-developed treatise on the gender of race and nation.

In another century, and from a very different political perspective, Ann Laura Stoler also elaborates on the pointed truth that the intimate arrangements of domestic life are more than just a template for private behavior. In her essay "Tense and Tender Ties" she argues that domestic arrangements are a primary structural component of public life and a vehicle for the creation and enforcement of colonial hierarchy and postcolonial social formations.[7] Stoler writes that her own research on Dutch Indonesia has centered on the "relation between prescription and practice, in those frequently-entered-into domestic arrangements that could blur distinctions of color and culture but also those that reiterated relations of dominance in kitchens, bedrooms, and nurseries—and behind the barely screened partitions of the colonial army's 'family' barracks."[8] But in "Tense and Tender Ties" she calls for the creation of a larger comparative field that would investigate such arrangements for both blurring and highlighting the color line as they function in colonizing projects as distinct from the Indies as the U.S. Southwest, British India, and the Caribbean. Crucially, Stoler is inviting historians of the United States to consider sexuality and gender as a postcolonial feminist anthropologist might, as vectors of power, inseparable from one another, state, and military interests, posing as the merely sentimental while dissimulating their role in selecting, regulating, erasing, and enforcing race. They are implements of social control, like a gun or a law, and North American history, she believes, would benefit from more comparative studies of their uses.[9]

I agree. But I intend in this chapter to raise a further concern about such a comparative methodology, using as an example how considerations of intimacy impact my own research in late-nineteenth-century and early-twentieth-century U.S. cultural history. First, while the *spheres* of comparison in colonial and postcolonial theory have become wonderfully fluid—so that in contemporary scholarship metropole and colony, colonizer and colonized, public and private, whiteness and blackness no longer designate rigid binaries but unstable, dialectical spheres—the *substantive content* of those spheres often still remains deceptively inert, at least in Americanist scholarship. That is to say, while many colonial and postcolonial scholars now articulate these binaries one with the other, we may not yet have sufficiently appreciated that the extent to which what *counts as* "metropole" or "colony" or "colonizer" or "colonized" and so forth—or, indeed, as "gender" and "sexuality"—is also volatile.[10] And just as, for instance, we now understand that we ought not to presume a consistent, sharp delineation between metropole and colony, neither can we presume beforehand what is meant by "sex" or "domesticity" or "child rearing," or even by the relations between and among them. Instead, if scholars of North American history are to take up Stoler's challenge to do more comparative antiracist work, we will need to make use of the best available historical, theoretical, and linguistic insights simply *to find out* what constituted the content of the fluid category of intimacy in each and every instance and to determine if and how it undergirded the racist projects of the nation. Otherwise, we run the risk of assuming what we need to prove and repeating a prescriptive framework of integrating public and private that can be as useful to reactionary forces as to progressive, as the example of Grady shows.

Intimacy is not a simple descriptive noun: it designates complicated and often contested connections. Consider the "relations of dominance in kitchens, bedrooms, and nurseries" that form the centerpiece of Stoler's argument. What relations of dominance are we talking about? Slavery? Indenture? Wage labor? Or prostitution? Incest? Rape? How about heteronormativity? The missionary position? The cold shoulder? Or how about the limitation of the franchise? All of these kinds of arrangements suffused the atmosphere of early-twentieth-century U.S. domestic life; all were deeply political and productive of power. May we imagine only one as intimate? And perhaps more to the point, *ought* we to imagine any one without the suite of others?

U.S. feminists and other scholars of this period have recently been at pains to uncover the dimensions of sexual domination understood as interracial rape. This work is focused on historically charged instances of white against black violence and weighs in against white allegations of black male criminality. Because of this work, the lynching era in the United States has been rightly recentered as the pivot of late-nineteenth-century and early-twentieth-century U.S. cultural theory. But *intra*racial violence, including white on white dominance behavior such as harassment and domestic abuse, is not generally discussed in the same breath as interracial sexual violence. Yet such violence also helped maintain bourgeois white male control within the family. It was the same men in each instance—Ida B. Wells-Barnett's point precisely.[11]

The paradigm-shifting research that Stoler calls for will fail to reach to the core of the racial system if it does not disaggregate, rename, and rearticulate all the aspects of such violence with one another. During and after Reconstruction, without being necessarily congruent or equal to one another, each form of abuse was nonetheless part of the underlying effort to protect what Henry Grady called, "the supremacy of the white race of the South."[12] For Grady, too, the big house and the back house existed in a rich relation to one another. The metaphor of nursing blood, and the violence implied by the marrow and the bones, is an intimate, family-centered ferocity.

In addition, other types of harassment have not held the attention of scholars to the same degree as heterosexual rape.[13] Although threatening behavior on a day-in, day-out basis surely came as an array of practices within the home, in much research it is as if *intimacy* is merely a euphemism for *sexuality*, which in turn is a name only for genital penetration. But in the post–Civil War South, white male strategies of control were all linked pursuant to unifying "the white race" in "resistance to its domination" by the newly freed black population and took on different aspects in different social locations and at different times. To focus exclusively on the genital aspect of white male rage is to miss the entire pattern. Again, it is this nexus to which Grady refers when he calls for "maintenance . . . at all points and at all hazards."

None of this is simple. Indeed, perhaps the most predatory aspect of nineteenth-century domesticity was exactly the mutual interconnection it fostered among race *and* sexuality *and* other intimacies. Etienne Balibar was struggling to describe such a complex cultural shape when he wrote that "the phenomenon of 'depreciation' and 'racialization' which is directed simultaneously against different social groups which are quite different in 'nature' (particularly 'foreign communities,' 'inferior races,' women and 'deviants') does not represent a juxtaposition of merely analogous behaviors and discourses applied to a potentially indefinite series of objects independent of each other, but *a historical system of complementary exclusions and dominations which are mutually interconnected.*"[14] Americanist scholars answering Stoler's call for new comparative work on colonial histories can take from Balibar not only that the "out there" was intimately related to "in here" but also that constructions of the intimate in the late nineteenth century and early twentieth in the United States were not *parallel* sets of race and sex effects. Instead, they form a messier, and ultimately more sinister, sexual and nonsexual repertoire. Simultaneously enacted, these complementary dominations buoyed the asymmetries of white supremacy; but separately understood, they may appear only as localized pathologies without an underlying drift.

And finally, there are important implications for comparative U.S. women's history, as well as for general comparative North American history in Stoler's thesis. Given the entanglements of gender and race, it is a scandal that it is so difficult to find clear white antiracist women writers' voices before Jesse Daniel Ames launched an antilynching campaign in 1930.[15] By that time thousands of African American men and women had already been murdered in the wave of disenfranchisement and dispossession that saw the ex-Confederacy rewrite state constitutions to constrict black citizenship. Countless others were mortally threatened, yet the Stoler thesis is suggestive of the possibility that domestic violence was an intimate concern that also raised the race issue. Such reservations as white women held toward the brutal means that their men took to reassert white supremacy in the former Confederacy were often overtly couched as anxiety over the possible "degeneration" of white masculinity through its "descent" into mob violence. But the historical problem may be to distinguish the race-loyal aspects of white female rebellion against "relations of dominance in kitchens, bedrooms, and nurseries" from the fissures in white supremacist solidarity that also—at least potentially—appeared in the privacy and isolation of domestic abuse.

In other words, despite what propagandists like Grady would have us believe, white women were by no means sanguine about all they saw and endured from their own men as they "cut up their dresses and made breeches for their husbands, and, with a patience and heroism that fit women always as a garment, gave their hands to work" while the land still ran red with the blood of fathers, brothers, and sons. Men returned changed from the war, as they always do. Some of them were violent. The theme of the difficulty of renewing white masculinity in a postwar, postslavery era runs in one way or another through the entire literature by white women of the 1880s and 1890s. It is likely that the missing white southern woman's protest against the campaign of plunder, rape, and murder of freedmen and women in the Jim Crow era, if there is one, will be located at her assigned place within the domestic apparatus, when what she knew as intimacy was also a form of violence.

In this proposition I am following the lead of Sandra Gunning, who has made the point that "when we begin consistently to examine turn-of-the-century white women writers as female subjects already racialized (as indeed black women writers have always been considered), the question of how such women and their contemporaries might have participated—overtly or not—in discussions of race may become answerable."[16] Arguing for a comparative treatment of black and white literary canons, Gunning observes that for both black and white male writers of antilynching texts, the "black rapist, the white rape victim, the white avenger, and the black woman as prostitute operate together with differing resonances" and that "these stereotypes also operate together in texts by black and white women." She concludes, however, that among the women writers,

> definitions of what constitute racial violence and its consequences are at times profoundly different. For example, women's texts engage not with male access to citizenship and property, but rather with the problem of establishing female subjectivity within a public debate whose terms are universally established by men; with the political and personal consequences of rape; with the attraction and repulsion of fantasies of sexual desire; and with the need for sexual recovery. Thus we must re-imagine the discourse on racial violence as including not just men and women writing, but men *and* women writing in different tonalities, with different strategies, and with different concerns. . . . In the 1880's and 1890's, the years of greatest violence (and thus the years of the highest number of assaults on white women, if white supremacists are to be believed), white women certainly had something to say about racial violence and its impact on their communities; however we need to recognize that, as was the case for black women, their angle of vision and, therefore, their very mode of address would necessarily have been different from those of their men.[17]

Gunning's comparative method speaks to Stoler's formulation in a nuanced way, that neither predetermines the content nor the vectors of white or black female racial discourse. Rather it seeks to find them out in situ and to name them in relation to a broader politics. In recognizing that in texts by black and white women "the definitions of what constitute racial violence and its consequences are at times profoundly different," Gunning suggests a way to hear white female gender protest for what it was—and wasn't. Like Albert Memmi's attempt, in *The Colonizer and the Colonized*, to anatomize "the colonizer who refuses" and "the colonizer who accepts," the mapping of these differences opens potential space.[18]

Specifically, I would like to consider the role played by domestic violence in the life and writings of Kate Chopin, one of the southern white women writers of that period with whom Gunning is also concerned. In *Race, Rape, and Lynching* Gunning suggests that "the value of Chopin as a middle-class white woman writing primarily about the South comes precisely in the complexity and contradiction of her position on race, specifically on whiteness as a racialized category, and in the ways in which that complexity and that contradiction texture and shape her considerable literary achievements."[19] I will argue that "the complexity and contradiction of her position on race" results in part from the fact that Chopin experienced domestic violence in relation to racial affiliation, as well as to her gender. In other words, the use of the example of Kate Chopin for expanding the comparative project does not end with her written words.

A HAUNTING STORY COMES DOWN to us about Kate Chopin in St. Louis in 1904. Chopin was actually born in St. Louis, Missouri, in 1851, the same year that Henry Grady was born in Athens, Georgia. The South was her, as well as his, lifelong literary obsession. Unlike Grady, however, Chopin chose to write not as a journalist but as a novelist and author of short stories. Married soon after the war to a cotton factor, Oscar Chopin, she moved from St. Louis to New Orleans in 1870, where the young couple initially prospered. But Oscar soon went bankrupt in the chaotic postwar economy. She and their rapidly growing family were forced to relocate in 1879 to rural northwest Louisiana, where Oscar's family retained some plantation property. Kate chafed at the narrow boundaries of rural respectability while ill luck continued to plague her husband, and when he died prematurely in 1883, she moved as rapidly as possible back to her mother's home in St. Louis. Living once again in the city of her birth, she learned to exploit the vogue of plantation fiction, and throughout the late 1880s and 1890s she put her observations of New Orleans and Nachitoches to work in many widely popular tales of the Old South, as well as in her scandalous 1899 masterpiece, *The Awakening*.

Chopin's local fiction depends on but far exceeds the simpleminded formula of "moonlight and magnolias." Both more violent and more sexual than was the norm, her writing opposes the saccharine perspective of a gender apologist like Grady without challenging directly the concomitant white supremacy. By the time the World's Fair opened in St. Louis in 1904, Chopin was a famous—some said infamous—author of two novels and more than one hundred short stories that chronicled the Civil War and Reconstruction from an elite southern white woman's point of view. She retained her interest in, and sense of entitlement to, the stories of the lives of persons very different from herself. We might surmise that a spectacle such as the St. Louis

World's Fair would have been particularly compelling to someone of that temperament.

And, in fact, we know that as soon as season tickets went on sale for the St. Louis World's Fair of 1904, Kate Chopin secured one for herself. Her biographer Emily Toth reports that the fifty-six-year-old writer attended the fair several days each week from late April to mid-August, deep into the long, hot, muggy St. Louis summer. She took a trolley or walked the six blocks from her house, whether or not anyone was free to accompany her.[20]

This last remark implies that something was not entirely conventional about her independence. Chopin was eccentric in a society that still expected public deference and discretion from respectable ladies. Practically speaking, Kate Chopin had long since left such strictures behind. But the power of the norm was such that a sense of transgression must still have been attached to stepping so far out of one's "proper sphere" as repeatedly to attend the fair alone, to stare and be stared at in public. In 1904 such boundary crossing would have reminded Kate Chopin — and the myriad other middle-class women who also tasted similar freedoms at the fair — that her curiosity was a gendered pleasure not to be taken for granted.

Although the St. Louis World's Fair invited this sort of gender insubordination, it did so ambivalently, and its managers attempted to recuperate the liberated female spectator into an overarching plan. Like the Chicago Exposition a little more than a decade earlier, and like the Paris Exposition of the recent past, the St. Louis World's Fair offered a stimulating environment where classes, races, and ethnic groups from all over the world could mix in social spaces designed for that purpose. But simultaneously it tried to control the thrills and dangers of such seeing and being seen by the presentation of strictly regulated exhibits of "exotic" peoples or by "concessions" (interesting word) on the Pike that highly policed cross-class, racial, and gender interactions.[21]

Film critic Lauren Rabinovitz has analyzed journalists' drawings of the Chicago Exposition, noting that they show that such displays constructed "a *triangulated* rather than reciprocal relationship of women seeing and being seen." The drawings of these exhibitions indicate that white women might "look at both white and nonwhite men, but they do so only while they simultaneously are held as the unaware objects of other men's gazes, both passersby as well as the sketch artist."[22] To Rabinovitz this "pictorial triangle" suggests two possibilities: "first, that the fantastically theatricalized space itself and its spectacular displays of consumption were themselves complicit in this extension of a *sexualized* gaze to passersby made over into spectacle and, second, that the wandering sketch artists implicitly used such representational conventions because they understood the fair as an excuse for and containment of that kind of authorized voyeurism. The sketches made by journalists depict human figures as the subjects and the objects of each other's gazes. The journalists dramatize the way that oversight overlapped with spectacle."[23] That is to say, in Chicago the fair surveilled the viewer. Inside the theatrical space of the fairgrounds the white female gaze was relatively free. But this liberty was won by substituting the symbolic panoptical presence of a white male point of view for the literal necessity of a white male chaperone.

At St. Louis, also, this type of oversight was delivered by means of a vast educational program embedded in the exhibitions, the vistas, and the very architecture of the entire fairgrounds. The spectacle was framed as a display of white male supremacy that obviated the necessity of an actual male counterpart to signal the protected place on the sexual hierarchy represented by the white woman. Once within the gates, a white woman was free to wander, so long as the white man "owned" the civilizations that she saw.

The St. Louis World's Fair was also composed in very material ways as a story of the triumph of a new formation of United States power. America's recent victory in the war with Spain in Cuba, seizure of the Philippines from Spain, and annexation of Hawaii highlighted the global economic ambitions of the newly reunited nation. Displays of newly colonized populations signified American acceptance of "the White Man's Burden." The nationalist fervor of this new imperial order transformed both the resistant sectionalism of the Old South and the resilient commercialism of the New beyond all possibility of imagining in the nineteenth century.

Not all who attended bought the myth of progress and the place of the United States within it. The historian Henry Adams, for instance, was only partly won over. In a certain way he was drawn to what he saw. In *The Education of Henry Adams* he observed, only half ironically, that "the world had never witnessed so marvelous a phantasm. By night Arabia's crimson sands had never returned a glow half so astonishing as one wandered among long lines of white palaces, exquisitely lighted by thousands on thousands of electric candles; soft, rich, shadowy, palpable in their sensuous depths."[24] But although entranced by the electricity, Adams was also disturbed by the philistinism of the exhibits and by the mobs of common people who came to see the fair, for they undercut the cultural rewards of American power and progress. "Had there been no exhibits at all and no visitors," he wrote, "one would have enjoyed it only the more." At the earliest possible moment, Adams fled the St. Louis World's Fair, and what it prophesied about the coming mass culture of the twentieth century, for France and the cathedrals of Normandy, Rouen, and Amiens. Adams found in the medieval Catholic monuments to the Virgin, "World's Fairs of thirteenth-century force" that "turned Chicago and St. Louis pale."[25]

Kate Chopin, on the other hand, eagerly consumed the exposition of a new American dream, a mass culture intertwined with the politics of white supremacy. Chopin, along with many others of her day, had been an avid reader of such European social theorists as Darwin, Spencer, and Huxley. The Social Darwinism of this generation dissociated the unequal distribution of American goods and social power from social causes and effects and projected it onto a mythic screen of natural selection. It presented as a fixed law of nature the highly political struggles of the former slave masters and newly dominant businessmen, and it saw no contradiction — because there was no contest — between mass culture and white supremacy.

It may be important that most of the literary figures who influenced Chopin were European, not American — Molière, Alphonse Daudet, Maupassant, George Sand — for the Eurocentrism of her education also abetted this kind of abstraction, which Adams, with a fuller education and broader experience, could not abide. Chopin admired, for instance, the irony of French realists like Maupassant but was repelled by the acid social realism of American writers like Hamlin Garland and Frank Norris or the racial jeremiads of George Washington Cable. These men gave voice to literal, rather than figurative, contradictions and focused on trenchant social disjunctions. Unlike Adams, but like many of the white women writers of her era (and like Grady), Chopin preferred to figure the problem of social conflict through the sexual and gender issues of private life. Above all else, Chopin, like most of the rest of the "New Women" and "New Men" of the early twentieth century, wanted to believe that her own personal freedom was an avatar of social progress. The rest of the world would naturally come to desire just the personal liberties that they themselves pioneered.

The social vision that linked personal goals of a selective few with general historical advancement of the entire world was the secret fantasy that made St. Louis so "fair." Kate Chopin, and millions more, thrilled at the sight. In a Chopin family memoir, recorded after her death, it is said that Chopin was particularly interested in "the fair *ensemble* in a certain magical, semi-

mystical light."[26] That is to say, her attraction to the fair was especially pronounced when its allure was the most general and she could see the whole
"ensemble."

But this is a curious remark. There is little mysticism anywhere else in
Chopin's character. On the contrary, when faced with the numerous challenges and setbacks of her marriage and early widowhood, she sold the plantation, cleared the debt, and moved her family back to her birthplace, St.
Louis, in very rapid order. It was a clear-eyed and courageous pragmatism
that guided Chopin's actions.

White supremacy, however, *was* a mystical idea, as we learn once more
from Henry Grady:

> The Indian, the Malay, the Negro, the Caucasian, these types stand as
> markers of God's will. Let not man tinker with the work of the Almighty.
> Unity of civilization, no more than unity of faith, will never be witnessed
> on earth. No race has risen or will rise above its ordained place. Here is
> the pivotal fact of this great matter—two races are made equal in law, and
> in political rights, between whom the caste of race has set an impassable
> gulf. This gulf is bridged by a statute, and the races are urged to cross
> thereon. This cannot be. The fiat of the Almighty has gone forth, and in
> eighteen centuries of history it is written.[27]

Chopin's tropism to the fair indicates that she submitted to this seductive
mythology. At the fair the Anglo-Saxon claim to the dawning of the twentieth century would have appeared so similar to the Anglo-Saxon mythos of
the antebellum South that the violent convulsions of murder and rebellion
characterizing the two moments might be seen to have worked not tragedy,
after all, but a remarkable synthesis.

From this perspective the racial symbolism of the St. Louis World's Fair
united both the antebellum period and the fin de siècle, the plantations
of the Old South and the racial panoramas of the American empire. The
nearly universal white supremacy that found expression in St. Louis in 1904
would finally redeem the Confederacy from the defeat of the Civil War by
making southern expertise useful to the next generation of capitalists, northern and southern, and their new plantations. Disfranchisement of blacks
in the South, functionally nearly complete by the end of the nineteenth
century, could even function as a new model of colonial administration.
Thus framed, the national obsession—and Chopin's own personal habit—

of looking backward to a southern past was both a practical and a visionary politics that offered new meaning to southern populism.

What this meant in practice, C. Vann Woodward has explained in *Origins of the New South*:

> The North had taken up the White Man's Burden, and by 1898 was looking to Southern racial policy for national guidance in the new problems of imperialism resulting from the Spanish war. Commenting on the Supreme Court's opinion upholding disfranchisement in Mississippi, the *Nation* pronounced it "an interesting coincidence that this important decision is rendered at a time when we are considering the idea of taking in a varied assortment of inferior races in different parts of the world" — races "which, of course, could not be allowed to vote." Senator Morgan of Alabama was chairman of the committee of the Hawaiian Commission that framed the voting restrictions for one "assortment of inferior races." To reject the property and literacy tests recommended for Hawaiians, reported the Senator, would be to "turn the legislature over to the masses." Senator Morgan's advice was also sought by the white-supremacy advocates of his own state who were currently debating additional franchise restrictions for Alabama. A speech in defense of American imperialism by George F. Hoar "most amply vindicated the South," said Senator John L. McLaurin of South Carolina. He thanked the Massachusetts statesman "for his complete announcement of the divine right of the Caucasian to govern the inferior races." The Boston *Evening Transcript* reluctantly admitted that the Southern way was "now the policy of the Administration of the very party which carried the country into and through a civil war to free the slave."

Events in the Philippines soon indicated that the Mississippi Plan had become the American Way. "If the stronger and cleverer race," said an editorial in the Boston *Atlantic Monthly*, "is free to impose its will upon 'new-caught, sullen peoples' on the other side of the globe, why not in South Carolina and Mississippi? The advocates of the 'shotgun policy' are quite as sincere, and we are inclined to think quite as unselfish, as the advocates of 'benevolent assimilation.' The two phrases are, in fact, two names for the same thing." Professors John W. Burgess and William A. Dunning of Columbia University brought academic authority to the support of Southern policy. Burgess thought "that the Republican party, in its work of imposing the sovereignty of the United States upon eight millions of Asiatics, has changed its view in regard to the political relations of races and has at last virtually accepted the ideas of the South upon that subject." He assured the South that the leaders of the part of emancipation would never "again give themselves over to the vain imagination of the political equality of man."[28]

And so, apparently, visiting the fair moved Kate Chopin closer to the central contradiction of American culture: race versus democratic rights.

It may also have moved her closer to death. On August 20, despite the punishing heat and many cases of heat prostration, Kate Chopin could not resist returning once again to view the "mystical ensemble." August 20 was Pennsylvania Day. It featured the opening of the International Congress of the Deaf, where Helen Keller and her teacher, Annie Sullivan, were representatives. Native American schoolchildren from the Carlisle Indian School and elsewhere put on a program at the Model Indian School, which simultaneously showed off their accomplishments and attested to the widely appreciated capacity of American education to "elevate the lower races." There were military band concerts and military drills. And Pennsylvania military companies staged a spectacular martial display, in full military dress, to "illustrate the function and administrative faculty of the Government in time of peace and its resources as a war power," as the congressional act providing for their funding established.[29]

That day, however, Chopin returned home from the fair exhausted and, complaining of a headache, went to bed. Later that evening she suffered a massive cerebral hemorrhage, and she died on August 22 without regaining consciousness. By the dazzling, "magical, semi-mystical light" of the St. Louis World's Fair, the South was reflected back to her as the pivot of world history. It was virtually the last light she ever saw.

HOW ARE WE TO THINK about this story? I propose that the very repetition of Chopin's attendance at the St. Louis World's Fair is *symptomatic evidence*, a performance to be analyzed. And in addition I want to propose that repetition on this scale, as Freud and others tell us, is likely to be related to repression. Chopin's obsession with attending the fair indicates something left unfinished or forgotten but not left behind. Was there unexpressed ambivalence toward the spectacle of white supremacy? And at the heart of this ambivalence, was there an interrogation of white male supremacist discourses that—like the visual politics of the Fair—confined even when they were supposed to liberate?

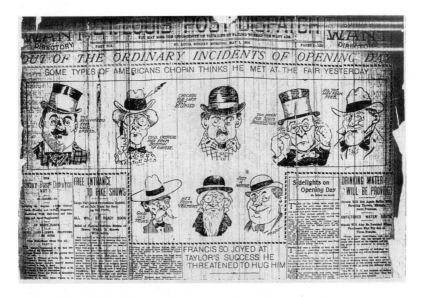

Oscar Chopin, "Out of the Ordinary Incidents of Opening Day: Some Types of Americans Chopin Thinks He Met at the Fair Yesterday," *St. Louis Post-Dispatch*, May 1, 1904, 1-D.

Chopin died before she could record her own impressions of the fair. Nevertheless, there is one compelling piece of material evidence that may suggest her point of view. Chopin's son, Oscar, an editorial cartoonist of some note, worked for the *St. Louis Post Dispatch*. In 1904 he was living with his mother, and he as well as she attended the opening of the fair on Saturday, April 30; mother and son probably attended together. The next day, Sunday, May 1, Oscar published a very clever drawing in the morning paper. It is Oscar's drawing, and not Kate's, of course, but it does give some feeling for what drew their attention and suggests what he felt deserved comment.

The drawing takes looking itself as its text, just like the other journalists' drawings of the Chicago World's Fair studied by Lauren Rabinovitz. In his cartoon Oscar comments satirically on the different kinds of looking that different "types of Americans" practiced at the fair.[30] Entitled "Out of the Ordinary Incidents of Opening Day," and subtitled "Some Types of Americans Chopin Thinks He Met at the Fair Yesterday," the entire drawing is a composite impression of looking relations, politically conceived. Eight separate figures are arranged across the top of the newspaper page, and each figure is labeled as a distinct "type." The point of the captions is to mock visitors from the rest of the country who might have felt superior to home-town folks from St. Louis.

There is "the New Yorker," whose "eyes were opened" by the splendor of the St. Louis fair. There is a fussy lady with a lorgnette who is "cold, critical and from Boston, of course"; a brash but abashed looking midwesterner from Chicago who "for once felt eclipsed"; a man in a top hat with his fingers stuck in his ears because the St. Louis fair was "too much for staid Philadelphia"; a slick-looking character who has arrived "all the way from Pike"; an unassuming-looking little man in a large ten-gallon hat from "good old Texas"; a dumb and dumbfounded-appearing character whose puzzlement can only be explained by the fact that "he's from Vermont"; and a salesman type who refuses all identity beyond the observation that he's "just a native." Taken all together, the group represents Oscar's feeling that fairgoers fell back on their regional identities while trying to cope with the magnitude of the task of viewing the fair. His humor turns on a kind of U.S. tribalism that in fact subtly subverts the very message of the fair as an anthropological display of "Others."

Cleverly, Oscar situates the reader as the object of the gaze of most of these figures. Those who are not directly looking at the reader are glancing away, as if they had either only just become distracted and will return their eyes to ours momentarily or as if they had some reason for deliberately avoiding our look. The result is that even though the viewer is on display, he or she is also turning the tables on the "gawkers" by scrutinizing and labeling them too. Like the journalists Rabinovitz examined, Oscar Chopin depicts the experience of looking at the fair as a hierarchy of surveillance. But at the same time he is rendering this hierarchy ironic. The drawing is a record of triangulated looking but of a different sort than that which Rabinovitz described, in which the joke turns as much on race and section as on gender and sexuality. In Oscar's drawing we can clearly see what Judith Butler means when she argues that the visual field is always already a political field, and we can see how Oscar was refusing the official line.[31]

Kate Chopin surely saw this drawing and understood its force. Were there ways that she, too, might have resisted the fair's governing perspective even while transfixed by the spectacle? Encountering its many public representations of the old slave economy as a fit foundation for the new imperial order, might Chopin even have come face-to-face with intimate knowledge of the past that upset the public story? I believe so. For example, on display at the St. Louis World's Fair was a log cabin taken from the McAlpin plantation and said to be the home of Uncle Tom himself. Kate Chopin's father-in-law owned that plantation after McAlpin. This "Uncle Tom's Cabin" display would therefore have recalled her father-in-law's widely known cruelty to his slaves, from which her husband as an adolescent had fled. It also might have brought to mind her father-in-law's beating of her mother-in-law with a leather strap until she, too, fled from the plantation. The fair's insistence on racial order may also have recalled the violence she herself had lived though during Reconstruction, when her own husband and many of her male associates were participating members of white terrorist organizations in the struggle for white supremacy in northwestern Louisiana and in New Orleans. And the parading of U.S. militarism would have rested uneasily alongside the memory of the hypermasculinism of a suitor of her own, whom she left after learning he had threatened and beaten his estranged wife.[32]

The "tense and tender ties" of empire laced displays of the domestic life of the native populations of new American colonies. But Kate Chopin's own intimate experience made plain the hypocrisies of the plantation and the violence of empowered white men. Despite the strenuous efforts of official voices to cloak a new American hegemony in the sunny mythology of a past plantation culture, domestic violence in Chopin's own past provided an alternate perspective. My hypothesis is that perhaps she could not stop attending the fair because she could not ultimately secure its vision "ensemble," as she would have liked. Rather, its public face kept devolving into an uncanny private fragmentation.

The story of Chopin at the fair gets at something even more ineffable than racial mysticism, although equally material and real: the division by gender of a "structure of feeling," as Raymond Williams put it, that pitted racial conservatism against sexual liberation and revealed the contradictions of each.[33] By my reading, Chopin's obsession with the St. Louis World's Fair suggests the complications that domestic abuse in intimate life could bring to the orchestration of consent in the consolidation of the United States' twentieth-century empire.

THERE IS ONE MORE HISTORICAL SOURCE: Kate Chopin's own fiction. Edna Pontellier, the heroine of Kate Chopin's 1899 novel, *The Awakening*, struggles also with unprocessed knowledge. Her thoughts often become suddenly perilous, or insistent, intrusive, and fixed. Her vision also grows dramatically unstable. The thirty-something wife of a New South businessman and mother of two little boys, Edna Pontellier tries throughout the novel to shed what feels to her like a false self, to claim control of her own sexuality, and to gain freedom of choice and freedom of movement in her daily domestic life. The effort makes her moody, impulsive, and sometimes irritable:

> There were days when she was very happy without knowing why. She was happy to be alive and breathing, when her whole being seemed to be one with the sunlight, the color, the odors, the luxuriant warmth of some perfect Southern day. She liked then to wander alone into strange and unfamiliar places. She discovered many a sunny, sleepy corner, fashioned to dream in. And she found it good to dream and to be alone and unmolested.
>
> There were days when she was unhappy, she did not know why,— when it did not seem worth while to be glad or sorry, to be alive or dead; when life appeared to her like a grotesque pandemonium and humanity like worms struggling blindly toward inevitable annihilation. She could not work on such a day, nor weave fancies to stir her pulses and warm her blood.[34]

Also, Edna's memory is volatile. In one of the pivotal scenes in the novel Edna feels an overwhelming terror while she is actually sitting safely at her friend's bedside while her friend gives birth. At first she is "seized with a vague dread." Then the present "scene of torture" raises distant recollections, which seem "far away, unreal, and only half remembered . . . an ecstasy of pain, the heavy odor of chloroform, a stupor which had deadened sensation, and an awakening to find a little new life to which she had given being, added to the great unnumbered multitude of souls that come and go" (104).

There follow greater inroads on Edna's composure, as deeper conflicts emerge: "And are you going abroad?" the doctor asks. "Perhaps," she first replies, but then: "No, I am not going. I'm not going to be forced into doing things. I don't want to go abroad. I want to be let alone. Nobody has any right—except children, perhaps—and even then, it seems to me—or it did seem—." And in answer to his concerned inquiry Edna explains:

> "Some way I don't feel moved to speak of things that trouble me. Don't think I am ungrateful or that I don't appreciate your sympathy. There are periods of despondency and suffering which take possession of me. But I don't want anything but my own way. That is wanting a good deal, of

course, when you have to trample upon the lives, the hearts, the prejudices of others—but no matter—still I shouldn't want to trample upon the little lives. Oh, I don't know what I'm saying, Doctor. Good night. Don't blame me for anything." (105)

Ultimately, in the final moments before she commits suicide by drowning herself in the Gulf of Mexico the next morning, Edna is able to think only in flashbacks and fragments: "She looked into the distance, and the old terror flamed up for an instant, then sank again. Edna heard her father's voice and her sister Margaret's. She heard the barking of an old dog that was chained to the sycamore tree. The spurs of the cavalry officer clanged as he walked across the porch. There was the hum of bees, and the musky odor of pinks filled the air" (109).

In *Trauma and Recovery* psychologist Judith Herman writes that "the traumatic moment becomes encoded in an abnormal form of memory, which breaks spontaneously into consciousness, both as flashbacks during waking states and as traumatic nightmares during sleep. Small, seemingly insignificant reminders can also evoke these memories, which often return with all the vividness and emotional force of the original event. Thus, even normally safe environments may come to feel dangerous, for the survivor can never be assured that she will not encounter some reminder of the trauma."[35] This seems an accurate description of Edna's consciousness near the end of her life. But what trauma would be haunting her?

Others have suggested the trauma of childbirth, or rejected love, but I think not, or at least not simply. To me, the key point about trauma is that it has a repetitive, retrospective structure. According to Freud and most investigators after him, trauma consists in two parts: first the event, and second the memory. Between the two is a negative space, an interlude, that represents the subject's retreat from the pain of consciousness. Trauma is only manifest when a bridge over this space is crossed and the subject looks back and reengages this forgotten pain, newly understanding what happened.

Edna Pontellier's own name means "bridge maker," and in the course of the novel she does in fact cross over. To read *The Awakening* as a traumatic narrative is to recognize, therefore, that her friend's labor and her lover's desertion may be necessary, but neither reaches to the level of sufficient cause of Edna's suicide. They are merely new shocks that have engaged with something else dredged up from the past.

Rather, the source of Edna's despair would have to have been a prior blow.

That is, Adèle's suffering may cause Edna to remember her own pain in labor, but the intensely abnormal perceptions of the childbirth scene make it plausible also to propose that what Edna is suffering from is memory. It could be the thought of mothers in general or of her own dead mother specifically. But recalling the figure of the mother apparently unmasks the domestic violence that Edna saw but did not comprehend as a child and that, as an adult, herself in labor, she had new reason to understand, and repress.

That is to say, witnessing childbirth as nature's "torture" gives Edna access also to another kind of "torture," this time administered by men. "Think of the children, Edna. Oh think of the children! Remember them," Edna's friend begs, just before Edna leaves her bedside (104). And, "she meant to think of them," writes Chopin; "that determination had driven into her soul like a death wound" (106). Adèle's request is similar to the patronizing and disparaging command that Edna's husband, Léonce, has earlier voiced when he drunkenly criticizes her supposed lack of attention to the children. Generations of elite white women must have been instructed to "remember the children," and Edna's mother would have heard much the same words. With this command Adèle polices Edna for the "sake" of the children: she is speaking the patriarchal tongue.

Notoriously, however, patriarchal language can have one meaning for a woman contented in marriage, like Edna's friend Adèle, and quite another for a woman like Edna's mother, married to a Confederate veteran who both gambled and drank. Chopin does not specify exactly what Edna's mother may have been asked to give up "for the sake of her children." But the text makes it clear that children could be used to extort sacrifice from their mothers: "The children appeared before her like antagonists who had overcome her; who had overpowered and sought to drag her into the soul's slavery for the rest of her days" (108). The daughter of a mother who *had* been forced "to sacrifice herself for the sake of her children," Edna swears she will never succumb. But her mother's death resonates in the words of Edna's lover: "I love you. Goodbye, because I love you" (106).

What, then, haunts Edna Pontellier in my reading of the novel is reminiscence, as Freud says is true of all "hysterics." Edna remembers the trauma of family life during and directly after the Civil War: "At a very early age, —perhaps it was when she traversed the ocean of waving grass—she remembered she had been passionately enamored of a dignified and sad eyed cavalry officer who visited her father in Kentucky. She could not leave his presence when he was there, nor remove her eyes from his face, which was something like Napoleon's with a lock of black hair falling across the forehead. But the cavalry officer melted imperceptibly out of her existence" (18). It is noteworthy that Edna remembers this man who moved her so deeply as the "cavalry officer." Like her father, a former Confederate soldier who is still called "the Colonel," for her it is as if the war is still in the present tense.

Later in the novel we learn that "the Colonel" lost his Kentucky property, her family's home, at the race track: "His race horses literally ran away with the prettiest bit of Kentucky farming land I ever laid eyes upon," says her husband, Léonce (63). After her father lost the bluegrass farm, the family moved to a plantation in Mississippi, where Edna spent her teenage years. Edna's mother died soon after, when Edna and her younger sister were still "quite young." Edna remembers that her death had a chilling effect on herself and her two sisters: "She and her younger sister, Janet, had quarreled a good deal through force of unfortunate habit. Her older sister, Margaret, was matronly and dignified, probably from having assumed matronly and housewifely responsibilities too early in life, their mother having died when they were quite young. Margaret was not effusive; she was practical. Edna had had an occasional girl friend, but whether accidentally or not, they seemed to have been all of one type—the self-contained" (17).

The girls suffered not only from their mother's death but also from the sadistic way that their father oversaw their lives. "Likely as not it was Sunday," Edna laughs at another memory of her childhood; "and I was running away from prayers, from the Presbyterian service, read in a spirit of gloom by my father that chills me yet to think of" (17). Edna's memories directly contradict Grady's sentimental tales.

Both the husband and the doctor in *The Awakening* are well aware of the existence of violence against women in their society. "What have you been doing to her, Pontellier?" the doctor asks when the husband consults him about marital problems. "Doing! *Parbleu!*" the husband replies, by which we are to know that he personally is not physically abusive (68). Nevertheless, he is having difficulty in managing Edna, and he cannot persuade her to come with him to her own sister's wedding: "'She says a wedding is one of the most lamentable spectacles on earth. Nice thing for a woman to say to her husband!' exclaimed Mr. Pontellier, fuming anew at the recollection" (63). Léonce is fearful that Edna might turn against him personally, as well as against marriage in general by redefining it as a "lamentable spectacle." But Léonce is not really the target of her fury; he is too easily disposed of. It is Edna's own father who is at the core of the issue:

"You are too lenient, too lenient by far, Léonce," asserted the Colonel. "Authority, coercion are what is needed. Put your foot down good and hard; the only way to manage a wife. Take my word for it."

The Colonel was perhaps unaware that he had coerced his own wife into her grave. Mr. Pontellier had a vague suspicion of it, which he thought it needless to mention at that late day. (68)

So that there will be no mistaking it, the shocking information that the Colonel "had coerced his own wife into her grave" is stated as a fact by the narrator, not as a matter of opinion by Léonce, who admits only to "a vague suspicion of it." The narrator does not divulge exactly how Edna's mother died. It is something that Edna cannot bear to remember. Léonce suppresses what he suspects: "he thought it needless to mention at that late date." But Edna, in a classic response to trauma, *represses* it. Henceforth, her memory will return only in condensed, abnormal fragments.

The point is that *The Awakening* narrates a story of post–Civil War white male violence that does not take the form of systematic sexual exploitation of women of color that most scholars so far have studied. Edna Pontellier's traumatic childhood suggests that domestic violence was a specific and localizable, if unspeakable, regularity within the planter patriarchy, affecting the lives of its "own" women, as well as women of color.[36] Furthermore, as Edna begins to realize, during her explorations of the interlocking social circles of New Orleans, each "type" of victim was "intensely tied" to the others in a "historical system of complementary exclusions and dominations which are mutually interconnected."[37] Before the war the master had absolute rights over the lives and bodies of female slaves: but law and social custom gave him also absolute rights over his own wife and daughters. Edna remembers that he regularly abused them all. And after the war, it was these same ex-masters and veterans — men just like and including Chopin's male family members and acquaintances — who used the carefully constructed "innocence" of their own wives and daughters as a transparent pretext for the spectacle of murder as lynching.

Remembering this violence is threatening to the fictional Edna because she knows the violence is still going on. "The old terror flamed up for an instant, then sank again" (109). Swimming in the Gulf becomes an experience of déjà vu. Edna hears "the barking of an old dog that was chained to the sycamore tree." She hears the spurs of the cavalry officer "that clanged as he walked across the porch." And she hears "the hum of bees, and the musky odor of pinks filled the air." Redolent of her father's world, and her mother's death, these spurs "clang" just like the iron chain of the protesting old dog, chained to the sycamore tree. As Edna sinks to her death in the Gulf, her head starts to hum with a sound like that of the bees and fills with the funereal smell of flowers. From the ringing in her ears, we know that the master's boot from that Mississippi plantation has come down "good and hard" one more time.

But remembering would have been threatening as well for the author of *The Awakening*, who also had domestic violence in her past. I believe that Kate Chopin lost herself at the fairgrounds much as her fictional heroine wandered the Kentucky bluegrass fields. Caught and transfixed by uncanny comparisons and the double of the moment, Kate Chopin returned repeatedly to the displays, as Edna Pontellier returned to the Gulf. And as it became inescapable to both that the new ways would be used to justify the same old reign of domestic terror, each died, as it were, of the blow.

IN AN EXCELLENT INTRODUCTION to the recent Barnes and Noble Classics edition of *The Awakening* Rachel Adams also notes the "ironic" fact that Kate Chopin collapsed and died after spending the day of August 20, 1904, at the St. Louis World's Fair. "An author with a flair for the coincidental, Chopin probably would have appreciated the ironic overlap between the end of her own life and the arrival of the world's largest international exposition in her hometown," she writes.[38] Adams sees the perspective of the fair as similar to Edna's:

> The Fair spoke to Americans' thirst for knowledge about the rest of the world. At the same time, its allegedly wide-angle vision was actually a telescope that used other nations as a reference point to establish American superiority. As much as it addressed the desire to learn about and collaborate with a global community, it was also designed to parade the nation's cultural advancement and growing economic and military might on a world stage. The sad irony that with supremacy come loneliness and isolation is crystallized in the image of Edna's favored musical composition, "Solitude," which evokes a man standing desolate and despairing before the sea. In addition to its many other accomplishments, *The Awakening* succeeds in illustrating the alienation that results from having the best that the world can offer, but existing under conditions that make it impossible to give of oneself in return.[39]

But at the same time, Adams cautions the reader *not* to compare Edna with Chopin herself:

> Chopin, who read widely, traveled to Europe, and witnessed pivotal events of her time, should not be confused with her protagonist. A widow, single mother, and professional writer, she lived her life fully and to its end. Such experience grants the far more worldly author the insight to depict a character whose lack of reciprocity is less an individual flaw than a flaw of a culture that treated women as property and maintained rigid racial and class structures. There are good reasons for keeping the fictional character and the real woman separate, including the narrowed appreciation it might bring for Chopin's art. The two should not be confused.[40]

However, I am proposing not that they might be confused but that they should be compared. Such a strategy reveals the "tense and tender ties" that Stoler highlights in her essay. It is true, as Adams points out, that unlike the suicidal Edna Pontellier, Kate Chopin lived widely and freely in the public world. But it is also true that her domestic life held secrets not easily available to her public — secrets that could have affected the ways that women like herself experienced "the pivotal events of her time." Considering the secrets of Edna's emotional life is one of the few ways to access the *meaning* of being white to Chopin herself, as well as her community. Stoler has thus sounded a complicated challenge to American historians: to read what empire intimates, as well as what it says.

NOTES

1. Turpin, "Henry Grady: His Life and Work," 8.

2. Harris, quoted in Turpin, "Henry Grady: His Life and Work," 10–11.

3. Grady, "The New South," 30–31.

4. Ibid.

5. Grady, "The South and Her Problems," 54, 55.

6. Ibid., 55.

7. Stoler has been a primary and powerful exemplar of intersectional research in colonial and postcolonial studies among a growing field of practitioners. Examples of her books that have influenced my own thinking include *Race and the Education of Desire*, *Carnal Knowledge and Imperial Power*, and her collection of essays, coedited with Frederick Cooper, *Tensions of Empire*.

8. Stoler, "Tense and Tender Ties," 6.

9. Any list of major works that already make use of a similar perspective on gender and sexuality would include Scott's "Gender: A Useful Category of Historical Analysis," 28–50. The additional challenge of Stoler's essay is to place North American studies within a colonial and postcolonial intersectional frame.

10. I think it is important to point out here that scholars in the fields of lesbian, gay, bisexual, and transgender studies, as well as sexuality studies, have also long taken on the task of disseminating this crucial insight. See, e.g., Rubin, "Thinking Sex," in which Rubin announces at the outset that "the time has come to think about sex" (267).

11. See Wells-Barnett, *Southern Horrors and Other Writings*, 80.

12. Grady, "The South and Her Problems," 53.

13. I am thinking in particular here of the brilliant work on street harassment by Cathy de La Aguilera, in "Disrupting Street Harassment," her senior thesis for the Women's and Gender Studies major at Yale University, 2004 (manuscript in possession of the author).

14. Balibar, "Racism and Nationalism," 49.

15. See Hall, *Revolt against Chivalry*. See also Carby, *Reconstructing Womanhood*; and Gilmore, *Gender and Jim Crow*.

16. Gunning, *Race, Rape, and Lynching*, 11.

17. Ibid.

18. Memmi, *The Colonizer and the Colonized*, 19, 45.

19. Gunning, *Race, Rape, and Lynching*, 13.

20. Toth, *Kate Chopin*, 391.

21. See, e.g., Rydell, *All the World's a Fair*.

22. Rabinovitz, *For the Love of Pleasure*, 66.

23. Ibid.

24. Adams, *The Education of Henry Adams*, 466–67.

25. Ibid., 469.

26. Toth, *Kate Chopin*, 391.

27. Grady, "The South and Her Problems," 54.

28. Woodward, *Origins of the New South, 1877–1913*, 324–25.

29. Government bulletin quoted in Rydell, *All the World's a Fair*, 3.

30. Oscar Chopin, "Out of the Ordinary Incidents of Opening Day; Some Types of Americans Chopin Thinks He Met at the Fair Yesterday," *St. Louis Post-Dispatch*, May 1, 1904, 1-D.

31. See Butler, "Endangered/Endangering."

32. Toth, *Kate Chopin*, 178–81.

33. See Williams, *Marxism and Literature*, 132.

34. Chopin, *The Awakening*, 56. Subsequent quotations from Chopin's novel are cited parenthetically in the text.

35. Herman, *Trauma and Recovery*, 37.

36. On the other hand, see Nell Painter's exceptional study *Soul Murder and Slavery*.

37. Balibar, "Racism and Nationalism," 49.

38. Adams, introduction, xv.

39. Ibid., xxxvi.

40. Ibid., xxxi.

12

GWENN A. MILLER

"The Perfect Mistress of Russian Economy":

Sighting the Intimate on a Colonial Alaskan

Terrain, 1784–1821

In a remote colonial outpost in the American Northwest, European fur traders and indigenous women lived together with their children in semisubterranean homes. These dwellings were constructed of wood and mud and
then covered with sod, probably by male members of the woman's extended
family. Thatched roofs sometimes protected the ceiling, as Europeans had
adapted some of their own building traditions to these abodes. Inside, the
corners were probably slightly rounded, and the walls were embedded with
inlaid rocks. A cooking fire in a sunken pit warmed the central room, which
served as a dining area, place of work, and at times a stage.[1] Smaller spaces
that the inhabitants used as sleeping quarters and storage rooms were off
to the side. Traditionally, indigenous people in the region had entered these
dwelling places either through a ventilation hatch in the roof or through
very small side doors. One European naturalist wrote that his back had suffered from bending to climb in through the small holes.[2] Other European
men must have suffered as well, for they altered the traditional structures by
enlarging the front door. Some also added windows. Objects made by indigenous women, such as mats, small animal-skin window covers, animal-
skin rugs, animal-oil lamps, and some wall hangings, served both practical and ornamental needs. Archaeological evidence suggests that at various
sites near this main outpost, European materials, such as gun parts, musket
balls, and iron objects "commingled" with those that were clearly aboriginal, such as slate knives, cobble fishing weights, and bottle-glass pendants.[3]
Perhaps this description of converging lifestyles in close proximity sounds
easily recognizable to readers familiar with the history of the westward-
moving American fur trade. But the Europeans who dwelled in these particular intimate spaces were Russians, the indigenous people were Alutiiqs,

and the dwellings themselves were located on Kodiak Island, Alaska: the easternmost reach of the Russian Empire, and the western edge of America.

The story of U.S. expansion westward across the continent is often stereotyped and romanticized. Nevertheless, it is a canonical mainstay of American history. Far less familiar is its eastward-moving counterpart: the story of Russia's expansion out from Muscovy, first over the Ural Mountains and across Siberia and then across the Pacific to Kodiak Island, Alaska. There the ambitious head of a large fur-trading company, Grigorii Shelikhov, arrived in 1784 to establish a permanent settlement.

For many Americans raised during the cold war, the news that Russians colonized part of North America may come as a rude surprise. But Russians did colonize on American shores — first at Kodiak Island, Alaska, and then along the continental seaboard to California. Certain aspects of the late-eighteenth-century encounters between Russians and Alaska's native people will seem like other colonial episodes. These encounters entailed adaptation to alien environments, the "discovery" and exploitation of natural resources, relations between indigenous peoples and colonizing Europeans, the developing technologies of an imperial state in attempts to moderate those relations, and a web of Christianizing practices. However, common ground with other American colonies should not be overstated. Russian colonization in Alaska began some two hundred years later than the first phases of Spanish, English, Dutch, and French colonization of North America. Russians began setting up colonies in the Pacific at the very same time that the American and French Revolutions consumed the Atlantic American coast and the Western European world; it was a moment just before new forms of European imperialism gained momentum in the 1830s.

The initial period of Russian colonization fell between two modes of colonialism. The Alaskan enterprise marked a convergence of early "New World" colonial projects, from the fifteenth century through the eighteenth, with the bureaucratic age of high empire in modern Europe. For historians it also marks a convergence of two previously divergent bodies of scholarship: that of early America and that of Imperial Russia. Early American history has been moving toward multiethnic and transcontinental perspectives for some time. Alan Taylor's 2001 history of early North America heralded a new and growing wave of continental scholarship that included, but also looked beyond, the eastern seaboard and its Atlantic connections. Taylor answered the question of "what counts" as colonial America by including in his framework not only the British "thirteen colonies," as we might expect, but also Spanish, French, Dutch, and even Russian settlements as significant sites of early American encounters.[4] It may turn out that "what's colonial" about this period is most visible in sites that scholars earlier excluded from the traditional rubric of colonial America.[5]

Indeed, colonial sites beyond the confines of traditional early America do not bear the conventional national narrative of a developing Anglo-American polity in the wake of the pathogenic annihilation of Indians and building on the transportation of African labor forces bound within a closed system of slavery. In Russian Alaska colonizers consciously acknowledged the skills and ways of knowing possessed by native peoples. This acknowledgment accompanied their coercion of these local labor forces. Degrees of acknowledgment and use of local skills is a critical issue in a wide range of other colonial contexts. For instance, late-seventeenth-century Frenchmen in the Great Lakes region also recognized and drew on the skills of local peoples. However, the French fur trade, at least in its beginning stages, was based more on trade for pelts than on consciously coerced labor.

Because most early European colonial outposts were largely male enclaves, indigenous women often found themselves uniquely positioned as mediators. Like New France, Alaska was no exception in this regard. It was through Aleut and Alutiiq women that Russians gained access to the marine hunting skills of Aleut and Alutiiq men. The Russian Empire in Alaska was driven by the collection of furs. However, this fur trade differed significantly from those established by the English and French in North America. In fact, it was not really a trade at all, at least not in the beginning. The distinctive process of Russian colonization along contiguous borders eastward into Siberia had already set a precedent for tributary fur payment procured *from*, instead of bartered *with*, indigenous peoples.[6]

As scholarship on early America has expanded, so has English-language scholarship on Imperial Russia and its shifting borderlands to the East. It would be impossible to overstate the impact that the breakup of the Soviet Union has had on this work, particularly from the perspective of scholars who have hoped to recover the multiethnic nature of the tsarist empire.[7] At the beginning of the twenty-first century, Russian archives (at least for now) are more accessible, and historians are delving into new material on populations at the outer reaches of empire and asking new questions about their status in the Imperial Russian regime. In a move that "has come late to students of Russian history," shifting away from 1917-centered analyses and drawing on the terrain of colonial studies and American Indian studies has allowed some researchers to explore the complex history of people who had been passed over as active participants in this vast empire that covered more than eleven time zones.[8] This belated thinking makes it no surprise that the majority of this work is still in a phase of recovery and delineation, highlighting for the first time the very existence and agency of indigenous peoples in outlying regions.[9] This work in itself has elicited new questions, and scholars have recently begun to unravel the varied textures of indigenous interactions with European Russians. Indigenous peoples, from Buryats to Kamchadals, met European Russians, from missionaries to land-cultivating peasants, on a variety of terrains, ranging from the grasslands of the Steppe to the frozen tundra of Siberia.[10] Recent work has certainly drawn on some familiar concepts, but scholars have rarely brought the resonant gender history into this conversation.

The particular story of late-eighteenth-century and early-nineteenth-century colonization that follows builds on the convergence of these recent shifts in early American and Imperial Russian scholarship. Some intimacies of empire are familiar ones—for example, those that emerge out of physical sexual encounters. But other close relationships—of learning, living, and labor—that are about mutual dependence also resonate with those in diverse colonial contexts. In the case of colonial Kodiak Island, such mutual dependence was at the center of interaction between Russian fur-trading men and Aleut and Alutiiq people, both men and women. By attending to the range of ways in which these people met face-to-face, what is colonial about Russian America comes into relief in new ways. As we will see, even seemingly familiar categories such as "creole" take on a completely new meaning in the Alaskan context.

The evidence is both scarce and elusive; nevertheless, it indicates that the control of close encounters was a critical key to the development of a remote colonial project. As the arbiters of Russian rule plotted the Alaskan terrain onto the maps of their extending empire, they also plotted a course for what kinds of interactions would be condoned in those lands. They carefully calculated how relationships would foster a colony that could sustain itself and considered how it would compare and rival, perhaps even surpass, the successful American colonies of other European empires. Comparison was an important element of Russian colonial planning.

The documents used here range from imperial decrees, official government reports, and Russian Orthodox missionary records to early ethnographies and travel journals written by Russian, French, German, Spanish,

English, and American adventurers, as well as by fur-trade company administrators. The fur traders, or *promyshlenniki*, who formed unions with native women and supervised native men, came from families of peasants who had worked the land. They were usually illiterate and almost never left written records behind. Similarly, Alutiiq men and women did not produce written records. But, as we have seen in the dwelling described earlier, these Russian fur traders and Alutiiq people did leave behind material artifacts, evidence of the proximity in which they lived. A close reading of the physical and scripted evidence that survives, however limited it may be, can show how close relationships between Russians and Alutiiqs affected the form of colonialism that emerged in Alaska at the beginning of the nineteenth century.[11] Naval officers, merchants, scientific experts, missionaries, and fur traders were all agents and brokers of Russian empire who brought to Alaska distinctive forms of knowledge about colonization. That knowledge came directly from the uneven successes of Siberian ventures.

THE RUSSIAN FUR TRADE: FROM SIBERIA TO THE ALEUTIAN CHAIN AND KODIAK

The Russian advance from the Kamchatka Peninsula of Siberia through the Islands of Alaska was only the last phase of a conquest that had been launched by Muscovy in the mid–sixteenth century.[12] This conquest was driven by the one resource that the sparsely populated and inhospitably frigid forest expanses produced in abundance: furs. These furs were one of the main sources of Russian state revenue through the early eighteenth century; there was a high demand for the luxuriant furs of the Far North in the markets of Europe and Asia. In Siberia Russian Cossacks and promyshlenniki did some trapping themselves but did not "trade" goods for the bulk of furs that the government received from indigenous peoples. Rather, they participated in what one might call an economy of confiscation. They seized both produce and people, disrupting the lives of indigenous Siberians. Russians took some hostages (usually women and children) and demanded furs as a form of state tribute, or *iasak*, in exchange for which they promised to provide "protection."[13] After they had "subjugated" indigenous people and drained the fur supplies in one area, the Cossacks and promyshlenniki moved on, always in search of new pelts. Beginning in the 1600s, once these men claimed "new" territories in the name of the empire, Russian leaders decreed that Slavic peasants should be sent to Siberia to cultivate the land

and provide food for the newly established towns on the eastern side of the Ural Mountains.[14] Unlike other regions of the Russian Empire settled during this time, Siberia was distinct in that there were no nobles or large landed estates. Some of the descendants of this Slavic-Siberian peasantry would become the promyshlenniki who carried the *iasak* tradition all the way to the Pacific Ocean and through the Aleutians to the western coast of North America. They were the ones who would later come into direct contact with the people of Kodiak.

In Siberia, eighteenth-century Russian travelers, newly exposed to a culture of scientific reason, drew on a vocabulary that allowed them to distinguish between European Russian "perfection" and the "crudity" of indigenous Siberian peoples. As in so many other colonial contexts, they feared that the very act of colonizing would turn their foot soldiers of empire — Cossacks, traders, and peasant settlers — into persons too akin to the colonized.[15] In the 1770s one visiting Russian officer disdainfully commented that the Kamchadals (of the Kamchatka Peninsula of Siberia) "do not keep themselves clean at all, do not wash their hands and faces. . . . All smell like fish, as do the birds, [and they] do not comb their hair."[16] On direct and sensory contact with these people, he was both repulsed by and fascinated with their lifestyle.

These various components of the Siberian models of colonization — fur tribute, settlement, missionary enterprise, and distinctions between European Russians and indigenous peoples — were grafted onto the Alaskan terrain in noteworthy ways. They were directly related to the specific demands of the coastal North American environment, the form of fur trade that developed, and the mixed families that emerged in this remote overseas locale.

SEA OTTER HUNTS AND KODIAK UNIONS

The emergence of mixed Russian-Alutiiq families was spawned in the shifting tides of the fur hunt at the end of the eighteenth century. During the 1720s Tsar Peter the Great had instigated Vitus Bering's expeditions into the North Pacific Ocean. The Russian ruler wanted Bering to find out whether Russia's far eastern shore was connected to North America and then to forge a path for Russian expansion into that remote region, which held the interest of so many European leaders. On his first voyage Bering sailed through the strait that now bears his name, thus showing that the Asian and American continents did not connect. During his second voyage the explorer reached

Alaska in 1741 but died on the way home. The survivors of his second expedition returned to Siberia bringing news of "a great land" beyond the eastern ocean. They also brought samples of exquisite sea otter furs — the softest pelts they had ever encountered.

When Russians introduced these dense furs into the China market in the mid-eighteenth century, they discovered that they could reap profits from sea otter pelts that were well beyond those gained from the skins of other animals, including the fast-diminishing Siberian sable. The rarity and richness of sea otter fur quickly made it a mark of prestige among Mandarin nobles. Their demand for the fur drove the prices of this "soft gold" increasingly higher during the late 1700s.[17] In Russia, news of the profits to be made soon sparked a rush of fur traders across the Kurile and Commander islands, directly off the coast of Kamchatka, the southern peninsula that hangs down from Siberia. Once Russian fur traders had depleted the resources in these islands near the coast, they extended the hunt farther east to the Aleutians and, finally, by the 1760s, to Kodiak Island.[18] Thus, Russians had a head start over other European colonial powers in this part of the world; their Western European competitors did not venture into northern Pacific waters for another generation.[19] One of the greatest challenges for the Russians who participated in this venture was shifting from land-based to sea-based hunting.

The marine environment of sea otter hunting dramatically changed the nature of the Russian fur trade. Promyshlenniki were familiar with the boreal forests of Siberia and adept at the land-based hunting techniques needed to catch the Siberian sable. However, the sea otters of the North Pacific were an entirely different matter. These marine creatures spent little, if any, time on land and had to be hunted in the water.[20]

This type of hunting was an integral element of Aleut and Alutiiq culture; fathers trained boys of a young age to spear animals while they balanced small canoes and kayaks in chilling waters. In the meantime, women and girls prepared these and other animal skins for food, clothing, and supplies. The maritime hunt was marked by distinct gender roles, as it required a well-coordinated effort utilizing specialized tools and the skills of many individuals.[21] Russians arrived without these necessary skills and quickly recognized that they would gain the greatest profit if they could convince local men to do the work for them. Of course, there was a precedent for such "collection" of furs from the aboriginal peoples of Siberia. Thus, as they moved through the Aleutians, the promyshlenniki, employees of the individual merchant companies that sponsored hunting expeditions with permission from the Russian Crown, took native women and children as hostages while they forced fathers, brothers, sons, and husbands to bring them the precious sea otter pelts. In the 1770s two Russian officers described the situation in the following manner: "They [promyshlenniki] drag their vessels on to shore and try to take as hostages children from the island or nearby islands. If they cannot do this peacefully they will use force. . . . No matter where the Natives hunt . . . they are forced to give everything to the *promyshlenniki*."[22] The success of the fur trade enterprise in Alaska hinged on local male labor and access to that labor through women and children.

In August of 1784 the Alutiiq men of Kodiak staged a resistance that some said lasted a month. The promyshlenniki, with their Russian arms, eventually overpowered the Alutiiq, but the duration and violence of this standoff is essential to our understanding of colonial Kodiak.[23] Years later, an Alutiiq man reported his own recollections of the events to a visiting scientist. When his people revisited the place the following summer, "the stench of the corpses lying on the shore polluted the air so badly that none could stay there."[24]

From their first arrival on Kodiak, promyshlenniki continued the practice of taking hostages in exchange for furs. Company men eventually enforced obligatory work on all Alutiiq men between the ages of eighteen and fifty while they held many family members of these men hostage in long cabins along the shore.[25] Whether or not Alutiiq women were raped in these cabins, the people of Kodiak must have lived in fear of these Russian invaders. But at the same time, the Russians relied on the local knowledge of these people for survival.

For the Russians, control of Alutiiq men was critical to the success of the fur trade and the new colony. Certainly, they wanted the furs that these men could so adeptly capture. In addition, placing colonized men's lives at risk by putting them to work was one of the ways that colonial control operated. Many Alutiiq men drowned as the Russian promyshlenniki forced them to travel farther and farther away from the island and for progressively longer periods even under weather conditions in which they would never have gone out themselves.[26] This control and movement of Alutiiq men was directly linked to the delicate environmental balance that Russian demands disturbed. At Kodiak the sea otter population rapidly diminished because the Russians demanded more and more furs as prices escalated in the China market.

Keeping men at risk also kept the women and children under Russian

Gwenn A. Miller

control. For every Alutiiq man whose life was upset by these extended and often perilous hunting expeditions, there were women whose usual responsibilities of preparing food and clothing for their families were made more onerous when they did not receive help for work traditionally performed by men. Russian presence on the island thus completely disordered both Alutiiq men's and women's daily lives but in different ways. Alutiiq people had been accustomed to working together in partnerships; now the demands imposed by Russians tore those partnerships apart. Not only were women left at home, but they were also often held hostage for weeks at a time and had to scramble to gather enough food for their families. Thus, many Alutiiq people almost starved during the first winters of Russian presence, as neither men nor women had time to provision their own families properly.

The intimate violence that Russians inflicted on Alutiiq people took on many forms, from hunger and starvation to fear of physical aggression. In 1789 one woman and two men from nearby islands testified to Russian governmental inspectors that they suffered cruel treatment under some of the trading companies and that they were forced "against our will to hunt and to provide food and do domestic work without pay . . . [and] although we see our women forced to become sexual partners and treated cruelly . . . we have to go on because we fear what might happen."[27]

Faced with such conditions, some Alutiiq women may very well have felt forced to surrender, while others may have chosen to form close liaisons with Russian hunters in an effort to survive. Whether it was the stench of corpses rotting in the bay or the fear that their families would die of starvation that drove their decisions, within a few years of the Russians' arrival, some Alutiiq women married Russian men. Reading histories in which indigenous women "took up" with European men sometimes gives a seamless sense of the initiation of these relationships. But the notion of choice takes on a whole different meaning in the context of violence and despair. If Russian men could provide access to food and clothing, and sometimes gifts, it seems likely that at least some Alutiiq women would have chosen to form unions with them, even though many of these women's lives had been made more difficult with the Russians' arrival. Other women may have been encouraged to marry Russians by family members, particularly fathers who acted as community leaders and wished to establish amicable ties with Russians.

The promyshlenniki inevitably approached these unions in their own distinctive way. As low-ranking Siberian peasants the fur traders undoubtedly felt the scorn of those Russians higher up on the social ladder. Indeed, company leaders, missionaries, and naval officers often reported that the promyshlenniki were the most crude of anyone living in the new outpost *including* indigenous people. Some promyshlenniki felt at home in Alaska, so much so that a leading hunter, who had a sense of his cohort's attitudes, said that those men who had married indigenous women and had children with them might wish to remain on the island permanently.[28] However, these unions could have easily been emotionally tense and economically convenient, or expedient and loving, at the same time. Such concerns never arose among Russian colonial leaders who crafted plans for what they hoped would become a full-fledged colonial capital on the mainland.[29]

RUSSIAN OFFICIALS AND THEIR COLONIAL COMPARISONS

As the first permanent Russian settlement at Kodiak was taking shape in the late 1780s, the company leader, Grigorii I. Shelikhov, wrote letters to empress Catherine II from his company's central offices in Irkutsk, the administrative center of Siberia. He beseeched her to allow a monopoly on the fur trade and advocated for military and financial aid for the burgeoning colony at Kodiak.

A second phase of limited colonization on Kodiak began when this newly approved group of immigrants including 121 workmen, 45 artisans and farmers, 9 Russian missionaries, as well as provisions, seeds, and cattle, finally arrived at Kodiak on the ship *Ekaterina* in 1794.[30] They would find St. Paul's Harbor (present-day Kodiak), or Pavlovsk, located on the northeastern shore of the island, a nativized Russian settlement as much as it was a Russianized native settlement; it was not entirely one or the other. In the same year the famous English explorer George Vancouver wrote that Russian promyshlenniki "appeared to be perfectly content to live after the manner of the native indians of the country; partaking with equal relish and appetite their . . . food, adopting the same fashion, and using the same materials for their apparel."[31] Numerous sources describe promyshlenniki "living like the natives."[32] But they were not only living *like* Alutiiq people on Kodiak; they were living *with* them. Specifically, they were living with Alutiiq women and having children. Some Russian fur hunters were also living with Alutiiq men temporarily when they went out on expeditions for months at a time.

In the same way that they adopted Alutiiq living spaces, Russian men adopted some Alutiiq clothing styles that their female companions sewed from the furs and animal remains that the promyshlenniki received as pay from the fur-trade company.[33] Inside the semisubterranean homes these couples and their children ate a combination of roots, berries, fish, and whale fat, which, according to the English scientist Archibald Menzies, "they devoured with uncommon relish."[34]

Russian men adopted local food and clothing because their Alutiiq companions had learned to prepare these items from the animal and plant life available on and around the island from childhood; their ancestors had gained this knowledge over centuries. Alutiiq women, on the other hand, altered the traditional form of their houses in small ways and started using the few imported Russian tools available to them. Such concrete accommodations in these zones of colonial contact suggest how much Russian men depended on Alutiiq women. They also point to the ways in which Alutiiq women were willing to make calculated changes in their lives to increase the range of options available to them—options that, though construed differently, were also on the minds of imperial officials in Siberia and St. Petersburg.

Appreciating what mixed unions looked like on the ground is quite different from understanding those that existed in the minds of imperial officials. These officials were shaping their imperial policy through a surprisingly wide range of comparisons. What is striking is how often this comparative frame that focused on intimate relations—of domestic space, marriage, sexual contact, parenting—returned again and again in imperial documents in a way that touched on people's habits, bodies, and tastes.

Along with whatever material baggage new settlers brought in 1794 from Siberia aboard the ship *Ekaterina*, they also arrived with cultural baggage about marriage and legitimate unions. Imperial officials' detailed descriptions of how the new colony should be governed traveled in carefully stocked trunks most likely secured in the ship captain's stateroom. In those papers were the Siberian governor Ivan Pil's recommendations on marriage among members of the new colony at Kodiak. It is easily understandable that government directions to colonial leaders would have included prescriptions on methods of fur collection, treatment of indigenous populations, the planting of crops, symbolic land claims, mapping regions, and foreign competition. But why did they also put so much stock in intimate relations?

On the one hand, Russian officials had their own models of colonial rule that had been established in Siberia. On the other hand, it was precisely during the time that fur traders were arriving in Alaska that Catherine the Great was focused on proving that Russia could be a great, even *the* great, empire rather than a curious and backward oddity in the eyes of Western Europeans.

Indeed, Catherine was the self-proclaimed successor to Peter I (1682–1725) in his effort to claim Russia's place as a civilized member of Western Europe.[35] During the eighteenth century, then, comparisons between Russia and the West were a continued subject of inquiry for Russian intellectuals and for members of the state apparatus.[36] Leaders at this time did not simply want to secure Russian society; they wanted to make it appear more cosmopolitan.[37]

Catherine was a Francophile. Not only did French become the language of the nobility under her reign, but French enlightenment thinking also seeped into her understanding of how her empire should be administered. She was an avid reader of the French philosophes and was known in Western European circles for her "unabated zeal for education, toleration, and material progress."[38] In the Alaskan records Catherine's "intentions . . . that the welfare and peace of the aborigines should be maintained" and that they should be educated and "enlightened" emerge repeatedly.[39]

Thus, by 1794, when the settlers and missionaries arrived at Kodiak under direct order from the empress, Siberian governor General Pil recommended that single male settlers should be encouraged to marry native women legally, within the Russian Orthodox Church. As in other colonial contexts, such as British India and the Dutch Indies, the fur-trade company had succeeded in setting up the original colony, and soon afterward the government took a greater interest. In this particular case members of the autocratic Russian court viewed the colony as a reflection of their own civilities in the eyes of Western Europeans — Spanish, French, British, and "Boston men" among them — who roamed the American North Pacific coast in ever-increasing numbers by the end of the eighteenth century. Indeed, one Englishman who visited the region in 1785 and 1786 thought the following of Russians whom he felt had so brazenly claimed the Alaskan Coast: "nothing can be more rude and barbarous than themselves."[40] A Russian post at Alaska might be the only piece of the Russian Empire that some Europeans would ever see. Thus, these architects of developing policy became increasingly weary that Russian citizens might slip into states of "incivility" and be poor representatives of the empire.

It was Alutiiq women who were to learn "civilizing" domestic tasks with the help of the few newly arrived women settlers. They could then help turn the colony into a place where Europeans from everywhere would arrive and be pleasantly surprised to find the intimate comforts of home and the marks of European progress. Sitting around the table in the house of the company manager on Kodiak in 1805, Nikolai Rezanov, an ambitious Russian gentleman, husband to a daughter of Shelikhov, and shareholder in the company, "often imagined" that a new Alaskan city would become a showcase of Imperial Russia; he relished the possible "surprise of future seafarers arriving and totally unexpectedly finding a well planned, magnificent city, a large school, a well stocked library, an electrical machine, a magnificent mineral collection, good cooks and a midday meal prepared in the European manner."[41] Alutiiq women, this man imagined, would learn to prepare and serve those midday meals.

As much as fur-trade company leaders wanted to impress other Europeans, they also wanted to protect their trade. Influential Russians were keenly interested in the activities of the "North American Republicans," and numerous reports regarding American movements traveled from Alaska to Siberia to St. Petersburg.[42] Lewis and Clark's famous transcontinental expedition to the Pacific Ocean in November of 1805 troubled the Russian leaders.[43] They looked to other European colonial practices as models of how to protect their territorial claims and trades. For example, company directors worried that U.S. captains were undercutting their trade on the Alaskan coast. They thought the imperial government should make a formal decree that "foreigners" should not be able to trade directly with Alaskan peoples. They wrote, "A similar situation exists in all other European colonies, in both Indies, where no [foreigner] may trade with the savages, but only with the colonizing company."[44]

While they protected Russian trade, imperial leaders also wanted to be sure that indigenous Alaskans would become "civilized" subjects of the Russian Empire, and only the Russian Empire. Governor Pil, under the auspices of the imperial government, hoped to achieve a "transformation of natives from savage to civilized persons . . . to turn them into Christians. In short, [it sought] to bring them into a state of awareness and instill in them a feeling for the work Russians perform. . . . Americans are by nature quick-witted; they understand well, are dexterous and have strong constitutions."[45]

The managers of Shelikhov's company, as well as members of the imperial government, viewed Alutiiqs as morally and culturally inferior, yet they encouraged Russian men to live with and marry these women. Perhaps Russian leaders subscribed to a notion that the children of mixed unions would be the most resilient members of a new colonial society.[46] Supposedly, these children would embody the best traits of Russian fathers, who represented the "civilizing" regime in this remote locale, and Alutiiq mothers, who were equipped with deep knowledge of the locality.

With no intention of returning to Russia, as we know, many promysh-lenniki sought to have their companions, their children's mothers, baptized by the missionaries who first arrived at Kodiak in 1794, ten years after the initial settlement.[47] Many promyshlenniki did not strictly follow all the mores of the church when they were so far from European Russia. They certainly mixed Christian and pre-Christian folk beliefs in practice.[48] Nevertheless, they carried miniature painted icons of saints among their sparse belongings and considered sanction by the church important.[49]

As they had in Siberia, Russian Orthodox Missionaries followed on the heels of the promyshlenniki. There they had baptized some indigenous peoples, but this baptism did not automatically make the people Russian. In the imperial vocabulary they were clearly marked as "*iasak* people" (tribute-paying people), distinct from the Slavic peasant families of Siberia. Like other Russians, missionaries brought ideas about who could be converted and in what way, ideas that they carried with them from Siberia.

Baptism is an indication of the types of relations in which people were willing to invest on colonial Kodiak. This is not to say that promyshlenniki behavior always pleased men of the cloth. In fact, the missionary Ioasaf complained that promyshlenniki took women only as "companions." The church had specific definitions of marriage before God. By the end of the eighteenth century, as a nationalist movement started to emerge in Russia, members of the government were beginning to insist that church marriage was the one and only form of marriage that they would officially sanction. Previously, the imperial government had accepted traditional peasant marriage as official in the eyes of the law whether or nor it included a ceremony in the church.[50] When missionaries arrived at Kodiak, church marriage became mandatory.

However, men and women already living together may well have perceived relationships that the clergy saw as mere "companionship" differently. By Alutiiq custom, women and men were united when the man came to the woman's house, stayed with her for one night, and then gave presents to her and her family.[51] Therefore it is likely that many women who lived with promyshlenniki before the arrival of missionaries thought that they were married to these men. Even when these women went through the rituals of baptism and marriage by missionaries, it is doubtful that they would have construed this form of union as different from that earlier formed with promyshlenniki and that members of their own society considered legitimate.

Because they embraced accommodation in the everyday — in the food they ate, the clothes they wore, and the style of their homes—Alutiiq women who married Russian men were probably more acutely aware of the contradictions of colonial contact than anyone else on Kodiak at the time. These conflicts became even more pronounced once Russian naval officers and missionaries actively tried to change the ways in which these women dressed, cooked, and behaved. One young and impressionable Russian officer who visited Kodiak briefly in 1802 wrote that Alutiiq women were "immoral," with "loose," "unrespectable" sexual tendencies. He prescribed European norms of moral "femininity" as the ideal to which they should aspire. Yet when native women adopted European clothing, and combined that with traditional forms of dress, he complained that these clothes "seemed not to suit them at all." Still, he noted, "Like women everywhere, they love dressing up."[52] Through such mixed-style dress, however, Alutiiq women integrated and redefined elements of the unfamiliar culture they encountered. On some level the Russian officer hoped that they were indeed like women everywhere, and he had no trouble praising "fashionable" native women's custom of washing their faces in urine, the contemporary acid peel of choice, in order to make them whiter and clearer.[53] Still, such an officer would never recognize them as members of Russian society.

These comments not only underscore how Alutiiq women could be incorporated into Russian society but also raise the question of whether they should be. Could these women, like the "perennial outsiders" of Siberia, marry Russian men and become something else?[54] Could they and their children become Russian when the men they married, who at times were called "the scum of Siberian criminals and adventurers," remained on the margins of Russian society?[55] If the naval officer admitted that they were "like women everywhere," did he allow them entry into his own social realm? If he emphasized their difference, did he lower his own prestige by admitting that other Russians had formed intimate unions with "savage" people? Though almost all the men who formed unions with these women were members of the Siberian peasantry, some possibly even children of mixed marriages themselves, they were still identified by members of the state apparatus as Russians.

These contested notions of marriage, femininity, and social standing provide a context for understanding the apparently ambiguous identity of one Alutiiq woman who had lived with a Russian officer for some time before marrying him in 1790. The English secretary to a Russian naval expedition described her as "handsome, but perforated in the skin," or tattooed.

She also had a customary bone with beads piercing her bottom lip, and she wore Siberian dress. Her children were healthy, her house was extremely clean, and she "seemed the perfect mistress of Russian economy."[56] The Englishman admitted that he was surprised to find that when he dined in her home, he "was very well satisfied with the treatment" he received there. This woman's display of hospitality and unique blend of Russian and native qualities might be read as a sign of cultural accommodation within a colonial context, but it was one the colonizers found unsettling.

KREOL CHILDREN — NEWLY DEFINED SOCIAL KINDS

However ambiguous their status, native women parented children with Russian men, and their children eventually became the leading literate labor source for the Russian American Company (RAC), which was incorporated in 1799. By the beginning of the nineteenth century there was a substantial core of these children, and perhaps even some adults, living in and around the settlement at St. Paul's Harbor on Kodiak. Fathers of some of these children were sending their sons to Siberia to be educated. The company leaders, as well as the imperial government, encouraged this practice because they saw the opportunity to train capable employees for new settlements. Cultural biases clearly made Russians believe that these children were more capable than were their native counterparts. One missionary noted that while native people "lacked variety of character," this was not evident in children of mixed descent.[57] He also seems to have believed that kreol children naturally displayed great gifts. To his mind the very blood of these ethnically mixed children, and its distinction from the blood of "clean," or "pure," native children, made them innately more "gifted."

All known English-language scholarly work and English translations of Russian archival documents refer to the Russian-Alaskan population of mixed ancestry as "creoles," but this is somewhat of a misnomer.[58] Although the Russians purposefully adopted the French and Spanish terms *creole* and *crioli* to refer to the children of Russian and Native Alaskan parentage, they did not use these terms to identify children born of two European parents in the colonies as did these other Europeans. Instead, the Russian American Company charter of 1821 specifically identified the children of Russian fathers and native mothers as *kreol*.[59]

In the 1821 charter of the RAC (a monopolistic extension of the original company whose leaders settled Kodiak in 1784), the Russian government codified a new legal category for kreol children.[60] This category applied only in Russian America. The legal rights of these children included membership in their father's estate (class). However, if they had been educated at the expense of the company, they were required to serve the colony for at least ten years. Unlike all other Russians, they paid no taxes, nor were they required to enter into military service as long as they remained in the colonies. Regardless of the privileges accorded to kreol people in Alaska, Russian imperial leaders clearly marked them as a category of citizen distinct from Russians. As in other colonial contexts, moreover, there were always exceptions to these rules. There were undoubtedly some people of Russian and native Alaskan parentage who became members of their mothers' villages. In addition, some kreols moved to mainland Russia and registered as members of their fathers' estates.[61] Nonetheless, these examples are the exceptions to the definitions set out in the 1821 charter. It is clear that Russian officials viewed and wanted to label people of mixed ancestry as a particular social kind in the taxonomy of the empire. The mere fact that a new legal category was created to identify them demonstrates that officials worked to mark them as different from ordinary Russian citizens of any rank.[62] In 1825 Kirill T. Khlebnikov, a governmental official and longtime administrator of the RAC, characterized the kreol position as follows: "They constitute a link uniting Russians and islanders, humanity and savagery, and education and ignorance."[63]

Scholars of the late nineteenth century may seek to compare Russian Alaskan kreols to colonial mixed populations elsewhere in the world, but Stoler's warning that there were many different meanings for "mixedness" in colonial contexts is pertinent here.[64] We must consider the specific surroundings in which the term emerged. By the first decades of the nineteenth century the Russian Empire constituted the largest contiguous series of states in the world. To the west it reached as far as Finland and the Crimea; to the east it extended to America and even briefly to the Hawaiian Islands. The geography and climate of these vast expanses made the state difficult and costly to govern and protect.[65]

In the early 1800s, imperial officials were preoccupied with resettling and improving the state of peasant lives within the contiguous borders of the far-reaching empire. Officials clearly had something specific in mind when they drafted the addendum to the RAC charter of 1821. Because the state retained Slavic peasants to cultivate and inhabit the contiguous Russian borderlands, and reports had surfaced of the hardships of life in Russian America, developing a Slavic Russian population there would have been difficult. Hence, at the time that the 1821 charter was drafted, government and company officials realized that they would never achieve a sustained Russian population in Alaska. Instead, they focused on articulating a social stratum with loyalties both to Alaskan land and to Russian culture and state; the children of Alutiiq women and promyshlenniki served this purpose in the Russian officials' designation of them as *krioli*.

THE CASE OF RUSSIAN ALASKA points to the importance of attending to the intimate spaces people inhabit and the ways they do so in order to understand the making of overseas imperial regimes. Unlike the French and British fur-trade companies in North America, the operations of which were conducted mostly on land, the Russian fur trade focused almost exclusively on the maritime hunt. In these other North American fur trades, Indians and Europeans traded with each other on relatively level ground, at least initially. Members of the Imperial Russian government were mindful of Western European modes of empire; many even sought to emulate those models. And at the end of the eighteenth century Catherine the Great was particularly mindful of all things French.[66] However, Russian awareness of Western European models did not exist in a vacuum. With the Russian fur trade, the imperial government had a long-established system of tribute payment in Siberia, which informed how the fur-trade companies venturing into the waters of the North Pacific would interact with indigenous people they met there. Russians disrupted the lives of Aleut and Alutiiq families as they took women and children hostage and forced thousands of men into frigid weather and the dangers of the sea, where they often met death in the icy waters. Their superior talent in the hunt, as well as Russian men's unwillingness to acquire the necessary skills, made the labor and control of Alutiiq men an extremely lucrative means of production for the Russian fur trade.

The consequent absence of Alutiiq men often caused Alutiiq women to become overextended in their own responsibilities and helps us understand their decisions to enter into mutually dependent relationships with Russian men early on. Women do not seem to have served as guides or traders themselves; rather, they, too, were coerced into working for the company to provide food and clothing for all.[67] On Kodiak Island a handful of Alutiiq women married company administrators, but most others who married European men formed unions with promyshlenniki. There certainly was no single uniform "experience" of mixed union in Russian Alaska. While some Alutiiq women may have wanted to form unions with Russian men, others were probably abducted as hostages and forced to live with promyshlenniki. Likewise, some promyshlenniki were probably brutish and needy at the same time. Some may have only wanted sexual and material favors from women. Others formed unions that made them want to stay on Kodiak for a variety of reasons, even when their contracts were over and they were supposed to return to Siberia.

The experience of Alutiiq women, Russian men, and their kreol children on Kodiak Island points to a complexity that encompasses exploitation as well as "tenderness" rather than a clear demarcation between the two. In Alaska Russian fur traders drove Alaskan men to hunt at sea, where they perished frequently. At the same time, many Russian men formed permanent relations with Alaskan women. These Russian men and Alutiiq women had children who became the backbone of the Russian enterprise in North America. The kreol children of Russian America remained the core of the Russian subject population in the remote colonial settlements right up until Russian imperial officials finally decided to sell Alaska to the United States in 1867.

Attention to these varied domains of the intimate underscores that cultural fusion, material deprivation and dependence, and emotional ambiguity do not exceptionally converge in the Alaskan context. Rather, that is what colonialism is about. In colonial contexts the very acts of clothing families, finding and eating food, parenting children, building houses, and laboring for foreign companies encompass both violence and dependence; the tension between the two is part and parcel of colonial ties. They can, and often do, go hand in hand.

NOTES

I wish to thank Ann Stoler for her constant encouragement and close reading of my work. I am also indebted to the following readers for their insightful comments on earlier versions of this chapter: Deborah Breen, Elizabeth Fenn, Parker Goyer, Nancy Hewitt, Amy Kaplan, Noleen McIlvenna, Martin Miller, Catherine Phipps, Peter Wood, and all of the contributors to this volume.

1. Lisiansky, *Voyage Round the World*, 212–13.

2. Merck, *Siberia and Northwestern America*, 100.

3. In his archaeological study of a Russian fur trader's dwelling at Three Saints Harbor, on Kodiak Island, Aron Crowell found European and indigenous items completely

"commingled." He concluded that the structure probably revealed either "an ethnically mixed household . . . [and] extensive adoption of indigenous material culture" (Crowell, *Archeology and the Capitalist World System*, 105, 151–52).

4. Taylor titled the book *American Colonies*, not *Colonial America*. It explores large geographical regions over time, arguing against a historical tradition that has highlighted a "fundamentally happy story of 'American exceptionalism': the making of a new people, in a new land" (Taylor, *American Colonies*, x). Taylor argues, instead, for the significance of multiple colonial situations in North America. This work is a synthesis; however, the very fact that it is a synthesis, an attempt by a highly respected historian to bring together this period of American history, indicates that these changes were already established in the scholarly literature on which he drew for his analysis.

5. See Warner, "What's Colonial about Colonial America." Also see Stoler's take on this point in "Tense and Tender Ties."

6. This process is reminiscent of the way that the English took lessons learned from their invasion and colonization of Ireland to the Americas during the Elizabethan era. See Canny, *Making Ireland British, 1580–1650*; and Canny, "The Ideology of English Colonization."

7. Architects of the Soviet state had sought to eradicate differences among the many peoples of the USSR, for example, by enforcing the exclusive use of Russian language in schools throughout Siberia while permitting limited zones of cultural autonomy. This policy is similar to what architects of the U.S. government did in Indian schools in the late nineteenth century and the early twentieth. Early Soviet ethnographies of indigenous peoples treated them as monolithic groups while criticizing coercive systems of tsarist rule.

8. Brower and Lazzerini, *Russia's Orient*, xi. See introductions to Brower and Lazzerini, *Russia's Orient*, and to Burbank and Ransel, *Imperial Russia*, for detailed overviews of the state of the field. See also Fitzhugh and Crowell, *Crossroads of Continents*; Slezkine, *Arctic Mirrors*; Sunderland, "Making the Empire"; Balzer, *The Tenacity of Ethnicity*; Barrett, *At the Edge of Empire*; Geraci and Khodarkovsky, *Of Religion and Empire*; Rethman, *Tundra Passages*; Reid, *The Shaman's Coat*; Kertula, *Antler on the Sea*; American Society for Ethnohistory, panel on "Northern Shamanism and Its Observers and Interpreters," Oct. 17, 2002; Sunderland, *Taming the Wild Field*.

9. Thomas Sanders has even declared that this "subterranean" field of inquiry "is the strongest historiographical force at work in Russia today" (Sanders, introduction to *Historiography of Imperial Russia*, 12). At the forefront of this work Yuri Slezkine traced the story of indigenous Siberians all the way to the twentieth century. Throughout all of his work he gave a sense of native, as well as Russian, actions and perceptions without making indigenous people seem passive in their relations with European Russians.

10. Both Thomas Barrett and Willard Sunderland use important concepts that have developed in the study of Native American history over the past decade. Barrett draws

on Daniel Usner's concept of "frontier exchange" and on Richard White's concept of a "middle ground" to explore the frontiers of the Northern Caucasus as he asserts the usefulness of conceptions of American frontiers. See Barrett, "Lines of Uncertainty." Willard Sunderland looks to Paul Carter, Greg Dening, James Scott, Richard White, and Mary Louise Pratt as he argues that the relations between Russian peasants and indigenous people all over the empire were much more complicated than they have thus far been presented in historical writings. See Sunderland, "An Empire of Peasants"; and Sunderland, "Making the Empire."

11. Many records were lost or destroyed when Russia sold Alaska to the United States for seven million dollars in 1867. According to some archivists in St. Petersburg, some documents from the Imperial era were used as scrap paper or as fuel for fires during the early Soviet era.

12. These Russians had a long history of involvement in the fur trade that went back as far as the late eleventh century. In fact, the fur trade became the driving force behind the emergence of Russian principalities. As early as 1096 people of Novgorod reported men in far-off lands who spoke a different language and gave furs in exchange for the iron they desired. See Slezkine, *Arctic Mirrors*, 11. Novgorod (the dominant northern Russian principality until the sixteenth century) gained its wealth by exporting furs to Bulgur, Kiev, and even Byzantium.

13. This tributary mode of the production of furs is distinct from those modes that were used in non-Russian North American fur-trade situations. British, French, some Spanish, and Dutch (until the mid-1600s) fur traders all practiced the exchange of commodities with Native Americans. In fact, in many cases Native Americans became important market consumers for expanding European industries. In Canada and the Old Northwest, French and British fur traders did not subjugate the native peoples with whom they traded under their own crowns but recognized these groups as independent nations. Europeans even sought out these Native American nations as allies against rival Europeans.

14. Russian attitudes toward populating this land were similar to those of the English populating the New World. "Russians like Anglo-Saxons celebrated the courage and back-breaking labour of the farmer-colonist struggling in a hostile wilderness against an unfamiliar climate in order to bring improvement and civilization to the vast 'empty' regions of the earth" (Lievin, *Empire*, 208).

15. Slezkine, *Arctic Mirrors*, 56.

16. Krasheninnikov, *Opisanie zemli Kamchatki s*, 366–68 (author's translation).

17. By 1775 a sea otter skin could fetch fifty to eighty rubles, while a sable skin could only fetch two to two and a half rubles. See Gibson, *Feeding the Russian Fur Trade*, 29. By 1790 a single sea otter pelt was worth between eighty and one hundred dollars in the China market. See Ogden, *The California Sea Otter Trade, 1784–1848*, 6. That amount would be equivalent to between fifteen hundred and twenty-three hundred U.S. dollars in today's terms.

18. By the 1750s sea otters had vanished from the coast of Kamchatka, by the 1780s from the Kurile Islands, and by 1789, they were hardly ever seen in the Aleutians. See Gibson, *Feeding the Russian Fur Trade*, 31.

19. Still, Russian fur-gathering expeditions faced numerous obstacles in these literally uncharted waters. Vessels that carried these expeditions commonly went down in the high seas and on average approximately one-quarter to one-third of each venture's crew perished through disease, warfare, or accident. See Gibson, *Feeding the Russian Fur Trade*, 31.

20. Bodkin, "Sea Otters," 74.

21. Aleut and Alutiiq men would go out in one- and two-person skin-covered boats. As soon as one hunter saw an otter, he would spear the animal, which would plunge into the sea. The hunter then let the others know by raising his paddle quietly in the air. The entire group formed a circle around the area where the animal had submerged, awaiting its return to the surface. The process was repeated until the animal became so exhausted that it could no longer dive into the water. In May 1805 Lisiansky wrote, "I was told by very expert hunters, that these animals were sometimes easily caught; whereas at other times, twenty bidarkas would be employed half a day in taking a single otter: and that this animal has been known to tear the arrow from its body in order to escape" (Lisiansky, *Voyage Round the World*, 203). Also see Bodkin, "Sea Otters," 80–81, for a description of early hunting methods and value of sea otter fur.

22. "Ekstrak iz zhurnalov flota kapitana P. K. Krenitsyna i kapitan leitenanta M. D. Levashova, 1771 g" (Extract from the journals of Captain Krenitsyna and Captain Lieutenant Levashova), 357 (author's translation).

23. The fur-trade company leader, Shelikhov, sent reports back to Catherine the Great saying that he had been able to "pacify the savages" with relative ease, and though he had fear in his heart, he had done it all in the name of the empress, for the glory of Russia (Shelikov, *A Voyage to America, 1783–1786*, 40–41).

24. In 1854 the ethnographer H. J. Holmberg wrote that according to this Alutiiq man, Arsenti aminak, the Russians had an interpreter from Unalaska with them. The interpreter was able to speak Kodiak Alutiiq because he had been taken as a slave from Kodiak to the Fox Islands as a young child. Through this interpreter the Russians demanded hostages from the Alutiiq chiefs, who would not give them any. Arminak told an early German ethnographer working for a Russian expedition that the Island of Sitkalidak (off the southeast end of Kodiak) had many Alutiiq settlements at that time. and people living there gathered together at one settlement on a high cliff because they feared attack by the Russians. "The Russians went to the settlement and carried out a terrible blood bath. Only a few [Alutiiq] men were able to flee . . . [and] 300 Koniagas were shot by the Russians. This happened in April, and since then the island [Sitkalidak] has been uninhabited. After this every chief had to surrender his children as hostages" (Holmberg, *Holmberg's Ethnographic Sketches*, 59).

25. Merck, *Siberia and Northwestern America*, 97.

26. Khlebnikov, *Colonial Russian America*, 145.

27. "Complaints of the Natives of Unalaska District, 1790," 2.

28. "Hunter Egor Purtov, being questioned . . . ," June 25, 1790. Yudin Collection, Box 1, folder 23. Library of Congress, Manuscripts Division. Washington, D.C.

29. It was to be a capital in which "it will be possible to boast" to other Europeans that "the Russians [in America] live in good order" (Shelikov to Baranov [1794], 33).

30. See "Pis'mo Shelikhova I Polevago k Baranovu" [Shelikhov in a letter to Baranov, 1794], 2:67–77. Tikhmenev's 1863 collection of reprinted documents, an appendix to his (the first published) history of Russian America, contains many letters and government directives that are not found elsewhere because they were probably destroyed after the Russian government sold Alaska to the United States. Many scholars agree that the collection remains an important source on the early period of Russian presence in Alaska.

31. Vancouver, *A Voyage of Discovery to the North Pacific Ocean and Round the World*, 207. See also Menzies, *The Alaska Travel Journal of Archibald Menzies, 1793–1794*, Volume 2, where Menzies observes that "Russians in their clothing food and manner of living, differed very little from the Natives of the Country" (99).

32. See, e.g., Davydov, *Dvukratnoe puteshestvie*; Gedeon, *Ocherk is Istorii Amerikanskoi Pravoslavoi Dukhovnoi Missii*; Langsdorff, *Remarks and Observations on a Voyage around the World from 1803 to 1807*; Khlebnikov, *Colonial Russian America*, and *Russkaia Amerika v neopublikovannykh zapiskakh K. T. Khlebnikova.*

33. The payment system changed to a wage system when the Russian American Company monopoly was formed in 1799. See Arndt, "Memorandum of Captain 2nd Rank Golovin," 70.

34. Menzies, *The Alaska Travel Journal of Archibald Menzies*, 99.

35. It was Diderot who recommended to Catherine that she commission his protégé Falconet to sculpt the famed *Bronze Horseman* statue in honor of Peter (with the emblematic inscription in Latin, as well as in Russian, "To Peter I from Catherine II"). See Malia, *Russia under Western Eyes*, 50–51. To this day the statue remains the most well-known symbol of St. Petersburg and is the subject of an epic poem by Pushkin, *The Bronze Horseman.*

36. Bassin, *Imperial Visions*, 37; Greenfield, *Nationalism*, 189–274.

37. Whittaker, "The Idea of Autocracy among Eighteenth-Century Russian Historians," 19.

38. Malia, *Russia under Western Eyes*, 54.

39. Tikhmenev, *Istoricheskoe obozrenie*, 59; see also ibid., 22. It is important to note that these were intentions only and part of her hope to be a "benevolent monarch" in the European fashion. However, Catherine's intentions did not always coincide with her desires for imperial grandeur nor with the realities of a remote colonial outpost such as Kodiak Island.

40. Walker, *An Account of a Voyage to the North West Coast of America in 1785 and 1786*, 148.

41. Langsdorff, *Remarks and Observations on a Voyage around the World from 1803 to 1807*, 42–43. What are we to make of the electrical machine? As with displaying knowledge

of science, perhaps it would prove that Russia was right in step with the technological advances toward modernity taking place in Western Europe. It would show not only that Russians were sophisticated enough to know of such technology but also that the government considered it important enough to maintain this technology halfway round the world from the imperial capital.

42. "Ministerstvo inostrannykh del sssr," 241–43.

43. "Captain Winship [American] has told Baranov that last fall 60 American men were sent overland to the Columbia River to establish a settlement there, but we could have occupied that region easily. The American states have claimed their right to this coast, stating that the headwaters of the Columbia River rise in their territory. Using the same argument they can claim their possessions also extend over all territories where they do not encounter European settlements" ("Ministerstvo inostrannykh del sssr," f. St. P. Glavnii arkhiv, 1–7, op. 6, 1802 g. d.1). Indeed, the U.S. government declared Manifest Destiny not long after, in 1823.

44. "Ministerstvo inostrannykh del sssr," 241–43.

45. "Instruktsia Shelikhovy 12 Maya 1794." By "Americans," Pil meant indigenous Alaskans, not citizens of the United States.

46. Jean Taylor has made this claim for the children of ethnically mixed descent in Batavia. See Taylor, *The Social World of Batavia*, 16.

47. "A Report from Arkhimandrit Ioasaf to His Archbishop Concerning Conditions in the Russian Settlement of Kodiak Island," 38–39.

48. Matossian, "The Peasant Way of Life," 23.

49. See Smith and Barnett, introduction to *Russian America*, 15. See also Black, *Orthodoxy in Alaska*, 13.

50. Peasant marriage ceremonies in the seventeenth century comprised both Christian and pre-Christian rituals. First, the potential groom visited the bride's home, bringing presents. Then friends and family participated in separate "bachelor" and "maiden" parties. Finally, the groom led the bride away from her parents' house for a ceremony in the local church (often located in another larger town). After an Orthodox Church ceremony the couple went to the man's home, where the husband's father traditionally removed the wife's veil. The newly married couple then sat in the icon corner while the husband's family welcomed them with a huge feast for many relatives and friends. Finally, the woman would take off the man's boots as a sign of submission, and the two were led to bed amidst the sound of bawdy songs sung by friends. See Matossian, "The Peasant Way of Life," 23. This change in the government's policy demonstrates how meanings of marriage are not static. Marriage is not a definitive ritual that is universally transferable but rather a regulative tool of human societies that acts through exclusionary practices. See Borneman, "Until Death Do Us Part," 215–16. Even within those societies there can be multiple versions of marriage, and when they meet at the interface of divergent cultures, definitions become blurred even further.

51. Lisiansky, *Voyage Round the World*, 198–99.

52. Davydov, *Dvukratnoe puteshestvie*, 18.

53. Ibid., 68. The note on washing the face with urine might seem a facetious remark on the part of this naval officer. However, it was a concept with which he might have been familiar. Nadya Peterson notes that in Russian peasant tradition, where cleanliness was synonymous with purity, urine was considered to have medicinal value; it could even enhance the skin's elasticity. See Peterson, "Dirty Women." Other Russian observers also remarked that Alutiiq women washed themselves with urine. See Lisiansky, *Voyage Round the World*, 214.

54. Stoler addresses this issue in "Sexual Affronts and Racial Frontiers." Slezkine suggests that by the nineteenth century, elite Russians believed that the indigenous people in Siberia, who had originally been redeemable by baptism in the seventeenth century, could never become "Russians." They remained "perennial outsiders." See Slezkine, *Arctic Mirrors*, 52.

55. Langsdorff, *Remarks and Observations on a Voyage around the World from 1803 to 1807*, 35–36.

56. Sauer, *An Account of a Geographical and Astronomical Expedition to the Northern Part of Russia*, 173. Billings, one of the leaders of this expedition, was an astronomer who had traveled to the Northwest with Cook in 1778. Catherine II enlisted him to explore the so-called uncharted Chukotski Peninsula for Russia in 1791. In 1793 the primary meaning of the term *mistress* was "head of household" (*Oxford English Dictionary*, 2003 online ed., s.v. "mistress").

57. Gedeon, *Ocherk is Istorii Amerikanskoi Pravoslavoi Dukhovnoi Missii*, 20.

58. The original use of the term *creole* to describe the children of Russian men and Native Alaskan women is unclear; it appeared in the official documents of the Russian American Company in the second decade of the nineteenth century. The meaning of the term in Russian America was very specific and based, not surprisingly, on a French and Spanish model. Rezanov used the term in 1805 to refer to the children of Russian fathers and Native Alaskan mothers in the Russian colony. Arkhiv Vneshne Politiki Rossiiskoi Imperii, Moscow. f.342, d.277, ll.1–3. It appeared in a population table in a notation that read, "Following the example of Europeans who hold colonies in the West Indies, the company calls children of Russians and [Native] American women creoles" (Golovin, *Puteshestvie vokrug sveta*). The Russian navy officer V. M. Golovin, who traveled in Alaska in 1818, identified the term in print during the 1820s. According to eminent Russian America scholar Lydia Black, the term first emerged in the Sitka parish Orthodox Church records in 1816. See Black, "Creoles in Russian America," 143. Prior to this written use of the term *kreol*, many terms were used for mixed-union children, including, *illegitimate, colonial youth*, and even Baranov's pejorative *Russian bastard*. See Tikhmenev, *Istoricheskoe obozrenie*, 98.

59. Thus, I use the term and spelling *kreol* to identify children of mixed Russian–Native Alaskan descent.

60. *Polnoe sobranie zakonov rosiiskoi imperii s 1649 goda*, 756, 842–54.

61. Black, "Creoles in Russian America," 152.

62. Black argues that class, not race, determined the status of kreol children. Certainly class was indeed supremely significant in this colonial context because of the intricate class rank system that existed in Russia. However, I would argue that given the prejudices toward indigenous Alaskans outlined earlier in this chapter, the issue is more complicated; both race and class together were important factors in the ordering of colonial status in Russian Alaska.

63. Khlebnikov, *Russkaia Amerika v neopublikovannykh zapiskakh K. T. Khlebnikova*, 67. Khlebnikov wrote these notes on Russian America from 1818 to 1832, during his stay in Alaska as manager at Sitka.

64. See Stoler, "Tense and Tender Ties."

65. Russian leaders did whatever they could to promote the colonization of "unpopulated and uncultivated" lands. See Chechulin, *Nakaz imp. Ekateriny II. dannyi kommisii o sochinenii proekta novogo ulozheniia* (cited in Sunderland, *Taming the Wild Field*, 77–85). See also Paul Duke's English translation, *Catherine the Great's Instruction (Nakaz) to the Legislative Commission, 1767*, 77–81. Of course these lands were actually inhabited by indigenous peoples.

66. At the same time, she was certainly terrified of French revolutionary tendencies.

67. In the French and English trades Sylvia Van Kirk and Richard White have both suggested that women's burdens were often alleviated by the arrival of European hunters. See Van Kirk, *"Many Tender Ties"*; and White, *The Middle Ground*.

Circuits of
Knowledge
Production

13

ALEXANDRA MINNA STERN

An Empire of Tests: Psychometrics and the

Paradoxes of Nationalism in the Americas

In the fall of 1996, thousands of people took to the streets in Mexico City. Over the course of several weeks they marched to the presidential palace, blocked traffic downtown, and shut down the Ministry of Public Education.[1] Mexican students, parents, researchers, and even several members of Congress were protesting a new and abruptly decreed federal policy requiring every fifteen-year-old to take a standardized test, consisting of 128 multiple-choice questions, in order to enroll in the second phase of high school. Faced with such broad-based opposition, the Ministry of Public Education made a few concessions, altering some cumbersome bureaucratic and administrative procedures, but the placement test became a permanent facet of Mexico's educational system.

At the time, critics linked the expansion of standardized testing to the waves of privatization that were "liberalizing" previously state-controlled institutions and industries in the wake of the North American Free Trade Agreement.[2] Following the U.S. model of the Educational Testing Service, elite Mexican educators, many of them working in the upper echelons of the Ministry of Education, had created a secretive for-profit company to design and mass-produce standardized tests for all classroom levels. For many teachers who believed in the promise of high quality and low cost public schooling, a right guaranteed all citizens in the 1917 Constitution, such developments were anathema to what they considered the core principles of education and citizenship in Mexico. One of the most commonly heard criticisms was that standardized testing was new to the country, a corrosive import fresh off the shelves of U.S. corporations.

However, the demonstrations that began in 1996, and that have continued sporadically to the present, are part of a much longer history of imperialism, psychometrics, and nationalism. In her work on empire and the intimate Ann Stoler examines the intelligence surveys administered by the Carnegie Foundation in multiple sites, including the southern United States and South Africa, and outlines how a specific technology of racialization and difference-making resonated in distinct national and colonial contexts. In this chapter I expand on her insights by focusing on the mechanics, content, and logic of early-twentieth-century mental tests, paying attention to how they moved—linguistically and ideationally—across national lines. I do so by telling a story unique to the Americas, first, of the arrival and reformulation of intelligence tests to the United States from France and, second, of the development of mental tests in Mexico during the decades of heightened nationalism and civic reconstruction that followed the 1910 revolution. This story illustrates an understudied dimension of the asymmetrical power dynamics of inter-American relations and suggests a fruitful port of entry into the "politics of comparison." In Mexico and the United States, intelligence tests promoted the shared goals of modernizing and standardizing education. However, despite the fairly static architecture of mental tests, their effects varied greatly in each country, reflecting and promoting divergent ideas about the cognitive and rational capacity of distinct ethnic and racial groups and the body politic as a whole.

Standardized tests are an ensemble of homogenizing, rigidly scripted, and narrow inductive exercises administered by experts—usually on behalf of state agencies—to designated subject groups. In most respects they function quite circularly, first and foremost, by evaluating an individual's cognitive skills and acquired knowledge according to norms that have been already preestablished by the aggregation and statistical calculation of results from previous tests. As Geoffrey C. Bowker and Susan Leigh Star have argued, one of the hallmarks of effectively universalized classification schemes is their invisibility; they are "boundary objects" creating silent infrastructures that can stretch out over seemingly incommensurate domains.[3] This silence is broken when the process of negotiation over meaning and organization spills out of bounds and is contested by social actors and institutions. This noisy "torque" can betray the underlying assumptions and outer limits of taxonomic systems. Given the high stakes involved in standardized testing, it is not surprising that such disruptions are not uncommon, as evidenced by recent battles in the United States over the validity of the Scholastic Aptitude Test (SAT) for college admissions.

Psychometrics was one of many medical and psychological technologies that helped to give rise to modern biopower: mental tests generated diagnostic and prognostic knowledge about polities and populations at the same time that they insinuated new notions of subjectivity and "interiority."[4] Administered as a series of regimented and tightly contained exercises, intelligence tests were geared toward the absorption and internalization of norms, in terms of content as well as form.[5] As such, they produced a certain brand of intimacy, embodied by the hierarchically charged relationship of student and teacher and, more important, by the birth of a reflexive psychological awareness often linked to self-monitoring and the instillation of self-discipline. Furthermore, the hidden economy of intelligence tests also imbued them and their results with a sense of intimacy, the clandestine, and revelation.

Intelligence testing emerged in the early twentieth century, in tandem with similar endeavors, such as anthropometrics and better-baby contests, which were focused on the measurement of human bodies and capacities. In contrast to such biometrics, however, which gauged externalities, the aim of psychometrics was to label and calculate what was *inside*.[6] Like Freudian psychoanalysis, intelligence testing was driven by the urge to elucidate the submerged realities of the human mind.[7] In addition, it was influenced by pathbreaking discoveries in health and medicine, above all bacteriology and germ theory, which traced diseases not to stinky and unsightly filth and miasma but to unseen microorganisms that were responsible for diseases such as typhus, cholera, and bubonic plague.[8]

The scientific desire to probe the enigmatic workings of the mind had begun a century earlier with craniometry, which ostensibly calculated brain volume by packing the cerebrum with substances such as mustard seed and gunpowder.[9] It was superseded by phrenology, which interpreted personality profiles by reading the protrusions on a skull's exterior, and criminology, founded by the Italian Cesare Lombroso, who thought that criminals could be identified by the stigmata of atavistic "races." Intelligence testing went one step beyond these earlier practices. Instead of deciphering the epidermis or manipulating skulls, it sought to conjure cognitive ability through two- and three-dimensional problems and puzzles that ranged from simple geometric wooden games to lengthy pencil-and-paper exams. Test results were then quantified according to statistical rules about deviations, sample size, and permissible data variation and were represented pictorially with bell curves, pie charts, and graphs.

Intelligence testing incited and continues to incite controversy because it claims to transparently measure something—mental capacity—that has been defined differently across time, space, and culture. Indeed, a closer look at the transnational circuit of standardized testing in the early twentieth century demonstrates many instances of dissonance, when tests bristled and broke against the pressures of historical specificity and contingency. In the context of U.S.-Mexican relations intelligence tests can be conceptualized as mobile "boundary objects" that traveled in a manner that was sometimes smooth, sometimes haphazard, and constantly pulled by the undertow of imperial definitions of science and objectivity.

THE MAKING OF THE INTELLIGENCE TEST

At the outset of the twentieth century, mental tests, reproduced in the millions, were formulated by psychologists across the globe, usually working in governmental agencies of education and health. These tests were administered to subjects, most frequently students, in the form of a fastidiously timed exam requiring a lead pencil and adherence to a strict and precise set of verbal instructions. Tests devised to rank students and assess them vis-à-vis one another were a significant component of the modernization of education, which included the establishment of graded classrooms, standardized textbooks, mandatory physical education, and school hygiene. However, while the classificatory impulse, prompted by the taxonomic concerns of the nascent field of psychology and an ever-increasing number of schoolchildren, might have been shared by educators worldwide, tests did not arise autonomously and organically in each distinct country. Instead, intelligence testing became global through uneven, imperial trajectories that wove a web of "technology transfer" from Europe and the United States to other parts of the world.[10]

What we think of as the modern intelligence test (for example, the Weschler, Binet-Simon, Otis, and several sections of the hotly contested SAT) took its foundational form in France. In the first decades of the 1900s the director of the psychology laboratory at the Sorbonne, Alfred Binet, began to seek out methods for determining the aptitudes of the human mind—separate from the physiological and ergonomic workings of the entire body. In 1904 the French Ministry of Public Education asked him to come up with pedagogical tools for "identifying mildly retarded and learning-disabled children."[11] Significantly, Binet did not view his scores and scales as devices "for ranking normal children" but rather as indicators of a child's intellectual potential.[12] Although Binet quantified his results by noting both the chronological and the "mental" age of schoolchildren for purposes of subtraction and comparison, he consistently asserted that intelligence was too complex to be captured by a number alone. Once imported into the United States, however, Binet's initially flexible understanding was replaced by the notion of innate intelligence, a change spurred by the German psychologist William Stern's concept of intelligence quotient or IQ, articulated in 1912. As opposed to Binet, who subtracted mental age from chronological age to obtain a general gauge of the recommended classroom level for children, Stern argued that mental age should be *divided* by chronological age to produce a *quotient*, a number that could serve as a permanent marker of an individual's innate intelligence.[13]

Introduced at the same time that the eugenics movement was becoming consolidated, intelligence tests rapidly became central to arguments about racial, ethnic, class, and gender differences. In France and Latin America the natural sciences tended to be influenced by Lamarckism, which posited that heredity could be gradually transformed through environmental modifications. This meant that test results and scores were more likely to be interpreted as malleable to change and improvement. Although Lamarckism was popular in the United States at the beginning of the twentieth century, Mendelianism, which upheld that hereditary material was transmitted intact and inalterably down the family line, predominated by the mid-1910s.[14] One of the hallmarks of the U.S. eugenics movement was a generalized belief in the existence of simplistic Mendelian ratios and genes, often described as solitary "unit characters."[15] A one-on-one correlation was presumed to exist between such unit characters and emotional, mental, and physiognomic traits. Once merged with evolutionary theories of human difference and types, the eugenic reasoning of Mendelianism then projected these attributes onto "races," which were depicted as singular, hierarchically arranged groups.

Henry H. Goddard, research director at the Vineland Training School for Feeble-Minded Girls and Boys in New Jersey, became intrigued by Binet's research and by 1910 had brought the Frenchman's tests across the Atlantic, translated them into English, and started to administer them at his institution.[16] As he reformulated the tests for utilization in the United States, he applied Mendelian logic, asserting that intelligence was a singular "unit character" that could be measured and ranked. As Stephen Jay Gould demonstrates in *The Mismeasure of Man*, Goddard and the psychologists who followed in his footsteps committed one of the grossest fallacies of modern science: they reified and fabricated intelligence, "assumed it was largely inherited, and developed a series of specious arguments confusing cultural differences and innate properties."[17] Goddard promoted intelligence tests to ascertain fine gradations of mental deficiency—coining the category "moron" to define "borderline" persons. Like many eugenicists, he evinced great anxiety about the rising presence of the "feebleminded," who, he and an expanding nativist chorus averred, were contaminating the nation both from within and without.[18]

In order to recraft the intelligence tests for the United States and, above all, to be able to discern the extent to which an influx of diseased and "feebleminded" immigrants threatened the nation's sanguinity, in 1913 and 1914 Goddard carried his test kits to Ellis Island. He was especially interested in determining the "degeneracy" of the so-called new—Italian, Greek, and Turkish—immigrants that had been disembarking on U.S. shores in growing numbers since the 1890s. These arrivals were given written tests if they spoke English, and if they did not, they were given a host of nonverbal exams, including cube tests, counting and mathematical problems, copying exercises, and puzzles. Results of these and similar tests, which "proved" the lower intelligence of "new" immigrants, were integral to the passage of the exceedingly restrictive National Origins Act of 1924, which set a 2 percent quota on Southern and Eastern European immigrants (based on the 1890 census) and banned virtually all immigration from Asia.[19]

If Goddard initiated the task of recalibrating Binet's test for use in the United States, the prominent Stanford psychologist Lewis Terman completed it. In the late nineteenth century, while writing a dissertation under the guidance of psychologist G. Stanley Hall at Clark University, Terman became convinced that intelligence could be quantified: "the nature of intelligence could best be explained through the use of mental tests by which an individual's performance could be quantified and compared to the 'normal' performance of the population at large."[20] Furthermore, early in his career Terman embraced the idea that mental levels varied from race to race and were all but fixed at birth. In 1905 a tuberculosis infection prompted him to move west, where he eventually found a home in the Psychology Department at Stanford University. There he embarked on a systematic revision of the Binet-Simon test; in order to craft a test suitable for U.S. children that could, with some precision, distinguish the mental abilities of different "races," Terman and his protégés began to administer hundreds of exams in California schools.

In 1915, when he spoke at the American Association for the Advancement of Science meeting at the Panama Pacific International Exposition in San Francisco, Terman had completed his revision of the Binet test, which he called the Stanford-Binet. Terman's multipronged testing program involved increasing the number of tests given to children at each age, thoroughly incorporating the concept of IQ, and, most important, standardizing results by establishing a numerical index to classify pupils as idiots, imbeciles, morons, borderline deficients, feebleminded, dull normal, normal, superior, very superior, or geniuses.[21] Before his audience at the fair, Terman shared one of the principal arguments of his forthcoming book: that a definite correlation existed between intelligence and "race."[22] In the first chapter of the tract to which he referred, *The Measurement of Intelligence*, published the following year, Terman expounded on the many virtues of IQ tests, which could single out delinquent, retarded, diseased, and otherwise unfit individuals. In this influential book Terman enmeshed the doctrine of white supremacy into the circular reasoning of modern statistics to explicate direct links between scores, normalcy, and the capacities of racial groups. His conclusions were sanctified and hardened by the impartial neutrality of numbers, above all, the perfect figure of 100 which represented the score of the average, almost always white, child.[23] Terman's "Normal Curve"—employed to calculate the results of test takers—placed the IQs of Mexicans, Indians, and "Negroes" in the borderline ranges of 70 to 90. According to his didactic scale Mexicans—the largest immigrant group in California—hovered between high-grade deficiency and somewhat more able groups "usually classed as normal but dull."[24]

These norms were bolstered by another psychologist-eugenicist, Robert Yerkes, who spawned the first wave of mass testing in 1917 when he and a cadre of psychologists devised the Army Alpha (verbal) and Beta (nonverbal) exams to determine the IQs of 1.75 million World War I recruits.[25] Yerkes's findings revealed not only the mental impotence of most European immigrants and "Negroes" but also that "the average mental age of white American adults stood just above the edge of moronity."[26] Such startling findings catapulted many psychometricians into a frenzy of test drafting and preparation in order to measure and ultimately improve the fitness and virility of the nation. In 1919, riding the success of the army tests, Terman and Yerkes were awarded funds from the General Education Board of the Rockefeller Foundation to formulate what would become the National Intelligence Test (NIT).[27] Published in 1920, this test measured children and adolescents for what by then had become known as "g" or general factor of intelligence; these tests spread like wildfire throughout the nation's school system. Over half a million copies of the NIT were sold in the first year and by the mid-1920s a whole array of spin-off tests such as the Dearborn Intelligence Test and the Myers Pantomime were selling in the millions.[28] It was during this psychometric flurry that Carl C. Brigham, author of the 1923 *Study of American Intelligence* and a vocal proponent of Nordic and Aryan superiority, designed the SAT, which is still the most popular test for college entrance. By the late 1920s, intelligence testing, in its many guises, had become the bedrock of the modern U.S. educational system, used to evaluate the grade level, retardation, and giftedness of tens of thousands of students.[29]

TESTS IN TRANSLATION: THE PARADOXES AND
POLITICS OF INTELLIGENCE TESTING IN MEXICO

As in the United States, the explosion of mental testing in Mexico was preceded by the growing interest in school hygiene, physical education, and modern pedagogy that emerged in the late nineteenth century. By the early 1900s educators and scientists had launched anthropometric surveys, relying on an armamentarium of instruments to measure indicators such as height, weight, reflex time, and lung capacity. One maverick went so far as to invent his own device, the "cirtometrograph," to size the thoraxes of schoolchildren.[30] As these hygienists gathered variables in the hopes of establishing statistical baselines and improving national health, they became increasingly eager to assess what still eluded them: the human mind. By the 1910s many Mexican psychologists had begun to search out scales for separating normality from abnormality.

It was not until after the armed phase of the revolution had ended and Binet's tests had inspired dozens more in Europe and the United States that Mexican educators began to traffic in intelligence tests.[31] In the early 1920s Rafael Santamarina, a physician and psychologist, chaired a commission entrusted with deciding which tests could be most easily incorporated into Mexico's educational system. The commission did not turn to the United States but, rather, in accordance with Mexico's long-held scientific and medical alliances, to France. In fact, Santamarina explicitly rejected the models utilized in the United States, which he judged as suitable only for "anglo-saxon children and difficult to apply among us." After having reviewed all the European alternatives, he and his team concluded: "we can concretely say that in order to understand the mental development of Mexican children we will use the Binet-Simon and Descoeudres scales and hope to be able to formulate a special test for the children of our country."[32]

The initial rejection of U.S. tests was rooted in the anti-Yankee sentiment of many Mexican intellectuals, who were fiercely nationalistic and scorned the crass capitalism of their northern neighbor, as well as its system of racial apartheid. As intelligence tests moved along an inter-American circuit of knowledge production freighted by U.S. economic and cultural hegemony, their adaptation and translation in Mexico sparked controversy. For example, in 1927, at the First Panamerican Congress of Eugenics and Homiculture, held in Havana, Santamarina adamantly expressed his disapproval of U.S. tests and scales.[33] Santamarina had recently been appointed director of the pioneering Department of Psychopedagogy and Hygiene (Departamento de Psicopedagogía e Higiene, DPH) at the Mexican Ministry of Public Education (Secretaría de Educación Pública, SEP). Founded in 1925, as part of the multifaceted project of political and civic reconstruction that followed the revolution, the DPH symbolized the postrevolutionary government's commitment to creating new citizen-subjects through applied science and education.[34] As soon as it was established, the DPH began testing thousands of Mexican children. In 1926, for example, the department sought to determine levels of mental retardation by administering exams to more than fifteen thousand pupils.[35] Its efforts led to an exponential growth of testing over the next two decades; by the early 1930s, between ninety thousand and two hundred thousand students were being tested per year, and by the late 1930s, testing was becoming routinized in public education.[36]

Like the majority of the twenty-eight delegates in attendance, Santamarina supported eugenics but not as defined by Charles B. Davenport, head of the influential Eugenic Records Office (ERO) located in Cold Spring Harbor, New York, and the key U.S. organizer of the conference. After Davenport delivered two lectures in which he warned against the dangers of miscegenation, discussed the biological undesirability of mestizos and mulattos, and advocated stricter immigration exclusion, Santamarina voiced his disagreement.[37] He denounced Davenport's address as "a hysterical exposition of the development of immigration laws in the United States" and rebuked Davenport's pronouncements about superior and inferior "races," contending that one of the methods most commonly used in the United States to measure the fitness of individuals and groups—mental testing—was biased and inadequate.[38] Santamarina was particularly incensed that Mexican schoolchildren in the Southwest and California were being given only English-language tests and scored according to U.S. standards. Clearly aware of recent surveys, many conducted by Terman's protégés, that placed the IQ of Mexican children between 65 and 85, at least fifteen points below the average 100 of their Anglo counterparts, Santamarina inveighed against those "preeminent psychologists who have had no scruples in classifying Mexican children as mentally inferior, something that is completely false."[39] Subsequently, in a brief evening address Santamarina, reflecting the strong current of indigenism and the celebration of the "cosmic race" that was integral to postrevolutionary nation-building, glorified the hybrid figure of the mestizo, a product of the "indomitable courage of the ancestral peoples [of Mexico] and the quixoticism and gallantry of the Spanish race."[40] He described his department's successful educational activities at indigenous training schools, which had demonstrated the "striking adaptability" of "pure" Indians to civilization, a fact that undermined the "humiliating idea that the indigenous race was an inferior race" incapable of change.[41] Wary of the underpinnings and goals of U.S. mental tests, Santamarina claimed that Mexican students could only be judged fairly by Mexican norms—that physical, mental, and moral means varied from nation to nation and could not be ascertained from afar.

While Santamarina was in charge of the DPH, the tracking of students into homogeneous groups—a key policy of the SEP—was carried out *without* the calculation of a child's IQ.[42] From the inception of his directorship Santamarina had rejected the concept of IQ, as elaborated by Stern and Terman, stating that it was useless given the variability of children's intelligence; instead, he consistently embraced Binet's notion of retardation (chronological age minus mental age), which he believed was more than sufficient to separate the imbeciles from idiots and the feebleminded from the normal.[43] Until the early 1930s this more flexible logic prevailed. One of the most popular tests, for example, the Descoeudres, did not demand a true or false answer, permitting students to engage with the question in an open-ended fashion. Unlike the U.S. tests, which often asked about multiple consumer products and brand names, the questions on the Descoeudres were self-referential and required simple handwritten answers to a range of straightforward questions. Including queries such as "who cleans the streets?" and "who cures the sick?," the Descoeudres offered latitude in terms of response; for example, doctor, nurse, or pharmacist would all garner points for the latter. The Fay, a nonverbal test, was similar. It asked young schoolchildren to draw a cumulative sequence of figures that began with a woman, then depicted her walking down the street, next added landscape and rain, and ultimately included protection from the rain. If, for instance, the student drew a lady with an umbrella at her side instead of raised over her head (the ideal response) while under the rain, he or she would receive at least a quarter or half point, not zero.[44]

Driven by the spirit of functionalism and organicism, the Descoeudres and Fay reinforced the notion that societies were entities in which each person and object had a specific role and position.[45] This reasoning meshed well with Mexico's long-standing affair with Comtean positivism as well as a neo-Lamarckian bent toward progress that embraced environmental reforms and envisioned the possibility of social cohesion through the gradual assimilation of "backward" social groups, especially Indians, into a modern mestizo nation. Ironically, despite Santamarina's general preference for European tests and his confrontation with Davenport, one of his greatest contributions to Mexican psychometrics was the translation and adaptation of the Stanford-Binet intelligence test, as reconfigured by Terman in the mid-1910s. He and his colleagues at the DPH administered the Santamarina-Stanford-Binet to students who had been categorized as potentially retarded or "abnormal" by an initial battery of tests. Santamarina's simultaneous rejection of the concept of IQ and embrace of Terman's signature test, which relied on this same concept, illustrate the insidious patterns of technology transfer that unfolded between the United States and Mexico. In the early-twentieth-century international world of psychometrics, many of the mental tests elaborated by U.S. psychologists held a claim on objectivity that even Santamarina could not ignore. When these "boundary objects" and their inventors traveled across national borders and from one racial regime to the next, tensions surfaced. Indeed, over the next decade, as the DPH expanded its mission and sought greater professional legitimacy, such contradictions became more visible.

In the early 1930s, after Santamarina ceded the directorship of the DPH, open-ended tests such as the Descoeudres began to fall out of favor, and the authoritative pull of U.S. tests grew stronger. For example, by 1933, in large part because a new cadre of DPH educators wanted to become more "scientific" and "objective," the more malleable French and Belgian tests were replaced by verbal and nonverbal U.S. tests.[46] In 1935, for example, the DPH prepared a new battery of elementary-school tests consisting solely of the Detroit-Engel, Pinter-Cunningham, and Otis. It was designed for regular use by schoolteachers, who were being primed to assume testing procedures from the DPH's psychometricians, and underscored that the placement of children should be based on the statistical correlation between chronological and mental age.[47] Although the concept of IQ was never explicitly endorsed by the DPH in the 1930s, Binet's idea of retardation disappeared from the department's tests and publications. Instead of seeking to divide the abnormal from the normal by determining mental age, DPH educators assembled "students according to similar mental level" regardless of age.[48] As José Gómez Robleda, the head of the DPH's Psychological and Anthropological Research Service, explained, "Earlier groups were formed based solely on chronological age; experience has clearly demonstrated the error of this method, for which reason chronological age now only serves as a point of comparison."[49] Moreover, this transformation was also accompanied by the thorough incorporation of a uniquely U.S. product: the multiple-choice question. According to its inventor, Kansas educator Frederick J. Kelly, the multiple-choice question was "subject to only one interpretation," called "for but one thing," and was "wholly right or wholly wrong, and not partly right and partly wrong."[50] In addition to forbidding any deviation, multiple-choice exams drew from a variegated symbolic field, requiring students to make connections between random external signifiers. Thus, instead of responding to more fungible questions about the functioning of modern society, as in the Descoeudres, children now had to answer with exactitude 85 multiple-choice questions, many of which were translated literally from English to Spanish and oft times quite confusing. For example, students were asked whether "islands" were "lands, boats, soldiers, time, waters" but also whether "to mix" was "to make a mistake, to return, to sanction, to yell, or to hurry." In the sentence comprehension section children faced about 75 true/false questions such as "Are rocks hard?" and "Is the idea of a burial attractive?"[51]

As this quiet transformation was occurring, Lázaro Cárdenas became president and initiated sweeping cultural and social reforms aimed at completing the process of postrevolutionary reconstruction. In 1938 he expropriated the country's petroleum holdings out of the hands of foreign, primarily U.S., hands. Nowhere was Cárdenas's radicalization more evident than in the realm of education.[52] Soon after taking office in 1934, he mandated a program of socialist education, which was to be based first and foremost on scientific knowledge. While never totally abandoning the work of their predecessors, DPH psychologists and educators now declared that in its earlier incarnation the department had been "from every point of view deficient" and would have been "unable to respond to the new exigencies" of socialist education.[53] To remedy this situation, the National Institute of Psychopedagogy (NIP) was founded in 1936; by the late 1930s it had completely absorbed the DPH. It included a host of original services, including psychophysiology, professional placement, and pedagogical analysis. This same year its staff established the Mexican Society of Psychopedagogy, which was devoted to an analogous agenda within the nongovernmental domains of pediatrics, psychology, and medicine.[54]

By the late 1930s, at the zenith of the socialist education plan, all of the French tests introduced during Santamarina's tenure had been supplanted by exams designed by U.S. psychometricians and based on experiments in cities such as Detroit and Minneapolis; this intellectual reorientation was accompanied by a heightened emphasis on the role heredity played in producing delinquent and problem children.[55] While Mexican psychometricians had always perceived of intelligence as biologically determined — either by direct familial transmission or neo-Lamarckian environmental alterations — explanations of the mental and physical capacities of children became increasingly informed by strict biological determinism in the late 1930s. Reports issued by the NIP frequently advocated in-depth "studies of heredity," which would "have an indisputable social transcendence," and reminded readers that "it should not be forgotten that many traits of our most recent traits are susceptible of being inherited."[56] Many schoolchildren performed poorly on the overhauled, U.S.-inspired, battery of tests — above all those including multiple-choice questions. In 1934, for example, one educator, after having tested forty-seven girls between the ages of seven and eight, found an "inferiority complex" to be the most pronounced trait of the group as a whole.[57] This was a conclusion reached by many DPH testers. In a 1936 study of two hundred "proletarian school children" that involved anthropometric, physiological, mental, and affective tests, José Gómez Robleda and his team found this "class" of youngsters to be abnormal and deficient in almost every way. On one hand, psychologists claimed that their weak performance was the result of poverty and that it was the state's moral duty to improve the lot of the working class. On the other, the team identified many of the gravest "somatic abnormalities" of proletarian children as constitutional, in other words, as hereditary and inalterable.[58]

Thus, in a twisted configuration a nationalistic program of socialist education, which in principle sought distance from capitalist, especially Yankee, influence, embraced U.S. intelligence tests and their hard-line biological determinism because they carried the imprimatur of science and objectivity. Once on the desks of Mexican school children, the tests that originated in the United States, even if modified by DPH psychologists, produced unpleasant results, such as inferiority complexes and constitutional abnormalities.

Popular literature on Mexican nationalism, culture, and education during this period suggests that the subtle impact of this ideological imperialism might be greater than we have yet acknowledged, and in addition, may have shaped leading intellectuals' ideas about the capacity of the self and the bounds of the intimate. Indeed, it can be argued that the deep psychology of inferiority that a midcentury generation of men of letters, such as Samuel Ramos and Octavio Paz, began to diagnose as a debilitating pathology of the national psyche was manufactured in part by the ripple effects of European and U.S. testing regimes.[59] Paz traced the genesis of this inferiority complex back to the humiliating and emasculating impact of a conquest in which an Indian woman (Malinche) was "screwed" (*chingada*—literally and figuratively raped and betrayed) by a Spaniard man (Cortes) and the sanctity and purity of the Mexican forever bastardized.[60] Paz also, however, stressed the potential that education held for decolonizing Mexican manhood and enabling Mexicans to break away from the intellectual domination of Europe and the United States. Ramos was more explicit. Influenced by the theories of Alfred Adler, he called on the postrevolutionary generation of educators to gather authentic, not foreign-derived, "knowledge of Mexico" and to "Mexicanize knowledge" in order to transcend the perpetual maladjustment and sense of inferiority that scarred his countrymen.[61]

"BOUNDARY OBJECTS" AND THE POLITICS OF COMPARISON

This volume challenges us to embark on novel research itineraries that transcend, traverse, and link state-bounded archives while not forsaking state actors or ignoring the centripetal force of the nation-state as the favored object of narration and periodization.[62] Tracking the history of intelligence testing between the United States and Mexico takes us on a journey through a transnational circuit of knowledge production that demonstrates one way in which U.S. history and American studies might engage with some of the conceptual touchstones of (post)colonial studies. As "boundary objects" passing from the hands of one psychometrician to another, intelligence tests can serve "as a window onto *specific* exchanges, interactions, and connections" that shaped inter-American relations.[63]

The popularization of psychometrics in the early twentieth century was a global process hinged on the solidification of a new metasystem of classification whose key components — multiple-choice questions, statistical rules, and pictorial models — were swiftly integrated into varied nationalistic and educational projects. Like Möbius strips, intelligence tests functioned recursively, spawning findings about "race," class, and difference that were embedded a priori in the tests' scales and spectrums. In the United States in the 1920s and 1930s, for example, mental tests reinforced racial segregation and exclusion by repeatedly "proving" the diminished cognitive capacity of Mexicans, African Americans, and some immigrant groups. In Mexico, however, where the same decades were characterized by an impulse toward national homogeneity that centered on the icon of the mestizo, tests were used to argue for the innate promise of indigenous peoples and the potential of working-class children. Nevertheless, adapting U.S. tests to Mexico, a project that was completed by the late 1930s, generated "torque" and friction as the underlying social assumptions of U.S. psychometrics clashed with the vision of modernity and society endorsed by Mexican postrevolutionary educators such as Santamarina and Robleda. This "torque" sheds light on the thorny terrain that Mexican psychometricians encountered when they procured "scientific objectivity" from their powerful northern neighbor, a country that little more than fifty years earlier had acquired close to half of Mexico's original territory through war and treaty.

NOTES

1. "Protests against Teaching in Mexico," *FairTest Examiner*, http://www.fairtest.org/examarts/fa1196/k-mextst.htm (accessed July 11, 2005).

2. See Méndez and Díaz-Barriga, *Evaluación académica*.

3. Bowker and Star, *Sorting Things Out*, 16.

4. See Foucault, *The History of Sexuality*; Rabinow, *Michel Foucault*; Steedman, *Strange Dislocations*, 222–41.

5. See Turner, "The Rationalization of the Body"; Corrigan, *Social Forms/Human Capacities*.

6. See Stoler, "Racial Histories and Their Regimes of Truth."

7. See Hutton, "Foucault, Freud, and the Technologies of Self."

8. See Rosen, *A History of Public Health*; and Kraut, *Silent Travelers*. For an excellent

study of the ways in which the discourses of medicine and engineering underwrote the profession of IQ testing see Brown, *The Definition of a Profession*. For more on IQ testing see Evans and Waites, *IQ and Mental Testing*; and Hothersall, *History of Psychology*. On mental retardation in the United States see Trent, *Inventing the Feeble Mind*.

9. See Gould, *The Mismeasure of Man*.

10. My knowledge of this process encompasses Western Europe, the United States, and several countries in Latin America. Fascinating questions remain about the emergence of intelligence testing in the colonial contexts of Africa, Eastern Europe, the Soviet Union, and East Asia (especially Japan vis-à-vis China and Korea). For an insightful overview of the relationship between standardization, eugenics, and statistics, and the "avalanche of numbers" that was instrumental to nineteenth-century governmentality, see Hacking, *The Taming of Chance*. Claudio Lomnitz's concept of contact frames and contact zones is particularly relevant for this kind of analysis; see Lomnitz, *Deep Mexico, Silent Mexico*.

11. Gould, *The Mismeasure of Man*, 185.

12. Ibid.

13. Ibid., 180.

14. See Cooke, "The Limits of Heredity."

15. See Kevles, *In the Name of Eugenics*; Wier, Lawrence, and Fales, *Genes and Human Knowledge*; Kitcher, *The Lives to Come*.

16. Goddard's life and career are superbly reconstructed in Zenderland, *Measuring Minds*.

17. Gould, *The Mismeasure of Man*, 187.

18. Wendy Kline argues that the category "moron" was gendered female and usually applied to "wayward" girls, many of whom got trapped in county facilities and were frequently sterilized. See Kline, *Building a Better Race*. For an interesting article on lesser-known parts of Goddard's career see Ryan, "Unnatural Selection." For an analysis of the invention of categories of social deviants at the start of the twentieth century see Geld, "Social Deviance and the 'Discovery' of the Moron," 247–58. Goddard was involved in the eugenics movement from its inception; he was a member of the Eugenics Committee of the American Breeders' Association in the 1910s and served on the advisory council of the American Eugenics Society from 1925 to 1935.

19. See Higham, *Strangers in the Land*.

20. Chapman, *Schools as Sorters*, 24. On Terman's early studies see ibid., chap. 1. For an insightful discussion of the role of G. Stanley Hall in early-twentieth-century notions of civilization, manliness, and evolution see Bederman, *Manliness and Civilization*.

21. Terman, *The Measurement of Intelligence*, 79. The classifications he formulated are as follows: "25 or below = idiot; 25–50 = imbecile; 50–70 = moron; 70–80 = borderline deficiency sometimes classifiable as dullness often as feeblemindedness, below 70 definite feeblemindedness; 80–90 = dullness rarely classifiable as feeblemindedness; 90–110 = normal or average intelligence; 110–120 = superior intelligence; 120–140 = very superior intelligence; above 140 = 'near' genius or genius."

22. See Chapman, *Schools as Sorters*.

23. See Gould, *The Mismeasure of Man*, 207.

24. Terman, *The Measurement of Intelligence*, 87.

25. Gould, *The Mismeasure of Man*, 207; and Carson, "Army Alpha, Army Brass, and the Search for Army Intelligence."

26. Gould, *The Mismeasure of Man*, 226.

27. See Chapman, *Schools as Sorters*, 77–82; Gould, *The Mismeasure of Man*, 204–10.

28. Chapman, *Schools as Sorters*, 77–82.

29. On the recent history of standardized testing, and the debt its development owes to the military, see Lemann, *The Big Test*. For a glimpse into the anxiety that test taking produces in high school students see Michael Chandler's documentary, inspired by Lemann, *Secrets of the SAT*.

30. See, e.g., González, *Higiene escolar*, 308–11.

31. Apparently, David Pablo Boder, a professor affiliated with Mexico City's Psychotechnic Division, made the first attempt to translate the Binet-Simon, as revised by Terman, for use in Mexico. Boder's version was largely ignored by Mexican educators. See Boder, *La B-S-T-M*.

32. Commission to the Director of the Service of School Hygiene, Aug. 26, 1922, Box 3, Folder 20, Servicio de Higiene Escolar, Salubridad Pública, Archivo Histórico de la Secretaría de Salubridad y Asistencia, Mexico City. Alice Descoeudres was a French educator who used the Binet-Simon as a template for elaborating primary and secondary school tests. At some point in the 1910s she incorporated the notion of a fixed intelligence or IQ into her tests. See Descoeudres, *L'Année psychologique* (1914–1919), 485; and Descoeudres, *L'Année psychologique* (1920–1921), 303. Santamarina published his first version of the Binet-Simon (1911) in 1922, although he was quite unsatisfied with it; see Santamarina, "Untitled."

33. For an analysis of this conference see Stepan, *"The Hour of Eugenics,"* chap. 6.

34. For the history of education in Mexico, especially in relation to the postrevolutionary period, see Vaughan, *The State, Education, and Social Class in Mexico, 1880–1928*; Vázquez de Knauth, *Nacionalismo y educación en México*; Loyo, "Popular Reactions to the Educational Reforms of Cardenismo"; Rockwell, "Schools of the Revolution."

35. A figure of 21,387 was reported in "Sección de Higiene." Exact figures are difficult to calculate because reports were submitted by several psychometricians, and the number of tests administered was much higher than the number of students since some students were given many or repeated exams.

36. In 1932, 180,673 students were tested (see Secretaria de Educación Pública, *Memoria de la SEP* [1932]: 304); the figure of 93,385 is given by the SEP for 1935, but this was after the Departamento de Psicopedagogía e Higiene had trained many schoolteachers to administer tests themselves. See Secretaria de Educación Pública, *Memoria de la SEP* 1 (1935): 249–53.

37. Davenport, "'Race Crossing.'" Santamarina's participation in the conference is de-

tailed in III-36–10, Archivo Histórico de la Secretaría de Relaciones Exteriores, Mexico City.

38. "Primera sesión de la Primera Conferencia Panamericana de Eugenesia y Homicultura."

39. Ibid.

40. Santamarina, Transcription of evening address.

41. Ibid.

42. For an excellent analysis of tracking see Vaughan, *The State, Education, and Social Class*, esp. chap. 5.

43. Santamarina, "Standardización de la definición de la debilidad mental y sus diferentes grados."

44. *Pruebas colectivas para medir el desarrollo Mental I.*

45. "Tests parciales de lenguaje 'Alicia Descoeudres,' adaptación del Dr. Rafael Santamarina."

46. See Robleda, "Pruebas mentales de clasificación escolar."

47. Secretaria de Educación Pública, *Pruebas mentales colectivas para realizar una clasificación escolar.*

48. Robleda, "Pruebas mentales de clasificación escolar," 15.

49. "Datos que intervienen en la clasificación."

50. Cited in Samelson, "Was Early Mental Testing, (a) Racist Inspired, (b) Objective Science, (c) A Technology for Democracy, (d) The Origin of Multiple-Choice Exams, (e) None of the Above, (Mark the RIGHT Answer)." According to Samelson, the multiple-choice question first appeared in 1914 and became standard in mental testing following World War I.

51. "Estudio de Adaptación de los Stanford Achievement Test."

52. See Vaughan, *Cultural Politics in Revolution*; for an excellent description of the projects of socialist education see Knight, "Popular Culture and the Revolutionary State in Mexico, 1910–1940."

53. "Informe de las labores desarroladas durante los dias que van transcurrindo del presente año, por el DPH."

54. See *Statutes of the Mexican Society of Psychopedagogy.*

55. During the 1938–39 academic year, for example, no French tests were administered at all; instead, educators utilized the Stanford Achievement, Pinter, Otis, and National Intelligence tests.

56. Secretaria de Educación Pública, *Memoria de la SEP* (1936–37): 237.

57. See Enriquez, "Report by Dr. Raul González Enriquez."

58. Robleda et al., *Características Biológicas de los Escolares Proletarios.*

59. See Ramos, *Profile of Man and Culture in Mexico*; and Paz, *The Labyrinth of Solitude*. For insights into how Mexican intellectuals framed and constructed "Mexico" as an analytical and readable object (whether as Nation, Psychology, or People) see Lomnitz, *Deep Mexico, Silent Mexico.*

60. Chicana feminists were the first to interrogate the misogyny that characterizes much of Paz's writings. See Alarcón, "Traddutora, Traditora."

61. Ramos, *Profile of Man and Culture in Mexico*, 129. These are jeremiads delivered to a male audience with a presumed male subject.

62. See Stoler, "Tense and Tender Ties," 847. On the mutual and deeply entrenched symbiosis of the nation-state and linear history, see Duara, *Rescuing History of the Nation*.

63. Stoler, "Tense and Tender Ties," 847.

14

LAURA BRIGGS

Making "American" Families: Transnational Adoption and U.S. Latin America Policy

During the NBC coverage of the Summer 2000 Olympics, a major market for TV advertisers to tell sentimental stories of liberal internationalism, two separate corporate sponsors showed ads telling stories of Asian children being adopted by U.S. families. Retailer J. C. Penney interpellated the "Asian baby" story into a familiar narrative, in which a composed woman tells her frantic husband, "It's time." The ad gestures toward a genre of late-night labor-and-delivery stories; the husband rushes around ineffectually, while competent women personifying "J. C. Penney" put up cribs and assemble other baby paraphernalia. The punch line, a final shot of a Chinese girl toddler, is meant to surprise, and it effectively completes the tale of how young heterosexual couples make a "new" American family.[1] The second ad, by the insurance company giant John Hancock, tells another liberal story of the "new" American family, but this one was controversial because the parents it portrayed were lesbians. It was first aired during the pre-Olympic gymnastic trials and then became the site of a struggle between the Christian right and gay and gay-friendly activists. While right-wing groups urged boycotts, the email that circulated on left and liberal listservs urged recipients to contact Hancock over its "courageous" ad and described the ad this way: it "shows 2 women at the airport where they are just bringing home their newly adopted Asian baby. They are so loving and it is so sweet you can't help but cry. They congratulate each other on what great moms they'll be, etc." Hancock compromised; the company showed its ad once during the Olympics. This paradoxical conjuncture—of a lesbian, cross-racial-baby story that the conservative right hates, sponsored by a Fortune 500 global corporation—begs for analysis, mapping as it does startlingly contrasting narratives of what constitutes a "real" American family.

In an incisive article, "Why Daughters Die," Nancy Armstrong argues that from the earliest moments of U.S. nation-making, there have been two textual traditions for understanding family: one, a sentimental tradition of racial purity, in which daughters in particular bear the burden of carrying forward a "pure" culture in the form of a "pure" (racial) body embedded in a heterosexual nuclear family. This daughter is always endangered, and the strength of Armstrong's account is that it notices the way the imperial problem of "going native" (cultural impurity), the national problem of "miscegenation" (racial impurity), and the gender problem of female-headed households are collapsed, symbolically and materially, into the problem of the reproduction of the pure (English) family. She argues that beginning with seventeenth-century captivity narratives—stories about white women being kidnapped by Native Americans—we in the region that became the United States have been working out this problem of "pure" races, families, and nations through the textual problem of the "pure" daughter, counterpoised against a potentially more liberatory possibility of nonnuclear, racially heterogeneous families.[2]

There is much to be said for Armstrong's account. It pulls together the reviled families of the Moynihan Report (in which Black men's underemployment was blamed on their emasculating mothers, the "Black matriarchs"), the fictional single motherhood of TV character Murphy Brown, and all those whom demographers continue to point out are the majority—nonnuclear, not white, immigrant, or other, not necessarily "pure," American families. Furthermore, it confirms our common sense about transracial and transnational family making, that because it does not look like a white, suburban, heterosexually produced nuclear family ideal, it is an intrinsically radical cultural practice. But what of the "Chinese" girl toddler in the J. C. Penney ad? What cultural weight is she made to carry? What does it mean to say that this is a new "American" family? I want to suggest that the narrative tradition Armstrong identifies is undergoing revision in ways related to how the historical "other" of racial minorities inside the United States, and "foreign" elites elsewhere, is also being rewritten. International adoption, cathected through a sentimental liberal internationalism and an increasingly emphatic demand that citizens be parents, has made some transnational and transracially composed families "pure," or at least pure enough. Free trade and globalization have produced a growing internationalization of the middle and elite classes in the United States (as elsewhere), a changing complexion of wealth that has made it possible to imagine raising dark-skinned children in white families. At the same time, in ways I later discuss, another narrative of domesticity is emerging that centers on hybridity, difference, and the violence of the processes through which children come to be adopted. These two positions — on the one hand imagining that internationally adopted children can become the inheritors of their adoptive parents' national culture and, on the other hand, understanding them as exilic, diasporic refugees whose inheritance is necessarily plural and ambivalent — have, I will argue, replaced this older set of dualisms: pure/impure, white/racially mixed, and heteronormative/not heteronormative. To show what I mean, let me turn to intercountry adoption narratives, specifically with reference to Latin America. Transnational adoption is a surprisingly literary affair, as adoptive parents, in particular (but also their children), struggle to make this unusual event make sense by narrativizing it. One strain of such narratives, I would suggest, manages the potential contradictions of these stories in the same way that Armstrong's captivity narratives organized the meanings of racial and national domination: through the sentimental, by invoking endangered children and desperate (adoptive) parents. For example, one of the best-known and most influential accounts of international adoption in recent years is a book called *Family Bonds*, by Harvard law professor Elizabeth Bartholet. Bartholet tells the story of how she left for Lima, Peru, in the fall of 1985 to adopt the first of two Peruvian infants she would raise and how she simultaneously launched a career as a policy analyst on matters of adoption, family, and race whose positions on adoption put her regularly in the company of the neoconservative American Enterprise Institute. Her subsequent authority as a participant in policy making that would make it easier for white families to raise black and brown children (and provide them massive tax breaks, upward of nine thousand dollars) — and for these children's birth parents to lose them, some would say, even if their only crime was being poor or nonwhite — was not yet evident in her story of this and a subsequent trip to Peru. She wrote that she worried about whether her clothes were appropriate; she struggled to prove herself competent as a potential parent to lawyers and officials and was terribly frightened that she would lose "her" children to a legal system she did not understand, communicating in a language she does not speak. She wrote, "I am now engaged in what will be an eight-week process of legalizing our bond, our connection. This process of making him 'my child' as a matter of law will be an agonizing one, in large part because of the threat that this person who already feels like part of me will be taken from me."[3] She tells a vulnerable and moving narrative and returns to argue (uphill, she would say) for the legitimacy of her family-by-adoption in the face of overwhelming bias for biological bonds.

Yet there is something off about this narrative, something too quick about the scare quotes that designate the legal work of making him "my child" essentially superfluous to the emotional bond that has already, after ten days, made him "part of me." The child, whom she calls Michael, has birth parents, though she never refers to them; the legal process, as Bartholet well knows, is at least theoretically intended to ensure that their rights are respected and to provide a forum for any grievance or objection they might raise. And despite Bartholet's sense of vulnerability, her status as a Harvard law professor, and a United States citizen in Latin America at the height of U.S. cold war preoccupation with the region, defines power relations between her and the birth parents that are uneven in a much different direction from the one she maps. In the opening pages of the book she writes of her vulnerability with reference to a night in which she fearfully carried "her" two-week-old child down thirteen flights of stairs in the dark, with far too much cash in her pocket to feel safe from thieves, with the electricity out as a result of a bombing near her apartment by the Maoist guerrilla group *sendero luminoso* (the shining path).[4] Without minimizing the real fear that sendero luminoso has inspired in Peru, it is possible to notice that invoking Latin American Marxists imperiling U.S. mothers and children is hardly an original trope — it reads, rather, as an effort to incorporate brown children born in Peru into a familiar account about endangered Americans. And, indeed, this sets up the narrative structure of the book (as it opens onto policy pronouncements): Peruvian children are innocent, vulnerable, sick, crying; Peruvian adults are threatening, corrupt, takers-of-bribes, thieves, or terrorists. In the one passage where Bartholet does acknowledge the existence of birth mothers, some are portrayed as "having no good choices," whereas others take pleasure in their decision to send their child to the "land of opportunity." Yet even this marginally sympathetic characterization of birth mothers is cut short — managing one clause of one sentence in a 276-page book — and immediately contrasted with young children in Peruvian foster care, crying alone after being knocked down on a playground, with "birth parents who may never visit and have no apparent ability to function as parents," and the grief of a would-be adoptive parent whose child was taken away a few days later, ostensibly because the birth parent wanted her back but probably, Bartholet thinks (with no evidence), because some Peruvian official was not given a bribe.[5] Feminist scholar Rickie Solinger points out that "Americans who have portrayed ICA [intercountry adoption] as primarily a child rescue mission have tended to define the situation in ways that insist that the biological mother doesn't really count."[6] She then cites Bartholet as a key example. One might add that adoptive parents are portrayed as vulnerable, endangered, and fearful, while birth parents are portrayed as cold, indifferent, or (at best) happily sending their children off to a land where they will have more material benefits.

None of this is particularly new. As Ann Stoler has continued to remind us, raising the "orphans" of colonized people is a very familiar practice. From nineteenth-century French orphanages in Indochina to early-twentieth-century U.S. children's homes in Puerto Rico, managing orphans and raising youth to belong to a culture different from that of their ancestors has a history. Indeed, the white settler colonies of the British Empire — the United States, Canada, Australia — made acculturating native children in boarding schools as indispensable a part of their policies toward indigenous people as war and reservations, beginning in the eighteenth century and continuing through the 1970s. By providing them with industrial education, teaching them how to farm or to clean other people's homes as domestic laborers, such policies sought to bring civilization to indigenous people. In all three nations, too, the decline of boarding schools was accompanied by a growing practice of adoption of native children by white families. These practices created the conditions of possibility for transnational adoption and begin to make Bartholet's and Hancock's representational practices less mystifying. Governments and missionaries in these settler-states long believed that it was possible to bring colonized people into the fold, make them part of colonial society — although always with a difference.[7]

Bartholet's invocation of *sendero luminoso* suggests something of how invoking threats and danger serves to obfuscate and indeed reverse the actual power relations at work in transnational adoption. An analysis of this rhetoric offers a strategy for framing the ways transnational adoption is invested with colonial legacies and can be allied with U.S. state power and other kinds of violence. International adoption from Latin America to the United States became more than an occasional practice beginning in the 1980s, at the same moment that the Reagan administration made of Latin America a proving ground that cold war anticommunist military interventionism was not over. In response to what its conservative critics called the "Vietnam syndrome" — the left and liberal call for the U.S. to abandon its imperial military role overseas — the Reagan administration instead pursued an aggressive policy of intervention in Nicaragua, El Salvador, and elsewhere in Latin America, even illegally continuing support for the contras' war against the elected government of Nicaragua in the face of an outright ban on such activities by Congress.[8] After the collapse of the Soviet Union, U.S. military interventionism intensified in Latin America and Asia, promoting U.S. strategic and economic interests under the name of antiterrorism and a war on drugs. This aggressive U.S. internationalism continued under the leadership of conservative Democrats like Clinton, who maintained the U.S. military role but also more explicitly began promoting economic interests through free trade agreements (embodied in treaties like NAFTA), neoliberalism, and the backing of what came to be called "globalization." State policies related to free trade turned U.S. citizen-consumers into participants in this kind of globalization, which in turn shored up consent for interventionism abroad. International adoption was a good fit with the broad thrust of these policies, producing and relying on a renewed sense of American responsibility for those outside its borders and an easing of the movement of money and (some) people.

Bartholet's two ideological moves engage, with the discounting of birth parents and identifying the children politically with the interests of the United States. These are at the heart of how they become part of an "American" family. In an intriguingly pro-"nurture" move in this genetic age writers, parents, and policy makers like Bartholet systematically erase all but the most innocuous traces of the child's origins. These children become American in a very old sense: their biographies begin the day they come to the United States. Whether this forcible dehistoricizing works is of course another question; the prevalence of the "search for lost origins" stories among adoptees suggests something of its failures.[9] Indeed, there is plenty of evidence that trying to imagine internationally adopted children as the inheritors of their adoptive parents' culture and privilege is deeply problematic in a society stratified by race and national origin.[10] The failures of these erasures may constitute them as intrinsically unstable. These difficulties do not make them any the less powerful, but may rather go a long way toward explaining how Bartholet became a crusader against family reunification efforts in foster care policy and a passionate advocate for adoption as a solution to poverty.[11]

In Latin America, in contrast, no negative characterizations of intercountry adoption would sound surprising or excessive. International adoption with the United States has often been characterized as an extension of U.S.

economic and military power and is frequently contextualized in a way that would be incomprehensible to most U.S. Americans—in relation to child kidnapping, prostitution, murder, and organ theft. In 2002, for example, Juan Díaz González, a commissioner of the Mexico City Legislative Assembly, proposed a reform of police procedures to address child disappearances, telling a reporter with the newspaper *Reforma*, "This is a very serious problem because beyond the [child] theft, we are also dealing with issues related to the child pornography network, the trafficking of organs and the sale of children into illegal adoptions."[12] He warned readers and officials that twenty thousand children disappear each year from Mexico City. Although his numbers may be hard to verify, Díaz González's statements entered a familiar and extensive public discourse throughout Latin America about child kidnapping, illegal adoption, sexual exploitation, and a traffic in children's organs. As anthropologist Nancy Scheper-Hughes has argued, a rumor of a grisly international traffic in the body parts of children who have been kidnapped, killed, and mutilated has been called an "urban legend" and vigorously refuted by the U.S. State Department, but official denunciations have only carried this tale further, and thus a story that began in the shantytowns of Latin America and Asia is now discussed seriously in official circles, including the Mexican legislature.[13] It stands in sharp contrast to much of the literature for potential intercountry adopters in the United States, which describes orphanages full of unwanted children and invites American families to imagine making space in their home and hearts for an unloved, racially and culturally different, child with little or no future in his or her home country—adapting the classic U.S. sentimental narrative of what "we" do abroad.[14]

This disjuncture, between Latin American ideologies of U.S. exploitation and a U.S. belief in our capacity to rescue "them," is both a set of competing stories about what happens to actual children and, implicitly, an allegory for all of U.S. foreign policy. Díaz González's account and Elizabeth Bartholet's are mirror opposites. Bartholet's Latin Americans are soul-murderers, leaving parentless children crying on playgrounds; Díaz González's U.S. Americans are child-murderers, mutilating their bodies for organs. Bartholet's Latin Americans are terrorists, thieves, and communists; Díaz González's U.S. Americans are heartless capitalists, child rapists, and kidnappers. Bartholet's Latin Americans are too poor to raise children properly; Díaz González's U.S. Americans are too rich to love anybody. Such caricatures are not entirely false. Bartholet's account tracks the disrupted state of families, economies, and states, resulting in some measure from U.S. cold war anticommunist foreign policy and post-1989, neoliberal economics. These have eliminated many social services and given rise to antiterrorism and antidrug policies that have supported right-wing military dictatorships and death squads. Díaz González's account tracks Latin American blame of the United States for the widespread violence and upheaval of the post–World War II period. Neither position—that the United States is innocent or that the United States is responsible for all bad things in Latin America—is particularly accurate, but both carry rhetorical force.

ALTERNATIVE NARRATIVES

There are, however, more than these two opposing positions, in which U.S. families work through the sentimental on the one hand to deny the fact that they are "taking" Latin American children, and on the other to ignore the demands of Latin American officials to return the children. U.S. individuals' and families' choices to adopt transnationally also arise from and produce dissent about U.S. foreign policy and hegemonic racial formations. The creation of racially "mixed" families was also a goal of the civil rights movement, fought most forcefully in *Loving v. Virginia*, a case argued in the Supreme Court to allow interracial marriage. The disruptive potential of international and interracial adoption to a nation foundationally wedded to beliefs about cultural and racial purity—rooted in the family—cannot be entirely papered over. Moreover, there are revealing moments when those who believed in sentimental child-saving narratives abandoned them.

David Kruchkow tells such a story in *When You Wish upon a Star*. His narrative is a study in contrasts to Bartholet's. His book-length manuscript was published on the Internet, not by Houghton-Mifflin; he is a used car salesman who did not finish college; the child adopted by him and his wife, Sara, has health problems; but, most significant, it turns out that the child was not legally available for adoption, though her birth family was never found. Kruchkow emerges with a sharp critique of international adoption protocols, charging that international adoption agencies are profiteers and that the State Department is not particularly interested in investigating potential illegalities. His narrative is ultimately both compassionate about the hard choices made by birth parents and angry that his adoptive child will not have any future opportunity to have contact with hers.

His account begins in a fairly typical way, positioning him and Sara as consumers choosing from an internationalized market in children and race, with a sense that children's origins were fairly interchangeable and that the culture and inheritance the child would bear would be theirs. He began, as many U.S. adopters do, with little knowledge about opposition to and controversy over U.S. adoption of "third world" children, an easy sense of doing good by alleviating overpopulation, and an acute and hypervigilant sense of the domestic politics of race:

> Neither of us wanted to deal with the social issues of being white parents of an adopted black child, so we looked in the direction of Eastern Europe and Latin America. . . . Sara felt she would be comfortable parenting a Latin American child as she has a dark enough complexion to pass as Hispanic. My degree in Anthropology focused on the peoples, cultures, and prehistory of the Western Hemisphere, so I had no objections and felt that I could help our child stay connected with its culture and heritage.[15]

Unfortunately, Kruchkow's confident sense that he learned everything he needed to know about Latin America in a few anthropology courses was profoundly disrupted by his subsequent experience in adopting from Mexico. After a referral from a local adoption facilitator, he and Sara Kruchkow poured tens of thousands of dollars into an attempt to adopt, and they ultimately went to Mexico, where they took custody of an undocumented child. With an ignorance of immigration law at once privileged and tragic, they essentially smuggled her across the border and wandered unwittingly into an international controversy. The Kruchkows subsequently became better acquainted with the politics of international adoption, when they, along with sixteen other Long Island, New York, families, became the focus of an INS investigation of an illegal adoption operation between Mexico and the United States—and, Kruchkow charges, though the allegations were not investigated, several other Latin American countries as well.[16]

WRITING AND ERASING THE TRACES OF VIOLENCE

Mexican journalists have struggled to document and tell the story of illegal adoption, and this, in fact, is how the Kruchkow's case began. In October of 1998 Mexican newspapers began to report on an illegal adoption network operating along the Mexico-U.S. border, for the most part through the contiguous cities of Agua Prieta, Sonora, and Douglas, Arizona.[17] The U.S. Immigration and Naturalization Service (INS) investigated the allegations circulating in Mexican newspapers, and in March 1999 a woman named Margarita Soto was arrested crossing the border into Douglas for transporting an unrelated child whom she claimed was hers. Soto worked for a lawyer named Mario Reyes, who practiced on the Agua Prieta side of the border but lived in Douglas. He was arrested shortly thereafter (and was probably lucky to be arrested and tried by U.S. authorities rather than Mexican ones, who accused him of smuggling five hundred unlawfully obtained children and angrily demanded his extradition).[18] The INS accused Reyes of mail fraud, wire fraud, and illegally transporting seventeen children and placing them with U.S. adoptive families. Two Long Island women, Arlene Lieberman and Arlene Reingold, were held on similar charges for their roles in acting as go-betweens with New York families and Reyes.[19]

The Agua Prieta–Douglas area made an ideal site for an illegal adoption network. It is essentially a single city divided by an international border, and people on either side are linked through ties of friendship, family, and commerce. There is an extensive, daily, circular traffic across the border, with people living on one side or the other but crossing to shop, socialize, and engage in political and business transactions, taking advantage of differences in law, opportunity, and costs that the border produces. In recent years Agua Prieta–Douglas has been transformed from a quiet desert town into a booming border city by the establishment of *maquiladoras* on the Agua Prieta side, and Agua Prieta has grown from eighteen thousand people to a population of more than ninety thousand, drawn from all over Mexico by the promise of factory work; as often as not these people end up jobless residents in the city's growing shantytowns. Average wages at the maquiladoras are about seventy-three cents an hour, according to those promoting business investment in the area.[20] In Agua Prieta, social workers told the *New York Times*, wealthy lawyers regularly offer cash for children, and while most parents refuse, a handful, with few other prospects for earning money, accept.[21] An international airport in nearby Tucson makes it easy to transport an illegally procured child to a waiting family anywhere who is willing to pay twenty or thirty thousand dollars. This was, essentially, what happened with the Long Island cases.[22]

Illegal adoption cases, in the rare instances in which they are pursued and prosecuted, present a formidable narrative problem for a rescue story. In the Long Island cases there were at least two responses: those that insisted ever more strongly that the children were "really" American and those that worked out more complex answers. The INS apparently assured the Long

Island families from the very beginning of the investigation that they would be able to keep "their" children,[23] and seemingly made no effort to locate the birth parents, even refusing to allow a group in Mexico dedicated to finding kidnapped children to obtain photos of the Long Island adoptees.[24] On the other hand, one Long Island family, the Libertos, returned their adoptive child, nine-year-old Flor Azucena, to the birth mother the child missed fiercely even before the illegalities of the adoption ring were revealed. Reyes had apparently persuaded the mother to relinquish her child for a few hundred pesos for food and grandiose promises, never kept, of building her and her family a decent house. The Libertos told the *New York Times* that they decided to return their child to her family because Mrs. Liberto understood, firsthand, how painful it could be to be "rescued" from one's working-class family: "Mrs. Liberto cried when she was asked why she agreed to let Flor Azucena go. The decision, she said, arose from memories of growing up poor and being sent every year to a summer camp in Pennsylvania. It was the most beautiful place she had ever seen, Mrs. Liberto said. But after a few days, she recalled, she was crying and pleading to go home. 'A family bond is something you cannot break,' she said."[25] For her, it was not self-evident that poverty was a reason to separate children from their birth families nor that the child was "really" hers or "really" American. At the same time, the Libertos' response was decidedly ambivalent; they got drawn into the INS case because they subsequently adopted Flor Azucena's little sister.

Yet most press coverage of these cases refused any kind of complexity, relying instead on Bartholet-style accounts that rendered the birth parents unfit and discountable and the adoptive parents as heroic rescuers. An article in the *Arizona Republic*—with similar intent but more flourishes than a great many similar news articles about the Reyes case—uses the Kruchkows to suggest the logic of keeping the children in the United States and, implicitly, points to the common rhetorical features that produce transnationally adopting families as undoubtedly U.S. American:

> Sara and David Kruchkow . . . fear the child they adopted from Mexico may be taken from them. . . . The couple already has been through an emotional wringer. . . . Twice, the adoption group told the couple there was a child available, only to dash their hopes a few months later. [Sara is] happy to tell how delighted the Kruchkows were a year and a half ago, when they met a bright 20-month-old girl with a sense of humor. They named her Shelly, and "she took to us immediately," Kruchkow said. A

few things about her new life in New York startled the little girl at first. "When she saw running water, she started screaming and jumping up and down and saying, '*Agua, agua*,' so evidently where she was there wasn't running water," Kruchkow said. . . . Now, she said, "My biggest fear is I'm not going to be able to keep the child I was meant to have."

The article goes on to explain that the couple spent thirty thousand dollars on the adoption and that Reyes operated from a desire to help children and from an opposition to abortion.[26] The ideological work of estranging "Shelly" (previously known as María Soledad) from her birth parents is accomplished in multiple ways in this article. First, she lived in Mexico, did not have running water, and has asthma. Although this is not an account of child neglect, for U.S. Americans schooled by organizations like UNICEF and the Christian Children's Fund in saving children from generic third world poverty, the narrative mobilizes pity as it begins to account for why "Shelly" belongs with her adoptive parents. Second, the Kruchkows are American, middle class, were childless before her adoption, and have ordinary service-sector jobs—they are constituted as solidly within a nationalist narrative of "American" domesticity, except for their childlessness, which the article produces as an urgent problem to remedy. The article says nothing about "Shelly's" birth parents, maquiladoras, or U.S. foreign policy; by its end the only important question the article has considered is whether a worried and vulnerable Sara, who has already "been through an emotional wringer," will "be able to keep the child [she] was meant to have."

Another, similar story of smuggled children made headlines in Mexico in 1997, when editorials and articles argued that dollars and practices of globalization emanating from the United States were illegally separating children from their birth parents. This one involved documentation of the transport of Mexican children to "orphanages" in Guatemala, with no record of how the children were obtained. Journalist Karina Avilés, working for the Mexico City paper, *La Jornada*, wrote a series of articles detailing the traffic in children in Guatemala, including a report that at least twenty Mexican children had been smuggled across the mountainous border between Mexico and Guatemala. She identified a network of eighty Guatemalan professionals and officials—lawyers, social workers, judges—who benefited from these operations. Avilés told stories of kidnappers, birth mothers who sold children for as little as $250, homes where women stayed through their pregnancies with the understanding that their newborns would be adopted, and even prostitutes who "rented their wombs," in her phrase, becoming repeatedly pregnant and being paid for their offspring. She quoted Carmela Curup, of the Procuría General de la Nación of Guatemala, describing the difficulty of proving the existence of an international traffic in children but acknowledging that everyone knows about it and that "everything [about the operation] is legal, all, in inverted commas, is 'legal.'" She added, "We see with concern the number of people who get here, into Guatemala who, for a few quetzales, manage to procure a child."[27] Avilés also wrote of the other side of the equation, a fantastic account of a hotel full of foreigners, each carrying an about-to-be-adopted, brown-skinned infant, an image worthy of Borges and repeated daily in Guatemala.[28] Jorge Camil, commenting on Avilés's investigation, found in the tragedy of the whole affair "the disembodied specter of the U.S. dollar," a traffic in human beings for sale. For Camil it was easy enough to understand U.S. adopters, raised on images of large-eyed children in magazines asking to be "saved" by Americans, and not too difficult to understand the corrupting influence of twenty thousand U.S. dollars per infant.[29]

Guatemala is currently the largest exporter of children per capita (the fifth largest by nation), with 90 percent of the infants being adopted internationally going to the United States.[30] Adoption is also one of the largest economic sectors in Guatemala, at fifty million dollars in 2001. Adoption from Guatemala takes place directly, with the heads of "orphanages" placing children with overseas families with no legal regulatory process intervening, except the U.S. embassy, which grants visas to these infant immigrants.[31] While U.S. adopters imagine themselves as benefactors — one Internet-based organization for U.S. would-be adopters from Guatemala, Precious.org, titles its ad on Google.com, "Save a Child — Adopt" — Guatemalans, like Mexicans, believe the fundamental issue to be violence and theft. In 1994 two U.S. visitors to Guatemala were beaten nearly to death by mobs following accusations that they were trafficking in children.[32]

An article in the July 15, 2002, issue of *Newsweek* recontextualized the Mexican story of the corrupt effect of American dollars in Guatemala by rendering transnationally adopted children American, surrounding them with nationalist symbols of an American family. The article begins with Kathleen and Richard Borz, who adopted a child, Fabiola — whom they renamed Holly — even after her birth mother told U.S. embassy officials that she had been paid to relinquish her child and had understood that she could expect to see Fabiola monthly. The director of the orphanage, Susana

Luarca, paid working-class families to relinquish, as both embassy officials and the Borzes understood; in addition, Luarca was at that time married to the chief justice of the Guatemalan Supreme Court. Not only did they keep Fabiola, but the Borzes mounted a campaign with their congressman to take her brother as well. Two years later, they did succeed in adopting "Holly's" brother, as well as seven-year-old "Rico," after a Guatemalan judge found that his mother neglected and abused Rico, charges she disputed. The judge found the maternal grandmother an unsuitable parent because she was a lesbian, and a maternal aunt was rejected because, it was said, her husband had hit the child. Whatever the accuracy of the abuse and neglect charges, and letting pass the familiar official homophobia, no one inquired after the biological father. When he resurfaced, Casa Alianza, an international children's rights group that has been outspoken on issues of illegal adoption, charged that the child's "abandonment" order was improper, but no judge would agree to rehear the case. Furthermore, the birth father told *Newsweek* that he was attacked on a bus by two machete-wielding men who told him to stop trying to reclaim his child.[33]

Yet the *Newsweek* article casts the adoptive parents as beleaguered innocents, duped citizen-consumers in a globalized marketplace perhaps, but also, importantly, parents who should raise this child in an American family:

With dad proudly watching and the coach shouting his name, "Rico! Rico!" a scrawny 12-year-old crouches at second base. . . . With his team up 8–0, Rico glances over to the first-base line. Dad smiles. What could be more perfect than a father and son at a Little League game in the Pittsburgh suburbs? Every few months, however, the bliss is shattered when yet another reporter calls wanting to know if it is true: was Rico stolen? Kathleen and Richard Borz, Rico's parents, almost always refuse to comment and hang up the phone. Like the growing number of Americans who go overseas to fulfill their dreams of parenthood, they believe that adoption—especially from an impoverished country—is inherently a good thing for the child.

The article tells of the couple's loss of a birth child to a brain seizure, Rico's good grades, and some difficult, postinstitutional behavior problems like hoarding food. It quotes Rep. Henry Hyde: "There is nothing to be gained by forcing innocent babies to spend the rest of their childhood in orphanages instead of with loving parents in the United States." In this narrative the Borzes are located within two nationalist rhetorics—domestic family values of baseball, concerned parenting, and good schoolwork on the one hand, and an officially sanctioned, liberal internationalist concern about "innocent babies" on the other. Birth parents once again are discounted. While the article urges prospective international adopters to "do their homework" as consumers, it never suggests that Rico ought to live with his birth father. Rather, it implies that poverty itself is a sufficient reason to estrange Rico from his country and parents of origin, as in the following passage: "[Rico's birth mother, Flor] earned less than $50 a month handing out food samples in grocery stores. Home was a one-room cardboard-and-corrugated-tin shack. Rico attended school sporadically. Flor had little choice but to leave him in charge of his baby half brother, Jeffrey." Poverty, here, rather than being a problem of international capital or a civil war in which the United States was anything but innocent, is reduced to a symptom of bad parenting, from which U.S. families can rescue children.[34]

TRUTH COMMISSIONS AND ACTIVISTS

The origins of unregulated Guatemalan adoption lie in this violence. During the thirty-year civil war, children were abducted by the military and forced to be soldiers or servants. Sometimes Mayan youngsters were given to the families of the ladino soldiers who were systematically exterminating their people and were subsequently raised by them, according to reports by both the Catholic Church's Project to Recover Historical Memory (REHMI) and by the U.N.-sponsored truth commission, the Commission for Historical Clarification.[35] According to one army officer, "The families of many army officers have grown with the adoption of victims of the violence since, at certain times, it was popular among army soldiers to take responsibility for little three or four year olds found wandering in the mountains."[36] The Commission for Historical Clarification report also documents, in twelve volumes, the role of the United States in the human rights abuses of those years: the war was sparked by the CIA's overthrow of the elected Arbenz government in 1954 and continued through the 1960s, 1970s, and 1980s through U.S. funding, direct CIA involvement, and training for the Guatemalan military in "counterinsurgency" tactics that included disappearances, torture, and murder of civilians — all part of an attempted genocide of Mayan populations.[37] Although the civil war officially ended with the peace accord of 1996, violence and disappearances have continued. Even documenting illegal adoption and other human rights abuses in Guatemala is a dangerous occupation. Bishop Juan Gerardi Covedera, who oversaw the production of the REHMI report, was bludgeoned to death two days after its release.[38] According to human rights groups and even the U.S. State Department a Universidad de San Carlos professor, Mayra Gutierrez, disappeared in April 2000, probably because of her research on illegal adoption.[39] The office of Casa Alianza has been repeatedly burglarized, and its director, Bruce Harris, has been charged with libel in Guatemalan court for his outspokenness about shady adoption practices.[40]

Any account of illegal adoption in Latin America must also mention Argentina, which has an early and tangled history with exploitative adoption that is still being unraveled. During the Argentine Dirty War the military kept alive pregnant women who had been "disappeared" and forced into camps. Some were pregnant when arrested or abducted by the military; others were raped. These leftist women prisoners were allowed to live until the birth of their children, then killed. Their infants were adopted by families and friends of the ruling junta. The most persistent critics of the military dictatorship in those years, Las madres de la plaza de Mayo, have in recent times shifted their activism and, calling themselves the Abuelas [grandmothers] de la plaza de Mayo, have sought to locate and return what they say are the more than five hundred illegally adopted children of the disappeared. Throughout the 1980s the child kidnapping charges were officially denied, although a film, La Historia oficial, and an anthropologists' account confirmed them.[41] The Abuelas de la plaza de Mayo and other relatives mounted a fifteen-year campaign to establish their relationship to the adopted children of prominent families through DNA testing and trying to prosecute adoptive parents through the Argentine courts.[42] It was not until June 1998, when former president Jorge Rafael Videla was arrested and charged with running a government-sponsored illegal adoption operation during the Dirty War, that these claims gained official status.[43] The U.S. government supported the Argentine military junta throughout the Dirty War through a variety of means, including training military and junta leaders at the U.S. School of the Americas, maintaining close diplomatic ties (except during the Carter administration), and encouraging their support of the Nicaraguan contras. Recently declassified documents suggest that shortly after the Argentine military coup in 1976, Henry Kissinger directly assured members of the military junta that there would be no interference from the United States in the Dirty War campaign of assassination and torture.[44]

SINCE THE ADVENT OF less repressive regimes in Argentina, it is still not clear that illegal adoption has entirely disappeared or that the United States' role in sponsoring less-than-consensual transfer of children from their birth families has ceased. José Steinsleger, a Mexican journalist who has written extensively about illegal adoption, quotes Atilio Alvarez, president of Argentina's National Council for Minors, in a 1997 article as saying, "In this country, kidnapping of children does not usually exist because the trafficker doesn't need to steal them. They can get them, sometimes, for a bag of food. But if someone takes a child, nobody denounces or accuses them, and on top of that, if they are put in prison, the judge that punished them is questioned for having punished someone who possibly had an altruistic goal. But whether an object of exchange or product of theft, the child is equally a victim."[45]

Anthropologist Nancy Scheper-Hughes has documented illicit adoption practices in Brazil. "In the shantytowns of Brazil I encountered several cases of coerced adoption and (in 1990 alone) two cases of child stealing by wealthy 'patrons,'" she writes, one of whom was a boss who requested the presence of a worker's child overnight "for [her] amusement." When the child failed to return, the *patrón* told the parents that the child had been adopted by an American couple and that their objections were "selfish" because they would deny the child an opportunity for a better life in the United States. In the context of pressure, threats, and the omnipresent reality of paramilitary murder of shantytown residents who cause too much trouble, the parents let the matter drop, though years later, Scheper-Hughes writes, they still mourned. At the other end of the adoption business, in 1989 Scheper-Hughes spoke to staff at an "orphanage" run by American missionaries. "When I asked, directly, about the Brazilian 'traffic in babies,' the director admitted that aspects of the adoption process were murky. Sometimes, she had to fight with mothers to release their children. Some birth mothers resisted signing the adoption papers even when they know it would be best for their child."[46] Why adoption was "best" for their child is left unstated, as if it were simply a given that any working-class, shantytown resident parents in Brazil were intrinsically worse than middle-class or wealthy parents in the United States, Europe, Israel, or Australia.

The activities of these many activists and U.N.-sponsored truth commissions have had an effect; there have been efforts at the level of international law to clean up transnational adoption. In 2000 an international treaty, the Hague Convention on Protection of Children and Co-operation in Respect of Intercountry Adoption, proposed to remedy some abuses. It requires that the birth family be shown to be unable to care for the child—not just impoverished relative to potential adoptive parents; that consent for relinquishment be freely and irrevocably given; that the relationship of those claiming to be the relinquishing parents to the child be clearly demonstrated, preferably through DNA testing; and that both sending and receiving countries have a central authority that regulates international adoption. Mexico and many other nations promptly ratified it. However, neither the United States nor Guatemala did. The United States promised (and failed) to implement it by 2004, following the enactment of legislative and administrative measures that would make kidnapped or coercively obtained children ineligible for adoption—a chilling acknowledgment of the past and current state of U.S. international adoption law.[47] Guatemala began the process of ratifying and coming into compliance with the convention, only to abruptly decide not to sign the treaty. That neither nation can readily agree to these terms speaks volumes about the nature of the adoption traffic between them and suggests that considerable enforcement measures are needed to ensure an end to illegal and abusive transnational adoption practices, even if laws are changed to ensure conformity with treaty terms.

CONCLUSION

I have been arguing that the development of new "American" families through transnational adoption may be considerably less transgressive than it first appears, that for some adoptive parents and policy makers its justifications rely on a structure of erasing children's origins and the violence encompassed within U.S. foreign policy. In such accounts international adoption to the United States operates in much the same way that U.S. foreign policy works—through a strategic forgetting that makes it possible to ask, "Why do they hate us?" as so many have done in the post-9/11 United States, to assume a posture of hurt or bewildered innocence. In this sense adoption not only echoes but reinforces the broader cultural management of representing U.S. military and economic policy—the symbolic "rescue" of national policy becomes the literal raising of "third world" children by U.S. families. And sometimes, as the Kruchkows' and many similar cases make clear, the Latin American charge that U.S. Americans are not rescuing children but violently destroying families is also literalized. Adopted children "saved" from the poverty and violence of Latin American nations may in fact be protected with the complicity of U.S. state power from repatriation in cases of kidnapping or unlawful relinquishment—a definition of "saving" that might justifiably be understood as having something to do with "taking." While individual parents or families may, understandably enough, believe that they are making a difference in the life of a child, feel attached to children they have raised for years, and be resistant to any calls to repatriate a child whom they love and for whom they experienced great hardship to bring him or her into their family, it also bears noticing that sentimental narratives, as told in the popular press, work in only one direction. The pain felt by U.S. adoptive parents over previous childlessness or over the thought of losing their child is not weighed against an equally emotive story that one might tell of the loss felt by birth parents or the desperate choices that individuals might make to feed some members of their family at the cost of losing another.

Far from being a challenge to the white heterosexual reproduction of "Americanness" in the representational tradition that Armstrong identifies with captivity narratives, transnational adoption can be simply an expansion of who and what gets to count as a "real" American family. One sentimental narrative should not replace another. All adopted Latin American infants and children were not plucked from the arms of their victimized parents. Children may be separated from their birth parents, in Latin America as elsewhere, for reasons that include abuse, neglect, death, and disability. Disrupted families in Latin America and unlawful adoption have a history rooted in a U.S. foreign policy that has made Latin America one of its battlegrounds for more than half a century. Sentimental narratives of child-saving acts cannot entirely be disentangled from that history.

However, there is also another, subordinated but existing, practice and narrative at work here, one that embodies strategies for understanding family and nationality that is not about producing a pure or nationalist domesticity. For the Libertos, complexity and multivocality are at the heart of their understanding of adoption—imagining the little girl they adopted for thirty thousand dollars not to be "theirs," in the sense of owning or buying, nor even U.S. American in any exclusive sense. They imagined her as potentially living in their family or with her birth family, as Mexican or U.S. American. In 2002 David Kruchkow wrote a conclusion and postscript to the narrative that he first posted to the Internet the year before. In it he railed against the corruption of the high-profit intercountry adoption industry, raised questions about coercion and illegitimate pressure on birth parents in places like Guatemala and Mexico to relinquish their children, and mourned the loss of the possibility of contact with his daughter's birth parents as a result of the shady dealings of Mario Reyes and his associates. He wrote about the local politics in Agua Prieta that had first allowed Mexican officials to ignore Reyes's illegal trafficking in children and then to demand his prosecution. He had, in a few years, moved from being a naive (if powerful) consumer of the goods of transnational adoption markets to a close analyst of the political and affective economies of intercountry adoption.[48] He is not alone among U.S. adoptive parents in calling for reform or in tacking steadily to the left with respect to the politics of developing countries or adoption—these kinds of sentiments are regularly raised on adoptive parents' listservs and in their books and stories. Raising an adoptive child born outside the United States sometimes seems to bring U.S. parents into complex, critical relationship with conditions in the adoptees' home countries and U.S. foreign policy. For all their power in mobilizing potential parents to consider "saving" a child, or to account for why and how they ought to adopt from overseas, complicit sentimental narratives seem to do a surprisingly poor job of providing a satisfying narrative of how to raise them. And this unexpected outcome, of the very heterogeneous politics of *raising* adopted children, perhaps leaves the door open for more critical accounts of how the process of getting them could be different.

NOTES

1. *American* here—as in the title and throughout the chapter—carries for me a heavy sense of irony. Many Latin American critics have pointed to the arrogance implicit in the use of the name for the whole continent—"America"—to refer to the inhabitants of one nation within it, the United States. My use of *American* to refer to a narrative about a hegemonic family formation is in precisely this sense—a U.S. family, understood in relationship to a U.S. nationalism that relies on a tremendous sense of U.S. entitlement and power.

2. See Armstrong, "Why Daughters Die."

3. Bartholet, *Family Bonds*, 40.

4. Ibid., 17–18.

5. Ibid., 42–44.

6. Solinger, *Beggars and Choosers*, 28.

7. Almost the same, but not quite, in Homi Bhabha's formulation. Bhabha, "Of Mimicry and Man," 85–92.

8. See LeoGrande, *Our Own Backyard*, 6–7.

9. See, e.g., Gail Dolgin's and Vicente Franco's excellent documentary, *Daughter from Danang*.

10. See, e.g., Patton, *Birthmarks*.

11. See, e.g., Bartholet's crusader book, *Nobody's Children*.

12. Quoted in Bordon, "Advierten robo de 6 niños al día."

13. See Scheper-Hughes, "Theft of Life"; Leventhal, "The 'Baby Parts' Myth"; Martín Medem, *Niños de repuesto*.

14. See Martin and Groves, *Beating the Adoption Odds*.

15. Kruchkow, *When You Wish upon a Star*.

16. Although it was never mentioned in the indictment, some believed that the seventeen Long Island children were the tip of the iceberg. Kruchkow cites evidence for believing that Reyes was involved in illegal adoption from Columbia and Peru; the Mexican parents' group FIND charges that he was involved in five hundred illegal adoptions from Mexico. Although neither source is conclusive, they certainly raise interesting questions.

17. David Halbfinger, "U.S. Accuses 3 of Smuggling Mexican Babies," *New York Times*, May 28, 1999, A1, B5.

18. Christina Ortiz, "Identifican a traficante de menores," *La Reforma*, Jan. 13, 2000.

19. Mike Allen, "Women Accused of Smuggling Used a Friendly Approach," *New York Times*, May 31, 1999, B1, B5; Jim Cason and David Brooks, "Tres detenidos en eu acusados de tráfico de bebés Mexicanos," *La Jornada*, May 28, 1999; Halbfinger, "U.S. Accuses 3 of Smuggling Mexican Babies," *New York Times*, May 28, 1999, A1, B5; Ginger Thompson, "In Mexico, Children, and Promises, Unkept," *New York Times*, June 2, 1999, A1, B4.

20. Douglas, *Discover Douglas, Arizona*, http://www.discoverdouglas.com/EconDev/Agua%20Prieta.htm, accessed June 1, 2003.

21. Thompson, "In Mexico, Children, and Promises, Unkept," *New York Times*, June 2, 1999, A1, B4.

22. Ibid.

23. Kruchkow, *When You Wish upon a Star*, chap. 11.

24. Viana, "Presentarán Queja."

25. Thompson, "In Mexico, Children, and Promises, Unkept," *New York Times*, June 2, 1999, A1, B4.

26. "Adoption Suspect Ordered to NY; Douglas Man Had Good Intentions, Lawyer Says," *Arizona Republic*, June 1, 1999, B1.

27. Karina Avilés, "Desde Guatemala, red internacional de tráfico de niños," *La Jornada*, Sept. 22, 1997.

28. "Todo es legal, entre comillas, es legal. Nosotros vemos con preocupación la cantidad de gente metida aquí en Guatemala que por unos cuantos quetzales logra sustraer al menor." Jaime Avilés, "El tonto del pueblo: Beneplácito un nuevo Pinochet," *La Jornada*, April 12, 1997; Karina Avilés, "Desde Guatemala, red internacional de tráfico de niños," *La Jornada*, Sep. 22, 1997; Karina Avilés, "En Quetzaltenango, 29 niños en calidad de productos caducos e inservibles," *La Jornada*, Sept. 21, 1997; Karina Avilés, "Impunes, tratantes de niños en Guatemala," *La Jornada*, Sept. 2, 1997; Karina Avilés, "Robo de infante, delito común en ese país: Casa alianza, Ong internacional," *La Jornada*, Sept. 23,

1997; Karina Avilés, "Se utilizó el hospital de Malacatán, en Guatemala, como expendio de menores," *La Jornada*, Sept. 24, 1997.

29. Jorge Camil, "Tráfico de niños," *La Jornada*, Sept. 25, 1997.

30. U.S. Department of State, *Immigrant Visas Issued to Orphans Coming to the U.S.*

31. Zarembo, "A Place to Call Home."

32. One of the women, June Weinstock, returned to her home state of Alaska in a coma and never recovered. According to some Internet sources she was a leftist who had gone to the region to support the Zapatista uprising in Chiapas (Gutierrez, *June Weinstock*). The other woman's name was Janice Vogel (Edward Orlebar, "Child Kidnaping Rumors Fuel Attacks on Americans; Guatemala: Military May Be Fomenting Fear of Foreigners. Hysteria May Invite Hard-Liner Backlash," *Los Angeles Times*, April 2, 1994, A1).

33. Zarembo, "A Place to Call Home."

34. Ibid.

35. Comisión para el Esclarecimiento Histórico, *Guatemala: Memoria del silencio*, 3:71–78; Recovery of Historical Memory Project, *Guatemala: Never Again*, 37–38.

36. Recovery of Historical Memory Project, *Guatemala: Never Again*, 38.

37. Comisión para el Esclarecimiento Histórico, *Memoria del silencio*.

38. Serge F. Kovaleski, "In Guatemala, Grief Grows into Suspicion: Many Feel Bishop's Killing Was Motivated by Politics," *Washington Post*, April 30, 1998, A23.

39. Human Rights Groups like the Lawyers Committee for Human Rights, Amnesty International, and the Grupo de Apoyo Mutuo have championed Gutierrez's case for years. Even the skeptical U.S. State Department admitted as "credible" the political motivation of her disappearance. See U.S. Human Rights Bureau of Democracy, Human Rights, and Labor, "Guatemala: Country Reports on Human Rights 2000," 13.

40. Casa Alianza, *They Shoot Children, Don't They?*

41. Puenzo, *La Historia Oficial* (*The Official Story*); Suarez-Orozco, "The Treatment of Children in the Dirty War."

42. See Abuelas de la Plaza de Mayo, *Abuelas de la plaza de Mayo*.

43. Clifford Krauss, "Ex-Argentine Junta Leader Held in 70's Kidnapping," *New York Times*, June 10, 1998, A3.

44. Hitchens, *The Trial of Henry Kissinger*, xii–xiv.

45. José Steinsleger, "Lo Que El Diablo Se Llevó," *La Jornada*, Aug. 8, 1997. "En este país no existe habitualmente la sustracción de los chicos porque el traficante no necesita robarlos. Los consigue, a veces, por una bolsa de comida. Pero si alguien consigue un chico, nadie lo denuncia ni lo acusa y encima, si lo meten preso, el juez que lo castiga es cuestionado por haber castigado a su vez a alguien que posiblemente tuvo una finalidad altruista. Por lo que sea, objeto de trueque o producto de robo, el niño es igualmente víctima."

46. Scheper-Hughes, "Theft of Life," 9.

47. U.S. Department of State, *Hague Convention on Intercountry Adoption*.

48. Kruchkow, *When You Wish upon a Star*.

15

PAUL A. KRAMER

The Darkness That Enters the Home:

The Politics of Prostitution during

the Philippine-American War

Major Owen Sweet's war against prostitutes began shortly after his arrival in Jolo, in the southern Philippines, in May 1899. It was a war within a war: specifically, a war to prevent the opening of a second, Muslim-American front in the three-month-old war against the Philippine Republic. Having taken control from Spanish forces, the 23rd Infantry had, according to Sweet, fallen "heir to the lax moral conditions incident to the Philippines and Oriental countries generally." Lacking barracks space, they had been forced to live "in close contact" with "mixed races," and Sweet had found himself "confronted with the same status of immoralities and the lawless community" as commanders had elsewhere. A "personal" investigation in November, for example, involving a "house to house examination and inspection," had revealed gambling houses, grog-shops, saloons, "joints where the vilest drugs were dispensed," and "several resorts of prostitution," inhabited primarily by Chinese and Japanese but also by Filipinos, Moros, and "other immoral women scattered throughout the villages."[1]

In a report to his superiors, who demanded a full account of his conduct at Jolo following his service, Sweet recounted his energetic uprooting of vice.[2] In the interests of "morality, discipline and good administration," he had acted to "limit, restrict, control, and finally if possible, eliminate the unbriddled [sic] status of drunkenness, gambling, smuggling and prostitution that prevailed." He raided "gambling resorts" through occasional raids, "regulated" liquor traffic, destroyed bino stocks, and closed down all liquor dealers and saloons in early 1900. Facing "an almost wholly immoral woman community," Sweet had given "these women and their keepers" a "course of regulation, restriction and control heretofore unknown in their lifetime." What he called "noted women" were "watched, restrained and examined." Regarding brothels, he at once "instituted a system of strict surveillance, exacting restriction, inspections and control and punishments and medical examinations by the [army] Surgeons." While a "Detention Camp" was established for diseased soldiers, Sweet had incarcerated "all women in Jolo known to be diseased" in a special hospital wing, and he "deported" those found infected with "so-called Asiatic diseases." Together these policies constituted a "system of attrition" that "tended to reduce the number in various ways." Sweet had first "rid the towns of the Chinese then the miscellaneous nationalities," then Moro women "in the most quiet way conceivable," and "from time to time the more objectionable Japanese women." He then "gradually drove out the Visaya and Filipino women." Proceeding gradually toward what he called "eventual elimination," Sweet's system of fees, inspections, incarcerations, and deportations, directed against the "commoner women," had by his own measure succeeded by June 1900 in Jolo, where "only some twenty odd women remained." Had he remained in command a few months longer, 1901 would have seen the "social evil" there "eradicated."[3]

Sweet's campaign was only one instance in a much larger, transnational story of the politicization of prostitution during the Philippine-American War.[4] There is perhaps some irony in the fact that the investigation into Sweet's conduct had been prompted by the collective anger of reformers who thought that, in allowing more than thirty Japanese prostitutes to remain in Jolo, his repression of vice had not gone far enough. It was not Sweet's war against prostitutes but his regulations mandating their medical inspection that would become the subject of intense debate in the United States. His project was part of a more extensive one. During the Philippine-American War the U.S. Army would undertake the broadest program for the venereal inspection of prostitutes conducted by the military to that time.[5] It would be set in place just months into the U.S. occupation of Manila and, over the course of the war, be elaborated there and differently in local army commands. In these many settings, systems of regulation institutionalized gendered and racialized notions of morality and disease, casting "native women" as the "source" of venereal disease and the exclusive objects of inspection, treatment, and isolation.

The inspection system went undetected in the United States for nearly two years, but its discovery by a prohibition journalist in June 1900 triggered an almost instant mobilization by diverse reform groups and campaigns for "abolition" that would reach their height over the next two years. Different groups constructed the issue differently, each attempting to employ it to advance its own agenda. For social purity activists the problem was that regulation "licensed" vice in several senses, threatening soldiers' moral and physical health and that of the society to which they would return. Suffragists cast the policy as the natural by-product of a state without women's moralizing influence. "Anti-imperialists" connected it to broader fears of bodily and political "corruption." For all of them, adoption of regulation signaled a tragic collapse of national exceptionalism, as the United States adopted British or "continental methods." After initial denials the War Department and the U.S. Army admitted regulation and eventually condemned it rhetorically, while allowing its continuance in modified, and less domestically visible, form. Among these modifications the army formalized and universalized the inspection of its soldiers in the Philippines after May 1901.

This study has two historiographic objectives. The first is to situate the history of U.S. empire within a larger, transnational field from which it has too long been isolated and exceptionalized.[6] This broader effort will involve the careful reconstruction of highly specific, historically grounded connections between societies, states, and empires, connections that involve not the study of "transplants" and "exports" but of interpretations, recontextualizations, and debates on the character and meaning of connection itself.[7] When historians establish "connections" based on perceived structural similarities, they risk obstructing the actual ways that historical actors compared, contrasted, and connected their own and other societies, substituting for these criteria ones that are artifacts of the contemporary sociology of knowledge.[8] This chapter is not a comparative history but, in part, a history of comparisons: it demonstrates that both advocates and opponents of regulation made frequent reference to British imperial precedents, for example, but shows both conflicting interpretations and readings tailored to historically specific conflicts.[9] The second of my objectives is to explore the politics of gender in the making of U.S. empire. This is a project well under way, with new literatures emerging that treat both the role that empire played in elaborations of U.S. gender politics and the gendered understandings that informed twentieth-century U.S. global power.[10] This chapter draws on this literature in interpreting the politics of prostitution during the Philippine-American War, situating debates over prostitution in the colonies within a particular moment in the history of U.S. gender politics. Rather than a generic analysis of the "intimate" — an ahistorical category that often conflates gender, the domestic, the familial, the emotional, and the sexual — as the irreducible ground of empire, it is a history of debates over articulations of gender and empire that were contingent and shifting.

BY 1898 THE STATE REGULATION of prostitution through systems of coerced medical inspection had become a crucial element of municipal policy, sanitary strategy, and moral reform projects throughout the globe, although its particular institutional practices varied widely both between and within states.[11] These systems were first developed in continental Europe in the mid-nineteenth century, but as documented by Philippa Levine, their widest and most varied projections were in the British Empire. By 1870 "contagious diseases" ordinances were in place in more than a dozen of Britain's colonies, treaty ports, and the United Kingdom itself.[12] Although their institutional forms and procedures varied, these ordinances provided for the mandatory medical inspection of prostitutes and the incarceration of those found with venereal disease in lock hospitals; they institutionalized the double standard by not providing for the inspection or incarceration of men.[13] By the last decades of the nineteenth century the state regulation of prostitution was part of what defined a modern empire and was instituted in far smaller and weaker colonial empires, such as Spain's.[14] In the 1880s and 1890s Spain's colonial government in the Philippines, for example, had medically inspected Manila's prostitutes.[15]

These projects also gave rise, almost instantaneously, to movements aimed at their abolition, especially in the Anglo-American world. As Ian Tyrrell has shown, these movements brought together the forces and discourses of evangelical Christianity, feminism, and suffragism in an assault on regulation as the state "toleration" of "vice." As state regulation traveled outward on imperial channels, these campaigns played out on a global terrain. Organizations such as the World Woman's Christian Temperance Union (WWCTU) and the International Federation for the Abolition of the State Regulation of Vice enlisted the support of an Anglo-American, and often self-consciously "Anglo-Saxon," constituency.[16] Connected by long-standing transatlantic reform networks—hence their adoption of the name "abolitionist"—British and American "social purity" reformers traded campaigns, personnel, and literature in the last two decades of the nineteenth century. Americans, however, occupied a distinct position within the organizations: the United States, they did not tire of pointing out, was "pure" of "regulation" apart from a few notable municipal experiments, such as that of St. Louis, which had been quickly crushed.[17] The high point of Anglo-

American cooperation along these lines was reached in the struggle to abolish regulation in India. Two Americans, Katherine Bushnell and Elizabeth Andrew, were enlisted to investigate regulation practices in India in 1897 over the course of a year and a half. Their report, *The Queen's Daughters in India*, was a scathing indictment that, following their testimony before Parliament, was instrumental in achieving the abolition of the Contagious Diseases Acts in India, eleven years after their abolition in the British metropole.[18]

THE U.S. OCCUPATION OF MANILA in August 1898, which blocked the entry of Philippine Revolutionary forces, did permit another, secondary occupation: that of hundreds of prostitutes who entered the city from innumerable ports of call. Imperial war had brought together the sex workers of the world in one dense capital city. Numerous commentators were startled at the rapid influx of what one called a "cosmopolitan harlotry."[19] "With the advent of the American troops, there came abandoned women from every corner of the earth," wrote H. S. Neuens of the Purity Society of India.[20] They were part and parcel of what evangelist Rev. Arthur Judson called "the scum which is ever cast up by the advancing waves of civilization."[21] The largest numbers of foreign prostitutes were Japanese: prostitution networks from Japan had extended to the Philippines as early as the 1880s but expanded massively and simultaneously with the U.S. occupation. Motoe Terami-Wada estimates that there were 167 Japanese prostitutes in the Philippines in 1900 and 2,435 in 1905. Even accounting for the widening power of data collection during this period, this marks an increase of almost fifteen times.[22] But more shocking to the U.S. military authorities were white women. While numbers were likely to shift rapidly and subsequent hospital records represented only a highly imperfect statistical measure, a November 1901 report included among the "inmates" of a hospital ward for prostitutes one Spaniard, one Hungarian, one Australian, two Italians, two "Europeans," twelve Russians, and fourteen Americans.[23] This last group, most alarming to U.S. authorities, should not have been surprising: as Eileen Scully has shown, American prostitutes were also present in the outposts of the United States' informal empire such as the treaty ports of China.[24] The vast majority of Manila's prostitutes were, however, Filipinas. Rural families in the Philippines in the late nineteenth century, displaced by rising rents, export agriculture, or Spanish repression, had sent daughters to Manila to work; many were coerced into and trapped in prostitution.[25] The U.S. occupation of Manila, then, not only ushered the

United States into the ranks of military powers in Asia, but it also gathered together into the city a genuinely international, imperial working class of sexual laborers.

The inspection regime was instituted in the context of a perceived moral and medical crisis.[26] According to Provost Marshall General Robert Hughes, the city had "but few white families of bad character," and together the military Board of Health and police had made "strenuous efforts" to "prevent any increase of this class of people from foreign ports." But it was nearly impossible "to locate the native females of bad character" and "to prevent communication between them and our soldiers by the police force." For a peseta, a "native" would bring "the female" to "any designated locality" to meet a client; experience showed "the evil" could only be prevented "by making prisoners of the females." This "evil" manifested itself in another way: by October there were three hundred men in the hospital for venereal disease, specifically syphilis and gonorrhea, and fifty operations had been conducted. Without reserves, and fearing that the disease might leave military efforts "seriously crippled," Hughes felt compelled to act to "jealously guard the man behind the gun."[27]

Although U.S. officials would later invoke the British example, the U.S. Army's inspection program did not involve the "import" of the Contagious Diseases Acts but the continuation of local practices conducted first by the Spanish and, briefly, by the revolutionary government under Emilio Aguinaldo.[28] Nonimportation is suggested by the very different political processes by which inspection was authorized in the two cases. Unlike the Contagious Diseases Acts, for example, Philippine inspections were not initiated by metropolitan authorities or formally enacted by legislation but were the creation of U.S. military orders in the Philippines. General MacArthur's favorable February 1901 citation of regulation in British India in defense of U.S. policies would be striking in its vagueness. While "books containing reference to this matter" could "not be obtained in Manila," MacArthur was certain there existed works demonstrating "that in Asia unusually strong measures have been taken to protect the English speaking soldier from the result of temptations which confront him."[29]

To be sure, U.S. Army doctors who inaugurated the inspection program were in all likelihood far better versed on the Contagious Diseases Acts. With that in mind, what is telling is not the structural similarity of U.S. and British regulation systems but continuities with practices on the ground between Spanish, Philippine, and U.S. regimes. A Spanish regulatory system had been put into effect in Manila in the late 1880s under a liberal governor, apparently based on Madrid regulation; in 1897 a Public Hygiene section of the Department of Health enforced the mandatory registration of brothels and the prostitutes that lived and worked in them and the reportage of changes in residence, along with compulsory medical inspection and incarceration in hospitals and treatment in the case of illness. Health authorities were given substantial power to close brothels and to fine brothel keepers or prostitutes in cases of violations.[30] Given the tumultuous shifts in Manila's governance in mid-1898, however, what is striking is the apparent continuity in practices of inspection. On the day of the U.S. occupation of Manila, for example, Aguinaldo and Leandro Ibarra, the revolutionary government's Secretary of the Interior, authorized the continuation of Spain's regulatory program "to prevent the contraction of syphilitic and venereal diseases."[31]

The U.S. inspection regime drew on the basic outlines of the existing Spanish program, including its most innovative feature, its funding by compulsory fees and penalties paid by prostitutes themselves. The U.S. employment of a "native physician (Spanish)" to carry out medical inspections suggests further continuities.[32] There were, of course, also discontinuities: U.S. inspections took place weekly rather than biweekly; U.S. inspectors were not ordered (although some would undertake) to counsel prostitutes against their trade. Despite the rhetorical use of the British example, policies themselves appear to have evolved based on these and other local institutions. When civilians took over the Board of Health, and the regulation project, from the army in 1901, for example, it rehearsed the idea of borrowing policies—from U.S. rather than British sources—only to reject the strategy in favor of ongoing directions. While "the regulations of Honolulu and St. Louis on prostitution" were "now on the file in this office," army surgeon and board member Charles Lynch noted, "no changes were deemed necessary in the methods pursued."[33] The notion that U.S. Army officials "imported" the Contagious Diseases Act to the Philippines should be viewed as part of a genealogy that dates back to regulation's critics rather than as a historically accurate characterization of the evolution of regulation policies.

By late 1898 the military's inspection regime was well under construction. By November 2, just under three months into the occupation, the board had established a "womans [sic] hospital" for the isolation and "treatment" of all prostitutes found diseased, in a wing of San Lazaro leper hospital. Emphasizing the institution's local origins, Hughes claimed that the decision was "entirely my own" but taken in consultation with Board of Health director

Frank Bourns and the board's other "medical gentlemen."[34] The Bureau of Municipal Inspections employed a physician who made daily visits, a male orderly, two female nurses, two servants, and a cook. The board had also, according to Bourns, "taken possession" of a former vaccination center at 24 Calle de Iris, and turned it into an "office of inspection" where certificates were issued to those women found free of disease. Those found diseased were "compelled to go to the hospital for treatment." Bourns also requested the assistance of the Manila police force "to guard detained (sick) persons and conduct them to the hospital" and to visit "every known house of prostitution" at least once a week to check that the certificates of "inmates" were current. If certificates were not current, the house in question was to be "closed until every inmate has been properly examined."[35]

The first principle of the system was that the prostitute was the perpetual and exclusive source of contagion. Since their beginning, efforts to control venereal disease through state medical inspections had instituted a rigid gender double standard that both explicitly and implicitly attributed venereal epidemics to prostitutes and rationalized the nonexamination of men. In colonial contexts this double standard was often intertwined with racialized medical assumptions that colonized peoples were reservoirs of dangerous tropical disease.[36] The U.S. Army's inspection system in the Philippines was, at first, no different, with heightened concern for the health of U.S. troops unaccompanied by mandatory systems to inspect them. As in the British regulation system, subjecting men to venereal inspection was believed to be intrusive, humiliating, and dishonorable, a force for "demoralizing" troops; prostitutes at home or abroad apparently had none of this burdensome honor to lose. This gendered inattention is suggested by the absence of venereal disease information in studies conducted among soldiers until mid-1901. When Simon Flexner and L. F. Barker, professors at the Johns Hopkins University, were sent to the Philippines in March 1899 as a "medical commission" to study "all cases of illness occurring within the territory embraced by the American military lines," they entirely passed over the question of venereal disease among U.S. troops.[37] Their first report, delivered in December, contained accounts of ongoing U.S. efforts against beriberi, dysentery, typhoid fever, and malaria, "the principal diseases from which the Americans suffered"; but even their secondary list, "tuberculosis, diphtheria, and scarlet fever," did not include venereal disease.[38]

Over the next two and a half years the inspection program became more systematized and intensive. As it evolved, the system apparently incorporated many of the functions originally assigned the police: a "native physician (Spanish)" was employed as "medical inspector" to make "house-to-house" inspections of "all known brothels" in the city on a weekly basis and to examine each of their "inmates." Instead of issuing weekly certificates, the board issued "inspection-books" to be retained by each woman; if the inspector found a woman free from disease, he registered this in her book; if not, "she was placed in the hospital." In support of the medical inspector, a "lay inspector" was given wide latitude, tracing the "whereabouts of women not found by the doctor, locating new houses, taking or sending women to hospital whose books were in arrears." This lay inspector was "an enlisted man detailed," and after fall 1900, the same man was hired as a civilian.[39] Until early 1901 the system brought into the hospital between twenty and ninety women, most of them Filipinas. To reduce inefficiencies and expenses of transportation and surveillance, the cost of examinations was Mex$1 for on-site exams in the hospital, Mex$2 for exams done in brothels. (The estimated cost of an inspection was forty-seven cents per woman.) Fees were set on a racial sliding scale, doubled for white women. These funds remained apart from other army budgets in a "special fund"; between mid-1899 and early 1901 the bureau turned an impressive 23 percent profit.[40]

In early March 1901 the inspection regime was reorganized and placed under the authority of the Board of Health. The reason for this change may have been revelations about the program, about which more later. In addition, a separate "Bureau of Municipal Inspection" might have been seen as more politically exposed than an embedded function of what, by 1901, was a complex bureau charged with numerous sanitary and health-related tasks. It was also likely related to broader public health concerns. When bubonic plague had struck Manila in January 1900, the board had inspected all brothels, "as it was believed that plague might spread from such foci"; this surveillance had been kept up subsequently. According to Maj. Charles Lynch, the surgeon and Board of Health member in charge of the hospital, the board understood that "no method of control" would be effective without "competent executive force." This "force" was racialized: the board had hired an American physician "who does the work of the two former native physicians." In terms of sheer numbers inspected, the board was, indeed, capable of greater "executive force": just two months into its takeover, it was incarcerating 86 percent more women than previously; it had registered 115 percent more. It aspired, half-heartedly, to widen the inspection regime to include soldiers—whose inspection was not formalized—and teamsters employed by the quartermaster, "among whom there is much venereal disease."[41] It also attempted to enlist the help of missionaries in a broader work of "uplift." Dr. Foxworthy, a physician formerly in charge of the hospital, had attempted "to use his influence for the reform of individual prostitutes," although his efforts had resulted only in a reduction in drinking among American and European prostitutes, "probably but temporary." There was a "wide field for missionary work" in the hospital for women versed in Spanish or Tagalog, who were "not afraid of moral contamination from these prostitutes." Lynch believed Filipinas especially reformable, "being not drunken" and entering "through necessity" or because of "the cupidity of parents" rather than, as Americans, Europeans, and Japanese, out of hard-core professionalism.

Despite their increasing energy and self-confidence, inspectors ran into myriad problems of enforcement, almost exclusively regarding Filipino prostitutes.[42] As both the program's aggressive surveillance and fee incentives suggested, prostitutes were resistant to medical inspection. Officials felt a need to "disassociate their minds from the idea that the hospital is a prison."[43] By mid-1901 the hospital was offering to treat prostitutes' "other complaints," and although few had taken advantage, it was hoped that "from time to time many will avail themselves of this privilege, as there is no other place where they can obtain good treatment." Most of the system's difficulties revolved around the problems of identifying brothels in the first place. The fee-driven system of inspection and registration guaranteed that new, uninspected brothels would constantly spring up on the outskirts of the districts surveyed, and enormous possibilities for bribery assured that they would spring up inside the system itself.[44] In May 1900 Dr. Ira Brown, then Board of Health president, suggested the formation of a strictly bounded red-light district. Such a district would be policed in part through existing incarceration mechanisms; any prostitutes doing business apart from this section would be "deprive[d] . . . of their liberty" to reinforce the point that they "cannot mingle with outside society."[45] Such a district would allow respectable Manila residents to avoid encounters with vice. The city's people, he stated, "should be protected from houses springing up here and there in their midst; especially should the child be protected."[46] Districting would also help prospective clients identify brothels; "frequently men suffering from acute alcoholism" had apparently "entered respectable houses located near those occupied by prostitutes."[47]

The biggest problems of identification were, however, at the level of individuals. At the crux of Sweet's category of a "noted woman" was a fundamental paradox, that a "prostitute" was in many ways indistinguishable from someone who was not. This paradox frequently confounded the inspection system. When "[s]everal men go into a place where there are but two or three women," noted Brown with dismay, "the enterprising women send out to a neighbor and ask her to come in and help out." This neighbor was "not regularly in the business, and escapes examination, and it is in such instances that disease is spread."[48] But along with the difficulty of policing the line around "prostitution," it was difficult to identify even those individual women registered within the system. For over a year the program had functioned using either certificates or inspection books bearing only names and identification numbers. But just as they avoided inspection and its costs, Manila's prostitutes had quickly developed a vigorous trade in up-to-date, disease-free inspection books. This trade was the foreseeable by-product of the sheer costs of inspection and incarceration, the difficulty of avoiding disease, and the elasticity of demand. It is unclear how this exchange functioned: the inspection of entire brothels at one sitting would have made such deception difficult, but the deceit was perhaps more easily carried out in the more individualized hospital setting. Knowledge of evolving inspection patterns in the city may have allowed coordination of the trade on a much broader scale than the individual brothel itself. Perhaps, accompanied with bribes beneath the existing fee structure, it gave inspectors adequate reason to willfully ignore deception. At some point in 1900, however, inspectors received orders to begin photographing individual prostitutes.[49] One copy of this photograph was placed on an index card with a name and number so that "any woman's exact status may be determined at a glance." A number linked this card to "numbers on leaves of a book." Another photograph was placed in her inspection book "so that one woman cannot substitute [an] examination or book for another."[50] Despite inspectors' confidence in the power of photo identification, one is left to speculate what games prostitutes might have played with commercially available photographs.

While regulation's biggest and most complex institutional manifestation was in Manila, smaller-scale efforts were also undertaken at the local level in provincial cities, a process enabled by the decentralized nature of the U.S. command structure in general. The nature and extent of these practices remains hard to assess, but the case of the project at Jolo—of which Sweet had been the architect—suggests the variable and contextual nature of inspection regimes. Regulation projects varied not only between the Philippines and other colonies but within the Philippines itself, operating with a range of resources and subject to diverse political forces. According to Captain R. R. Stevens, when U.S. forces had taken Jolo from the Spanish in mid-May 1899, there was a "large influx of both Asiatics of both sexes and of many nationalities and of the usual oriental standard of morality, including Cingalese, East Indians, Chinese, Japanese and Filipinos."[51] U.S. soldiers had quickly begun "mixing" with the women, he maintained, and thereafter developed venereal disease; worst of all had been Chinese and Moro prostitutes living outside the walls of Jolo. Sweet, as we've seen, had undertaken a largely successful process of "elimination" aimed at these "native women" who were, as one second lieutenant put it, "according to common report almost universally affected with venereal disease."[52] At least some streams of this "influx," however, had occurred with official military approval. Maj. E. B. Pratt recalled that shortly after the U.S. occupation, he was informed that "some Japanese women (prostitutes)" then in North Borneo wished to come to Jolo. After "considering the subject carefully," Pratt had "decided to grant the permission." After learning of their arrival and settlement on "one of the principal streets," he had directed that they relocate "near the outskirts in the vicinity of the walls." They did so, taking up four houses—one of them designated as a hospital—on a "back street" of the city.[53]

While both Pratt and Sweet would deny charges of "licensing" or "encouragement," the Jolo brothels were in many ways projects of state. Patrols and sentinels stationed near the brothels were given orders to segregate them racially, "to allow no persons but soldiers to enter the premises."[54] According to one soldier, "[n]atives, Chinese and casual visitors were excluded as a necessary sanitary precaution."[55] Against the grain of the system elsewhere, U.S. soldiers were inspected once a month themselves, and were prohibited from entering the brothel during the conduct of inspections, if found diseased, or after the playing of "taps," "except by written pass signed by the Company commander."[56] While male ingress was heavily controlled, the prostitutes were also strictly forbidden "to advertise themselves by parading the streets."[57] The prostitutes were required to submit to weekly medical inspection by a U.S. Army surgeon, paid for by the brothel keeper; in case of disease a woman was to be confined to the hospital for treatment. More than one officer testified that the army surgeon conducted these exams for private gain, "in the nature of outside practice."[58] Many saw the system as successful because of its virtual invisibility. "A person could live in Jolo a year and not know there was a Jap prostitute in the town unless told of the fact," marveled Capt. W. H. Sage.[59] One lieutenant suggested that "any lady could have lived there the whole time" of the U.S. occupation and "never have known that such places existed."[60] What "disorder" there was belonged to U.S. soldiers, including "fighting and breaking furniture," stealing from the prostitutes, and assaulting them.[61] This invisibility was in part attributed to the compliance of the Japanese prostitutes, who were "perfectly amenable" to regulations, which "could hardly be said of the various other women."[62]

But the Jolo inspection regime was very much a response to local politico-military contingencies: the 23rd Infantry was charged with preventing an outbreak of hostilities with the predominant Moro population, which would have opened a disastrous southern front in the Philippine-American War. According to Capt. C. E. Hampton, "the report was by Sulu women that some of the soldiers had made improper advances to them."[63] This was, for U.S. commanders, an extremely flammable situation. Hampton, having made an "intimate investigation of the character and habits of the Sulu people," concluded that prostitution was "practically unknown among them." Any "interference, however slight," with Moro women would be "resented in the hottest and most savage manner."[64] Maj. W. A. Nichols stated that "the reason understood for permitting these houses to exist" was that "the Moro men exhibited great solicitation for their women"; some had "stated that trouble would arise between the Moros and Americans should the soldiers consort with the Moro women."[65] As a result, as one captain recalled, "soldiers were forbidden to cohabit with Moro women or others outside the walls of the town."[66] In this light the inspection regime not only prevented the spread of disease but the advent of war. One captain recalled that when the Japanese prostitutes arrived, "our relations with the moros [sic] were very uncertain."[67] The "toleration" of the brothels had "not only promoted the health and contentment of the enlisted men" but "also avoided unfortunate complications with the moros [sic] outside the walled town," where "our men would undoubtedly have gone in violation of orders."[68]

Although the inspection regime was meant to protect U.S. soldiers, the war itself accelerated the spread of venereal disease in the rural Filipino population. Despite the assumption in practice that disease inhered in Filipinos' bodies, U.S. troops left North America heavily infected with venereal disease (as many U.S. Army doctors would concede). According to Ken De Bevoise, seventeen of every one thousand candidates for enlistment had been rejected on these grounds; venereal disease rates rose during training as brothels and dives grew up around U.S. bases. Troops at the Presidio in

San Francisco were examined for venereal diseases, given medicine, and returned to duty; one army official who sailed with one of the first regiments to depart, in mid-1898, reported that 480 of the unit's approximately 1,300 men had been "registered for venereal disease" before departing. This rate, as we've seen, leapt again following the landing of U.S. troops in Manila. But as De Bevoise observes, the rapid dispersal of U.S. troops into the Philippine countryside after 1900 provided ideal conditions for the explosive spread of venereal disease. The deliberate destruction of rural resources, especially the burning of crops and killing of carabao by U.S. troops, and the massive dislocation and starvation among Filipino villagers that ensued, greatly reduced disease immunity in general.[69]

At the same time, guerrilla war meant close social contact between U.S. troops and Filipino villagers in garrisoned towns, contacts that included sexual liaisons. Survival strategies among uprooted rural families included sending daughters to towns and cities in search of work. In this sense the U.S. invasion not only provided demand for sexual laborers but also spurred their supply. In larger towns brothels developed to serve U.S. garrisons, becoming dense in disease vectors. In smaller ones, with more temporary U.S. occupations, prostitution took the form of what one medical officer called "a transient class of native women who are infected [and who] travel from one post to another spending a few days at each garrison."[70] Few Americans noted the possibility that Filipinos might contract disease, although Maj. F. A. Meacham of the Manila Board of Health observed in mid-1901 that syphilis was "spreading among the native population of these islands," with results that he believed would repeat "the history of this disease among primitive peoples."[71]

Medical officers lamented these sexual encounters in their own right. One surgeon complained that "consorting with native women can not be controlled when the troops are stationed in scattered town quarters."[72] The fact that this was itself imagined as a medical problem — apart from an explicit disease context — suggests the ways in which fears of disease and miscegenation intersected.[73] Given that Filipinos were in many cases believed to be inherently diseased, miscegenation meant contagion; whether or not specific Filipino women were believed to be diseased, miscegenation was often imagined as both a sign and trigger of physical and moral "degeneration" among white American soldiers. For some, contracting venereal disease and engaging in sex with "native women" constituted different but related forms of "treason." When commanders suggested that venereal disease was primarily a problem of troop strength, and that soldiers' immorality and recklessness was its cause, they made the act of contraction a sort of bodily treason, a partial denial of one's physical constitution to the state.

IT WAS A SIGN OF THE army's care in masking it, the logistical difficulties of transpacific communication, and, possibly, the success of U.S. Army censorship that the Manila inspection system apparently went entirely undetected outside the Philippines for its first two years of operation. What made this most surprising was the growing presence of Protestant missions in the islands during precisely this period. The U.S. Army's occupation of Manila had been accompanied not only by hordes of camp followers but also by optimistic Protestant missionaries.[74] According to missionary Charles Briggs, mission board representatives in Singapore and Canton "had long looked wistfully toward Manila, and prayed the more earnestly that the everlasting doors might be lifted up there and let the King of Glory come in."[75] Commodore Dewey's victory at Manila Bay in May 1898 had been "taken by the Evangelical Mission Boards in America as a summons to enter the field, now for the first time open."[76] The first Protestant missionary, a Presbyterian, had arrived in April 1899; by mid-1901 six other denominations would branch out from Manila, which would remain common ground as they divided the archipelago into "comity" zones. Given their zeal, it is surprising in retrospect that these missionaries allowed "regulated vice" to gain much headway. Perhaps the reason was the limited information networks of new arrivals, or perhaps regulated vice failed to stand out on such an immense canvas of sin.

On June 27, 1900, William B. Johnson, a correspondent for the *Chicago New Voice*, a prohibition newspaper, filed a sensationalist report whose outraged details would echo, with further distortion, through the social purity, suffrage, and "anti-imperialist" presses over the next two years. The piece began ominously, with Johnson's visit to Manila's First Reserve Hospital, which served 40 percent of the army's sick, and where a head surgeon had noted more than three thousand cases of venereal disease among soldiers, about one of six on the sick list. Johnson also reported being shown the "national cemetery" at Malate, where, according to his guide, an American editor, more of "our boys" had been sent "through bad women and drink than through the bullets of the Filipinos." Behind this dark curtain of disease and death stood a governmental machinery of vice. Through "newspapermen, police reports and officials," Johnson had learned that there were "about 200 regularly licensed houses of prostitution in the city," containing about six hundred prostitutes "under direct control of the military authorities, who represent American 'Christian' civilization here." (This number did not include "the swarms of loose women who have rooms and prowl around the streets.") Prostitution in the city, he charged, was "conducted under the supervision of a regular department of the military government," which he called the "'department of prostitution.'" The Bureau of Municipal Inspection, which ran on "alleged scientific principles," possessed a "big staff of assistants, inspectors, doctors and flunkies of various sorts." According to Johnson, women could only open a brothel with "the express permission of the military authorities," after paying for a one-hundred-peso wine-and-beer license. Johnson accurately described the inspection and incarceration system; when he had asked why hospitalized women were "compelled to pay their way," he had been told that it was "'official business'" and of "'no concern to the public.'"[77]

Like other social purity reformers, Johnson tended to see the regulation system, and the sexual markets he believed flourished under its protection, as both Europeanizing and Orientalizing. For this reason he found disturbing how "thoroughly American" the "whole situation" was. In the red-light district of Sampaloc, a "settlement of lust," there was "scarcely a house of prostitution which is not decorated with American flags," an adornment he had observed both "inside and out." Some had American flags "painted clear across the front of their establishments." Sampaloc was, indeed, a "concrete revel of 'American civilization.'" To emphasize his point about the "official" character of Manila prostitution, Johnson adorned his own report with two photographs he had taken at different sites, each captioned "Licensed House of Prostitution in Sampalog [sic] District, Manila." The bold-faced message that accompanied these descriptions — "Who Will Haul This Flag Down?" — was telling. Republican imperialists were at that moment accusing their critics of desiring to "haul down the flag," signaling a withdrawal of imperial prestige, honor, and masculinity. Johnson's ironic commentary threw this flag patriotism back on itself: the Republicans' "flag" of imperial sovereignty came with another, more sordid, one. Perhaps pulling down the one was the only way to remove the other.

Immediately following these revelations, the issue of regulated vice was taken up by a wide array of reformers. Directly cited, plagiarized, or paraphrased, details from the Johnson report — reproduced with varying degrees of accuracy — immediately appeared beneath indignant headlines in the social purity, suffrage, and "anti-imperialist" presses. (In the latter category Mark Twain would eventually include in his unpublished February 1901 satiric revision of "The Battle Hymn of the Republic" the verse: "We have legalized the strumpet and are guarding her retreat" with an accompanying explanatory note that "in Manila the Government has placed a certain industry under the protection of our flag.")[78] Each of these groups had its own agenda to advance and coalition to build, and each seized on the issue with varying degrees of emphasis and by focusing on different elements. In doing so, they prioritized, in moral and causal terms, war, militarism, empire, prostitution, immorality, and disease, in highly divergent ways. Ultimately, the combined force of these campaigns would compel the War Department and the U.S. Army to reform the inspection regime.

First and foremost among those who politicized regulated vice were the social purity activists, who had been active in fighting the Contagious Diseases Acts in a self-consciously Anglo-American arena since at least the 1880s.[79] In the present crisis organizations like the American Purity Alliance (APA) and Woman's Christian Temperance Union (WCTU) widely circulated the Johnson report and mobilized petitions and letter-writing campaigns.[80] Their critiques were consistent with earlier campaigns against regulated vice in Europe and its colonies. Central to them was an erotic theory of the state: "the social evil" was itself enabled by state approval through regulation. While they could not account for prostitution in unregulated environments, social purity advocates emphasized the ways that regulation increased prostitution by making vice "safe." This theory could be said to rely on the causal relationship between "license" — as state sanction — and "license" — understood as unregulated sexual expression. When the state approved vice externally, critics maintained, the internal self was denied the privilege of repressing itself.

Even prior to Johnson's revelations, the Anglo-American connections of social purity politics had been strong enough that American purity reformers interpreted the Spanish-Cuban-American War and the acquisition of Caribbean and Pacific colonies almost reflexively in terms of European colonial experiences, prophesying the perfectly coterminous arrival of regulated vice to the United States' new colonies. Their discourse was one of tragic analogy, in which the United States, once exceptional without overseas colonies, would through colonialism inevitably — but perhaps not irreversibly — immerse itself in the fouling waters of both vice and regulation. "We may be reasonably sure that the same problems as to the morality of the soldiers and

Paul A. Kramer

the degradation of womanhood will stare us in the face as disturb the English people in reference to their army in India," wrote Dr. O. Edward Janney, future APA president, of the Philippine campaign.[81] Mariana W. Chapman wrote that "it will be a shameful record for our army to make, if we repeat East Indian conditions in relation to the native women. . . . The Filipinos may combine for us all the unfortunate situations in which Great Britain has found herself in India and Hong Kong."[82] Speaking from within a self-consciously global opposition movement, APA president Aaron Powell emphasized what he called the "kindred grave problems" that confronted "France in Africa, Holland in her Dutch colonies, Germany and Russia in their vast military areas." But rather than urging opposition to imperialism, Powell merely sounded a cautionary note. He urged Americans, "many of whom appear latterly dazzled with the prospect of enlarged colonial possessions," to "be made more thoughtful as to the grave responsibility involved," a responsibility both for the "moral and physical health" of soldiers and for the "ignorant, undisciplined natives of these tropical islands."[83]

Missionaries and social purity reformers visiting American army encampments and touring naval vessels in mid-to-late 1898 found their darkest fears confirmed: hordes of camp followers gathering under the tolerant eye of officers. Josiah W. Leeds had years earlier read of an English naval officer who had allowed prostitutes onto his ship, and Leeds had told himself "in the spirit of thankfulness, that such things at least were not tolerated in the navy of this nation." But he noted ominously that "since our navy and army witnessed expansion under the new empire, that the same debaucheries of the Old World powers prevail in the American services."[84] William Lloyd Garrison Jr. reported a conversation he had had with a YMCA worker returning from Camp Chickamauga in Tennessee, his response suggesting the intensity of Anglo-American reform networks and ideologies. Almost instantaneously his mind shifted from Tennessee to the lock hospitals of India. "Saddened by this revelation," he wrote, "my mind reverted to the horrors of the British camps in India, whereof I had been reading in Mrs. Josephine Butler's pathetic appeal for aid to prevent the re-enactment of the Contagious Diseases Acts."[85]

Although they shared common theories of state, desire, and sexual commerce, American social purity activists departed from their English counterparts in asserting national-exceptionalist claims against regulation in the Philippines. U.S. national exceptionalism had long been a part of Anglo-American social purity discourse, which touted Americans' unique success in largely keeping regulated vice from their shores. As Antoinette Burton has shown, Josephine Butler and other British feminist social purity activists had made their claims on the discursive ground of empire: ending regulated vice in the colonies would assert women's claims to participate in, moralize, and improve the British Empire.[86] While this was certainly true of many American social purity activists, many also relied on national-exceptionalist "anti-imperialist" discourses that suggested that regulated vice was a tragic and inevitable by-product of "empire" itself. The formula was borrowed from earlier social purity logic, crossed with republican antimilitarism: colonies meant standing armies, standing armies meant prostitution, and prostitution meant officers' attempts to regulate vice in the interests of disease control. As an American clergyman reported of Barbados, "social and sexual demoralization is one of the conditions incident to militarism."[87] The formula also relied on a geography of moral restraint: the farther armies were projected outward from the metropole, the farther they were from "restraining home influences" that were the proper, nonstate means for "regulating vice." The social purity press quoted Sergeant Oscar Fowler, recently returned from Manila, along these lines. "The social evil and other iniquities find congenial environment," he wrote, "in the atmosphere of a militarism existing far from the seat of the home government."[88]

While social purity advocates on occasion expressed concern for the morality—and, still less frequently, the health—of colonized peoples, they were most preoccupied with imperial soldiers and the domestic society to which they would eventually return. In mid-1899 Powell conveyed his fears that "some of these soldiers and sailors, without moral restraint, and contaminated in their new environment," would return and "in turn also contaminate our home population."[89] On another occasion, he instructed readers in "Lessons from India" along these lines, observing that "American advocates of colonial expansion frequently cite, by means of precedent and justification, English experience in India and other colonial dependencies."[90] It was a sign of how powerful these connections remained that Powell himself felt compelled to cite British authorities against regulation. He quoted Lord George Hamilton, secretary of state for India, for example, who opposed regulation for its domestic impact, medical and nonmedical, on British society. Under regulation, British soldiers returned, "bringing with them the debasing sentiments and habits acquired during their Indian training, and infecting our industrial communities with a moral pestilence more destructive of the national stamina" than venereal disease itself. Powell also quoted a London review on the problem of "imbecility" among returning imperial soldiers, as reported by "police magistrates, poor-law guardians and matrons of workhouses, educational authorities, and all the philanthropies." The problem was "surely due to vice in the sufferer or his parents"; when a soldier reentered civilian life he brought with him "for good or evil, the habits and ideas he has learned in the army." The "morality of civil life" would be threatened until "this 'return of the native' can be reckoned a positive gain."[91]

From this view regulated vice in the colonies not only promoted actual disease in the metropole but was itself a kind of contagion that would spread from the colonies inward. During the Philippine-American War this "contagion" was said to run in two directions. The first of these was from Europe to the United States. If regulation was, on the one hand, a natural by-product of militarism in whatever form, it was also (as militarism itself) continually associated with Europe, known especially as the "continental system"; adopting it meant surrendering U.S. national-exceptional virtue. The "contagion" of regulation also ran in another direction: from colony to metropole. Social purity advocates feared that the colonies would be the opening wedge permitting the entry of "regulation" into the United States. Whereas Fowler had located "militarism" "far from the seat of home government," others witnessed its emergence in the metropole. Speaking before the London Congress of the International Federation for the Abolition of State Regulation of Vice, Powell observed "indications of the danger of a revival here of regulation propagandism," due in part to "the prevalence of vice in connection with army life, away from home restraints."[92] A September 1900 APA memorial to McKinley emphasized the risk of "enactment of a similar regulation system by State Legislatures, incited by the example of the [national] government."[93]

Just as social purity activists saw Europe as a source of corruption, they also turned to British precedents for inspiration. Along with British repeal of the Contagious Diseases Acts in both the metropole and India, there was, more recently, the April 28, 1898, order by Lord Wolseley, commander-in-chief of the British Army. The order, printed copies of which were forwarded through Anglo-American reform networks to War Department officials, was a stern and repressive warning to officers to keep their men away from "vice" and, because it failed to mention regulation, was read as a rejection of it. Wolseley lamented that many men spent "a great deal of their short term of service" in military hospitals, a large number of them "permanently disfigured and incapacitated" by vice. To avoid such losses, officers were to convey to their men, "and particularly to young soldiers," the "disastrous effects of giving way to habits of intemperance and immorality." A soldier who led a "vicious life" of drink and debauchery "enfeebles his constitution," exposed himself to diseases "of the kind which has of late made terrible ravages in the British Army." Men "tainted with this disease" were "useless to the State" and a "source of weakness." Officers were urged to "exercise a salutary influence in these matters," providing "example and guidance" to men far "from the restraints and influences of home." Moral influence of this kind, combined with punishment, would allow the army to "compare favorably with other classes of the civil population" in terms of morality.[94] It was unsurprising that the order circulated as widely and rapidly as it did; it not only failed to mention "regulation" but also proffered social purity understandings of sexuality, morality, and the state articulated by the British Army itself.

Although social purity activists most ardently claimed regulated vice as their issue, it was also taken up in a secondary way by the suffragists with whom they were closely allied.[95] It was a commonplace of much social purity activism that granting women the vote would be one way to strengthen political forces against regulated vice, a policy no self-respecting woman was believed capable of supporting. The Woman's Christian Temperance Movement was one of the chief organizations promoting women's suffrage, and membership in it and suffrage organizations like the National American Woman Suffrage Association (NAWSA) in many cases overlapped.[96] According to Kristin Hoganson, woman suffragists were divided around the question of colonial empire. Like British imperialist feminists, some saw in empire an opportunity to assert white women's political power over and above that of racialized colonial subjects. Others, far fewer in number, made common cause with the Philippine Revolution and condemned patriarchy as "domestic imperialism."[97] Suffrage alliances with "anti-imperialists" were fraught, however, not only by suffrage imperialism but also by "anti-imperialist" patriarchy: while some among the "anti-imperialist" leadership supported woman suffrage, the vast majority were preoccupied with critiques of colonial empire that often began from masculinist presuppositions about honor and national duty.[98] To an important extent suffrage perspectives on colonial empire were opportunistic; with "anti-imperialist" ranks swelling to three times suffrage numbers at the beginning of the twentieth century, suffragists sought a means to participate in the "Philippine question," which William Jennings Bryan would declare the "paramount issue," according to the *New York Times* on July 28, 1900. Although regulated vice in the Philippines enlisted only a small fraction of suffrage energy, it allowed suffragists to argue that such moral lapses were the necessary by-products of an exclusively male electorate. It also allowed suffragists to engage in the politics of colonialism without committing themselves to anti-imperialism. As with social purity advocates, eliminating regulated vice, under women's guidance, might enhance the United States' moral imperium.

When the Johnson exposé surfaced just prior to the 1900 NAWSA convention in Rochester, New York, concerns such as these prompted a September 1, 1900, resolution, which was "adopted by a unanimous vote" and subsequently submitted to McKinley. The resolution "earnestly protested" the introduction of the "European system of State regulation of vice" into Manila on three grounds. First, such a policy was "contrary to good morals" and appeared to give "official sanction to vice" before "both our soldiers and the natives." Second, there was the double standard, the "violation of justice" that applied to "vicious women" compulsory exams "not applied to vicious men." Third, the system was ineffective and, it maintained, currently being abandoned everywhere it had been attempted. "The United States should not adopt a method that Europe is discarding," read the resolution, "nor introduce in our foreign dependencies a system that would not be tolerated at home." The resolution issued its protest "in the name of American womanhood," believing its sentiments represented "the opinion of the best American manhood." The *Woman's Column* asked that "every woman who reads this article write a letter of protest to Mr. McKinley" or that each get her husband to do so since, it noted bitterly, "the protests of voters have more weight than those of women."[99] The following February, the Mississippi Woman Suffrage Association followed this advice, submitting its own five-point resolution to McKinley. While sharing NAWSA's preoccupations with moral messages and double standards, it also called regulation "an insult to womanhood" and expressed concern that it "breeds a moral and physical degeneration that will avenge itself upon our American society when these soldiers shall have been recalled to their native country."[100]

The broader "anti-imperialist" movement also turned the issue of regulated vice to its own purposes, although less consistently than either social purity reformers or suffragists. "Anti-imperialist" argumentation was as diverse as the strange political bedfellows—liberal Republicans, white supremacist Democrats, organized labor—it brought into alliance.[101] Among their other concerns, "anti-imperialists" condemned the impact of "militarism" on domestic republican institutions and the risk of "mongrelization" that colonialism posed to the U.S. body politic.[102] Many of these fears hinged on notions of "corruption": the decay of republican virtue before imperial tyranny and arrogance; the sinister hands of "trusts" in promoting overseas annexation; the scams of distant "carpet-bagging" officials in the new colonies; the degradation of individual white bodies through miscegenation and of a collective, national white body through potential colonial immigration and labor competition. As reports of high troop sickness rates cycled back to the United States, disease proved a powerful metaphor that condensed and concretized these various forms of "corruption." A January 1899 political cartoon in the *New York World* showed Columbia recoiling from an opened urn labeled "The Philippines Treaty," from which vapors emerged labeled not only "Imperial Standing Army," "Despotic Rule," and "A War Against Freedom" but "Leprosy" and "Fevers."[103] More directly still, one before-and-after cartoon showed Uncle Sam prior to "his wish for expansion" in a condition of robust "Prosperity," overlooking smoke-belching factories. In a subsequent panel, representing its aftermath, he is an invalid, both ill and emasculated, confined to looking out a window at closed plants.[104]

It was through these broader discourses of disease as "corruption" that concerns with regulated vice entered "anti-imperialist" discourse. The most direct example was Edward Atkinson's 1899 pamphlet *The Hell of War and Its Penalties.* Among "anti-imperialists," Atkinson was as fervent as he was confrontational, challenging U.S. military censorship by sending his inflammatory homegrown publications directly to U.S. soldiers in the Philippines.[105] In *The Hell of War and Its Penalties* he turned to the subject of venereal disease as corruption, taking on the issue with a specificity and indelicacy not present in the social purity press.[106] As Atkinson knew from the British imperial experience, venereal disease was one of empire's greatest evils. The "records of the British army in India and China," and "the condition of the English troops in Hong Kong," were "horrible in the extreme." According to one "English gentleman" Atkinson had met, 50 percent of British troops in Hong Kong were infected. Atkinson emphasized that the disease would, like imperialism, make its way from the new colonies to the metropole as soldiers conveyed it back to their homes. "It is well known that while there may be an apparent cure," he wrote, "this disease works corruption of the blood to the third and fourth generation, ending in degeneracy."[107] Importantly, however, Atkinson made no mention of either prostitution or its regulation as mechanisms of transfer; rather, he connected venereal disease and colonial empire together as related — and inseparable — processes of bodily and political corruption.

THE STATE'S FIRST RESPONSE to spiraling accusation was denial. With apparent, bewildered sincerity War Department officials barraged with correspondence and petitions, especially from local WCTU chapters, responded that they had no knowledge of the inspection program. In October 1900, for example, the acting secretary of war informed the president of the WCTU that "so far as this Department is advised no such conditions obtain as set forth in your letter." But he also promised that General MacArthur had been instructed "to investigate the subject fully, and to make full report on the subject matter of your resolutions."[108] The War Department was, at that moment, particularly vulnerable to sensationalist criticism of this kind, as officials sought the passage of the Army Reorganization Bill toward the end of 1900. Secretary of War Elihu Root complained to William Howard Taft, head of the second Philippine Commission in the Islands, that "yellow journal hypocrites, posing as fanatics" had "created an impression among millions of good people that we have turned Manila into a veritable hell"; letters had inundated the War Department "by the thousands."[109] The city of Manila, whose proliferating saloons filled with American soldiers always accompanied reports of "licensed" brothels, became a powerful symbol for temperance reformers opposing provisions in the bill for an army canteen.[110] Indeed, the canteen provision went down on January 10 in a hail of speeches regarding what Senator Teller called the "curse" of "Government encouragement of drinking among the soldiers of the American army and the Filipinos."[111] Root expressed frustration that the Senate had "delayed the progress of the army bill" to discuss the issue, as well as amendments prohibiting the importation and sale of liquor to the Philippines.[112]

Eager to sideline moral objections to the Army Reorganization Bill, Root requested a full accounting from Taft on January 15, and the army forwarded a similar request to General MacArthur.[113] It was a sign of ongoing civilian/military clashes that their answers diverged greatly in degree of disclosure. MacArthur's was a terse and telegraphic denial: "Houses of prostitution are not licensed, protected or encouraged."[114] Taft admitted that the inspection system existed and described its value in "maintain[ing] effectiveness of army" by "subject[ing] known loose women to certified examination"; it had, he claimed, "greatly reduced percentage of disability from this cause."

Nonetheless, Taft thought it necessary to distance himself from it: it was an "army police measure outside our jurisdiction; military necessity." He also argued for situational context: the policy was "better than futile attempts at total suppression in oriental city of 300,000, producing greater evil."[115] According to purity reformer Wilbur Crafts, Taft's admission had been deliberately withheld from the War Department for six days, thereby allowing MacArthur's denial to command headlines.[116]

By the early months of 1901 the War Department adopted a policy of engagement with the social purity activists, meaning an open admission and defense of inspection. MacArthur's carefully worded reply came only on February 4 and, "in view of the very considerable number of . . . protests," was "put in type" for mass circulation. He accused the critics of regulation of being "misled as to the facts upon which they comment," with "a very imperfect information of general conditions in the Orient," and of failing to take into consideration "the disturbed conditions incident to military occupation and the state of war here prevailing." Prostitutes were not "licensed" in the Philippines, he stated, nor charged for a landing permit upon entry. Indeed, women "discovered to be prostitutes" were prohibited from landing unless they could demonstrate "a prior legal residence" and prove that they would "not be a cause of disorder in the community." Against the accusation that the army had actively facilitated the immigration of prostitutes, MacArthur boasted that "many prostitutes have been deported from the islands."[117]

MacArthur dedicated only four extremely delicate sentences to a description of what he admitted was the military's medical inspection of prostitutes. But he cast these inspections in the light of other "sanitary regulations particularly necessary in the tropics," such as those directed against smallpox and bubonic plague. It was a sign of his relative embattledness that MacArthur did not defend inspections in principle but resourcefully accumulated protective layers of exception around them. There was temporal exception, the fact that the wartime military government had been "necessarily one of emergency." There was situational exception, the fact that Manila, as the army's central entry and departure point, housed sixty-five thousand soldiers "in the prime of life" and "remotely removed from the restraining influences that might be exercised over them by their home surroundings." U.S. colonial exceptionalism with respect to the rest of Asia provided MacArthur a way to refocus attention away from Manila, a city whose condition was "more remarkable in view of the general lack of moral tone pervading the seaports of the East."

While employing these exceptions, however, MacArthur insisted on the ubiquity and banality of the army's dilemma. Where critics had attempted to see in regulation a tragic and novel Europeanization and Orientalization of the United States, MacArthur recast it as the virtually universal solution to a virtually universal problem. "We have been confronted with a problem which has vexed modern civilization in both Europe and America," he wrote. The ongoing fact of conquest and "the method of life in Asiatic cities" had "furnished difficulties" in solving it that were "not so easy to overcome as those encountered in the United States or elsewhere where conditions are more settled." On the other hand, he claimed that comparable conditions in the Philippines and the United States justified the army's policies. Where reformers complained that the Manila police knew the locations of brothels, for example, this was "as true of Manila as of any city in the United States." MacArthur was "convinced that the city of Manila may to-day challenge a comparison as to its moral and orderly condition with any city of the United States." Indeed, he asserted, policies in Manila were superior to those in domestic U.S. municipalities. "No city in America and Europe, certainly none in Asia, can today vie with Manila in the good order and morality which have resulted from the practical measures adopted." MacArthur invited the army's critics to investigate "social conditions" in the Islands themselves, but he insisted that if they did so, they must "also visit other ports on the Asiatic coast for purpose of comparison." They should also, before leaving home, "acquaint themselves with the statistics and conditions in regard to the social evil[s] which obtain in cities of the United States of the same population as Manila." Having done so, he was sure they would reassess the U.S. Army as a "civilizing agent" and come to accept "temporary expedients to . . . meet the emergent conditions presented."

In the wake of MacArthur's announcement the "abolition" campaign reached a standstill in mid-1901. Social purity, suffrage, and "anti-imperialist" petitioning against regulated vice together had achieved only a public admission, if one that wore its rhetorical weakness on its sleeve. Early 1902, however, would see changes underway in the metropole, largely brought about by the Washington-based efforts of suffragist and social purity activist Margaret Dye Ellis. Ellis had made appeals before the Woman's National Council and Suffrage Association to secure strong antiregulation resolutions and combined these appeals with a dramatic new tactic. At both meetings she widely circulated what she claimed was the "official registration book issued by the U.S. authorities" to a "child prostitute" with the somewhat implausible name "Maria de La Cruz" (which reformers were careful to translate). According to the suffrage press, the book contained regular inspection records and a photograph, "the portrait of a girl seemingly about twelve years old, with a childlike face and big, pathetic dark eyes." Around February 17, 1902, Ellis apparently left copies of "this dreadful little book" with every member of the Congressional Committee on the Philippines. Emphasizing women's political participation, suffrage editors claimed that "circulars left at the homes of the Congressmen fell into the hands of their wives and stirred them to womanly indignation."[118] More probably, they had been widely circulated among social purity networks and provoked an avalanche of letters to the War Department.

Over the next two months Root and Roosevelt would both appear to dramatically reverse course, from one of defensive admission to one of forthright condemnation. In March 1902 the opponents of regulated vice at last got their American Wolseley order, from Roosevelt himself. On March 18 he issued an order directed to the attention of "the officers and enlisted men in the army, especially those serving in the tropics." Roosevelt's conclusion was identical to Wolseley's and some of the latter's statements directly cribbed; Roosevelt was, however, far less elliptical and euphemistic than Wolseley on the centrality of venereal disease to the politics of vice. Roosevelt declared forthrightly that "the only really efficient way in which to control the diseases due to immorality is to diminish the vice which is the cause of these diseases." Venereal disease could be prevented through a sexually restrained and self-disciplined masculinity. It was the duty of regimental and company officers "to try by precept and example" to point out to soldiers "the inevitable misery and disaster which follow upon intemperance and upon moral uncleanliness and vicious living." Officers must themselves, of course, be models of "temperate and cleanly living." They must suggest, "using the utmost tact, discretion and good sense," that venereal disease was "almost sure to follow licentious living" and that it was "criminal folly" to believe that "sexual indulgence is necessary to health." The masculine honor, virtue, and purity of both the soldiers themselves and the nation that they represented were at stake. "As a nation we feel keen pride in the valor, discipline, and steadfast endurance of our soldiers," he concluded. Along with these virtues must go those of "self-restraint, self-respect, and self-control."[119]

Roosevelt's order was taken as a victory by the opponents of regulated vice. "The Administration has issued through the Secretary of War a stinging rebuke to the army officials who have introduced in the Philippines the European method of making social vice safe," crowed the *Outlook*. This "wholesome order," it anticipated, would "put an end to a scandal that existed of which we could scarcely credit when it was first charged two years ago."[120] Writing in July, the president of the APA declared that although the order was largely intended for soldiers abroad, "it will apply equally well to the soldiers at home, and equally, also, to people at home who are not soldiers." It would "apply to Washington as well as Manila."[121] Maurice Gregory, a London-based antiregulationist, called the Roosevelt order a "powerful memorandum." It was "a matter of congratulation" to antiregulationists "throughout the world" that there was "so much activity of thought on our question in the North American Continent at the present moment." Asserting Euro-American reform connections, Gregory opined it "cannot fail to re-act with highly beneficial effects on opinion in the Old World."[122]

The combination of domestic U.S. pressures and local resistance gave rise to the most sweeping transformation of the inspection system: the formalization of the regular inspection of U.S. soldiers. While this had been undertaken earlier in places like Jolo, it was made general policy on May 21, 1901, with General MacArthur's General Order No. 101, mandating the venereal inspection of U.S. soldiers in the Philippines for the first time. Commanding officers were to direct medical officers to make a "thorough physical inspection" of enlisted men twice a month, with "constitutional and local evidence of venereal infection . . . especially sought for." The men "must be stripped" for these exams, and those found infected with syphilis or "incapacitated" as a result of other venereal diseases would be sent to a hospital. Those still capable of service would be kept on a list and ordered to receive treatment "until cured." At the same time, the inspection of women would continue. In towns and barrios where "an infectious disease prevails in the command," army surgeons would be sent "to ascertain, if possible, its source," and "all women found infected" would be "placed under surveillance as will prevent the spread of the disease." The orders specifically called on the "aid of local municipal authorities" in carrying out the instructions; it should be "made plain" to these largely Filipino authorities that "by their hearty co-operation they will improve the hygienic conditions of their people."[123]

But acquiring elites' "hearty co-operation" was often difficult: the shift toward the inspection of U.S. soldiers had been undertaken at least in part because Filipino officials would not comply with U.S. medical mandates. When asked to answer for a disproportionately large number of venereal disease cases among U.S. troops in Dagupan in February 1903, for example,

Dr. M. A. De Laney conceded that he had found it nearly impossible to enforce existing ordinances on the "segregation" and "treatment" of prostitutes. He had informed the municipal *presidente* of the names and locations of prostitutes and had been "assured" that the presidente "would order the police to drive all infected women from the town." But no action had been taken; De Laney "received no reply" in response to subsequent inquiries. U.S. soldiers emerged, then, as the only remaining diseased population that medical officers could fully supervise.[124]

By mid-1902 it appeared that "regulated vice," as the reformers understood it, had ceased to exist. In reality, however, Root had merely discovered through Ellis the key to ending the issue: making regulation invisible. From the beginning, critics had had difficulty representing state "sponsorship" of vice symbolically. Crafts noted the ambiguities of "licensing" itself in his response to MacArthur's claim that prostitution was not "licensed, protected or encouraged"; the statement, he observed resentfully, "may have been true in a Pickwickian sense," given that prostitutes in Manila were "only certified and superintended."[125] Johnson's images of flag-draped brothels was seized on precisely because it seemed to make regulation powerfully visible, but even this was problematic. As one Lutheran minister who had worked in the islands, an army ally, had apparently noted, even if U.S. flags often did drape Manila's brothels (which he believed they did not), such a use was "not forbidden by law in the home land." Besides, "wherever our flag may be thus used it does not in any way signify that such houses were licensed by the Government."[126]

President Roosevelt himself was concerned by questions of visible vice and apparent government sponsorship. In mid-March 1902 he requested information from Manila authorities regarding the use of flags in brothels with the aim of curtailing such uses.[127] He received back word that Manila's chief of police, George Curry, had already acted. Recently seeing an American flag painted on the front of a brothel under renovation, he had ordered all precinct commanders "to see that the same was removed or obliterated at once and also to strictly prohibit the flying of flags or the painting of flags on any of the houses of ill-repute." Curry proudly reported that "there are no flags or paintings of flags at the present time in or on any houses of ill-fame in this city."[128] Where reformers made the regulation of prostitution a symbol for what was wrong with colonial empire in general, hauling down U.S. flags from brothels was a small price to pay for not having to pull them down from the Philippines as a whole.

Paul A. Kramer

If removing flags from brothels was one way to remove visible (if false) signs of regulated vice, another was to do away with other material signs of the system, such as inspection booklets. On February 19 Root cabled Luke Wright, governor-general of the Philippines, stating that he "considered [it] advisable" that "no fees be charged" to inspected prostitutes and "no certificates of examination given." Medical officers could "keep their own records of names, descriptions, residences, and dates of examination," and the system could continue "without the liability of a misunderstanding and the charge of maintaining a system of licensed prostitution."[129] This reform appears to have been widely adopted in the Philippines: as the General Order No. 101 made explicit, the inspection of women would be continued if the double standard had been surmounted. Social purity advocates noted this fact: the October 1902 report "More Trouble in Manila" contrasted Roosevelt's "admirable preachment" with the continuing "tacit toleration" of prostitution in Manila.[130]

Although it did not die out entirely, protest regarding regulation in the Philippines declined precipitously following the Roosevelt order. Part of the explanation for decreasing attention to the issue can be found in the character of lobbying that led up to the Roosevelt order. Ellis had, for example, apparently agreed to trade an end of agitation for Roosevelt's "preachment." Following a meeting with Secretary of War Root, J. T. Ellis jotted a memo to the effect that his wife "will be glad to make public the favorable showing you have so kindly given me regarding this whole Philippines business." By public "I mean through the W. C. T. U. organ & by circulating to her state superintends."[131] The following April, Bureau of Insular Affairs director Clarence Edwards confirmed the agreement with Ellis herself. Edwards understood that WCTU activists "now realized and appreciated that much misinformation from prejudiced . . . sources had gone abroad on this subject" and that Ellis was "today only anxious to gain the facts," facts that he openly admitted involved the continuation of inspection without fees or certificates.[132] The price of public victory, it appeared, had been failure in terms of actual "abolition."

But there were other contributing factors in the disappearance of the issue from public debate. First among these was an additional declaration made by Roosevelt, on July 4, 1902: a preemptive declaration of an "end" to the Philippine-American War. Social purity, suffragist, and "anti-imperialist" criticisms had defined empire in terms of "militarism," and militarism in terms of war and the mobilization of troops for war. Even though the most intrusive U.S. presence in the Philippines was still to come, the declaration of war's end and the return of a majority of U.S. troops curtailed many of these criticisms. Regulation and venereal disease had always been marginal to "anti-imperialist" criticism, and in the postwar period "anti-imperialists" would continue to criticize U.S. colonization on other grounds. For social purity advocates and suffragists it was perhaps seen as better strategy to prophesy darkly what soldiers would carry home with them before they actually returned. War Department defenders of regulation also took advantage of the shift from war to "peace." Edwards wrote Ellis, for example, that while the policy had been a military necessity during wartime, "when peace conditions bettered, the question resolved itself into one of sanitation and the application of sanitary law."[133] It was also no longer a "national" policy, exercised through the army—a main source of criticism—but a "municipal" one undertaken by specific city governments. Regulation in the Philippines was no longer the Contagious Diseases Acts, a national-imperial target, but a kind of St. Louis in Southeast Asia, whose government was far less subject to pressures from inside the United States.

In some ways the decline of purity activism on the issue was not so surprising. Reformers had won an important rhetorical concession from the president and the War Department; they had ended the double standard in medical inspections in the Philippines. To the extent that social purity activism had been opportunistic, chances to press the issue declined as the still-ongoing war dropped out of U.S. newspapers and public debate. At the same time, the civilian regime mobilized the very terms reformers themselves had held up against the army's inspection regime: the colonial state itself—even while it continued inspections—would be the guarantor of uplift, morality, and national exceptionalism.[134]

The intertwined histories of military occupation, sexual labor, disease control, and moral politics were central to the advent of U.S. overseas empire. They would continue to unfold together darkly across the "American century." From Puerto Rico to South Korea, military empire would both outrun America's moral imperium and undermine many of its foundations.[135] The military-prostitution complex would continue to be marginalized in an effort to protect moral justifications of U.S. power overseas, although a critical awareness of its character and costs would develop under the impetus of anticolonial and feminist movements.[136] The necessary entanglements of sexual and imperial politics had been foretold at the turn of the century by a grim soldiers' joke. U.S. soldiers found with venereal disease in the Philippines had been given a nickname by their comrades: "Rough Riders."[137] The joke turned potential emasculation by disease into a marker of masculinity and, possibly, legitimated aggressive or coerced sex. But it also suggested that these soldiers connected the politics of sexuality to the politics of empire. In renaming their comrades in this way, soldiers also cast the invasion of Cuba during the Spanish-Cuban-American War and, presumably, the invasion of the Philippines in which they were engaged, as acts of "rough" sex. While not without their pleasures for imperial soldiers and nations, such invasions also brought with them innumerable dangers. The character of those dangers, and the question of who would suffer them, would continue to haunt the rough ride of empire.

NOTES

My thanks to Judith Walkowitz, Richard Meixsel, Martha Hodes, Dirk Bönker, Gabrielle Spiegel, Philippa Levine, Ann Stoler, Nancy Cott, Daniel Rodgers, Ken DeBevoise, Caleb McDaniel, and Katherine Hijar for their comments and criticisms. Any errors are my own.

1. The southern Philippines, never fully conquered by the Spanish, remained under the control of powerful Muslim datus; U.S. military strategy against the Philippine Republic depended in part on the prevention of war between U.S. and Muslim forces until after the Republic had been defeated.

2. On March 5, 1902, the adjutant of the 23rd Infantry sent excerpts from reports by Rev. C. Guy Robbins, Private Adrian B. Trench, William B. Johnson, and Rev. A. B. Leonard pertaining to regulation in Jolo, with requests for a response; approximately thirty officers responded, including Sweet. The facts surrounding Sweet's removal remain unclear. Sweet's self-defense was accompanied by the claim this "most annoying and aggravating trial" had led to "mental, physical nervous strain and overwork," health breakdown and a return to the United States "to save my life" (Owen J. Sweet to Commanding Officer [23rd Infantry], March 12, 1902, RG 94/417937/B, National Archives and Records Administration, Washington, D.C. [hereafter NARA]).

3. Owen Sweet to Adjutant General, Feb. 6, 1902, RG 94/417937/B, NARA.

4. The existing literature on the Philippine-American War details both combat history and the politics of the war, but it contains little or nothing regarding on-the-ground issues of gender, sex, and prostitution. See Miller, *"Benevolent Assimilation"*; Shaw and Francia, *Vestiges of War*; Linn, *The Philippine War, 1899–1902*; Linn, *The United States Army and Counterinsurgency in the Philippine War, 1899–1902*. For an account of venereal disease among U.S. troops at Camp Stotsenburg in the early twentieth century see Meixsel, *Clark Field and the U.S. Army Air Corps in the Philippines, 1919–1942*, 78–85.

5. According to one account regulations mandating the venereal inspection of prosti-

tutes had been imposed during the Civil War among Union troops stationed in Memphis and Nashville. See Siler, *The Prevention and Control of Venereal Diseases in the Army of the United States of America*, 72. My thanks to Richard Meixsel for identifying this source.

6. For a review of the literature on exceptionalism see Rodgers, "Exceptionalism." For recent efforts to internationalize the study of U.S. history see Bender, *Rethinking American History in a Global Age*.

7. On interimperial connection see Kramer, "Empires, Exceptions, and Anglo-Saxons"; Bönker, "Admiration, Enmity, and Cooperation." On the need to examine metropole and colony in a single analytic field see Stoler and Cooper, "Between Metropole and Colony." For an exemplary transnational history of the social welfare state see Rodgers, *Atlantic Crossings*.

8. Ann Laura Stoler draws such "indirect" connections between historical forms and argues for the irreducibility of "the intimate" in the making of empire in her "Tense and Tender Ties." For a critique see Kramer, "Are All Unhappy Families Alike?"

9. For a comparative, rather than interimperial, perspective on regulation see Pivar, "The Military, Prostitution, and Colonial Peoples."

10. See esp. Rosenberg, "Gender"; Kaplan, "Manifest Domesticity"; Hoganson, *Fighting for American Manhood*; Renda, *Taking Haiti*; Wexler, *Tender Violence*. Vicente Rafael discusses intersections of domesticity and imperialism in the Philippines in "Colonial Domesticity: Engendering Race." Laura Briggs explores the politics of prostitution and regulation in the context of Puerto Rico in *Reproducing Empire*, chap. 2.

11. For a useful survey of the historiography of prostitution see Gilfoyle, "Prostitutes in History."

12. For the definitive work on the politics of prostitution and regulation in the British Empire see Levine, *Prostitution, Race, and Politics*. See also Ballhatchet, *Race, Sex, and Class under the Raj*.

13. Walkowitz, *Prostitution and Victorian Society*; Spongberg, *Feminizing Venereal Disease*. On the treatment of venereal disease see Brandt, *No Magic Bullet*.

14. For prostitution policy in Puerto Rico during this period, for example, see Findlay, *Imposing Decency*, chap. 3.

15. For the best accounts of venereal disease and prostitution in the Philippines see De Bevoise, *Agents of Apocalypse*, 69–93; De Bevoise, "A History of Sexually Transmitted Diseases and HIV/AIDS in the Philippines."

16. See Tyrrell, *Woman's World/Woman's Empire*, esp. chap. 9.

17. On attempts at municipal regulation in the nineteenth-century United States see Burnham, "Medical Inspection of Prostitutes in America in the 19th Century."

18. See Andrew and Bushnell, *The Queen's Daughters in India*. On the investigation and its impact see Burton, *Burdens of History*, 157–64.

19. See Sawyer, *The Inhabitants of the Philippines*, 114.

20. Neuens, quoted in Shibley, *Momentous Issues*, 180.

21. Judson, *The New Era in the Philippines*, 107.

22. Terami-Wada, "Karayuki-San of Manila: 1890–1920," 287–316.

23. Quoted in Hazlett, "A View of the Moral Conditions Existing in the Philippines."

24. Scully, "Prostitution as Privilege"; Scully, "Taking the Low Road to Sino-American Relations."

25. On prostitution in the nineteenth-century Philippines see Camagay, *Working Women of Manila in the 19th Century*; Dery, "Prostitution in Colonial Manila"; Bankoff, *Crime, Society, and the State in the Nineteenth-Century Philippines*, 26–27, 41–44.

26. The regulation of prostitution took place within a broader context of ad hoc medical and public health institution building. By September 1898 the U.S. Army had established two reserve hospitals in Manila, and an interim Board of Health under military authorities would begin establishing sanitation and health-care policies, overseeing special hospitals for smallpox and leprosy, as well as venereal disease. See Anderson, "Colonial Pathologies," esp. chaps. 1–2.

27. Robert Hughes to Adjutant General, U.S. Army, Feb. 7, 1902, RG 350/2039/8 ½ (Box 246), National Archives and Records Administration, College Park, Md. [hereafter NARA-CP].

28. Philippa Levine similarly argues for the local adaptations of venereal inspection regimes in the British Empire and important variations between them. See Levine, *Prostitution, Race, and Politics*, 51.

29. Maj. Gen. Arthur MacArthur to Adjutant General of the Army, Feb. 4, 1901, RG 94/343790 (Box 2307), NARA.

30. De Bevoise, *Agents of Apocalypse*, 80–81.

31. Taylor, *The Philippine Insurrection against the United States, 1899–1903*, 194–95.

32. Albert Todd to Acting Adjutant General, May 16, 1901, in Davis, *Report on the Military Governor of the City of Manila, P.I., from 1898–1901*, 264.

33. Charles Lynch to President, Board of Health, May 18, 1901, ibid., 267.

34. Robert Hughes to Adjutant General, U.S. Army, Feb. 7, 1902, RG 350/2039/8 ½ (Box 246), NARA-CP.

35. Frank S. Bourns to R. P. Hughes, Nov. 2, 1898, Enclosure 41, in Davis, *Report on the Military Governor of the City of Manila, P.I., from 1898–1901*, 261–62.

36. Warwick Anderson emphasizes the notion of Filipinos as "reservoirs" of disease; see Anderson, "Immunities of Empire."

37. Flexner, "Medical Conditions Existing in the Philippines." This was also true of their longer report, published in the following year: Flexner and Barker, "Report of a Special Commission Sent to the Philippines by the Johns Hopkins University to Investigate the Prevalent Diseases of the Islands."

38. They did make passing reference to the San Lazaro hospital, with its "one ward devoted to the treatment of venereal diseases among the native prostitutes" (Flexner, "Medical Conditions Existing in the Philippines," 166).

39. Albert Todd to Acting Adjutant General, May 16, 1901, in Davis, *Report on the Military Governor of the City of Manila, P.I., from 1898–1901*, 264–66.

40. Between March 1 and May 15, 1901, the Board of Health reported a 52 percent profit. Maj. Charles Lynch to President, Board of Health, May 18, 1901, ibid., 269.

41. Ibid., 267–68.

42. According to U.S. Army doctors, European and American prostitutes largely avoided what they perceived as stigmatizing inspection by U.S. Army doctors, preferring instead to be inspected by private physicians.

43. Maj. Charles Lynch to President, Board of Health, May 18, 1901, in Davis, *Report on the Military Governor of the City of Manila, P.I., from 1898–1901*, 268.

44. Philippa Levine emphasizes the ambiguities of brothels as spaces; see Levine, "Erotic Geographies."

45. Maj. Ira C. Brown to Acting Adjutant General, May 16, 1900, in Davis, *Report on the Military Governor of the City of Manila, P.I., from 1898–1901*, 276.

46. Ibid., 275.

47. Ibid. This effort was undertaken shortly afterward, and a vice district was inaugurated. See "Must Move Out to Adjust Social Evil," *Manila Freedom*, Aug. 31, 1900, RG 350/2039 (Box 246), NARA-CP. On the district and its eventual suppression see Dery, "Prostitution in Colonial Manila," 481–82.

48. Brown to Acting Adjutant General, May 16, 1900, in Davis, *Report on the Military Governor of the City of Manila, P.I., from 1898–1901*, 276.

49. The origins of this policy in the U.S. colonial context remain obscure. Prostitutes in Singapore were also photographed by officials there for purposes of identification, although more research is needed before any conclusions about intercolonial borrowing can be made. See Warren, *Ah Ku and Karayuki-San*, 100–101, 108–9.

50. Maj. Charles Lynch to President, Board of Health, May 18, 1901, in Davis, *Report on the Military Governor of the City of Manila, P.I., from 1898–1901*, 266–67.

51. R. R. Stevens to Adjutant, March 25, 1902, RG 94/417937/B, Enclosure 3, NARA.

52. J. A. Moore to Adjutant, March 7, 1902, RG 94/417937/B, Enclosure 13, NARA.

53. E. B. Pratt to Adjutant, March 11, 1902, RG 94/417937/B, Enclosure 17, NARA. See also C. E. Hampton to Adjutant, March 14, 1902, RG 94/417937/B, Enclosure 19, NARA. One civilian physician in Zamboanga complained for years that this lucrative source of revenue was a corrupt monopoly, but he was rebuffed by army officials; see letter from Dr. A. T. Short, October [no date] 1908, RG 94/1481399, NARA.

54. R. R. Stevens to Adjutant, March 25, 1902, RG 94/417937/B, Enclosure 3, NARA.

55. C. E. Hampton to Adjutant, March 24, 1902, RG 94/417937/B, Enclosure 19, NARA.

56. R. C. Croxton to Adjutant, March 10, 1902, RG 94/417937/B, Enclosure 21, NARA.

57. W. H. Sage to Adjutant, March 13, 1902, RG 94/417937/B, Enclosure 5, NARA.

58. W. A. Kent to Adjutant, March 6, 1902, RG 94/417937/B, Enclosure 27, NARA.

59. W. H. Sage to Adjutant, March 13, 1902, RG 94/417937/B, Enclosure 5, NARA.

60. H. C. Bonnycastle to Adjutant, March 8, 1902, RG 94/417937/B, Enclosure 28, NARA.

61. D. B. Devore to Adjutant, March 13, 1902, RG 94/417937/B, Enclosure 24, NARA; J. H. Sutherland to Adjutant, March 6, 1902, RG 94/417937/B, Enclosure, NARA. For reference

to an assault charge see R. C. Croxton to Adjutant, March 10, 1902, RG 94/417937/B, Enclosure 21, NARA.

62. R. R. Stevens to Adjutant, March 25, 1902, RG 94/417937/B, Enclosure 3, NARA.

63. C. E. Hampton to Adjutant, March 14, 1902, RG 417937/B, Enclosure 19, NARA.

64. Ibid.

65. W. A. Nichols to Commanding Officer, March 10, 1902, RG 94/417937/B, Enclosure 7, NARA.

66. R. C. Croxton to Adjutant, March 10, 1902, RG 94/417937/B, Enclosure 21, NARA.

67. H. G. Cole to Adjutant, March 12, 1902, RG 94/417937/B, Enclosure 22, NARA.

68. Ibid.

69. On the cholera epidemic that immediately followed the war see De Bevoise, *Agents of Apocalypse*, 175–84; Ileto, "Cholera and the Origins of the American Sanitary Order in the Philippines."

70. Quoted in De Bevoise, *Agents of Apocalypse*, 89.

71. Ibid., 90.

72. Quoted ibid., 89.

73. U.S. missionaries in the Philippines, for example, often complained of the "querida problem," the widespread cohabitation of U.S. soldiers with Filipino women during and after the war. The issue involved inseparable race, gender, and class elements: ordinary U.S. soldiers were forbidden from bringing over U.S. wives, while Filipino-American unions raised fears of moral and racial degeneration through "miscegenation." This topic, related to but also distinct from the present one, deserves treatment elsewhere. For a path-breaking exploration of these themes in the context of colonial Southeast Asia see Stoler, "Sexual Affronts and Racial Frontiers."

74. On Protestant missions to the Philippines see Clymer, *Protestant Missionaries in the Philippines, 1898–1916*.

75. Briggs, *The Progressing Philippines*, 122.

76. Ibid., 112.

77. See Johnson, "The Administration's Brothels in the Philippines." Johnson was a "Special Commissioner" for the *New Voice*. Information from this article was used by the American League in its pamphlet *The Crowning Infamy of Imperialism*, RG 94/417937 (Box 2307), NARA. Critics of the Philippine-American War identified themselves using "anti-imperialist" and "anti-imperialism," terms conceived in both negation and U.S. national exceptionalism that defined "imperialism" narrowly as territorial conquest. While I use their own term here, my own definition of imperialism includes broader forms of non-territorial control.

78. Twain, "Battle Hymn of the Republic (Brought Down to Date)," 41.

79. On social purity in this earlier period see Pivar, *Purity Crusade*. For the early twentieth century see Pivar, *Purity and Hygiene*. For a brief account of social purity protest regarding licensed vice in the U.S. colonies, see Tyrell, *Woman's World / Woman's Empire*, 213–17.

80. For moral reformers as pioneers of new lobbying tactics see Foster, *Moral Reconstruction*.

81. Janney, "Letter from Dr. O. Edward Janney."

82. Chapman, "The New Militarism and Purity," 2, 3.

83. Powell, "Lessons from India," 11.

84. Leeds, "Letter from Josiah W. Leeds," 7.

85. "The Schooling of a Camp," 24. The article quoted a letter from Garrison to the October 18, 1898, issue of the *Woman's Journal*.

86. See Burton, *Burdens of History*, chap. 5.

87. "Notes and Comments," *Philanthropist* 17, no. 2 (July 1902): 1.

88. "Notes and Comments," *Philanthropist* 15, no. 4 (Jan. 1901): 1.

89. Powell, "Appeal for Purity," 13.

90. Powell, "Lessons from India," 10.

91. *London Contemporary Review*, quoted in Powell, "Lessons from India," 11.

92. "London Congress of the International Federation for the Abolition of State Regulation of Vice," 18.

93. September 27, 1900, American Purity Alliance memorial to McKinley, RG 350/2045 (Box 246), NARA-CP.

94. "Memorandum Issued by the Commander-in-Chief," April 28, 1898 (London: Harrison and Sons, St. Martin's Lane, 1898), RG 94/343790 (Box 2307), NARA.

95. On the suffrage movement and feminism see Cott, *The Grounding of Modern Feminism*; and Kraditor, *The Ideas of the Woman Suffrage Movement, 1890–1920*.

96. See Tyrrell, *Woman's World/Woman's Empire*.

97. Hoganson, "As Bad Off as the Filipinos," 9–33. See also Sneider, "The Impact of Empire on the North American Woman Suffrage Movement"; Newman, *White Women's Rights*.

98. On imperialist attacks on "anti-imperialist" masculinity see Hoganson, *Fighting for American Manhood*, esp. chap. 7.

99. "A National Disgrace," 1–3.

100. Resolution by the Mississippi Woman Suffrage Association to William McKinley (circa Feb. 11, 1901), RG 94/343790 (Box 2307), NARA.

101. On "anti-imperialism" see Schirmer, *Republic or Empire*; Welch, *Response to Imperialism*; Zwick, *Anti-Imperialism in the United States*.

102. On "anti-imperialist" racism see Lasch, "The Anti-Imperialists, the Philippines, and the Inequality of Man." On "degeneration" in the debate on the Philippine-American War, see Hoganson, *Fighting for American Manhood*, chap. 6.

103. "It Yields Too Much!" *New York World*, Jan. 27, 1899. My thanks to Bonnie Miller for identifying this image.

104. "Uncle Sam before and after His Wish for Expansion," in Hoganson, *Fighting for American Manhood*, 182.

105. On Atkinson see Beisner, *Twelve against Empire*, chap. 5.

106. Atkinson was charged with indelicacy and inaccuracy and his pamphlet condemned as "The Venereal Disease Libel" in Chamberlin, *The Blow from Behind*, 83–91.

107. Atkinson, *The Cost of a Nation Crime*, 18.

108. Acting Secretary of War to Lillian Stevens, Oct. 8, 1900, RG 94/343790, NARA.

109. Elihu Root to William Howard Taft, Jan. 21, 1901, William H. Taft Papers, microfilm ed. M1584, ser. 21, special correspondence, vol. 2 (1900–1901), reel 640. My thanks to Richard Meixsel for identifying this source.

110. There were profound connections between the politics of antiregulation and temperance that cannot be fully explored here. Brothels and saloons were strategically conflated in ways that brought temperance and social purity reformers together: brothels would attract soldiers to drink, and saloons would attract soldiers to prostitution. "Regulated" brothels in the Philippines were imagined as parallel to the army canteens that permitted the sale of alcohol to soldiers. On the army canteen see Coffman, *The Old Army*, 359–61. On subsequent debates on opium traffic in the Philippines and its prohibition see Foster, "Models for Governing."

111. Teller, quoted in "No Beer for the Nation's Defenders," *New York Times*, Jan. 10, 1901, 5.

112. Root to Taft, Jan. 21, 1901 (see note 109).

113. Root to Taft, telegram, Jan. 15, 1901, Taft Papers, reel 640; H. C. Corbin to A. MacArthur, telegram, Jan. 16, 1901, Taft Papers, reel 640.

114. MacArthur, quoted in "Moral Conditions in the Philippines," 8.

115. Taft, quoted in "Moral Conditions in the Philippines," 9.

116. See "Moral Conditions in the Philippines," 8.

117. Maj. Gen. Arthur MacArthur to Adjutant General of the Army, Feb. 4, 1901. Quotations from MacArthur in this and the following two paragraphs are from this communiqué.

118. "Against 'Regulated' Vice," 1.

119. Roosevelt, quoted in "For Social Purity in the Army," 944–45.

120. "For Social Purity in the Army," 944–45.

121. Editorial, *Philanthropist*, 4.

122. "Conditions in America," 6–7.

123. General Order No. 101, issued May 21, 1901, RG 350/2039/26 (Box 246), NARA-CP. The mandated venereal inspection of U.S. soldiers would begin in the Philippines, Cuba, and Puerto Rico and later be institutionalized within the U.S. Army as a whole. See Maus, "A Brief History of Venereal Diseases in the United States Army and Measures Employed for their Suppression"; and Siler, *The Prevention and Control of Venereal Diseases in the Army of the United States of America*. This would be merely one instance in which reforms undertaken in colonial settings had implications for the formation of U.S. institutions more generally. See Kramer, "The World's Work."

124. M. A. De Laney to Chief Surgeon, Feb. 18, 1903, RG 112/26/88939/B (Box 614), NARA.

125. "Moral Conditions in the Philippines," 9.

126. Quoted in Geo. Davis to F. H. Maddocks, Nov. 24, 1900, RG 350/2045 (Box 246), NARA-CP.

127. George Cortelyou to Elihu Root, March 21, 1902, RG 350/2045/26 (Box 246), NARA-CP.

128. George Curry, report, May 6, 1902, quoted in W. Cary Langer to George Cortelyou, June 11, 1902, RG 350/2045/28 (Box 246), NARA-CP.

129. Elihu Root to Luke Wright, Feb. 18, 1902, RG 350/2039 (Box 246), NARA-CP.

130. "More Trouble in Manila," 4.

131. Secretary to the President to Elihu Root, note enclosed, Feb. 6, 1902, RG 350/2039/17 (Box 246), NARA-CP.

132. Clarence Edwards to Mary Dye Ellis, April 3, 1902, RG 350/2039/after-20 (Box 246), NARA-CP.

133. Ibid.

134. See Kramer, *The Blood of Government*.

135. See esp. Moon, *Sex among Allies*; and Bailey and Farber, *The First Strange Place*.

136. See esp. Sturdevant and Stoltzfus, *Let the Good Times Roll*; and Enloe, *Bananas, Beaches, and Bases*.

137. De Bevoise, *Agents of Apocalypse*, 86.

16

EMILY S. ROSENBERG

Ordering Others: U.S. Financial Advisers
in the Early Twentieth Century

Sidney De La Rue, a specialist in finance, led a substantial American advisory team that operated as a quasi-colonial administration in Liberia in the 1920s. His memoir, *Land of the Pepper Bird*, is primarily a tender description of Liberia's geography and diverse cultures. "The big house in Monrovia where I lived," he recalled, "stood high on the rocky ridge which forms the backbone of the city, and from the wide, three-storied verandas, one could look over most of the town."[1] Taking for granted that Liberia was America's territory, to be compared with the French and British colonial presence in neighboring areas of West Africa, De La Rue's imperial gaze produced intimate descriptions of West Africa; he exuded knowledge about Liberia and affection for its people.

The memoir provides only a brief glimpse of De La Rue's work as financial adviser. He writes that because of the country's foreign-debt burden and its World War I–related decline in exports, the Liberian treasury, which he oversaw, had "so little money that every dollar was earmarked months in advance and the possible revenues calculated to the last cent. Expenditures were administered with rigid economy and every necessary expense cut to the bone." He explains that Liberia's financial measures went beyond "better administration in collection and expenditure of revenue." Export duties on rubber, for example, were removed in an attempt to attract U.S. investment.[2]

De La Rue provides no further detail, however, about the financial authority he exercised in Liberia, about the large U.S. advisory presence there, or about any of the conflicts over power or money that arose among advisory personnel, the two governments involved, and the powerful U.S. banking and rubber interests. He does not mention, for example, that in 1926 private bankers, working with both the State Department and Firestone Rubber, refunded Liberia's debt or that this controversial refunding loan entrenched the Liberian government's indebtedness while helping Firestone establish its huge rubber-growing plantations, which became Liberia's main source of employment and exports for decades to come. Within his nostalgic rendering of Liberia, as in so much colonialist literature, memory has left traces of tender familiarity but has silenced discord, travail, or exploitation.[3] In his book De La Rue's personal breakdown, which ended his job there in 1929, has no mention.[4]

This chapter focuses on U.S. international financial advisers, such as De La Rue, who became influential purveyors of economic knowledge and practice during the first three decades of the twentieth century. In constructing their new profession, which specialized in the financial oversight of foreign countries, some of these advisers occupied positions analogous to that of colonial administrators.

The chapter weaves two themes. The first, which Ann Stoler has called the "politics of comparison," examines the process of financial advising as it spanned the boundaries of the "domestic" and the "foreign" and as it circulated among different kinds of territories and states.[5] Noticing the comparisons and models invoked in international financial work undertaken by Americans, I investigate some of the circuits of knowledge by which expert advisers attempted to order the affairs of others and some of the discourses within which they understood such ordering to be a scientific endeavor undertaken from benevolent and progressive motives. By employing the word *ordering*, I mean to suggest the twin goals of American financial administrators abroad: ordering in the sense of commanding and trying to assume custodial power, and ordering in the sense of seeking to impart rationalized systems of governance and production through various institutional mechanisms based upon standardization, classification, and hierarchy.

The chapter also analyzes how financial oversight in certain countries floundered on the frustrations of personal encounters in situations of unequal power and unclear authority. It explores the dilemmas arising from the close, yet inevitably distanced and hierarchical, relationships between advisers and the countries that hosted them. Most advisers, who were operating in unfamiliar political cultures, became entrapped in the contradictions of being both intimates and strangers. Their initially benevolent and scientific aspirations became overlaid with day-to-day tensions, political intrigue, and backlash. In a paradoxical process that never seemed anticipated or understood, ordering could breed disorder.

Emily S. Rosenberg

During the early twentieth century a diverse group of countries and territories came to be advised, administered, and sometimes policed by the United States. Desiring to stabilize strategic areas but wary of outright colonialism, U.S. administrations from Theodore Roosevelt through Warren G. Harding turned to financial receiverships to gain the benefits of fiscal control without incurring the burdens of empire.[6] The practice of using a receivership to install an advisory regime may be better understood by emphasizing the comparative contexts in which it arose.

Receiverships did not emerge as unusual, or even particularly innovative, forms of managerial control. Especially during the 1880s and the severe global downturn of the 1890s, installing receiverships had become a rather common way to deal with entities in financial distress. Receiverships offered mechanisms for insisting on fiscal reorganization, installing new forms of accounting, and establishing expert oversight. As part of what Alfred Chandler called the "managerial revolution," they were widely used in the domestic arena to bring order to bankrupt businesses.[7] Likewise, European imperial powers used receiverships to supervise collection of customs revenue and to impose fiscal restraints on dependent foreign territories. In cases of default on private loans in China, Turkey, Greece, and elsewhere during the late nineteenth century, for example, Britain helped create international debt administrations to collect revenue and administer payments to creditors.[8] In Egypt, which both Theodore Roosevelt and Woodrow Wilson regarded as a model of progressive colonialism, Britain responded to loan default and antiforeign demonstrations by having a British financial adviser assume control over all governmental operations. Receiverships were constructed within a discourse of assistance: foreign experts were supposed to fix insolvencies and institute sound fiscal and budgetary practices.

Like their European counterparts, U.S. leaders sought to improve order and discipline in what they regarded as unruly areas in their broadening sphere of influence. A receivership with a strong financial adviser provided the custodial institution that they hoped would oversee economic (and, therefore, social) uplift. In 1905, for example, U.S. policy makers, bankers, and Dominican officials worked out a financial receivership for the Dominican Republic, which was deeply in debt to European creditors. This "Dominican model," initially presented as a successful alternative to colonialism, was invoked subsequently in designing other financial supervisory missions.[9] American bankers were, of course, familiar with the legal form of a receivership from domestic experience, and it seemed no great leap to treat insolvent governments with the prescription used for insolvent companies.

The model for a receivership involved convincing an American private bank (or consortium) to extend a loan to a country that was a poor credit risk (perhaps in default) but that needed to borrow new money to consolidate debt and reorganize its finances. The loan would be secured by customs revenue, the primary source of income for most governments. To guarantee regular repayment of the debt, a financial adviser would be appointed and approved by the president of the United States as a condition of the loan, a stipulation that the bankers wanted because it seemed to indicate that the U.S. government itself would enforce repayment in case of future default. This official would collect the nation's receipts (hence the word *receivership*), presumably ensuring an honest accounting and loan payback. If the loan could cover past indebtedness and also provide for new expenditures on, say, public works and infrastructure, it might promote investment, economic growth, and social improvements. Refunding debt and having new money to spend could seem attractive to political elites, whose desire to spread patronage and influence could well outweigh their dislike for a foreign receivership.

Architects of this model for putting a country in receivership expressed their justifications in terms of rationality and benevolence. In their view receiverships represented an ordering that was the antithesis of imperialism, arising from markets and morality rather than from an imperial state's designs for territorial aggrandizement. President Roosevelt explicitly rejected any idea of turning the Dominican Republic into a colony, and many anti-imperialist newspapers endorsed his plan to help the country work its way out of default through a receivership.

Such receivership-and-advisory relationships on the Dominican model were subsequently installed in Liberia, Nicaragua, and Haiti before World War I. They were also pressed, though unsuccessfully, on China, Guatemala, Mexico, and several states in South America. With the economic dislocations of World War I, however, a customs receivership with limited power hardly seemed enough. Woodrow Wilson, embracing the British model of installing a strong financial adviser, demanded that the receiverships in Haiti, the Dominican Republic, Liberia, and Nicaragua all move beyond the collection of customs revenue to assume complete fiscal (and, in effect, governmental) authority. The attempt to expand the powers of financial advisers in Haiti and the Dominican Republic led to such civic unrest in those

Emily S. Rosenberg

countries that Wilson gained acquiescence only after establishing U.S. military rule over both countries. In Nicaragua and Liberia pliant governments accepted the enlarged advisory presence, which was then kept in power by the training and arming of local constabularies.[10] What had begun as a rather simple office, collecting customs revenue and making regular payments on a consolidated debt, expanded in these four countries into a full-fledged (except in name) colonial apparatus.[11]

After World War I a newly created post in the Department of State called the Economic Advisor worked tirelessly to use the receivership–financial adviser formula to stabilize additional foreign economies. In the early 1920s the idea of spreading economic expertise and currency stabilization through the receivership model seemed so familiar and promising that it became the principal U.S. foreign-policy strategy for dealing with a world recovering from the immense global disruption of the Great War. During the mid-1920s, U.S. experts, attached as a condition to loans, took advisory positions in Germany (under the Dawes Plan) and Poland. Bolivia contracted a loan attached to a three-person receivership. The other Andean countries (Colombia, Ecuador, Peru, and Chile) reversed the process and *invited* American advisers during the 1920s in hopes that the appearance of U.S. supervision over customs collection, taxation, banking, and currency would entice higher levels of private lending to their central governments. Although these four countries did not sign formal receivership agreements, which became increasingly controversial in Latin America, the idea that foreign loans and advisers went together had become so widespread that U.S. advisers (especially if they were known to have links to willing banks) were in great demand from foreign states seeking to float bonds.[12]

The justifications for introducing foreign advisers attached to loans emphasized the capacity of these experts to insure order and progress. The new field of international economics, shaped within discourses of professionalism, objectivity, science, and manliness, assumed that standard accounting-style solutions could be applied fairly uniformly across time and space.[13] Financial advisers seemed to represent a new, helping relationship that could benefit everyone by forging a stable international order.

In articulating these assumptions, economists often drew analogies between their profession and the medical profession, another science-based and increasingly masculinized domain. Inflation, like germs, could infect a body politic and sap its vigor. Indeed, American advisers regarded the dirty, inflated paper currencies that circulated in many poor countries to be, both literally and figuratively, an infectious agent that "money doctors" needed to address. The "sickness" involved the interrelated afflictions of excessive government debt, runaway inflation, default, and corruption of budgetary processes. The proposed antidotes were the establishment of gold-standard currencies strictly regulated by new central banks, a receivership for the collection of customs revenue, and strict oversight to ensure foreign-debt repayment. Generally, financial advisers sought greater administrative centralization and new accounting procedures, both essential to monitoring tax collection and expenditures.

By the 1920s the medical discourse for curing financial disarray had become so widespread that it framed nearly every discussion of advising. Edwin Kemmerer, who held a chair in international economics at Princeton University, was almost always introduced to a country as the "famed money doctor," and one can scarcely find any contemporary or academic treatment of Kemmerer that does not discuss his missions by using medical analogies. In 1926 the national secretary of the YMCA in Poland, for example, reported in his newsletter that "Dr. Kemmerer of Princeton has just been called in and he has made his report. The patient is by no means dead and with good nursing will soon be round and about as usual. The doctor prescribes remedies which will doubtless be taken."[14] Arthur Millspaugh's account of his advisory experience in Persia in the 1920s also invoked the familiar trope. "Persia's condition has often been likened to a disease," wrote Arthur Millspaugh. He recounted that a newspaper in Teheran greeted his mission with these words: "You are a physician called to the bedside of a very sick person. If you succeed, the patient will live. If you fail, the patient will die." He quoted a Persian radio speaker announcing that his country presented Millspaugh with a "wound worthy of a doctor like you and your American mission to operate on and cure." And he remembered proudly that, years later, President Franklin Roosevelt had referred to his mission as a "clinic."[15] It helped, perhaps, that advisers such as Kemmerer and Millspaugh held PhDs and, therefore, used the title of "Dr."

The casting of financial advising within a medical discourse had profound implications. It suggested the intimacies, yet the hierarchies, that might arise between doctor and patient. It drew a picture of a dependent relationship, fashioned with the patient's consent and for the patient's own good. It implied a tender ethic of caring and of curative powers.

The advisory discourse, in emphasizing the need to submit to the presumably universal medicine of fiscal discipline, however, also implied the incapacities of benighted others. By standardizing fiscal practices, advisers were to bridge the gulf between nations that seemed "civilized" and those that seemed "backward" or incompetently administered. The very presence of these foreign "doctors" therefore inscribed and reinforced cultural difference, especially where perceptions of racial difference came into play. The standardization implied in economic ordering and the bifurcation of cultural othering became twin processes that were, at once, both complementary and contradictory. The very notion of a profession of international economics arose, after all, simultaneously with the imperial mentality that characterized the early twentieth century.[16]

A QUESTION OF EMPIRE

Were financial receiverships and advising relationships the equivalent of empire? Where was the U.S. empire during this era? The answer, of course, depends on the discursive tradition within which the word *empire* is invoked. To most late-nineteenth-century Americans, the term *empire* involved overt control over and governance of territory; it conjured up images of an observable and named imperial presence. Various European countries, after all, had built and attempted to govern empires in the Americas since the sixteenth century. The United States itself had been born as part of a revolt against imperial taxes and restrictions on production and trade. Empire seemed to be an attribute of Old World mercantilism and represented much of what the United States, with its commitment to free-trade and limited government, stood against.

The expansion of globalized networks of trade and investment by the late nineteenth century prompted alternative ways of invoking the idea of empire. In America Charles Conant wrote that overcapacity in production, by necessitating larger markets to absorb excess investment capital and exports, established the "economic basis of imperialism." In Britain Hobson made (or borrowed) a similar argument, and V. Lenin turned the idea into a cardinal principle of Marxist theory. The equation between imperialism and the ever-expansionist needs of capitalism established a discourse of empire within an economic, rather than a strictly political, military, and territorial, context.

Although describing these two traditions of empire as "territorial" and "economic" greatly oversimplifies complex bodies of thought and historically contingent nuances in usage, it may provide one starting point for discussing American empire. I sometimes ask history students whether or not the United States had an empire. Almost all say yes. Then I ask them to locate and "name" it. I have a checklist that includes California, Puerto Rico, the Philippines, the Dominican Republic, Nicaragua, Mexico, Brazil, Standard/Exxon Oil facilities, Ford Motor plants, McDonalds franchises, the Internet, and so forth. No list of what constituted imperialism and what did not is the same, and for pretty obvious reasons. In America the word *imperialism* fails to convey any common meaning at all. Worse still, even if all respondents could agree to define *empire* as strictly a matter of territory, there would still be no consistency in response. Most students, like most Americans generally, have no idea at all which territories might or might not have had a heavy administrative presence exercised by the United States. Almost any citizen of England would know that India was part of the British Empire; almost any Dutch citizen would name Indonesia. But how many Americans would list Puerto Rico or the Philippines, both of which were colonies in name and law? How many understand that Cuba and Panama were protectorates? How many might claim that the United States had no empire at all? Or how many might claim that U.S. empire is everywhere? Being nowhere or everywhere, of course, both render the notion of empire so vague as to be nearly useless. And, in the middle of nowhere and everywhere, there is nothing even close to a map or chronology of U.S. empire on which citizens — or scholars — would agree.

The imprecision in the common understanding of the phrases "U.S. empire" or "U.S. imperialism" complicates how comparative imperial studies may be applied to the United States. Can the word *imperialism* stand for the expansion of U.S. influence, both public and private, anywhere on the globe? Where is the line dividing "influence" and "hegemony," on the one hand, from "empire," on the other? How might one untangle the discursive threads in words such as *imperialism, internationalism,* and *modernization*? Each of these terms may describe a similar interaction but cast it within a different narrative tradition. For example, the influence of international financial advisory missions may be described within a history of U.S. imperialism, of the spread of internationalist impulses, or of a modernizing and developmental ethos. Moreover, the word *empire* seems to be constituted in race and geography. Financial adviserships, for example, could be designed for any area of the world, including Europe, but they seem most akin to an imperial presence when they were located in tropical climates and among darker-skinned peoples. Would there be any way to sort out which of the many varied advisory arrangements in different places should fall under the term *imperialism* and which under the rubric of "international development"?

Within this complex tapestry of meanings the word *empire* appears and disappears and was invoked inconsistently by U.S. citizens of the early twentieth century.[17] Many proponents of financial advising, for example, styled themselves as anti-imperialists, claiming that they were substituting benign, uplifting commercial connections for imperialistic military force. Their critics (at home and abroad), who embraced the name "anti-imperialists," however, charged them with spearheading an "imperialistic" administrative presence that, in some cases, veered into military involvement. In short, a vigorous U.S. foreign-policy debate over imperialism, which reemerged during the 1920s, revolved around the definition of the term and around establishing who—those enabling financial receiverships and advisers or those opposing such arrangements—could claim the legacy of the nation's anti-imperialist heritage.[18] And this debate over whether financial advisory teams exemplify modernization or imperialism continues to shape historical scholarship as well. World-systems and dependency theorists have tended to label the economic ordering that integrated peripheral areas into capitalist metropoles "imperialism"; liberal or neoliberal theorists incline toward using the words *modernization* or *development*.

To map the invocations and refusals to invoke the word *imperialism* must remain beyond the scope of this essay. The complexity of drawing such a discursive map, however, helps highlight the challenges involved in bringing comparative colonial or postcolonial studies into U.S. history and the special advantages of looking, instead, toward what Stoler calls the transnational "circuits of knowledge production." Without getting unduly entangled in naming the time and place of the U.S. empire, one can examine the groups of Americans—such as the new professionals in the field of international finance—who sought to effect administrative changes around the world. A comparative perspective may highlight connections and comparisons that invoking the word *empire* might obscure.

THE DIFFICULTIES OF CLOSE ENCOUNTERS

Shelves of books and diverse interpretive schools have surrounded the advent of American overseas expansion during and after the War of 1898, particularly the acquisition of Hawaii; the establishment of formal colonies in

Puerto Rico, the Philippines, and Guam; and the imposition of protectorates in Cuba and Panama.[19] There are few historical studies or theoretical works, however, that broadly examine whatever happened to this enthusiasm for acquisition. Financial adviserships (which policy makers styled as anti-imperial because they did not involve possession or protection) were a seemingly more benign and certainly less controversial method of ordering others. Still, even these experiments in tutelage did not last. The various financial receivers and advisers that had been introduced from 1905 through the mid-1920s withered and were put aside, and the push to establish more of them, which had been so strong just after World War I, lasted only a few years. From about 1927 on, the administrations of Calvin Coolidge, Herbert Hoover, and Franklin Roosevelt backed away from pursuing new advisory commitments, sought to distance public policy from both private bankers and financial advisers, and tried to extricate the United States from commitments that had been made in more optimistic times. Why?

A variety of circumstances may help contextualize the U.S. government's ever-greater reluctance to introduce supervision through financial advisers attached to private loans.[20] One was related to what economists call the "lending cycle." Loan and advisory arrangements obviously spread more rapidly during the early uptick and middle stages of the cycle, as foreign governments sought to attract U.S. investment bankers by offering greater security for their loans and as bankers sought to find risk-reduced outlets for excess capital. This upward movement in the lending cycle coincided with an optimism about the benefits and transformative potential of foreign supervision. In the late 1920s, however, a weakening bond market and an increasingly shaky global economy accompanied worries about overextended levels of international indebtedness and the potential for loan default. With financial supervisors beginning to fear possible insolvency in their various countries, the relationships between government policy makers, international banking houses, and advised governments all became strained, as each sought to deflect blame onto the other.

In addition, domestic and transnational opposition to economic oversight of foreign territory grew. America's own anti-imperial heritage provided a language that oppositional elements adapted in order to shape a new anti-imperialist movement. Socialist ideologies, which identified bankers and economic supervision with imperialism, also contributed to a growing transnational anti-imperialist impulse. Advisory regimes had joined the fates of diverse peoples in the United States and in the far-flung jurisdictions in which advisers operated. Although no simple formula captured the nature of transnational coalitions that either supported or assailed these financial interconnections, homegrown and international anti-imperialists joined together in varied coalitions to argue that the United States had become deeply implicated in imperial control.[21] Just as they denounced British colonial presence in India, anti-imperialists of the 1920s also spoke out particularly against U.S. involvement in the Dominican Republic, Haiti, Nicaragua, and Liberia.

Moreover, resistance in various supervised countries also raised the moral and monetary costs of maintaining advisory missions. In Haiti, the Dominican Republic, and Nicaragua marines were called on to maintain control, and these military costs together with the costs of training local constabularies weighed on budgets. In the mid and late 1920s the dispatch of military forces to pacify Nicaragua and to bolster the position of U.S. administrators there began to claim American lives and to focus attention on the supervisory relationships that had been implanted largely out of the public eye. Many members of Congress responded by threatening to cut off funds for further military action. In the late 1920s, as anti-imperialist coalitions presented Nicaragua as the poster-child for an exploitative "dollar diplomacy," rising opposition among Congress, the public, and various transnational anti-imperialist groups forced President Calvin Coolidge to seek ways to lessen the direct involvement of the U.S. government in supervisory arrangements.[22]

There was also a less obvious, but perhaps more important, dynamic that I would like to explore at greater length. Simply put, after some years of experience with direct economic supervision over countries deemed to be economically and administratively unstable, policy makers concluded that advisory regimes did not work and, indeed, may have induced more instability than they cured. This conclusion remained almost completely invisible in public policy at the time and has hardly been emphasized in later historical accounts. To uncover it, we must look away from the public justifications for supervision and turn to reports (often confidential) about implementation. Examination of the close encounters involved in ordering others will help suggest what went wrong.[23]

Supervision involved face-to-face relationships among those, from both sides, who sought to guide the terms of governance. At this microlevel, what U.S. proponents of financial advisory regimes regarded as the scientific "reform" of economic systems became embedded in specific cultural interactions among people of often vastly different backgrounds and incommensurable circumstances. Economic supervision turned out to be not a matter of objective and universalized science, as the professionals had thought, but of the contingencies and the coercions of cultural encounter.[24]

These close encounters among *persons*—all trying to enlist others in whatever social, economic, or political project they sought to advance—show financial supervisory regimes as both tender and tense personal interactions. Initially cast as sympathy rather than power, advisers and their hosts spoke the language not of coercion but of assistance. Yet in the private and often hidden arena of personal connection, people on all sides maneuvered to convince or force culturally different associates to change their ways. When these interactions faltered, and they often did for a variety of obvious and not-so-obvious reasons, supervision became dysfunctional, and the entire project of uplift and stability began to break apart.

In looking at financial advisory regimes as close personal encounters in the wide variety of foreign territories in which they operated, the politics of comparison is again evident. Although foreign policy histories are generally organized according to regional geography, seeing the circuits that were designed to spread economic knowledge from a globalized, comparative perspective can reveal hitherto unnoticed networks. Advisers went from place to place. Arthur Millspaugh headed the advisory team in Persia and then in Haiti; Sidney De La Rue got his start leading the advisory mission in Liberia, and he also later went to Haiti. William Wilson Cumberland helped design and run the Central Bank in Peru, and he, too, then had stints in both Nicaragua and Haiti. The financial team of Edwin Kemmerer, which conducted the economic assessments leading to advisers in most Andean countries, also conducted missions in South Africa and Poland (and was besieged for advice by many others around the globe). Kemmerer and many others gained initial experience in the U.S. colony of the Philippines, which became an incubator and laboratory for America's globally oriented technical experts. Lesser accountants and financial experts of various kinds (taxation advisers, railroad engineers, customhouse managers, central bank and currency advisers, and the like) appear again and again in different places and circumstances.[25] Often military and policing advisers sent by the War Department accompanied the financial missions. An American (Colonel H. Norman Schwartzkopf) commanded the gendarmerie that U.S. army officers trained in Persia; U.S. commanders trained a "frontier force" to quell rebellion in Liberia and formed constabularies in Nicaragua, the Dominican Republic, and Haiti.[26]

Emily S. Rosenberg

U.S. financial and military advisers moved from continent to continent, apparently seeing their expertise as essentially detached from culture and applicable anywhere. In these endeavors advisers drew from, and often saw their motives as more benevolent than, the colonial agents of other powers.

After examining the many and diverse places that hosted receivership-advisory missions, a rather consistent pattern of complications emerges. Close encounters (especially when national revenues and expenditures were involved) seldom bred mutual respect or good working relationships. Comparative international histories (and histories of comparative colonialism) may be illuminated by examining the common irritants and failures that recurred in the private diplomatic reports related to supervisory regimes. Policy makers came to question whether on-the-spot supervision accomplished the initial goals of spreading "scientific" fiscal reforms, advancing economic and social stability, and cementing friendly ties with the United States. A few of the recurrent tensions may be detailed.

Advisers tended to emphasize the irresponsibility of the governmental personnel whom they advised. Most advisers complained about "graft" both in customs collection and in expenditures on public works. Venal, backward governments, in their reports, frustrated efficient and scientific accounting and administrative methods. Almost all denounced what they regarded as excessive spending and the continual pressure to use borrowed money for "unproductive" purposes. The view that host governments were not sufficiently appreciative and receptive to the help offered by advisory regimes often prompted a kind of personal anger and resentment on the part of supervisory personnel. Millspaugh in Persia complained that his advice was generally disregarded and that his mission was "worse than useless" because it provided "window dressing" giving the "false impression that reform has been undertaken."[27] These emotions frequently surfaced in the rather constant demands that the U.S. government should take a more active and public role in forcing obedience and respect. The strains between advisers and host countries could easily become displaced into stresses between demanding advisers and more distanced State Department personnel.[28]

Alongside the generally derogatory views of host governments that advisory personnel often voiced in their reports, however, are traces of a very different interpretation. State Department files are replete with charges leveled against the advisers themselves, including incompetence, overpayment, and corruption. Motivations for such charges (as for the charges leveled against host countries) may have been politically self-serving, of course, but the larger context of such complaints should be considered. There was a great shortage in the United States of people skilled in the emerging professional fields of accountancy and finance, and there were, as yet, few measures of professional accreditation for advisory work.[29] Talented economists who specialized in finance were in strong demand as teachers and consultants domestically, and few wanted to derail their careers by going to some remote outpost where language, climate, culture, and often appearance (the State Department maintained a policy of appointing only white advisers, even in Liberia, which was ruled by descendants of American slaves) ensured that life might be lonely and accomplishments professionally unrecognized. One of the reasons why advisers recycled through many positions in different countries was precisely because there were so few people available at all for such positions. In theory we might label advisory personnel as carriers of "circuits of knowledge," but it is very hard to ascertain the value of the "knowledge" those circuits really carried.

There are many examples. A large private bank loan to Bolivia in 1922 installed a three-man receivership appointed by the bankers (and not approved by the president of the United States, as was done in some other loans). Later, when Bolivia could not meet its payments on the loan, an internal State Department investigation reported that all three men lacked rudimentary knowledge of accounting and were incompetent. A similar internal review of personnel in the large advisory regime that a U.S. Marine guard kept installed in Nicaragua came to similar conclusions. It privately reported to the department that the administration of the U.S. high commissioner in Nicaragua, Roscoe Hill, was defective and exercised little audit control. In Persia the U.S. chargé reported that most of the advisory mission staff had no previous experience in the offices they filled, and three of them held military titles, a connotation that reportedly infuriated many Persians.[30]

Sometimes the State Department reluctantly supported these unpopular or incompetent advisers out of fear that not doing so would damage U.S. prestige. Despite extremely negative reports about Arthur Millspaugh in Persia, for example, the State Department continued publicly to support his mission because officials feared that U.S. economic interests in the region might otherwise suffer. And the shortage of advisers who would go to Haiti was so severe that despite Millspaugh's questionable performance, the department subsequently hired him to become Haiti's financial adviser. There he fought bitterly with the head of the U.S. military government, as he had with the Shah in Persia, and was finally quietly removed. The department delayed removal of Hill in Nicaragua for years on the grounds that it needed to stand fast and show no weakness in face of Nicaraguan demands for his ouster.[31]

The fact or the appearance of profiteering by advisers presented yet another problem. Although many of the advisers preached economy to the governments they advised, their own salaries, perks, and severance packages seemed unbelievably lavish to their hosts. Some of this problem, of course, stemmed from the differentials in pay scales between the United States and poorer nations. The collector-general in Nicaragua made the huge (even in the United States) salary of fifteen thousand dollars per year and enjoyed commodious housing and lengthy all-expense-paid leaves of absence each year. A State Department consultant, in a personal, confidential letter to the secretary of state wrote that the collector-general "performs comparatively little work" and "on no conceivable grounds" can justify his high compensation.[32]

Even where there were no charges of corruption and where salaries did not become an issue, cultural and/or policy differences could limit the effectiveness of advisory missions. The American agent general attached to the Dawes loans of 1924 in Germany, S. Parker Gilbert, reportedly established few social connections in five years' time in office. Dispatches to the State Department described him as having learned little German and living in relative isolation, even from British officials. Part of this characterization, however, might have stemmed from his earnest effort to staunch the huge flow of lending into Germany, a stimulant that many Germans welcomed but that Gilbert rightly predicted would lead eventually to default and collapse. Relative isolation may have allowed him greater freedom to speak his mind and (in his view) do his job. Nevertheless, by the end of the 1920s the Office of the Agent General was terminated as the bankers, the State Department, and even Gilbert himself had come to believe it was ineffective. Gilbert felt that German critics of his office had been able to use him as a scapegoat for economic problems rather than taking responsibility themselves for necessary (but unpopular) measures.[33]

In Liberia, especially, cultural and climatic differences took their toll. Here, as elsewhere, the large U.S. administrative presence fought with local officials over who had ultimate authority for budgetary and administrative decisions. Advising turned into a fight over jurisdiction. More important, advisers lasted only a short time before suffering nervous breakdowns, chronic illness, or such severe alcoholism that they had to return home.[34]

As advisers cycled in and out of Monrovia, always at the expense of the Liberian government, State Department officials clearly grew exasperated and sought ways to terminate the advisory regime (whose existence, like so many others, was prescribed by the terms of a long-term loan contract with bankers). In 1929, after De La Rue had experienced a nervous breakdown, the incoming financial adviser reported that incompetents filled most advisory jobs. The auditor, he wrote, had no auditing experience, was an alcoholic, and his only financial records were a list of bank deposits. Next to this information the assistant secretary of state wrote "damn!"[35]

There were, of course, many differences among the advisory structures and personal advisory relationships that came into being between 1905 and 1930 and then mostly dissolved during the turmoil of the 1930s. But one similarity emerges from nearly all: the circuits of financial knowledge and uplifting economic "science," which were assumed to be part of an enlarging structure of international financial advising, did not work well. Strained by the variety of tensions emerging from close cultural encounters, loan-advisory relationships produced neither the anticipated economic benefits (namely stability) nor the bonds of sympathy that assistance had been presumed to forge. Anti-U.S. sentiments often intensified the condition of chronic instability, and vice versa.[36]

THIS CHAPTER, FOCUSING on U.S. financial advisory regimes that operated internationally during the first three decades of the twentieth century, has examined some of the processes and problematics involved in ordering others. It advances the framework of "ordering"—taking on administrative duties (both command and rationalization) developed through a politics of comparison within global networks of knowledge that accentuated particular ideas (and hierarchies) of expertise, science, race, and gender. The word *imperialism* is an insufficient analytical category for this investigation because it often acts discursively to separate the domestic from the foreign; because, in U.S. history, it designates no commonly understood time and space; and because it may keep historical discussions about U.S. relations with some states (in Europe, for example) deceivingly distanced from those involving relations with others (for example in the Caribbean).

The face-to-face encounters of these ordering relationships, although predicated on notions of science, objectivity, and universalism, sharpened problems arising from national, ethnic, and cultural difference. They invariably gave rise to contests over power and provoked resentments about who

Emily S. Rosenberg

wielded authority. The initially tender, but increasingly tense, personal encounters between advisers and their hosts in diverse countries located in Latin America, Africa, and Europe help to explain the rather rapid demise of U.S. advisory structures after the mid-1920s and, perhaps, the subsequently broad support for the internationalized bodies that were created in 1944 to help "stabilize" the post–World War II world. Those postwar institutions, the International Monetary Fund and the International Bank for Reconstruction and Development (later called the World Bank), still sought to order the globe to facilitate trade and investment; they still had U.S. capital at their center; and they, too, slowly evolved elaborate systems through which loans leveraged supervisory authority. They offered, however, the buffer of a more internationalized, more bureaucratic, and less personalized approach. U.S. financial receiverships of the first three decades of the twentieth century provided a kind of halfway house between the territorial imperialism of the turn of the century and the American economic hegemony that a new variety of national and international institutions helped spread globally after World War II.

NOTES

1. De La Rue, *Land of the Pepper Bird*, 47.

2. Ibid., 236–38.

3. Buell, *The Native Problem in Africa*, by contrast, presented a scathing indictment of Liberia's exploitation and touched off considerable controversy about America's role in Liberia in the late 1920s. Sundiata, *Black Scandal*, 44–47, summarizes the controversy.

4. Trouillot, *Silencing the Past*, presents a broader examination of how power shapes remembering and forgetting.

5. See Stoler, "Tense and Tender Ties." On placing U.S. expansion in a global context see also Bender, *Rethinking American History in a Global Age*; Adas, "From Settler Colony to Global Hegemon"; Tyrrell, "American Exceptionalism in an Age of International History"; and Go and Foster, "Introduction." Rodgers, *Atlantic Crossings*, examines the intellectual and institutional exchanges related to early-twentieth-century social politics, including models that affected imperial practices.

6. This chapter involves a reconceptualization of some of the material in my book *Financial Missionaries to the World*. For more extensive citations, particularly to archival material, please see the portions of the book cited below.

7. Chandler, *The Visible Hand*. See also Skowronek, *Building a New American State*, on government's embrace of administrative expertise; and Sklar, *The United States as a Developing Country*. Although improving the management in bankrupt domestic compa-

nies had certain superficial similarities to stabilization programs carried out by financial advisers abroad, there were significant differences. Unlike companies, after all, countries had citizens. Business receiverships did not have to worry about national welfare or political process. Moreover, domestic business receiverships generally provided temporary assistance to people who were culturally similar to the overseeing experts. Advisers to the treasuries of foreign countries, by contrast, sought long-term oversight that could expand into more and more administrative areas and open the charge of "imperialism."

8. Feis, *Europe, the World's Banker, 1870–1914,* 289–92, 313–15, 383–97.

9. See Veeser, *A World Safe for Capitalism,* 126–54; and Rosenberg, *Financial Missionaries to the World,* 31–60.

10. Were those who fought against the United States and its client regimes "bandits" (as U.S. officials called them), or were they factions participating in localized contests over land or power, or were they "patriots" upholding the sovereignty of their nation against invasion? Framing and labeling the actors in these early-twentieth-century military actions raises important issues about history and memory. Examples of contrasting frames may be found in Boot, *The Savage Wars of Peace,* which presents a relatively positive view of American "peacekeeping"; Langley, *The Banana Wars,* which is more critical of the United States; and Calder, *The Impact of Intervention;* Plummer, *Haiti and the Great Powers;* and Schroeder, "The Sandino Rebellion Revisited." Calder, Plummer, and Schroeder present anti-U.S. movements in the Dominican Republic, Haiti, and Nicaragua, respectively, less as "banditry" or heroic "nationalism" than as phenomena rooted in longer-standing local and regional rivalries. For a relevant reflection on "banditry" see Ileto, "Outlines of a Nonlinear Employment of Philippine History."

11. Rosenberg, *Financial Missionaries to the World,* 61–96. For an examination of various forms of colonial control, placed in comparative perspective, see Osterhammel, *Colonialism.*

12. Rosenberg, *Financial Missionaries to the World,* 97–121; Feis, *The Diplomacy of the Dollar.*

13. On the structure and importance of the economics profession at home see esp. Ross, *The Origins of American Social Science;* and Bernstein, *A Perilous Progress.* Scott, *Seeing Like a State,* suggests a critique that is relevant to financial oversight. On the role of "manliness" in constructing both the order and the other see Rosenberg, "Revisiting Dollar Diplomacy." The connections between masculinity and the rise of statistical practices are highlighted in Hannah, *Governmentality and the Mastery of Territory in Nineteenth-Century America;* and Folbre, "The 'Sphere of Women' in Early-Twentieth-Century Economics." On colonialism and gender, generally, see Burton, *Gender, Sexuality, and Colonial Modernities.*

14. "January 1926 News Letter of Paul Super, National Secretary of the Y.M.C.A. in Poland," in Poland: Correspondence and Reports, 1926–1930, File 1926, Jan.–March, Kautz Family YMCA Archives, University of Minnesota. See also Drake, *The Money Doctor in the Andes;* Drake, *Money Doctors, Foreign Debts, and Economic Reforms in Latin*

America from the 1890s to the Present; and Eichengreen, "House Calls of the Money Doctor."

15. Millspaugh, *Americans in Persia*, 8.

16. See Rosenberg, *Financial Missionaries to the World*, 187–218.

17. Salman, *The Embarrassment of Slavery*, provides a relevant discussion of the similarly movable discourses of "slavery" and "freedom" within the imperial debate.

18. For opposing postures in this debate see Inman, "Imperialist America"; and Welles, "Is America Imperialistic?" For a larger perspective see Johnson, *The Peace Progressives and American Foreign Relations*; and Salisbury, *Anti-Imperialism and International Competition in Central America, 1920–29*. An insightful meditation on the meanings and "absence of empire" in the study of American culture is Kaplan, "'Left Alone with America.'"

19. Ninkovich, *The United States and Imperialism*, stresses the modernizing discourses in Progressive-Era American imperialism; LaFeber, *The New Empire*, emphasizes economic interest; Challener, *Admirals, Generals, and American Foreign Policy, 1898–1914*, examines strategic goals; May, *American Imperialism*, presents evidence of transatlantic influences; Hoganson, *Fighting for American Manhood*, looks at policy makers' concerns over declining manhood; two works—Jacobson, *Barbarian Virtues*; and Kramer, "Empires, Exceptions, and Anglo-Saxons"—stress race and ethnicity; Zimmermann, *First Great Triumph*, accentuates the role of self-confident individuals.

20. For a more detailed discussion of the decline of supervisory regimes see Rosenberg, *Financial Missionaries to the World*, 219–52.

21. For development of this point see Renda, *Taking Haiti*; and Go, "The Chains of Empire."

22. Rosenberg, *Financial Missionaries to the World*, 230–40.

23. I use the term *close encounters* in the sense suggested by Joseph, "Close Encounters," 15: aiming to "at once validate the unequal nature of Latin America's encounter with the United States and write a history that is culturally sensitive, multivocal, and interactive."

24. For a broader view of the contingencies and varieties of localized cultural encounters see Appadurai, *Modernity at Large*.

25. Rosenberg, *Financial Missionaries to the World*, 193.

26. On military training and its larger contexts in several countries in this era see, e.g., Millspaugh, *Americans in Persia*, 44; Bermann, *Under the Big Stick*; Millett, *Guardians of the Dynasty*; Schmidt, *The United States Occupation of Haiti, 1915–1934*; Calder, *Impact of Intervention*; Buell, *The Native Problem in Africa*.

27. Millspaugh, *Americans in Persia*, 52.

28. Rosenberg, *Financial Missionaries to the World*, 221–22.

29. See Cary, *The Rise of the Accounting Profession*.

30. Rosenberg, *Financial Missionaries to the World*, 222–23.

31. Ibid., 223–24.

32. Ibid., 224–25. Quote is from W. W. Cumberland to Secretary of State, March 10, 1928, Department of State, National Archives, RG 59, 817.51/1921.

33. Rosenberg, *Financial Missionaries to the World*, 166–76; McNeil, *American Money and the Weimar Republic*, 28–30, 92, 165–68, 175–76.

34. Rosenberg, *Financial Missionaries to the World*, 227–28. For a broader perspective on reports of such afflictions see Anderson, "The Trespass Speaks." Anderson also discusses a similar pattern of ineptitude among health professionals in the colonial Philippines in "Going through the Motions." Fabian, *Out of Our Minds*, provides a suggestive interpretation of a different set of "scientists" (anthropologists) operating in Africa.

35. Rosenberg, *Financial Missionaries to the World*, 226–27. Quote is from Loomis to Secretary of State, March 22, 1929, Department of State, National Archives, RG 59, 882.51A/59.

36. The idea that economic penetration into less-developed areas created instability rather than the promised stability is a general theme in the works of, among others, Adas, *Prophets of Rebellion*; LaFeber, *The American Search for Opportunity, 1865–1913*; and Hobsbawm, *The Age of Empire*.

REFRACTIONS

17

LINDA GORDON

Internal Colonialism and Gender

The stimulus for this book has been Ann Stoler's important and original work on "intimacies of empire," particularly her lucid essay—a letter to American historians—on how these ideas could be brought to bear on U.S. history. I was originally asked to comment on the papers as a group but found myself unable to suppress my own small response to this intellectual agenda. So instead I offer a hybrid contribution: another look at the concept of "internal colonialism," followed by an attempt to elucidate themes common to this volume as a whole. Employed and elaborated by students of many regions of the world, internal colonialism was a concept used in the United States in 1960s' and early 1970s' leftist and/or Marxist theoretical discourse, but it has been discarded or at least neglected by Americanists since then; this disregard, I think, impoverishes our understanding. For the internal colonialism concept to be productive, however, it must take on a gender analysis. (The same goes for most social-theoretical concepts.) So in what follows, part 1 sketches the origin and career of the internal colonialism concept in U.S. scholarship, then suggests a context in which it may still be a useful notion, and illustrates how gender analysis makes it a more effective concept. Part 2 identifies some themes that run through this volume and then considers one group of papers more closely.

ORIGINS AND FUNCTIONS OF THE CONCEPT

The concept of internal colonialism arose from within the Marxist tradition (although it was opposed by many orthodox Marxists), used by Lenin and Gramsci, for whom it came to characterize intersecting economic exploitation and political exclusion of a subordinated group that differed racially or ethnically from the dominant group—and all this within a polity rather than across oceans or borders. Internal colonialism was above all a metaphor, calling attention to similarities between classic colonialism—in which countries of the global north occupied and exploited "Third World" developing regions and peoples—and intranational relations of domination in which exploitation coincided with racism and national chauvinism. Internal colonialism typically calls attention to the role of racism in creating supplies of especially cheap labor; the concept often rests on the view that racism is at root an economic phenomenon, produced by capital's search for profit. Thus one reason the concept has been largely discarded and little used by younger scholars in the United States is the cultural turn in history and other social studies, a turn that often ignores or even erases the economic. But the concept of internal colonialism need not exclude the material force of cultural and ideological forms of domination. Another reason for the concept's disuse is that it is often employed as a blanket and static generalization, insensitive not only to diversity and historical change but also to the multiple forms of conflict that are always present in situations of domination. Thus the concept has sometimes become reified and treated as if it were a general descriptor rather than an axis of analysis.

If we can keep these complexities in mind, and recall that internal colonialism is a metaphor and an analytic abstraction, I believe it remains a concept valuable precisely because it is rich, capacious, flexible, and connotative rather than denotative. At the same time, it is more precise than racism or exploitation in general. It can help distinguish different forms of domination. For example, in what follows I will suggest that internal colonialism can help delineate the position of Mexican Americans but not that of African Americans.

Starting from Stoler's expanded notion of how empire works, I would identify (at least) three layers on which internal colonialism operates. It calls attention, first, to imperial exploitation and colonial relationships within a single polity and asks us to consider these processes as having been central to the historical development of the United States. Internally colonial practices have shaped American racisms and nationalism. In this sense of *internal* the concept compares relations labeled "domestic" to others labeled "foreign," those labeled "internal" to others labeled "external," and the comparison can reveal hidden aspects of both sides of the analogy. By refusing to naturalize national boundaries as the proper and inevitable demarcations of fields of power — or fields of study, teaching, or theorizing — the concept anticipated later understandings of globalization. Indeed, by asking those who study borders, liminal sites, and global circulation of cultural technologies to consider colonialism, it draws attention not just to power but also to struggles for power.

As a metaphor, internal colonialism calls attention to the fact that the very distinction between the domestic and the foreign in U.S. history has been an ideological one. Its transformation into common sense stemmed from the doctrine of "Manifest Destiny," which rationalized and institutionalized the "domestic United States" as that region contained between two oceans and the borders with Canada and Mexico. (Alaska was slipped in so smoothly that few notice the inconsistency it created.) In 1845 Democrat John O'Sullivan proclaimed that the United States had a "Manifest Destiny" "to over spread and to possess the whole of the continent which Providence has given us for the development of the great experiment of liberty and . . . development of self government entrusted to us. It is [a] right such as that of the tree to the space of air and the earth suitable for the full expansion of its principle and destiny of growth."[1] O'Sullivan's justification for conquering land all the way to the Pacific was a hawkish policy argument and by no means a description of the inevitable. After U.S. might created "facts on the ground," however, a hindsight discourse made its expansion into its current borders seem ineluctable, "natural." But California was no more "internal" or less "external" then than Hawaii or the Philippines. Did not the Monroe Doctrine argue to consider all of Latin America as "internal" to the United States?

Internal colonialism can also serve, second, to evoke realms of colonial relations that Stoler has called intimate. These are realms sometimes referred to as domestic, homely in the sense of the Yiddish *haimish*. After all, the term *domestic* functions not only to define *foreign* by posing as its opposite but also to define *public* by similar opposition; it also aligns itself with the terms *private* and *female* in the closely related binaries private/public and female/male. That is, colonial dimensions of the familial, the household, the relational, the "private," and even that territory (the subconscious?) within the personalities and character structures of both subjects and objects of colonialism[2] — or internalized colonialism, in the words of Cherríe Moraga.[3] If we are to prevent the obliteration of gendered and racialized aspects of colonialism, we must include these dimensions.

Third, the discursive construction of these intimate colonial practices takes us into matters of official and mainstream culture, high and low, of the professions, the educational system, the intellectual and cultural paradigms through which colonial domination is maintained, reproduced, and reshaped to meet new conditions.

All three meanings of *internal colonialism* connect. They ask us to interrogate colonial processes and relations from a variety of perspectives. But when we do so, we must remain aware of two dangers: defining the phrase so broadly that it includes all forms of inequality or so narrowly that it excludes the social and cultural forms, the intimate arenas and relations, that make colonialism go.

The internal colonialism metaphor arose from an intellectual desire to construct comparisons with foreign colonialism. Like all comparisons, as Ann Stoler has pointed out, these are unavoidably political, and that is how I use them. In what follows I begin with the economic, political, and public and move toward the social, cultural, and "domestic." I do so with full awareness that these distinctions are also ideological, a trait demonstrated repeatedly by the feminist scholarship of the late twentieth century. The social construction of such distinctions, their capacity to create as well as reflect ideology, is illustrated by the notion of gender itself. Although gender is a vital analytic concept, in real time the boundaries between it and class, race, or sexual identity are not fixed or given but always in every context interflowing. Most social meaning, and language itself, rests on comparison, or taxonomy, and its constituent decisions about what is comparable and what is not. Logically, anything can be compared to anything — eggs to elephants, astronomical stars to movie stars — if we are specific about what features we are comparing. Ideologies constructed through comparison and differentiation shape and rationalize racial and political domination. But they can also work subversively. They can challenge mystifying ideologies and practices by bringing functional similarities and dissimilarities into view. By the last quarter of the twentieth century, the very act of naming U.S. foreign policy as imperialist, a naming effectuated through comparison to "traditional" European imperialism, contributed to debunking claims of U.S. exceptionalism, and to illuminating the nature of U.S. power in the world.

American Application

The concept of internal colonialism was used by Lenin and his followers to describe uneven development and distribution of rights and resources *within* a sovereign state.[4] By decentering geographical division between colonizer and colonized, it directed our attention to relations not always visible to those for whom neoclassical economics had become an ideology. It also emphasized the imbrication of racial domination and class exploitation: a colonized group within a state was typically differentiated and stigmatized by "race" or religion or ethnicity, and its demarcation allowed a superexploitation of its labor by capital. Scholars and theorists have used and developed the concept to understand relations such as that between England and its "Celtic fringe," between Latin American countries and their native (Indian) populations, between Canada and the Inuit, between the Soviet Union and indigenous Siberian peoples, and between Australia and its Aborigines. The African National Congress of South Africa rested a great deal of its analysis on the notion that internal colonialism was a useful way to think about relations between Europeans (whites) and Africans in that republic.[5]

In the United States, civil rights activists and later black (and Chicano/a and American Indian) nationalists appropriated the concept not only as a way of understanding American racism but also as a means of associating the African American struggle for equality with national liberation struggles in the Third World. The Vietnam War greatly intensified the identification of radical Americans of color with colonized peoples and spurred the development of internal colonialism theory in the United States. Internal colonialism provided an ontologically objective ground for that solidarity but in doing so often got used as a literal rather than a metaphoric characterization.

In American academic sociology the term was applied to the situation of African Americans in the 1960s and 1970s by Bob Blauner and others. They emphasized that U.S. racism and the colonialism of the imperialist era both developed from the same historical situation and that racism and colonialism shared basic components. These included, for Blauner, the fact that the colonized underwent (1) a forced, involuntary entry into the dominant society, (2) the erosion or even outright suppression of indigenous cultures, (3) subjection to administration by representatives of the colonial power, (4) subjection to racist ideology, and (5) subordination within a division of labor.[6] Following this early work came many critiques of internal colonialism, also focusing on African Americans. The critiques are right: the theory does not explain much about white racism against blacks or about the specific position of African Americans. Nevertheless, taking note of some of the intellectual and political work it has done is important here. With respect to the narrative of U.S. history, the internal colonialism theory challenged an approach that once dominated the teaching of U.S. diversity, in which blacks, Mexicans, Filipinos, and Chinese were understood as waves of immigrants who, like the Irish, Italians, or Jews, would eventually be assimilated. By treating racism and even exploitation as matters of passing prejudice, this historical story explained the economic success and failure of the racial and ethnic groups on the basis of characteristics internal to the groups rather than on the basis of their relations to a larger political economy. In this respect the "whiteness" studies of the past several decades have offered a similar challenge, albeit from an alternate starting place—that race is a historical structural matter and that by studying the historical process by which some groups became white, we better understand the structural positions of those who remained nonwhite.

Part of what kept America's internally colonized groups from becoming white was the construction of a racialized labor system. It featured a labor market so segregated that jobs themselves appeared racially specialized and publicly earmarked to a degree that almost rivaled the gendering of jobs. Just as preschool teaching was female and truck driving was male, so Pullman porters were black; within meatpacking there were white jobs and black jobs; in department stores whites worked out front with customers, and nonwhites worked in back in packaging, shipping, cleaning. The fact that such labeling could easily shift under economic pressure—for example, agricultural work that "no white man would do," such as picking strawberries, became flooded with white laborers when the Depression and the dust bowl drove many whites from the plains states into California's agricultural fields and California deported several hundred thousand Mexicans—did not prevent the development of new, equally racialized, job labels. Once domestic servants were, almost by definition, Irish, until they became, almost by definition, black or Latina. Above all, in the colonial culture of work certain dirty and servile jobs could no longer be done by whites, on the penalty of losing their whiteness.

But this usage of internal colonialism, as developed in the 1960s, tended to derive racism "ultimately" from economic exploitation.[7] It explained white supremacy on the basis of economic self-interest, an explanation that left unexplained some of the irrational aspects of racism and colonialism. It was vulnerable to the critiques directed against Marxist theories that imperialism did not produce net profits for the metropoles and that imperialism was often enthusiastically supported by those who had nothing economic to gain from it. By using "race" or "nation" as its fundamental category, it seemed to reify those concepts even as it reduced them to effects of the pursuit of economic self-interest. It was unable to see race as in itself a complex, changing, and frequently contested historical and ideological construction.

Internal colonialism theory also, like leftist theory of imperialism itself, neglected the intimate, social, and cultural aspects of domination. It was blind to gender or, at best, treated it, like race, as an artifact of independent economic imperatives—which it conceived in narrow terms. It neglected even economic aspects of the familial and the intimate, such as household labor and reproductive labor, and it failed to examine the circulation of resources among kinfolk. It thereby missed vital dimensions of domination and control, those that took place in families, households, and schools as opposed to factories, mines, or fields.

Internal colonialism theory in the United States was killed off, in large part, by the centrality of the African American experience to U.S. history. The theory could not bear the weight of having to explain the evolution, operation, appeal, dominance, and persistence of racism against blacks in the United States.

Perhaps most fatally, the theory lost its usefulness as activists appropriated it to take in diverse forms of domination. All groups with grievances became "colonized." A good example is the "Fourth World Manifesto," issued by a group of cultural feminists in 1971 to compare women's oppression to that of the third world and male dominance to imperialism.[8] The limits of the metaphor got lost in the desire to share in the clout of such a vivid concept.

But precision was not the point. Political mobilization was. Internal colonialism theory worked most effectively as an analogy to classical colonialism and as a call for international solidarity with, for example, the Vietnamese NLF, Cuban revolutionaries, and African liberation movements such as those in Angola, Mozambique, the Congo, and South Africa. Moreover, it provided an analytical rationale for these solidarities, although it tended simultaneously to obscure any bases for coalitions with whites. It was primarily an instrumental concept. Ronald Bailey and Guillermo Flores defined internal colonialism in part as "the *process* [my emphasis] by which oppressed people of a given geo-political unit come to comprehend and internalize the experiences of other oppressed people. . . . [But] identity alone, although a necessary condition for the important process of decolonization within the US, is by no means . . . sufficient. . . . Required is a deep understanding both of the social conditions . . . and of the forces that have conditioned the development or parallel social conditions."[9] In this respect the internal colonialism concept gained political utility at a historical moment, but it soon lost relevance.

The concept was, I think, discarded too soon and for the wrong reasons. It remains fruitful as a means of exploring and interpreting some relations of domination within the United States. Consider the case of Mexicans and Mexican Americans. About eighty thousand became U.S. residents by the treaties of 1848 and 1853, when the United States annexed half of Mexico. Many more came to the United States voluntarily. But internal colonialism theory rightly draws our attention away from the circumstances of incorporation and directs it toward ongoing *relations* between the dominated and dominating groups after incorporation. After all, were Mexicans who had been driven to the United States by economic need any less powerless than those annexed militarily? Neither group sought at first to become "Americans." All sought to share in U.S. resources as a way to advance their well-being within Mexico or "Mexico afuera," as they often called the southwestern United States. Their labor, however, was vital to the development of several regions and economic sectors crucial to the U.S. economy, notably hard-rock mining, railroad construction, and industrial agriculture.[10] Moreover, the concept draws our attention to the many ways in which colonial relations between U.S. capital and Mexican Americans parallel those between the United States and Mexico.

In the southwestern United States Mexican and Chicana/o workers were successfully—albeit conflictedly—established as a reserve army of labor, providing corporations access to a workforce at times of peak demand without having to make possible year-round subsistence for those workers and their families. There is a strong parallel here to how the South African black labor force was constructed. From the late nineteenth century on, in agriculture, mining, and railroad construction, Mexican workers were alternately recruited and expelled according to employers' needs; this was done sometimes informally and "privately," through direct recruitment and word of mouth, and sometimes formally by the state, as in the *bracero* program and the deportation (often titled repatriation) during the Depression of the 1930s. This process did not characterize all subordinated groups. The reserve-army-of-labor notion did not fit African Americans well, as they were not so easily deported or made to appear "alien" as Mexicans. Similarly, sociologist Ruth Milkman showed that the reserve-army-of-labor concept failed to explain women's subordinate position in the labor force: sex segregation has been so extreme that women could not easily be shifted in and out of jobs according to men's availability.

A further limitation of internal colonialism theory is that it cannot work strictly internally, that is, unconnected to international imperialism. External military and economic conquest helps construct race and class systems domestically, and vice versa. This relation sets limits on the applicability and value of the theory because some groups are more tightly and enduringly tied to international power relations than others. For example, the status of African Americans in the United States is not primarily dependent on twentieth-century developments in Africa, but the status of Mexican Americans cannot be explained without reference to developments in Mexico. The development of the Mexican and Chicana/o labor force derived from U.S. imperialism in Mexico. The in-and-out migration of Mexicans across the border was produced by Mexico's economic subordination to the United States. By 1910 U.S. capital controlled Mexican railroads, by 1912 Mexican mines, and soon thereafter Mexican oil, finance, communications (telegraph and telephone), and urban transport systems. Indeed, Mexico became the first foreign country to fall into U.S. economic control without losing its political sovereignty; it was the pilot model — or guinea pig — for a new form of transnational colonial power.[11] This economic annexation has shaped the status of Mexican Americans ever since, including even those who have been U.S. citizens for a century and a half. Mae Ngai has characterized this relation as "imported colonialism," a phrase that points to a set of relations both within and without the United States.[12]

The internal colonialism concept is most illuminating when it rests on spatial as well as racial and ethnic and class bases. Some who applied it to African Americans slid into the "black nation" argument and strategy, proposing an independent African American state. Others focused on urban black ghettos. But the Mexican American case is stronger. Mexican Americans differed in religion and language, as well as looks, from dominant groups. For well over a century most Mexican Americans considered themselves a nation, and most continued to reinforce that identity through a degree of political identification with Mexico. This identification was continually solidified by cross-border movement, and that movement was made possible by geographical concentration and proximity, by, that is, the fact that most Mexican Americans lived in segregated communities near the U.S.-Mexico border. Large numbers of Mexican Americans built binational, transnational lives. As the original possessors and/or owners of much of the land annexed (notably in California, New Mexico, and Texas), they were expropriated by legal as well as illegal means, but the "legal" means included refusing to honor titles valid under the Mexican legal system.[13] Moreover, white male intermarriage with Mexican women was one of the crucial means by which land was appropriated. Some Mexican elites held on to a modicum of economic and even political power; others earned a living, and occasionally prospered, through the development of business enterprises that served the growing Mexican American population in the twentieth century. As in all colonial situations, members of the subordinated group participated in the exploitation and domination of these subjects, in positions ranging from foremen to labor subcontractors to large ranchers. These relationships made it possible for many Mexicans to live in all-Mexican enclaves within the United States.

The position of Mexican Americans is also shaped by U.S. cultural influence on Mexico. Internal colonialism theory was sometimes reductively economic, an approach that weakened the usefulness of the concept. Rather, internal colonialism worked through a "pincer-like squeeze," as Bailey and Flores put it, "of the penetration of national economic systems by the developed, capitalist superpower . . . coupled with the superordinate position of scientism and Euro-American 'world culture.'"[14] In that latter form of domination we have to include, for example, baseball, noticing how it came to overtake bullfights as the favorite sport in Mexico, just as beer became more popular than tequila, American-style trousers came to replace Mexican pantalones, shoes replaced huaraches, and coats replaced serapes.[15] We must remember, however, not to treat these as unwanted impositions. The Mexican families of migrant workers, especially the women, longed for American cooking ranges, roofs that did not require rethatching every few years, and cotton mattresses. And all this is part of a two-way process. Mexican Americans created large communities and infrastructures — churches, stores, fraternal and sororal organizations, kinship networks — in which they lived inside the United States as if in a more prosperous Mexico, using their native language, eating their native food, buying from Mexican merchants. And non-Mexicans living in those areas took in Mexican commodities and styles with alacrity. These relationships, too, can be usefully compared to other historical experiences of colonialism. By this two-way process, David Gutiérrez writes, Mexicans created a "distinct, if syncretic, variant of Mexican culture in what had become part of the United States."[16]

Some argue that a theory of internal colonialism is not necessary because identifying the mesh of race and class is sufficient to explain Mexican American history. Perhaps, but only if concepts of race are employed with more nuance than the term usually allows. The stipulations of the Treaty of Guadalupe Hidalgo granting Mexicans citizenship led a federal court to rule in 1897 that Mexicans were "white." Moreover, the domination of the U.S. binary, black-white racial system led Mexican Americans struggling for rights and acceptance to insist that they were white. The virulence of southwestern white racism against Mexican Americans is more fully explained if we add to race and class their connection to a conquered nation, their geographical concentration next to that nation, and the way that U.S. employers made of them a reserve army of labor.

I am not suggesting that internal colonialism is an exact or sufficient analysis of Mexican Americans' position in the United States and certainly not that it fits other subordinated groups equally well. I am suggesting merely that it is a fruitful metaphor, an invitation to comparison with external colonialism. But even as a metaphor, internal colonialism theory needs gendered and "intimate" dimensions. Many economic structures rest on gendered structures. South African apartheid, for example, was a deeply gendered system. It built gender relations that were distinct both from the traditional African and from those that were normative for the dominant European population. To summarize just one aspect of the system: South African segregation was based on geographical separation of racial groups but only for part of the working population. Individual African (black) workers were licensed and required to carry passes that legitimated their entry into "white" areas for work, while their families—wives, children, parents, siblings—were confined to the poor rural areas reserved for Africans or other legally defined racial groups. This setup allowed many African families to survive, barely, on the sub-subsistence wages of their members in the wage-labor force in the white areas because of the contributions to the family economy of other members' small-time gardening, trading, commerce, and wage work in the African areas. Preventing family co-residence for huge proportions of the population, the apartheid system heightened gender antagonism, intensifying male cultures of heavy drinking, sex with multiple partners, and violence, including sexual assault, in the townships and hostels—which weakened African resistance to colonialism, of course. Apartheid institutionalized "single" motherhood and female-headed households even as it confronted the inferiority of these kinship forms both as a matter of ideology and as a matter of physical survival. These women who so often supported families bore not only the double burden of wage work and domestic labor but also the burden of coping with the instability of their relations with male family members. At this point it becomes impossible to distinguish the economic from the cultural. It is not a matter of including women in the analysis; it is a matter of considering the "intimate," "personal," aspects of men's lives as well. These gender systems are structural as well as cultural, although that divide, too, is illusory. The more one works at understanding the "intimate" and the "personal," the more they spill into the allegedly public, economic, and political.

The U.S.-Mexican system had its own unique history and less brutality; nevertheless, it displayed some striking parallels to the South African. The territory taken from Mexico by the United States in the mid–nineteenth century became a region whose economic development depended on Mexican labor. All of those native to the annexed regions were automatically awarded U.S. citizenship. But many of these workers so crucial to the U.S. economy were Mexican citizens, at first usually male, who periodically crossed the border (a border that was entirely unmarked in most areas for many decades) to earn, while those who remained resident in areas now joined to the United States found their status defined not by their U.S. citizenship but by their co-nationality with Mexican citizens. The common southwestern distinction between "Americans" and "Mexicans" exemplified the ironic situation of Mexican American people: rendered as alien by gringos regardless of their citizenship—"foreigners in their native land," as David Weber put it.[17] Yet this language was adopted by Mexican Americans themselves and furthered by continuing involvement in social movements in Mexico rather than those in the United States—such as the Mexican revolutionary conflicts and Mexican labor unions early in the twentieth century. In other words, Mexican Americans constructed political subjectivities as colonized people, in part, as an aspect of resistance to colonialism.

As in South Africa, these developments rested on a gender system and changed it. Mexicans' ability to work as migrants in the United States typically depended on extended familial economies in Mexico, on kinfolk who continued to farm and earn within Mexico. When Mexican women's migrant labor began on a large scale, probably in the 1920s, it often depended on women leaving their children to be cared for in Mexico. Many women resident in the United States returned to Mexico in order to give birth among kinfolk. Mexican migrant workers' goals were constructed in the context of these family economies—often they hoped to earn enough in the United States to be able to return to Mexico and succeed as a farmer or small entrepreneur. At the same time, many Mexican migrant women's aspirations in the United States were prominently influenced by the ways in which American family expectations and commercial culture seemed to them to promise greater freedom and security. The capacity of Mexican American populations to engage in economic, cultural, and political struggle for respect and equality, when civil rights campaigns arose in the early twentieth century, depended to a significant degree on women's community-building labor in the United States. At all times patterns of Mexican-"white" sexual relationships and marriage profoundly affected the degree to which Mexicans could get respect and political rights. In the nineteenth century, "mixed" marriages between white men and Mexican women typically produced families integrated into white communities. By the early twentieth century, however, the imposition of segregation and disfranchisement tended to push such families into Mexican neighborhoods. Furthermore, white women pioneered this segregation and often regarded it as a progressive reform analogous to similar moral cleansing campaigns in overseas colonies.[18]

Gendered understandings of both *Mexican* and *American* pervade the culture of the Southwest and will increasingly affect the cultures of other parts of the United States as the in-migration and internal migration continue. These understandings must become part of how we think about internal colonialism. Consider "intermarriage" and other cross-race relationships, for example. These took place almost always between white men and Mexican women (the opposite of black-white relationships), for a set of reasons all highly gendered. An "Orientalist" construction of Mexican women made them seem simultaneously submissive and exotically sexually attractive.[19] But this white male perception of Mexican women intersected with the status of Mexican women handsomely dowried with property, or even as property heirs under the Spanish-Mexican law that governed southwestern real property in the nineteenth and early twentieth centuries, so that they became also economically attractive partners for the ambitious white men who were migrating to the Southwest in the nineteenth century. Moreover, Mexican women were not merely exchanged. They often preferred or even sought out marriages with white men because of their reputation of being more egalitarian, less controlling than Mexican men and because of their better jobs and greater resources. The transborder life lived by so many working-class Mexican *norteños* in the twentieth century produced gendered effects, such as the separation of husbands and wives. In Mexico women became more often acting heads of household, for example. Men's return brought money and gifts but often also tension. Mexican religiosity was intensely gendered, not only theologically in its Mariolatry but also in the greater attachment of women than men to the church. The current appeal of evangelical Protestantism among Mexicans also has gendered meanings, idealizing a considerably different family norm.

Elite reform campaigns for the benefit of these colonial subjects produced further gendered complications. Like metropolitan and settler women in transoceanic colonies, white elite women in internal colonies frequently interpreted the alleged benefits of imperialism in terms of the gender system in which they functioned. They championed their dominion over underdeveloped populations as a necessary historical process of female emancipation and uplift. They subscribed to claims both Marxist and liberal—marking both intellectual traditions as equally Eurocentric—that the status of women was a measure of "civilization." They lamented male brutality and rituals of mastery in allegedly backward cultures. Yet they typically overlooked, misunderstood, and/or disdained the household, familial, and communal cultures created by these supposedly powerless women. And they opposed most aspects of women's economic independence of men. Female elite discourse treated "native" women as alternately victimized or morally "fallen," but in either case low (an attitude that harmonized, perhaps significantly, with the fact that the elite women were often taller). It is hardly surprising that projects to "rescue" colonized women from their patriarchies were not strikingly successful.

The mixed results of such efforts flowed also from elite women's own conflicts of interest, because female elites depended on the cheap domestic labor of colonized women to buy their own leisure and freedom of movement, within as well as outside the United States. Indeed, the relation between mistress and domestic was in some ways as central to the colonial relation as was that between landlord and peasant or overseer and plantation laborer. To a degree, colonizer wives' relations with their privileged husbands, as well as their female virtue and self-esteem, also depended on the division of labor that positioned colonized women as sex workers. In both domestic service and prostitution, therefore, elite women held a vested interest in securing the subordinate status of the colonized women. Some of these elites took organized action to prevent colonized women from escaping these fates—as when white women insisted that schools train girls for domestic service, complained that welfare programs created a scarcity of domestics, or initiated zoning to keep sexual commerce remote from their own spheres but protected at the same time. Some of these reformers identified with women's-rights campaigns in their own cultures, and some did not. But for both groups the subordination of colonized women served as a foil that justified self-congratulatory confidence in the superiority of European civilization. (To call this subordination a foil does not mean that it was "unreal" or a discursive construction by outsiders. A fundamental aspect of the power of colonialism, internal and external, was that it often brought cultural forms simultaneously desirable to colonized women and disruptive of their security.)

Masculinity has been an equally contested internal colonial ground. In general the most effectively hegemonic colonial strategies of rule involved providing room for masculine pride among the colonized, but this was not easily accomplished. Since masculine pride is so widely assimilated to domination, those men subordinated to colonial power often responded defiantly. Moreover, colonialists frequently expressed their own sense of the vulnerability of their control through attributing hypermasculinity—a.k.a. uncivilized masculinity—to their male subjects. This attribution allowed a self-justifying understanding of resistance, of course, through which they imagined anticolonial opposition as neither manly striving for independence nor organized, strategized opposition but merely savage rejection of civilization. It also provided an arena in which male and female colonialists could act out benevolence through uplift projects, sometimes educational and recreational programs that resembled what labor historians call "corporate welfare," sometimes protocols of dress and demeanor that were at once symbols of Westernization and of subordination, as in the case of servants, managers, and clerks. And these protocols were sometimes enforced equally rigorously by "native" employees.[20]

Colonialists produced gendered readings of diverse masculinities, which they deployed to justify policies of control. Since colonial politics was mainly a set of relations among men, their confrontations and interpretations of these confrontations were, for all sides, personally gripping and challenging. "Patriarchy" is first a hierarchical relation among men.[21] These complexities did not, of course, assume identical patterns across different societies, and in studying them, the goal is not to make transcultural, transhistorical generalizations but to better analyze these relations of control and resistance.

THE CONTRIBUTIONS OF THIS VOLUME

This list could continue, but I mean it only as an elementary sketch of how a gendered notion of internal colonialism might be employed. One of the casualties of the gendered structure of academic research has been the loss of further development of internal colonialism theory. That is, those who study labor markets and migration patterns synthetically rarely consider gender, kinship, or community structures; they often count women workers and migrants but don't analyze the gendered and kinship and domestic systems in which everyone lives, male as well as female. On the other side, those who do study gender increasingly focus on cultural and social practices and often fail to incorporate them into the organization of labor and political power.

So my hope for these chapters is that they encourage multiple discussions in a variety of contexts. They should be incorporated into economics discourse about labor markets, sociological discussions of race and intermarriage, historical scholarship about corporate and labor history, anthropological work about kinship and household, and educational studies about racial, national, and cultural difference and disadvantage. I read these chapters as contributing to colonial, postcolonial, and internal colonial studies. They contribute in the complex, unsystematic way that examining the world typically does, and with the specificity of the deep research that their scholarship requires, so that my responses may not reflect the authors' agendas.

Several themes and fruitful contradictions arise from the juxtaposition of these chapters. One theme concerns the flow of first-world social science and the professions into the colonies where they, on the one hand, contribute to the colonial structures and, on the other, influence anticolonial resistance and shape postcolonial societies. Often hidden within the ideology of "modernization," these scholarly, technical, and intellectual developments operate on multiple sides of colonial struggles—maintaining domination, challenging domination, reshaping domination on the part of new elites. Moreover, in examining these changing methods, several authors show how professionals and managers generate their own imperatives and dynamics so that the colonial agents are by no means limited to state bureaucrats. At the same time, we can see in these chapters how the state is often implicated in constructing intellectual and cultural paradigms even when it may seem uninvolved.

A second contradiction, one that is closely related and also often packed unnoticed into modernization boxes, appears in relation to cultural norms, both popular and elite. Several authors show how *both* colonialism and anticolonialism make use *both* of recognition and rejection of *both* traditional and transgressive norms—in a system of operations more complex than could be easily diagramed.

Linda Gordon

A third theme is the fundamental importance of "personal," "private" (once considered historically inconsequential except among men of great power) relationships in constructing, maintaining, and/or undermining colonialism. Exploring these relationships creates another sort of contradiction: that the supposedly private is often also very public. And although studying the private brings women into view, it also reveals male actors in activities once hidden from the historical record, as Emily Rosenberg shows in this volume. Some of the best scholarship has already begun to demonstrate women's part in constructing and maintaining colonial power, and vice versa, the empire's influence on gender formation; several articles in this collection continue this line of inquiry. Paul Kramer focuses our attention on sexual activity as part of imperialism. And, as Laura Briggs shows, studying the intimate can also expose how children have been made to function in imperial culture.

Fourth, examining these spheres requires a rethinking of what is accommodation and what is resistance — and what might be called "reaccommodation." These categories have been applied by scholars and political thinkers since the radical challenges laid down in many disciplines by New Left intellectuals. Today, happily, many scholars are wary both of romanticizing subaltern behavior, such that mere survival strategies get the imprimatur of resistance, and of erasing agency and activity, such that domination appears as a totalizing, perfectly entrapping discursive corral. That notion of a total domination is analytic, not descriptive, for such never existed. Indeed, the intricacies of colonial management, from the law courts to the sports fields, show that there has been no perfect domination or control (except possibly for very short stretches) and that those who wish to rule protractedly must adjust to some degree to the ruled. Likewise most forms of resistance involve some degree of conformity to rulers. Examining the "intimate," the internal in colonialism, leads to no precision or resolution in the definition of resistance but does broaden the universe of its possible forms while simultaneously advancing a model that is always two-sided — about conflict and negotiation rather than simply domination and social control.

A fifth general theme is empire's relation to how race is constructed — within intimate relationships as well as larger ones. The renascence of race scholarship in the last few decades has already demonstrated both the (limited) fluidity and the (relative) stability of race categories and hierarchies. But not enough of that work has been comparative, and Martha Hodes offers here a vivid and productive comparison. We need a fuller range of comparisons, especially on the question of race, even within the United States, since Americanists have tended to overgeneralize the black-white system. U.S. historians need to study Ireland, not only as a colony of immigrants but as a colony of England, a polity colonized by others of the same "race." Few U.S. historians make use of the history of European anti-Semitism or the race relations within the old Russian and Ottoman empires. Moreover, much of the scholarship on race is too detached from its relation to economic and political power. The whiteness studies have been instructive, but they sometimes imply that race is something that can be voluntarily accepted or rejected. Framing race studies within the rubric of internal colonialism might obviate this misimpression. But as Hodes has reminded us, race talk and race thought are inseparable from questions of gender, sexuality, and reproduction. It is in these dimensions that race is at once most passionately enforced and most actively transgressed.

Finally, there is the matter of what is not here, the silence that, as in an interview, often tells us as much as the noise. Despite the original impulse behind these papers, gender analysis is not their major common denominator. In understanding this gap, we need to consider whether gender is simply not influential in some aspects of colonial relations or whether we need to dig deeper to find it.

Yet it seems to me that these papers provide ample evidence and/or questions with which to pursue a gender analysis. Some take that analysis quite a distance; others do not. Let me reflect on how such an analysis might proceed in relation to one grouping of essays in this volume: those that discuss technologies of control.

Psychometric testing has functioned to establish and maintain social stratification (a.k.a. "gatekeeping") in the United States for more than a century. It has been well established that the notion of IQ is phony, supposedly measuring an innate, biological capacity. In fact, IQ scores can be radically changed through education. Alexandra Stern takes us on an international voyage and not in a straight line, either, as we see how Mexican professionals appropriated U.S. and French testing technologies under circumstances and with intentions that radically changed their meanings. Acting on an anti-imperialist and antiracist perspective, Mexicans planned to reject U.S. tests in favor of French. But under the influence of the then-dominant socialist ideology—Marxian "scientific" socialism, with its faith in technology and progress—Mexican professionals turned back to U.S. testing instruments because they were more quantitative and disallowed flexibility and multiple readings. This move back toward accepting an area of U.S. authority was not only consistent with but also part of President Cárdenas's program of "Socialist Education . . . based . . . on science and precision." It is not hard to see how these tests helped configure Mexican stratification and even contributed to the allegations of Mexican cultural inferiority by some Mexican liberal intellectuals. The problem, however, is not easily transcended because meritocracy itself, once called "careers open to talent" and intended to democratize politics and society, becomes part of the technology of domination, and the search for "objective" ways to measure talent only deepens the embeddedness of that domination. In Brazil a similar trajectory produced at first the "finding" that Brazilians were less intelligent than recent European immigrants, a finding subsequently quashed by limiting the sample to urban residents. This limitation probably improved the "objectivity" of the findings, given what we know about cities and the diverse experiences to which they expose their residents; but the point here is simply the professionals' willingness to revise "findings" to make them concur with political preferences—much as school systems in the United States today are revising achievement tests because so many children fail them. Did these ratings of intelligence produce a gendered breakdown? Is it not likely that the tests themselves have considerable gendered content and gender bias, as they have been shown to include in the United States? (But the U.S. critique has remained mainly quantitative, and a more fundamental set of questions, like those Stern asks, about the gendered meanings of testing itself, need to be asked.) And how was the discourse of Mexican cultural inferiority gendered?

Systems of racial classification are just as evidently bizarre, because "race" is just as vague and unscientific a notion as IQ. But while the South African racial system has long seemed absurd to many Americans because of its legalistic and nakedly discriminatory character and purpose, it is only quite recently that scholars, stimulated by critical race theory, have fully understood the extent to which the U.S. racial system was similarly legalistic and explicitly discriminatory. Martha Hodes reveals this and more: she exposes the contradictions in the pseudoscience of race classification. The men who designed these censuses included some of the leading social scientists of their time, but, like the psychometricians, they were unable to avoid collisions among their desire to collect data, their own understandings of race, and the political burdens that racial systems always carry. The most striking of these contradictions resulted, Hodes points out, from the racial and gendered imperative to prevent any honest official recognition of sex across the color line. The "honest" is important because a mythology about black rape of white women was officially recognized and acted on savagely through the quasi-official use of lynching.[22] Meanwhile the extent of voluntary and coerced sexual relations (and it could be difficult to tell the difference) between white men and black women was, literally, unspeakable. The problem was not only that the continued practice of measuring fractions between the mythic "pure" black and "pure" white subverted the imperative to be silent about mixed-race sex. The problem was also that offspring of such unions were overwhelmingly born to black mothers, not to black fathers, but carried the same "mixed blood" whether from black male–white female or white male–black female relationships. (The gendering of "interracial" sexual relationships requires much further study. Hodes's comparison to the way that census race categories treated American Indians is particularly valuable and argues for the importance of further comparative studies.) Why then, Hodes asks, the "proliferation of labels"? Her answer—marginal to her paper but strikingly consonant with Stern's argument—is that the professionals who develop and administer these technologies develop their own inertia, their own drive to pursue the potentialities of the technologies they have generated. This evident tension between the logic of social science and the logic of domination reminds us of why theories that treat controlling agents—or colonial technologies—as homogeneous, or as mere agents of ruling groups, are so often inadequate.

Emily Rosenberg's chapter puts the brakes on any tendency to coast toward overrating "expertise," however. It turns out that the "receivers" assigned to guide the economies of weaker nations were often anything but expert. Indeed, a litany of complaints about the incompetence of "native" administration served partly to obscure the incompetence of U.S. administration (which Rosenberg found in confidential reports).[23] It appeared that U.S. administrations, despite an allegedly corruption-free civil service system, appointed political cronies and supporters rather than experts to these jobs. If we consider these receivers as agents of the state, we are introduced to yet more complexity in understanding what imperialism or colonialism is. We may need a category in-between "external" and internal colonialism —or perhaps a continuum rather than a category, since these receiverships ranged from takeovers to advice. Rosenberg's subject is so new that we can only begin to compile the questions: Did the receivers have individual interests, investments, and so forth in the places they advised? Did they do favors for their cronies? And what were the gendered ideas and practices within this arrangement?

Courts, too, are supposed to operate on the basis of expertise, in this case legal. But in Nayan Shah's essay there is very little to suggest that any body of legal knowledge contributed to a decision based instead on various sorts of commonsense ideology. Shah's two cases illuminate multiple intersections, among the racial, national, familial, gendered, and sexual, as "Hindu marriage" got construed so differently in his two cases. In Oregon, legal marriage was able to overcome evidence of sexual deviance, and the customs of the Hindus could be invoked to legitimize suspicious behavior. There is a kind of Orientalism here, in that the "Hindu customs" are accepted by the court as so binding, so locked in collective tradition, that the possibility of individual deviance was unimaginable. Yet in New Mexico another court refused to recognize a Hindu marriage. That marriage not being Christian, and based on "repugnant" customs, an appellate court ruled against the Indian wife—essentially denying the legality of "Hindu marriage." What was deviant here were the Indian customs themselves, a kind of twist or inversion of the Oregon finding. Yet the cases have in common the fact that neither was decided on legal grounds. There is a hint of a hierarchy of colonials, with the American legal system ultimately favoring the internal colonial subject over the external one, the subject of U.S. power over the subject of British power, and, perhaps most important, the nearby over the distant, thus preventing the alienation of valuable land into the hands of a foreign citizen. One wonders if the Mexican American widow's immediate remarriage disturbed the judges—in other words, was Soledad Jubala really an actor in this play? Don Sing's wife was not; she served only as an embodied proof of marriage that ipso facto legitimated his sexual activity. But Soledad might well have been an actor, presumably along with her relatives and future second husband, deploying their U.S. residence so as to control Jubala's property.

Shannon Dawdy considers expertise in the management of slave labor, showing how transparently flexible it could become in the context of the goal, which was, of course, productivity and docility. She highlights the interplay between two seemingly opposite principles of management: a rationalist segregation and a paternalist intimacy. In fact, rationalism and paternalism worked in such close partnership that the distinction between them begins to dissolve—just as the public/private or external/internal distinctions break down. The paternalists were rational and instrumental, while the rationalists made use of anomalies such as "tender caresses." Wet-nursing provides a vivid example of such inconsistency, inasmuch as it represented the most complete violation of segregation, the greatest intimacy, in the interest of protecting slave-owning women from labor, possible pain, and . . . sexual exposure? The contradictory principles of slave handling appear also in the design of slave housing and in the recommended responses to bodily contact with slaves. Dawdy captures the owners' response to the smell of sweaty blacks in a revealing phrase, "disguised as disgust," implying that the alleged disgust may have arisen as a mask, conscious or unconscious, for something else—but we will have to wait for more of her work to see what might be beneath the mask.

Kathleen Brown examines the management of servants who were legally free, setting up thereby a striking comparison with Dawdy's chapter—another example of the productivity of comparison. In her early-nineteenth-century sources she finds the same acceptance of physical intimacy, an unavoidable aspect of the master-servant relation as it was understood at the time. Indeed, it may well be that before the advent of fully modern biologistic racism in the late nineteenth century, such intimacy did not seem repellent or troublesome to the masters. But the most revealing aspect of Brown's chapter is another type of comparison: between the perspective of an upper-class mistress and a black male servant. Here, three-quarters of a century after Dawdy's sources, the contradictions of bodily intimacy between master and servant have become a major theme: "struggles over the cleanliness of servant bodies . . . that inevitably became soiled as they labored to meet . . . elite and bourgeois domestic standards." Among the servants' tasks, therefore, is to hide their own labor—surely an imperative integral to modern urban domesticity and one put forward notably by women.

Brown herself is uncomfortable with applying the label "colonial" to her material, so she may be equally uncomfortable with my analysis. Yet surely one would be surprised to find this discomfort with dirt and smell between master and servant in premodern societies, and Brown is clear that the world in which her sources are situated—and the "world" comes to the diary writer through her husband and father—is one of empire in which the imposition of modern domesticity is central. Brown is clear that associating "black," "savage," and "dirt" was a crucially (though not uniquely) imperial understanding. Is there a historical change here or only a regional or cultural difference? Dawdy's slave manager believed the smells to be biologically emanating uniquely from certain racial groups, while the New Englanders were confident that servants could be trained to get rid of these smells. We might call this New England confidence in education one of the values of modern imperialism, with its justifications based on raising up, civilizing, the natives. Only in such a context does it make sense that the servant author, Robert Roberts, who so thoroughly agreed with his masters in his emphasis on the shamefulness of dirt and the obligation, even moral obligation, of servants to present themselves to their masters as clean and sweet — this author was an antislavery activist, identifying with New England's bourgeois abolitionists.

What could be more gendered than attitudes toward dirt, smell, and servitude? Roberts considered, Brown tells us, "the career servant as dignified, professional, and self-disciplined." What sorts of masculinity, we might ask, does this self-perception involve and what sorts does it occlude? What kinds of family are available to a manservant? Was acceptable masculinity in servitude fit only for a man of color? And what would the self-esteem and pride of a female servant look like? In some ways Brown's evidence exposes a contradiction in norms of femininity: the ascendant bourgeois norm required delicacy, but Lawrence had trouble holding servants because the labor was too heavy for them. Similar double-binds may have developed even among elite women in imperial situations, where life was hard for everyone and everyone struggled against hostile animal life, intemperate climates, and the absence of high culture, reliable legal systems, and decent transportation, for example.

Paul Kramer offers a detailed account of the battle over regulated prostitution after the United States took over the Philippines. The situation there directly challenged Americans' fond belief in the exceptionally moral character of their nation, as compared to decadent Europe. Governing the Philippines also challenged the relative strength of organized feminism in the United States, in contrast to that in Europe. (Kramer points out that from the American moralists' perspective, Oriental norms were close to European norms.) The controversy identifies a concrete instance of how U.S. domestic matters were ineluctably entangled in U.S. foreign involvements: imperialism became polluting to the mother country through a blowback from colonial immorality. Anti-imperialists could thus argue that imperialism was dangerous to the national health and the health of its citizenry. Moreover, attempting to protect the nation through inspection for venereal disease was dangerous in another way, because the civilized ego required the challenge of self-regulation for its health. In these conundrums we see one aspect of the complex relation between metropolitan feminists and the colonies.

All of this discourse was deeply gendered, of course, and warrants further examination. The burden of self-regulation was in theory laid only on men, white men of course, while women, native women of course, did not require an internalized morality but could be controlled through external regulation. Meanwhile, the sexual inspection of native women was difficult to administer not for administrative reasons but because of the gender system itself. To take money for sex, or to offer sex for money, was an option so universal among poor women that it could not easily be delimited. Wherever there were poor women, within as well as without the United States, there were "kept" women, street girls who could be used in return for small gifts, mothers needing additional income.

One major theme in this book, thus, has to be dragged out from behind screens or the screens overturned in order for us to see what they are hiding: gender. It hides itself so easily, standing so often behind racial and national and class conflicts, allowing those more assertive squabblers the spotlight. Gender disguises itself so well. Like a chameleon it colors and recolors itself so as not to stand out against a background, especially a background to which the viewer is habituated. Indeed, one has to dehabituate oneself to find gender—that is, to reject common sense, to take nothing for granted, even to examine most closely that which seems most familiar.

NOTES

1. O'Sullivan, "The Great Nation of Futurity," 426–30. The ideological implications of the "internal colonialism" metaphor extend, no doubt, to many other histories as well.

2. My friend and colleague Martha Hodes uses the phrase "domestic colonialism" in her contribution to this volume. It has the virtue of multiple meanings, just like "internal colonialism"; I stick with the latter because it has the richer legacy of previous theoretical work.

3. Moraga, "From Inside the First World, Foreword 2001," xvi.

4. For a review of its uses see Hind, "The Internal Colonial Concept."

5. See African National Congress, "Colonialism of a Special Type."

6. Blauner, Racial Oppression in America, chap. 3.

7. See Harris, "The Black Ghetto as Internal Colony."

8. See Burris, "Fourth World Manifesto."

9. Bailey and Flores, "Internal Colonialism and Racial Minorities in the U.S."

10. My discussion of internal colonialism in relation to Mexicans comes primarily from Barrera, Race and Class in the Southwest; Almaguer, "Toward the Study of Chicano Colonialism"; Almaguer, "Historical Notes on Chicano Oppression"; Almaguer, Racial Fault Lines; Montejano, Anglos and Mexicans in the Making of Modern Texas, 1836–1986. Other

sources for my comments include Bonacich, "A Theory of Ethnic Antagonism"; Blauner, *Racial Oppression in America*, chap. 2; Bonilla and Girling, *Structures of Dependency*; Bailey and Flores, "Internal Colonialism and Racial Minorities in the U.S."; Jacobson, "Internal Colonialism and Native Americans"; Murguia, *Assimilation, Colonialism, and the Mexican American People*; Chaloult and Chaloult, "The Internal Colonialism Concept"; Love, "Modeling Internal Colonialism"; Sheridan, *Arizona*; Cooper and Stoler, *Tensions of Empire*.

11. González and Fernandez, "Empire and the Origins of Twentieth-Century Migration from Mexico to the United States."

12. See Ngai, *Impossible Subjects*.

13. Ibid.; Montejano, *Anglos and Mexicans in the Making of Texas*; Monroy, *Thrown among Strangers*.

14. Bailey and Flores, "Internal Colonialism and Racial Minorities in the U.S.," 157.

15. Sanchez, *Becoming Mexican American*, 23; Park, "History of Mexican Labor," 223; Ruíz, *The People of Sonora*, 195–96.

16. David Gutiérrez, *Walls and Mirrors*, 37.

17. See Weber, *Foreigners in Their Native Land*

18. Gordon, *The Great Arizona Orphan Abduction*; Benton, "What about Women in the White Man's Camp?"

19. The geographical misfit here in my use of Said's label suggests, again, the fruitfulness of comparison—if it is not used to erase complexity.

20. See Brown, this volume.

21. See "Forum: What Comes after Patriarchy."

22. I label lynching quasi-official because of the voluminous evidence showing the participation and cooperation of officials of the state.

23. The structure of this system, in which public complaints about incompetence among subordinates veiled private acknowledgments of one's own incompetence, reminds me in its form of the way in which southern white hysteria about black men raping white women veiled the real rape of black women by white men.

18

CATHERINE HALL

Commentary

Ann Stoler's essay, "Tense and Tender Ties," has provided a powerful stimulus. Reading and thinking about it, and about the other chapters written for this volume, from the perspective of a British historian of empire has been a challenging task. As the only author writing from outside U.S. studies and the U.S. context, broadly defined, my aim is to reflect on the questions addressed in these pages from the British context. In my commentary the map of comparison is widened and connections made with what is sometimes called, not always with the degree of distance and irony one might hope for, "the British world."

The 1990s saw the emergence in Britain of "new imperial history," now a rapidly growing body of work influenced by postcolonial and feminist theory. It was born of Britain's postcolonial moment, the moment after decolonization, when large numbers of erstwhile colonized men and women "came home" and settled in the metropole. The recognition of a permanent African and Asian presence, people who had come to stay for good and to have children and grandchildren who were born in Britain, provoked a profound disruption in a society that had long imagined itself as homogeneous and white. Colonized peoples lived out there, in the empire. They might visit the metropole, but then they went home. The gap between metropole and colony was critical to the way in which metropolitan power was conceptualized: "they" were over there, different from "us," not capable of ruling themselves. "Home" and "away" were understood as incommensurable, and the distinction between them structured the manner of governance both at home and in the empire. "Race" belonged to the empire and was lived at a distance. The disintegration of this split between colonizing self and colonized other, the recognition of "race" *within* the society, marked a significant shift in patterns of racial thinking within the United Kingdom. The increasingly vocal claims made by Britons of color, the challenges they mounted to what it meant to be British, to belong in this society, opened up new thinking about race and nation and a critical return to the empire and its legacies. Scholars working in the field of British history turned to questions about the connections between metropole and colony, questions that have had a persistent life in the undercurrents of imperial and anti-imperial thought but have been consistently sidelined from the mainstream of British culture and historiography. They deconstructed the separation made between domestic and imperial history, a separation that has both mirrored and actively constituted notions of "home" and "away." The return to empire, as Antoinette Burton argues, can be seen as "one symptom of the pressure of postcolonial social, political and demographic realities on the production of modern knowledge."[1]

The new research agenda that came out of Britain's postcolonial moment has been an interdisciplinary venture from the beginning. Cultural critics, anthropologists, historical geographers, and historians have begun to recover Britain as an imperial space. The traces of empire have been documented in every sphere of metropolitan life, from the material culture of the everyday to the imaginative, spiritual, commercial, and political worlds of the men and women of the past. The presence of colonized "others," and their sometimes disruptive impact, has been traced across generations. Following Said's call for the need to examine the classificatory conventions of colonial knowledge, shifting constructions of colonizer and colonized have been investigated both within and across metropolitan and colonial sites. A central concern for some has been to disrupt the narratives of "the island story," Britain's version of U.S. exceptionalism that has dominated British history for so long. They have engaged in the writing of national histories through the webs of connection across the empire, telling the stories of the colonial relations across which both metropole and colony were constituted. Others have investigated the empire as a spatialized terrain of power, a space in which geographies of connection between peoples and places contributed to the formulation and reformulation of colonial discourses. Attention has been paid to the ways in which gender and sexuality have been critical arenas for the articulation of colonial power. Challenging the old paradigm of "center and periphery," the empire has been conceptualized as an "imperial social formation" or as a web of relations that brought disparate regions, commodities, and individuals into contact through systems of mobility and exchange, always in unequal relations of power.[2]

The emergence of this body of work owes as much to practitioners of British history in the United States and other parts of the world as it does to those in Britain. This new historiography is a crisscrossing business, building on the insights of critical thinkers across the globe and connecting history writing to postcolonial issues in India, the Caribbean, Australia, New Zealand, South Africa, and Ireland, to name just some of the places in which rethinkings of empire are taking place. There are obvious points of connection between this venture and the essays in this volume, not least the work of Ann Laura Stoler herself, which has been a constant point of reference for many of those writing in the field. Her insistence on the ways in which sexuality was managed and racial categories produced; on the connections between "the broad-scale dynamics of colonial rule and the intimate sites of implementation"; on affective attachments as critical to the making of colonial categories and "the conceptual fixity of categories and the fluidity of their context" have all stimulated scholars working on the British Empire.[3]

The purpose of this volume, as Stoler argues, is to focus on the intimacies of empire and the circuits of knowledge production that transcend national boundaries and confined frames—the global circuits through which gendered and racialized selves are constituted. The authors collectively propose a reconfigured field of U.S. history (to call it North American would involve engaging with Canadian material)—a history that is more attentive to the colonial aspects of its formation and that focuses on transnational movements and trajectories rather than on national narratives. The essays range widely in their spatial and temporal concerns—from eighteenth-century Alaska to the twentieth-century Philippines, nineteenth-century St. Louis to twentieth-century New Mexico, to name but a few of the locations. All circle conceptually around questions of race and racial classification, gender, intimacy, and knowledge production. Stoler's respondents question and situate the relevance of empire, which, it should be noted, does not feature as a key conceptual tool in some of the essays. Stoler herself, as a historian of empire, is interested in the "domains of overlap and difference" involved in "becoming colonial," the patterns that are particular to time and place but "resonate with practices in a wider global field."[4] She looks to the mutual relevance of U.S. history and (post)colonial studies. Let me add something of the British Empire into this rich mix.

Stoler's argument is that "the intimate frontiers" of empire are the social and cultural spaces where racial classifications were "defined and defied" and where "relations between colonizer and colonized could powerfully confound or confirm the strictures of government and the categories of rule." Her interest is explicitly comparative and theoretical. She is pursuing the connections between "the broad-scale dynamics of rule and the intimate domains of implementation." "Sexual and affective intimacies," she suggests, "are a privileged site," "dense transfer points of power" in Foucault's terms, "sites of production of colonial inequities and therefore of tense ties as well."[5] The tenseness of the "tender ties" were effects of their being locked into the violence of conquest and dispossession and the daily practices of intimate inequalities, as Gwenn Miller explores in her work on Alaska in this volume.

As a historian of the British Empire my question is how a focus on discourses of affect and the livedness of emotional life might have an impact on the upholding, mediating, or transgressing of colonial relations? What difference might it make to the histories we already have when we interrogate them through questions of intimacy and emotion? What might an emphasis on affect and feeling open up?

THE TITLE OF STOLER'S ESSAY draws on Sylvia Van Kirk's classic study of fur-trade society, *"Many Tender Ties." Women in Fur-Trade Society in Western Canada, 1670–1870*, first published in 1980, when women's history was in its infancy. Van Kirk's own title utilized an evocative passage from James Douglas, a company official of the North West Company who eventually rose to become a chief factor of the Hudson's Bay Company. "There is indeed no living with comfort in this country," Douglas wrote in 1843, "until a person has forgot the great world and has his tastes and character formed on the current standard of the stage.... Habit makes it familiar to us, softened as it is by the many tender ties, which find a way to the heart."[6] Douglas had married Amelia Connolly, the child of a British fur trader (who was Douglas's own immediate superior) and a Cree mother. His "comfort" in the harsh world of the Northwest depended on his adaptation to the mixed world of fur traders and hunters, "the current standard" of his stage, and on the emotional connections he made with the indigenous peoples he encountered, the "tender ties" that found a way to his heart. Van Kirk was interested in exploring the role of First Nations, "mixed-blood," and white women in the development of fur-trade society, and the archives provided a rich source from which to explore the human dimension of the colonial encounter and the changes across time as colonialism developed. Her work has continued to focus on these issues, though it has grown more inflected by questions of gender, race, and cultural difference, as might be expected. She, along with other scholars, has produced a rich body of scholarship on the development of the Canadian West in its colonial context. Stoler, however, has not gone beyond Douglas's phrase to explore the relevance of this work to her concerns. What might that scholarship tell us of the significance of affective intimacies in confirming, mediating, or transgressing colonial classifications?

The body of feminist scholarship on western Canada allows us to investigate the relation between the "broad-scale dynamics of rule" and the "intimate domains of implementation" very effectively. It points us to the critical importance of the social, economic, and legal contexts in which "tender ties" were made and different forms of intimacy legitimated. It reminds us of the significance of historical change over time, of generation as well as gender, of the flow of possibility across time that was never simply linear, of what might be possible for mothers but not daughters or for sons but not fathers, how attempts were made at different levels to regulate patterns of intimacy.[7] But addressing this work through the lens of "affect" could take us into yet further dimensions of the lived relations of colonialism. The story of James Douglas and his family offers an instructive case study. Born in Demerara in 1803, he was the son of a Scottish sugar merchant and a free woman of color. His father had later married a Scot, and James was educated in Scotland and then sent to make his fortune in the Northwest, a suitably distant outpost of empire as Adele Perry notes.[8] In 1828 he married Amelia Connolly according to the "custom of the country," the fur-trade marriage rite that combined European and Aboriginal traditions. As Van Kirk documented, in the first phases of fur-trade activity it was common for European traders to marry indigenous women, establish households, and raise families. The fur trade generated a distinctive culture, one "based on a commodity exchange between two divergent groups of people" living in a mutually dependent set of relations. Aboriginal women had much to offer for they brought contacts and economic possibilities. By the early nineteenth century, however, the traders were tending to marry "mixed-blood" wives, as did Douglas, rather than "Indians." By the 1830s and 1840s the increasing numbers of white women coming to the region, this in-migration a strategic policy to reduce the threat of miscegenation, meant that many of the traders abandoned their Aboriginal families and sought white wives to improve their status. Marriage according to the "custom of the country" was attacked by the missionaries who were now establishing themselves across the Northwest. Young "mixed-blood" girls, brought up to expect marriage, found themselves reduced to the status of mistress, a humiliating experience and one that locked them into the racialized category of the promiscuous native woman, a stereotype that was increasingly utilized in the Canadian West. Company officers who had Aboriginal wives were criticized and found themselves in danger of prejudicing their careers.[9] Douglas, however, renewed his commitment to Amelia, and they were married again in 1838, this time in an Anglican ceremony.[10]

Early forms of colonial encounter, dominated by exploration and commercial exploitation, were structured through dependence between fur traders and indigenous peoples. The shift to settler colonialism involved the expropriation of the land and the claim that the land belonged to the colonizers. The association between dispossession, colonization, and migration was critically made through gender, as Adele Perry argues so eloquently in *On the Edge of Empire*. Settler colonies like British Columbia were organized, she demonstrates, "around the double need to dispossess indigenous societies and build a settler population in their stead. . . . Gender is where the abiding bonds between dispossession and colonisation become most clear."[11] If a white society was to be built, white women must bear legitimate heirs and be "the mothers of the race"; white men would claim and cultivate the land, and Aboriginal peoples would be marginalized.

As the new colony of Vancouver Island, soon to be merged into British Columbia, developed, prominent fur-trading families bought land and moved in to Fort Victoria, the heart of the new crown colony. The men aimed to become part of the colonial elite, but those, like Douglas, whose wives and children were "mixed-blood" found they faced particular challenges. For Douglas, forgetting "the great world" became more difficult as British Columbia became a colony; local connections to the metropole were strengthened, and new colonists arrived, strengthening both cultural and emotional ties to the mother country. The increased mobility of the mid-nineteenth century, the improved communications, the move from trading posts to settlements with missionaries and teachers, the more effective knowledge circuits of the nineteenth-century empire all brought the once isolated world of the fur trader into closer proximity with the metropole. All this had its affective dimensions. Family affections were threatened as, for example, daughters became embarrassed by the looks and manners of their mixed-blood or Indian mothers. Or British men, drawing on their emotive attachment to home, became enmeshed in the increased hostility to miscegenation. Racial thinking in the metropole was hardening in the mid-Victorian period as emancipated Africans in the West Indies proved to be less obliging than expected and indigenous peoples across the empire resisted colonialism.[12] A stress on racial belonging, for whites and others, produced a new economy of affect across the empire. In British Columbia increasingly harsh conflicts with indigenous peoples over land and resources as settlers tried to create a white colony, an offshoot of the mother country, fostered binary divisions between "them" and "us," divisions across which feelings of love and affection were not supposed to operate. Douglas himself was protected by his status; his African blood was much less an issue than his wife's Cree lineage. Amelia and their children were subjected to adverse comment despite the protection of their wealth.

Despite his mixed origins and those of Amelia, Douglas was to become the governor of British Columbia in 1850 and was knighted for his services in 1863. Hudson's Bay Company officers, argues Van Kirk, "never seem to have questioned the desirability of acculturating their families to British norms and customs." Their private correspondence is full of paternal concern for their children, and "this was posited in terms of negating the latter's Indianness."[13] Their sons and daughters were taught in English and learned the Bible; their dress was Anglicized, their habits made genteel. This was a project of sensibility: the making of certain kinds of feeling in young men and women. The four Douglas daughters made successful marriages by these standards, attaching themselves to colonial officials and members of the colonial elite. The demographics of British Columbia was critical to the "success" of young women such as these, for the paucity of white women meant that their class status was able to efface their lineage. This may be an instance of a failure to manage sexuality in the ways that were desired by architects of the colonial project who tried hard to persuade more respectable white women to go to British Columbia. Sons were more problematic. Men were expected to operate in the public world of work and politics, and racial stereotyping, casting young Aboriginal men as "naturally" rowdy and dissolute, meant that they were easily displaced by young emigrants from Britain. The successes of the men of the first generation who had made the transition from company officers to colonial elite were not mirrored in the careers of their sons. What were the states of feeling, it would be fascinating to know, of this second generation?

In her recent consideration of the larger colonial context of patterns of intermarriage, Van Kirk argues that between the early seventeenth century and the late nineteenth century the practice of marriage between Aboriginals and non-Aboriginals shifted from "marrying-in," that is staying in close proximity to the Aboriginal group, to "marrying-out." "Marrying-out" meant that if Aboriginal women married white men, and it was almost always this way round, they had to leave their own culture and attempt assimilation. This shift in marriage patterns was associated with a broader dynamic of rule—the end of coexistence between Euro-Canadian and Aboriginal societies in western Canada and the erection of spatial, social, legal, and emotional boundaries between Indians and whites.[14] This process could never be completed, for, as Perry argues in relation to British Columbia, "a number of profound and vexing contradictions lay at the heart of the settler colony's project."[15] Settlers were meant to be white but were often not. Native peoples were supposed to be marginal but constituted the majority of the population. Mixed-race men and women threatened the image of a colony supposedly divided between "them" and "us" and were the embodied expressions of at least some kind of affective ties across racial difference. What were the effects of these shifts in marriage pattern at the level of emotion? How were these changes lived?

The creation of a federal Canada brought new attempts at classification. And whatever the messiness that belied the neat categorizations, these new laws had real effects. The Indian Act of 1876, for example, made Aboriginal people minors—subjects, not citizens—under the guardianship of the new federal government.[16] Furthermore, it minimized the numbers of Aboriginal peoples who were able to make claims on the state. Mainstream discourse was focused on the clear division between "them" and "us," pathologizing or rendering invisible people of mixed origins in this process. In the prairies, as Sarah Carter has shown, métis challenged these constructions, claiming a legitimate, proud, and local identity. It is worth noting that this is a history that invites comparison across both imperial and other borders. In the early period the major impetus for marrying-in had come from Aboriginal groups who wanted to create a socioeconomic bond that would draw Euro-Canadian men into native kinship networks. By the end of the colonial period, dated in 1885, when Plains Indians had been subjugated, métis resistance defeated, and the Canadian-Pacific Railway built, intermarriage had been transformed by the development of settler society into marrying-out.[17] Passing as white was now the main hope for women of Aboriginal descent who had married Euro-Canadians. Their lineage was something to be erased. The attempted control of love, care, and sex became a central plank of governance, demonstrating the importance of affective relations to federal rule.

A number of critical legal cases about the nature of marriage marked the key shifts in this process. As Shah, Salesa, and Cott all argue in this volume, the regulation of marriage is a critical aspect of governing strategies on population. In 1867 the Superior Court of Lower Canada still accepted the practices of both Europeans and Aboriginal people as critical to marital union. Mutual consent, cohabitation, and public reputation as husband and wife were the essential components of marriage. Yet the process of intermarriage had already become effectively colonized, for it was seen as a way to remove Aboriginal women from their own cultures and make them as European as possible. Miscegenation, with all its negative associations, was increasingly thrown into disrepute, both in British Columbia and across the Prairie West.[18] Those of mixed-race were marginalized as settlers sought to insist on the making of a white society and emphasize the sharp distinction between themselves and Indians, who lived "naturally" on reserves. The Aboriginality of the Douglas daughters was lost as they were assimilated into the colonial elite, protected by their class position from the fate of their less-fortunate sisters. Aboriginal women were increasingly sexualized in negative ways. Whereas once they were constructed as wives bringing opportunities and contacts, now, unless they were safely married and assimilated, they were constructed in colonial discourse as dangerous and sinister concubines and prostitutes.[19] Aboriginal women, it might be suggested, became the containers for emotional displacement and disruption, a holding place for the tense ties associated with colonial violence.

A series of legal statutes attempted to define who was "Indian" and who was not. As Renisa Mawani notes, "Since inclusion and exclusion from the nation and access to land and resources were contingent upon defining who was 'white' and who was 'Indian,' it is hardly surprising that the prevalence of 'mixed-race' relations and peoples elicited such anxiety among government officials."[20] By 1886 a legal judgment on intermarriage negated the ruling of 1867, insisting that the cohabitation of a civilized man and a savage woman could not constitute a marriage. Amelia Connolly's mother and father would have been ruled out of court. Some intimacies were declared legally and socially possible, others not. Here the focus is on the legal boundaries that were drawn. But what was the undertow of affect associated with this? The control of marriage by the state was about regulating property and inheritance, racial and physical relations, gender codes and practices of childcare, and the organization of sexual conduct. If we add to this a concern with "affect," other questions arise: of forms of connection that are profoundly irrational, sentient, beyond control to an even greater extent than (although profoundly linked to) physical relationships. In postcolonial literature that concern for affect has been registered in terms of desire, but perhaps notions of sex have been more recognized than that ever-elusive domain of feeling that we need to try and uncover if we are to fully grasp the complex relations of colonialism. The "current standard" of Douglas's stage had shifted substantially as the broad dynamics of rule were geared to shaping the inclusions and exclusions of the new Canadian Federation. As the literature on western Canada shows us so well, "tense and tender ties" were always framed by the larger contexts of historical process and change.

Western Canada was locked into the webs of empire, and this example points to the interconnections between the dynamics of rule in the metropole and those in its far-flung outposts. The translation of metropolitan directives into local practice was always a messy and unfinished business in colonies of white settlement, for as in the North American colonies, colonizers were colonized too. White men in these colonies sought to translate the rights and liberties of free-born Englishmen into new locations, establishing white male suffrage and representative institutions. Their relation to the metropole was ambivalent at best, and often fraught, for the Crown and the imperial Parliament retained considerable powers throughout the nineteenth century — tying colonials into forms of subordination to imperial authority. This was always a cultural as much as a political, legal, or economic phenomenon. And it was an emotional phenomenon too. *Ambivalence* is a word laden with states of feeling and intimations of inner life. Subordination was played out in the bedroom and the kitchen, as well as in the courtroom or the representative assembly. Colonists were provincial, and the culture of the metropole continued to operate a powerful pull, constructing inferiorities and envies. The imperative of thinking across metropole and colony, I would suggest, should never be a reason to forget the salience of metropolitan power and its effects.

WHEREAS MY FIRST EXAMPLE has been focused on the questions that can begin to be addressed when thinking through the lens of affect, my second argues for a broadening of our definition of what might constitute the tense and tender ties negotiated in the making of racialized and gendered selves.

For Stoler there is something special about the arena of sexuality, domesticity, and intimacy — something particular happens in those terrains, which does not happen elsewhere and which makes sexual and domestic relations of power different, especially pertinent in defining relations between colonizer and colonized. "Sexual and affective intimacies are not the only sites," she grants (in response to a discussion with the historian James Vernon), "from which to explore the relationship between metropolitan and colonial histories. Studies in public health and histories of deportment, labor, communication, and transport provide other nodal points. . . . Still, I would argue that sexual and affective intimacies are a privileged site on which those other sites invariably turn back and converge."[21] But affective intimacies can take place in many domains. Take religion, a critical arena of intimacy with the self and a terrain in which affective channels, registers, and states were produced and lived. What part did religious institutions play in the circuits of colonial knowledge production through which new subjects were made? What is the significance of the missionary movement, a movement that had vast ramifications across the European empires, in this configuration? Nurseries and boarding schools are seen as key sites for comparison — but what of the religious and spiritual aspects of their practices and beliefs and the ways in which these shaped new subjectivities? What of the churches, chapels, and mission schools across the globe? Were relations between missionary and native sometimes intimate? And if not, how should they be characterized? What of the notions of the self fostered by different missionary projects? What feeling states did missionaries hope to evoke?

Feminist scholars and those influenced by postcolonial forms of analysis have turned to missionary archives as a rich source for the investigation of the relations between colonizer and colonized.[22] My own research has focused on missions as sites for the making of new subjects, both in the metropolitan and colonial contexts.[23] The missionary movement that developed in Britain from the 1790s was rooted in evangelical Christianity. Real Christianity, as it was called, to be distinguished from nominal Christianity, which was only concerned with the forms of religious belonging, depended on conversion. Classically associated with the experience of St. Paul on the road to Tarsus, conversion meant an individual's overpowering conviction of original sin and sense of the possibility of redemption through the divine mission of Christ. The soul was flooded with God's grace, and there was a melting of self or individual will, a renunciation and fusion with Christ, a new state of feeling. The soul was washed clean; the penitent was born anew in Christ.

Rebirth in Christ made possible a new man or woman. The "undivided surrender" of the heart to "holy obedience" was the aim of the serious Christian, matched by a constant fear of backsliding. From the concern with the pervasiveness of sin, the sense of oneself as depraved, weak, and inadequate, came the obsession with self-examination. Evangelicalism thus encouraged a powerful sense of self but a self that was transformed and made anew in God's image. This renewal demanded new codes of behavior, based on a new morality, and a new emotional life. Prayer was the key to the overlooking of the self, sometimes assisted by journal keeping, a record of the trials and tribulations of each day, the sins committed, the temptations refused. Individual introspection was a necessary part of religious practice. At the same time, Christians would engage in mutual supervision, the constant checking on each other by brothers and sisters in Christ. For evangelicals the family and household occupied a special place in their faith: given the assumptions as to the wickedness of the world, the home was the haven, the place of peace, the site of a proper religious life. Within the family the father would act as spiritual guide or monitor for his dependants and in the church or chapel the minister would act as spiritual father to his flock. In the struggle for the better self, constant vigilance was essential, and the Christian family was obligated to help in any way it could. The family must engage in the control, disciplining, ordering, and suppression of affective connections. A constant commentary on the most intimate practices of daily life was part of the evangelical agenda. How were men and women behaving? Were there signs of sin — in sexual immorality, indulgence in drink, the wrong kinds of feelings for unsuitable people, improper activities on the Sabbath or in the workplace?[24]

It was this evangelical code that was at the center of much of the missionary activity across the Empire that burgeoned from the 1790s. In the 1820s a renewal of antislavery activity in the metropole brought an increased interest in the West Indies, and enthusiastic young evangelicals were recruited to work on the plantations, taking advantage of the concessions that had been won in the Imperial Parliament, compelling plantation owners to make religious teaching available to the enslaved. The Baptist missionaries whose activities I have tracked in Jamaica had all experienced conversion themselves, struggled on a daily basis to live what they saw as a properly religious life, and devoted their lives to saving "the heathen," not in their own benighted country but in the more exotic settings of the Caribbean or India. Their task as they saw it was to teach Africans or Indians to be new men and women in Christ. In the process they constructed themselves as colonizers, not the same kind of colonizers as planters, colonial officials, or military or naval men but committed to a reforming colonial project, one that would create a humanitarian tutelary empire. The enslaved were "poor souls" to be rescued from sin and bondage. They were wretched victims locked in the double barbarisms of slavery and Africa. It was Britain's Christian duty, ordained by God in his providential plan for her empire, to save these sinners. The missionary vision was of a universal family of God: they themselves were the patriarchs, bringing leadership and guidance to those in need. They would be authoritative but tender with their charges, attempting to organize and legislate both their own emotional lives and those of their congregations — regularizing marriages in an attempt to stop intimacies "out of place," training wives and mothers to produce family meals so that food took its proper place in an economy of affect, disciplining when necessary by expulsion from the family of the church.

Missionaries were in constant need of financial, political, and moral support "at home." Their activities were initially funded by home societies. In the Caribbean in the early nineteenth century they were at loggerheads with the plantocracy, who saw their teachings as dangerous. They needed supporters at home to lobby the Colonial Office and the government, write letters to newspapers, circulate petitions, and mobilize public outrage. Through their letters and reports, their lectures when on furlough, their impassioned pleas for support in the heady years of the struggle against slavery, missionaries instructed the British public in the colonial order of things and argued for a particular vision of empire, one in which generous and liberty-loving Britons supported poor heathens in their efforts to become civilized. In this way missionary work contributed to the creation of a colonial frame of mind in the metropole. It played a significant part in the constitution of a particular cultural identity, in the making of a deep connection between being a colonizer and being English. And this was a state of feeling, a way of being in the world, a set of affective relations with others.

Missionary visions took many forms. There were differences between the societies, differences according to time and place, and differences between individual evangelists, whether male or female. In the period before emancipation was won in 1834 the project of the missionaries in the Caribbean was in many respects at odds with that of the colonial state. Between 1834 and the mid-1840s the humanitarian lobby — those in support of antislavery and of the necessity of protecting indigenous peoples from the depredations of settler colonialism — enjoyed its greatest period of influence. By the

1850s the power of these voices had waned as harsher rhetorics of racial difference and imperial authority became more widespread. The missionary movement was never simply an arm of the colonial state, and nonconformist societies, in particular, frequently occupied a critical stance in relation to imperial policies. In elaborating the relation between an imperial body politic and the making of racialized and gendered selves, it is important to recognize the mediating activities of those involved with the varied colonial projects that together made up the myriad activities of colonizers across the globe.[25] Each colonial project had its own relation to the state, and each produced particular ways of being a colonizer, with different imaginings of the colonized. Each was engaged in its own way in the making of an imperial social formation.[26]

In the Jamaica of the 1820s and 1830s Baptist missionaries subscribed to a notion of the universal family of God. Family was associated not simply with blood but with religious belonging, and it might also be used to connote membership of the church or chapel, brothers and sisters in Christ. Thus "native" Christians, African men and women, might be part of the wider Christian family. But racial hierarchies were inscribed into this notion of family, just as men and women were placed as spiritually equal but socially and politically different. St. Paul's much quoted dictum, "neither Jew nor Greek, neither male or female, ye are all one in Christ Jesus," was always in tension with the inscription of inferiority on bodies that were neither white nor male. Black people were "babes in Christ," children who must be led to freedom, and the missionaries were their parents, exemplars, guides, and educators on the road to civilization. While the father/patriarch might be a somewhat distant figure, the missionary wife was frequently more identified with her native protégés, caught in the complexities of a maternal or sisterly role that was rooted in a shared womanhood but marked by the axes of race and class.[27]

In the aftermath of the abolition of slavery Baptist missionaries enjoyed a rare moment of power. Freedmen and freedwomen were well aware of the contribution the missionaries had made to the winning of emancipation and rewarded them by flocking to their chapels in the thousands. The dual moments of emancipation and conversion, the unshackling of both body and soul, brought exceptional opportunities. Missionaries envisioned a new colonial order, with properly regulated gender relations and an industrious proletariat. They borrowed capital from Britain, bought land, and built villages, free villages as they were called, in which men and women could live away from the persecutions of the plantations. Black men would become responsible, industrious, independent, familial, and Christian. They would become citizens and vote. They would work for wages and survey their families with pride. Black women would be wives and mothers, freed from the degradation of concubinage and the unremitting labor of the plantation. The villages were designed with the chapel, mission house, and mission school in pride of place. Neat cottages were laid out around them, roses climbing around the doors, gardens fenced, plots of land large enough to grow vegetables for the family but not enough to support needs without the wage labor of the man. Relations between men and women and parents and children were especially subject to scrutiny, for proper families were seen as the bedrock of a good society. Did women clean their homes well? Were children sleeping separately from parents? What code of conduct regulated family meals? What arrangements were there for personal hygiene? What states of feeling were being lived in these homes? The free villages were to be model communities—the building blocks of a better empire. And the missionaries and their deputies would ensure the proper regulation of daily life, down to the last details of emotional life.

Such a vision was a fantasy. In imagining the possibility of starting anew, the tabula rasa made by emancipation and conversion, the missionaries denied the realities of an existing African culture. Once established, the free villages could not be maintained in their image. The fantasy of the all-seeing, all-regulating, all-supervising hand and eye—buying land, designing houses, marrying couples to legitimize their offspring, educating children—reckoned without the inhabitants. They were men and women who brought with them their own cultural knowledge, shaped by slavery, the middle passage, and the plantations, and they had been honed through their encounter with Christianity and the missionaries, to build their own syncretic forms of religion, their own rituals, their own practices, their own emotional economies, their own African Jamaican way of life.[28] The tensions produced by the intimate ties that missionaries established often erupted; missionary influence was challenged and gradually waned. Nevertheless, the histories of colonizers and colonized embedded in the missionary archives deserve a place in considerations of the affective structures of metropolitan and colonial societies. For an evangelical Christian there was no relation more intimate than that with God and his earthly protagonists.

There is much more that could be said in response to this volume and these essays and the echoes they evoke in the British colonial context. Lisa Lowe's reflections on the intimate connections across continents open up questions of the relation between the empire in her thinking—the project of enlightenment humanism and global capitalism—and the temporalities and characteristics of different European empires. Tiya Miles's essay points to the construction of racial hierarchies between African Americans and Native Americans—a distinction that comes up in other essays alongside that between slavery and dispossession, and the positioning of migrants who are not citizens—all critical tools for the colonizers in the workings of empire and central to British rule. Paul Kramer's discussion of gender and the politics of prostitution in the Philippines invites detailed comparison with Philippa Levine's new study of the management of intimacy through the regulation of venereal disease across both metropole and colony.[29] The list could go on. But finally, one last big question preoccupies me. Britain's empire was overseas— "away" —and the gap between metropole and colony was central to the system of colonial rule. "They" could never be quite like "us," and that is why "we" ruled "them." Complex hierarchies, demarcating subject and citizen, marking forms of inclusion and exclusion, provided the basis for the forms of governmentality that were seen as appropriate to particular colonial sites. The mapping of difference was an empirewide project, and those mappings were constantly articulated and rearticulated over the colonial period—and left vital postcolonial legacies. Did this work differently in the United States—where race was always within, not without? How did this work in the West, where Aboriginality, not slavery, was the key to racial thinking? Were the logics of racial thinking differently constructed in frontier territories? And was it different again from that of an empire? Like all good books this volume leaves us with a rich agenda for further work.

NOTES

Special thanks to Gail Lewis and Adele Perry for their suggestions on this commentary.

1. Burton, "Introduction: On the Inadequacy and Indispensability of the Nation," 2.

2. It is impossible to provide a bibliography of this work, but a brief selection of (for me) pathbreaking titles follows: Burton, *Burdens of History*; Burton, *At the Heart of the Empire*; Midgley, *Women against Slavery*; Coombes, *Reinventing Africa*; Sinha, *Colonial Masculinity*; Kale, *Fragments of Empire*; Thorne, *Congregational Missions and the Making of an Imperial Culture in Nineteenth Century England*; Lester, *Imperial Networks*; Collingham, *Imperial Bodies*; Wilson, *The Island Race*; Ballantyne, *Orientalism and Race*;

Fletcher, Mayhall, and Levine, *Women's Suffrage in the British Empire*; Levine, *Prostitution, Race, and Politics*.

3. Stoler, *Carnal Knowledge and Imperial Power*, 7, 8.

4. Stoler, "Tense and Tender Ties," 830.

5. Ibid., 831.

6. Van Kirk, *"Many Tender Ties"* (1980 ed.), title page. I am most grateful to Sarah Carter and Adele Perry for their support in my effort to begin to educate myself in the history of the Canadian West.

7. This account depends on the work of Van Kirk, Adele Perry, Sarah Carter, and other scholars of Canada. See Perry, "The State of Empire"; Van Kirk, "From 'Marrying-In' to 'Marrying-Out'"; Perry, *On the Edge of Empire*; Clayton, *Islands of Truth*; Carter, *Capturing Women*; Carter, *Aboriginal People and Colonizers of Western Canada to 1900*; Mawani, "In between and Out of Place."

8. See Perry, "The State of Empire."

9. Van Kirk, *"Many Tender Ties"* (1980 ed.), 3, 160–71.

10. Perry, "The State of Empire."

11. Perry, *On the Edge of Empire*, 19.

12. On this shift in metropolitan thinking see Hall, *Civilising Subjects*.

13. Van Kirk, "Tracing the Fortunes," 158.

14. Carter, *Capturing Women*.

15. Perry, "The State of Empire," 3.

16. Carter, *Aboriginal People*, 117.

17. See Van Kirk, "From 'Marrying-In' to 'Marrying-Out.'" This paragraph is drawn from Van Kirk's essay.

18. Perry, *On the Edge of Empire*; Carter, *Capturing Women*.

19. Barman, "Taming Aboriginal Sexuality"; Carter, *Capturing Women*.

20. Mawani, "In between and Out of Place," 53.

21. Stoler, "Tense and Tender Ties," 831n4.

22. For a comparative discussion of some aspects of this work see Hall, "Of Gender and Empire."

23. See Hall, *Civilising Subjects*. The details of the next pages draw on this work.

24. See Davidoff and Hall, *Family Fortunes*, esp. chap. 1.

25. For an excellent example of the workings of particular colonial projects see Clayton, *Islands of Truth*.

26. See Sinha, *Colonial Masculinity*.

27. On the complexities of the relation between missionary women and native subjects see Jolly, "Colonizing Women"; Haggis, "'Good Wives and Mothers.'"

28. See Besson, *Martha Brae's Two Histories*.

29. See Levine, *Prostitution, Race, and Politics*.

NANCY F. COTT

Afterword

Participants' rich and varied engagements with Ann Stoler's essay, "Tense and Tender Ties," testify to the depth of the vein she has been mining. Stoler intended to provoke others by confronting the United States in her probing of the intimacies of empire, and she succeeded. Yet her provocation has produced a collection different from what might have been envisioned at the outset. The participants sidled away from a direct focus on "empire" itself — or colonial relations as such — and embraced other parts of Stoler's conceptual vocabulary. The contents of the volume chorus in tune with Stoler's metathemes, without necessarily vindicating the rubric of empire as the most useful to aggregate or clarify disparate researches.

As a nation-state the United States has generally refused to name its exercise of power as that of an empire. (This is despite its conquest of a continent, its conversion of native groups into "dependent sovereigns," its acquisition of colonies and other island possessions in the Spanish-American and later wars.) When scholars apply the terminology of empire to U.S. history, it goes against the grain — but some have taken that critical approach since the 1960s. *The New American Empire: An Interpretation of American Expansion*, by Walter LaFeber (a student of William Appleman Williams's), led the way in 1963. The endeavor gained scope and particularity in the 1990s, especially following the stimulus of Amy Kaplan's *Cultures of United States Imperialism* (1993).

This collection of essays may indicate a new phase. In their effort to understand how the United States, with its ostensibly representative institutions, has wielded power and has sustained inequalities, the authors here tend to acknowledge the imperial model without adopting it. Emily Rosenberg faces the issue directly with her explicit cautions about imprecision in applying the words *empire* and *imperialism* to U.S. exertions of power and influence, while other essayists sidestep by focusing on concepts such as race, modernity, or governmentality.

Most of the attention here, understandably, alights on Stoler's dimension of "intimacies." The volume's kaleidoscope of responses hooks together conclusively, globally, the familial and sexual intimacies usually called private and the state governing functions usually called public. The two should not easily be separated again. The refusal to accept public and private "as is" has been characteristic of feminist scholarship since the 1980s — a principal feature of the larger project of analyzing how the sex/gender system operates in institutional structures and in social and political order. Stoler's books and articles showing how colonial selves are formed and colonial order implemented via the arena of intimacy have been an energetic part of this literature, as well as part of the literature on racial formation.

It should be impossible hereafter to assess governing strategies — including methods such as standardization, the making of classifications, the taking of statistics — without looking into the realm of "intimacies." Making this connection, linking this link, in the framework of empire is crucial to the aim of internationalizing U.S. history. But the connection is not *more* relevant to imperial management than to the nation-state. Hodes's chapter, on census categories and the indeterminacy of racial classification, is a case in point. That modern (or modernizing) governments drive this highway between the enumerations and classifications required for rule and the "intimate domains" of "sex, sentiment, domestic arrangement, and child rearing" (in Stoler's words) is the overarching point.

No modern nation ignores the intimate domain, because the population is composed and reproduced there. Marriage regulation provides the clearest instance. Legal marriage is only one form of intimacy, but it is the form of sexual and intimate relationship in which the state figures by definition. I became indebted to Stoler's insights when researching the history of marriage as a public institution in the United States. From the founding of this nation to the present, assumptions about marriage have been deeply embedded in public policy of governments at all levels. Monogamy on a Christian model prevailed among the diverse peoples in the United States in great part because political authorities endorsed and aimed to perpetuate it. Positive and punitive laws and government policy choices gave incentives for that model of marriage and prevented alternatives. The domain of sexual and familial intimacies mattered all the more to political authorities because the United States government was based on popular sovereignty. Where the people ruled, the composition and reproduction of the populace had political consequences. Without underrating the religious dimension of marriage, the importance of the political aspects of family formation have to be recognized and credited.

The multiracial character of the U.S. population and the constant incorporation of immigrants into the body politic have also freighted the intimate domain. Because the United States is a hybrid nation, its racial formation is as complicated as that in a European empire, and marriage regulations have registered some of these complications. By incriminating some marriages and encouraging others, marital regulations have drawn lines among the citizenry and defined what kinds of sexual relations and which families will be legitimate. Public policy on marriage has had a great impact not only on what *family* means but also on understandings of *race*. For example, the existence of laws in at least forty states and territories for some period of their histories, prohibiting and criminalizing marriage between a white person and a person of African (and in some fewer number of states, Asian and/or Native American) descent, had a profound influence on the way race itself was constructed and understood. By naming categories of persons who could not marry whites, marriage law constructed race difference and de-legitimated, prohibited, and punished "race mixture." Not until 1967 — at which point these bans were intact in sixteen states — did the U.S. Supreme Court declare this kind of law unconstitutional, for denying equal protection of the laws, and abridging freedom to marry.[1]

Centering on marriage amid the realm of intimacies brings economic attributes more immediately into view. Marriage and property are always linked. In legal cases on the validity of marriages, such as those discussed by Shah and Salesa, for instance, judges were usually aiming to keep dependent women and minor children from having to be supported by public funds, even if that was not mentioned in the opinions. As important as questions about mixedness were in marriage across the color line or across cultures, judges whose decisions pronounced on the morality, legality, and suitability of such unions often had equally in mind securing the putative husband's support for the wife and children. These essays, being drawn to the interface of imperial modalities and intimate lives, show less attention to property than they might — though no one would deny the bearing of sexual intimacy on descent of property as well as of race. (Like marriage, which embodies both public authority and private consent, "private" property, passed on through families, has doubled status, as the foundation of public exploit, entree, wealth, status. The world of privately owned commerce and business is the public world, of course.)

The chapters taken together suggest that the social formation of empire is one governmental version of larger historical developments in the relations between "the West and the rest." Empire as a social formation gives one extended application or illustration of the paradox of "Western civilization": that rationalization and uplift—the "taxonomic" and the "affective" aspects of government administration, in Stoler's words—are tied, twinned, despite their seeming opposition. Lisa Lowe's essay is a prime stimulus to widen the conceptual frame, while both Kathleen Brown's and Shannon Dawdy's confirm it at the very local level of the individual household. This paradox of Western civilization reverberates through the volume. Salesa's Samoan case, for example, illuminates the fundamental point that imperial states, if they are going to claim to protect a population, want to enumerate them. The twinning of motives and consequences reverberates historically around the globe, along the "circuits of knowledge production" that Stoler has brought to the forefront.

More than any other of Stoler's propositions, "circuits of knowledge production" are invoked again and again in these accounts, tellingly. By showing that transnational circuits of knowledge figured in U.S. policies and practices far more strategically than typical nation-bounded histories would grant, the volume distinctively advances a critical internationalism in American history.[2] Stern's essay on psychometrics provides one pattern. And Salesa's and Rosenberg's provide others, both of them emphasizing that the knowledge that travels these circuits can be maladaptive. The forceful presence of global circuits, for good or ill, stays in the mind. Methodologically, this will be a lasting contribution of the essays as a group.

NOTES

1. *Loving v. Virginia*, 388 U.S. 1 (1967), 6 n.5. See Cott, *Public Vows*.

2. See Desmond and Domínguez, "Resituating American Studies in a Critical Internationalism."

Aboriginal Affairs Planning Authority. *Aboriginal Welfare: The Initial Conference of Commonwealth and State Aboriginal Authorities.* Canberra: Government Printer, 1937.

Abuelas de la Plaza de Mayo. *Abuelas de la plaza de Mayo.* http://www.abuelas.org.ar/ (accessed July 13, 2005).

Adams, H. C. "How the People Are Counted." *Chautauquan* 12, Jan. 1891, 473–76.

Adams, Henry. *The Education of Henry Adams.* Boston: Houghton Mifflin, 1973.

Adams, Rachel. Introduction to *"The Awakening" and Selected Short Fiction,* by Kate Chopin. New York: Barnes and Noble Classics, 2003.

Adams, William Howard. *The Paris Years of Thomas Jefferson.* New Haven, Conn.: Yale University Press, 1997.

Adamson, Alan H. *Sugar without Slaves: The Political Economy of British Guiana, 1838–1904.* New Haven, Conn.: Yale University Press, 1972.

Adas, Michael. "From Settler Colony to Global Hegemon: Integrating the Exceptionalist Narrative of the American Experience into World History." *American Historical Review* 106, no. 5 (Dec. 2001): 1692–1720.

———. *Prophets of Rebellion: Millenarian Protest Movements against the European Colonial Order.* Chapel Hill: University of North Carolina Press, 1979.

Adelman, Jeremy, and Stephen Aron. "From Borderlands to Borders: Empires, Nation-States, and the Peoples in between in North American History." *American Historical Review* 104, no. 3 (June 1999): 814–41.

African National Congress. "Colonialism of a Special Type." http://www.anc.org.za/ ancdocs/history/special.html (accessed July 14, 2005).

"Against 'Regulated' Vice." *Woman's Column,* May 3, 1902, 1.

Alarcón, Norma. "Traddutora, Traditora: A Paradigmatic Figure of Chicana Feminism." In *Scattered Hegemonies: Postmodernity and Transnational Feminist Practices,* ed. Inderpal Grewal and Caren Kaplan, 110–33. Minneapolis: University of Minnesota Press, 1994.

Aldridge, William. Preface to "A Narrative of the Lord's Wonderful Dealings," by John Marrant. In Potkay and Burr, *Black Atlantic Writers of the Eighteenth Century,* 75–76.

Aleinikoff, T. Alexander. *Semblances of Sovereignty: The Constitution, the State, and American Citizenship.* Cambridge, Mass.: Harvard University Press, 2002.

Allen, Ann Taylor. "Gardens of Children, Gardens of God: Kindergarten and Daycare Centers in Nineteenth-Century Germany." *Journal of Social History* 19 (spring 1986): 433–50.

Almaguer, Tomás. "Historical Notes on Chicano Oppression: The Dialectics of Racial and Class Domination in North America." *Aztlán* 5, nos. 1 and 2 (spring 1974): 27–56.

———. *Racial Fault Lines: The Historical Origins of White Supremacy in California.* Berkeley: University of California Press, 1994.

———. "Toward the Study of Chicano Colonialism." *Aztlán* 2, no. 1 (spring 1971): 7–20.

America Society for Ethnohistory. Panel on "Northern Shamanism and Its Observers: Historical and Contemporary Perspectives." Quebec City. October 17, 2002.

American League. *The Crowning Infamy of Imperialism.* RG 94/417937 (Box 2307). National Archives and Records Administration, Washington, D.C.

Anderson, Benedict. *Imagined Communities: Reflections on the Origin and Spread of Nationalism.* London: Verso, 1991.

Anderson, James Douglas. "Education for Servitude: The Social Purposes of School in the Black South, 1870–1930." PhD diss., University of Illinois, 1973.

Anderson, Margo J. *The American Census: A Social History.* New Haven, Conn.: Yale University Press, 1988.

———. "Counting by Race: The Antebellum Legacy." In *The New Race Question: How the Census Counts Multiracial Individuals,* ed. Joel Perlmann and Mary C. Waters, 269–87. New York: Sage, 2002.

Anderson, Warwick. "Colonial Pathologies: American Medicine in the Philippines, 1898–1921." PhD diss., University of Pennsylvania, 1992.

———. *The Cultivation of Whiteness: Science, Health, and Racial Destiny in Australia.* New York: Basic Books, 2003.

———. "Going through the Motions: American Public Health and Colonial 'Mimicry.'" *American Literary History* 14 (2002): 686–719.

———. "Immunities of Empire: Race, Disease, and the New Tropical Medicine." *Bulletin of the History of Medicine* 70, no. 1 (1996): 94–118.

———. "Leprosy and Citizenship." *Positions: East Asia Cultures Critique* 6 (1998): 707–30.

———. "Postcolonial Histories of Medicine." In *Locating Medical History: The Stories and Their Meanings,* ed. John Harley Warner and Frank Huisman, 285–307. Baltimore: Johns Hopkins University Press, 2004.

———. "The Trespass Speaks: White Masculinity and Colonial Breakdown." *American Historical Review* 102, no. 5 (Dec. 1997): 1343–70.

———. "Where Is the Postcolonial History of Medicine?" *Bulletin of the History of Medicine* 72 (1998): 522–30.

Andrew, Elizabeth Wheeler, and Katharine Caroline Bushnell. *The Queen's Daughters in India.* London: Morgan and Scott, 1899.

L'Année psychologique 21 (1914–1919), 22 (1920–1921). Paris: Presses universitaires de France.

Appadurai, Arjun. *Modernity at Large: Cultural Dimensions of Globalization*. Minneapolis: University of Minnesota Press, 1996.

Appleton, Nathan. *Introduction of the Power Loom, and Origin of Lowell*. Lowell, Mass.: B. H. Penhallow, 1858.

Appleton, William. *Selections from the Diaries of William Appleton*. Boston: Merrymount Press, 1922.

Appleton, William, and Company Collection. Mss 766. Vols. 175–80. Harvard Business School Archives. Boston, Mass.

Appleton Family Papers. Massachusetts Historical Society, Boston.

Aptheker, Herbert. *Toward Negro Freedom*. New York: New Century Publishers, 1956.

Archivo Histórico de la Secretaría de Relaciones Exteriores, Mexico City.

Arendt, Hannah. *The Origins of Totalitarianism*. New York: Harcourt Brace, 1975.

Armstrong, Nancy. "Why Daughters Die: The Racial Logic of American Sentimentalism." *Yale Journal of Criticism* 7, no. 2 (fall 1994): 1–25.

Arndt, Katherine L., trans. "Memorandum of Captain 2nd Rank Golovin on the Condition of the Aleuts in the Settlements of the Russian-American Company and on Its Promyshlenniki." *Alaska History* 1, no. 2 (fall–winter 1985–86): 56–71.

Ashforth, Adam. *The Politics of Official Discourse in Twentieth-Century South Africa*. Oxford: Clarendon, 1990.

Atchison, Rena Michaels. *Un-American Immigration: Its Present Effects and Future Perils, a Study from the Census of 1890*. Chicago: Charles H. Kerr, 1894.

Atkinson, Edward. *The Cost of a Nation Crime. The Hell of War and Its Penalties. Two Treatises Suggested by the Appointment of a Day of National Thanksgiving by the President of the United States*. Boston: Rockwell and Churchill Press, 1898.

Attwood, Bain. *The Making of the Aborigines*. Sydney: Allen and Unwin, 1989.

Attwood, Bain, and Fiona McGowan, eds. *Telling Stories: Indigenous History and Memory in Australia and New Zealand*. Sydney: Allen and Unwin, 2001.

Austin, Tony. "Cecil Cook, Scientific Thought, and 'Half-Castes.'" *Aboriginal History* 14 (1990): 104–22.

———. *Never Trust a Government Man: Northern Territory Aboriginal Policy, 1911–1939*. Darwin: Northern Territory University Press, 1997.

Austrian, Geoffrey D. *Herman Hollerith: Forgotten Giant of Information Processing*. New York: Columbia University Press, 1982.

Axtell, James. *The Invasion Within: The Contest of Cultures in Colonial North America*. New York: Oxford University Press, 1985.

———. "The Power of Print in the Eastern Woodlands." In *After Columbus: Essays in the Ethnohistory of Colonial North America*, 86–99. New York: Oxford University Press, 1988.

Ayers, Edward L. "What We Talk about When We Talk about the South." In *All over the Map: Rethinking American Regions*, ed. Edward L. Ayers, Peter Onuf, Patricia Nelson Limerick, and Stephen Nissenbaum, 62–82. Baltimore: Johns Hopkins University Press, 1997.

Bailey, Beth, and David Farber. *The First Strange Place: The Alchemy of Race and Sex in World War II Hawaii*. New York: Free Press, 1992.

Bailey, Ronald, and Guillermo Flores. "Internal Colonialism and Racial Minorities in the U.S.: An Overview." In Bonilla and Girling, *Structures of Dependency*, 149–60.

Bailyn, Bernard, and Philip D. Morgan, eds. *Strangers within the Realm: Cultural Margins of the First British Empire*. Chapel Hill: University of North Carolina Press, 1991.

Baker, Ernest A., ed. *Cassell's French-English, English-French Dictionary*. New ed., revised by J. L. Manchon. New York: Funk and Wagnalls, 1951.

Bakhtin, Mikhail. *Rabelais and His World*. Bloomington: Indiana University Press, 1984.

Balandier, George. "'La situation coloniale': Approche théorique." (The colonial situation: Theoretical approaches.) *Cahiers internationaux de sociologie* 11 (1951): 44–79.

Balibar, Etienne. *Masses, Classes, Ideas: Studies on Politics and Philosophy before and after Marx*. Trans. James Swenson. New York: Routledge, 1994.

———. "Racism and Nationalism." In *Race, Nation, Class: Ambiguous Identities*, ed. Etienne Balibar and Immanuel Wallerstein, 37–67. London: Verso, 1992.

Ballantyne, Tony. *Orientalism and Race: Aryanism in the British Empire*. Houndmills: Palgrave, 2002.

Ballhatchet, Kenneth. *Race, Sex, and Class under the Raj: Imperial Attitudes and Policies and Their Critics, 1793–1905*. London: Weidenfeld and Nicolson, 1980.

Balzer, Marjorie M. *The Tenacity of Ethnicity*. Princeton, N.J.: Princeton University Press, 1999.

Bankoff, Greg. *Crime, Society, and the State in the Nineteenth-Century Philippines*. Quezon Hall: Ateneo de Manila Press, 1996.

Barman, Jean. "Taming Aboriginal Sexuality: Gender, Power, and Race in British Columbia, 1850–1900." *BC Studies* 115/116 (autumn/winter 1997–98): 237–66.

Barrera, Mario. *Race and Class in the Southwest*. Notre Dame, Ind.: University of Notre Dame Press, 1979.

Barrett, Thomas M. *At the Edge of Empire: The Terek Cossacks and the North Caucasus Frontier, 1700–1800*. Boulder, Colo.: Westview Press, 1999.

———. "Lines of Uncertainty: The Frontiers of the Northern Caucasus." In Burbank and Ransel, *Imperial Russia*, 148–73.

Bartholet, Elizabeth. *Family Bonds: Adoption and the Politics of Parenting*. Boston: Houghton Mifflin, 1993.

———. *Nobody's Children: Abuse and Neglect, Foster Drift, and the Adoption Alternative*. Boston: Beacon Press, 1999.

Bashford, Alison, and Maria Nugent. "Leprosy and the Management of Race, Sexuality and Nation in Tropical Australia." In *Contagion: Historical and Cultural Studies*, ed. Alison Bashford and Claire Hooker, 76–105. London: Routledge, 2001.

Bassin, Mark. *Imperial Visions: Nationalist Imagination and Geographical Expansion in the Russian Far East, 1840–1865*. New York: Cambridge University Press, 1999.

———. "Inventing Siberia: Visions of the Russian East in the Early Nineteenth Century." *American Historical Review* 96, no. 3 (June 1991): 763–94.

Bauman, Zygmunt. *Modernity and Ambivalence*. Cambridge: Polity Press, 1991.

Bayoumi, Moustafa. "Moving Beliefs: The Panama Manuscript of Sheikh Sana See and African Diasporic Islam." *Interventions* 5, no. 1 (April 2003): 58–81.

Bederman, Gail. "'Civilization,' the Decline of Middle-Class Manliness, and Ida B. Wells's Antilynching Campaign (1892–94)." *Radical History Review* 52 (winter 1992): 207–39.

———. *Manliness and Civilization: A Cultural History of Gender and Race in the United States, 1880–1917*. Chicago: University of Chicago Press, 1995.

Behlmer, George K. *Child Abuse and Moral Reform in England, 1870–1908*. Stanford, Calif.: Stanford University Press, 1982.

Beisner, Robert L. *Twelve against Empire: The Anti-Imperialists, 1898–1900*. New York: McGraw-Hill, 1968.

Bellingham, Bruce. "Waifs and Strays: Child Abandonment, Foster Care, and Families in Mid-Nineteenth Century New York." In *The Uses of Charity: The Poor on Relief in the Nineteenth-Century Metropolis*, ed. Peter Mandler, 123–60. Philadelphia: University of Pennsylvania Press, 1990.

Bender, Thomas, ed. *Rethinking American History in a Global Age*. Berkeley: University of California Press, 2002.

Benitez-Rojo, Antonio. *The Repeating Island: The Caribbean and Postmodern Perspective*. Durham, N.C.: Duke University Press, 1996.

Benton, Katherine. "What about the Women in the White Man's Camp?: Gender, Nation, and the Redefinition of Race in Cochise County, Arizona, 1853–1941." PhD diss., University of Wisconsin, Madison, 2002.

Berger, Peter, and Thomas Luckman. *The Social Construction of Reality*. New York: Anchor, 1967.

Berkhofer, Robert F. *The White Man's Indian: Images of the American Indian from Columbus to the Present*. New York: Knopf, 1978.

Berlant, Lauren, ed. *Intimacy*. Chicago: University of Chicago Press, 2000.

———. Introduction to *Intimacy*, ed. Lauren Berlant, 1–8. Chicago: University of Chicago Press, 2000.

Bermann, Karl. *Under the Big Stick: Nicaragua and the United States since 1848*. Boston: South End Press, 1986.

Bernstein, Michael A. *A Perilous Progress: Economists and Public Purpose in Twentieth-Century America*. Princeton, N.J.: Princeton University Press, 2001.

Berry, Mary Frances. *The Pig Farmer's Daughter and Other Tales of American Justice*. New York: Knopf, 1999.

Besson, Jean. *Martha Brae's Two Histories: European Expansion and Caribbean Culture-Building in Jamaica*. Chapel Hill: University of North Carolina Press, 2002.

Bhabha, Homi. "Of Mimicry and Man: The Ambivalence of Colonial Discourse." In *The Location of Culture*, 85–92. New York: Routledge, 1994.

Billings, John S. "The Diminishing Birth-Rate in the United States." *Forum* 15 (June 1893): 467–77.

Biolsi, Thomas. "The Birth of the Reservation: Making the Modern Individual among the Lakota." *American Ethnologist* 22, no. 1 (1995): 28–53.

Bird, Carmel, ed. *The Stolen Children: Their Stories*. Sydney: Random House, 1998.

Black, Lydia. "Creoles in Russian America." *Pacifica* 2, no. 2 (Nov. 1990): 142–55.

———. *Orthodoxy in Alaska: Christianization of Alaska, Veniaminov's Stewardship, Orthodoxy in Alaska after 1867.* Patriarch Athenagoras Orthodox Institute at the Graduate Theological Union. Distinguished Lecture series, no. 6. Berkeley, 1999.

Blake, Kellee. "'First in the Path of the Firemen': The Fate of the 1890 Population Census." *Prologue: Quarterly of the National Archives and Records Administration* 28 (spring 1996): 64–81.

Blauner, Robert. *Racial Oppression in America.* New York: Harper and Row, 1972.

Block, Sharon. "Lines of Color, Sex, and Service: Comparative Sexual Coercion in Early America." In Hodes, *Sex, Love, Race,* 141–63.

Boder, David Pablo. *La B-S-T-M: La escala Binet-Simon-Terman en su adaptación provisional para Mexico.* Mexico City: Talleres Graficos de la Nación, 1926.

Bodkin, James. "Sea Otters." *Alaska Geographic* 27, no. 2 (2000): 74–92.

Bonacich, Edna. "A Theory of Ethnic Antagonism: The Split Labor Market." *American Sociological Review* 37 (Oct. 1972): 547–59.

Bonilla, Frank, and Robert Girling, eds. *Structures of Dependency.* Stanford, mimeo, 1973.

Bönker, Dirk. "Admiration, Enmity, and Cooperation: U.S. Navalism and the British and German Empires before the Great War." *Journal of Colonialism and Colonial History* 2, no. 1 (spring 2001).

Boot, Max. *The Savage Wars of Peace: Small Wars and the Rise of American Power.* New York: Basic Books, 2002.

Bordon, Alejandro. "Advierten robo de 6 niños al día." *La Reforma,* April 24, 2002, online edition, http://busquedas.gruporeforma.com/utilerias/imdservicios3W.DLL?JSearchformatS&File=MEX/REFORM01/00247/00247571.htm&palabra=bordon&siteforma (accessed Aug. 23, 2005).

Borneman, John. "Until Death Do Us Part: Marriage/Death in Anthropological Discourse." *American Ethnologist* 23, no. 2 (spring 1996): 215–50.

Bowker, Geoffrey C., and Susan Leigh Star. *Sorting Things Out: Classification and Its Consequences.* Cambridge, Mass.: MIT Press, 1999.

Boym, Svetlana. "Diasporic Intimacy: Ilya Kabokov's Installations and Immigrant Homes." *Critical Inquiry,* no. 24 (winter 1998): 498–524.

Brace, Charles Loring. *The Dangerous Classes of New York and Twenty Years' Work among Them.* 1880. Reprint, Montclair, N.J.: P. Smith, 1967.

Brandt, Allan M. *No Magic Bullet: A Social History of Venereal Disease in the United States since 1880.* New York: Oxford University Press, 1985.

Breeden, James O. *Advice among Masters: The Ideal in Slave Management in the Old South.* Westport, Conn.: Greenwood Press, 1980.

Briggs, Charles W. *The Progressing Philippines.* Philadelphia: Griffith and Rowland Press, 1913.

Briggs, Laura. *Reproducing Empire: Race, Sex, Science, and U.S. Imperialism in Puerto Rico.* Berkeley: University of California Press, 2002.

Brooks, James, ed. *Confounding the Color Line: The Indian-Black Experience in North America.* Lincoln: University of Nebraska Press, 2002.

Brooks, Joanna. *American Lazarus: Religion and the Rise of African-American and Native American Literatures*. New York: Oxford University Press, 2003.

Brower, Daniel R., and Edward J. Lazzerini, eds. *Russia's Orient: Imperial Borderlands and Peoples, 1700–1719*. Bloomington: Indiana University Press, 1997.

Brown, JoAnne. *The Definition of a Profession: The Authority of Metaphor in the History of Intelligence Testing, 1890–1930*. Princeton, N.J.: Princeton University Press, 1992.

Brown, Kathleen M. *Good Wives, Nasty Wenches, and Anxious Patriarchs: Gender, Race, and Power in Colonial Virginia*. Chapel Hill: University of North Carolina Press, 1996.

Brown, Wendy. *States of Injury: Power and Freedom in Late Modernity*. Princeton, N.J.: Princeton University Press, 1995.

Brownell, Atherton. "Turning Savages into Citizens." *Outlook*, Dec. 24, 1910, 921–31.

———. "What American Ideas of Citizenship May Do for Oriental Peoples." *Outlook*, Dec. 23, 1904, 975–85.

Brubaker, Rogers. *Citizenship and Nationhood in France and Germany*. Cambridge, Mass.: Harvard University Press, 1992.

Brumberg, Joan Jacobs. "The Ethnological Mirror: American Evangelical Women and Their Heathen Sisters, 1870–1910." In *Women and the Structure of Society*, ed. Barbara J. Harris and JoAnn McNamara, 108–28. Durham, N.C.: Duke University Press, 1984.

Buckingham, Jane. *Leprosy in Colonial South India*. Basingstoke: Palgrave, 2002.

Buck-Morss, Susan. "Hegel and Haiti." *Unpacking Europe: Towards a Critical Reading*, ed. S. Hassan and I. Dadi, 42–70. Rotterdam: Museum Boijmans Van Beuningen, 2001.

Buell, Raymond Leslie. *The Native Problem in Africa*. Vol. 2. New York: Macmillan, 1928.

Bull, W. K. *A Trip to Tahiti and Other Islands in the South Seas*. Melbourne: Privately published, 1858.

Burbank, Jane, and David L. Ransel, eds. *Imperial Russia: New Histories for the Empire*. Bloomington: Indiana University Press, 1998.

Burgess, Perry. *Who Walk Alone*. New York: Henry Holt, 1940.

Burkitt, Ian. "Civilization and Ambivalence." *British Journal of Sociology* 47 (1996): 135–50.

Burnham, John C. "Medical Inspection of Prostitutes in America in the 19th Century: The St. Louis Experiment and Its Sequel." In *Paths into American Culture: Psychology, Medicine, and Morals*, 138–49. Philadelphia: Temple University Press, 1988.

Burnley, William Hardin. *Observations on the Present Condition of the Island of Trinidad and the Actual State of the Experiment of Negro Emancipation*. London: Longman, Brown, Green, and Longman, 1842.

Burris, Barbara. "Fourth World Manifesto." In *Dear Sisters: Dispatches from the Women's Liberation Movement*, ed. Ros Baxandall and Linda Gordon, 101–3. New York: Basic Books, 2000.

Burton, Antoinette. *At the Heart of the Empire: Indians and the Colonial Encounter in Late Victorian Britain*. Berkeley: University of California Press, 1998.

———. *Burdens of History: British Feminists, Indian Women, and Imperial Culture, 1865–1915*. Chapel Hill: University of North Carolina Press, 1994.

———, ed. *Gender, Sexuality, and Colonial Modernities*. New York: Routledge, 1999.

———. "Introduction: On the Inadequacy and Indispensability of the Nation." In *After the Imperial Turn: Thinking with and through the Nation*, 1–26. Durham, N.C.: Duke University Press, 2003.

———. "Introduction: The Unfinished Business of Colonial Modernities." In Burton, *Gender, Sexuality, and Colonial Modernities*, 1–16.

Bushman, Richard L. *The Refinement of America: Persons, Houses, Cities*. New York: Knopf, 1992.

Butcher, John G. *The British in Malaya, 1880–1941: The Social History of a European Community in Colonial South-East Asia*. Kuala Lumpur: Oxford University Press, 1976.

Butler, Judith. "Endangered/Endangering: Schematic Racism and White Paranoia." In *Reading Rodney King/Reading Urban Uprising*, ed. Robert Gooding-Williams, 15–22. New York: Routledge, 1993.

———. *Subjects of Desire: Hegelian Reflections in Twentieth-Century France*. New York: Columbia, 1987.

Butterfield, Kenyon L. *Report of Dr. Kenyon L. Butterfield on Rural Conditions and Sociological Problems in South Africa*. New York: Columbia University, 1929.

Bynum, Victoria E. *Unruly Women: The Politics of Social and Sexual Control in the Old South*. Chapel Hill: University of North Carolina Press, 1992.

Calder, Bruce. *The Impact of Intervention*. Austin: University of Texas Press, 1984.

Calhoun, Craig. *Critical Social Theory: Culture, History, and the Challenge of Difference*. Oxford: Blackwell, 1995.

Camagay, Maria Luisa. *Working Women of Manila in the 19th Century*. Manila: University of the Philippines Press, Center for Women's Studies, 1995.

Campbell, James T. *Songs of Zion: The African Methodist Episcopal Church in the United States and South Africa*. New York: Oxford University Press, 1995.

Canny, Nicholas. "The Ideology of English Colonization: From Ireland to America." *William and Mary Quarterly*, 3rd ser., 30 (1973): 575–98.

———. *Making Ireland British, 1580–1650*. Oxford: Oxford University Press, 2001.

———. "Writing Atlantic History; or, Reconfiguring the History of Colonial British America." *Journal of American History* 86, no. 3 (Dec. 1999): 1093–1114.

Carby, Hazel V. *Reconstructing Womanhood: The Emergence of the Afro-American Woman Novelist*. New York: Oxford University Press, 1987.

Carnegie Commission. *Joint Findings and Recommendations of the Commission, Report of the Carnegie Commission of Investigation on the Poor White Question in South Africa*. Stellenbosch: Pro Ecclesia-Drukkery, 1932.

Carroll, Charles. *The Negro a Beast, or, in the Image of God*. St. Louis: American Book and Bible House, 1900.

Carson, John. "Army Alpha, Army Brass, and the Search for Army Intelligence." *Isis* 84, no. 2 (June 1993): 278–309.

Carter, Sarah. *Aboriginal People and Colonizers of Western Canada to 1900*. Toronto: University of Toronto Press, 1999.

———. *Capturing Women: The Manipulation of Cultural Imagery in Canada's Prairie West*. Montreal: McGill-Queens University Press, 1997.

Cary, John. *The Rise of the Accounting Profession*. New York: American Institute of Certified Public Accountants, 1969–70.

Casa Alianza. *They Shoot Children, Don't They?* http://www.casa-alianza.org/EN/ human-rights/ (accessed Aug. 7, 2003).

Cashin, Joan E. "The Structure of Antebellum Planter Families: 'The Ties That Bound Us Was Strong.' " *Journal of Southern History* 56, no. 1 (1990): 55–70.

Castaneda, Antonia I. "Sexual Violence in the Politics and Policies of Conquest." In *Building with Our Hands: New Directions in Chicana Studies*, ed. Adela de la Torre and Beatriz M. Pesquera, 15–33. Berkeley: University of California Press, 1993.

Cell, John W. "Anglo-Indian Medical Theory and the Origins of Segregation in West Africa." *American Historical Review* 91, no. 2 (April 1986): 307–35.

———. *The Highest Stage of White Supremacy: The Origins of Segregation in South Africa and the American South*. New York: Cambridge University Press, 1982.

"The Census Muddle." *Nation*, Sep. 18, 1890, 223–24.

"The Census of the United States." *Scientific American* 63 (Aug. 30, 1890): 132.

"Certificate of Degree of Indian or Alaska Native Blood." *Federal Register* 65, no. 75 (April 18, 2000): 20775–87.

Cervantes, Fred. "Chicanos as a Post Colonial Minority: Some Questions Concerning the Adequacy of the Paradigm of Internal Colonialism." In *Perspectives in Chicano Studies*, ed. Reynaldo Flores, 123–35. Los Angeles: Chicano Studies Research Center, UCLA, 1977.

Chakrabarty, Dipesh. "Postcoloniality and the Artifice of History: Who Speaks for 'Indian' Pasts?" *Representations* 37 (winter 1992): 1–26.

———. *Provincializing Europe: Postcolonial Thought and Historical Difference*. Princeton, N.J.: Princeton University Press, 2000.

Challener, Richard. *Admirals, Generals, and American Foreign Policy, 1898–1914*. Princeton, N.J.: Princeton University Press, 1973.

Chaloult, Norma Beatriz, and Yves Chaloult. "The Internal Colonialism Concept: Methodological Considerations." *Social and Economic Studies* 28 (Dec. 1979): 85–99.

Chamberlin, Frederick C. *The Blow from Behind*. Boston: Lee and Shepard, 1903.

Chandler, Alfred D., Jr. *The Visible Hand: The Managerial Revolution in American Business*. Cambridge, Mass.: Harvard University Press, 1977.

Chandler, Michael, dir. and prod. *Secrets of the SAT*. Frontline, 1999.

Chapman, Mariana W. "The New Militarism and Purity." *Philanthropist* 14, no. 2 (April 1899): 2–3.

Chapman, Paul Davis. *Schools as Sorters: Lewis M. Terman, Applied Psychology, and the Intelligence Testing Movement, 1890–1930*. New York: New York University Press, 1988.

Chapman, Ronald Fettes. *Leonard Wood and Leprosy in the Philippines: The Culion Leper Colony, 1921–27*. Washington, D.C.: University Press of America, 1982.

Chatterjee, Indrani. "Colouring Subalternity: Slaves, Concubines, and Social Orphans in Early Colonial India." In *Subaltern Studies X: Writings on South Asian History and Society*, ed. Gautam Bhadra, Gyan Prakash, and Susie Tharu, 49–97. New Delhi: Oxford University Press, 1999.

Chatterjee, Partha. *The Nation and Its Fragments*. Princeton, N.J.: Princeton University Press, 1993.

Chechulin, N. D., ed. *Nakaz imp. Ekateriny II. dannyi kommisii o sochinenii proekta novogo ulozheniia*. St. Petersburg, 1907.

Chesnutt, Charles W. "What Is a White Man?" 1889. Reprinted in *Interracialism: Black-White Intermarriage in American History, Literature, and Law*, ed. Werner Sollors, 37–41. New York: Oxford University Press, 2000.

Chesterman, John, and Brian Galligan. *Citizens without Rights: Aborigines and Australian Citizenship*. Cambridge: Cambridge University Press, 1997.

Child, Brenda J. *Boarding School Seasons: American Indian Families, 1900–1940*. Lincoln: University of Nebraska Press, 1998.

Cho, Yu-Fang. "Narratives of Coupling in the Shadow of Manifest Domesticity: Women's Rights, Racialized Labor, and the Transnational Politics of U.S. Cultures of Benevolence, 1890s–1910s." PhD diss., University of California, San Diego, 2004.

Chopin, Kate. *The Awakening*. Ed. Margaret Culley. New York: Norton, 1976.

Churchill, Ward, and Glenn T. Morris. "Key Indian Laws and Cases." In Jaimes, *The State of Native America*, 13–21.

Churchward, William Brown. *My Consulate in Samoa: A Record of Four Years' Sojourn in the Navigators Islands*. London: R. Bentley and Son, 1887.

Cilento, R. W. *The White Man in the Tropics, with Especial Reference to Australia and Its Dependencies*. Melbourne: Government Printer, n.d. [c1925].

"Citizenship of Children Born Abroad and of Married Women." Feb. 10, 1855, 33rd Cong. Ch. 71; 10 Stat. 604.

Clancy-Smith, Julia, and Frances Gouda, eds. *Domesticating the Empire: Race, Gender, and Family Life in French and Dutch Colonialism*. Charlottesville: University Press of Virginia, 1998.

Clark, Elizabeth B. "'The Sacred Rights of the Weak': Pain, Sympathy, and the Culture of Individual Rights in Antebellum America." *Journal of American History* 82, no. 2 (Sep. 1995): 463–93.

Clark, Ira G. "The Elephant Butte Controversy: A Chapter in the Emergence of Federal Water Law." *Journal of American History* 61 (1975): 1006–33.

Clarke, Kamari Maxine. *Mapping Yoróba Networks*. Durham, N.C.: Duke University Press, 2004.

Clark, Robert Emmet. "Management and Control of Community Property in New Mexico." *Tulane Law Journal* 26 (1952): 324–43.

Clayton, Daniel W. *Islands of Truth: The Imperial Fashioning of Vancouver Island*. Vancouver: University of British Columbia Press, 2000.

Cleary, Richard Louis. *The Place Royale and Urban Design in the Ancien Régime*. New York: Cambridge University Press, 1999.

Clinton, Catherine. *The Plantation Mistress: Woman's World in the Old South*. New York: Pantheon, 1982.

Clinton, Catherine, and Michele Gillespie. *The Devil's Lane: Sex and Race in the Early South*. New York: Oxford University Press, 1997.

Clymer, Kenton J. *Protestant Missionaries in the Philippines, 1898–1916: An Inquiry into the American Colonial Mentality*. Urbana: University of Illinois Press, 1986.

Coffman, Edward. *The Old Army: A Portrait of the American Army in Peacetime, 1784– 1898*. New York: Oxford University Press, 1986.

Cohen, Patricia Cline. *A Calculating People: The Spread of Numeracy in Early America*. Chicago: University of Chicago Press, 1982.

Cohen, William B. *The French Encounter with Africans*. Bloomington: Indiana University Press, 1980.

Cohn, Bernard S. *An Anthropologist among the Historians and Other Essays*. Delhi: Oxford University Press, 1987.

Colley, Linda. *Captives: Britain, Empire, and the World, 1600–1850*. New York: Random House, 2002.

Collingham, E. M. *Imperial Bodies: The Physical Experience of the Raj*. Cambridge: Polity, 2001.

Collins, Patricia Hill. *Black Feminist Thought: Knowledge, Consciousness, and the Politics of Empowerment*. Boston: Unwin Hyman, 1990.

"The Columbian Exposition — IX." *Nation*, Sep. 28, 1893, 224–26.

Comaroff, Jean, and John Comaroff. *Ethnography and the Historical Imagination*. Boulder, Colo.: Westview Press, 1992.

Comaroff, John. "Reflections on the Colonial State, in South Africa and Elsewhere." *Social Identities* 4 (1998): 338–40.

Comisión Nacional sobre la desaparición de personas, Argentina. *Nunca más: Informe de la Comisión Nacional sobre la desaparición de personas*. Buenos Aires: EUDEBA, 1984.

Comisión para el Esclarecimiento Histórico. *Guatemala: Memoria del silencio*. 12 vols. Guatemala: Oficina de servicios para proyectos las naciones unidas, 1991.

Commager, Henry Steele. *The Empire of Reason: How Europe Imagined and America Realized the Enlightenment*. Garden City, N.Y.: Anchor Press, 1977.

———. *Jefferson, Nationalism, and the Enlightenment*. New York: G. Braziller, 1975.

Commission to the Director of the Service of School Hygiene, Aug. 26, 1922, Box 3, Folder 20, Servicio de Higiene Escolar (SHE), Salubridad Pública (SP), Archivo Histórico de la Secretaría de Salubridad y Asistencia (AHSSA), Mexico City.

"Complaints of the Natives of Unalaska District, 1790." [Zhaloby korennykh zhitelei unalashki]. *Meeting of Frontiers* online, Library of Congress, Manuscript Division, Yudin Collection, Digital id: yo010073, http://international.loc.gov/intldl/mtfhtml/ mfsplash.html (accessed June 20, 2002).

"Conditions in America." *Philanthropist* 17, no. 2 (July 1902): 67.

Cook, C. E. "Leprosy Problems." *Medical Journal of Australia* 2 (1926): 801–3.

Cook, C. E. "The Native in Relation to Public Health." *Medical Journal of Australia* 1 (1949): 569–71.

Cooke, Kathy J. "The Limits of Heredity: Nature and Nurture in American Eugenics before 1915." *Journal of the History of Biology* 31 (1998): 263–78.

Coombes, Annie E. *Reinventing Africa: Museums, Material Culture, and Popular Imagination in Late Victorian and Edwardian England.* New Haven, Conn.: Yale University Press, 1994.

Cooper, Frederick. "Le concept de mondialisation sert-il a quelque chose? Un point de vue d'historien." *Critique internationale* 10 (Jan. 2001): 101–24.

———. "Review Essay: Race, Ideology, and the Perils of Comparative History." *American Historical Review* 101, no. 4 (Oct. 1996): 1122–38.

Cooper, Frederick, Thomas C. Holt, and Rebecca J. Scott, eds. *Beyond Slavery: Explorations of Race, Labor, and Citizenship in Postemancipation Societies.* Chapel Hill: University of North Carolina Press, 2000.

Cooper, Frederick, and Ann Laura Stoler, eds. *Tensions of Empire: Colonial Cultures in a Bourgeois World.* Berkeley: University of California Press, 1997.

Coronil, Fernando. "Beyond Occidentalism: Toward Nonimperial Geopolitical Categories." *Cultural Anthropology* 11 (Jan. 1996): 51–87.

———. "Listening to the Subaltern: The Poetics of Neocolonial States." *Poetics Today* 15 (winter 1994): 643–58.

Corrigan, Philip R. *Social Forms/Human Capacities: Essays in Authority and Difference.* New York: Routledge, 1990.

Corssley, Ceri. "Using and Transforming the French Countryside: The 'Colonies Agricoles' (1820–1850)." *French Studies* 45 (Jan. 1991): 36–54.

Costigliola, Frank. "'Mixed Up' and 'Contact': Culture and Emotion among the Allies in the Second World War." *International History Review* 20 (Dec. 1998): 791–805.

———. "'Unceasing Pressure for Penetration': Gender, Pathology, and Emotion in George Kennan's Formation of the Cold War." *Journal of American History* 83, no. 4 (March 1997): 1309–39.

Cott, Nancy F. *The Bonds of Womanhood: "Woman's Sphere" in New England, 1780–1835.* New Haven, Conn.: Yale University Press, 1978.

———. *The Grounding of Modern Feminism.* New Haven, Conn.: Yale University Press, 1987.

———. "Notes toward an Interpretation of Antebellum Childrearing." *Psychohistory Review* 7 (spring 1978): 4–20.

———. *Public Vows: A History of Marriage and the Nation.* Cambridge, Mass.: Harvard University Press, 2000.

Crowell, Aron. *Archeology and the Capitalist World System: A Study from Russian America.* New York: Plenum Press, 1997.

Curtin, Philip D. *Atlantic Slave Trade: A Census.* Madison: University of Wisconsin Press, 1969.

———. "The Black Experience of Colonialism and Imperialism." In *Slavery, Colonialism, and Racism*, ed. Sidney W. Mintz, 17–29. New York: Norton, 1975.

Cuthbertson, Greg. "Racial Attraction: Tracing the Historiographical Alliances between

South Africa and the United States." *Journal of American History* 81, no. 3 (Dec. 1994): 1123–36.

Dabydeen, David, and Brinsley Samaroo, eds. *Across the Dark Waters: Ethnicity and Indian Identity in the Caribbean.* London: Macmillan Caribbean, 1996.

"Datos que intervenien en la clasificación." Departamento de Psicopedagogía e Higiene, Archivo Histórico de la Secretaría de Educación Pública, Box 5155, Folder 7, Mexico City.

Daunton, Martin, and Rick Halpern, eds. *Empire and Others: British Encounters with Indigenous Peoples, 1600–1850.* Philadelphia: University of Pennsylvania Press, 1999.

Davenport, C. B., and Morris Steggerda. *Race Crossing in Jamaica.* Washington, D.C.: Carnegie Institution of Washington, 1929.

Davenport, Charles. " 'Race Crossing,' and the Eugenical Principles of Immigration." Folder: Panamerican Conference (1st). Charles B. Davenport Papers, b/d27, American Philosophical Society, Philadelphia.

Davidoff, Leonore, and Catherine Hall. *Family Fortunes: Men and Women of the English Middle Class, 1780–1850.* Rev. ed. London: Routledge, 2002.

Davin, Anna. "Imperialism and Motherhood." In Cooper and Stoler, *Tensions of Empire,* 87–151.

Davis, George W., ed. *Report on the Military Government of the City of Manila, P.I., from 1898 to 1901.* Manila: Headquarters Division of the Philippines, 1901.

Davis, David Brian. *Slavery and Human Progress.* Oxford: Oxford University Press, 1984.

Davis, F. James. *Who Is Black? One Nation's Definition.* University Park: Pennsylvania State University Press, 1991.

Davis, Lois Wright Richardson. Papers. Rare Book, Manuscript, and Special Collections Library. Duke University.

Davydov, G. I. *Dvukratnoe puteshestvie v Ameriku morskikh Ofitserov Khvostova I Davydova, pisannoe sim poslednium, chast vtoraia.* St. Petersburg: Morskaia tipografiia, 1812.

Dawdy, Shannon Lee. "Enlightenment on the Ground: Le Page du Pratz' *Histoire de la Louisiane.*" *French Colonial History* 3 (2002): 17–34.

———. "*La ville sauvage*: 'Enlightened' Colonialism and Creole Improvisation in New Orleans, 1699–1769." PhD diss., University of Michigan, 2003.

Dayan, Joan. *Haiti, History, and the Gods.* Berkeley: University of California Press, 1995.

Deacon, Harriet Jane. "A History of the Medical Institutions on Robben Island, Cape Colony, 1846–1910." PhD diss., University of Cambridge, 1994.

De Bevoise, Ken. *Agents of Apocalypse: Epidemic Disease in the Colonial Philippines.* Princeton, N.J.: Princeton University Press, 1995.

———. "A History of Sexually Transmitted Diseases and hiv/aids in the Philippines." In *Sex, Disease, and Society: A Comparative History of Sexually Transmitted Diseases and hiv/aids in Asia and the Pacific,* ed. Milton Lewis, Scott Bamber, and Michael Waugh, 113–38. Westport, Conn.: Greenwood Press, 1997.

Degler, Carl N. *Neither Black nor White: Slavery and Race Relations in Brazil and the United States.* Madison: University of Wisconsin Press, 1971.

Dekker, Jeroen J. H. *Straffen, Redden en Opvoeden: Het onstaan en de ontwikkeling van de residentiele heropvoeding in West-Europa, 1814–1914, met bijzondere aandacht voor "Nederlandsche Mettray"* (To punish, save, and raise: The genesis and development of residential re-education in Western Europe, with special attention to "Dutch Mettray"). Assen: Van Gorcum, 1985.

De La Rue, Sidney. *Land of the Pepper Bird: Liberia.* New York: G. P. Putnam's Sons, 1930.

Deloria, Philip J. *Playing Indian.* New Haven, Conn.: Yale University Press, 1998.

Deloria, Vine, Jr. *Custer Died for Your Sins: An Indian Manifesto.* New York: Macmillan, 1969. Reprint, Norman: University of Oklahoma Press, 1988.

D'Emilio, John, and Estelle B. Freedman. "Commentary: A Response to Ann duCille's 'Othered' Matters." *Journal of the History of Sexuality* 1 (Jan. 1990): 128–30.

———. *Intimate Matters: A History of Sexuality in America.* New York: Harper and Row, 1988.

Demos, John. *The Unredeemed Captive: A Family Story from Early America.* New York: Vintage, 1995.

Dening, Greg. *Islands and Beaches: Discourse on a Silent Land: Marquesas, 1774–1880.* Carlton, Vic.: Melbourne University Press, 1980.

Denison, John H. "The Survival of the American Type." *Atlantic Monthly,* Jan. 1895, 16–28.

Dery, Luis C. "Prostitution in Colonial Manila." *Philippine Studies* 39 (1991): 475–89.

Desmond, Jane, and Virginia Domínguez. "Resituating American Studies in a Critical Internationalism." *American Quarterly* 48 (Sep. 1996): 475–91.

Deutsch, Sarah. "Landscapes of Enclaves: Race Relations in the West, 1895–1990." In *Power and Place in the North American West,* ed. Richard White and John M. Findlay, 110–31. Seattle: University of Washington Press, 1999.

———. *No Separate Refuge: Culture, Class, and Gender on an Anglo-Hispanic Frontier in the American Southwest, 1880–1940.* New York: Oxford University Press, 1987.

Dictionnaire de L'Académie française. 4th ed. Paris: Chez la Veuve de Bernard Brunet, 1762.

Dirks, Nicholas B., Geoff Eley, and Sherry B. Ortner, eds. *Culture/Power/History.* Princeton, N.J.: Princeton University Press, 1994.

Dirlik, Arif. "The Postcolonial Aura: Third World Criticism in the Age of Global Capitalism." *Critical Inquiry* 20 (winter 1994): 328–56.

Divin, V. A., ed. *Russkaia tikhookeanskaia epopeia.* Khabarovsk: Khabarovskoe Knizhnoe Izdatel'stro, 1979.

Dodge, Ernest S. *New England and the South Seas.* Cambridge, Mass.: Harvard University Press, 1965.

Dolan DNA Learning Center. *Image Archive on the American Eugenics Movement.* http://vector.cshl.org/eugenics (accessed July 17, 2001).

Dolgin, Gail, and Vicente Franco, dirs. *Daughter from Danang.* Waltham, Mass.: Balcony Releasing, 2002.

Dorsey, Bruce. *Reforming Men and Women: Gender in the Antebellum City.* Ithaca, N.Y.: Cornell University Press, 2002.

Douglas, City of. *Discover Douglas, Arizona.* Http://www.discoverdouglas.com (accessed Aug. 22, 2005).

Douglas, Mary. *Purity and Danger: An Analysis of Concepts of Pollution and Taboo.* New York: Praeger, 1966.

Douglass, Frederick. "Cheap Labor." In *The Life and Writings of Frederick Douglass.* Ed. Philip S. Foner. Vol. 4, *Reconstruction and After,* 246–66. New York: International Publishers, 1955.

———. "Coolie Trade." In *The Life and Writings of Frederick Douglass.* Ed. Philip S. Foner. Vol. 4, *Reconstruction and After,* 262–63. New York: International Publishers, 1955.

Drake, Paul W. *The Money Doctor in the Andes: The Kemmerer Missions, 1923–33.* Durham, N.C.: Duke University Press, 1989.

———, ed. *Money Doctors, Foreign Debts, and Economic Reforms in Latin America from the 1890s to the Present.* Wilmington, Del.: Scholarly Resources, 1994.

Dreyfus, Hubert L., and Paul Rabinow. *Michel Foucault: Beyond Structuralism and Hermeneutics.* Chicago: University of Chicago Press, 1982.

Dua, Enakshi. "Racialising Imperial Canada: Indian Women and the Making of Ethnic Communities." In Burton, *Gender, Sexuality, and Colonial Modernities,* 119–33.

Duara, Prasenjit. *Rescuing History of the Nation: Questioning Narratives of Modern China.* Chicago: University of Chicago Press, 1996.

Du Bois, Consul General Coert. "The European Population of Netherland India." Aug. 25, 1929 (856d, roll 33, M 682). Records Relating to the Internal Affairs of the Netherlands, 1919–1929. Records of the Department of State. Washington, D.C.

———. "The Problem of the Half Caste." Oct. 9, 1928 (856d.00–.40, roll 33, M 682). Records Relating to the Internal Affairs of the Netherlands, 1919–1929. Records of the Department of State. Washington, D.C.

Du Bois, W. E. B. *Black Reconstruction in America, 1860–1880.* 1935. Reprint, New York: Free Press, 1992.

———. "Darkater." In *The Oxford W. E. B. Du Bois Reader,* ed. Eric J. Sundquist, 481–623. Oxford: Oxford University Press, 1996.

———, ed. *Some Notes on Negro Crime, Particularly in Georgia.* Atlanta, Ga.: Atlanta University Press, 1904.

———. *The Souls of Black Folk.* 1903. Reprint, New York: Vintage, 1990.

DuBow, Saul. *Scientific Racism in Modern South Africa.* New York: Cambridge University Press, 1995.

duCille, Ann. "'Othered' Matters: Reconceptualizing Dominance and Difference in the History of Sexuality in America." *Journal of the History of Sexuality* 1 (Jan. 1990): 102–27.

Dudden, Faye E. *Serving Women: Household Service in Nineteenth Century America.* Middletown, Conn.: Wesleyan University Press, 1983.

Duke, Paul, trans. and ed. *Catherine the Great's Instruction (Nakaz) to the Legislative Commission, 1767.* Newtonville, Mass.: Oriental Research Partners, 1977.

Dussel, Enrique. *The Underside of Modernity: Apel, Ricoeur, Rorty, Taylor, and the Phi-*

losophy of Liberation. Ed. and trans. Eduardo Mendieta. Atlantic Highlands, N.J.: Humanities Press, 1996.

Editorial. *Philanthropist* 17, no. 2 (July 1902): 1.

Eichengreen, Barry. "House Calls of the Money Doctor: The Kemmerer Missions to Latin America, 1917–1931." In Drake, *Money Doctors, Foreign Debts, and Economic Reforms in Latin America from the 1890s to the Present*, 110–32.

Eley, Geoff, and Ronald Grigor Suny, eds. *Becoming National: A Reader.* New York: Oxford University Press, 1996.

Elias, Norbert. *State Formation and Civilization: The Civilizing Process.* Vol. 2. Oxford: Blackwell, 1982 [1939].

Elkin, A. P. "Anthropology and the Future of the Australian Aborigines." *Oceania* 5 (1934): 1–18.

———. *Citizenship for the Aborigines: A National Aboriginal Policy.* Sydney: Australasian Publishing, 1944.

Elkins, Stanley. *Slavery: A Problem in American Institutional and Intellectual Life.* Chicago: University of Chicago Press, 1959.

Ellinghaus, Katherine. "Taking Assimilation to Heart: Marriages of White Women and Indigenous Men in Australia and North America, 1870s–1930s." PhD diss., University of Melbourne, 2002.

Eltis, David. *Economic Growth and the Ending of the Transatlantic Slave Trade.* Oxford: Oxford University Press, 1987.

Eng, David, and David Kazanjian, eds. *Loss: The Politics of Mourning.* Berkeley: University of California Press, 2002.

Enloe, Cynthia H. *Bananas, Beaches, and Bases: Making Feminist Sense of International Politics.* Berkeley: University of California Press, 1989.

Enriquez, Raul González. "Report by Dr. Raul González Enriquez." 1934. Departamento de Psicopedagogía e Higiene, Archivo Histórico de la Secretaría de Educación Pública, Box 5131, Folder 15. Mexico City.

Espiritu, Yen. *Asian American Women and Men: Labor, Laws, and Love.* Thousand Oaks, Calif.: Sage, 1997.

"Estudio de adaptación de los Stanford Achievement Test." Departamento de Psicopedagogía e Higiene, Archivo Histórico de la Secretaría de Educación Pública, Box 5116, Folder 42. Mexico City.

Etherington, Norman. "Natal's Black Rape Scare of the 1870s." *Journal of Southern African Studies* 15 (Oct. 1988): 37–53.

Evans, Brian, and Bernard Waites. *IQ and Mental Testing: An Unnatural Science and Its Social History.* London: Macmillan, 1981.

Eze, Emmanuel Chukwudi. *Race and the Enlightenment: A Reader.* Cambridge, Mass.: Blackwell, 1997.

Fabian, Johannes. *Out of Our Minds: Reason and Madness in the Exploration of Central Africa.* Berkeley: University of California Press, 2000.

Fanon, Frantz. *Black Skin, White Masks.* Trans. Charles Lam Markmann. 1952. Reprint, London: Pluto, 1986.

Feis, Herbert. *The Diplomacy of the Dollar.* Baltimore: Johns Hopkins University Press, 1950.

———. *Europe, the World's Banker, 1870–1914: An Account of European Foreign Investment and the Connection of World Finance with Diplomacy before the War.* New Haven, Conn.: Yale University Press, 1930.

Ferguson, Roderick. *Aberrations in Black: Toward a Queer of Color Critique.* Minneapolis: University of Minnesota Press, 2004.

Fields, Barbara J. "Ideology and Race in American History." In *Region, Race, and Reconstruction: Essays in Honor of C. Vann Woodward,* ed. J. Morgan Kousser and James M. McPherson, 143–77. New York: Oxford University Press, 1982.

Findlay, Eileen J. Suárez. *Imposing Decency: The Politics of Sexuality and Race in Puerto Rico, 1870–1920.* Durham, N.C.: Duke University Press, 1999.

Finn, Janet. "Boarding Schools and the American Indian Education Experience: Lessons of Culture, Power, and History." Oct. 2000 (manuscript in Ann Laura Stoler's possession).

Fiske, John. *American Political Ideas Viewed from the Standpoint of Universal History.* New York: Harper, 1885.

Fitzhugh, William W., and Aron Crowell, eds. *Crossroads of Continents: Cultures of Siberia and Alaska.* Washington, D.C.: Smithsonian Institution Press, 1988.

Fitzpatrick, Tara. "The Figure of Captivity: The Cultural Work of Puritan Captivity Narrative." *American Literary History* 3 (1991): 1–26.

Fleming, E. McClung. "Symbols of the United States: From Indian Queen to Uncle Sam." In *Frontiers of American Culture,* ed. Ray Browne, Richard Crowler, Virgil Locke, and William Stafford, 1–24. West Lafayette, Ind.: Purdue University Studies, 1968.

Fletcher, Ian Christopher, Laura E. Nym Mayhall, and Philippa Levine, eds. *Women's Suffrage in the British Empire.* London: Routledge, 2000.

Flexner, Simon. "Medical Conditions Existing in the Philippines." *Transactions and Studies of the College of Physicians of Philadelphia,* 3rd ser., 21 (1899): 165–77.

Flexner, Simon, and L. F. Barker. "Report of a Special Commission Sent to the Philippines by the Johns Hopkins University to Investigate the Prevalent Diseases of the Islands." *Journal of the Military Service Institution* 26 (1900): 421–33.

Folbre, Nancy. "The 'Sphere of Women' in Early-Twentieth-Century Economics." In *Gender and American Social Science: The Formative Years,* ed. Helene Silverberg, 35–60. Princeton, N.J.: Princeton University Press, 1998.

Foley, Neil. *The White Scourge: Mexicans, Blacks, and Poor Whites in Texas Cotton Culture.* Berkeley: University of California Press, 1997.

Forbes, Jack D. *Africans and Native Americans: The Language of Race and the Evolution of Red-Black Peoples.* Urbana: University of Illinois Press, 1993.

———. *Black Africans and Native Americans.* Oxford: Blackwell, 1988.

"For Social Purity in the Army." *Outlook,* April 19, 1902, 944–45.

"Forum: What Comes after Patriarchy? Comparative Reflections on Gender and Power in a 'Post-Patriarchal Age.'" *Radical History Review* 71, no. 2 (spring 1998): 53–96.

Foster, Anne L. "Models for Governing: Opium and Colonial Policies in Southeast Asia, 1898–1910." In Go and Foster, *The American Colonial State in the Philippines*, 92–117. Durham, N.C.: Duke University Press, 2003.

Foster, Gaines M. *Moral Reconstruction: Christian Lobbyists and the Federal Legislation of Morality, 1865–1920*. Chapel Hill: University of North Carolina Press, 2002.

Foucault, Michel. *The Archaeology of Knowledge*. Trans. A. M. Sheridan Smith. New York: Pantheon, 1972.

———. *Discipline and Punish: The Birth of the Prison*. Trans. Alan Sheridan. Harmondsworth: Penguin, 1977, 1991.

———. "Faire vivre et laisser mourir: La naissance du racisme" (To make live and to let die: The birth of racism). *Temps Modernes* 535 (Feb. 1991): 37–61.

———. "Governmentality." In *The Foucault Effect: Studies in Governmentality*. Ed. Graham Burchell, Colin Gordon, and Peter Miller. London: Wheatsheaf, 1991.

———. *The History of Sexuality*. Vol. 1, *An Introduction*. New York: Vintage, 1980.

———. *"Society Must Be Defended": Lectures at the Collège de France, 1975–76*. Ed. Mauro Bertani and Alessandro Fontana. New York: Picador, 2003.

Fox-Genovese, Elizabeth. *Within the Plantation Household: Black and White Women of the Old South*. Chapel Hill: University of North Carolina Press, 1988.

Fraser, Nancy. "What's Critical about Critical Theory?" In *Unruly Practices: Power, Discourse, and Gender in Contemporary Social Theory*. Minneapolis: University of Minnesota Press, 1989.

Fredrickson, George M. *White Supremacy: A Comparative Study in American and South African History*. New York: Oxford University Press, 1981.

Friedman, Lawrence J., and Mark D. McGarvie, eds. *Charity, Philanthropy, and Civility in American History*. New York: Cambridge University Press, 2003.

Fu, May. "Rethinking Chinese Workers in Cuban History: Race and Labor in Transition from Slavery to Freedom, 1847–1899." Master's thesis, Department of Ethnic Studies, University of California, San Diego.

Fujitani, T., Lisa Yoncyama, and Geoffrey M. White, eds. *Perilous Memories: The Asia Pacific War(s)*. Durham, N.C.: Duke University Press, 2001.

Gabbacia, Donna. *From the Other Side: Women, Gender, and Immigrant Life in the U.S., 1820–1990*. Bloomington: Indiana University Press, 1994.

Gallay, Alan. "The Origins of Slaveholders' Paternalism: George Whitefield, the Bryan Family, and the Great Awakening in the South." *Journal of Southern History* 53, no. 3 (1987): 369–94.

Galloway, Patricia. "Rhetoric Difference: Le Page du Pratz on African Slave Management in Eighteenth-Century Louisiana." *French Colonial History* 3 (2003): 1–15.

Garcia, Cristina. *Monkey Hunting*. New York: Knopf, 2003.

Gates, Henry Louis. *The Signifying Monkey: A Theory of African American Literary Criticism*. New York: Oxford University Press, 1988.

Gatewood, Willard B., Jr. *Black Americans and the White Man's Burden, 1898–1903*. Urbana: University of Illinois Press, 1975.

Gauthier, Jason G. *Measuring America: The Decennial Censuses from 1790 to 2000*. Washington, D.C.: U.S. Census Bureau, 2002.

Gedeon, Davydov. *Ocherk is Istorii Amerikanskoi Pravoslavoi Dukhovnoi Missii.* St. Petersburg: M. Merkusheva, 1897.

Geld, Steven A. "Social Deviance and the 'Discovery' of the Moron." *Disability, Handicap, and Society* 3 (1987): 247–58.

Genovese, Eugene D. "Rebelliousness and Docility in the Negro Slave: A Critique of the Elkins Thesis." *Civil War History* 13 (1967): 293–314.

———. *Roll, Jordan, Roll: The World the Slaves Made.* New York: Pantheon, 1974.

Geraci, Robert P., and Michael Khodarkovsky, eds. *Of Religion and Empire: Missions Conversion, and Tolerance in Tsarist Russia.* Ithaca, N.Y.: Cornell University Press, 2001.

Gibson, James R. *Feeding the Russian Fur Trade.* Madison: University of Wisconsin Press, 1969.

Gilfoyle, Timothy. "The Hearts of Nineteenth Century Men: Bigamy and Working-Class Marriage in New York City, 1800–1890." *Prospects* 19 (1994): 135–60.

———. "Prostitutes in History: From Parables of Pornography to Metaphors of Modernity." *American Historical Review* 104, no. 1 (Feb. 1999): 117–41.

Gilmore, Glenda Elizabeth. *Gender and Jim Crow: Women and the Politics of White Supremacy in North Carolina, 1896–1920.* Chapel Hill: University of North Carolina Press, 1996.

Gilroy, Paul. *The Black Atlantic: Modernity and Double Consciousness.* Cambridge, Mass.: Harvard University Press, 1993.

Gilson, R. P. *Samoa 1830 to 1900: The Politics of a Multi-Cultural Community.* Melbourne: Oxford University Press, 1970.

Ginzburg, Lori. "Global Acts, Local Acts: Grass-Roots Activism in Imperial Narratives." *Journal of American History* 88, no. 3 (Dec. 2001): 870–73.

Gitlin, Jay. "On the Boundaries of Empire: Connecting the West to Its Imperial Past." In *Under an Open Sky: Rethinking America's Western Past,* ed. William Cronon, George Miles, and Jay Gitlin, 71–89. New York: W. W. Norton, 1992.

Glenn, Evelyn Nakano. "Racial Ethnic Women's Labor: Intersection of Race, Gender, and Class Oppression." *Review of Radical Political Economics* 17, no. 3 (1983): 86–108.

———. *Unequal Freedom: How Race and Gender Shape American Citizenship and Labor.* Cambridge, Mass.: Harvard University Press, 2002.

Go, Julian. "The Chains of Empire: State Building and Political Education in Puerto Rico and the Philippines." In Go and Foster, *The American Colonial State in the Philippines,* 182–216.

Go, Julian, and Anne L. Foster, eds. *The American Colonial State in the Philippines: Global Perspectives.* Durham, N.C.: Duke University Press, 2003.

———. "Introduction: Global Perspectives on the U.S. Colonial State in the Philippines." In Go and Foster, *The American Colonial State in the Philippines,* 1–42.

Godbeer, Richard. "Eroticizing the Middle Ground: Anglo-Indian Sexual Relations along the Eighteenth-Century Frontier." In Hodes, *Sex, Love, Race,* 91–111.

Goldberg, David Theo. *The Racial State.* Oxford: Blackwell, 2002.

———. *Racial Subjects: Writing on Race in America.* New York: Routledge, 1997.

Golovin, V. M. *Puteshestvie vokrug sveta.* St. Petersburg: Morskaia tipographiia, 1822.

González, Gilbert G., and Raúl Fernandez. "Empire and the Origins of Twentieth-Century Migration from Mexico to the United States." *Pacific Historical Review* 71, no. 1 (2002): 19–57.

González, José de Jesús. *Higiene escolar*. León, Mexico.

Gordon, Linda. *The Great Arizona Orphan Abduction*. Cambridge, Mass.: Harvard University Press, 1999.

———. *The Moral Property of Women: A History of Birth Control Politics in America*. Urbana: University of Illinois Press, 2002.

Gordon, Sarah Barringer. "'The Liberty of Self-Degradation': Polygamy, Woman Suffrage, and Consent in Nineteenth Century America." *Journal of American History* 83, no. 3 (Dec. 1996): 815–45.

———. *The Mormon Question: Polygamy and Constitutional Conflict in Nineteenth Century America*. Chapel Hill: University of North Carolina Press, 2002.

Gouda, Frances. "Nyonyas on the Colonial Divide." *Gender and History* 5 (Nov. 1993): 335–36.

Gould, Stephen Jay. *The Mismeasure of Man*. 2nd ed. New York: Penguin, 1996.

Grady, Henry Woodfin. "The New South." In Turpin, *The New South and Other Addresses*, 23–42.

———. "The South and Her Problems." In Turpin, *The New South and Other Addresses*, 43–91.

Gramsci, Antonio. *Selections from Prison Notebooks*. London: Lawrence and Wishart, 1971.

Gray, Geoffrey. "From Nomadism to Citizenship: A. P. Elkin and Aboriginal Advancement." In Peterson and Sanders, *Citizenship and Indigenous Australians*, 55–78.

Gray, J. A. C. *Amerika Samoa: A History of American Samoa and Its United States Naval Administration*. Annapolis: United States Naval Institute, 1960.

Great Britain Parliamentary Papers: Correspondence, Dispatches, and Other Communications Respecting the Emigration of Chinese Coolies, 1852–58. Shannon: Irish University Press, 1971.

Green, Rayna. "The Pocahontas Perplex: The Image of Indian Women in American Culture." *Massachusetts Review* 16 (1975): 698–714.

———. "The Tribe Called Wannabee: Playing Indian in America and Europe." *Folklore* 99 (1988): 30–55.

Greenberg, Stanley B. *Race and State in Capitalist Development: Comparative Perspectives*. New Haven, Conn.: Yale University Press, 1980.

Greene, Jack P., Rosemary Brana-Shute, and Randy J. Sparks. *Money, Trade, and Power: The Evolution of Colonial South Carolina's Plantation Society*. Columbia: University of South Carolina Press, 2001.

Greene, Jack P., and J. R. Pole, eds. *Colonial British America: Essays in the New History of the Early Modern Era*. Baltimore: Johns Hopkins University Press, 1984.

———. *The Intellectual Construction of America: Exceptionalism and Identity from 1492 to 1800*. Chapel Hill: University of North Carolina Press, 1993.

Greenfield, Liah. *Nationalism: Five Roads to Modernity*. Cambridge, Mass.: Harvard University Press, 1992.

Gregg, Robert. *Inside Out, Outside In: Essays in Comparative History*. New York: St. Martin's, 2000.

Gregory, J. W. *The Menace of Colour*. London: Seeley Service, 1925.

Gregory, Samuel. *Man-Midwifery Exposed and Corrected*. New York: George Gregory, 1848.

Grew, Raymond. "The Comparative Weakness of American History." *Journal of Interdisciplinary History* 16 (summer 1985): 87–101.

Griffin, Catherine Carrie. "'Joined Together in History': Politics and Place in African American and American Indian Women's Writing." PhD diss., University of Minnesota, 2000.

Grimshaw, Patricia. *Paths of Duty: American Missionary Wives in Nineteenth-Century Hawaii*. Honolulu: University of Hawaii Press, 1989.

Grinde, Donald A., Jr., and Bruce E. Johansen. *Exemplar of Liberty: Native America and the Evolution of Democracy*. Los Angeles: American Indian Studies Center UCLA, 1991.

Grossberg, Michael. *Governing the Hearth: Law and the Family in Nineteenth-Century America*. Chapel Hill: University of North Carolina Press, 1985.

Grove, Richard H. *Green Imperialism: Colonial Expansion, Tropical Island Edens, and the Origins of Environmentalism, 1600–1800*. New York: Cambridge University Press, 1995.

Gunning, Sandra. *Race, Rape, and Lynching: The Red Record of American Literature, 1890–1912*. New York: Oxford University Press, 1996.

Gutiérrez, David. *Walls and Mirrors: Mexican Americans, Mexican Immigrants, and the Politics of Ethnicity*. Berkeley: University of California Press, 1995.

Gutierrez, Jose. *June Weinstock*. Radio Farabundo Marti Australia, 1994. http://csf .colorado.edu/femisa/1994/mg00150.htm.

Gutiérrez, Ramón A. "What's Love Got to Do with It?" *Journal of American History* 88, no. 3 (Dec. 2001): 866–69.

———. *When Jesus Came, the Corn Mothers Went Away: Marriage, Sexuality, and Power in New Mexico, 1500–1846*. Stanford, Calif.: Stanford University Press, 1991.

Gutman, Herbert George. *The Black Family in Slavery and Freedom, 1750–1925*. 1st ed. New York: Pantheon, 1976.

Guy, Donna. "'White Slavery,' Citizenship, and Nationality in Argentina." In *Nationalisms and Sexualities*, ed. Patricia Yaeger, Doris Sommer, and Andrew Parker, 207–17. New York: Routledge, 1992.

Haag, Pamela. *Consent: Sexual Rights and the Transformation of American Liberalism*. Ithaca, N.Y.: Cornell University Press, 1999.

Habermas, Jürgen. *The Structural Transformations of the Public Sphere*. Cambridge, Mass.: MIT Press, 1989.

Hacking, Ian. "Making Up People." In *Reconstructing Individualism*, ed. Thomas Heller, Morton Sosna, and David Wellbery. Stanford, Calif.: Stanford University Press, 1986.

———. *The Social Construction of What?* Cambridge, Mass.: Harvard University Press, 1999.

Hacking, Ian. *The Taming of Chance*. New York: Cambridge University Press, 1990.

Haebich, Anna. *Broken Circles: Fragmenting Indigenous Families, 1800–2000*. Fremantle, Western Australia: Fremantle Arts Centre Press, 2000.

———. *For Their Own Good: Aborigines and Government in the South West of Western Australia, 1900–1940*. 3rd ed. Nedlands: University of Western Australia Press, 1998.

Haggis, Jane. " 'Good Wives and Mothers' or 'Dedicated Workers'? Contradictions of Domesticity in the 'Mission of Sisterhood,' Travancore, South India." In *Maternities and Modernities: Colonial and Postcolonial Experiences in Asia and the Pacific*, ed. Kalpana Ram and Margaret Jolly, 81–113. Cambridge: Cambridge University Press, 1998.

Hall, Anthony. *The American Empire and the Fourth World*. Montreal: McGill-Queen's University Press, 2003.

Hall, Catherine. *Civilising Subjects: Metropole and Colony in the English Imagination, 1830–1867*. Cambridge: Polity, 2002.

———, ed. *Cultures of Empire: A Reader: Colonizers in Britain and the Empire in the Nineteenth and Twentieth Centuries*. Manchester: Manchester University Press, 2000.

———. "Of Gender and Empire: Reflections on the Nineteenth Century." In *Gender and Empire*, ed. Philippa Levine, 46–76. Oxford: Oxford University Press, 2004.

Hall, Catherine, Keith McClelland, and Jane Rendall. *Defining the Victorian Nation: Class, Race, Gender, and the British Reform Act of 1867*. Cambridge: Cambridge University Press, 2000.

Hall, Jacquelyn Dowd. *Revolt against Chivalry: Jessie Daniel Ames and the Women's Campaign against Lynching*. New York: Columbia University Press, 1993.

Hall, Stuart. "Race, Articulation, and Societies Structured in Dominance." In *Sociological Theories: Race and Colonialism*. Paris: UNESCO, 1980.

Halttunen, Karen. "Humanitarianism and the Pornography of Pain in Anglo-American Culture." *American Historical Review* 100, no. 2 (April 1995): 303–34.

Hannah, Matthew G. *Governmentality and the Mastery of Territory in Nineteenth-Century America*. New York: Cambridge University Press, 2000.

Hansen, Karen Tranberg. *Distant Companions: Servants and Employers in Zambia, 1900–1985*. Ithaca, N.Y.: Cornell University Press, 1989.

Haraway, Donna. *Modest_Witness@Second_Millennium.FemaleMan©_Meets_Onco Mouse™: Feminism and Technoscience*. New York: Routledge, 1997.

———. *Primate Visions: Gender, Race, and Nature in the World of Modern Science*. New York: Routledge, 1989.

Harouel, Jean-Louis. *L'Embellissement des villes: L'Urbanisme français au XVIIIe siècle*. Paris: Picard, 1993.

Harris, Cheryl I. "Whiteness as Property." *Harvard Law Review* 106, no. 8 (1993): 1707–91.

Harris, Donald. "The Black Ghetto as Internal Colony: A Theoretical Critique and Alternative Formulation." *Review of Black Political Economy* (summer 1972): 3–33.

Harris, Leslie M. "From Abolitionist Amalgamators to 'Rulers of the Five Points': The Discourse of Interracial Sex and Reform in Antebellum New York City." In Hodes, *Sex, Love, Race*, 199–207.

Hartman, Saidiya. *Scenes of Subjection: Terror, Slavery, and Self-Making in Nineteenth-Century America*. New York: Oxford University Press, 1997.

Hazlett, Rev. A. Lester. "A View of the Moral Conditions Existing in the Philippines." RG 94/343790 (Box 2307), National Archives and Records Administration, Washington, D.C.

Hechter, Michael. *Internal Colonialism: The Celtic Fringe in Britain's National Development*. New Brunswick, N.J.: Rutgers University Press, 1999.

Hegel, Georg Wilhelm Fredrick. *Phenomenology of Spirit (Phänomenologie des Geistes)*. 1807. Trans. A. V. Miller. Oxford: Oxford University Press, 1977.

———. *Philosophy of Right (Philosophie des Rechts)*. 1821. Ed. Allen Wood. Cambridge: Cambridge University Press, 1991.

Heidegger, Martin. "The Thing." In *Poetry, Language, Thought*. Trans. Albert Hofstadter, 161–84. New York: Harper and Row, 1971.

Heiser, Victor G. *An American Doctor's Odyssey: Adventures in Forty-five Countries*. New York: Norton, 1936.

———. "The Culion Leper Colony: One of the Outgrowths of Our Occupation of the Philippine Islands." Dec. 14, 1914. Typescript, B:H357. Heiser Collection, American Philosophical Society, Philadelphia.

———. Diaries. July 13, 1914. B:H357. Heiser Collection, American Philosophical Society, Philadelphia.

———. "Fighting Leprosy in the Philippines." *World's Work* 31 (1916): 310–20.

———. "Leprosy in the East: Its Treatment and Prevention." Nov. 3, 1915. Typescript, B:H357. Heiser Collection, American Philosophical Society, Philadelphia.

Helly, Denise. *The Cuba Commission Report: A Hidden History of the Chinese in Cuba*. Baltimore: Johns Hopkins University Press, 1993.

Hempenstall, Peter J. *Pacific Islanders under German Rule: A Study in the Meaning of Colonial Resistance*. Canberra: Australian National University Press, 1978.

Herman, Judith. *Trauma and Recovery: The Aftermath of Violence—from Domestic Abuse to Political Terror*. New York: Basic Books, 1997.

Herzfeld, Michael. *Cultural Intimacy: Social Poetics in the Nation-State*. New York: Routledge, 1997.

Hesse, Barnor. "Writing Racialized Modernity: 'Europe/Non-Europe,' Undecidable." *tRACES*, ed. David Theo Goldberg and Kim Furumoto. Durham, N.C.: Duke University Press, forthcoming.

Higham, John. *Strangers in the Land: Patterns of American Nativism, 1860–1925*. 1955. Reprint, New Brunswick, N.J.: Rutgers University Press, 2002.

Hill, Ernestine. *The Great Australian Loneliness*. London: Jarrolds, 1937.

Hind, Robert J. "The Internal Colonial Concept." *Comparative Studies in Society and History* 26, no. 3 (July 1984): 543–68.

Hine, Darlene Clark. "Rape and the Inner Lives of Black Women in the Middle West: Preliminary Thoughts on a Culture of Dissemblance." *Signs* 14, no. 4 (summer 1989): 912–20.

Hirschman, Albert. *The Passions and the Interests: Political Arguments for Capitalism before Its Triumph*. Princeton, N.J.: Princeton University Press, 1971.

Hirschman, Charles. "The Meaning and Measurement of Ethnicity in Malaysia: An Analysis of Census Classifications." *Journal of Asian Studies* 46 (Aug. 1987): 555–82.

Hitchens, Christopher. *The Trial of Henry Kissinger.* Paperback ed. New York: Verso, 2002.

Hobsbawm, Eric. *The Age of Empire, 1875–1914.* New York: Pantheon, 1987.

Hodes, Martha Elizabeth. "Color, Classification, and Manhood: An Exploration across Borders." Keynote address, German Association of American Studies, Tutzing, February 2004.

———. "The Mercurial Nature and Abiding Power of Race: A Transnational Family Story." *American Historical Review* 108, no. 1 (Feb. 2003): 84–118.

———, ed. *Sex, Love, Race: Crossing Boundaries in North American History.* New York: New York University Press, 1999.

———. *White Women, Black Men: Illicit Sex in the Nineteenth-Century South.* New Haven, Conn.: Yale University Press, 1997.

Hodges, Graham Russell. Introduction to Roberts, *The House Servant's Directory,* xi–xlii.

Hoffman, Frederick L. *Race Traits and Tendencies of the American Negro.* New York: Macmillan, 1896.

Hofstadter, Richard. *Social Darwinism in American Thought.* 1944. Reprint, Boston: Beacon Press, 1992.

Hoganson, Kristin. "As Bad Off as the Filipinos: U.S. Women Suffragists and the Imperial Issue at the Turn of the Twentieth Century." *Journal of Women's History* 13, no. 2 (summer 2001): 9–33.

———. *Fighting for American Manhood: How Gender Politics Provoked the Spanish-American and Philippine-American Wars.* New Haven, Conn.: Yale University Press, 1998.

Holmberg, H. J. *Holmberg's Ethnographic Sketches.* Trans. Fritz Jaensch. Ed. Marvin W. Falk. Fairbanks: University of Alaska Press, 1985.

Holt, Thomas. *The Problem of Freedom: Race, Labor, and Politics in Jamaica and Britain, 1832–1938.* Baltimore: Johns Hopkins University Press, 1992.

Holt, W. Stull. *The Bureau of the Census: Its History, Activities, and Organization.* Washington, D.C.: Brookings Institution, 1929.

Horst, D. W. "Opvoeding en onderwijs van kinderen van Europeanen en Indo-Europeanen in Indies" (Raising and educating children of Europeans and Indo-Europeans in the Indies). *Indische Gids* 2 (1900): 989–96.

Hosmer, James K. *A Short History of Anglo-Saxon Freedom: The Polity of the English-Speaking Race.* New York: Charles Scribner's Sons, 1903.

Hothersall, David. *History of Psychology.* Philadelphia: Temple University Press, 1984.

Howe, Renate, and Shirlee Swain. "Saving the Child and Punishing the Mother: Single Mothers and the State." *Journal of Australian Studies* 37 (1993): 31–46.

Hsu, Madeline. *Dreaming of Gold, Dreaming of Home: Transnationalism and Migration between the United States and South China, 1882–1943.* Stanford, Calif.: Stanford University Press, 2000.

Hu-DeHart, Evelyn. "Chinese Coolie Labor in Cuba and Peru in the Nineteenth Century: Free Labor or Neoslavery?" *Journal of Overseas Studies* 2 (1992): 149–81.

Human Rights and Equal Opportunity Commission. *Bringing Them Home: National Inquiry into the Separation of Aboriginal and Torres Strait Islander Children from Their Families*. Sydney: Commonwealth of Australia, 1997.

Hunt, Nancy. "'Le Bébé en Brousse': European Women, African Birth-Spacing, and Colonial Intervention in Breastfeeding in the Belgian Congo." In Cooper and Stoler, *Tensions of Empire*, 287–321.

Hunter, Jane. *The Gospel of Gentility: American Women Missionaries in Turn-of-the-Century China*. New Haven, Conn.: Yale University Press, 1984.

Hurtado, Albert L. *Intimate Frontiers: Sex, Gender, and Culture in Old California*. Albuquerque: University of New Mexico Press, 1999.

Hutton, Patrick. "Foucault, Freud, and the Technologies of Self." In *Technologies of the Self*, ed. Luther H. Martin, Huck Gutman, and Patrick H. Hutton, 121–45. Amherst: University of Massachusetts Press, 1988.

Ignatieff, Michael. "The American Empire: The Burden." *New York Times Magazine*, Jan. 5, 2003, 22–54.

Ileto, Reynaldo C. "Cholera and the Origins of the American Sanitary Order in the Philippines." In *Imperial Medicine and Indigenous Societies*, ed. David Arnold, 125–48. Manchester: Manchester University Press, 1988.

———. "Outlines of a Nonlinear Employment of Philippine History." In *The Politics of Culture in the Shadow of Capital*, ed. Lisa Lowe and David Lloyd, 98–131. Durham, N.C.: Duke University Press, 1997.

"Informe de las labores desarrolladas durante los dias que van transcurriendo del presente año, por el DPH." Departamento de Psicopedagogía e Higiene, Archivo Histórico de la Secretaría de Educación Pública, Box 5123, Folder 56. Mexico City.

Inglis, Amirah. *The White Women's Protection Ordinance: Sexual Anxiety and Politics in Papua*. London: Chatto and Windus, 1975.

Inman, Samuel Guy. "Imperialist America." *Atlantic Monthly*, July 1924, 107–16.

"Instruktsia Shelikhovy 12 Maya 1794" (Instructions to Shelikhov 12 May 1794). *Meeting of Frontiers* online. Library of Congress, Manuscript Division, Yudin Collection, Digital id: y0010006, http://international.loc.gov/intldl/mtfhtml/mfsplash.html (accessed June 2002).

In the Matter of the Estate of Julio Jubala. Supreme Court of New Mexico, No. 4137. New Mexico Supreme Court Law Library and Archives, Santa Fe, New Mexico.

Iriye, Akira. *Cultural Internationalism and World Order*. Baltimore: Johns Hopkins University Press, 1997.

Jacobs, Patricia. *Mister Neville*. Fremantle, Western Australia: Fremantle Arts Centre Press, 1990.

———. "Science and Veiled Assumptions: Miscegenation in W.A., 1930–1937." *Australian Aboriginal Studies* 2 (1986): 15–23.

Jacobson, Cardell K. "Internal Colonialism and Native Americans: Indian Labor in the United States from 1871 to World War II." *Social Science Quarterly* 65, no. 1 (March 1984): 158–71.

Jacobson, Matthew Frye. *Barbarian Virtues: The United States Encounters Foreign Peoples at Home and Abroad, 1876–1917*. New York: Hill and Wang, 2000.

———. *Whiteness of a Different Color: European Immigrants and the Alchemy of Race*. Cambridge, Mass.: Harvard University Press, 1998.

Jaimes, M. Annette. "Federal Indian Identification Policy: A Usurpation of Indigenous Sovereignty in North America." In Jaimes, *The State of Native America*, 123–38.

———, ed. *The State of Native America: Genocide, Colonization, and Resistance*. Boston: South End Press, 1992.

James, C. L. R. *The Black Jacobins: Toussaint L'Ouverture and the San Domingo Revolution*. 1938. Reprint, New York: Random House, 1963.

Jameson, Elizabeth, and Susan Armitage, eds. *Writing the Range: Race, Class, and Culture in the Women's West*. Norman: University of Oklahoma Press, 1997.

Jameson, Fredric. *The Political Unconscious: Narrative as Socially Symbolic Act*. Ithaca, N.Y.: Cornell University Press, 1981.

Janara, Laura. *Democracy Growing Up: Authority, Autonomy, and Passion in Tocqueville's Democracy in America*. New York: State University of New York Press, 2002.

Janney, O. Edward. "Letter from Dr. O. Edward Janney." *Philanthropist* 14, no. 2 (April 1899): 6.

"January 1926 News Letter of Paul Super, National Secretary of the Y.M.C.A. in Poland." In *Poland: Correspondence and Reports, 1926–1930*. File 1926, Jan.–March, Kautz Family YMCA Archives, University of Minnesota.

Jefferson, Thomas. "Extract and Notes on Louisiana." Thomas Jefferson Papers. Series 1: General Correspondence, 1651–1827. Library of Congress, Washington, D.C.

———. *Notes on the State of Virginia*. 1785. Reprint, Ed. Frank Shuffleton. New York: Penguin, 1999.

———. *The Works of Thomas Jefferson*. Ed. Paul Leicester Ford. 12 vols. New York: G. P. Putnam's Sons, 1904.

Jenks, Albert E. "Assimilation in the Philippines, as Interpreted in Terms of Assimilation in America." *American Journal of Sociology* (1912): 773–91.

Jennings, Francis. *The Creation of America: Through Revolution to Empire*. New York: Cambridge University Press, 2000.

Jensen, Joan. "Farm Families Organize Their Work, 1900–1940." In *Essays in Twentieth Century New Mexico History*, ed. Judith Boyce De Mark, 13–28. Albuquerque: University of New Mexico Press, 1994.

———. *Passage from India: Asian Indian Immigrants in North America*. New Haven, Conn.: Yale University Press, 1988.

Johnson, Robert David. *The Peace Progressives and American Foreign Relations*. Cambridge, Mass.: Harvard University Press, 1995.

Johnson, Sara. "Migrant Recitals: Pan Caribbean Interchanges in the Aftermath of the Haitian Revolution." PhD diss., Stanford University, 2001.

Johnson, Walter. *Soul by Soul: Life inside the Antebellum Slave Market*. Cambridge, Mass.: Harvard University Press, 1999.

Johnson, William E. "The Administration's Brothels in the Philippines." *New Voice Leaf-*

lets, vol. 1, no. 26 (Aug. 18, 1900), RG 350/2045/10 (Box 246), National Archives and Records Administration, College Park, Md.

Johnston, W. Ross. *Sovereignty and Protection: A Study of British Jurisdictional Imperialism in the Late Nineteenth Century*. Durham, N.C.: Duke University Press, 1973.

Jolly, Margaret. "Colonizing Women: The Maternal Body and Empire." In *Feminism and the Politics of Difference*, ed. Sneja Gunew and Anna Yeatman, 103–27. St. Leonards: Allen and Unwin, 1993.

Jones, Robert W. "Ruled Passions: Re-Reading the Culture of Sensibility." *Eighteenth-Century Studies* 32, no. 3 (1999): 395–402.

Jordan, Winthrop D. *White over Black: American Attitudes toward the Negro, 1550–1812*. Chapel Hill: University of North Carolina Press, 1968.

Joseph, Gilbert M. "Close Encounters: Toward a New Cultural History of U.S.–Latin American Relations." In Gilbert M. Joseph, Catherine C. LeGrand, and Ricardo D. Salvatore, eds. *Close Encounters of Empire: Writing the Cultural History of U.S.–Latin American Relations*, 3–46. Durham, N.C.: Duke University Press, 1998.

Joseph, Gilbert M., Catherine C. LeGrand, and Ricardo D. Salvatore, eds. *Close Encounters of Empire: Writing the Cultural History of U.S.–Latin American Relations*. Durham, N.C.: Duke University Press, 1998.

"Judge Lynch as an Educator." *Nation*, Sep. 28, 1893, 222–23.

Judson, Arthur. *The New Era in the Philippines*. New York: Fleming H. Revell, 1903.

Jung, Moon-Ho. *"Coolies" and Cane: Race, Labor, and Sugar Production in the Age of Emancipation*. Baltimore: Johns Hopkins University Press, forthcoming.

Kakar, Sanjiv. "Leprosy in British India, 1860–1940: Colonial Politics and Missionary Medicine." *Medical History* 40 (1996): 215–30.

Kale, Madhavi. *Fragments of Empire: Capital, Slavery, and Indian Indentured Labor Migration in the British Caribbean*. Philadelphia: University of Pennsylvania Press, 1998.

———. "Projecting Identities: Empire and Indentured Labor from India to Trinidad and British Guiana, 1836–1885." In *Nation and Migration: Politics of Space in the South Asian Diaspora*, ed. Peter Van Der Veer, 73–92. Philadelphia: University of Pennsylvania Press, 1995.

Kame'eleihiwa, Lilikala. *Native Land and Foreign Desires: Pehea La E Pono Ai? How Shall We Live in Harmony?* Honolulu: University of Hawaii Press, 1992.

Kammen, Henry. *The Spanish Inquisition: A Historical Revision*. New Haven, Conn.: Yale University Press, 1998.

Kaplan, Amy. *The Anarchy of Empire in the Making of U.S. Culture*. Cambridge, Mass., Harvard University Press, 2002.

———. "'Left Alone with America': The Absence of Empire in the Study of American Culture." In *Cultures of United States Imperialism*, ed. Amy Kaplan and Donald E. Pease, 3–21. Durham, N.C.: Duke University Press, 1993.

———. "Manifest Domesticity." *American Literature* 70, no. 3 (1998): 581–606.

Kelley, Robin D. G. "How the West Was One: African Diaspora and the Re-mapping of U.S. History." *Rethinking American History in a Global Age*, ed. Thomas Bender, 123–47. Berkeley: University of California Press, 2002.

Kelly, George Armstrong. *Idealism, Politics, and History: Sources of Hegelian Thought.* Cambridge: Cambridge University Press, 1969.

Kelly, John D. *A Politics of Virtue: Hinduism, Sexuality, and Countercolonial Discourse in Fiji.* Chicago: University of Chicago Press, 1991.

Kennedy, Dane. "Imperial History and Post-Colonial Theory." *Journal of Imperial and Commonwealth History* 24 (May 1996): 345–63.

Kennedy, Paul M. "Bismarck's Imperialism: The Case of Samoa, 1880–1890." *Historical Journal* 15, no. 2 (1972): 264–67.

———. *The Samoan Tangle: A Study in Anglo-German Relations, 1878–1900.* St Lucia: Queensland University Press, 1974.

Kennedy, Rosanne. "The Affective Work of Stolen Generations Testimony: From the Archives to the Classrooms." *Biography* 27, no. 1 (winter 2004): 48–77.

Kertula, Anna. *Antler on the Sea.* Ithaca, N.Y.: Cornell University Press, 2000.

Kevles, Daniel J. *In the Name of Eugenics: Genetics and the Uses of Human Heredity.* 2nd ed. Cambridge, Mass.: Harvard University Press, 1995.

Khan, Aisha. *Callaloo Nation: Metaphors of Race and Religious Identity among South Asians in Trinidad.* Durham, N.C.: Duke University Press, 2003.

Khlebnikov, K. T. *Colonial Russian America: Kyrill T. Khlebnikov's Reports, 1817–1832.* Trans. and ed. Basil Dmytryshyn and E. A. P. Crownhart-Vaughn. Portland: Oregon Historical Society, 1976.

———. *Russkaia Amerika v neopublikovannykh zapiskakh K. T. Khlebnikova.* Leningrad: Izdatel'stvo "Navka," 1979.

Kidd, Rosalind. *The Way We Civilise: Aboriginal Affairs—The Untold Story.* St Lucia: University of Queensland Press, 1997.

Kidwell, Clara Sue. "What Would Pocahontas Think Now?" *Callaloo* 17 (winter–summer 1994): 149–59.

King, Anthony D. "Writing Colonial Space: A Review Article." *Comparative Studies in Society and History* 37, no. 3 (1995): 541–54.

Kipp, Rita Smith. "The Evangelical Uses of Leprosy." *Social Science and Medicine* 39, no. 2 (1994): 165–78.

Kitcher, Philip. *The Lives to Come: The Genetic Revolution and Human Possibilities.* New York: Penguin, 1997.

Klein, Herbert. *Slavery in the Americas.* Chicago: University of Chicago Press, 1967.

Kline, Wendy. *Building a Better Race.* Berkeley: University of California Press, 2001.

Klor de Alva, J. Jorge. "The Postcolonization of the (Latin) American Experience: A Reconsideration of 'Colonialism,' 'Postcolonialism,' and 'Mestizaje.'" In *After Colonialism: Imperial Histories and Postcolonial Displacements*, ed. Gyan Prakash, 241–78. Princeton, N.J.: Princeton University Press, 1997.

Knapman, Claudia. *White Women in Fiji, 1835–1930: The Ruin of Empire.* Boston: Allen and Unwin, 1986.

Knight, Alan. "Popular Culture and the Revolutionary State in Mexico, 1910–1940." *Hispanic American Historical Review* 4, no. 3 (1994): 393–444.

Kojève, Alexandre. *Introduction to the Reading of Hegel: Lectures on the Phenomenology of Spirit* [*Introduction à la Lecture de Hegel*, 1947]. Trans. James H. Nichols Jr. New York: Basic Books, 1969.

Kolodny, Annette. *The Land before Her: Fantasy and Experience of the American Frontiers, 1630–1860*. Chapel Hill: University of North Carolina Press, 1984.

———. *The Lay of the Land: Metaphor as Experience and History in American Life and Letters*. Chapel Hill: University of North Carolina Press, 1975.

Kraditor, Aileen S. *The Ideas of the Woman Suffrage Movement, 1890–1920*. New York: Columbia University Press, 1965.

Kramer, Paul A. "Are All Unhappy Families Alike? A Critique." Paper presented at the "Tense and Tender Ties" workshop, Ann Arbor, Michigan, December 2003. Manuscript in possession of the author.

———. "Empires, Exceptions, and Anglo-Saxons: Race and Rule between the British and U.S. Empires, 1880–1910." *Journal of American History* 88, no. 4 (March 2002): 1315–53.

———. *The Blood of Government: Race, Empire, the United States and the Philippines*. Chapel Hill: University of North Carolina Press, 2006.

———. "The Pragmatic Empire: U.S. Anthropology and Colonial Politics in the Occupied Philippines, 1898–1924." PhD diss., Princeton University, 1998.

———. "Reflex Actions: Reform and Colonialism in the U.S. Empire." Working paper (manuscript in possession of the author).

Krasheninnikov. *Opisanie zemli Kamchatki s prilozheniem raportov, donesenii I drugikh neopublikovannik materialov*. Moscow: Izdatel'stvo Glavsevmorputi, 1949.

Kraut, Alan M. *Silent Travelers: Germs, Genes, and the "Immigrant Menace."* Baltimore: Johns Hopkins University Press, 1995.

Kruchkow, David. *When You Wish upon a Star: An Adoption Story*. http://www.adoption agencychecklist.com/page655.html (accessed Aug. 23, 2005).

Kupperman, Karen Ordahl. *Settling with the Indians: The Meeting of English and Indian Cultures in America, 1580–1640*. Totowa, N.J.: Rowman and Littlefield, 1980.

Kutzinski, Vera M. *Sugar's Secrets: Race and the Erotics of Cuban Nationalism*. Charlottesville: University Press of Virginia, 1993.

La Aguilera, Cathy de. "Disrupting Street Harassment: Performance, Gender, Race, and Resistance." Senior thesis for the Women's and Gender Studies major at Yale University, 2004.

La Brack, Bruce. *The Sikhs of Northern California, 1904–1975*. New York: AMS Press, 1988.

La Cadena, Marisol de. *Indigenous Mestizos: The Politics of Race and Culture in Cuzco, Peru, 1919–1991*. Durham, N.C.: Duke University Press, 2000.

LaFeber, Walter. *The American Search for Opportunity, 1865–1913*. Vol. 2 of *Cambridge History of American Foreign Relations*. New York: Cambridge University Press, 1993.

———. *The New Empire: An Interpretation of American Expansion, 1860–1898*. Ithaca, N.Y.: Cornell University Press, 1963.

Lagemann, Ellen Condliffe. *The Politics of Knowledge: The Carnegie Corporation, Philanthropy, and Public Policy*. Middletown, Conn.: Wesleyan University Press, 1992.

Lai, Walton Look. *Chinese in the West Indies, 1806–1995.* Mona: University of West Indies, 1998.

———. *Indentured Labor, Caribbean Sugar: Chinese and Indian Migrations to the British West Indies, 1838–1918.* Baltimore: Johns Hopkins University Press, 1993.

Lamar, Howard, and Leonard Thompson, eds. *The Frontier in History: North America and Southern Africa Compared.* New Haven, Conn.: Yale University Press, 1981.

Landers, Jane, ed. *Against the Odds: Free Blacks in the Slave Societies of the Americas.* London: Frank Cass, 1996.

Landsman, Gail. "The 'Other' as Political Symbol: Images of Indians in the Woman Suffrage Movement." *Ethnohistory* 39, no. 3 (1991): 247–84.

Langley, Lester D. *The Banana Wars: An Inner History of American Empire, 1900–1934.* Lexington: University Press of Kentucky, 1983.

Langsdorff, Georg Heinrich. *Remarks and Observations on a Voyage around the World from 1803 to 1807.* Trans. Victoria Joan Moessner. Ed. Richard A. Pierce. Kingston, Ontario: Limestone Press, 1993.

Larsen, Nella. *Passing.* 1929. Reprint, New York: Modern Library, 2000.

Lasch, Christopher. "The Anti-Imperialists, the Philippines, and the Inequality of Man." *Journal of Southern History* 24 (Aug. 1958): 319–31.

Lasser, Carol. "The Domestic Balance of Power: Relations between Mistress and Maid in Nineteenth-Century New England." In *Women and Power in American History: A Reader,* Vol. 1: 5–22, ed. Kathryn Kish Sklar and Thomas Dublin. Englewood Cliffs, N.J.: Prentice Hall, 1991.

Laurence, K. O. *A Question of Labour: Indentured Immigration to Trinidad and British Guiana, 1875–1917.* New York: St. Martin's, 1994.

"Law of November 8, 1867." In *A Collection of the Diplomatic and Consular Laws and Regulations of Various Countries,* ed. Abraham Howard Feller and Manley Ottmer Hudson, 1:552. Washington: Carnegie Endowment for International Peace, 1933.

Lawrence, Sarah E. Diaries and Account Book. 14 vols. Amos A. Lawrence Papers. Massachusetts Historical Society. Boston.

Lawrence, William R. *Extracts from the Diary and Correspondence of the Late Amos Lawrence; with a Brief Account of Some Incidents in His Life.* Boston: D. Lothrop, 1856.

———. *Life of Amos A. Lawrence: With Extracts from His Diary and Correspondence.* Boston: Houghton Mifflin, 1888.

Leacock, Eleanor. "Montagnais Women and the Jesuit Program for Colonization." In Leacock and Etienne, *Women and Colonization,* 25–42.

Leacock, Eleanor, and Mona Etienne, eds. *Women and Colonization: Anthropological Perspectives.* New York: Praeger, 1980.

Le Conte, Joseph. *The Race Problem in the South.* 1892. Reprint, Miami: Mnemosyne, 1969.

Lee, Robert. *Orientals.* Philadelphia: Temple University Press, 1999.

Leeds, Josiah. "Letter from Josiah W. Leeds." *Philanthropist* 14, no. 2 (April 1899): 7.

Legassick, Martin. "British Hegemony and the Origins of Segregation in South Africa,

1901–1914." In *Segregation and Apartheid in Twentieth-Century South Africa*, ed. William Beinart and Saul DuBow, 43–59. London: Routledge, 1995.

Lemann, Nicholas. *The Big Test: The Secret History of the American Meritocracy.* New York: Farrar, Straus and Giroux, 2000.

LeoGrande, William M. *Our Own Backyard: The United States in Central America, 1977–1992.* Chapel Hill: University of North Carolina Press, 1998.

Leonard, Karen. *Making Ethnic Choices: California's Punjabi Mexican Families.* Philadelphia: Temple University Press, 1992.

Le Page du Pratz, Antoine Simon. *Histoire de la Louisiane.* Paris: De Bure, 1758.

———. *The History of Louisiana.* London: T. Becket and J. S. W. Harmanson, 1774. Reprint, Baton Rouge: Louisiana State University Press, 1975.

Lepore, Jill. *The Name of War: King Philip's War and the Origins of American Identity.* New York: Knopf, 1998.

Lester, Alan. *Imperial Networks: Creating Identities in Nineteenth-Century South Africa and Britain.* London: Routledge, 2001.

Leventhal, Todd. "The 'Baby Parts' Myth: The Anatomy of a Rumor." http://tafkac.org/medical/organ.theft/baby.parts/baby_parts_myth.html (accessed Aug. 23, 2005).

Levine, Philippa. "Erotic Geographies: Sex and the Managing of Colonial Space." In *Nineteenth-Century Geographies: The Transformation of Space from the Victorian Age to the American Century*, ed. Helena Michie and Roland R. Thomas, 149–60. New Brunswick, N.J.: Rutgers University Press, 2003.

———. "Orientalist Sociology and the Creation of Colonial Sexualities." *Feminist Review* 65 (summer 2000): 5–21.

———. *Prostitution, Race, and Politics: Policing Venereal Disease in the British Empire.* New York: Routledge, 2003.

Lewis, Charlene M. Boyer. *Ladies and Gentlemen on Display: Planter Society at the Virginia Springs, 1790–1860.* Charlottesville: University Press of Virginia, 2001.

Lewis, Jan, Joseph Ellis, Lucia Stanton, Peter S. Onuf, Annette Gordon-Reed, Andrew Burstein, and Frasier D. Norman. "Forum: Thomas Jefferson and Sally Hemings Redux." *William and Mary Quarterly* 57, no. 1 (2000): 125–210.

Lewis, Jan Ellen, and Peter S. Onuf, eds. *Sally Hemings and Thomas Jefferson: History, Memory, and Civic Culture.* Charlottesville: University Press of Virginia, 1999.

Library of Congress. *Catalogue of the Library of Thomas Jefferson 4.* Washington, D.C.: Library of Congress, 1955.

Lievin, Dominic. *Empire: The Russian Empire and Its Rivals.* New Haven, Conn.: Yale University Press, 2000.

Limerick, Patricia Nelson. *The Legacy of Conquest: The Unbroken Past of the American West.* New York: Norton, 1987.

———. *Something in the Soil: Legacies and Reckonings in the New West.* New York: Norton, 2000.

Limón, José E. *American Encounters: Greater Mexico, the United States, and the Erotics of Culture.* Boston: Beacon, 1998.

Lindsey, Donal. *Indians at Hampton Institute, 1877–1923.* Urbana: University of Illinois Press, 1995.

Linn, Brian McAllister. *The Philippine War, 1899–1902*. Lawrence: University Press of Kansas, 2000.

———. *The United States Army and Counterinsurgency in the Philippine War, 1899–1902*. Chapel Hill: University of North Carolina Press, 1989.

Linnekin, Jocelyn. "'Mornings of the Country': Centering the Nation in Samoan Historical Discourse." In *Narratives of Nation in the South Pacific*, ed. Ton Otto and Nicholas Thomas, 189–209. Amsterdam: Harwood Academic Publishers, 1997.

Lionnet, Françoise. "Narrating the Americas: Transcolonial Métissage and Maryse Condé's 'La migration des coeurs.'" In *Mixing Race, Mixing Culture: Inter-American Literary Dialogues*, ed. Monika Kaup and Debra J. Rosenthal, 65–87. Austin: University of Texas Press, 2002.

Lisiansky, Urey. *Voyage round the World in the Years 1803, 1804, 1805, and 1806*. London: J. Booth, 1814.

Little, Ann M. "'Shoot That Rogue, for He Hath an Englishman's Coat On!' Cultural Cross-Dressing on the New England Frontier, 1620–1760." *New England Quarterly* 74, no. 2 (June 2001): 238–73.

Littlefield, Daniel F., Jr. *Africans and Seminoles: From Removal to Emancipation*. Westport, Conn.: Greenwood Press, 1977.

Litwack, Leon F. *Trouble in Mind: Black Southerners in the Age of Jim Crow*. New York: Knopf, 1998.

Lomawaima, Tsianina. *They Called It Prairie Light: The Story of Chilocco Indian School*. Lincoln: University of Nebraska Press, 1994.

Lomnitz, Claudio. *Deep Mexico, Silent Mexico: An Anthropology of Nationalism*. Minneapolis: University of Minnesota Press, 2001.

"London Congress of the International Federation for the Abolition of State Regulation of Vice." *Philanthropist* 14, no. 1 (Jan. 1899): 18.

Lopez, Ian F. Haney. *White by Law: The Legal Construction of Race*. New York: New York University Press, 1996.

Love, Joseph L. "Modeling Internal Colonialism: History and Prospect." *World Development* 17 (June 1989): 905–22.

Lovett, Laura. "'African and Cherokee by Choice': Race and Resistance under Legalized Segregation." In *Confounding the Color Line: The Indian-Black Experience in North America*, ed. James Brooks, 192–222. Lincoln: University of Nebraska Press, 2002.

Lowe, Lisa. *Immigrant Acts: On Asian American Cultural Politics*. Durham, N.C.: Duke University Press, 1996.

———. "Race from Universalism." In *traces*, ed. David Theo Goldberg and Kim Furumoto. Durham: Duke University Press, forthcoming.

Loyo, Engracia. "Popular Reactions to the Educational Reforms of Cardenismo." In *Rituals of Rule, Rituals of Resistance: Public Celebrations and Popular Culture in Mexico*, ed. William H. Beezley, Cheryl English Martin, and William E. French, 247–60. Wilmington, Del.: Scholarly Resources, 1994.

Makdisi, Ussama. "Bringing America Back into the Middle East: A History of the First American Missionary Encounter with the Ottoman Arab World." In *Im-*

perial Formations beyond Europe, ed. Ann Laura Stoler, Peter Perdue, and Carole McGranahan. Santa Fe: School of American Research, forthcoming.

Malia, Martin. *Russia under Western Eyes*. Cambridge: Belknap Press of Harvard University Press, 2000.

Mandell, Daniel R. "Shifting Boundaries of Race and Ethnicity: Indian-Black Intermarriage in Southern New England, 1760–1880." *Journal of American History* 85, no. 2 (Sep. 1998): 466–501.

Manderson, Leonore, and Margaret Jolly, eds. *Sites of Desire/Economies of Pleasure: Sexualities in Asia and the Pacific*. Chicago: University of Chicago Press, 1997.

Mangum, Charles S., Jr. *The Legal Status of the Negro*. Chapel Hill: University of North Carolina Press, 1940.

Mani, Lata. *Contentious Traditions: Debate on Sati in Colonial India*. Berkeley: University of California Press, 1998.

Manne, Robert. "In Denial: The Stolen Generations and the Right." *Australian Quarterly Essay* 1 (2001): 1–113.

Markus, Andrew. *Governing Savages*. Sydney: Allen and Unwin, 1990.

Marrant, John. "A Narrative of the Lord's Wonderful Dealings with John Marrant, a Black (Now Going to Preach the Gospel in Nova Scotia) Born in New York, in North America." In Potkay and Burr, *Black Atlantic Writers of the Eighteenth Century*, 75–105.

Marshall, T. H. "Citizenship and Social Class." 1950. Reprinted in T. H. Marshall and Tom Bottomore, *Citizenship and Social Class*. London: Pluto, 1992.

Martin, Cynthia, and Dru Martin Groves. *Beating the Adoption Odds: Using Your Head and Your Heart to Adopt*. New York: Harcourt Brace, 1998.

Martinez-Alier, Verena. *Marriage, Class, and Colour in Nineteenth-Century Cuba: A Study of Racial Attitudes and Sexual Values in a Slave Society*. London: Cambridge University Press, 1974.

Martín Medem, José Manuel. *Niños de repuesto: Tráfico de menores y comercio de órganos*. Madrid: Editorial Complutense, 1994.

Massachusetts Vital Records. Dracut, 1869, vol. 218. Massachusetts State Archives, Boston.

Matossian, Mary. "The Peasant Way of Life." In *Russian Peasant Women*, ed. Beatrice Farnsworth and Lynne Viola, 11–40. New York: Oxford University Press, 1992.

Matsumoto, Valerie J., and Blake Allmendinger, eds. *Over the Edge: Remapping the American West*. Berkeley: University of California Press, 1999.

Maus, L. M. "A Brief History of Venereal Diseases in the United States Army and Measures Employed for Their Suppression." American Social Hygiene Association, June 14, 1917, Box 131, File 3, ASHA Collection, University of Minnesota.

Maushart, Susan. *Sort of a Place Like Home: Remembering the Moore River Native Settlement*. Fremantle, Australia: Fremantle Arts Centre Press, 1993.

Mawani, Renisa. "In between and Out of Place: Mixed-Race Identity, Liquor, and the Law in British Columbia, 1850–1913." In *Race, Space, and the Law: Unmapping a White Settler Society*, ed. Sherene H. Razack, 47–70. Toronto: Between the Lines, 2002.

May, Ernest R. *American Imperialism: A Speculative Essay*. New York: Atheneum, 1968.

May, Gita. "Tocqueville and the Enlightenment Legacy." In *Reconsidering Tocqueville's Democracy in America*, ed. Abraham S. Eisenstadt, 25–42. New Brunswick, N.J.: Rutgers University Press, 1988.

McClintock, Anne. *Imperial Leather: Race, Gender, and Sexuality in the Colonial Contest*. New York: Routledge, 1995.

———. "Pitfalls of the Postcolonial." In McClintock, *Imperial Leather*, 9–17.

McFerson, Hazel M. *The Racial Dimension of American Overseas Colonial Policy*. Westport, Conn.: Greenwood Press, 1997.

McGowen, Randall. "Power and Humanity, or Foucault among Historians." In *Reassessing Foucault: Power, Medicine, and the Body*, ed. Colin Jones and Roy Porter, 107–10. New York: Routledge, 1994.

McGranahan, Carole. "Arrested Histories: Between Empire and Exile in Modern Tibet." PhD diss., University of Michigan, 2001.

McGregor, Russell. "An Aboriginal Caucasian: Some Uses for Racial Kinship in Early Twentieth-Century Australia." *Australian Aboriginal Studies* 11 (1996): 11–20.

———. *Imagined Destinies: Aboriginal Australians and the Doomed Race Theory*. Melbourne: Melbourne University Press, 1997.

———. "Representations of the Half-Caste in the Australian Scientific Literature of the 1930s." *Journal of Australian Studies* 36 (1993): 51–64.

McKenzie, Kirsten. *The Making of an English Slave-Owner: Samuel Eusebius Hudson at the Cape of Good Hope, 1796–1807*. Cape Town: UCT Press, 1993.

McKeown, Adam. "Ritualization of Regulation: The Enforcement of Chinese Exclusion in the United States and China." *American Historical Review* 108, no. 2 (April 2003): 377–403.

McMichael, Philip. "Incorporating Comparison within a World Historical Perspective: An Alternative Comparative Method." *American Sociological Review* 55 (June 1990): 385–97.

McNeil, William C. *American Money and the Weimar Republic: Economics and Politics on the Eve of the Great Depression*. New York: Columbia University Press, 1986.

Mehta, Uday Singh. *Liberalism and Empire: A Study in Nineteenth-Century British Liberal Thought*. Chicago: University of Chicago Press, 1999.

———. "Liberal Strategies of Exclusions." In Cooper and Stoler, *Tensions of Empire*, 59–86.

Meinig, D. W. *The Shaping of America: A Geographical Perspective on 500 Years of History*. Vol. 2, *Continental America, 1800–1867*. New Haven, Conn.: Yale University Press, 1993.

Meixsel, Richard B. *Clark Field and the U.S. Army Air Corps in the Philippines, 1919–1942*. Quezon City: New Day Publishers, 2001.

Meleisea, Malama, and Penelope Schoeffel Meleisea, eds. *Lagaga: A Short History of Western Samoa*. Suva: University of the South Pacific, 1987.

Melish, Joanne Pope. *Disowning Slavery: Gradual Emancipation and "Race" in New England, 1780–1860*. Ithaca, N.Y.: Cornell University Press, 1998.

Memmi, Albert. *The Colonizer and the Colonized*. Trans. Howard Greenfield. Boston: Orion Press, 1965.

Méndez, Teresa Pacheco, and Angel Díaz-Barriga. *Evaluación académica*. Mexico City: UNAM, Centro de Estudios sobre la Universidad: Fondo de Cultura Económica, 2000.

Menzies, Archibald. *The Alaska Travel Journal of Archibald Menzies, 1793–1794*. Ed. Wallace M. Olson. Fairbanks: University of Alaska Press, 1999.

Merck, Carl Heinrich. *Siberia and Northwestern America, 1788–1792: The Journal of Carl Heinrich Merck, Naturalist with the Russian Scientific Expedition Led by Captains Joseph Billings and Gavriil Sarychev*. Trans. Fritz Jaensch. Ed. Richard A. Pierce. Kingston, Ontario: Limestone Press, 1980.

Merrell, James H. *Into the American Woods: Negotiators on the Pennsylvania Frontier*. New York: Norton, 1999.

———. "The Racial Education of the Catawba Indians." *Journal of Southern History* 50 (Aug. 1984): 363–84.

Merriam, W. R. "The Evolution of American Census-Taking." *Century Magazine*, April 1903, 831–42.

Merry, Sally Engle. *Colonizing Hawai'i: The Cultural Power of Law*. Princeton, N.J.: Princeton University Press, 2000.

Michelet, Jules. "25 août 1850." *Journal*. Vol. 2. Paris: Gallimard, 1959.

Midgley, Clare. *Women against Slavery: The British Campaigns, 1780–1870*. London: Routledge, 1992.

Mignolo, Walter D. *Local Histories/Global Designs: Coloniality, Subaltern Knowledges, and Border Thinking*. Princeton, N.J.: Princeton University Press, 2000.

Mihesuah, Devon A. *Cultivating the Rosebuds: The Education of Women at the Cherokee Female Seminary, 1851–1909*. Urbana: University of Illinois Press, 1993.

Miles, Tiya. "Uncle Tom Was an Indian: Tracing the Red in Black Slavery." In *Confounding the Color Line: The Indian-Black Experience in North America*, ed. James F. Brooks, 137–60. Lincoln, University of Nebraska Press, 2002.

Miller, Gwenn Alison. "She Was Handsomed but Tatooed: Communities of Empire in Early Russian Alaska, 1784–1820." PhD diss., Duke University, 2004.

Miller, Kelly. *The Everlasting Stain*. Washington, D.C.: Associate Publishers, 1924.

Miller, Roberta Balstad. "Science and Society in the Early Career of H. F. Verwoerd." *Journal of Southern African Studies* 19 (Dec. 1993): 634–61.

Miller, Stuart Creighton. *"Benevolent Assimilation": The American Conquest of the Philippines, 1899–1903*. New Haven, Conn.: Yale University Press, 1982.

Millett, Richard. *Guardians of the Dynasty: A History of the U.S.-Created Guardia Nacional de Nicaragua and the Somoza Family*. Maryknoll, N.Y.: Orbis, 1977.

Milloy, John S. *A National Crime: The Canadian Government and the Residential School System, 1879–1986*. Winnipeg: University of Manitoba, 1999.

Millspaugh, Arthur C. *Americans in Persia*. Washington, D.C.: Brookings Institution, 1946.

Ming, Hanneke. "Barracks-Concubinage in the Indies, 1887–1920." *Indonesia* 35 (April 1983): 65–93.

"Ministerstvo inostrannykh del sssr." In *Vneshniaia politika Rossii XIX i nachala XX veka. Sbornik Dokumenty Rossiiskogo Ministerstva Inostrannyk Del* (Foreign Policy of Russia in the Nineteenth and Early Twentieth Century. Documents of the Russian Ministry of Foreign Affairs). Ser. 1, Vol. 4, Doc. 104 (April 21, 1808).

Mintz, Sidney. *Sweetness and Power: The Place of Sugar in Modern History.* New York: Viking, 1985.

"The Misfortune of the Census." *Nation,* July 23, 1891, 63–64.

Missionary Record of the United Presbyterian Church. 10 (Nov. 1, 1855). Edinburgh.

Mitchell, Harvey. *America after Tocqueville: Democracy against Difference.* Cambridge: Cambridge University Press, 2002.

Mitchell, Michelle. "Silences Broken, Silences Kept: Gender and Sexuality in African-American History." *Gender and History* 11 (Nov. 1999): 433–44.

Mitchell, Timothy, ed. *Questions of Modernity.* Minneapolis: University of Minnesota Press, 2000.

Mongia, Radhika. "Always Nationalize: Or, Some Methodological Considerations on Analysis of the Nation State." Lecture, Feminist Interventions: Rethinking South Asia, University of California, Santa Cruz, May 3, 2002.

Monnereau, Élie. *The Complete Indigo-Maker.* London: P. Elmsly, 1769.

Monroy, Douglas. *Thrown among Strangers.* Berkeley: University of California Press, 1990.

Montejano, David. *Anglos and Mexicans in the Making of Texas.* Austin: University of Texas Press, 1987.

Montgomery, Benilde. "Recapturing John Marrant." In Shuffleton, *A Mixed Race,* 105–15.

Moon, Katharine H. S. *Sex among Allies: Military Prostitution in U.S.-Korea Relations.* New York: Columbia University Press, 1997.

Moore, Donald S., Anand Pandian, and Jake Kosek, eds. *Race, Nature, and the Politics of Difference.* Durham, N.C.: Duke University Press, 2003.

Moraga, Cherríe. "From inside the First World, Foreword 2001." In *This Bridge Called My Back: Writings by Radical Women of Color,* ed. Cherríe Moraga and Gloria Anzaldúa, xv–xxxiii. 1981. Reprint. Berkeley: Third Woman Press, 2002.

"Moral Conditions in the Philippines." Report included with Wilbur Crafts to Theodore Roosevelt, Jan. 22, 1902. RG 94/416181A, National Archives and Records Administration, Washington, D.C.

Moreau de Saint-Méry, M. L. E. *Description topographique et politique de la partie espagnole de l'isle Saint-Domingue.* Philadelphia: Chez l'auteur, 1796.

"More Trouble in Manila." *Philanthropist* 17, no. 3 (Oct. 1902): 4.

Morgan, Edmund. *American Slavery, American Freedom: The Ordeal of Colonial Virginia.* New York: Norton, 1975.

Morgan, Jennifer L. "'Some Could Suckle over Their Shoulders': Male Travelers, Female Bodies, and the Gendering of Racial Ideology, 1500–1700." *William and Mary Quarterly* 54 (Jan. 1997): 167–92.

Morgan, L. "'Some Could Suckle over Their Shoulder': Male Travelers, Female Bodies, and the Gendering of Racial Ideology, 1500–1770." In *Skin Deep, Spirit Strong: The*

Black Female Body in American Culture, ed. Kimberly Wallace-Sanders, 37–65. Ann Arbor: University of Michigan Press, 2002.

Morner, Magnus. *Race Mixture in the History of Latin America*. Boston: Little, Brown, 1967.

Morrell, W. P. *Britain in the Pacific Islands*. Oxford: Oxford University Press, 1960.

Mrázek, Rudolf. "'Let Us Become Radio Mechanics': Technology and National Identity in Late-Colonial Netherlands East Indies." *Comparative Studies in Society and History* 39 (Jan. 1997): 3–33.

Mullin, Michael. *Africa in America: Slave Acculturation and Resistance in the American South and the British Caribbean, 1736–1831*. Urbana: University of Illinois Press, 1992.

Munasinghe, Viranjini. *Callaloo or Tossed Salad? East Indians and the Cultural Politics of Identity in Trinidad*. Ithaca, N.Y.: Cornell University Press, 2001.

Murguia, Edward. *Assimilation, Colonialism, and the Mexican American People*. Austin: University of Texas Press, 1975.

Murray, Archibald Wright. *Forty Years' Mission Work in Polynesia and New Guinea, from 1835 to 1875*. London: J. Nisbet, 1876.

Murray, W. A. *Health Factors in the Poor White Problem*. Vol. 4 of *The Poor White Problem in South Africa; Report of the Carnegie Commission*. Stellenbosch: Pro Ecclesia-Drukkery, 1932.

"Must Move Out to Adjust Social Evil." *Manila Freedom*, Aug. 31, 1900. RG 350/2039 (Box 246), National Archives and Records Administration, College Park, Md.

Nash, Gary. "The Hidden History of Mestizo America." *Journal of American History* 82, no. 3 (Dec. 1995): 941–62.

———. "The Image of the Indian in the Southern Colonial Mind." *William and Mary Quarterly* 29, no. 2 (April 1972): 197–230.

Nathans, Eli. *The Politics of Citizenship in Germany: Ethnicity, Utility, and Nationalism*. Oxford: Berg, 2004.

"A National Disgrace." *Woman's Column*, Nov. 17, 1900, 1–3.

"Native Peoples and Colonialism." Special Issue, *British Columbian Quarterly* 115/116 (1997).

Nelson, Dana. *The Word in Black and White: Reading "Race" in American Literature, 1638–1867*. New York: Oxford University Press, 1992.

Nelson-Erichsen, Jean, and Heino R. Erichsen. *How to Adopt from Latin America*. Austin, Tex.: Niños International Adoption Center, 1987.

Neville, A. O. *Australia's Coloured Minority: Its Place in the Community*. Sydney: Currawong Publishing, n.d. [c1947].

Newman, Louise Michele. *White Women's Rights: The Racial Origins of Feminism in the United States*. New York: Oxford University Press, 1999.

Ngai, Mae M. *Impossible Subjects: Illegal Aliens and the Making of Modern America*. Princeton, N.J.: Princeton University Press, 2004.

Nielsen, Waldemar A. *The Big Foundations*. New York: Columbia University Press, 1972.

Ninkovich, Frank. *The United States and Imperialism*. Malden, Mass.: Blackwell, 2001.

Niranjana, Tejaswini. "'Left to the Imagination': Indian Nationalisms and Female Sexuality in Trinidad." In *A Question of Silence? The Sexual Economies of Modern India*, ed. Mary John and Janaki Nair, 111–38. London: Zed, 2000.

Nobles, Melissa. *Shades of Citizenship: Race and the Census in Modern Politics*. Stanford, Calif.: Stanford University Press, 2000.

"Notes and Comments." *Philanthropist* 15, no. 4 (Jan. 1901): 1.

"Notes and Comments." *Philanthropist* 17, no. 2 (July 1902): 1.

Nott, Josiah. "The Mulatto a Hybrid—Probable Extermination of the Two Races if the Whites and Blacks Are Allowed to Intermarry." *American Journal of the Medical Sciences* 6 (July 1843): 252–56.

Oakes, James. *The Ruling Race: A History of American Slaveholders*. New York: Knopf, 1982.

Oberly, John H. "Indian Commissioners' Reports." In *The American Indian and the United States: A Documentary History*, ed. Wilcomb E. Washburn, 416–541. New York: Random House, 1973.

Obregón, Diana. *Batallas contra la lepra: Estado, medicina y ciencia en Colombia*. Bogotá: Banco de la República, 2002.

O'Brien, Jean M. *Dispossession by Degrees: Indian Land and Identity in Natick, Massachusetts, 1650–1790*. New York: Cambridge University Press, 1997.

Ogden, Adele. *The California Sea Otter Trade, 1784–1848*. Berkeley: University of California Press, 1941.

Okihiro, Gary. *Margins and Mainstreams*. Seattle: Washington State University Press, 1997.

Olsen, Otto H., ed. *The Thin Disguise: Turning Point in Negro History—"Plessy v. Ferguson": A Documentary Presentation*. New York: Humanities Press, 1967.

Ortiz, Fernando. *Cuban Counterpoint: Tobacco and Sugar*. 1940. Reprint, Durham, N.C.: Duke University Press, 1995.

Osborne, Thomas J. "Empire Can Wait." *American Opposition to Hawaiian Annexation, 1893–1898*. Kent, Ohio: Kent State University Press, 1981.

Osorio, Jon Kamakawiwo'ole. *Dismembering Lahui: A History of the Hawaiian Nation to 1887*. Honolulu: University of Hawaii Press, 2002.

Osterhammel, Jürgen. *Colonialism: A Theoretical Overview*. Trans. Shelley L. Frisch. Princeton, N.J.: M. Wiener, 1997.

O'Sullivan, John. "The Great Nation of Futurity." *The United States Democratic Review* 6, no. 23 (Nov. 1839): 426–30.

Owen, Charlie. "'Mixed Race' in Official Statistics." In *Rethinking "Mixed Race,"* ed. David Parker and Miri Song, 134–53. London: Pluto, 2001.

Oyono, Ferdinand. *Houseboy*. Trans. John Reed. 1960. Reprint, London: Heinemann, 1987.

Padover, Saul K., ed. *The Complete Jefferson*. New York: Duell, Sloan, and Pearce, 1943.

Painter, Nell Irvin. *Soul Murder and Slavery*. Waco, Tex.: Baylor University Press, 1995.

———. *Standing at Armageddon: The United States, 1877–1919*. New York: Norton, 1987.

Paisley, Fiona. "Unnecessary Crimes and Tragedies: Race, Gender, and Sexuality in Australian Policies of Aboriginal Removal." In Burton, *Gender, Sexuality, and Colonial Modernities*, 134–47.

Papli'i, Aumua Mata'itusi Simanu. *'O Si Manu a Ali'i*. Auckland: Pasifika Press, 2002.

Park, Joseph Franklin. "The History of Mexican Labor in Arizona in the Territorial Period." PhD diss., University of Arizona, 1961.

Parry, Suzanne. "Identifying the Process: The Removal of 'Half-Caste' Children from Aboriginal Mothers." *Aboriginal History* 19 (1995): 141–53.

———. "Tropical Medicine and Northern Identity." In *Migration to Mining: Medicine and Health in Australian History*, ed. Suzanne Parry, 89–98. Darwin: Historical Society of the Northern Territory, 1998.

Pascoe, Peggy. "Miscegenation Law, Court Cases, and Ideologies of 'Race.'" In Hodes, *Sex, Love, Race*, 464–90.

———. "Race, Gender, and the Privileges of Property: On the Significance of Miscegenation Law in the U.S. West." In Matsumoto and Allmendinger, *Over the Edge*, 201–14.

Pateman, Carole. *The Sexual Contract*. Stanford, Calif.: Stanford University Press, 1988.

Patterson, Orlando. *Sociology of Slavery: An Analysis of the Origins, Development, and Structure of Negro Slave Society in Jamaica*. Rutherford, N.J.: Fairleigh Dickinson University Press, 1975.

Patton, Sandra. *Birthmarks: Transracial Adoption in Contemporary America*. New York: New York University Press, 2001.

Paz, Octavio. *The Labyrinth of Solitude: Life and Thought in Mexico*. New York: Grove, 1961.

Perdue, Theda. *Cherokee Women: Gender and Culture Change, 1700–1835*. Lincoln: University of Nebraska Press, 1998.

———. *Slavery and the Evolution of Cherokee Society, 1540–1866*. Knoxville: University of Tennessee Press, 1979.

Perry, Adele. *On the Edge of Empire: Gender, Race, and the Making of British Columbia, 1849–1871*. Toronto: University of Toronto Press, 2001.

———. "The State of Empire: Reproducing Colonialism in British Columbia, 1849–1871." *Journal of Colonialism and Colonial History* 2, no. 2 (2001): 1–23.

Peterson, Nadya L. "Dirty Women: Cultural Connotations of Cleanliness in Soviet Russia." In *Russia, Women, Culture*, ed. Helena Goscilo and Beth Holmgren, 188–201. Bloomington: Indiana University Press, 1996.

Peterson, Nicolas, and Will Sanders, eds. *Citizenship and Indigenous Australians*. Cambridge: Cambridge University Press, 1998.

Phillips, Charles. Journal. London Missionary Society, South Seas Journals. School of Oriental and African Studies Library, London.

Pigeaud, J. J. *Iets over kinderopvoeding: Raadgevingen voor moeders in Indie* (Something on raising children: Advice for mothers in the Indies). Semarang, 1898.

Pilkington, Doris. *Follow the Rabbit-Proof Fence*. St Lucia: University of Queensland Press, 1996.

Pitts, Jennifer. Introduction to *Writings on Empire and Slavery*, by Alexis de Tocqueville. Ed. and trans. Jennifer Pitts. Baltimore: Johns Hopkins University Press, 2001.

Pivar, David J. "The Military, Prostitution, and Colonial Peoples: India and the Philippines, 1885–1917." *Journal of Sex Research* 17 (Aug. 1981): 256–69.

Pivar, David J. *Purity and Hygiene: Women, Prostitution, and the "American Plan,"* *1900–1930*. Westport, Conn.: Greenwood Press, 2002.

———. *Purity Crusade: Sexual Morality and Social Control, 1868–1900*. Westport, Conn.: Greenwood Press, 1973.

Plane, Ann Marie. *Colonial Intimacies: Indian Marriage in Early New England*. Ithaca, N.Y.: Cornell University Press, 2000.

———. "Legitimacies, Indian Identities, and the Law: The Politics of Sex and the Creation of History in Colonial New England." In Daunton and Halpern, *Empire and Others*, 217–37.

Plummer, Brenda Gayle. *Haiti and the Great Powers*. Baton Rouge: Louisiana State University Press, 1988.

Polansky, Lee. "I Certainly Hope You Will Be Able to Train Her: Reformers and the Georgia Training School for Girls." In *Before the New Deal: Social Welfare in the South, 1830–1930*, ed. Elna C. Green, 138–59. Athens: University of Georgia Press, 1999.

"Political Report No. 6." July 16, 1929. American Consulate, Medan, Sumatra (microfilm: roll 51, M 682), Records Relating to the Internal Affairs of the Netherlands, 1919–1929, Records of the Department of State, RG 59, National Archives and Records Administration, Washington, D.C.

Polnoe sobranie zakonov rosiiskoi imperii s 1649 goda. First Series, Vol. 37, no. 28.

Porter, R. P. "The Eleventh Census: An Address Delivered before the American Statistical Association." Quoted in "The United States Census of 1890," 326–33.

Potkay, Adam, and Sandra Burr. "About John Marrant." In Potkay and Burr, *Black Atlantic Writers of the Eighteenth Century*, 67–74.

———, eds. *Black Atlantic Writers of the Eighteenth Century*. New York: St. Martin's, 1995.

Powell, Aaron M. "Appeal for Purity." *Philanthropist* 14, no. 3 (July 1899): 13.

———. "Lessons from India." *Philanthropist* 14, no. 3 (July 1899): 11.

Powell, J. W. "Are Our Indians Becoming Extinct?" *Forum* 15 (May 1893): 343–54.

Powell, Patricia. *The Pagoda*. San Diego, Calif.: Harcourt Brace, 1998.

Pratt, Mary Louise. *Imperial Eyes: Travel Writing and Transculturation*. London: Routledge, 1992.

Price, A. Grenfell. *White Settlers in the Tropics*. New York: American Geographical Society, 1939.

"Primera sesión de la primera conferencia panamericana de eugenesia y homicultura" (unauthorized transcript of meeting). Folder: Panamerican Conference (1st), CBD, B/D27, American Philosophical Society Libraray.

"Property Settlement Agreement between Julio Jubala and Maria P. Jubala." Feb. 12, 1929. In *In the Matter of the Estate of Julio Jubala*, 218–19.

"Protests against Teaching in Mexico." *FairTest Examiner*. http://www.fairtest.org/examarts/fa1196/k-mextst.htm (accessed July 29, 2005).

Pruebas colectivas para medir el desarrollo Mental I: Test de Fay. Departamento de Psicopedagogía e Higiene, Archivo Histórico de la Secretaría de Educación Pública, Box 5114, Folder 4. Mexico City: Talleres Graficos de la Nación, 1926.

Puenzo, Luis, dir. *La Historia Oficial* (*The Official Story*). Buenos Aires: Historias Cinematograficas Cinemania, 1985.

Putnam, Lara. "Public Women and One-Pant Men: Migration, Kinship, and the Politics of Gender in Caribbean Costa Rica, 1870–1960." PhD diss., University of Michigan, 2000.

Rabinovitz, Lauren. *For the Love of Pleasure: Women, Movies, and Culture in Turn-of-the-Century Chicago.* New Brunswick, N.J.: Rutgers University Press, 1998.

Rabinow, Paul, ed. *Michel Foucault: Ethics, Subjectivity, and Truth.* New York: New Press, 1994.

Rafael, Vicente. "Colonial Domesticity: Engendering Race at the Edge of Empire, 1899–1912." In *White Love and Other Events in Filipino History*, 52–75. Durham, N.C.: Duke University Press, 2000.

———. "Colonial Domesticity: White Women and United States Rule in the Philippines." *American Literature* 67 (Dec. 1995): 639–66.

Rai, Amit. *The Rule of Sympathy: Sentiment, Race, and Power, 1750–1850.* New York: Palgrave, 2002.

Ralston, Caroline. *Grass Huts and Warehouses: Pacific Beach Communities of the Nineteenth Century.* Canberra: Australian National University Press, 1977.

Ramos, Samuel. *Profile of Man and Culture in Mexico.* Translated by Peter G. Earle. Austin: University of Texas Press, 1962.

Raynal, Abbé. *Histoire Philosophique et politique des éstablissemens et du commerce des Européens dans les deux Indes.* Geneva: Chez J. L. Pellet, 1780.

Recovery of Historical Memory Project. *Guatemala: Never Again. The Official Report of the Human Rights Office, Archdiocese of Guatemala.* Abridged English ed. Maryknoll, N.Y.: Orbis, 1999.

"Register of British Subjects Residing in the Samoan Islands, 1878–1882." Film 1130492, Family History Center, Salt Lake City, Utah.

Reid, Anna. *The Shaman's Coat.* New York: Walker, 2002.

Reinhard, Kenneth. "Freud, My Neighbor." *American Imago* 54, no. 2 (1997): 165–95.

Renda, Mary. "Sentiments of a Private Nature." *Journal of American History* 88, no. 3 (Dec. 2001): 882–87.

———. *Taking Haiti: Military Occupation and the Culture of U.S. Imperialism, 1915–1946.* Chapel Hill: University of North Carolina Press, 2001.

"A Report from Arkhimandrit Ioasaf to His Archbishop Concerning Conditions in the Russian Settlement of Kodiak Island." Library of Congress, Manuscript Division. Yudin Collection, Archive of the Holy Synod, Box 643.

Report on Population of the United States at the Eleventh Census: 1890, 2 vols. Washington, D.C.: Government Printing Office, 1895–97.

Report on Indians Taxed and Not Taxed in the United States (Except Alaska) in the Eleventh Census: 1890. Washington, D.C.: Government Printing Office, 1894.

Rethman, Petra. *Tundra Passages: History and Gender in the Russian Far East.* University Park: Pennsylvania State University Press, 2001.

Richter, Daniel K. *Facing East from Indian Country: A Native History of Early America.* Cambridge, Mass.: Harvard University Press, 2001.

Rintoul, Stuart. *The Wailing: A National Black Oral History*. Port Melbourne: Heine-mann, 1993.

Roberts, Robert. *The House Servant's Directory, or a Monitor for Private Families: Comprising Hints on the Arrangement and Performance of Servants' Work*. 1827. Reprint, Armonk, N.Y.: M. E. Sharpe, 1998.

Robinson, Cedric. *Black Marxism*. Chapel Hill: University of North Carolina Press, 1983.

Robleda, José Gómez. "Pruebas mentales de clasificación escolar: Ideas fundamentals." Departamento de Psicopedagogía e Higiene, Archivo Histórico de la Secretaría de Educación Pública, Box 5134, Folder 6. Mexico City.

Robleda, José Gómez, Carlos Busauri, J. de Jesús Núñez, and Benjamín A. Martínez. *Características Biológicas de los Escolares Proletarios*. Mexico City: DAPP, 1937.

Rockwell, Elsie. "Schools of the Revolution: Enacting and Contesting State Forms in Tlaxcala, 1910–1930." In *Everyday Forms of State Formation: Revolution and Negotiation of Rule in Modern Mexico*, ed. Gilbert M. Joseph and Daniel Nugent, 170–208. Durham, N.C.: Duke University Press, 1994.

Rodgers, Daniel T. *Atlantic Crossings: Social Politics in a Progressive Age*. Cambridge, Mass.: Belknap Press of Harvard University Press, 1998.

———. "Exceptionalism." In *Imagined Histories: American Historians Interpret Their Past*, ed. Anthony Molho and Gordon S. Wood, 21–40. Princeton, N.J.: Princeton University Press, 1998.

Rodney, Walter. *A History of the Guyanese Working People, 1881–1905*. Baltimore: Johns Hopkins University Press, 1981.

Rose, Willie Lee. "The Domestication of Domestic Slavery." In *Slavery and Freedom*, ed. William W. Freehling, 18–36. New York: Oxford University Press, 1982.

Rosen, George. *A History of Public Health*. Expanded edition. Baltimore: Johns Hopkins University Press, 1993.

Rosenberg, Charles. *The Cholera Years: The United States in 1832, 1849, and 1866*. 1962. Reprint, Chicago: University of Chicago Press, 1987.

Rosenberg, Emily S. *Financial Missionaries to the World: The Politics and Culture of Dollar Diplomacy, 1900–1930*. Cambridge, Mass.: Harvard University Press, 1999; paperback edition, Durham, N.C.: Duke University Press, 2004.

———. "Gender." *Journal of American History* 77, no. 1 (June 1990): 116–24.

———. "Revisiting Dollar Diplomacy: Narratives of Money and Manliness." *Diplomatic History* 22 (spring 1998): 155–76.

Ross, Dorothy. *The Origins of American Social Science*. New York: Cambridge University Press, 1991.

Rothenberg, Diane. "The Mothers of the Nation: Seneca Resistance to Quaker Intervention." In Leacock and Etienne, *Women and Colonization*, 63–87.

Rothmann, M. E. *The Mother and Daughter of the Poor Family*. In Vol. 5 of *The Poor White Problem in South Africa; Report of the Carnegie Commission*. Stellenbosch: Pro Ecclesia-Drukkery, 1932.

Rowlandson, Mary. "The Sovereignty and Goodness of God, Together with the Faithfullness of His Promises Displayed; Being a Narrative of the Captivity and Restauration of Mrs. Mary Rowlandson." In *Held Captive by Indians*, ed. Richard VanDerBeets, 41–90. Knoxville: University of Tennessee Press, 1994.

Rubin, Gayle. "Thinking Sex: Notes for a Radical Theory of the Politics of Sexuality." In *Pleasure and Danger: Exploring Female Sexuality*, ed. Carol Vance, 267–319. New York: Routledge, 1984.

Ruddick, Daisy (as told to Kathy Mills and Tony Austin). "'Talking about Cruel Things': Girls' Life in the Kahlin Compound." *Hecate* 15 (1989): 8–22.

Ruíz, Ramon Eduardo. *The People of Sonora and Yankee Capitalists*. Tucson: University of Arizona Press, 1988.

Ryan, Mary P. *Civic Wars: Democracy and Public Life in the American City during the Nineteenth Century*. Berkeley: University of California Press, 1997.

———. *The Empire of the Mother: American Writing about Domesticity, 1830 to 1860*. New York: Institute for Research in History and Haworth Press, 1982.

Ryan, Patrick J. "Unnatural Selection: Intelligence Testing, Eugenics, and American Political Cultures." *Journal of Social History* 30, no. 3 (1996): 669–86.

Rydell, Robert W. *All the World's a Fair: Visions of Empire at American International Expositions, 1876–1916*. Chicago: University of Chicago Press, 1984.

Ryden, George Herbert. *The Foreign Policy of the United States in Relation to Samoa*. New Haven, Conn.: Yale University Press, 1933.

Sabioni, Jennifer, Kay Schaffer, and Sidonie Smith, eds. *Indigenous Australian Voices: A Reader*. New Brunswick, N.J.: Rutgers University Press, 1998.

Said, Edward W. *Culture and Imperialism*. New York: Vintage, 1993.

———. *Orientalism*. New York: Pantheon, 1978.

———. "Secular Interpretation, the Geographical Element, and the Methodology of Imperialism." In *After Colonialism: Imperial Histories and Postcolonial Displacements*, ed. Gyan Prakash, 21–39. Princeton, N.J.: Princeton University Press, 1995.

Saillant, John. "Remarkably Emancipated from Bondage, Slavery, and Death: An African American Retelling of the Puritan Captivity Narrative, 1820." *Early American Literature* 29 (1994): 122–40.

———. "Slavery and Divine Providence in New England Calvinism: The New Divinity and a Black Protest, 1775–1805." *New England Quarterly* 68 (1995): 584–608.

Saldivar, Jose David, ed. *Border Matters: Remapping American Cultural Studies*. Berkeley: University of California Press, 1997.

Salesa, Damon Ieremia. "Race Mixing: A Victorian Problem in Britain and New Zealand." D.Phil. diss., University of Oxford, 2000.

———. "'Travel Happy' Samoa: Colonialism, Samoan Migration, and a 'Brown Pacific.'" *New Zealand Journal of History* (2003): 171–88.

———. "'Troublesome Half-Castes': Tales of a Samoan Borderland." Master's thesis, University of Auckland, 1997.

Salisbury, Richard V. *Anti-Imperialism and International Competition in Central America, 1920–29*. Wilmington, Del.: Scholarly Resources, 1989.

Salman, Michael. *The Embarrassment of Slavery: Controversies over Bondage and Nationalism in the Colonial Philippines*. Berkeley: University of California Press, 2001.

Salmon, Marylynn. "The Cultural Significance of Breastfeeding and Infant Care in Early Modern England and America." *Journal of Social History* 28, no. 2 (1994): 247–69.

Salmond, Anne. *Two Worlds: First Meetings between Maori and Europeans, 1642–1772.* Auckland: Viking, 1991.

Samelson, Franz. "Was Early Mental Testing, (a) Racist Inspired, (b) Objective Science, (c) A Technology for Democracy, (d) The Origin of Multiple-Choice Exams, (e) None of the Above, (Mark the RIGHT Answer)." In *Psychological Testing and American Society, 1890–1930,* ed. Michael M. Sokal, 113–27. Piscataway, N.J.: Rutgers University Press, 1987.

"The Samoan Trouble." *Harper's Weekly,* Feb. 2, 1889, 82.

Sanchez, George. *Becoming Mexican American: Ethnicity, Culture, and Identity in Chicano Los Angeles, 1900–1945.* Oxford: Oxford University Press, 1995.

Sanders, Thomas, ed. Introduction to *Historiography of Imperial Russia: The Profession and Writing of History in a Multinational State.* Armonk, N.Y.: M. E. Sharpe, 1999.

Sangari, Kumkum, and Sudesh Vaid, eds. *Recasting Women: Essays in Indian Colonial History.* New Brunswick, N.J.: Rutgers University Press, 1990.

Santamarina, Rafael. "Standardización de la definición de la debilidad mental y sus diferentes grados." Departamento de Psicopedagogía e Higiene, Archivo Histórico de la Secretaría de Educación Pública, Box 5114, Folder 15. Mexico City.

———. Transcription of evening address. Folder: Pan American Congress (1st), Papers of Charles B. Davenport, B/D27, American Philosophical Society Library, Philadelphia.

———. "Untitled." Departamento de Psicopedagogía e Higiene, Archivo Histórico de la Secretaría de Educación Pública, Box 5119, Folder 85. Mexico City.

Sauer, Martin. *An Account of a Geographical and Astronomical Expedition to the Northern Part of Russia . . . by Commodore Joseph Billings, in the Years 1785, &C to 1794: The Whole Narrated from the Original Papers.* London: T. Cadell, 1802.

Saunders, Kay, ed. *Indentured Labour in the British Empire, 1834–1920.* London: Croom Helm, 1984.

Saunders, Suzanne. "Isolation: The Development of Leprosy Prophylaxis in Australia." *Aboriginal History* 14 (1990): 168–81.

Sawyer, Frederic H. *The Inhabitants of the Philippines.* New York: C. Scribner's Sons, 1900.

Scarborough, William K. "Slavery—The White Man's Burden." In *Perspectives and Irony in American Slavery: Essays,* ed. Harry P. Owens, 103–35. Jackson: University Press of Mississippi, 1976.

Scheper-Hughes, Nancy. "Theft of Life: The Globalization of Organ Stealing Rumors." *Anthropology Today* 12, no. 3 (1996): 3–11.

Schirmer, Daniel. *Republic or Empire: American Resistance to the Philippine War.* Cambridge, Mass.: Schenkman, 1972.

Schmidt, Hans. *The United States Occupation of Haiti, 1915–1934.* New Brunswick, N.J.: Rutgers University Press, 1971.

"The Schooling of a Camp." *Philanthropist* 14, no. 1 (Jan. 1899): 24.

Schrauwers, Albert. "The 'Benevolent' Colonies of Johannes van den Bosch." *Comparative Studies in Society and History* 43 (April 2001): 298–328.

Schroeder, Michael J. "The Sandino Rebellion Revisited." In Joseph, LeGrand, and Salvatore, *Close Encounters of Empire*, 208–68.

Schultz-Ewerth, Erich Bernhard Theodor. *Samoan Proverbial Expressions: Alaga'upu Fa'a—Samoa.* Auckland: Polynesian Press and Institute of Pacific Studies, 1980.

Schwartz, Stuart. "Spaniards, *Pardos*, and the Missing Mestizos: Identities and Racial Categories in the Early Hispanic Caribbean." *New West Indian Guide* 71, nos. 1 and 2 (1997): 5–20.

Schwartz, Stuart, and Frank Salomon. "New Peoples and New Kinds of People: Adaptation, Readjustment, and Ethnogenesis in South American Indigenous Societies (Colonial Era)." In *The Cambridge History of the Native Peoples of the Americas.* Vol. 3, *South America, Part II*, ed. Frank Salomon and Stuart Schwartz, 443–501. Cambridge: Cambridge University Press, 1996.

Scott, James C. *Domination and the Arts of Resistance: Hidden Transcripts.* New Haven, Conn.: Yale University Press, 1990.

———. *Seeing like a State: How Certain Schemes to Improve the Human Condition Have Failed.* New Haven, Conn.: Yale University Press, 1998.

Scott, Joan. "Gender: A Useful Category of Historical Analysis." In *Gender and the Politics of History*, ed. Joan Wallach Scott, 28–52. New York: Columbia University Press, 1988.

Scott, Julius Sherrard, III. "The Common Wind: Currents of Afro-American Communication in the Era of the Haitian Revolution." PhD diss., Duke University, 1986.

Scott, Rebecca J. "Fault Lines, Color Lines, and Party Lines: Race, Labor, and Collective Action in Louisiana and Cuba, 1862–1912." In Cooper, Holt, and Scott, *Beyond Slavery*, 61–106.

———. *Slave Emancipation in Cuba: The Transition to Free Labor, 1860–1899.* Princeton, N.J.: Princeton University Press, 1985.

Scully, Eileen P. *Bargaining with the State from Afar: American Citizenship in Treaty Port China, 1844–1942.* New York: Columbia University Press, 2001.

———. "Prostitution as Privilege: The 'American Girl' of Treaty-Port Shanghai, 1860–1937." *International History Review* 20, no. 4 (1998): 855–83.

———. "Taking the Low Road to Sino-American Relations: 'Open Door' Expansionists and the Two China Markets." *Journal of American History* 82, no. 1 (June 1995): 62–83.

"Sección de Higiene: Estudio sobre el desarrollo mental de niños mexicanos." In *Boletín de la SEP* 2 (Feb. 1926): 93–94. Departamento de Psicopedagogía e Higiene, Archivo Histórico de la Secretaría de Educación Pública, Box 5119, Folders 78 and 15,535. Mexico City.

Secretaria de Educación Pública. *Memoria de la SEP* 1 (1935): 249–53.

Secretaria de Educación Pública. *Pruebas mentales colectivas para realizar una clasificación escolar.* Mexico City: Talleres Gráficos de la Nación, 1935. Departamento de

Psicopedagogía e Higiene, Archivo Histórico de la Secretaría de Educación Pública, Box 5155, Folder 7. Mexico City.

Seed, Patricia. *American Pentimento*. Minneapolis: University of Minnesota Press, 2001.

———. *To Love, Honor, and Obey in Colonial Mexico: Conflicts over Marriage Choice, 1574–1821*. Stanford, Calif.: Stanford University Press, 1982.

Sekora, John. "Black Message/White Envelope: Genre, Authenticity, and Authority in the Antebellum Slave Narrative." *Callaloo* 10 (summer 1987): 482–515.

———. "Red, White, and Black: Indian Captivities, Colonial Printers and Early African American Narrative." In Shuffleton, *A Mixed Race*, 92–104.

Senior, Nancy. "Aspects of Infant Feeding in Eighteenth-Century France." *Eighteenth-Century Studies* 16, no. 4 (1983): 367–88.

"Several references to Le Page du Pratz's work appear in the journals of the expedition." To the Western Ocean: Planning the Lewis and Clark Expedition. http://www.lib.virginia.edu/speccol/exhibits/lewis_clark/planning2.html (accessed Aug. 22, 2005).

Seville, Armand. *"Les métis parias de l'Indo-Chine: Appel au peuple français"* (The pariah métis of Indochina: An appeal to the French people). *Annales Diplomatiques et Consulaires*, March 5, 1905.

Shah, Nayan. *Contagious Divides: Epidemics and Race in San Francisco's Chinatown*. Berkeley: University of California Press, 2001.

Shapiro, Michael Steven. *Child's Garden: The Kindergarten Movement from Froebel to Dewey*. University Park: Pennsylvania State University Press, 1983.

Shaw, Angel Velasco, and Luis H. Francia, eds. *Vestiges of War: The Philippine-American War and the Aftermath of an Imperial Dream, 1899–1999*. New York: New York University Press, 2002.

Shelikov, Grigorii I. "Pis'mo Shelikhova I Polevago k Baranovu" (Shelikhov in a letter to Baranov, 1794). In *Istoricheskoe obozrenie obrazovanie Rosiisko-Amerikanskoi kompanii*. Ed. P. A. Tikhmenev. 2 vols. 2: Appendix. St. Petersburg: E. Veimara, 1863.

———. Shelikov to Baranov [1794]. Quoted in S. B. Okun, *Rosiisko-Amerikanskaia kompaniia*. Moscow: Gosudarstvennoe Sotsial'no-ekonomicheskoe izdatel'stvo, 1939.

———. *A Voyage to America, 1783–1786*. Trans. Marina Ramsay. Ed. Richard A. Pierce. Kingston, Ontario: Limestone Press, 1981.

Shell, Marc. *Children of the Earth: Literature, Politics, and Nationhood*. New York: Oxford University Press, 1993.

Sheridan, Alan. *Michel Foucault: The Will to Truth*. New York: Tavistock, 1980.

Sheridan, Thomas E. *Arizona: A History*. Tucson: University of Arizona Press, 1995.

Sherman, Daniel. "Quatremère/Benjamin/Marx: Art Museums, Aura, and Commodity Fetishism." In *Museum Culture: Histories, Discourses, Spectacles*, ed. Daniel Sherman and Irit Rogoff, 123–43. Minneapolis: University of Minnesota Press, 1994.

Shibley, George. *Momentous Issues: Competition in Business, Stable Price Level, Prosperity and Republic vs. Trusts, Falling Price Level, Depression, Empire, Militarism, and Concentration of Wealth*. Chicago: Schulte Publishing, 1900.

Shoemaker, Nancy. "The Census as Civilizer: American Indian Household Structure in the 1900 and 1910 U.S. Census." *Historical Methods* 25 (winter 1992): 4–11.

———, ed. *Negotiators of Change: Historical Perspectives on Native American Women.* New York: Routledge, 1995.

Shryock, Andrew. *Off Stage/On Display: Intimacy and Ethnography in the Age of Public Culture.* Stanford, Calif.: Stanford University Press, 2004.

Shuffleton, Frank. *The American Enlightenment.* Rochester, N.Y.: University of Rochester Press, 1993.

———, ed. *A Mixed Race: Ethnicity in Early America.* New York: Oxford University Press, 1993.

Siler, Col. Joseph F. *The Prevention and Control of Venereal Diseases in the Army of the United States of America.* Army Medical Bulletin No. 67. Carlisle Barracks, Pa.: Medical Field Service School, May 1943.

Silverblatt, Irene. *Modern Inquisitions: Peru and the Colonial Origins of Western Civilization.* Durham, N.C.: Duke University Press, 2004.

Sing, Don. Washington State Penitentiary Inmate File #6453. Department of Corrections, Washington State Archives, Olympia, Wash.

Sinha, Mrinalini. *Colonial Masculinity: The "Manly Englishman" and the "Effeminate Bengali" in the Late Nineteenth Century.* Manchester: Manchester University Press, 1995.

Sklar, Martin. *The United States as a Developing Country.* New York: Cambridge University Press, 1992.

Skowronek, Stephen L. *Building a New American State: The Expansion of National Administrative Capacities, 1877–1920.* New York: Cambridge University Press, 1982.

Skurski, Julie. "The Ambiguities of Authenticity and National Ideology in Latin America: Doña Bárbara and the Construction of National Identity." In Eley and Suny, *Becoming National,* 371–402.

Slezkine, Yuri. *Arctic Mirrors: Russia and the Small Peoples of the North.* Ithaca, N.Y.: Cornell University Press, 1994.

Slotkin, Richard. *Regeneration through Violence: The Mythology of the American Frontier, 1600–1800.* Middletown, Conn.: Wesleyan University Press, 1973.

Smallwood, Stephanie. *Saltwater Slavery: A Narrative of Captivity and Diaspora in the Anglo-Atlantic World.* Cambridge, Mass.: Harvard University Press, forthcoming.

Smith, Barbara Sweetland, and Redmond J. Barnett, eds. Introduction to *Russian America: The Forgotten Frontier,* 9–15. Tacoma: Washington State Historical Society, 1990.

Smith, Carl. *Urban Disorder and the Shape of Belief: The Great Chicago Fire, the Haymarket Bomb, and the Model Town of Pullman.* Chicago: University of Chicago Press, 1995.

Smith, Lillian. *Killers of the Dream.* 1949. Reprint, New York: Norton, 1961.

Smith, Neil. *American Empire: Roosevelt's Geographer and the Prelude to Globalization.* Berkeley: University of California Press, 2003.

Smith, Shawn Michelle. *American Archives: Gender, Race, and Class in Visual Culture.* Princeton, N.J.: Princeton University Press, 1999.

Smits, David D. "'Abominable Mixture': Toward Repudiation of Anglo-Indian Intermarriage in Seventeenth-Century Virginia." *Virginia Magazine of History* 95 (April
1987): 157–92.

Sneider, Alison L. "The Impact of Empire on the North American Woman Suffrage
Movement: Suffrage Racism in an Imperial Context." UCLA *Historical Journal* 14
(1994): 14–32.

Snipp, C. Matthew. "American Indians: Clues to the Future of Other Racial Groups."
In *The New Race Question: How the Census Counts Multiracial Individuals*, ed. Joel
Perlmann and Mary C. Waters, 190–99. New York: Sage, 2002.

Snodgrass, John E. *Leprosy in the Philippine Islands*. Manila: Bureau of Printing, 1915.

Solinger, Rickie. *Beggars and Choosers: How the Politics of Choice Shapes Adoption,
Abortion, and Welfare in the United States*. New York: Hill and Wang, 2001.

Somers, Margaret R. "'We're No Angels': Realism, Rational Choice, and Relationality in
Social Science." *American Journal of Sociology* 104 (Nov. 1998): 722–84.

Sommer, Doris. *Foundational Fictions: The National Romances of Latin America*. Berkeley: University of California Press, 1991.

Sparks, Carol Douglas. "The Land Incarnate: Navajo Women and the Dialogue of
Colonialism, 1821–1870." In Shoemaker, *Negotiators of Change*, 135–56.

Spear, Jennifer. "Colonial Intimacies: Legislating Sex in French Louisiana." *William and
Mary Quarterly*, 3rd ser., 60, no. 1 (2003): 75–98.

———. "'They Need Wives': Métissage and the Regulation of Sexuality in French
Louisiana, 1699–1730." In Hodes, *Sex, Love, Race*, 35–59.

———. "Whiteness and the Purity of Blood: Race, Sexuality, and Social Order in
Colonial Louisiana." PhD diss., University of Minnesota, 1999.

Spongberg, Mary. *Feminizing Venereal Disease: The Body of the Prostitute in Nineteenth-
Century Medical Discourse*. Washington Square, N.Y.: New York University Press,
1997.

Stallybrass, Peter, and Allon White. *The Politics and Poetics of Transgression*. Ithaca,
N.Y.: Cornell University Press, 1986.

Stanley, Amy Dru. *From Bondage to Contract: Wage Labor, Marriage, and the Market in
the Age of Slave Emancipation*. Cambridge: Cambridge University Press, 1998.

Starr, Paul. "The Sociology of Official Statistics." In *The Politics of Numbers*, ed. William
Alonso and Paul Starr, 7–57. New York: Sage, 1987.

Statutes of the Mexican Society of Psychopedagogy. Departamento de Psicopedagogía e
Higiene, Archivo Histórico de la Secretaría de Educación Pública, Box 5155, Folder 7.
Mexico City.

Steedman, Carolyn. *Strange Dislocations: Childhood and the Idea of Human Interiority,
1780–1930*. Cambridge, Mass.: Harvard University Press, 1995.

Steggerda, Morris. *Anthropometry of Adult Maya Indians: A Study of Their Physical and
Physiological Characteristics*. Washington, D.C.: Carnegie Institution of Washington,
1932.

Stepan, Nancy Leys. *"The Hour of Eugenics": Race, Gender, and Nation in Latin America*.
Ithaca, N.Y.: Cornell University Press, 1991.

———. "Race, Gender, Science, and Citizenship." In *Cultures of Empire: Colonizers in*

Britain and the Empire in the Nineteenth and Twentieth Centuries, ed. Catherine Hall, 61–86. New York: Routledge, 2000.

Stern, Alexandra. "Buildings, Boundaries, and Blood: Medicalization and Nation-Building on the U.S. Mexican Border, 1910–1930." *Hispanic American Historical Review* 79 (Feb. 1999): 41–81.

————. "Responsible Mothers and Normal Children: Eugenics, Nationalism, and Welfare in Post-Revolutionary Mexico." *Journal of Historical Sociology* 12 (Dec. 1999): 369–97.

Stevenson, Robert Louis. *The Letters of Robert Louis Stevenson.* Ed. Bradford Allen Booth and Ernest Mehew. 8 vols. New Haven, Conn.: Yale University Press, 1994.

St. George, Robert Blair. Introduction to *Possible Pasts: Becoming Colonial in Early America*, ed. Robert Blair St. George, 1–29. Ithaca, N.Y.: Cornell University Press, 2000.

Stinchcombe, Arthur L. *Sugar Island Slavery in the Age of Enlightenment: Political Economy of the Caribbean World.* Princeton, N.J.: Princeton University Press, 1995.

Stoler, Ann Laura. "Affective States." In *A Companion to the Anthropology of Politics*, ed. David Nugent and Joan Vincent, 4–20. Oxford: Blackwell, 2005.

————. *Along the Archival Grain: Colonial Cultures and Their Affective States.* Princeton, N.J.: Princeton University Press, forthcoming.

————. *Capitalism and Confrontation in Sumatra's Plantation Belt, 1870–1979.* New Haven, Conn.: Yale University Press, 1985; 2nd ed., with new preface, Ann Arbor: University of Michigan Press, 1995.

————. "Carnal Knowledge and Imperial Power." In *Gender at the Crossroads of Knowledge: Feminist Anthropology in a Postmodern Era*, ed. Micaela di Leonardo, 55–101. Berkeley: University of California Press, 1991.

————. *Carnal Knowledge and Imperial Power: Race and the Intimate in Colonial Rule.* Berkeley: University of California Press, 2002.

————. "Colonial Archives and the Arts of Governance." *Archival Science* 2 (2002): 87–109.

————. "Developing Historical Negatives: Race and the (Modernist) Visions of a Colonial State." In *From the Margins: Historical Anthropology and Its Futures*, ed. Brian Axel, 156–85. Durham, N.C.: Duke University Press, 2002.

————. "Genealogies of the Intimate: Movements in Colonial Studies." In Stoler, *Carnal Knowledge and Imperial Power*, 1–21.

————. "Introduction: Reassessing Imperial Terrain." In Stoler et al., ed., *Imperial Formations and Their Discontents.*

————. "On Degrees of Imperial Sovereignty." *Public Culture*, 18, no. 1, winter 2006.

————. Preface to *Capitalism and Confrontation in Sumatra's Plantation Belt, 1870–1979.* 2nd ed. Ann Arbor: University of Michigan Press, 1995.

————. "[P]Refacing Capitalism and Confrontation in 1995." In Stoler, *Capitalism and Confrontation in Sumatra's Plantation Belt, 1870–1979*, 2nd ed., vii–xxxiv.

————. *Race and the Education of Desire: Foucault's "History of Sexuality" and the Colonial Order of Things.* Durham, N.C.: Duke University Press, 1995.

————. "Racial Histories and Their Regimes of Truth." *Political Power and Social*

Theory 11 (1997): 183–206. Reprinted in *Race Critical Theories*, ed. Philomena Essed and David T. Goldberg, 369–91. Malden, Mass.: Blackwell, 2002.

———. "Refractions off Empire: Untimely Comparisons in Harsh Times." *Radical History Review*, forthcoming, spring 2006.

———. "A Sentimental Education: Native Servants and the Cultivation of European Children in the Netherlands Indies." In *Fantasizing the Feminine in Indonesia*, ed. Laurie J. Sears, 71–91. Durham, N.C.: Duke University Press, 1997.

———. "Sexual Affronts and Racial Frontiers: European Identities and the Cultural Politics of Exclusion in Colonial Southeast Asia." *Comparative Studies in Society and History* 34 (Oct. 1992): 514–51. Reprinted in Cooper and Stoler, *Tensions of Empire*, 198–237; and in Eley and Suny, *Becoming National*, 286–322.

———. "Tense and Tender Ties: The Politics of Comparison in North American History and (Post) Colonial Studies." *Journal of American History* 88, no. 3 (Dec. 2001): 829–65.

Stoler, Ann Laura, and Frederick Cooper. "Between Metropole and Colony: Rethinking a Research Agenda." In Cooper and Stoler, *Tensions of Empire*, 1–56.

Stoler, Ann Laura, Carole McGronahan, and Peter Purdue, ed. *Imperial Formations and Their Discontents*. Santa Fe: School of American Research, forthcoming, 2006.

Stoler, Ann Laura, and Karen Strassler. "Castings for the Colonial: Memory Work in 'New-Order' Java." *Comparative Studies in Society and History* 42 (Jan. 2000): 4–48.

Stone, Henry. "The Census of 1880." *Lippincott's Magazine*, July 1878, 108–13.

Strong, Josiah. *Our Country: Its Possible Future and Its Present Crisis*. New York: Baker and Taylor, 1885.

Sturdevant, Saundra Pollock, and Brenda Stoltzfus. *Let the Good Times Roll: Prostitution and the U.S. Military in Asia*. New York: New Press, 1993.

Stutzman, Ronald. "El Mestizaje: An All-Inclusive Ideology of Exclusion." In *Cultural Transformations and Ethnicity in Modern Ecuador*, ed. Norman E. Whitten Jr., 45–94. Urbana: University of Illinois Press, 1981.

Suarez-Orozco, Marcelo. "The Treatment of Children in the Dirty War." In *Child Survival*, ed. Nancy Scheper-Hughes, 227–46. Dordrecht: D. Reidel, 1987.

Sunderland, Willard. "An Empire of Peasants: Empire-Building, Interethnic Interaction, and Ethnic Stereotyping in the Rural World of the Russian Empire, 1800–1850s." In Burbank and Ransel, *Imperial Russia*, 174–98.

———. "Making the Empire: Colonists and Colonization in Russia, 1800–1850s." PhD diss., Indiana University, 1997.

———. *Taming the Wild Field: Colonization and Empire on the Russian Steppe*. Ithaca, N.Y.: Cornell University Press, 2004.

Sundiata, I. K. *Black Scandal: America and the Liberian Labor Crisis, 1929–1936*. Philadelphia: Institute for the Study of Human Issues, 1980.

Sunia, Tauese. "Statement by Governor Tauese P. F. Sunia on the Status and Wishes of the People of the United States Territory of American Samoa." Talk at UN Seminar on Decolonization, Havana, May 23–25, 2001.

Sunley, Robert. "Early Nineteenth-Century American Literature on Childrearing." In

Childhood in Contemporary Cultures, ed. Margaret Mead and Martha Wolfenstein, 150–67. Chicago: University of Chicago Press, 1955.

Swaan, Abram de. *In Care of the State: Health Care, Education, and Welfare in Europe and the USA in the Modern Era*. New York: Oxford University Press, 1988.

Sweet, John Wood. *Bodies Politic: The Colonial Origins of the American North, 1730–1830*. Baltimore: Johns Hopkins University Press, 2003.

Synnott, Anthony. "Little Angels, Little Devils: A Sociology of Children." *Review of Canadian Sociology and Anthropology* 20 (Jan. 1983): 79–95.

Taguieff, André-Pierre. *La force du préjugé: Essai sur le racisme et ses doubles* (The force of prejudice: On racism and its doubles). Paris: La Découverte, 1988.

Takaki, Ronald T. *Iron Cages: Race and Culture in Nineteenth-Century America*. New York: Knopf, 1979.

Tamanoi, Mariko. "Knowledge, Power, and Racial Classifications: The 'Japanese' in 'Manchuria.'" *Journal of Asian Studies* 59, no. 2 (May 2000): 248–76.

Tamasese, TuiAtua Tupua. "The Riddle in Samoan History: The Relevance of Language, Names, Honorifics, Genealogy, Ritual, and Chant to Historical Analysis." *Journal of Pacific History* 29, no. 1 (1994): 65–79.

Tannenbaum, Frank. *Slave and Citizen, the Negro in the Americas*. New York: Knopf, 1947.

Tate, Thad W., Winthrop Jordan, and Sheila L. Skemp. *Race and Family in the Colonial South*. Jackson: University Press of Mississippi, 1987.

Tatupu Fa'afetai Mataa'afa Tu'i. *Lauga: Samoan Oratory*. Suva, Fiji: University of the South Pacific and the National University of Samoa, 1987.

Taussig, Michael. "Culture of Terror–Space of Death: Roger Casement's Putumayo Report and the Explanation of Torture." *Comparative Studies in Society and History* 26, no. 3 (1984): 467–97.

———. *Shamanism, Colonialism, and the Wild Man: A Study in Terror and Healing*. Chicago: University of Chicago Press, 1987.

Taylor, Alan. *American Colonies*. New York: Viking, 2001.

Taylor, Charles. *Modern Social Imaginaries*. Durham, N.C.: Duke University Press, 2004.

Taylor, Diana. *Disappearing Acts: Spectacles of Gender and Nationalism in Argentina's "Dirty War."* Durham, N.C.: Duke University Press, 1997.

Taylor, Jean Gelman. *The Social World of Batavia: European and Eurasian in Dutch Asia*. Madison: University of Wisconsin Press, 1983.

Taylor, John R. M. *The Philippine Insurrection against the United States, 1899–1903: A Compilation of Documents with Notes and Introduction*. Pasay City: Eugenio Lopez Foundation, 1971–3.

Tennert, Robert A. "Educating Indian Girls at Nonreservation Boarding Schools, 1878–1920." *Western Historical Quarterly* 13 (July 1982): 271–90.

Terami-Wada, Motoe. "Karayuki-San of Manila: 1890–1920." *Philippine Studies* 34 (1986): 287–316.

Terman, Lewis. *The Measurement of Intelligence*. New York: Houghton Mifflin, 1916.

"Tests parciales de lenguaje 'Alicia Descoeudres,' adaptación del Dr. Rafael Santamarina." Mexico City, 1926. Departamento de Psicopedagogía e Higiene, Archivo Histórico de la Secretaría de Educación Pública, Box 5155, Folder 53. Mexico City.

Thelen, David, ed. "Interpreting the Declaration of Independence by Translation: A Round Table." *Journal of American History* 85, no. 4 (March 1999): 1279–1460.

———, ed. "The Nation and Beyond: Transnational Perspectives on United States History." Special issue, *Journal of American History* 86, no. 3 (Dec. 1999): 965–1307.

———, ed. "Rethinking History and the Nation-State: Mexico and the United States as a Case Study." Special Issue, *Journal of American History* 86, no. 2 (Sep. 1999): 439–697.

Thomas, Howard Elsworth. *A Study of Leprosy Colony Policies.* N.p.: American Mission to Lepers, 1947.

Thorne, Susan. *Congregational Missions and the Making of an Imperial Culture in Nineteenth-Century England.* Stanford, Calif.: Stanford University Press, 1999.

———. "Missionary-Imperial Feminism." In *Gendered Missions: Women and Men in Missionary Discourse and Practice,* ed. Mary T. Huber and Nancy C. Lutkehaus, 39–66. Ann Arbor: University of Michigan Press, 1999.

Thornton, Russell. *American Indian Holocaust and Survival: A Population History since 1492.* Norman: University of Oklahoma Press, 1987.

Tilton, Robert. *Pocahontas: The Evolution of an American Narrative.* Cambridge: Cambridge University Press, 1994.

Tinker, Hugh. *A New System of Slavery: Export of Indian Labour Overseas, 1830–1920.* Oxford: Oxford University Press, 1974.

Tocqueville, Alexis de. *Democracy in America.* Volume 1. New York: Vintage, 1990.

———. *Writings on Empire and Slavery.* Ed. and trans. Jennifer Pitts. Baltimore: Johns Hopkins University Press, 2001.

Todorov, Tzvetan. *Conquest of America: Question of the Other.* New York: Harper, 1984.

Tomich, Dale. *Slavery in the Circuit of Sugar.* Baltimore: Johns Hopkins University Press, 1990.

———. *Through the Prism of Slavery: Labor, Capital, and World Economy.* Lanham, Md.: Rowman and Littlefield, 2004.

Toth, Emily. *Kate Chopin: A Life of the Author of "The Awakening."* New York: William Morrow, 1990.

Treckel, Paula A. "Breastfeeding and Maternal Sexuality in Colonial America." *Journal of Interdisciplinary History* 20, no. 1 (1989): 25–51.

Trent, James W., Jr. *Inventing the Feeble Mind: A History of Mental Retardation in the United States.* Berkeley: University of California Press, 1994.

Trexler, Richard C. *Sex and Conquest: Gendered Violence, Political Order, and the European Conquest of the Americas.* Ithaca, N.Y.: Cornell University Press, 1995.

Trollope, Frances. *Domestic Manners of the Americans.* Ed. John Larson. St. James, N.Y.: Brandywine Press, 1993.

Trouillot, Michel-Rolph. *Silencing the Past: Power and the Production of History.* Baltimore: Johns Hopkins University Press, 1995.

Truesdell, Leon E. *The Development of Punch Card Tabulation in the Bureau of the Census, 1890–1940.* Washington, D.C.: Department of Commerce, 1965.

Turner, Bryan S. "The Rationalization of the Body: Reflections on Modernity and Discipline." In *Max Weber: Rationality and Modernity*, ed. Sam Whimster and Scott Lash, 222–41. London: Allen and Unwin, 1987.

Turner, Frederick Jackson. "The Significance of the Frontier in American History." *Annual Report of the American Historical Association for the Year 1893*, 197–227. Washington, D.C.: Government Printing Office, 1894.

Turpin, Edna Henry Lee. "Henry Grady: His Life and Work." In Turpin, *The New South and Other Addresses*, 3–19.

Turpin, Edna Henry Lee, ed. *The New South and Other Addresses: With Biography, Critical Opinions, and Explanatory Note*. New York: Gordon Press, 1972.

Twain, Mark. "Battle Hymn of the Republic (Brought Down to Date)." February 1901. In *Mark Twain's Weapons of Satire: Anti-Imperialist Writings on the Philippine-American War*, ed. Jim Zwick, 40–41. Syracuse, N.Y.: Syracuse University Press, 1992.

Tyrrell, Ian. "AHR Forum: American Exceptionalism in an Age of International History." *American Historical Review* 96, no. 4 (Oct. 1991): 1031–55.

———. "American Historians in the Context of Empire." *Journal of American History* 86, no. 3 (Dec. 1999): 1015–44.

———. *Woman's World/Woman's Empire: The Woman's Christian Temperance Union in International Perspective, 1880–1930*. Chapel Hill: University of North Carolina Press, 1991.

"The United States Census of 1890." *Journal of the Royal Statistical Society* 55 (June 1892): 326–33.

U.S. Bureau of the Census. *Census of the Population: 1960*. Washington, D.C.: Government Printing Office, 1964.

———. *Negro Population, 1790–1915*. Washington, D.C.: Government Printing Office, 1918.

U.S. Bureau of Democracy, Human Rights, and Labor. "Guatemala: Country Reports on Human Rights 2000." Washington, D.C.: State Department, 2001.

U.S. Census Office. *Abstract of the Eleventh Census: 1890*. Washington, D.C.: Government Printing Office, 1896.

———. *Compendium of the Eleventh Census: 1890*. Prepared by Robert P. Porter. Washington, D.C.: Government Printing Office, 1892–97.

———. *Report on Crime, Pauperism, and Benevolence in the United States at the Eleventh Census: 1890*. Prepared by Frederick H. Wines. Washington, D.C.: Government Printing Office, 1895.

———. *Report on Population of the United States at the Eleventh Census: 1890*. Washington, D.C.: Government Printing Office, 1895–97.

———. *Report on the Insane, Feeble-Minded, Deaf and Dumb, and Blind in the United States at the Eleventh Census: 1890*. Prepared by John S. Billings. Washington, D.C.: Government Printing Office, 1895.

———. *Report on Vital and Social Statistics in the United States at the Eleventh Census: 1890*. Prepared by John S. Billings. Washington, D.C.: Government Printing Office, 1894–96.

U.S. Census Office. *Statistical Atlas of the United States Based upon Results of the Eleventh Census.* Prepared by Henry Gannett. Washington, D.C.: Government Printing Office, 1898.

———. *Vital Statistics of Boston and Philadelphia.* Prepared by John S. Billings. Washington, D.C.: Government Printing Office, 1895.

U.S. Congress. *Congressional Globe.* 46 Vols. Washington, D.C.: Government Printing Office, 1834–73.

———. *Congressional Record.* 50th Cong., 2nd sess., 1889. Vol. 20, pt. 3.

———. *Permanent Census Bureau.* 52nd Cong., 2nd sess., Feb. 1, 1893, H. Rep. 2393.

U.S. Department of State. Bureau of Consular Affairs, Overseas Citizens Services, and Office of Children Issues. *Hague Convention on Intercountry Adoption.* U.S. Department of State, June 2002.

———. *Immigrant Visas Issued to Orphans Coming to the U.S.* http://www.travell.state .gov/family/adoption/stats/stats_451.html (accessed Aug. 22, 2005).

Vancouver, George. *A Voyage of Discovery to the North Pacific Ocean and Round the World.* 6 Vols. London: John Stockdale, 1801.

VanDerBeets, Richard, ed. *Held Captive by Indians: Selected Narratives, 1642–1836.* Knoxville: University of Tennessee Press, 1994.

———. "Introduction." In VanDerBeets, *Held Captive by Indians*, 177–78.

Van Heyningen, Elizabeth. "The Social Evil in the Cape Colony, 1868–1902: Prostitution and the Contagious Diseases Acts." *Journal of Southern African Studies* 10 (April 1984): 170–97.

Van Kirk, Sylvia. "From 'Marrying-In' to 'Marrying-Out': Changing Patterns of Aboriginal/Non-Aboriginal Marriage in Colonial Canada." *Frontiers: A Journal of Women's Studies* 23, no. 3 (2002): 1–11.

———. *"Many Tender Ties": Women in Fur-Trade Society in Western Canada, 1670–1870.* Winnipeg: Watson and Dwyer, 1980. Reprint, Norman: University of Oklahoma Press, 1983.

———. "Tracing the Fortunes of Five Founding Families of Victoria." *BC Studies*, no. 115/6 (autumn/winter 1997/8): 149–79.

Van Krieken, Robert. "The Barbarism of Civilization: Cultural Genocide and the 'Stolen Generations.'" *British Journal of Sociology* 50 (1999): 295–313.

———. *Children and the State: Social Control and the Formation of Australian Child Welfare.* Sydney: Allen and Unwin, 1992.

Vaughan, Mary Kay. *Cultural Politics in Revolution: Teachers, Peasants, and Schools in Mexico, 1930–1940.* Tucson: University of Arizona Press, 1997.

———. *The State, Education, and Social Class in Mexico, 1880–1928.* DeKalb: Northern Illinois University Press, 1982.

Vaughan, Megan. "Without the Camp: Institutions and Identities in the Colonial History of Leprosy." In *Curing Their Ills: Colonial Power and African Illness*, 77–99. Stanford, Calif.: Stanford University Press, 1991.

Vázquez de Knauth, Josefina. *Nacionalismo y educación en México.* Mexico City: El Colegio de Mexico, 1970.

Veeser, Cyrus. *A World Safe for Capitalism: Dollar Diplomacy and America's Rise to Global Power*. New York: Columbia University Press, 2002.

Vergès, Françoise. *Monsters and Revolutionaries: Colonial Family Romance and Métissage*. Durham, N.C.: Duke University Press, 1999.

Viana, Virginia de. "Presentarán queja: La Secretaría de Relaciones Exteriores no ha respondido a la Fundación Nacional de investigaciones de niños robados." Aug. 31, 1999. http://www.ElImparcial.com (accessed Aug. 11, 2003).

Viswanathan, Gauri. *Masks of Conquest: Literary Study and British Rule in India*. New York: Columbia University Press, 1989.

Vlach, John Michael. *Back of the Big House: The Architecture of Plantation Slavery*. Chapel Hill: University of North Carolina Press, 1993.

Volpp, Leti. "American Mestizo: Filipinos and Anti-Miscegenation Laws." *U.C. Davis Law Review* 33, no. 4 (summer 2000): 795–835.

———. "Dependent Citizens and Martial Expatriates." Unpublished manuscript, in possession of the author.

———. "Dependent Citizens and Martial Expatriates." Rethinking Asian American History Conference, Los Angeles, May 2002.

Wade, H. W., and José Avellana Basa. "The Culion Leper Colony." *American Journal of Tropical Medicine* 3 (1923): 395–417.

Walker, Alexander. *An Account of a Voyage to the North West Coast of America in 1785 and 1786*. Ed. Robin Fisher and J. M. Bumsted. Seattle: University of Washington Press, 1982.

Walker, Francis A. "The Great Count of 1890." *Forum* 11 (June 1891): 75–83.

———. "Immigration and Degradation." *Forum* 11 (Aug. 1891): 634–44.

Walkowitz, Judith R. *Prostitution and Victorian Society: Women, Class, and the State*. Cambridge: Cambridge University Press, 1980.

Wareham, Evelyn. *Race and Realpolitik: The Politics of Colonisation in German Samoa*. Frankfurt: Peter Lang, 2002.

Warner, Michael. "What's Colonial about Colonial America?" In *Possible Pasts: Becoming Colonial in Early America*, ed. Robert Blair St. George, 49–70. Ithaca, N.Y.: Cornell University Press, 2000.

Warren, James Frances. *Ah Ku and Karayuki-San: Prostitution in Singapore, 1870–1940*. Singapore: Singapore University Press, 2003.

Washington, Booker T. *Tuskegee and Its People: Their Ideals and Achievements*. New York: D. Appleton and Company, 1905.

Watson, Christine. "'Believe Me': Acts of Witnessing in Aboriginal Women's Autobiographical Narratives." *Journal of Australian Studies* 64 (2000): 142–52.

Weber, David J., ed. *Foreigners in Their Native Land: Historical Roots of the Mexican Americans*. Albuquerque: University of New Mexico Press, 1973.

Weinter, James. *Tree Leaf Talk: A Heideggerian Anthropology*. New York: Berg, 2001.

Welch, Richard E., Jr. *Response to Imperialism: The United States and the Philippine-American War, 1899–1902*. Chapel Hill: University of North Carolina Press, 1979.

Welles, Sumner. "Is America Imperialistic?" *Atlantic Monthly*, Sep. 1924, 412–23.

Wells-Barnett, Ida B. *Southern Horrors and Other Writings*, edited and with an introduction by Jacqueline Jones Royster. Boston: Bedford/St. Martin's Press, 1997.

———. *On Lynchings*. 1892, 1895. Reprint, Salem, N.H.: Ayer, 1991.

Wendt, Albert. "Tattooing the Post-Colonial Body." In *Inside Out*, ed. Vilsoni Herenilco and Rob Wilson, 399–412. Lanham, Md.: Rowan and Littlefield, 1999.

Wexler, Laura. *Tender Violence: Domestic Visions in an Age of U.S. Imperialism*. Chapel Hill: University of North Carolina Press, 2000.

Weymouth, Lally. *Thomas Jefferson: The Man, His World, His Influence*. London: Weidenfeld and Nicolson, 1973.

Wheeler, L. R. "The Intelligence of East Tennessee Mountain Children." *Journal of Educational Psychology* 23 (May 1932): 351–70.

White, Luise. *The Comforts of Home: Prostitution in Colonial Nairobi*. Chicago: University of Chicago Press, 1990.

White, Richard. *The Middle Ground: Indians, Empires, and Republics in the Great Lakes Region, 1650–1815*. Cambridge: Cambridge University Press, 1991.

Whittaker, Cynthia. "The Idea of Autocracy among Eighteenth-Century Russian Historians." In Sanders, *Historiography of Imperial Russia*, 17–44.

Wier, Robert F., Susan C. Lawrence, and Evan Fales, eds. *Genes and Human Knowledge: Historical and Philosophical Reflections on Modern Genetics*. Iowa City: University of Iowa Press, 1994.

Wilcocks, R. W. "On the Distribution and Growth of Intelligence." *Journal of General Psychology* 6 (April 1932): 233–75.

———. *The Poor White*. vol. 2 of *The Poor White Problem in South Africa; Report of the Carnegie Commission*. Stellenbosch: Pro Ecclesia-Drukkery, 1932.

———. "Psychological Observations on the Relation between Poor Whites and Non-Europeans." *Social and Industrial Relations* 50 (May 1930): 3941–50.

———. "Rural Poverty among Whites in South Africa and in the South of the United States." April 5, 1933. Kenyon Butterfield Papers. Manuscript Division, Library of Congress, Washington, D.C.

Wilder, Gary. "The Politics of Failure: Historicising Popular Front Colonial Policy in French West Africa." In *French Colonial Empire and the Popular Front: Hope and Disillusion*, ed. Tony Chafer and Amanda Sackur, 33–55. New York: St. Martin's, 1999.

William, Walter. "United States Indian Policy and the Debate over Philippine Annexation: Implications for the Origins of American Imperialism." *Journal of American History* 66, no. 4 (March 1980): 810–31.

Williams, Eric. *Capitalism and Slavery*. Chapel Hill: University of North Carolina Press, 1944.

Williams, Raymond. *Marxism and Literature*. Oxford: Oxford University Press, 1977.

Williams, William Appleman. "The Frontier Thesis and American Foreign Policy." *Pacific Historical Review* 24 (Nov. 1955): 379–95.

Williamson, Joel. *New People: Miscegenation and Mulattoes in the United States*. New York: Free Press, 1980.

Wilson, Douglas L. "Thomas Jefferson's Library and the French Connection." *Eighteenth-Century Studies* 26, no. 4 (1993): 669–85.

Wilson, Kathleen. *The Island Race: Englishness, Empire, and Gender in the Eighteenth Century*. London: Routledge, 2003.

Wilson, Terry P. "Blood Quantum: Native American Mixed Bloods." In *Racially Mixed People in America*, ed. Maria P. P. Root, 108–25. Newbury Park, Calif.: Sage, 1992.

Winichakul, Thongchai. *Siam Mapped: A History of the Geo-Body of a Nation*. Honolulu: University of Hawaii Press, 1994.

Wishy, Bernard. *The Child and the Republic: The Dawn of Modern American Child Nurture*. Philadelphia: University of Pennsylvania Press, 1967.

Wolfe, Patrick. "Land, Labor, and Difference: Elementary Structures of Race." *American Historical Review* 106, no. 3 (June 2001): 866–905.

Wolff, Janet. *Feminine Sentences*. Oxford: Blackwell, 1990.

Wood, Donald. *Trinidad in Transition: The Years after Slavery*. London: Oxford University Press, 1968.

Wood, Gordon S. "The Relevance and Irrelevance of American Colonial History." In *Imagined Histories: American Historians Interpret the Past*, ed. Anthony Molho and Gordon S. Wood, 144–63. Princeton, N.J.: Princeton University Press, 1998.

Wood, Peter H. *Black Majority: Negroes in Colonial South Carolina from 1670 through the Stono Rebellion*. New York: Knopf, 1974.

Woodward, C. Vann. *Origins of the New South, 1877–1913*. Baton Rouge: Louisiana State University Press, 1971.

———. *The Strange Career of Jim Crow*. New York: Oxford University Press, 1955.

Wright, Carroll D. *The History and Growth of the United States Census*. Washington, D.C.: Government Printing Office, 1900.

———. "How a Census Is Taken." *North American Review* 148 (June 1889): 727–37.

———. "Lessons from the Census." *Popular Science Monthly*, 39 (Oct. 1891): 721–28; 40 (Nov. 1891): 75–83.

Wright, Gwendolyn. *The Politics of Design in French Colonial Urbanism*. Chicago: University of Chicago Press, 1991.

———. "Tradition in the Service of Modernity: Architecture and Urbanism in French Colonial Policy, 1900–1930." In Cooper and Stoler, *Tensions of Empire*, 322–45.

Wright, J. Leitch, Jr. *The Only Land They Knew: The Tragic Story of the American Indians in the Old South*. New York: Free Press, 1981.

Yanow, Dvora. "American Ethnogenesis and Public Administration." *Administration and Society* 27 (Feb. 1996): 495–96.

Yelvington, Kevin, ed. *Trinidad Ethnicity*. Knoxville: University of Tennessee Press, 1993.

Yoneyama, Lisa. *Hiroshima Traces: Time, Space and the Dialectics of Memory*. Berkeley: University of California Press, 2000.

Yu, Henry. "Mixing Bodies and Cultures: The Meaning of America's Fascination with Sex between 'Orientals' and 'Whites.'" In Hodes, *Sex, Love, Race*, 444–63.

Yun, Lisa. "'Coolie': From under the Hatches into the Global Age." Book manuscript.

———. "Under the Hatches: American Coolie Ships and Nineteenth-Century Narratives of the Pacific Passage." *Amerasia Journal* 28, no. 2 (2002): 38–61.

Yung, Judy. *Unbound Feet: A Social History of Chinese Women in San Francisco.* Berkeley: University of California Press, 1995.

Zafar, Rafia. "Capturing the Captivity: African Americans among the Puritans." *MELUS* 17 (1991–92): 19–35.

———. *We Wear the Mask: African Americans Write American Literature, 1760–1870.* New York: Columbia University Press, 1997.

Zarembo, Alan. "A Place to Call Home: The Anger, Tears, and Frustrating Runarounds of a Guatemalan Adoption Case." *Newsweek,* July 15, 2002, 27.

Zenderland, Leila. *Measuring Minds: Henry Herbert Goddard and the Origins of American Intelligence Testing.* New York: Cambridge University Press, 1998.

Zimmermann, Warren. *First Great Triumph: How Five Americans Made Their Country a World Power.* New York: Farrar, Straus and Giroux, 2002.

Zogbaum, Heidi. "Herbert Basedow and the Removal of Aboriginal Children of Mixed Descent from their Families." *Australian Historical Studies* 34 (2003): 112–38.

Zwick, Jim, ed. *Anti-Imperialism in the United States.* http://www.boondocksnet.com/ai/index.html (accessed July 20, 2005).

CONTRIBUTORS

WARWICK ANDERSON is the Robert Turell Professor in Medical History and Population Health Sciences and chair of the Department of Medical History and Bioethics at the University of Wisconsin, Madison. He is the author of *The Cultivation of Whiteness: Science, Health, and Racial Destiny in Australia* (2002).

LAURA BRIGGS is associate professor in the Women's Studies Department at the University of Arizona. She is the author of *Reproducing Empire: Race, Sex, Science, and U.S. Imperialism in Puerto Rico* (2002).

KATHLEEN BROWN is associate professor of History at the University of Pennsylvania. She is the author of *Good Wives, Nasty Wenches, and Anxious Patriarchs: Gender, Race, and Power in Colonial Virginia* (1996).

NANCY F. COTT is the Jonathan Trumbull Professor of American History at Harvard University and faculty director of the Schlesinger Library on the History of Women; her most recent book is *Public Vows: A History of Marriage and the Nation* (2000).

SHANNON LEE DAWDY, assistant professor of anthropology at the University of Chicago, is an archaeologist and historical ethnographer focusing on the colonial South and the Caribbean.

LINDA GORDON is professor of history at New York University. Her most recent book, *Dear Sisters*, edited with Ros Baxandall (2000), offers a historical introduction to the women's movement of the 1970s through essays and documents.

CATHERINE HALL is professor of history at University College, London. Her research focuses on rethinking the relation between Britain and its empire in the nineteenth and twentieth centuries. Her most recent book is *Civilising Subjects: Metropole and Colony in the English Imagination, 1830–1867* (2002).

MARTHA HODES, associate professor of history at New York University, is the author of *White Women, Black Men: Illicit Sex in the Nineteenth-Century South* (1997); and editor of *Sex, Love, Race: Crossing Boundaries in North American History* (1999).

PAUL A. KRAMER is assistant professor of history at Johns Hopkins University. He is currently completing a monograph entitled *The Blood of Government: Racial Politics in the American Colonial Philippines*.

LISA LOWE is professor of Comparative Literature at the University of California, San Diego. She is the author of *Immigrant Acts: On Asian American Cultural Politics* (1996).

TIYA MILES is assistant professor in the Program in American Culture, the Center for Afroamerican and African Studies, and the Native American Studies Program at the University of Michigan.

GWENN A. MILLER is assistant professor of history at The College of the Holy Cross in Worcester, Massachusetts.

EMILY S. ROSENBERG is the DeWitt Wallace Professor of History at Macalester University. Her book *Financial Missionaries to the World: The Politics and Culture of Dollar Diplomacy, 1900–1930* was reissued in paperback in 2004.

DAMON SALESA is assistant professor of history and American culture at the University of Michigan.

NAYAN SHAH is associate professor of history at the University of California, San Diego. He is the author of *Contagious Divides: Epidemics and Race in San Francisco's Chinatown* (2001).

ALEXANDRA MINNA STERN is associate director of the Center for the History of Medicine and assistant professor in the Department of Obstetrics and Gynecology and the Program in American Culture at the University of Michigan.

ANN LAURA STOLER, Willy Brandt Professor of Anthropology and Historical Studies at the New School for Social Research, is author of *Carnal Knowledge and Imperial Power: Race and the Intimate in Colonial Rule* (2002); and *Race and the Education of Desire: Foucault's "History of Sexuality" and the Colonial Order of Things* (1995). She is also coeditor with Frederick Cooper of *Tensions of Empire: Colonial Cultures in a Bourgeois World* (1997).

LAURA WEXLER is professor of American Studies and chair of the Women's and Gender Studies Program at Yale University. She is the author of *Tender Violence: Domestic Visions in an Age of U.S. Imperialism* (2000) and *Pregnant Pictures* (2000), coauthored with Sandra Matthews.

INDEX

Aborigines, 95, 103–5, 107–8, 109
Adams, Henry, 280–81
Adams, Rachel, 293–94
Adoption, 345–63; domestication of poverty and, 350–51, 357–58; imperialism and, 361–62; interpretations of, 349–51; truth commissions and, 358–61
African Americans: internal colonialism and, 431–41; literature of, 180–81; Native Americans and, 154–55, 165–74, 185 n.30. See also Race; Racial classification
Alaska, 297–98, 301–15
Alien Land Law (1921), 130–31
America as category, 363 n.1
Anderson, Benedict, 12, 31, 241
Anderson, Warwick, 15, 19, 20
"Anglo-Saxon," 249–51, 257, 264–65, 282, 369. See also Race; Whiteness; White supremacy
Anti-imperialist movement. See Social reform
Archeology, 297, 301
Archives: colonial Russia and, 299–300; constraints of national, 19–20, 55; construction of new, 135; household guides as, 215–16, 236–37; missionaries and, 462, 466; as site of knowledge production, 196, 203, 455–56
Arendt, Hannah, 9

Argentina, 359–60
Armstrong, Nancy, 345, 362
Atlantic slave trade, 191–92. See also Slavery
Australia, 95, 104–5, 109, 111, 112 n.8, 348

Balibar, Etienne, 275
Bartholet, Elizabeth, 346–51
Belonging, 3, 13, 132, 458, 462, 465. See also Citizenship
Benevolence, 97, 166, 408, 441. See also Sympathy
Bhabha, Homi, 31
Binet, Alfred, 328–29
Biopolitics: as an analytic, 13–14; in colonial education, 101–2, 106–8; in imperial formations, 25–26; psychometrics and, 326–27
"Black," 153, 259, 260, 263–65. See also Race; Racial classification
Blauner, Bob, 431
Blood, 13, 107–8, 149–50, 245, 247–48, 263–64
Boarding schools: colonization and, 348; Native Americans and, 46, 48–50, 284. See also Education; Reformatory; Vocational schools
Bodies: "body work" and, 214–15, 236; cartographies of, 214–16, 219–22, 234–36, 448–49; imperial formations and,

Jefferson, Thomas, 143–44, 150, 152–58, 166–70, 173, 183–84; on Louisiana Purchase, 142–43
Johnson, William B., 380–81, 387, 394, 401 n.77
Jubala, Julio, 117–26
Jubala, Soledad Garcia, 117–26, 447

Kaplan, Amy, 26–27, 30, 41, 216–17, 469
Kelley, Robin D. G., 205
Kemmerer, Edwin, 410, 416
Kindergarten: as microcosm of liberal state, 45. *See also* Nurseries
Kissinger, Henry, 359
Knowledge, politics of, 196, 206. *See also* Comparison; Politics of comparison
Kramer, Paul, 14, 443, 449–50, 467
Kruchkow, David, 351–52, 362–63, 364 n.16

Language: imperial classification and, 87; of liberal humanism, 206–8
La Rue, Sidney De, 405–6, 416, 420
Latin America: financial advising and, 408–9; international adoption and, 346–51; U.S. policy toward, 348–49
Lawrence, Sarah E., 215–19, 223–33, 233–38
Le Page du Pratz, Antoine Simon, 140, 144–58
Leprosy, 99–100. *See also* Disease; Hygiene
Liberalism, 11, 192–93, 206–7, 413
Liberia, 405–6, 408–9, 415–16, 419–20
"Literary imperialism," 177
Louisiana, 141
Lowe, Lisa, 11, 19, 467, 472

MacArthur, General Arthur, 371, 389–91, 394
Malherbe, E. G.: 50–51
Manifest Destiny, 141, 177, 216–17, 429
Marrant, John, 163–66, 174–84
Marriage: circuits of knowledge pro-

duction and, 124; in colonial Canada: 459–61; colonialism and, 132, 195, 456–60, 470–71; in Hegel, 201; mixed, as site of cultural exchange, 310–12; politics of, 125–26; production of citizenship and, 117–18, 126, 135–36; property and, 122, 471; racial classification and, 119–20, 260; in Russian colonization of Alaska, 305–6, 306–7, 308, 309, 310–12; Russian empire and, 307–8; in U.S. law, 80–82, 351
Masculinity, 276, 441
Medicine, as metaphor for progressive colonialism, 409–11. *See also* Hygiene
Memmi, Albert, 6–7, 31, 36, 54, 277
Memory, 6, 206–8
Mestizos, 28–29. *See also* Mixedness; Racial classification
Methodism, 184 n.2
Mettray, 44, 46–50
Mexican Americans: internal colonialism and, 434–41
Mexico: intelligence tests and, 325, 332–39, 444–45; United States and, 436–37, 438
Miles, Tiya, 16, 467
Miller, Gwenn, 455
Millspaugh, Arthur, 410, 416, 417, 418
"Miscegenation," 28, 81–82, 96, 109, 333, 379–80, 387–88, 401 n.73, 457–58, 460. *See also* Mixedness
Missionaries: in colonial Alaska, 310–11; colonialism and, 464–65; colonial marriage and, 456–57; intimacy and, 462–67; in the Middle East, 6; in the Philippines, 98, 380, 383, 401 n.73
"Mixed-bloods," 3, 6, 47–48, 56, 58, 446, 455–61. *See also* Blood; Mixedness; Racial classification
Mixedness: architectural prevention of, 145–46, 148–49; in British West Indies, 251–52; Enlightenment and, 156; fractions and, 244–45; local knowledge in

colonization and, 301–6, 306–7, 309, 310–12, 312–14; longevity and, 246–47; marriage and, 351, 439, 471–72; in Mexican intelligence tests, 338–39; offspring and, 79–81, 312–14; political relevance of, 259–60; politics of comparison and, 56; racial governmentality and, 197; reproduction and, 107–8, 246–48, 262–63, 265–66, 266 n.4, 379–80, 401 n.73, 445–46; as site of imperial anxiety, 28–30; "tender ties" in colonial Canada and, 455–61; in U.S. Census of 1890, 241–42. *See also* Race; Racial classification

"Modernization," 412–13, 442

Moore River Native Settlement, 95, 103, 106

Morgan, Edmund, 11

Mormons, 117, 125

"Mulatto," 243–45, 259–60, 263, 264. *See also* Mixedness; Racial classification

Narratives: of adoption, 346–47, 351–52, 352–58, 362–63; of U.S. family, 345. *See also* Colonialism: discursive qualities of

Nash, Gary, 27–30

National Intelligence Test (NIT): 331–32

National Origins Act (1924): 243, 330

Native Americans: African Americans and, 154–55, 165–74, 185 n.30; census and, 248–49, 265; colonial perspectives on, 179–80, 186 n.32, 188 n.71; Natural History and, 153; as Noble Savages, 169–70, 172

Neville, A. O., 95, 96, 103–4, 106

New England: attitudes toward race, 252; attitudes toward servants, 214–17, 226–27, 233–35

New Mexico, 120, 132; State Supreme Court, 123–25

New Orleans, 144–46

Nicaragua, 408–9, 415, 418–19

Normalization, through hygiene, 101–2

Nursemaids. *See* Breastfeeding

Nurseries: imperial anxiety and, 43–46; racial identity and, 45

Objectivity, politics of, 339, 420, 445

Pascoe, Peggy, 119–20

Paternalism: hygiene and, 97, 103–4; slavery and, 150–53, 155–58, 447

Patriarchy, 441

Paz, Octavio, 338

Perry, Adele, 457–61

Persia, 410, 416, 417, 418

Philippine-American War, 366–68, 370–97, 449

Philippines: as laboratory for financial advising, 416; as leper colony, 94–95, 98–103, 109–12; U.S. empire and, 27

Pocahontas, 179–80, 188 n.70

Poland, 409

Politics of comparison: as historical project, 1–2, 11, 39–42, 55, 57–58, 135, 273–74, 326, 406; as imperial program, 5–7, 55–57, 75, 167–69, 416; in North American history, 30–31, 32–46; pedagogy of empire and, 46–50; poor whites and, 50–54. *See also* Circuits of knowledge production; Comparison

Polygamy, 125–26, 134

Poor whites, 50–54, 66 n.69, 66 n.71

Postcolonial studies, 59 n.1

Postmodernism: transnationalism and, 40

Power: intimacy and, 274, 303–12, 314–15; proximities of, 177, 216–17; racial classification and, 258, 266

Property: citizenship and, 130–32; Hegel and, 200–210; marriage and, 122, 471

Prostitution, 44, 55; colonial regulation of, 367–97, 399 n.26, 449–50; patriotism and, 381, 396–97; Philippine-American War and, 366–68, 370–97, 449; politicization of, 367; temperance movement and, 403 n.110

Library of Congress Cataloging-in-Publication Data
Haunted by empire : geographies of intimacy in
North American history / edited by Ann Laura Stoler.
p. cm. — (American encounters/global interactions)
Includes bibliographical references and index.
ISBN 0-8223-3737-1 (cloth : alk. paper) —
ISBN 0-8223-3724-X (pbk. : alk. paper)
1. United States—Territories and possessions—History.
2. Intimacy (Psychology)—Political aspects—United
States—History. 3. Intimacy (Psychology)—Social
aspects—United States—History. I. Stoler, Ann Laura.
II. Series.
F970.H26 2006
973'.01—dc22   2005031722